OFF-BROADWAY MUSICALS SINCE 1919

From *Greenwich Village Follies* to *The Toxic Avenger*

Thomas S. Hischak

THE SCARECROW PRESS, INC.
Lanham • Toronto • Plymouth, UK
2011

Published by Scarecrow Press, Inc.
A wholly owned subsidiary of The Rowman & Littlefield Publishing Group, Inc.
4501 Forbes Boulevard, Suite 200, Lanham, Maryland 20706
http://www.scarecrowpress.com

Estover Road, Plymouth PL6 7PY, United Kingdom

British Library Cataloguing in Publication Information Available

Library of Congress Cataloging-in-Publication Data

Hischak, Thomas S.
  Off-Broadway musicals since 1919 : from Greenwich Village follies to the toxic
avenger / Thomas S. Hischak.
    p. cm.
  Includes bibliographical references and index.
  ISBN 978-0-8108-7771-9 (hardback : alk. paper) — ISBN 978-0-8108-7772-6
(ebook)
  1. Musicals—New York (State)—New York. 2. Off-Broadway theater. I. Title.
ML1711.8.N3H57 2011
792.609747'1—dc22   2010037326

Printed in the United States of America

For Greg, who has the spirit of Off Broadway

Contents

Acknowledgments

I WOULD LIKE TO EXPRESS MY THANKS to Mark Robinson, Bill Whiting, and Cathy Hischak who helped in the preparation of the manuscript; to the editors at Scarecrow Press; and to Ron Mandelbaum at Photofest.

Introduction: *Much More*

CONSIDER TWO MEMORABLE MOMENTS in the American musical theatre that occurred within a year of each other:

On May 21, 1959, the opening night of *Gypsy*, one of Broadway's biggest stars, Ethel Merman, launched into the song "Some People" about fifteen minutes into the show. With her bold and thrilling voice filling the Broadway Theatre, the largest venue in the Theatre District at the time, Merman's Rose proclaimed that she was not like other people and boasted how she was determined to make her young kids into stars. It was a brassy, unforgettable Broadway moment.

On May 3, 1960, about fifteen minutes into the opening night of the Off-Broadway musical *The Fantasticks*, the unknown ingénue Rita Gardner sang the plaintive song "Much More," a naive but heartfelt number in which the Girl vows not to be like other people and exclaims how her life will be filled with romance and adventure. There was no need to belt in the 144-seat Sullivan Street Playhouse, but Gardner's direct plea not to be "normal" was enthralling all the same. It was a charming, disarming Off-Broadway moment.

The difference between Broadway and Off Broadway can be understood from these two contrasting moments. In both cases the female lead sings her revealing "I am" song but each goes about it in her own unique way, influenced by the theatrical venue where the production takes place. Broadway musicals are bigger than life and offer outsized emotions expressed in large theatres; Off-Broadway musicals are smaller in scale and explore emotions that are more life-size as they are enacted in more intimate venues. When Broadway offers musical comedy, the songs, the dancing, the laughs, even the tears are big enough to fill a large and elaborate theatre. Off Broadway cannot afford such a scale and instead offers simpler productions and a more direct kind of music, dance, and comedy. The satire of Off Broadway is usually sharper than the large-scale spoofs of Broadway. The more serious musical plays sometimes have a greater intensity in the small Off-Broadway playhouses than they can on Broadway. Is one venue superior to the other? Of course not. Their uniqueness makes comparisons futile. The American theatre is richer for the contrasts and much of the diversity in our current musicals can be attributed to these two very different approaches.

Yet the Off-Broadway musical has always received much less attention than Broadway. This is understandable. Broadway is about fame, glory, and success. Off Broadway is about smart, sharp, little shows that make a personal impact. Many actors, writers, and directors first find critical acclaim Off Broadway, but only Broadway can make stars and super showmen. In these days when many Off-Broadway musicals make the transition to Broadway, it is easy to forget that Off Broadway began and found its identity as an *alternative* to Broadway. It has always been less expensive to produce an Off-Broadway musical than one on Broadway, and today it often seems that Off Broadway is a discount venue used to find fodder for Broadway. This was hardly the case in the 1950s. An Off-Broadway musical didn't want to go anywhere but Off Broadway. It was written and produced with Off Broadway in mind. In fact, it defied Broadway, often made fun of it, and took pride in not being big and glossy. As Broadway got more diverse in the 1960s, presenting rock, ethnic, and other kinds of musicals outside the mainstream, it made sense that successful Off-Broadway shows would aim for Broadway. Yet as the variety of musicals on Broadway widened, Off Broadway suffered. Off Broadway's costs escalated, actors with marquee value were sought, and the musicals became expensive enterprises. By the 1980s one had to go to Off Off Broadway to find the true alternative to Broadway. "Much More" became "Too Much," and the experimental nature of Off Broadway diminished.

Yet there are still fundamental differences between the two venues, and that is the focus of this critical look at 381 Off-Broadway musicals over the decades. This is neither a chronicle nor a detailed history of Off-Broadway musicals, though the book is arranged by decades and all the major musical works are discussed. The goal here is to look at the most representative Off-Broadway musicals over the years: remembered hits, forgotten failures, escapist musical comedies, demanding musical dramas, revues, and musical tributes to singers or songwriters. Revivals of Broadway musicals produced Off Broadway are not included in this discussion. The nature of an Off-Broadway musical is determined by attitude not venue. So when the 1934 Cole Porter success *Anything Goes* and the 1938 Rodgers and Hart hit *The*

Boys from Syracuse were given smart and small-scale revivals Off Broadway in the early 1960s, they were still Broadway musicals; they were just reimagined for Off Broadway. There is often a fuzzy line between Off and Off Off Broadway, and only important musicals in the latter classification are discussed, particularly if they later moved up to Off-Broadway status by change of venue or contract. The Off-Broadway musicals covered here include both long runs and short flops, for that is the nature of the theatre season in New York. Short runs included in this book sometimes had notable cast members, noteworthy artistic staff, or were just unusual enough to be considered.

Often Off-Broadway musicals accurately reflected what was going on musically and culturally in this country, as seen in productions ranging from satiric revues to passionate antiwar musicals to early and important musical works dealing with race, feminism, and sexual identity. Off Broadway sometimes picked up on the pulse and temperament of the nation in a way that Broadway could not or would not. Also, some Off-Broadway products have been very influential in determining the direction of the American musical theatre even though they may not enjoy the popularity and recognition of the bigger, brighter Broadway shows. There is so "Much More" to Off-Broadway musicals than has been given credit. This alternative venue is not a subplot in the story of the American musical; it is often the heart of this uniquely American art form.

Alphabetical List of Off-Broadway Musicals

- *A . . . My Name Is Alice*
- *A . . . My Name Is Still Alice*
- *Adding Machine*
- *Adrift in Macao*
- *After the Fair*
- *Ain't Misbehavin'*
- *Alice in Concert*
- *All in Love*
- *Altar Boyz*
- *Always . . . Patsy Cline*
- *American Rhapsody*
- *The Amorous Flea*
- *. . . And in This Corner*
- *And the World Goes 'Round*
- *Angry Housewives*
- *Annie Warbucks*
- *Assassins*
- *Avenue Q*
- *Babes in the Wood*
- *Bad Habits of 1926*
- *Baker's Dozen*
- *Balancing Act*
- *Ballad for a Firing Squad (Mata Hari)*
- *Ballad for Bimshire*
- *The Banker's Daughter*

- *The Contrast*
- *Cotton Patch Gospel*
- *Cowgirls*
- *The Cradle Will Rock*
- *Curly McDimple*
- *Dames at Sea*
- *Das Barbecü*
- *Debbie Does Dallas*
- *The Decline and Fall of the Entire World as Seen through the Eyes of Cole Porter Revisited*
- *Demi-Dozen*
- *Dessa Rose*
- *Diamonds*
- *Diamond Studs*
- *Dime a Dozen*
- *Dinah Was*
- *Dispatches*
- *Diversions*
- *Doctor Selavy's Magic Theatre*
- *The Donkey Show*
- *Dressed to the Nines*
- *The Drunkard*
- *Eating Raoul*
- *El Bravo*
- *Elegies: A Song Cycle*
- *El Grande de Coca-Cola*
- *Ernest in Love*
- *Evil Dead: The Musical*
- *The Faggot*
- *Fallout*
- *Falsettoland*
- *Fame on 42nd Street*
- *A Fantastic Fricasse*
- *The Fantasticks*
- *Fashion*
- *Fela!*
- *First Lady Suite*
- *Five Course Love*
- *Floyd Collins*
- *Fly Blackbird*
- *Forbidden Broadway*

- *Forever Plaid*
- *Four Below*
- *Four Below Strikes Back*
- *4 Guys Named José . . . and Una Mujer Named Maria!*
- *Frankenstein*
- *Further Mo'*
- *The Game Is Up*
- *Genesis*
- *Gertrude Stein's First Reader*
- *The Gifts of the Magi*
- *The Glorious Ones*
- *Goblin Market*
- *God Bless You, Mr. Rosewater*
- *Godspell*
- *The Golden Apple*
- *The Golden Land*
- *Graham Crackers*
- *The Grand Street Follies*
- *The Great American Trailer Park Musical*
- *The Great Macdaddy*
- *Great Scot!*
- *Greenwich Village Follies*
- *Greenwich Village Follies of 1920*
- *Greenwich Village, U.S.A.*
- *Grey Gardens*
- *Groucho: A Life in Revue*
- *Groundhog*
- *Gutenberg! The Musical!*
- *The Haggadah, a Passover Cantata*
- *Hair*
- *Half-Past Wednesday*
- *Hank Williams: Lost Highway*
- *Hannah . . . 1939*
- *Happiness*
- *Happy End*
- *Hark!*
- *Harlem Song*
- *Have I Got a Girl for You!*
- *Hedwig and the Angry Inch*
- *Hello Again*
- *Hello Muddah, Hello Fadduh*

- *The Last Sweet Days of Isaac*
- *Laughing Matters*
- *Let My People Come*
- *Lies & Legends: The Musical Stories of Harry Chapin*
- *Listen to My Heart: The Songs of David Friedman*
- *Little Fish*
- *Little Ham*
- *Little Mary Sunshine*
- *Little Shop of Horrors*
- *The Littlest Revue*
- *Livin' the Life*
- *Look Me Up*
- *Love (What about Luv?)*
- *Love, Janis*
- *Lovers*
- *Lovesong*
- *Lucky Stiff*
- *Madame Aphrodite*
- *The Mad Show*
- *Mahagonny (The Rise and Fall of the City of Mahagonny)*
- *Make Me a Song: The Music of William Finn*
- *A Man of No Importance*
- *Man with a Load of Mischief*
- *March of the Falsettos*
- *Marry Me a Little*
- *The Marvelous Wonderettes*
- *Mata Hari*
- *Mayor*
- *The Me Nobody Knows*
- *Menopause: The Musical*
- *The Middle of Nowhere*
- *Mixed Doubles*
- *The Musical of Musicals–The Musical*
- *My Life with Albertine*
- *My Old Friends*
- *The Mystery of Edwin Drood*
- *Naked Boys Singing!*
- *National Lampoon's Class of '86*
- *The National Lampoon Show*
- *National Lampoon's Lemmings*
- *A New Brain*

- *Newsical*
- *Next to Normal*
- *Nightclub Cantata*
- *Nite Club Confidential*
- *No for an Answer*
- *The No-Frills Revue*
- *No Shoestrings*
- *Now*
- *No Way to Treat a Lady*
- *Now Is the Time for All Good Men*
- *Nunsense*
- *Nunsense Ah-Men!*
- *Nunsense 2: The Sequel*
- *Of Mice and Men*
- *Oh! Calcutta!*
- *Oh Coward!*
- *Oil City Symphony*
- *Olympus on My Mind*
- *O Marry Me!*
- *Once on This Island*
- *Once Upon a Mattress*
- *One Mo' Time*
- *Our Sinatra*
- *Pageant*
- *Parade*
- *Passing Strange*
- *Peace*
- *Personals*
- *Pete 'n' Keely*
- *The Petrified Prince*
- *Philemon*
- *Phoenix '55*
- *Piano Bar*
- *Pick a Number, XV*
- *Pieces of Eight*
- *Pins and Needles*
- *Polly*
- *Preppies*
- *The Prince and the Pauper*
- *Privates on Parade*
- *Promenade*

- *Prom Queens Unchained*
- *Provincetown Follies*
- *Pump Boys and Dinettes*
- *Putting It Together*
- *Radiant Baby*
- *Radio Gals*
- *Rainbow*
- *Rap Master Ronnie*
- *Really Rosie*
- *Reefer Madness*
- *Rent*
- *Return to the Forbidden Planet*
- *Riverwind*
- *Road Show*
- *Roadside*
- *Rollin' on the T.O.B.A.*
- *Romance in Hard Times*
- *Romantic Poetry*
- *Runaways*
- *Ruthless!*
- *Salad Days*
- *Salvation*
- *Sandhog*
- *The Sap of Life*
- *Sarafina!*
- *Saturday Night*
- *Saturn Returns*
- *Scrambled Feet*
- *The Secret Life of Walter Mitty*
- *Secrets Every Smart Traveler Should Know*
- *See What I Wanna See*
- *Sensations*
- *Seven Comes Eleven*
- *Sex Tips for Modern Girls*
- *Shades of Harlem*
- *Shakespeare's Cabaret*
- *She Shall Have Music*
- *Shockheaded Peter*
- *Shoestring '57*
- *Shoestring Revue*
- *Shout!*

- *The Show Goes On*
- *Showing Off*
- *Shuffle Along*
- *Simply Heavenly*
- *Sing Muse!*
- *Smiling the Boy Fell Dead*
- *Smoke on the Mountain*
- *Snoopy*
- *Song of Singapore*
- *Songs for a New World*
- *Songs of Paradise*
- *The Spitfire Grill*
- *Spring Awakening*
- *Staggerlee*
- *Stag Movie*
- *Starting Here, Starting Now*
- *The Streets of New York*
- *Suds*
- *Sunset*
- *Sweethearts*
- *Swingtime Canteen*
- *The Taffetas*
- *Take Five*
- *Taking a Chance on Love*
- *Taking My Turn*
- *Tallulah*
- *Ten Percent Revue*
- *That's Life!*
- *The Thing about Men*
- *3 Guys Naked from the Waist Down*
- *Three Mo' Tenors*
- *The Threepenny Opera*
- *Three Postcards*
- *Tick, Tick . . . Boom!*
- *Time, Gentlemen Please*
- *Tintypes*
- *[title of show]*
- *Tomfoolery*
- *Touch*
- *To Whom It May Concern*
- *The Toxic Avenger*

Chronological List of Off-Broadway Musicals

1919

- *Greenwich Village Follies*

1920

- *Greenwich Village Follies of 1920*

1921

- *Shuffle Along*

1922

- *A Fantastic Fricasse*

1924

- *The Grand Street Follies*

1925

- *The Grand Street Follies*
- *Polly*

1926

- *Bunk of 1926*
- *Bad Habits of 1926*
- *The Grand Street Follies*

1927

- *The Grand Street Follies*

1934

- *Kykunkor (The Witch Woman)*

1935

- *Provincetown Follies*

1937

- *Pins and Needles*
- *The Cradle Will Rock*

1941

- *No for an Answer*

1954

- *The Threepenny Opera*
- *The Golden Apple*
- *I Feel Wonderful*
- *Sandhog*

1955

- *Shoestring Revue*
- *Phoenix '55*

1956

- *Four Below*
- *The Littlest Revue*
- *Shoestring '57*

1957

- *Livin' the Life*
- *Simply Heavenly*
- *Kaleidoscope*
- *Take Five*

1958

- *Demi-Dozen*
- *Diversions*
- *Salad Days*
- *Of Mice and Men*

1959

- *Fashion*
- *She Shall Have Music*
- *Once Upon a Mattress*
- *Fallout*
- *The Billy Barnes Revue*
- *Pieces of Eight*
- *Little Mary Sunshine*

1960

- *Parade*
- *Four Below Strikes Back*
- *The Fantasticks*
- *Ernest in Love*
- *Greenwich, U.S.A.*
- *Dressed to the Nines*
- *Valmouth*

1961

- *Smiling the Boy Fell Dead*
- *The Sap of Life*
- *Seven Comes Eleven*
- *O Marry Me!*
- *Time, Gentlemen Please*
- *All in Love*
- *Sing Muse!*

- *Black Nativity*
- *Madame Aphrodite*

1962

- *The Banker's Daughter*
- *Fly Blackbird*
- *Half-Past Wednesday*
- *King of the Whole Damn World*
- *No Shoestrings*
- *Dime a Dozen*
- *Riverwind*

1963

- *Graham Crackers*
- *The World of Kurt Weill in Song*
- *Ballad for Bimshire*
- *The Streets of New York*
- *Trumpets of the Lord*

1964

- *Baker's Dozen*
- *Jericho-Jim Crow*
- *. . . And in This Corner*
- *Jo*
- *The Amorous Flea*
- *Cindy*
- *The Game Is Up*
- *Bits and Pieces, XIV*
- *The Secret Life of Walter Mitty*
- *Babes in the Wood*

1965

- *The Decline and Fall of the Entire World as Seen through the Eyes of Cole Porter Revisited*
- *Pick a Number, XV*
- *Just for Openers*
- *Great Scot!*

1966

- *The Mad Show*
- *Below the Belt*
- *Mixed Doubles*
- *Man with a Load of Mischief*
- *Viet Rock*

1967

- *You're a Good Man, Charlie Brown*
- *Now Is the Time for All Good Men*
- *Hair*
- *In Circles*
- *Curly McDimple*

1968

- *Your Own Thing*
- *Jacques Brel Is Alive and Well and Living in Paris*
- *The Believers*
- *Now*
- *Walk Down Mah Street!*
- *How to Steal an Election*
- *Ballad for a Firing Squad (Mata Hari)*
- *Dames at Sea*

1969

- *Peace*
- *Promenade*
- *Oh! Calcutta!*
- *Salvation*
- *Gertrude Stein's First Reader*

1970

- *The Last Sweet Days of Isaac*
- *Joy*
- *Billy Noname*
- *The Drunkard*
- *Mahagonny (The Rise and Fall of the City of Mahagonny)*

- *Colette*
- *The Me Nobody Knows*
- *Sensations*
- *Touch*

1971

- *Stag Movie*
- *Godspell*
- *Two Gentlemen of Verona*
- *Look Me Up*

1972

- *Wanted*
- *Hark!*
- *Joan*
- *Berlin to Broadway with Kurt Weill*
- *Oh Coward!*
- *Doctor Selavy's Magic Theatre*
- *The Contrast*
- *Rainbow*

1973

- *National Lampoon's Lemmings*
- *El Grande de Coca-Cola*
- *What's a Nice Country Like You Doing in a State Like This?*
- *The Faggot*
- *Candide*

1974

- *Let My People Come*
- *The Great Macdaddy*
- *Fashion*
- *I'll Die If I Can't Live Forever*

1975

- *Diamond Studs*
- *Lovers*

- *The National Lampoon Show*
- *Be Kind to People Week*
- *Philemon*
- *A Chorus Line*
- *Boy Meets Boy*
- *Christy*
- *Tuscaloosa's Calling Me . . . But I'm Not Going!*

1976

- *Lovesong*
- *The Club*
- *Joseph and the Amazing Technicolor Dreamcoat*

1977

- *Nightclub Cantata*
- *Starting Here, Starting Now*
- *Happy End*

1978

- *Ain't Misbehavin'*
- *Runaways*
- *The Best Little Whorehouse in Texas*
- *I'm Getting My Act Together and Taking It on the Road*
- *Piano Bar*
- *A Broadway Musical*
- *In Trousers*

1979

- *My Old Friends*
- *The Umbrellas of Cherbourg*
- *Dispatches*
- *Scrambled Feet*
- *Big Bad Burlesque*
- *The King of the Schnorrers*
- *God Bless You, Mr. Rosewater*
- *One Mo' Time*

1980

- *Shakespeare's Cabaret*
- *The Housewives' Cantata*
- *Blues in the Night*
- *The Haggadah, a Passover Cantata*
- *Tintypes*
- *Really Rosie*
- *Ka-Boom!*
- *Trixie True, Teen Detective*
- *Alice in Concert*

1981

- *Marry Me a Little*
- *I Can't Keep Running in Place*
- *March of the Falsettos*
- *El Bravo*
- *Pump Boys and Dinettes*
- *Cotton Patch Gospel*
- *Tomfoolery*

1982

- *Forbidden Broadway*
- *Herringbone*
- *Little Shop of Horrors*
- *Charlotte Sweet*
- *Upstairs at O'Neals'*
- *Snoopy*

1983

- *Taking My Turn*
- *Preppies*
- *Tallulah*
- *Sunset*
- *The Human Comedy*

1984

- *A . . . My Name Is Alice*
- *Hey, Ma . . . Kaye Ballard*

- *Love*
- *Nite Club Confidential*
- *Shades of Harlem*
- *Rap Master Ronnie*
- *Kuni-Leml*
- *Diamonds*

1985

- *3 Guys Naked from the Waist Down*
- *Lies & Legends: The Musical Stories of Harry Chapin*
- *Mayor*
- *The Mystery of Edwin Drood*
- *Yours, Anne*
- *The Golden Land*
- *Personals*
- *Nunsense*
- *To Whom It May Concern*

1986

- *Beehive*
- *Goblin Market*
- *National Lampoon's Class of '86*
- *Olympus on My Mind*
- *Lady Day at Emerson's Bar and Grill*
- *Angry Housewives*
- *Sex Tips for Modern Girls*
- *Groucho: A Life in Revue*
- *Brownstone*
- *Have I Got a Girl for You!*

1987

- *The Knife*
- *Staggerlee*
- *Three Postcards*
- *No Way to Treat a Lady*
- *Bittersuite*
- *Sarafina!*
- *Birds of Paradise*

- *Oil City Symphony*
- *The No-Frills Revue*

1988

- *Ten Percent Revue*
- *Lucky Stiff*
- *Urban Blight*
- *Suds*
- *The Taffetas*
- *The Middle of Nowhere*
- *Sweethearts*

1989

- *Genesis*
- *Songs of Paradise*
- *Laughing Matters*
- *Showing Off*
- *Privates on Parade*
- *Closer Than Ever*
- *Up Against It*
- *Romance in Hard Times*

1990

- *Hannah . . . 1939*
- *Once on This Island*
- *Further Mo'*
- *Forever Plaid*
- *Falsettoland*
- *Broadway Jukebox*
- *Smoke on the Mountain*
- *The Gifts of the Magi*

1991

- *Assassins*
- *And the World Goes 'Round*
- *Pageant*
- *Song of Singapore*

- *Prom Queens Unchained*
- *Return to the Forbidden Planet*

1992

- *Groundhog*
- *Ruthless!*
- *Eating Raoul*
- *Balancing Act*
- *Weird Romance*
- *Hello Muddah, Hello Fadduh*

1993

- *Wings*
- *Putting It Together*
- *Howard Crabtree's Whoop-Dee-Doo!*
- *Annie Warbucks*
- *First Lady Suite*

1994

- *Hello Again*
- *That's Life!*
- *Jelly Roll!*
- *Nunsense 2: The Sequel*
- *Das Barbecü*
- *The Petrified Prince*

1995

- *Jack's Holiday*
- *Swingtime Canteen*
- *john & jen*
- *Zombies from Beyond*
- *Songs for a New World*
- *Bring in 'da Noise Bring in 'da Funk*

1996

- *Rent*
- *Cowgirls*

- *Floyd Collins*
- *Zombie Prom*
- *I Love You, You're Perfect, Now Change*
- *When Pigs Fly*
- *Radio Gals*
- *A Brief History of White Music*

1997

- *Violet*
- *Always . . . Patsy Cline*
- *The Last Session*
- *Secrets Every Smart Traveler Should Know*
- *The Show Goes On*

1998

- *Hedwig and the Angry Inch*
- *Saturn Returns: A Concert*
- *Dinah Was*
- *A New Brain*
- *Nunsense A-Men!*

1999

- *Rollin' on the T.O.B.A.*
- *Bright Lights Big City*
- *It Ain't Nothin' But the Blues*
- *If Love Were All*
- *After the Fair*
- *Naked Boys Singing!*
- *The Donkey Show*
- *Contact*
- *Shockheaded Peter*
- *James Joyce's The Dead*
- *Our Sinatra*

2000

- *Saturday Night*
- *The Wild Party*

- *Taking a Chance on Love*
- *The Bubbly Black Girl Sheds Her Chameleon Skin*
- *4 Guys Named José . . . and Una Mujer Named Maria!*
- *A Class Act*
- *American Rhapsody*
- *Pete 'n' Keely*

2001

- *Bat Boy: The Musical*
- *Love, Janis*
- *The IT Girl*
- *Urinetown*
- *Tick, Tick . . . Boom!*
- *The Spitfire Grill*
- *Reefer Madness*
- *Roadside*

2002

- *The Last Five Years*
- *Menopause: The Musical*
- *The Prince and the Pauper*
- *Harlem Song*
- *Little Ham*
- *Jolson and Company*
- *A Man of No Importance*
- *Debbie Does Dallas*

2003

- *Little Fish*
- *Radiant Baby*
- *My Life with Albertine*
- *Avenue Q*
- *Zanna, Don't!*
- *Elegies: A Song Cycle*
- *Hank Williams: Lost Highway*
- *Boobs! The Musical*
- *The Thing about Men*
- *Listen to My Heart: The Songs of David Friedman*

- *Fame on 42nd Street*
- *Caroline, or Change*
- *The Musical of Musicals—The Musical*

2004

- *Johnny Guitar*
- *bare*
- *Newsical*

2005

- *The 25th Annual Putnam County Spelling Bee*
- *Altar Boyz*
- *Dessa Rose*
- *Captain Louie*
- *The Great American Trailer Park Musical*
- *Five Course Love*
- *See What I Wanna See*

2006

- *Bernarda Alba*
- *I Love You Because*
- *Grey Gardens*
- *Spring Awakening*
- *[title of show]*
- *Shout!*
- *Evil Dead: The Musical*

2007

- *Gutenberg! The Musical!*
- *In the Heights*
- *Adrift in Macao*
- *Passing Strange*
- *Walmartopia*
- *Celia: The Life and Music of Celia Cruz*
- *Three Mo' Tenors*
- *Frankenstein*
- *The Glorious Ones*
- *Make Me a Song: The Music of William Finn*

2008

- *Next to Normal*
- *Adding Machine*
- *Bash'd! A Gay Rap Opera*
- *Fela!*
- *What's That Smell: The Music of Jacob Sterling*
- *The Marvelous Wonderettes*
- *Romantic Poetry*
- *Road Show*

2009

- *Happiness*
- *The Toxic Avenger*

Chapter One

———————◯———————

Broadway's Stepchild:
Beginnings

ALTHOUGH THE TERM "OFF BROADWAY" would not be readily used until the late 1930s, Off Broadway began much earlier in the century with the Little Theatre movement. In 1909 the playwright Percy MacKaye wrote in *The Playhouse and the Play* about a "theatre wholly divorced from commercialism" and termed it "civic theatre," though soon that expression was replaced by Little Theatre. In New York City this movement manifest itself in small, amateur theatre groups with radical ideas, often of a socialist nature. The Progressive Stage Society, the Liberal Club, the Theatre League, and the Socialist Press Club were among the short-lived organizations that sought to offer an alternative to the for-profit Broadway. By this time the Theatre District known as Broadway was centered on Longacre (later Times) Square, and these Little Theatres were housed outside of this area, many of them downtown. The Washington Square Players, an offshoot of the Liberal Club, was the most influential of the early Little Theatres, and some point to the company's 1915 inaugural production as the birth of Off Broadway. By now fully professional, the Players performed in the undesirable Bandbox Theatre on 57th Street and Third Avenue, geographically and philosophically removed from Broadway. New American works and rarely seen foreign plays were produced with growing success, promoting early works by playwrights such as Eugene O'Neill and Elmer Rice and introducing such performers as Katharine Cornell and Rollo Peters. The group disbanded in 1918 when most of its creative staff founded the Theatre Guild, a long-running theatre institution that flourished on Broadway for many decades. Other early Little Theatres to have an impact on the New York theatre scene included the Provincetown Players and the Neighborhood Playhouse, both founded in

1

1915 and located in Greenwich Village, Manhattan's Left Bank—the breeding ground for innovative creativity in all the arts.

Since Broadway was the reigning home of the American musical, the Little Theatres had little interest in presenting such entertainment. After all, they saw themselves as an alternative to the commercialism of the Street, and what was more commercial than a glitzy Broadway musical? Yet before long, both the Provincetown Players and the Neighborhood Playhouse put on musical revues, either to raise money at the end of a season of "serious" theatre or to have fun spoofing that same kind of drama. Such revues moving to Broadway for successful runs, it may seem like the Little Theatres were selling out. Yet there was still something "alternative" about these early musical revues. (The Theatre Guild would also offer a series of musicals over the years, but they all opened on Broadway.) Until the 1940s, the number of musicals away from Broadway remained very small. The emphasis was still on drama, and a notable Off-Broadway musical was more the exception than the rule until the 1950s. All the same, the story of the Off-Broadway musical starts with this handful of early revues and occasional book musicals.

If one wants to consider the spirit of the Off-Broadway musical, it is necessary to go back even further than the Washington Square Players and look at two very important African American musicals that predate 1915. These two works were curiosities in their day and, although they were presented in Broadway houses during the off-season, they illustrate the nature of the alternative musical. *Clorindy; or, The Origin of the Cake Walk* (1898) was a short musical "afterpiece" and was the first show written and performed by African Americans in a major Broadway house. Producer-director Edward E. Rice presented a vaudeville entertainment entitled *Rice's Summer Nights* for fifty-five performances on the rooftop of the Casino Theatre. Added during the run was *Clorindy* by Will Marion Cook (music) and Paul Lawrence Dunbar (book and lyrics). The "African singing and dancing novelty" featured such songs as "Every Coon Had a Lady Friend But Me," "Who Dat Say Chicken in Dis Crowd?," and "Darktown Is Out Tonight." The last song enjoyed some popularity at the time, and the show itself was well received as a delightful warm-weather diversion. (Dunbar would later become better known as a poet and civil rights advocate.) *In Dahomy* (1903) was a book musical also written and performed by African Americans and it played in the New York Theatre on the Street in the off-season. In the raucous libretto, Rareback Pinkerton (George Walker) goes to Florida to con an old millionaire out of his money, and he brings along his bumbling assistant Shylock Homestead (Bert Williams). Soon Rareback finds out that Shylock has a considerable fortune of his own, and Rareback bamboozles him, using the money to live a life of leisure in Florida and then in Africa until Shylock finally catches on.

Again Cook wrote the music and Dunbar provided the lyrics, but the songs took second place to the hilarious by-play of comics Walker and Williams who had first found success in vaudeville. White audiences were hesitant to attend, yet the musical managed to run a surprising fifty-nine performances. When Walker and Williams took the show to London where there was less prejudice, the musical ran seven months in 1904. Both *Clorindy* and *In Dahomy* would probably have been produced Off Broadway for longer runs if such a venue had existed.

The transition from Little Theatre to Off Broadway was gradual and vague enough that no one agrees on the exact date. By the mid-1930s the editor of the annual *Best Plays* added a section labeled "Off Broadway" to describe the season's productions that took place away from the Street. Many of these were still amateur or student productions, but they were admired for their ambitious repertoire, particularly classic and foreign works. Because there were a handful of leftist musicals on Broadway in the 1930s and 1940s, there seemed to be less pressure on Off Broadway to provide such hard-hitting shows. *Parade, Sing for Your Supper, Knickerbocker Holiday*, and *Johnny Johnson* were uncompromising musical works about war, unemployment, and racial inequality and, while none was a long-run hit, they managed to be noticed and to give Broadway a grittier edge at times. Add to these all the left-wing dramas by Clifford Odets and others during the Depression and one can see that Broadway was providing its own alternative. It wasn't until the conservative 1950s that Broadway eschewed controversy and it was left to Off Broadway to provide radical dramas and demanding musicals.

It is ironic that while the American musical was being rethought and redesigned in the 1940s thanks to *Oklahoma!* and the subsequent Rodgers and Hammerstein shows, Off Broadway had very few musical offerings. It seemed that the musical revolution on the Street meant that there was no need for such innovation Off Broadway. The scattered revues offered downtown were neither significant nor successful. Also, the war years were not ideal for leftist musicals and shows that criticized the system. The one exception to this, Marc Blitstein's blistering *No for an Answer*, was short-lived but potent all the same and is discussed in detail at the end of the chapter. The Off-Broadway musical during the years 1915 and 1949 can be represented by these sixteen productions. The total number of offerings was not much greater than this because, again, Off Broadway and musicals were not seen as compatible entities. The forces that propelled the Little Theatre movement and the early Off-Broadway years were not that interested in musicals. Despite such flashes of brilliancy as *Shuffle Along, Pins and Needles*, and *The Cradle Will Rock*, Off Broadway was not seen as a place for musicals. That was something for the future.

GREENWICH VILLAGE FOLLIES

[15 July 1919, Greenwich Village Theatre, Nora Bayes Theatre, 232 performances] a musical revue by John Murray Anderson, Philip Bartholomae. *Score:* A. Baldwin Sloane (music), John Murray Anderson (lyrics), various. *Cast:* Bessie McCoy Davis, Harry K. Morton, Harry Delf, Bobby Edwards, Cecil Cunningham, Ted Lewis and his Orchestra.

GREENWICH VILLAGE FOLLIES OF 1920

[30 August 1920, Greenwich Village Theatre, 24 performances; Shubert Theatre, 217 performances] a musical revue by Thomas J. Grey. *Score:* A. Baldwin Sloane (music), John Murray Anderson, Arthur Swanstrom (lyrics). *Cast:* Frank Crumit, Bert Savoy, Jay Brennan, Howard Marsh, Phil Baker, Mary Lewis, Harriet Gimbel.

The first Off-Broadway musical to gain wide recognition in New York was *The Greenwich Village Follies*, a revue that grew out of a cabaret-restaurant entertainment and later blossomed into a series of shows that were presented on Broadway. The cabaret venue was called Palais Royal, and it was run by Paul Salvin who commissioned the young John Murray Anderson to put together a musical show. Anderson, who began his career as a ballroom dancer, would go on to become a master of the Broadway revue, second only to Florenz Ziegfeld for his showmanship. His Continental-like shows at the Palais Royal were popular enough that Salvin and some other Greenwich Village businessmen and agents incorporated, called themselves The Bohemians, Inc., and raised $35,000 to produce *Greenwich Village Follies* far away from the Broadway district. Anderson wrote some sketches (with Philip Bartholomae) and the lyrics for various composers. More importantly, he staged the revue himself using his motto "simplicity and taste" and employed some of the scenic ideas he discovered in Europe, such as the unrealistic and evocative designs of Gordon Craig. One setting resembled a Toulouse-Lautrec poster, another a Japanese garden, and red roses filled the stage for another number. The decor was lavish through suggestion, and it was Anderson, working with various designers, who created a new look for the American musical. He even specified the subject matter for the overture curtain painted

by Reginald Marsh which illustrated all the notable Greenwich Village land-
marks (bookstores, eateries, taverns, artists' studios, Washington Arch, and
so on) seen on MacDougal Alley, Sheridan Square, 14th Street, and other
thoroughfares. Also pictured were street artists and musicians, poets, society
folks slumming, famous and struggling writers, and other "hobohemians." It
was evident to playgoers entering the theatre and seeing this complex cartoon
that they were not about to see a Broadway show but a Greenwich Village
musical.

Broadway star Bessie McCoy Davis was the name attraction of the revue,
but the real discovery in the show was singer-band leader Ted Lewis who
introduced his "When My Baby Smiles at Me" that caught on and served as
his theme song throughout his long career. Davis sang "I'm a Hostess of a
Bum Cabaret" about the upcoming Prohibition and danced as if she were a
marionette, complete with strings attached to her arms and legs. Other songs
included the catchy "I Want a Daddy Who Will Rock Me to Sleep" that lampooned Tin Pan Alley hits, and "The Critics' Blues" that mentioned the top
theatre reviewers of the day. Free love was satirized in "I'll Sell You a Girl,"
"My Little Javanese" was an Asian-flavored number, Bobby Edwards sang "I
Do Not Care for Women Who Wear Stays" as he accompanied himself on a
homemade ukulele fashioned from a cigar box, and Irving Berlin contributed
the Latin-flavored "I'll See You in C-U-B-A." The revue was titled *Greenwich
Village Nights* when it opened at the little venue on Sheridan Square, but
the producers, fearing the show might be thought of as another Palais Royal
nightclub entertainment, changed the title to *Greenwich Village Follies* so
that it was clear the musical was a full-scale revue. Ziegfeld protested vehe-
mently but was powerless to stop Salvin and Anderson because Ziegfeld did
not own the term "Follies"; he himself had stolen it from a 1906 Broadway
revue. The critics in their notices made comparisons to Ziegfeld's series,
most agreeing that Anderson's show was more brainy and wittier even and
as visually appealing as the *Ziegfeld Follies'* more elaborate decor. Word of
mouth gradually spread, and many playgoers made the trek downtown to
see for themselves. *Greenwich Village Follies* ran nearly two months before
transferring to a Broadway house where it stayed for another five and a half
months. Because the Off-Broadway venue did not fall under the rules of Actors' Equity, *Greenwich Village Follies* did not suspend performances during
the famous 1919 actors' strike and was able to perform when theatregoers
were desperate for entertainment. After the Broadway run, the revue had a
successful tour and plans for a new edition were made. Off Broadway had
its first musical hit.

The title *Greenwich Village Follies of 1920* made it clear that this was
going to be a series, another affront to Ziegfeld. Again Anderson directed,

provided lyrics, and hired the young designer James Reynolds who produced some dazzling visuals, such as a medieval Russian landscape, a colorful carnival, a birthday cake with human candles, a Valentine's Day number with a stage filled with lace, flowers, and cupids, and a perfume factory with girls as bottled scents. (Ziegfeld was either impressed or jealous because he hired Reynolds to design his next *Follies*.) The songs were not very memorable in this edition, and the emphasis seemed to be on sex and comedy. The former was evident in the provocative opening number "The Naked Truth" set in a Greenwich Village artists' studio overflowing with scantily clad models, art students, and gawkers. At the climax of the number, chorines dressed as body parts came together to create a huge Miss Greenwich Village. Equally sexy were the perfume-bottle girls who were poured into a giant pool of sandalwood and rose-scented elixir. The comedy team of Savoy and Brennan provided most of the laughs, particularly drag comic Bert Savoy who appeared as Lady Nicotine in a Village dive in a number titled "Come to Bohemia," and throughout the show he often popped up in female attire to join the chorus girls. Veteran vaudevillian Frank Crumit sang such ditties as "Just Snap Your Fingers at Care" and "I'm a Lonesome Little Raindrop," but the finest voice on the stage was that of young tenor Howard Marsh who first gained recognition in this show. (Marsh would later be the leading man in such Broadway hits as *Blossom Time*, *The Student Prince*, and *Show Boat*.) In addition to the studio and perfume numbers, the revue also boasted such show-stopping sequences as "Song of the Samovar" in which giant candelabras framed a Russian dance number; "The Krazy Kat's Ball" where comic strip characters came to life; "Just Sweet Sixteen" with the mammoth birthday cake with candles; and the first act finale "Tam (Tam, Tam, Tam, Tam, Tam)" in which the audience was provided with miniature tambourines and was asked to shake them during the number and as a way of applauding at the end of the act. *Greenwich Village Follies of 1920* featured the kind of spectacle only seen on Broadway, so it was not surprising that after a month Off Broadway it transferred to the Street for a healthy run of six months. By this time Anderson was staging shows on Broadway for others as well and was reluctant to keep returning to Off Broadway for future *Greenwich Village Follies*. Consequently the 1921, 1922, 1923, 1924, 1925, and 1928 editions all opened on Broadway, each one retaining the Off-Broadway venue's name. The shows continued to dazzle, and most of the subsequent editions were hits. Yet Greenwich Village was rarely the topic of the songs or the sketches, so the series became thoroughly Broadway in subject as well as look. The coming of the Depression finished off the series when the cost of a spectacular Broadway revue could not be met by dwindling audiences. Those first two Off-Broadway ventures were important milestones for the American theatre. The model of the sophisticated, irreverent Off-Broadway musical revue was established. The as-yet-unnamed Off Broadway was seen for the first time as an alternate to Broadway musicals as well as dramas.

SHUFFLE ALONG

[23 May 1921, 63rd Street Music Hall, 504 performances] a musical comedy by Flournoy Miller, Aubrey Lyles. *Score:* Eubie Blake (music), Noble Sissle (lyrics). *Cast:* Miller, Lyles, Sissle, Blake, Lottie Gee, Roger Matthews, Gertrude Saunders, Lawrence Deas, Paul Floyd, Mattie Wilks.

Not only the first successful full-length musical written, directed, and performed by African American artists, *Shuffle Along* was also one of the most joyous shows of the decade and it opened the door for other African American-created musicals. In the city of Jimtown, grocery store partners Steve Jenkins (Flournoy Miller) and Sam Peck (Aubrey Lyles) are each running for mayor, each promising the other that he will be made chief of police after the election. Steve wins and Sam heads the police department, but corruption sets in and the reform candidate Harry Walton (Roger Matthews) gets the people behind him. Soon Steve and Sam are back in the grocery store. A subplot concerned Harry and Jessie Williams (Lottie Gee), the daughter of one of Jimtown's richest citizens. Performers Miller and Lyles penned the risible libretto which was more a series of sketches and comic routines from vaudeville than a cohesive story. At one point in the second act, the plot was suspended and Lyles and Miller did one of their comedy routines. At another time, songwriters Eubie Blake (music) and Noble Sissle (lyrics) left the pit and did their musical act from the variety circuit. The production values for *Shuffle Along* were bargain basement and the cast was uneven, but it was the scintillating score that turned the low-budget, clumsy show into a hit. Ragtime, buck-and-wing dance steps, bluesy ballads, jazz, and an early version of the Charleston filled the vivacious score. The rapid fox-trot "I'm Just Wild about Harry" was the runaway hit and has survived to this day, but the rest of the score was also superior. The smooth romantic duet "Love Will Find a Way" was not only musically ahead of its time, its placement at the end of the act when it was sung by Harry and Jessie as a serious love song between two black characters was radically challenging for white audiences. The lusty celebration number "Bandana Days" was almost tribal in its vivacity, and the wry "If You Haven't Been Vamped By a Brownskin" was sassy and unapologetic. Other highlights included the joyous "(I'm) Simply Full of Jazz," the crooning "I'm

Craving for That Kind of Love," the jumping "Baltimore Buzz," and the giddy title number.

The four creators of *Shuffle Along* had a great deal of vaudeville experience and when performing together in Philadelphia, they started working on a full-length musical that showcased their various talents. The show tried out in various cities where they stayed just one step ahead of the bill collectors, and when Blake and his cohorts tried to bring the musical into New York, no producer would pick up the show despite the positive audience reaction it was receiving elsewhere. Finally Broadway producer John Cole and his son Harry took a risk and booked it in the dilapidated 63rd Street Music Hall far from the Theatre District. *Shuffle Along* opened to diverse reviews, some critics applauding the innovative score and bright performances but others dismissing the show as amateurish. Word of mouth was much more positive, and soon *Shuffle Along* became the must-see hit, particularly at its late-night Wednesday performances. The Coles also took a risk in desegregating the theatre, allowing African American patrons to buy up to one-third of the orchestra seats instead of being restricted to the balcony as was the current policy in first-class houses. The musical ran fifteen months and proved that all-black musicals could appeal to both white and black audiences. *Shuffle Along* also introduced many outstanding performers, not only in its original cast but in replacement casts and on tour. Paul Robeson, Adelaide Hall, Josephine Baker, Hall Johnson, and Florence Mills were among the African American performers who either made their stage debut or first found recognition in the show.

Other editions of *Shuffle Along* were presented in 1928 and 1932, both on Broadway, but neither was successful. In 1952 a new production of *Shuffle Along* opened on Broadway but with only two of the original score's songs and a whole new libretto. The production hardly qualified as a revival, though as a new musical it was also severely lacking. Flournoy Miller and Gerard Smith's new plot now concerned a group of African American soldiers in Italy at the end of World War II, in particular the WAC Lucy Duke (Dolores Martin) who, thinking her husband was killed in action, begins a new romance only to have her spouse (Miller) return. Noble and Sissle wrote some new numbers ("Swanee Moon," "Give It Love," "Rhythm of America," and "My Day") and appeared as themselves in the show which ran only four performances.

A FANTASTIC FRICASEE

[11 September 1922, Greenwich Village Theatre, 112 performances] musical revue by Marguerite Abbott Barker, various. *Score:* various. *Cast:* Bobby

Edwards, Jimmy Kemper, Jeanette MacDonald, Jay Strong, Jean White, Edwin Strawbridge, John Decker, Dorothy Smoller, Andre Chotin, Roy Shields and his orchestra.

Information on this revue is slight and the score is lost, yet the well-reviewed show managed to run a very profitable fourteen weeks at the Greenwich Village Theatre. Reviews from the time complimented the songs, in particular the witty lyrics by Robert Edwards, and the staging. Edwards was the cigar-box-ukulele player Bobby Edwards from the first *Greenwich Village Follies* in the same theatre, and he was a leading player this time as well. Yet by far the most famous performer to emerge from *A Fantastic Fricasse* was newcomer Jeanette MacDonald who later appeared in a handful of musicals on Broadway and on tour before going to Hollywood. Fellow cast member Andre Chotin directed the revue, which was deemed small-scale but impressive by the press. The most admired numbers were a soldier ballet, a satirical look at the newly termed "flappers," and a sequence involving marionettes that climaxed with Orlando Furioso fighting and slaying a dragon. *A Fantastic Fricasse* was a true Off-Broadway revue; not on the scale of the popular *Greenwich Village Follies*, but closer to the kind of shows Off Broadway would excel at in the 1950s and early 1960s.

THE GRAND STREET FOLLIES

[13 June, 1924, Neighborhood Playhouse, 5 performances; reopened 24 June 1924, 172 performances] a musical revue by Agnes Morgan, Dorothy Sands. *Score:* Albert Carroll, Lily M. Hyland (music), Carroll (lyrics), various. *Cast:* Carroll, Sands, Aline MacMahon, Helen Arthur, John F. Roche, Esther Mitchell, Joanna Roos, Dan Walker, Betty Prescott, Martin Wolfson, Adrienne Morrison, Paula Trueman, Edmond Rickett.

THE GRAND STREET FOLLIES

[18 June 1925, Neighborhood Playhouse, 148 performances] a musical revue by Agnes Morgan. *Score:* Lily Hyland (music), Morgan (lyrics), various.

Cast: Albert Carroll, Dorothy Sands, Helen Arthur, Whitford Kane, Edgar Kent, Irene Lewisohn, Paula Trueman, Ian Maclaren, Esther Mitchell, Marc Loebell, Dan Walker, Helen Mack.

The Neighborhood Playhouse, one of the ambitious Little Theatres that presented new works and classics away from the financial burdens of Broadway, was located far downtown at 466 Grand Street. It was founded in 1915 and soon established a reputation for its sterling George Bernard Shaw productions and early works by Eugene O'Neill. At the end of each season, the small and youthful company presented a spring show satirizing its own productions as well as those on the Street. The first *The Grand Street Follies* was presented in June of 1922 for twelve performances at the Neighborhood Playhouse for subscribers only. Self-described as a "low-brow show for High Grade Morons," it spoofed the theatre and used famous melodies which Albert Carroll set to new and irreverent lyrics. (The popular *Forbidden Broadway* series would do the same thing Off Broadway sixty years later.) It was a silly evening that concluded with the cast impersonating famous theatre folk as they left the theatre and made acid comments about the show. The Neighborhood Playhouse was so pleased with the response that after two years of these in-house entertainments they offered the first public edition of *The Grand Street Follies*. The format remained the same, though Lily Hyland and other composers came up with original music which often imitated the melodies of the day. Carroll again provided most of the wickedly funny lyrics, and the tone throughout was sassy, satirical, and playful. The Algonquin wits were seen on a ship heading out past the "three-mile limit bar" so they can drink booze; the Moscow Art Theatre was spoofed as the "Russian Art Players" as they performed a hillbilly melodrama; a musical version of *Hamlet* called "Who Killed the Ghost?" featured the cast impersonating famous actors; and poet William Butler Yeats was lampooned in "Play the Queen, or Old Irish Poker" which was awarded the Ignoble Prize. Most of the players were capable of doing hilarious impersonations of theatre stars, and almost every sketch and song was a celebrity roast of sorts. Everyone from John Barrymore and Jane Cowl to Elsie Janis and Fannie Brice was a target for the comedy. British players were also included; Aline MacMahon stopped the show singing "An English Favorite" as Gertrude Lawrence and newcomer Beatrice Lillie was also ribbed by Adrienne Morrison. Both playgoers and critics enjoyed the brash revue, and it ran over five months, helping the Neighborhood Playhouse financially and bringing Broadway audiences downtown to its space. Adding to the Bohemian nature of *The Grand Street Follies* was the decision to perform on Sundays, something no Broadway house would consider until four decades later.

In the fall of 1925, a new edition of *The Grand Street Follies* opened again at the Neighborhood Playhouse, and much of the cast and artistic staff was reunited in another evening of spoofing. In "They Knew What They Wanted under the Elms," Robert Edmond Jones's celebrated farmhouse set from *Desire under the Elms* was recreated, and a travesty of four recent melodramas were enacted in the four rooms. There was a cleaned-up version of the salty war drama *What Price Glory?* titled "What Price Morning-Glories?" in which the gruff military personnel spoke with dainty speech, and the hit comedy *Abie's Irish Rose* was turned into an Italian opera called "L'Irlandesa Rosa dell'Abie." Once again impersonation of stars ran rampant, climaxing in "Mr. and Mrs. Guardsman" with Carroll in drag doing a wild spoof of Lynn Fontanne. The songs for the show were less impressive than the comedy, especially in light of the Theatre Guild's recent musical revue *The Garrick Gaities* on Broadway, which boasted numbers by the unknown Richard Rodgers and Lorenz Hart. All the same, the second *The Grand Street Follies* was very popular, running over eighteen weeks.

POLLY

[10 October 1925, Cherry Lane Playhouse, 43 performances] a "ballad opera" by John Gay. *Score:* Gay (lyrics), various (music). *Cast:* Dorothy Brown, William S. Rainey, Geneva Harrison, Charles Trout, Edmund Forde, Maude Allan, Richard Abbott.

John Gay's 1728 "ballad opera" *The Beggar's Opera* is widely known today as a landmark in the history of musical theatre, but it is too often forgotten that it was a very controversial piece of theatre in its day. Gay was active in British politics and used the play to satirize his rival Sir Robert Walpole in the character of the mischievous Macheath. Walpole was furious when the piece became widely popular; therefore, when Gay penned a sequel titled *Polly*, Walpole used his considerable powers to have Lord Chamberlain refuse permission to have it performed. Gay's supporters had the play privately published, but there was no stage production until 1777, long after Gay had died. The plot of *Polly* follows directly after *The Beggar's Opera*. Having narrowly escaped the gallows, Macheath (William S. Rainey) abandons his wife Polly (Dorothy Brown) and sails to the West Indies with his prostitute-lover

Jenny Diver (Geneva Harrison). There he becomes a pirate and continues his rascally ways. Polly follows him to the New World and is content to take back the bigamist until he is caught and executed for his pirate crimes. After some bitter mourning, Polly weds the Indian chief Cawwawkee (Charles Trout). Even more outrageous than *The Beggar's Opera*, *Polly* was another attack on Gay's political adversaries, and the story is more far-fetched than the original. Again Gay took popular folk tunes and familiar melodies and turned them into opera "airs" which made the action even more exaggerated. The first New York production of *Polly* was seen Off Broadway in 1925, and it met with a mixed response. Although *The Beggar's Opera* was still regularly revived in Great Britain, the piece was not as popular in the States in the twentieth century and audience interest in its sequel was limited; *Polly* closed inside of six weeks. Yet this mounting is noteworthy because it helped define Off Broadway as a place where obscure European works could be presented in New York. This had been going on with plays for some time, but *Polly* was the first foreign musical to premiere away from the Street. Eventually Off Broadway would introduce or bring recognition to many non-American musical works, the most famous example being *The Threepenny Opera* in the 1950s.

BUNK OF *1926*

[16 February 1926, Heckscher Theatre, 38 performances; Broadhurst Theatre, 104 performances] a musical revue by Gene Lockhart, Percy Waxman. *Score:* Lockhart (music and lyrics), Waxman (lyrics). *Cast:* Lockhart, Jay Fassett, Carol Joyce, Hazel Shelley, Milton Reick, John Maxwell, Pauline Blair, Boots McKenna.

Roaring Twenties slang proliferated in revue titles on and Off Broadway. "Nifties," "Vogues," "Snapshots," "Brevities," "Revels," "Topics," and "Nix Nax" were among the catch phrases found on marquees. The Off-Broadway revue *Bunk of 1926* was similarly up-to-date, and the year in the title suggested that the show might lead to an annual series. The revue was successful enough to move to Broadway and return in the summer for a second edition, but subsequent *Bunks* did not surface. The revue was the brainchild of character actor Gene Lockhart, who would later enjoy a long career in talking pictures. In 1926 he wrote the sketches, music, and lyrics for this show, as well as staging it and performing in many of the skits and songs. The tone was silly and irreverent, the pacing was fast, and the thirty-five scenes were brief.

"Bunk" was the new slang term for empty talk or blarney, and some of the sketches employed double-talk, such as "Good Old Smill," which lampooned the idle conversation heard in British drawing room plays, or the political send-up "Vote for McGuff." Show business was the target of several songs and scenes, from the opening chorus number titled "You Never Hear a Word They're Singing" and the wry commentary on "Those Mammy Singers (Those Mammy Boys)" to the ballet satire "Aube—Un Ballet Fantastique (Dawn—A Fantastic Ballet)" and the silent film parody "A Movie Melodrama." The latest dance craze was ribbed in the song "Do You Do the Charleston?"; the sassy love song was called "You Told Me That You Loved Me But You Never Told Me Why"; and "The Amalgamated Rivetters' and Plume Knotters' Glee Club" presented singing union workers. (A decade later such a concept would lead to the long-running revue *Pins and Needles*.) *Bunk of 1926* was so well received by the public that, after running five weeks at the Heckscher Theatre downtown, Lockhart and his staff did some major rewriting and recasting and reopened on Broadway at the Broadhurst Theatre. Critics had been stingy in their praise Off Broadway but admitted the show was much improved the second time around. After running out the season, *Bunk of 1926* reopened again in a summer edition that consisted of mostly new material by new writers (Lockhart was out of the picture by this time) and a mostly new cast, which included Thomas "Fats" Waller and his partner Jo Trent in a few numbers. Hidden among the credits for the Broadway version of *Bunk of 1926* was young playwright Lillian Hellman as the production's press agent.

BAD HABITS OF 1926

[30 April 1926, Greenwich Village Theatre, 19 performances] a musical revue by Irving S. Strouse. *Score:* Manning Sherwin (music), Arthur Herzog (lyrics). *Cast:* Martin Wolfson, Robert Montgomery, Billy Murray, Flora Borden, Harriet and Katherine Hamill, Ralph Reader, Day Tuttle, Willard Tobias.

Also putting a year in its title, *Bad Habits of 1926* may have dreamt of becoming an annual affair, but instead it was a two-week flop. The critics who traveled down to the Village to see it gave the show some of the most vicious notices of the season despite some promising young talent in the cast. All the same, *Bad Habits of 1926* is worth at least a footnote here because it included a spoof of operetta that illustrated a satirical, very Off-Broadway attitude toward the Street. There had been similar parodies in Broadway revues in the 1920s, but this snide piece titled "The Student Robin Hood of Pilsen" was probably the most wicked. The Twenties being something of a golden age for American operettas, some critics may not have shared the revue's sense of humor about such lyrical hits as *Robin Hood*, *The Student Prince*, and *The Prince of Pilsen*. Judging from the reviews, the parody was not particularly witty, but it must have hit its marks. After the Depression pretty much killed off the old-time operetta on Broadway, such satires seemed toothless. Only in the 1940s and 1950s would Off-Broadway return to ribbing the long-gone genre, and by then it would be more nostalgic than vicious. The much later *Little Mary Sunshine* owes a passing nod to *Bad Habits of 1926*.

THE GRAND STREET FOLLIES

[15 June 1926, Neighborhood Playhouse, 55 performances] a musical revue by Agnes Morgan. *Score:* Lily Hyland (music), Morgan (lyrics), various. *Cast:* Morgan, Albert Carroll, Dorothy Sands, Helen Arthur, Marc Loebell, Paula Trueman, John Roche, Ian Maclaren, Jessica Dragonette, Tom Morgan.

THE GRAND STREET FOLLIES

[19 May 1927, Neighborhood Playhouse, 148 performances] a musical revue by Agnes Morgan. *Score:* Max Ewing (music), Morgan (lyrics), various. *Cast:* Morgan, Albert Carroll, Dorothy Sands, Marc Loebell, John Roche, Paula Trueman, Lois Shore, Aline Bernstein, Otto Hulicius, Junius Matthews, Lily Lubell.

The Neighborhood Playhouse continued its revue series at the end of each season, opening the shows in its downtown space even though the musicals were starting to look more and more like Broadway. The formula of play spoofs and impersonations of stars was repeated and, since there were always new dramas and new faces to parody, the revue was far from stale. Dorothy Sands took on Beatrice Lillie again, placing her at the North Pole, and did her own version of the villainous Mother Goddam in *The Shanghai*

Gesture, though here she was called Mother Goshdarn. *Uncle Tom's Cabin* was given a modern Russian interpretation with a constructivist setting (the dead characters went to heaven on an Otis elevator), *Jack and Jill* was given a weighty, symbolic approach by the Theatre Guild, and the Eugene O'Neill one-act tragedy *In the Zone* was turned into an Eskimo musical. (One of the numbers in this sequence, "Little Igloo for Two," was composed by beginner Arthur Schwartz.) Personages ranging from Al Smith to Irving Berlin were impersonated with uncanny accuracy, always a highlight of *The Grand Street Follies*. The revue ran through the summer and might have been able to continue on, but in the fall the Neighborhood Playhouse needed the theatre for its "serious" season.

At the end of the following season, the 1927 edition featured a new composer, Max Ewing, but the songs were always the least memorable aspect of *The Grand Street Follies* not changing the show all that much. Carroll and Sands were featured as they impersonated Mrs. Fiske, the Barrymores, Jane Cowl, and other stars. There was also a caricature of Calvin Coolidge, called Cautious Cal (Junius Matthews), caught up in a Gilbert and Sullivan-like operetta about a presidential press conference. "Stars with Stripes" was a prison spoof; "Jazz Baby Learns Aesthetic Dancing" satirized modern dance; "Close Harmony at Detroit" was a minstrel show parody; and academia was taken to task in the sketches "Why Girls Leave Home" and "A Morning Lecture and Its Results." Although this edition opened in the Neighborhood Playhouse's downtown venue, it moved to Broadway's Little Theatre after a few weeks and stayed for a very profitable four and a half months. This move allowed the revue to continue running into the fall without disrupting the regular Neighborhood Playhouse season. The plan worked so well that *The Grand Street Follies'* editions in May 1928 and May 1929 opened directly on Broadway and the series was no longer an Off-Broadway project. (Although no longer situated on Grand Street, the last two editions continued to use the title *The Grand Street Follies*.) The Depression put an end to the annual shows (as it did to most revue series), but the memory of the witty, up-to-date musicals by the Neighborhood Playhouse remained vivid for a whole generation of theatregoers who saw them in the 1920s.

KYKUNKOR (*THE WITCH WOMAN*)

[10 June 1934, Little Theatre, 65 performances] a musical dance drama by Asadata Dafora (Horton). *Score:* Dafora (music and lyrics). *Cast:* Dafora, Musu Esmai, Abdul Essen, Mirammu, Tuguese, Rimeru Shikeru.

By the mid-1930s the term "Off Broadway" was being used to denote small theatres and other performance venues away from the Theatre District. The African "dance opera" Kykunkor performed at a handful of these out-of-the-way places before arriving on Broadway and finding an audience for eight weeks. The unusual program was the work of the African American Asadtata Dafora (né Horton) whose ancestors were slaves brought to Nova Scotia four generations earlier. Dafora spent years studying the music and dance of Africa, transcribing tribal songs and notating traditional dance ceremonies. He put his knowledge of African life into a play that included chanted songs and lengthy dance rituals. The plot was simple and celebratory: the maidens of the Mendi tribe are taught by the chaperone Otobone (Rimera Shikeru) how to become good wives. When the young man Bokari (Dafora) arrives in the maiden village to choose a bride, the girls perform a ceremonial dance. He selects a beautiful bride (Musu Esmai), and preparations are made for the wedding. Bokari's father Chief Burah (Tuguese) arrives, and the son sings of his love for the bride. During the ceremony, the witch woman Kykunkor (Mirammu) enters, casts a spell on Bokari that leaves him on the brink of death, but a dance is performed to drive away the evil spell and the bridegroom recovers. The evening ended with a dance of joy as the couple was reunited. Dafora not only wrote the script and songs and played a major role, he directed and choreographed the piece and designed the sets and costumes. He was able to interest a small theatre company called the Unity Theatre Group in letting him and his performers (who used African names rather than their American ones) use the hall on East 23rd Street. The strange, hypnotic production ran thirteen performances and garnered enough interest that Dafora was able to secure an auditorium at City College for four more performances; it then went to the Chanin Auditorium high up in the Chanin Building for fifteen more showings. Finally Dafora was able to secure a Broadway house, the intimate Little Theatre, where the show was reviewed by all the major papers and was generally commended as a unique and enthralling theatrical experience. Interest in the African piece was such that in early 1935 Dafora and his company returned to the Chanin Building for a brief reprise. *Kykunkor* was certainly an unlikely entry in the New York theatre season but, because it first gained recognition Off Broadway, it survived and flourished.

PROVINCETOWN FOLLIES

[3 November 1935, Provincetown Playhouse, 63 performances] a musical revue by Frederick Herendeen, Gwynn Langdon, Barrie Oliver, George K.

Arthur. *Score:* Sylvan Green, Dave Stamper, Trevor Jones, Arthur Jones, Mary Schaeffer (music), Herendeen, Oliver, Arthur, Langdon (lyrics). *Cast:* Oliver, Beatrice Kay, Phyllis Austen, Billy Greene, Cyril Smith, Eileen Graves, Theodore Stanhope.

Just as the distinguished, very arty Neighborhood Playhouse had presented a series of *Follies* in the 1920s, the equally distinguished Little Theatre group, the Provincetown Players—which had first introduced Eugene O'Neill to theatregoers—produced its own revue in its Off-Broadway venue. The show did not spawn a series, but it was successful enough to run nearly eight weeks in Depression-era New York. Surprising for a company that prided itself on discovering American talent, the revue was decidedly British in tone. The show's host and narrator was Barrie Oliver, a continental favorite who was popular in both London and Paris nightclubs. Some of the most praised sketches and songs had a decided English flavor about them, such as comic Cyril Smith's hilarious monologue about a Cockney lion tamer. While some of the company was quite young, veterans sat on the creative staff, particularly composer Dave Stamper, who had scored several *Ziegfeld Follies'* entries decades before. The *Provincetown Follies* also boasted a superb comedienne in Beatrice Kay whose parody of a suicidal torch singer stopped the show. Several hands provided the music and lyrics for the score, but the only song to become popular was the interpolation "Red Sails in the Sunset." The ballad by Hugh Williams (aka Will Grosz) and Jimmy Kennedy was already popular in Great Britain, and when Phyllis Austen sang it in the *Provincetown Follies*, it soon became a hit in the States. Another pleasing aspect of the revue was the dancing staged by Mary Read. She had been a protégé of the innovative choreographer John Tiller and was able to recreate his distinctive, precision-style dance in this and other shows after Tiller's death a decade earlier. *Provincetown Follies* was one of the few Off-Broadway musicals in the 1930s to convince dwindling audiences to travel down to Greenwich Village for some alternative entertainment.

PINS AND NEEDLES

[27 November 1937, Labor Stage, 1,108 performances] a musical revue by Arthur Arent, Charles Friedman, Marc Blitzstein, Emanuel Eisenberg,

David Gregory. *Score:* Harold Rome (music and lyrics). *Cast:* Millie Weitz, Ruth Rubinstein, Al Levy, Lynne Jaffee, Hy Goldstein, Nettie Harary, Paul Seymour.

One of the longest-running revues in the American theatre, the smart little show started out as an amateur theatrical but eventually turned into a landmark of sorts. *Pins and Needles* was created as an amusement for members of the International Ladies Garment Workers' of America union (ILGWA). Louis Schaeffer, who was responsible for theatrical activities for the union, wanted a musical revue that would entertain current members and help recruit new members to the American Federation on Labor (AFL) organization. The union had recently bought the building housing the intimate 299-seat Princess Theatre and turned it into a recreation center for its members. Schaeffer renamed the auditorium the Labor Stage. He hired Charles Friedman to assemble and direct the revue using garment workers who would rehearse two nights a week. Friedman recruited a handful of writers for the sketches and unknown songwriter Harold Rome to write the score. The large cast of union workers, who had little or no stage experience, rehearsed nearly a year before the show was ready to be performed only for a few weekends. No critics came to the opening night of the amateur theatrical, but soon word of mouth hit the newspapers and glowing reviews followed. The demand for tickets meant *Pins and Needles* needed to play a regular performance schedule which caused a problem for the garment workers and their day jobs. A deal was made in which ILGWA members in the cast could temporarily leave their garment job and join another union, Actors' Equity, which belonged to rival Commission of Industrial Organizations (CIO), then return to their regular jobs after their participation in the revue was over. *Pins and Needles* later moved to the 849-seat Windsor Theatre and changed its title a few times: *New Pins and Needles*, *Pins and Needles of 1938*, and *Pins and Needles of 1939*. It also changed its songs and material throughout the three-year run to remain topical.

Despite its labor union agenda, *Pins and Needles* was far from ponderous or sermonizing. Instead the sketches and songs took a lighthearted look at labor relations, world affairs, and love. The cast may have been inexperienced, but the production was far from an embarrassing amateur affair, particularly with its first-class score. Rome's only experience had been writing songs and sketches for summer camp revues which Friedman had seen. He hired Rome for the ILGWA show, and the songs Rome provided were tuneful, satiric, leftist, yet pleasing. The theme song for the revue was "Sing Me a Song with

Social Significance" in which the cast proclaimed, with mock determination, that love without social impact was now *passé*. "One Big Union for Two" was a sly little ditty that used labor-management terminology in a love song format. "Doin' the Reactionary" was an acid number that encouraged a new dance step with sociopolitical bite. Not all of the songs referred to the union. Current events were spoofed in such songs as "Four Little Angels of Peace," which pictured Hitler, Mussolini, Anthony Eden, and a Japanese leader, all dressed as angels and justifying their aggressive takeovers with playful innocence. (Joseph Stalin and Neville Chamberlain were among the figures added to this number during the run.) Some numbers had no agenda at all and captured the everyday lives of the union workers: "Nobody Makes a Pass at Me" was the comic lament of a young lady who has bought and used all the beauty products she heard advertised on the radio, but her love life still hasn't picked up; "Chain Store Daisy" was a seriocomic character number about a Vassar grad who can only get a job selling ladies' foundation garments at Macy's; and "Sunday in the Park" was about Central Park as a haven for the working class who cannot afford to leave the city when a heat wave strikes.

Pins and Needles launched Rome's career, but few of the performers left the garment trade to become performers. For them the revue was a lark, and this may have added to the cozy and personal nature of the piece. The cast did a special performance to celebrate the twenty-fifth anniversary of the founding of the Department of Labor, and all the top officials attended the show which, by request of Labor Secretary Frances Perkins, was slightly censored to avoid offending certain political figures. But the company performed the unexpurgated version of *Pins and Needles* for a command performance at the White House for the Roosevelts, who quite enjoyed the show's slant to current events. Although its songs still hold up, *Pins and Needles* has rarely been revived because of this topicality. (There was no film version, but there was a television production in 1966 featuring Bob Dishy, Elaine Stritch, Josephine Premise, and Bobby Short.) Yet in its day *Pins and Needles* was a true alternative to what audiences were seeing in the big Broadway houses, and it foreshadowed the kind of irreverent wit and playfulness that would become the basis for Off-Broadway musical revues in the 1950s.

THE CRADLE WILL ROCK

[16 June 1937, Venice Theatre, 19 performances; Windsor Theatre, 108 performances] a musical play by Marc Blitzstein. *Score:* Blitzstein (music

and lyrics). *Cast:* Will Geer, Howard Da Silva, Olive Stanton, Edward
Fuller, Hiram Sherman, Blanche Collins, John Hoysradt, John Adair,
Peggy Coudray, Edward Hemmer, Bert Weston, Warren Goddard, Dulce
Fox.

A legendary music drama that is as famous for its opening night as it is for
itself, *The Cradle Will Rock* was a leftist work that broke the barriers of
the traditional musical and foreshadowed the later political musicals like
Cabaret, Hair, and *Assassins.* Marc Blitzstein wrote the score and the libretto,
which was set in Steeletown, U.S.A., a city run by Mr. Mister (Will Geer)
for the benefit of himself and his spoiled family and cronies. He controls the
press, overrides the church, and rules everything through his own Liberty
Committee. The upstanding labor organizer Larry Foreman (Howard Da
Silva) leads the steelworkers in a revolt and topples Mister and his gang. The
sung-through "opera" included commentary by various characters who sometimes served as narrators as well: the oppressed Harry Druggist (John Adair),
the knowing prostitute Moll (Olive Stanton), the pompous Reverend Shannon (Edward Hemmer), the corrupt doctor Mr. Specialist (Frank Marvel),
the toadying journalist Editor Daily (Bert Weston), and the self-absorbed "art
for art's sake" artists Dauber (Warren Goddard) and Yasha (Edward Fuller).
The characters were written in black and white, much as in a political cartoon, and there was no subtlety to the work. Yet it was powerful all the same
as it sneered, preached, protested, and cheered its way through its musical
episodes. The songs were harsh, tended to eschew melody, and often came
across as musical proclamations. There was no question that Blitzstein was
echoing the abrasive sound of the 1920s Bertolt Brecht–Kurt Weill music
dramas in Germany, though this form was not yet familiar to American audiences. (New York theatregoers would not discover those shows until the Off-
Broadway production of *The Threepenny Opera* which Blitzstein translated
and adapted in 1954.) Blitzstein himself described *The Cradle Will Rock* as
"a labor opera" that utilized "realism, romance, vaudeville, comic strip, Gilbert and Sullivan, Brecht, and agitprop." The realism and romance are hard
to find in the score, but there is surely an eclectic mix of the other forms in
the songs. The prostitute sang the searing indictment "Nickel under the Foot"
about how easy it is to have morals when one has money. When a worker
was hurt in a factory accident and he received no compensation because
the company bribed the doctor to say he was drunk at the time, his sister
(Blanche Collins) sang the seething "Joe Worker" asking when the average

Joe will get wise to the situation. In "Freedom of the Press," the editor argued that he was free to print the side of the truth that paid the best. Foreman led the cast in singing the title number at the finale, a rallying march that states the social system is changing, a storm is coming, and the cradle will rock. Other numbers were lighter in tone but had just as strident a subtext. The self-centered artists sang "Art for Art's Sake" encouraging one to be blind to reality; "Honolulu" was a South Seas parody that commented on the U.S. takeover of Hawaii; and "Croon Spoon" made fun of popular escapist music as it purposely kept hitting "wrong" notes in the melody. In 1938 members of the original cast recorded most of the score at a studio; the first attempt at a theatre cast recording of an American musical.

The story about the premiere of *The Cradle Will Rock* is much more interesting than the libretto of the musical itself. Blitzstein completed his "opera" in 1936, but Broadway producers were not interested in such an inflammatory piece. When the Actors' Repertory Company in New York agreed to produce it, John Houseman came on as producer and twenty-one-year-old Orson Welles was hired as director. In December 1936, union strikes in Flint, Michigan, led to riots that paralleled the events in *The Cradle Will Rock*. The Actors' Rep grew nervous and canceled the production. As a result Houseman and Welles went to the Federal Theatre Project. This was a government-sponsored program, Works Progress Association (WPA), that financed professional theatre to give employment to thousands of out-of-work theatre artists and to offer low-cost entertainment to Depression-stricken America. *The Cradle Will Rock* would be the first musical offering in the New York branch of the program, and the Maxine Elliott Theatre on Broadway was booked for the premiere. After strikes in Chicago led to another riot in which women and children were killed, the authorities at the Federal Theatre Project panicked and canceled the production. They also obtained a court injunction stating that the actors in *The Cradle Will Rock* could not perform the piece on any stage, and the musicians' union told its members that they could not play in any other venue without being paid Broadway wages, much higher than the agreed-upon Federal Theatre Project rates. Nonetheless, Houseman and Welles searched for another locale for the production as audiences gathered at the Maxine Elliott to see if the performance would go on. Police were stationed there to make sure no one entered and to see that no scenery or costumes were removed since they were government property. At the last minute, Houseman secured the out-of-the-way Venice Theatre, and Welles led the actors and audience for a twenty-block parade to the show's new home, gathering curious New Yorkers along the way, increasing the crowd size to over one thousand people by the time they arrived at the Venice. The cast was required to buy tickets and sit among the audience, and Blitzstein was the only one allowed on stage because he was not a member of the musicians' union. From his out-of-tune upright piano on the bare stage, Blitzstein pounded out the opening chords of the show and *The Cradle Will Rock* began, the actors caught in spotlights as they performed from the orchestra seats and the balcony. Blitzstein himself filled in, playing roles of actors who would not risk being seen in the renegade production. The unconventional presentation made the radical show seem even more daring, and the cheers and ovation at the end of the evening were overwhelming. The critics who joined the throng wrote about the unique event in their newspapers, and patrons clamored for tickets. Houseman was fired from the Federal Theatre Project for insubordination, and Welles quit; the two men then formed the Mercury Theatre Company. They repeated *The Cradle Will Rock* for nineteen performances at the Venice, then it played in various venues around New York before setting off to steel mill towns in Pennsylvania and Ohio. When the musical returned to Manhattan, it was presented on the bare stage of the Windsor Theatre. Although the actors performed from the stage, the only props were some chairs and the lone piano that served as the drugstore counter, the judge's bench, and other locales. Critics and several audience members thought the piece a simple-minded rant with clumsy writing and tuneless songs, but the vibrant cast and the electricity the whole experience conjured up each night was strong enough to attract playgoers. This version of the musical ran three months during which Welles even arranged for a radio broadcast of the show. Regional productions followed, causing controversy everywhere it was presented. The young writer Studs Terkel appeared in the Chicago version, and the Harvard student Leonard Bernstein directed and conducted a Cambridge production which was branded by civic leaders as an "indecent" Communist diatribe. New York heard Blitzstein's full orchestrations for the first time in a 1947 concert version conducted by Bernstein. That same year *The Cradle Will Rock* was revived for a month at the City Center with Alfred Drake as Foreman. The original Foreman, Howard Da Silva, directed both a 1960 production at the New York City Opera and a 1964 Off-Broadway revival featuring Jerry Orbach as Foreman and ran ten weeks. Houseman himself directed a 1983 revival by The Acting Company, featuring Patti LuPone as Moll, which toured the States, played in London and New York, and was filmed for PBS. The 1999 film *Cradle Will Rock* was more about the circumstances leading up to the opening night of the 1938 production than a movie version of the musical. The screenplay by director Tim Robbins mixes fact and fiction, yet the movie is an interesting depiction of the times, and scenes from the musical were shown near the end of the film. *The Cradle Will Rock* is still revived by colleges and regional theatres on occasion but usually proves more interesting historically than theatrically.

It is impossible now to recapture the excitement of that first performance. It was a landmark evening and a historic night in the chronicle of alternative theatre in America.

NO FOR AN ANSWER

[5 January 1941, Mecca Auditorium, 3 performances] a musical play by Marc Blitzstein. *Score:* Marc Blitzstein (music and lyrics). *Cast:* Carol Channing, Olive Deering, Bert Conway, Lloyd Gough, Martin Wolfson, Curt Conway.

The only noteworthy Off-Broadway musical of the 1940s was a three-performance flop titled *No for an Answer*, yet this seemingly minor footnote in the American musical theatre refuses to be forgotten or overlooked. The leftist music-theatre piece was by Marc Blitzstein who, as he had with *The Cradle Will Rock*, wrote the book, music, and lyrics. In fact, *No for an Answer* was written in 1937 right after that landmark production. At a 1930s Catskills resort, the workers are mostly Greek and Jewish immigrants from the city who are poorly paid but are given room and board for the summer. With the end of the season in sight and unemployment looming, the workers form the Diogenes Social Club at a Greek restaurant and begin a choral group, but the songs they sing are those of protest, and soon the organization attempts to form a union. Local officials manage to have the restaurant closed on a legal technicality forcing the workers to hold a demonstration on the steps of the town's courthouse. A mob of residents and the police attack the crowd killing some of the leaders, and the restaurant is burned to the ground. The next day the workers find that the mimeograph machine in the basement has survived the fire, and they vow to continue printing pamphlets and spreading the voice of the people. It was a heavy-handed piece of propaganda (Blitzstein was a known and very vocal Communist) and dealt in black and white except for the songs which sometimes overflowed with humanity. "Make the Heart Be Stone" and the title number are strident protest songs, but there is a lyrical quality to "Purest Kind of a Guy" and "Secret Singing." The song "Francie" is distinctive in that the melody is hummed without lyrics, but spoken prose interrupts the tune and conveys the message. The most enjoyable numbers are those that relieve the tension, such as the vaudeville turn "Penny Candy" and the satiric "Fraught" and "Dimples" which satirized the escapist pop songs of the day. These last two were sung by Bennington College student

Carol Channing who made her New York debut in the show. Blitzstein envisioned *No for an Answer* as a full-scale musical with orchestrations and highly trained singers. (He called the piece "an American opera.") After four years of being turned down by various producers, Blitzstein arranged for a bare-bones production with himself at the piano (as he had for *The Cradle Will Rock*), and it played on three successive Sunday nights at the Mecca Auditorium. His hope was that a producer would see the show and give it a full mounting. But in the months before America entered World War II, leftist ideas were losing potency and *No for an Answer* closed for, what seemed, forever. (Amazingly, an abridged original cast recording was made.) African American singer and activist Paul Robeson recorded "Purist Kind of Guy," and other parts of the score were performed on occasion in concert. Interest in Blitzstein was revived decades later, and there was a concert version of *No for an Answer* in 1960. Blitzstein's orchestrations were finally heard for the first time in the 2001 revival performed by the graduate students of San Francisco's American Conservatory Theatre's Master of Fine Arts program. The script had not only improved with time but there was a new appreciation for the score. While *The Cradle Will Rock* will always find the occasional revival, *No for an Answer* is an unlikely candidate for production. All the same, it is a noteworthy work by one of America's most unique theatre songwriters.

Chapter Two

———————○———————

A New Arena:
The 1950s

MANY THEATRE HISTORIANS POINT TO THE EVENING of April 24, 1952, as the date in which Off Broadway came into its own. On that night a revival of Tennessee Williams's *Summer and Smoke* opened downtown at the Circle in the Square Theatre with a luminous performance by Geraldine Page as the spinster Alma under the concise direction of Jose Quintero. The original 1948 Broadway production of the Williams drama had been a modest success (one hundred performances), but Off Broadway the play shone as it never had before. The intimate space, the revealing interpretation by the director and the cast, and the opportunity to revitalize an American play were not missed by the press or the public. *Summer and Smoke* was a hit (357 performances), making Page a star and Quintero a first-rank director, and turning Off Broadway into a destination for playgoers seeking quality theatre. That quality had been growing since 1949 when Actors' Equity Association ruled that its members could work in Off-Broadway theatres for a rate that, while less than Broadway scale, was fair and appealing. With many professional actors now at their disposal, Off-Broadway companies and producers were encouraged to improve the playhouses and the productions. No longer would Off Broadway have the taint of being amateur. Costs rose, as did ticket prices, but both were still far below those on the Street. Many movie theatres around town, which closed as the decade and the popularity of television progressed, were turned into playhouses, and by the end of the 1950s, there were about forty recognized venues for Off Broadway productions, totaling around one hundred productions each season. There were many other tiny and unofficial spaces with offerings that were less professional and far from commercial. (In the next decade they would eventually be labeled Off Off Broadway.) Each season brought more and more recognition to Off Broadway, and the alternative venue was helping to shape the nature of theatre in the city.

Among the new aspects of Off Broadway during the 1950s was the emergence of the musical. There were virtually none playing at the start of the decade, but by the end there were long-running musical hits and a wide variety of also-rans. Off Broadway was introducing new composer-lyricist talent and making musical stars. And this was done despite (or perhaps because of) a flourishing decade for musicals on Broadway. The 1950s may not have offered the high number of musicals on Broadway as in previous decades, but it was a golden age of sorts, introducing many musicals that are still in the revival repertory. *Guys and Dolls, The King and I, Wonderful Town, The Pajama Game, Peter Pan, The Boy Friend, Damn Yankees, My Fair Lady, West Side Story, The Music Man, Gypsy,* and *The Sound of Music* are among the 1950s' hits that are as familiar to audiences today as they were over half a century ago. There are few innovative or landmark shows on the list, but all of them are so well-crafted and so appealing that we will never see their like again. What did Off Broadway add during this period? Musicals that were often more demanding and not so worried about being appealing. Musicals that replaced spectacle with cleverness, belly laughs with wit, stars with promising newcomers, and popularity with bravado. Not that there were no musical hits Off Broadway in the 1950s. Some ran very long indeed, but their success was unexpected, a surprising accident that made them all the more exciting.

If the decade was a golden age for the traditional Broadway musical, the 1950s were also a high point for a genre that was rapidly disappearing on the Street: the musical revue. The few revues that opened on Broadway were either star-studded, such as *Two on the Aisle*, or hoping to make stars, as with the *New Faces* shows. Yet Off-Broadway musical revues proliferated. They were small-scale, highly satiric or even sarcastic, and filled with their own "new faces" on stage and back stage. The next generation of theatre performers and writers did not come from the book musicals but from these revues. The Off-Broadway revues were also very popular, offering audiences a kind of sass that could not be found in the Broadway musical comedies or dramas. Because these cabaret-like shows were timely and quickly dated, they are never revived and are mostly forgotten today. Yet the talent behind them would be the big players on Broadway in the next decade; therefore, the importance of the Off-Broadway revue cannot be overlooked.

Finally, an aspect of the 1950s Off Broadway that must be considered is the way the shows were proud of their alternative nature. The creators of both the revues and the book musicals often saw Broadway as too conventional, too predictable, and way too safe. They put together musicals that did not and could not belong on Broadway. They defied Broadway, made fun of it in their revues, and broke away from its format in many of its book musicals. A handful of 1950s shows attempted to transfer to Broadway but, at the end of the decade, *Once Upon a Mattress* was the only one to do so with financial success. For the most part, an Off-Broadway musical belonged Off Broadway, and it stayed there, even when it was popular enough to run several years, as in the case of *The Threepenny Opera*. One might say that the Off-Broadway musicals of the 1950s were the "purest" ever written for that venue. In succeeding decades the urge to move a successful show to Broadway would be very strong. But in the 1950s there was no reason for an Off-Broadway musical to feel inferior; a show was very happy to be Off Broadway and was proud of it.

THE THREEPENNY OPERA

[10 March 1954, Theatre De Lys, 95 performances; reopened 20 September 1955, 2,611 performances] a musical play by Marc Blitzstein based on Bertolt Brecht's *Die Dreigroschenoper*. *Score:* Kurt Weill (music), Blitzstein, Brecht (lyrics). *Cast:* Scott Merrill, Lotte Lenya, Jo Sullivan, Charlotte Rae, Leon Lishner, Beatrice Arthur, George Tyne, Gerald Price.

The Off-Broadway book musical, as we think of it today, begins with *The Threepenny Opera,* a major work of music theatre and one of the most influential of all foreign musicals. The piece has a long and interesting history, and the first time the musical was presented in New York, it was not welcomed. It was Off Broadway that turned *The Threepenny Opera* into a hit in America; and it was *The Threepenny Opera* that turned Off Broadway into a place for musical hits.

In Victorian England, the dashing villain MacHeath, better known to the police and the underworld as Mack the Knife, married Polly, the daughter of the crime syndicate boss Jonathan Peachum and his conniving wife. The parents convince the whore Jenny Diver to betray MacHeath to London police chief Tiger Brown. In jail MacHeath convinces his former lover Lucy, the daughter of Brown, to help him escape, but once again he is brought down by the jealous women in his life. About to be hanged, MacHeath is saved by a last-minute reprieve because of the Queen's coronation and is made a lord, a sarcastic ending that points out the irony of justice and goodness in the world. Based on John Gay's 18th-century ballad opera *The Beggar's Opera*, the 1928 German musical *Die Dreigoschenoper* by Kurt Weill (music) and

Bertolt Brecht (book and lyrics) was one of a handful of new versions of Gay's work that were inspired by a successful 1920 London revival of *The Beggar's Opera*. The Brecht-Weill version was first written by Elizabeth Hauptmann and utilized lyrics from Rudyard Kipling and Francois Villon in Gay's 1750 text. Brecht reworked the piece from a sly comedy of manners to a biting, scornful social drama with a sardonic sense of humor. He moved the time period of the play to Victorian England, toughened up the characters, and added a sense of menace to MacHeath's adventures, even the romantic ones. The young Weill's music was very German-sounding (despite the British characters and locale) and was often harsh and unmelodic, even as it was hypnotizing at times. Brecht was developing his theories of Epic Theatre and, although *The Threepenny Opera* was conventionally linear, the presentation was "historified" (removed in time from the audience's familiarity) and sometimes "alienated" (reminding the audience that this was a play and not reality). The numerous songs were meant to break the story line, serving as commentary rather than satisfying musical numbers, though often they were enthralling as set pieces that they broke the intellectual climate Brecht was striving for.

Die Dreigoschenoper opened in Berlin with a young Lotte Lenya playing Jenny, and the production was very successful. Subsequent productions were seen throughout Germany, as well as in Vienna, Budapest, Paris, and London. (The last was not popular; the British still preferring *The Beggar's Opera*.) The success of the piece disturbed Brecht because he felt *The Threepenny Opera* had become commercial entertainment and that the point of the music drama was lost. Against Weill's wishes, he revised his libretto and lyrics, making them more forceful and less literary. The result was an angry diatribe that was not much produced. Yet decades later new adaptations of *The Threepenny Opera* would return to this preachy version, and the results were some rather wooden and joyless theatre events. Which version Gifford Cochran and Jerrold Krimsky used for the 1933 Broadway debut of *The Threepenny Opera* is not clear, but it was a quick flop. Operetta favorites Robert Chisholm and Steffi Duna played MacHeath and Polly, generating a score that was probably more melodic than the European productions. All the same, some of the Brechtian elements must have survived because the critics described the musical as a puzzling, socialist piece and dismissed the show, though some complimented the strange but haunting Weill music. Since the production closed after twelve performances, most theatregoers were not even aware that the musical existed.

Not until after Weill's premature death in 1950 did producers look at the composer's German works, and in 1954 Carmen Capalbo and Stanley Chase presented Marc Blitzstein's translation and adaptation of the musical at the

Theatre de Lys Off Broadway. Blitzstein's own socialist musical *The Cradle Will Rock* seventeen years before was very much like the Brecht-Weill German musicals, both in the sound of the score and the approach to the drama. Blitzstein, who had been encouraged by Weill in the 1940s to translate his early German works, took a free hand with *Die Dreigoschenoper,* not worrying about a literal translation and thinking in terms of an intimate musical with a sting. His lyrics flowed more than Brecht's shouting, and often the satiric sense of humor was more accessible. Turning the grinding narrative song "Moritat: Und der Haifisch der hat Zähne" (which Cochran and Krimsky had translated as "The Legend of Mackie Messer") into the terse "(The Ballad of) Mack the Knife" was typical of Blitzstein's approach. The "Jealousy Duet" was still a battle of biting words but now with an alliterative punch that made the number funny. "Useless Song" developed from an angry list number in Brecht to a playfully sarcastic piece. MacHeath and Jenny's "Tango-Ballad" was still menacing but also very sexy. Polly and MacHeath's "Love Song" was still the most harmonious number in the score, yet Blitzstein's lyric never got saccharine. His translation of "Pirate Jenny" was chilling, yet the words flowed lyrically. All in all it was a masterful version of the score, remaining true to Brecht while finding a language that was potent and effective. Later detractors would complain that Blitzstein wasn't harsh enough and that his version was too pleasant. Brecht might have agreed. (And what he would think of Bobby Darin's best-selling pop recording of "Mack the Knife" is easy to guess.) Yet no one who saw *The Threepenny Opera* Off Broadway in the 1950s thought the show to be "pleasant." It was hard-edged, antiestablishment, and cynical as hell. Brecht's intentions had been realized.

The famous 1954 production at the Theatre de Lys, directed by Capalbo, featured an outstanding cast that included some promising new talents: Scott Merrill (MacHeath), Jo Sullivan (Polly), Beatrice Arthur (Lucy), Frederic Downs (Peachum), Charlotte Rae (Mrs. Peachum), Richard Verney (Tiger Brown), and Tige Andrews (Streetsinger). Lotte Lenya reprised her Jenny from the 1928 German original and was still as sultry and magnetic as ever. (Both Lenya and Merrill were nominated for Tony Awards, the first and only time Off-Broadway performances were included in the Broadway awards; Lenya won for Featured Actress in a Musical.) *The Threepenny Opera* was acclaimed by the press as a strange and fascinating "new" work, and the little show became the talk of the town. After its scheduled ninety-two performances, the production closed to make room for the next entry at the Theatre de Lys. The cry for tickets was such that the show reopened fifteen months later and ran just over six years, by far the longest running Off-Broadway production (musical or nonmusical) up to that time. Many playgoers who had never ventured beyond Broadway before had their first Off-Broadway experience with *The Threepenny Opera*. The musical helped define what the alternative venue could offer: intimacy that was also somewhat confrontational, a hard-edge that was still entertaining, and a spare production that was highly professional. The show was not a Broadway musical done in a small space; it was an Off-Broadway musical. In the past, size and attitude had demonstrated the difference between musicals on and off the Street. With *The Threepenny Opera*, the contrast with Broadway musicals was sharper. This slightly subversive, deliciously in-your-face show was a true alternative. It didn't belong on the Street, and its producers wisely kept it away from Broadway. Most subsequent revivals of the musical were on Broadway and, not coincidentally, were not successful.

In addition to the hundreds of productions over the years in colleges, regional theatres, and summer stock, there have been five major New York revivals of *The Threepenny Opera*. In 1966, the Stockholm Marionette Theatre of Fantasy visited Manhattan for two weeks and presented actors dressed as cutout puppets performing the text in Blitzstein's English version. A 1976 Lincoln Center production used a new and purposely unpoetic translation by Ralph Manheim and John Willett which used the word "shit" a lot so that audiences knew this was a new version. Most critics disdained the adaptation, but there was more approval for the very stylized production directed by avant-gardist Richard Foreman. The excellent cast included Raul Julia (MacHeath), Ellen Greene (Jenny), Caroline Kava (Polly), C. K. Alexander (Peachum), Elizabeth Wilson (Mrs. Peachum), and Blair Brown (Lucy). The Joseph Papp–produced mounting at the Vivian Beaumont Theatre was popular and was extended for a run of 307 performances. Rock star Sting was the attraction of the 1989 Broadway revival which, using Michael Feingold's adaptation, was billed as *3 Penny Opera*. The critics thought Sting's MacHeath a dull fellow, and the singer's fans could keep him on the boards for only sixty-five performances. John Dexter directed, and the cast also featured Alvin Epstein (Peachum), Georgia Brown (Mrs. Peachum), Maureen McGovern (Polly), Kim Criswell (Lucy), and Ethyl Eichelberger (Ballad Singer). *The Threepenny Opera* returned to Off Broadway in 2006 with a revival by the Jean Cocteau Repertory that ran ten weeks. The production featured Chad A. Suitts as MacHeath and used the Blitzstein translation. Unanimous pans greeted the 2006 Roundabout Theatre Company revival directed by Scott Elliott using a new version by Wallace Shawn. The main complaint concerned the vastly different acting styles used throughout the campy, overblown production which featured a bisexual MacHeath (Alan Cumming), a campy Jenny (Cyndi Lauper), a drag queen Lucy (Brian Charles Rooney), a shrill Mrs. Peachum (Ana Gasteyer), and a sly, understated Peachum portrayed by Jim Dale, who got the only good notices. There was no demand to extend the run beyond its scheduled seventy-seven performances. *The Threepenny Opera* was filmed in Germany in 1931 by G. W. Pabst with Rudolf Forster as Mackie Messer and Lotte Lenya as Jenny, and again in 1962 with Curt Jurgens as MacHeath, Hildegarde Kneff as Jenny, and Gert Frobe as Peachum. Raul Julia reprised his MacHeath in an English-language film titled *Mack the Knife* (1990) written and directed by Menahem Golan. The score was greatly abridged, but the cast was impressive: Julia Migenes (Jenny), Richard Harris (Peachum), Rachel Robertson (Polly), Julie Walters (Mrs. Peachum), Erin Donovan (Lucy), Bill Nighy (Tiger Brown), and Roger Daltry (Streetsinger).

THE GOLDEN APPLE

[11 March 1954, Phoenix Theatre, 173 performances; Alvin Theatre, 125 performances] a musical comedy by John Latouche based on Homer's *The Iliad* and *The Odyssey*. *Score:* Jerome Moross (music), Latouche (lyrics). *Cast:* Stephen Douglass, Priscilla Gillette, Kaye Ballard, Jack Whiting, Bibi Osterwald, Portia Nelson, Jerry Stiller, Jonathan Lucas, Dean Michener, Shannon Bolin, Julian Patrick.

One of the American musical theatre's most beloved failures, this sparkling and charming show has gained plenty of fans over the years. The witty and ingenious book and lyrics by John Latouche and the nimble pastiche music by Jerome Moross have given the show cult status, yet even the sets, costumes, and original performers have become the stuff of musical theatre legend. All the same, *The Golden Apple* has never entered the mainstream of revived shows. Some believe it is too clever, too brilliant, too original to have wide appeal. The musical, after all, is based on Homeric epics. Yet rarely has a *succes d'estime* been so much fun.

Soon after Ulysses (Stephen Douglass) and his men return from the Spanish-American War to their little town of Angel's Roost, Washington, the traveling salesman Paris (Jonathan Lucas) arrives in a hot air balloon from the neighboring town of Rhododendron. At the county fair, he is asked to judge the apple pie contest and chooses that of the mayor's wife Lovey Mars (Bibi Osterwald) because she promises to introduce him to Helen (Kaye Ballard), the sexy and bored wife of Sheriff Menelaus (Dean Michener). Helen seduces Paris and agrees to run off with him to Rhododendron just to cause a ruckus and get her name in the papers. The mayor Hector (Jack

Whiting) calls on Ulysses and the other war heroes and they follow in pursuit even though Ulysses does not wish to be separated again from his loving wife Penelope (Priscilla Gillette). In Rhododendron, Ulysses beats Paris in a boxing match, and the men from Angel's Roost win back Helen, but on their return are confronted by the evils of the big city, unscrupulous stockbrokers, seductive sirens and nymphs, and even a female scientist Miss Minerva (Portia Nelson) who sends some of the men into outer space. The witch Circe (Gillette) plots with Paris to murder Ulysses, but instead Paris kills Achilles (Julian Patrick), and Ulysses eventually returns home to his faithful Penelope. This retelling of *The Iliad* and *The Odyssey* tales was sung-through with no dialogue, and the score telling the story not so much in opera terms but more as a series of vaudeville numbers. With the men all away at war, the women lamented with "Nothing Ever Happens in Angel's Roost." Helen sang the languid blues number "Lazy Afternoon" as she undressed Paris, a dancing character who never spoke. Penelope sang the touching song of yearning "Windflowers" and joined her husband in the warm domestic duet "It's the Going Home Together." Lovey Mars stopped the show with the Hawaiian-flavored "By Goona-Goona Lagoon"; the men sang the lusty "Helen Is Always Willing"; and the sly stockbrokers (Michener and Whiting) did the vaudeville turn "Scylla and Charybdis," a dandy pastiche of Mr. Gallagher and Mr. Shean. Latouche's lyrics were scintillating throughout, and Moross's music toyed with all kinds of American idioms, from waltzes and vaudeville to ragtime and blues. It is a landmark score, but few have ever heard the whole thing. The original cast recording was so abridged that few songs come across very well, and the album featured rhymed narration by Whiting that was as irritating as it was unnecessary. Many point to the unsatisfying recording as one of the reasons *The Golden Apple* is not revived as much as it should be.

Although movie composer Moross and Broadway lyricist Latouche had some admirable credits, they had difficulty in finding someone to produce *The Golden Apple*. After being turned down by several Broadway presenters, the musical was picked up by the ambitious Off-Broadway Phoenix Theatre, which produced revivals and new works. It was the troupe's first musical venture, and the budget was limited to $75,000. Scenic designers William and Jean Eckart came up with a series of refreshing drops and set pieces that were very stylized, and Alvin Colt designed the colorful, cartoonish costumes. Norman Lloyd was the nominal director, but Hanya Holm staged and choreographed all the musical numbers which were, in fact, the whole show. The cast included the veteran Jack Whiting, but the rest of the company was young and up-and-coming talents, most memorably Kaye Ballad as a funny, sexy Helen, Stephen Douglass and Priscilla Gillette in full voice as

Ulysses and Penelope, and Bibi Osterwald as a handful of oversized characters. (Many of the cast members doubled to keep down expenses, and their performances were more enjoyable because of it.) Most of the reviews were highly enthusiastic, many using superlatives along the lines of "a milestone in the American musical theatre." The few naysayers found the show clever but hollow, yet audiences were willing to give the Off-Broadway musical a chance. (It should be pointed out that *The Golden Apple* opened the day after *The Threepenny Opera*. This may have taken attention away from the American work, but it also made it clear that Off Broadway was the place to see interesting and unusual musicals.) After doing brisk business for five months Off Broadway, *The Golden Apple* transferred to a large house on Broadway and struggled to last sixteen weeks; a hit Off Broadway had become a Broadway financial flop. There have been regional productions, and a 1962 Off-Broadway revival managed to find an audience for 112 performances, but *The Golden Apple* is still waiting for wide acceptance. In 1954 it was considered ahead of its time. Hindsight reveals it was one of the most unique musicals of the decade. When will it ascend from a cult favorite to a full-fledged hit?

I Feel Wonderful

[18 October 1954, Theatre De Lys, 48 performances] a musical revue by Barry Alan Grael. *Score:* Jerry Herman (music and lyrics). *Cast:* Grael, Phyllis Newman, Bob Miller, Nina Dova, Albie Gaye, Janie Janvier, John Bartis, Tom Mixon.

While a theatre major at the University of Miami in Ohio, Jerry Herman scored original musical revues, one of which was titled *I Feel Wonderful*. After graduation, Herman moved to New York City and produced and directed an Off-Broadway version of the student show. The cast of seventeen was comprised of young and promising talent, but the only member to go on to a substantial career was Phyllis Newman. The songs have not been recorded or published, but the critics who saw *I Feel Wonderful* all complimented Herman on the tuneful and catchy score. The lively little revue found an audience for six weeks, and Herman's New York theatre career was off and running. Interestingly, *I Feel Wonderful* was booked into the Theatre de Lys before its previous tenant, *The Threepenny Opera*, opened in March of 1954. Despite the rave reviews the German work received, it was forced to close in order to honor the contract with Herman. After *I Feel Wonderful* closed, *The Threepenny Opera* returned to the Theatre de Lys and stayed and stayed. The two musicals could not be more different since Herman's kind of optimistic and pleasurable musical was the antithesis of Brechtian theatre.

SANDHOG

[29 November 1954, Phoenix Theatre, 48 performances] a musical play by Earl Robinson, Waldo Salt based on Theodore Dreiser's story "St. Columbia and the River." *Score:* Robinson, Salt (music and lyrics). *Cast:* Jack Cassidy, Betty Oakes, Gordon Dilworth, David Brooks, Yuriko, Michael Kermoyan, Alice Ghostley, Eliot Feld, Paul Ukena.

This ambitious musical with the odd title was actually a traditional book musical based on a 1918 Theodore Dreiser short story and an attempt to create opera "for the people." From its three-act form to its integrated cast of black and white actors who actually performed together, *Sandhog* was different. Perhaps that is why it appealed to the Phoenix Theatre who had produced its first musical the previous year, the ingenious *The Golden Apple*. *Sandhog* did not measure up to that excellent show, but it had much to recommend it. A "sandhog" was slang for the men who worked below water building tunnels, and the musical took place mostly in such a tunnel beneath the Hudson River in the 1880s. Dreiser's story "St. Columbia and the River" concerned some of these workmen, and the libretto by Earl Robinson and Waldo Salt opened the action to include the nearby neighborhoods where these men lived. Irish immigrant Johnny O'Sullivan (Jack Cassidy) gets a job as a sandhog, but after several of his coworkers die in an avoidable accident, he quits. After marrying his sweetheart Katie (Betty Oakes), Johnny returns to work in the tunnel as a foreman, and during an explosion he is blown away from an accident and survives. The "ballad in three acts" was concerned with Johnny's relationship with the colorful "common people" of his neighborhood as well as with the traditional love story. The large cast included different ethnic types and a quintet of rambunctious kids who sang and danced. (Two of the youngsters were played by future dancer-choreographers Eliot Feld and Yuriko.) The streets of 1880s New York provided the color and light, but much of the musical was deep down in the tunnel where the men toiled, and the show often had the harsh, documentary feel of the Living Newspaper productions of the 1930s. Howard Bay, who had designed the most famous of those

Federal Theatre docudramas, did the sets and lights for *Sandhog,* and *The Cradle Will Rock* veteran Howard Da Silva directed it. Robinson wrote the stirring music for Salt's pungent lyrics, the songs shifting from light sing-along numbers like "Good Old Days" and "Song of the Bends" to the agitprop pieces like "Johnny's Cursing Song" and "Some Said They Were Crazy." The somber "Waiting for the Men" foreshadowed the tragedy which was mourned with "28 Men." Yet the *Sandhog* score was filled with life, and the boastful "Johnny O'" and the spirited quartets "T-w-i-n-s" and "Katie O'Sullivan" were quite joyous. The superior score was matched by the sterling cast. Cassidy was noticed and praised the most, but other new faces such as Betty Oakes, Alice Ghostley, Michael Kermoyan, and David Hooks were also commended. The reviews for *Sandhog* were mostly favorable, but the title and subject matter were both hard to sell, therefore the musical ran its scheduled six weeks and has rarely been heard of again. With the decade half over and with only a handful of musicals so far, Off Broadway was already getting a reputation for being the place where the most original and unconventional musicals in New York were to be found.

THE SHOESTRING REVUE

[28 February 1955, President Theatre, 96 performances] a musical revue by Ben Bagley, various. *Score:* various. *Cast:* Beatrice Arthur, Dody Goodman, Bill McCutcheon, Chita Rivera, Dorothy Greener, Arte Johnson, Mel Larned, Peter Conlow, Jon Sharpe, Maxwell Grant, Rhoda Kerns, Joan Bowman, Arthur Partington.

The brash and quixotic twenty-one-year-old Ben Bagley began his colorful theatre career producing this funny and tuneful revue that, as its title implied, was not big on spectacle but overflowing with promising young talent. Beatrice Arthur, Chita Rivera, Dody Goodman, and Bill McCutcheon would soon be Broadway regulars; Arte Johnson would find fame on television; and the unique comedienne Dorothy Greener would light up several Off-Broadway shows in her too-brief career. The young writers who contributed sketches and songs included such later successes as Sheldon Harnick, Michael Stewart, Charles Strouse, Lee Adams, Ronny Graham, and Arthur Siegel. But it was the wacky Bagley who assembled them all and left his mark on the whole silly enterprise. *The Shoestring Revue* was topical and enjoyed placing current celebrities and trends in classic works, such as "Medea in

Disneyland" and "Epic" in which Mike Todd tries to convince Marilyn Monroe to appear in his film version of *War and Peace*. Mel Larned sang the wry cowboy lament "WAbash 4-7473"; a waltzing Lady Godiva yearned for "Mink, Mink, Mink"; Dody Goodman complained that "Someone Is Sending Me Flowers"; a calypso version of Adam and Eve was featured in "Entire History of the World in Two Minutes and Thirty-Two Seconds"; *Hamlet* was retold as an ice show; and Beatrice Arthur sang the goofy torch song "Garbage" while Chita Rivera danced a tango in which she dove into a garbage bag to retrieve a cigarette. The rapid trio "Fresh and Young" written by Ronny Graham was a sort of theme song for the revue; the material and the performers were young and indeed fresh in both senses of the word. *The Shoestring Revue* was well reviewed and ran thirteen weeks, delighting audiences and launching several careers.

PHOENIX '55

[23 April 1955, Phoenix Theatre, 97 performances] a musical revue by Ira Wallach. *Score:* David Baker (music), David Craig (lyrics). *Cast:* Nancy Walker, Harvey Lembeck, Louise Hoff, Joshua Shelley, Bill Heyer, Elise Rhodes, Marge Redmond.

The Phoenix Theatre, the Off-Broadway troupe dedicated to revivals of the classics and new offbeat musicals, shifted gears at the end of the 1954–1955 season and presented a musical revue featuring Broadway comedienne Nancy Walker. Topical sketches and songs were not what the Phoenix did best, but the revue was enjoyable enough that after running a month the producers rewrote the contracts and, without changing theatres, *Phoenix '55* was considered a Broadway show. This allowed it to be in the running for the Tony Awards, and it did very well, Walker winning for best actress in a musical and awards going to Alvin Colt's costumes and Boris Runanin's choreography. The skits concerned life in the suburbs, newspaper items, the baby boom, and show business (particularly Method actors), and the songs were more showcases for the performers than anything much in themselves. Walker sold the silly ballad "Down to the Sea" and the torchy solo "A Funny Heart." There was a pleasing duet titled "Never Wait for Love," and Bill Hyer shone in both the demanding "This Tuxedo Is Mine!" and the circus-like number "The Charade of the Marionettes." Most critics thought Walker was the whole show (especially when she did a hilarious spoof of Method actors chewing the scenery) and audiences found her enough reason to see the revue, letting it run a total of three months.

FOUR BELOW

[4 March 1956, Downstairs Room, c. 50 performances] a musical revue by Julius Monk, various. *Score:* various. *Cast:* Dody Goodman, Jack Fletcher, Gerry Matthews, June Ericson.

While Ben Bagley and others were having a rollicking good time with the musical revue format, a different kind of Off-Broadway revue was being established by producer Julius Monk. These shows were intimate cafe revues with the male performers in tuxedos and the women in elegant cocktail dresses or evening gowns. There was no scenery or props except for some stools and a dark background that allowed the actors to quietly appear and disappear in and out of the lights. Monk himself served as host, or "regisseur" as he preferred to be called, and he welcomed audiences before the show and narrated or introduced the numbers. The dapper, impeccably dressed Monk (he was also a very highly paid model) set the tone for the evening. Although the revues were topical, the favorite targets being the theatre, movies, politicians, and current fads, the Julius Monk shows were never crude or outrageously wacky. He (and his audiences) preferred literate, sophisticated humor and pleasing music. This was not to say the shows were stuffy and high brow, but they were best enjoyed by knowledgeable New Yorkers than tourists looking for a hit show. Yet the revues were often hits because the production costs were minimal. An exact number of performances is difficult to determine since many of the revues did not perform on a traditional theatre schedule and there were many late-night performances.

When Monk was still a teenager, he got a job as pianist at the Ruben Blue nightclub in the late 1940s. He eventually took over the entertainment for the club and started producing his own shows. *Four Below* was his first venture at a location at the Downstairs Room at 51st Street. He later dubbed the venue Upstairs at the Downstairs and presented several revues there in the 1950s and early 1960s. The revue's title referred to the quartet of performers but also to indicate that this was Monk's fourth presentation. (All the subsequent revues would bear a succeeding number so that Monk's career was charted in the titles.) Bagley performer Dody Goodman was the standout member of the foursome but Jack Fletcher, Gerry Matthews, and

June Ericson were quick to pick up the Monk style of performing, and the little show ran several weeks. Arguments still persist over whether the Monk revues were technically Off-Broadway productions since the venue was not, strictly speaking, a theatre. Yet the shows were fully Off Broadway in attitude and format and were much more than a supper club act. Today Monk is mostly remembered for the writing and performing talent that he discovered over the years, but his impact on the revue genre is considerable. Also, most of the revues were recorded with a live audience, and these recordings serve as a valuable archive for demonstrating just what a 1950s Off-Broadway revue was like.

THE LITTLEST REVUE

[22 May 1956, Phoenix Theatre, 32 performances] a musical revue by Ben Bagley, various. *Score:* Vernon Duke, various (music), Ogden Nash, various (lyrics). *Cast:* Charlotte Rae, Tammy Grimes, Joel Grey, Larry Storch, George Marcy, Beverly Bozeman, Dorothy Jarnac, Tommy Morton.

SHOESTRING '57

[5 November 1956, Barbizon Plaza Theatre, 119 performances] a musical revue by Ben Bagley, various. *Score:* various. *Cast:* Dody Goodman, Fay DeWitt, George Marcy, Charlie Manna, Dorothy Greener, Paul Mazursky, Mary Ellen Terry, John Bartis, Bud McCreery.

Ben Bagley offered two revues within six months of each other and both were critical hits, though only one was a moneymaker. The Phoenix Theatre was looking for a light musical to end its season, and instead of concocting their own, the producers offered the venue to Bagley who was hoping to follow up his popular *Shoestring Revue* with another on-the-cheap show rich with new talent. Yet *The Littlest Revue* ended up being not so "shoestring," and the two primary songwriters were established Broadway figures, lyricist Ogden Nash and composer Vernon Duke. There were also contributions by well-known lyricists John Latouche and Sammy Cahn, acclaimed writer Eudora Welty, and some of Bagley's young talent from his earlier show: Sheldon Harnick, Michael Stewart, Charles Strouse, and Lee Adams. If the backstage artists were not beginners, the onstage talent was filled with new or recently discovered faces such as Joel Grey, Tammy Grimes, Larry Storch, and Charlotte Rae. The score was even stronger than that for *Shoestring Revue*, and it was delivered with panache by the superb cast. Grimes sang the breezy ballad "Madly in Love" and the risible feminist ditty "I'm Glad I'm Not a Man"; Rae was hilarious singing the geometric minuet "The Shape of Things" and lampooned an opera singer playing Las Vegas in "Spring Doth Let Her Colours Fly"; and Grey spoofed Harry Belafonte in the calypso number "I Lost the Rhythm" and crooned the deprecating "You're Far From Wonderful." Hedonism was celebrated in "Good Little Girls"; "Summer Is A-Comin' In" was a merry madrigal about seasonal lust; "Born Too Late" was an oddball ballad; and the Norman Vincent Peale best seller was ribbed in the idiotically happy "The Power of Negative Thinking." Among the other topics that came under fire were public toilets, fad diets, weird Off-Broadway shows, Noël Coward, and urban renewal that was tearing down admired old hotels. The critics were so enthusiastic about *The Littlest Revue* that it could have run longer than its one-month engagement.

But Bagley was back with another revue early the next season, and it was a fifteen-week hit. *Shoestring '57* reassembled many of the talents from his *Shoestring Revue*, both writers and performers, and there were also contributions by future notables Carolyn Leigh, Mark Charlap, Tom Jones, and Harvey Schmidt. Dody Goodman and Dorothy Greener were the comic standouts in the cast of twelve, and newcomers Fay DeWitt and Paul Mazursky were also complimented by the critics. The sketches took on the critics, Tennessee Williams, oddball encounters, psychiatrists, and mimes. A Parisian hussy complained about not being noticed by painters in the mock can-can "Renoir, Degas and Toulouse," and the cast poked fun at high-society small-talk rules in "Don't Say You Like Tchaikovsky." "At Twenty-Two" was a bittersweet song of resignation; the irregularity of city bus service was the subject of "Lament on Fifth Avenue"; "The Sea Is All Around Us" wryly pictured Manhattan completely underwater; "Family Troubles" was a Noël Cowardish number about some extreme domestic quirks; and in "The Arts" the mothers of Cole Porter, T. S. Eliot, and Ernest Hemingway grieved that their sons turned out so poorly. *Shoestring '57* had more dance than the previous Bagley shows, and the choreography by the up-and-coming Danny Daniels was roundly admired. The glowing reviews and Bagley's growing reputation helped the musical run longer than any of the previous editions.

LIVIN' THE LIFE

[27 April 1957, Phoenix Theatre, 25 performances] a musical play by Dale Wasserman, Bruce Geller based on Mark Twain's Missisippi River stories. *Score:* Jack Urbont (music), Geller (lyrics). *Cast:* Richard Ide, Timmy Everett, Lee Charles, Alice Ghostley, James Mitchell, Stephen Elliott, Patsy Bruder, Lee Becker, Edward Villella.

Instead of ending its season with a revue, the Phoenix Theatre offered an elaborate musical version of *Tom Sawyer* with a large cast, full score, and a very Broadway-like production. Dale Wasserman and Bruce Geller did the complete adaptation, taking characters from *The Adventures of Huckleberry Finn* but concentrating on the events in *Tom Sawyer*. Geller contributed the lyrics for Jack Urbont's music, and the score was pastiche Americana with more than a touch of Broadway in it. Tom (Timmy Everett) and Huck (Richard Ide) sang the freewheeling title song; the drunkard Muff Potter (James Mitchell) delivered the sloppy "Whiskey Bug" and sang about autumnal romance with Aunt Polly (Alice Ghostley) in "Late Love"; Tom reckoned he was "Probably in Love" and joined Becky Thatcher (Patsy Bruder) for the juvenile duet "All of 'Em Say"; the slave Jim (Lee Charles) sang "Jim's Lament"; and the townspeople kept returning to "River Ballad" as a leitmotif on the lines of "Ol' Man River." It was all efficiently done and satisfying without being particularly memorable. *Livin' the Life* boasted a strong cast and some fine dancing choreographed by John Butler; among the featured dancers were unknowns Edward Villella and Lee Becker (Theodore). Perhaps the Phoenix was hoping the show might be Broadway material, but after running three weeks Off Broadway, it closed. Coauthor Wasserman would have to wait a decade before he had a novel-to-musical hit with *Man of La Mancha*, and *Huckleberry Finn* would not be successfully musicalized until *Big River* in 1985.

SIMPLY HEAVENLY

[21 May 1957, 85th Street Playhouse, 44 performances; Playhouse Theatre, 62 performances; Renata Theatre, 63 performances] a musical comedy by Langston Hughes based on his novel *Simple Takes a Wife*. *Score:*

David Martin (music), Hughes (lyrics). *Cast:* Melvin Stuart, Ethel Ayler, Claudia McNeil, Marilyn Berry, Ray Thompson, Stanley Greene, John Bouie, Alma Hubbard.

A small but significant landmark in the history of African American musical theatre is this delightful show that found modest success and foreshadowed the black musicals of future decades. The renowned poet Langston Hughes was no stranger to Broadway, having written lyrics for Kurt Weill's *Street Scene* and having seen some of his dramas produced there. *Simply Heavenly* was much lighter than his previous theatre efforts, being based on a series of comic stories he wrote about the luckless, lovable Jess Simple (Melvin Stewart). When Simple loses his job in Harlem, he doesn't know how he is going to earn enough money to divorce his first wife so that he can marry the sweet Joyce Lane (Marilyn Berry). He walks his landlady's dog to pay his rent and drowns his troubles at Paddy's Bar where he has plenty of friends, including the seductive Zarita (Ethel Ayler) who lures Simple into trouble and temporarily causes a rift between Simple and Joyce. But Simple gets a job, promises to reform, and wins Joyce for good. In a subplot, the independent Mamie (Claudia McNeil) is pursued by Melon (John Bouie), a watermelon seller, and it takes all her energy to convince him she doesn't need a man. The plotting was thin and familiar, but Hughes's libretto was rich in characterization and there was a looseness and warmth in the show that had rarely been captured in an African American stage production. These characters were not afraid to be foolish, yet they didn't sacrifice their dignity in showing it. Simple had a handful of seriocomic monologues in which he complained about the plight of "colored people" or dreamed about a future when he will be a man of significance. The blues-and-jazz-flavored score also had a free-and-easy nature. Hughes penned the lyrics for David Martin's music, and the songs were often exhilarating and fun. Joyce sang the breezy title song about her love for Simple and joined him in the felicitous duet "Gatekeeper of My Castle"; Zarita offered the zesty "Let Me Take You for a Ride" and in a song of self-doubt wondered about "The Men in My Life"; Mamie and Melon sang the cross-purposes duet "When I'm in a Quiet Mood"; and bar patron Gitfiddle (Ray Thompson) insisted on singing the blues even though his guitar has "Broken Strings." Claudia McNeil as Mamie stopped the show twice, with her swinging song of independence "Good Old Girl" and when she joined Melon in the mellifluous "Did You Ever Hear the Blues?" It is a score that has lost none of its sass and charm over the years. Since no Broadway producer would consider *Simply*

Heavenly, Hughes and his company had to settle for the dilapidated 85th Street Playhouse. The reviews were encouraging enough that when the city condemned the theatre six weeks into the run, the show moved to Broadway, where it attempted to attract mainstream audiences. After eight weeks of spotty business, *Simply Heavenly* returned to Off Broadway and ran at the Renata Theatre for another eight weeks. Yet that was not the last of *Simply Heavenly*. In 1959 most of the original cast appeared in an abridged WNET-TV version, and that same year a London production opened. There have been regional productions over the years, and in 2003 Great Britain's Old Vic revived the musical; the one-month engagement was so popular that the next year it returned for a six-month run. *Simply Heavenly* may be considered a period piece today, but it still charms.

KALEIDOSCOPE

[13 June 1957, Provincetown Playhouse, c. 40 performances] a musical revue by Sig Altman, various. *Score:* various. *Cast:* Mickey Deems, Maria Karnilova, Kenneth Nelson, Tom Mixon, Penny Malone, Erin Martin, Bobo Lewis, Wisa D'Orso, Leonard Drum, John Smolko.

A handful of writers from the Ben Bagley revues were recruited for this ten-actor show that was filled with young talent. Sheldon Harnick, Michael Stewart, Tom Jones, and other Bagley veterans were joined by Martin Charnin, Louis Botto, David Rogers, and other new writers and, true to its title, *Kaleidescope* was a bright and colorful montage of anything and everything. It lacked the wit of the Bagley shows but made up for it in energy and verve. Air travel, babysitters, modern art, the military, suburbia, the New York subway, and contemporary love were among the topics covered in the sketches and songs. The cast was headed by the vaudeville-like comic Mickey Deems, and he was supported by such actors of future success as Kenneth Nelson, Bobo Lewis, and Maria Karnilova. There was also upcoming talent behind the scenes: actor Paul Mazursky started his new career when he directed the sketches and dancer Joe Layton was the assistant choreographer. *Kaleidoscope* was an unpretentious summer entertainment. It was the kind of show that, much earlier in the century, Broadway would offer on rooftop theatres for summer audiences. In the 1950s it was still possible to put together a low-cost revue, run a month or so, and not go deep in the red. Such a situation would not last much longer.

TAKE FIVE

[10 October 1957, Downstairs at the Upstairs] a musical revue by Julius Monk, various. *Score:* various. *Cast:* Ronny Graham, Ellen Hanley, Gerry Matthews, Jean Arnold, Ceil Cabot.

DEMI-DOZEN

[11 October 1958, Upstairs at the Downstairs] a musical revue by Julius Monk, various. *Score:* various. *Cast:* Ronny Graham, Jane Connell, Gerry Matthews, Jean Arnold, Ceil Cabot, Jack Fletcher, George Hall.

Ronny Graham, who had been contributing material to revues both on and Off Broadway for a few years, was the featured performer in Julius Monk's fifth show, *Take Five*. It was one of the very few times a single performer was spotlighted in a Monk show, but this edition lacked an outstanding female comic, so Graham took up the slack by writing and appearing in most of the sketches. He also penned the farcical hoedown number "Doing the Psycho-Neurotique" that never failed to stop the show each night. Other notable numbers included the felicitous ballad "Perfect Stranger," the busy "Gossiping Grapevine," and the satiric "Westport!" which took the Connecticut suburbs to task for its narrow-mindedness. Among the writers were lyricist Carolyn Leigh and composer Jonathan Tunick, who would go on to become a celebrated Broadway orchestrator and arranger.

Most of the cast returned a year later for Monk's *Demi-Dozen*; the most notable newcomer was the tiny comedienne Jane Connell who would become a Monk regular. Leigh also returned, this time providing songs with her new composer partner Cy Coleman. Tom Jones, Harvey Schmidt, Jay Thompson, Michael Brown, and Portia Nelson were among the other sketch and songwriters, and all were in top form because *Demi-Dozen* was perhaps the best of all the Monk revues. Most of the targets were New York City items (including Off Broadway itself), but there was also a funny number titled "Statehood Hula" about the battle to make Hawaii a state. Other highlights in the score included the beguiling ballad "You Fascinate Me So," the frantic "The Race of the Lexington Avenue Express," the "Seasonal

Sonatine" which melodically explored the clichés of the four seasons, the name-dropping "Guess Who Was There," the lilting "Sunday in New York," and a "Merrie Minstrel Show" finale. The Monk revues alternated between two performance spaces at 51st Street, and this one was done in the Upstairs at the Downstairs.

DIVERSIONS

[7 November 1958, Downtown Theatre, 85 performances] a musical revue by Steven Vinaver. *Score:* Carl Davis (music), Vinaver (lyrics). *Cast:* Nancy Dussault, Peter Friedman, Cy Young, Aline Brown, Thom Molinaro, Gubi Mann.

Critics thought that twenty-two-year-old Stephen Vinaver was someone to watch. He wrote the sketches and lyrics and directed the spirited little revue *Diversions* which found an audience for just over two months. But the one who really deserved watching was the composer of the show, Vinaver's college pal Carl Davis, who would go on to an illustrious career as a conductor and a film and television composer. *Diversions* was an unpretentious musical with quality material. The music was better than tuneful, and the comedy was more acid and witty than simple farce. Recent and old films, urban living, detective stories, and the inevitable song about the New York subway system were among the too-familiar subjects, yet *Diversions* had a cocky way of mocking itself and the revue genre in general. The amusing opening number "Hello" poked fun at the way such revues were to begin, "Five Plus One" introduced the six performers, and "Musicians" was a nod to the underappreciated music makers. When it was time for the expected ballad, the number was called "Here Comes the Ballad," and the second act opened with a splashy production number (done on the cheap) titled "Production Number." The cast donned different hats for different characters, while the scenery and props were minimal. The whole venture might have been dubbed "amateurish," but the performers were better than that and the material was too good to dismiss. Of the half-dozen performers, only Nancy Dussault went on to a substantial stage career. Vinaver and Davis brought *Diversions* to the Edinburgh Finge Festival in Scotland in 1961 where it was such a hit that it transferred to London and ran longer than in New York. Both men were hired for the new British television show *That Was the Week That Was*, Davis composing the theme song and Vinaver penning sketches. Neither ever returned to Off Broadway (or the States) again, spending the rest of their careers in England.

SALAD DAYS

[10 November 1958, Barbizon-Plaza Theatre, 80 performances] a musical comedy by Julian Slade, Dorothy Reynolds. *Score:* Slade (music and lyrics), Reynolds (lyrics). *Cast:* Barbara Franklin, Richard Easton, Mary Savage, Powys Thomas, Helen Burns, Eric Christmas, Jack Creley, Tom Kneebone, Gillie Fenwick.

If you are still under the delusion that Great Britain and the United States have similar tastes, *Salad Days* may come as a rude awakening. This featherweight, featherbrained musical opened in London in 1954 and ran 2,283 performances, the longest-running British musical until *Oliver!* came along. Deemed impossibly British, the show did not cross the Atlantic until 1958 when, hedging its bets, it opened Off Broadway. Some critics found it charming, most thought it too silly to contemplate, and a few said it was better than the London production. Audiences were curious enough to let it run ten weeks.

The story is set in London during a heat wave, which may account for the foolishness that follows. Sweethearts Timothy (Richard Easton) and Jane (Barbara Franklin) have just graduated from University and need to find jobs in a time of high unemployment. A Tramp (Powys Thomas) in the park offers the couple seven pounds a week for one month to look after his beat-up piano "Minnie," which sits outside near the university. With such a meager but guaranteed income, Timothy and Jane wed and, when checking on Minnie, they find that anyone who listens to the dilapidated instrument is overcome with a desire to dance. Soon anyone who comes within the sound of the piano, from businessmen and children to policemen and clergy, are dancing to its music. News of the piano's power upsets the Minister of Pleasure and Pastime (Gillie Fenwick), and he sends police to confiscate Minnie—but the piano has disappeared. Even Timothy and Jane do not know where it has gone. Timothy's mad scientist Uncle Zed (Jack Creley) takes the couple up over London in his flying saucer and they spot it: the Tramp has taken Minnie away for safety's sake. When the month ends, the piano is given to another young couple for guardianship, and Timothy and Jane bid Minnie goodbye with bittersweet affection. A plot this slight needed a score that was catchy and contagious enough to support such a thin and ridiculous story. For the most part it does. Julian Slade and Dorothy Reynolds came up with a set of songs that almost makes you believe in Minnie's powers. The opening number, "The Dons' Chorus (The Things That Are Done By a Don)," is a merry alma mater; the bubbly "Oh, Look at Me" is the musical realization of Minnie's power to inspire dancing; "We Said We Wouldn't Look Back" is a fox-trotting duet about looking forward; the diplomat's "Hush-Hush" is a Gilbert and Sullivan-like number about keeping mum at all costs; "It's Easy to Sing" is an idiotically happy sing-along; the tango "Cleopatra" is a farcical tribute to lavish living; the sprightly "We're Looking for a Piano" is a stiff-upper-lip can-can; "I Sit in the Sun" is a lilting number about enjoying nature while waiting for love to arrive; "The Saucer" is a sunny polka with a slapstick lyric; and the waltzing "The Time of My Life" is a gliding operatic air about enjoying one's youth (or salad days). If the score recalls any postwar musical at all, it is *The Boy Friend*, which was a gentle spoof of 1920s musical comedy. *Salad Days*, although it has a contemporary setting, has the same kind of nonsensical temperament which places a catchy song above all other elements.

Over the years *Salad Days* has remained a favorite in England. There was a television version and several London revivals, including a fortieth anniversary production that was very popular. Meanwhile, back in the States we are still scratching our heads. It is as difficult to explain why the Brits love *Salad Days* as it is to clarify why Americans don't. It helps to understand that in 1954 Great Britain was still in a deep recession and there was a shortage of goods because of the war. It also matters that in the 1950s, Broadway musicals were constantly crossing the ocean and boldly showing off on the West End. Then along came *Salad Days*, which was so merrily illogical and so contentedly un-American and un-Broadway. If the British were embarrassed that such a piece of fluff was their biggest musical hit of the decade, they didn't seem to show it. When Jerome Robbins was in London preparing the West End production of *West Side Story*, he was brought to see *Salad Days*. The somewhat paranoid Robbins thought the whole thing was a practical joke put together to make fun of him and his Broadway efforts. Not quite, but *Salad Days* would never be mistaken for a *West Side Story*-like musical, which might be why it is so essentially British and so boldly un-American.

OF MICE AND MEN

[4 December 1958, Provincetown Playhouse, 37 performances] a musical play by Ira J. Bilowit and Wilson Lehr based on the play by John Steinbeck.

Score: Alfred Brooks (music), Bilowit (lyrics). Cast: Leo Penn, Art Lund, Jo Sullivan, Tony Kraber, Byrne Piven, John F. Hamilton, Tom Noel.

The producers of this musical version of the powerful novel and play made it clear to the press that author John Steinbeck approved of the musical adaptation of his work. Unfortunately there was a newspaper strike in New York at the time, and few read about the show or the mostly positive reviews that the piece received. The libretto by Ira J. Bilowit and Wilson Lehr was deemed tasteful and accurate to the original, and the cast was similarly applauded. Leo Penn was the frustrated itinerant ranch hand George, Art Lund was his dim-witted friend Lennie who did not know his own strength, Byrne Piven was the foreman Curley who hired the two men, and Jo Sullivan was Curley's wife, who acted tenderly toward Lenny but tragically died when he accidently strangled her. George and Lennie sang the pathetically optimistic "We Got a Future," but by the end of the musical George must kill Lennie before the lynch mob finds him. The wizened African American Candy (John F. Hamilton), a secondary but memorable character in the novel, concluded the somber evening with "Candy's Lament." "Just Someone to Talk To" was a plaintive ballad of loneliness, and the aching "Is There Some Place for Me?" applied to both Lennie and the wife. Alfred Brooks composed the music for Bilowit's lyrics, and it was judged to be an atmospheric score that avoided verbal and musical clichés. A musical *Of Mice and Men* might not have been a popular attraction even if the word had gotten out, but it deserved better than a run of five weeks. The score was not recorded nor published but in 2007 the York Theatre Company presented a staged reading of the piece Off Off Broadway with a reputable cast, and it was clear that *Of Mice and Men* was a work of value.

FASHION

[20 January 1959, Royal Playhouse, 50 performances] a musical comedy based on Anna Cora Mowatt's play. Score: various. Cast: Enid Markey, Frederic Warriner, June Ericson, Will Geer, Rosina Fernhoff, Stanley Jay, Jonathan Abel.

One of the American theatre's best comedy of manners, Anna Cora Mowatt's 1845 *Fashion; or, Life in New York*, was ideal musical material. It is also arguably the oldest American play that can still be readily revived. The pretentious New Yorker Mrs. Tiffany (Enid Markey) has illusions of social grandeur and surrounds herself with culture, has an all-French staff, and entertains anyone she believes has aristocratic connections. Mrs. Tiffany insists that her daughter Serphina (June Ericson) wed the Count di Jolimaitre (Frederic Warriner) even though she does not love him. Mr. Tiffany (William Swetland) prefers more down-to-earth society and is often seen with Adam Trueman (Will Geer), a businessman with some sketchy legal episodes in his past. When the calculating Mr. Snobson (Stanley Jay) gets hold of damaging information, he tries to blackmail Trueman and aims to marry Serphina himself. A long-lost granddaughter of Trueman's helps him save his reputation, and she also exposes the count as nothing more than a French chef named Gustave Treadmill. Mr. Tiffany puts his foot down and sends his wife and daughter to stay in the simple and rustic country home of Trueman to learn less refined values. The witty and well-structured comedy is a masterwork of character, plot, and dialogue. The musical version listed no adaptor. The libretto was pretty much Mowatt's play interrupted by old-time song standards (though mostly forgotten today) such as "Come, Birdie, Come," "Walking Down Broadway," "The Independent Farmer," "Take Back the Heart," and "Down By the Riverside." Musicologist Deems Taylor selected and arranged the old tunes for the musical. Yet the real joy of the production was seeing the old play performed by such a superb cast. Veterans Enid Markey, William Swetland, Frederic Warriner, and Will Geer were joined by such young talents as June Ericson, Rosina Fernhoff, and Jonathan Abel. *Fashion* was well enough received to run six weeks. A very different musical version of *Fashion* would open Off Broadway in 1974 and run twice as long.

SHE SHALL HAVE MUSIC

[22 January 1959, Theatre Marque, 54 performances] a musical comedy by Stuart Bishop based on William Wycherley's comedy *The Country Wife*. *Score*: Dede Meyer (music and lyrics). *Cast*: Cherry Davis, Edgar Daniels, Lawrence Weber, Irene Perri, Barbara Pavell, Skedge Miller, Betty Oakes, Lawrence Chelsi.

William Wycherley's 1675 comedy of manners *The Country Wife* has always been considered the most risqué of the Restoration plays mainly because the immoral characters succeed and the innocents are converted to hedonism. The musical version titled *She Shall Have Music* that opened Off

Broadway softened some of the play's wickedness and dealt in plenty of double entendres. (The very title was a polite way of saying that the heroine discovers lust and likes it.) Stuart Bishop did the adaptation, which retained the seventeenth-century setting, characters, much of the story (with a more wholesome ending), and even some of the witty dialogue. The aging Pinchwife (Edgar Daniels) marries the young country girl Peg (Cherry Davis) and brings her to London, but he jealously keeps watch over her to prevent her from falling prey to the many young gallants about town. The philandering Horner (Lawrence Weber) has seduced many of the wives in London because he has sent out the rumor that he is a eunuch. Husbands trust him, and the ladies are not about to disclose Horner's sexual prowess. Horner has a difficult time seducing Margery because Pinchwife has not heard the rumor. After Horner succeeds, Margery nearly gives away his secret until her lady friends persuade her to leave well enough alone. The songs by Dede Meyer attempted to echo Wycherley's style, but "I Live to Love" and "Who Needs It" were more euphemistic than necessary. All the same, the press thought the score lively and the performances enjoyable, particularly Cherry Davis who was applauded for her dancing and comic timing and was dubbed by one critic as the "Off Broadway Gwen Verdon." *She Shall Have Music* managed to run seven weeks, but it has not been heard of since.

Once Upon a Mattress

[11 May 1959, Phoenix Theatre, 216 performances; Alvin Theatre, 460 performances] a musical comedy by Jay Thompson, Marshall Barer, Dean Fuller. *Score:* Mary Rodgers (music), Barer (lyrics). *Cast:* Carol Burnett, Jane White, Joe Bova, Jack Gilford, Anne Jones, Allen Case, Matt Mattox, Harry Snow.

This anachronistic musical version of the *Princess and the Pea* fairy tale was, despite its source material, a show for adults. It gently spoofed fairy tales even as it enjoyed being a costume musical comedy with more than a dash of vaudeville and burlesque. *Once Upon a Mattress* was also notable for introducing Carol Burnett and making her a stage star. Yet the musical has played effectively without stars in regional and educational theatre, and it is a solid piece of craftsmanship all around. In the libretto by Jay Thompson, Dean Fuller, and Marshall Barer, no one in the kingdom can marry until the hapless Prince Dauntless (Joe Bova) is wed, and his mother the Queen (Jane White) has seen to it that no girl is good enough for her boy. But the unconventional, spunky Princess Winifred (Burnett) outwits the Queen, passes her test of sensitivity even as she sleeps on a pile of mattresses, and there is a happy ending for everyone, including the once-mute King (Jack Gilford) who finally silences his bossy wife. The subplot regarding the dashing Sir Harry (Allen Case) and his pregnant but unmarried sweetheart Lady Larken (Anne Jones) was a bit daring for a fairy tale, but it lent an urgency to the situation: the two cannot wed until Dauntless does, and Larken will soon be starting "to show." It is a sly yet convivial script that is not afraid to stop for some charming commentary by the court Jester (Matt Mattox) and the court Minstrel (Harry Snow). Although it ended up being a showcase for Burnett's singing and comic talents, *Once Upon a Mattress* was not written that way. Instead it is a solid musical comedy with unpretentious hopes of entertaining on different levels.

Mary Rodgers and Barer wrote the merry score that is happily old-fashioned; not medieval old-fashioned but musical theatre old-fashioned. The opening narrative ballad "Many Moons Ago" has a touch of the middle ages in it, but after that the songs are in the Broadway style: the lively chorus number "An Opening for a Princess," the coy duet "In a Little While," the brazen "I am" song "Shy," the villainess' character number "Sensitivity," the tuneful charm songs "Normandy" and "Very Soft Shoes," the rowdy production number "Spanish Panic," the frustrated heroine's "Happily Ever After," and the mime duet "Man to Man Talk." Like her father Richard Rodgers, Mary Rodgers's music is strong on flowing melodic lines, and Barer's lyrics are comfortably pleasing without being too clever. Veteran director George Abbott staged the musical with his usual efficiency, and choreographer Joe Layton firmly established his career with his sprightly dances. Critical response was enthusiastic for all aspects of the show, though Burnett got the lion share of the praise. After running six and a half months Off Broadway, *Once Upon a Mattress* moved to the large Alvin Theatre on the Street and did very well for another fourteen months. An abridged television version of the show was made in 1964, and in 1972 Burnett reprised her Winifred in a slightly revised CBS broadcast. In the 2005 ABC version, Burnett graduated to the role of the Queen which was enlarged for her. *Once Upon a Mattress* has remained a favorite with regional, summer stock, community, and even school theatres (though high schools have to deal with the pregnancy issue). On Broadway, the musical requires a star. Sarah Jessica Parker was considered a bright and personable performer, but most critics felt her Princess Winifred was not raucous enough to hold together the 1996 Broadway revival which ran only six months.

Once Upon a Mattress proved to be an important turning point for Off Broadway. The Phoenix Theatre presented the show as the annual light musi-

cal offering to end their season, but it was such a success that it transferred
to Broadway where it was also a hit. *Once Upon a Mattress* looked fine on
Broadway because, frankly, it was put together like a Broadway show. One
doesn't hire Broadway's top director of musicals, George Abbott, and not
think beyond Off Broadway. The show was not as elaborate as its Broadway
neighbors *Flower Drum Song* or *Gypsy*, but neither was it small and intimate
as the still-running *The Threepenny Opera*. The Phoenix Theatre had previously sent their spring musical *The Golden Apple* to Broadway, but it failed
to run. *Once Upon a Mattress* did run, and an ominous precedent was set:
good Off-Broadway musicals should go to Broadway. This had happened a
few times earlier in the century, but now the economics were too appealing.
From this point on many, if not most, musicals that had Broadway potential
transferred to the Street. One might go so far as to say that after *Once Upon a
Mattress* many Off-Broadway musicals were created with the hope of moving
to Broadway. This would not happen overnight; but the trend was introduced,
and it would grow over the next few decades, and by the 1990s it seemed like
every Off-Broadway success was heading for the Street. *Once Upon a Mattress*
may have signaled the end of an era in the history of Off Broadway.

Fallout

[20 May 1959, Renata Theatre, c. 70 performances] a musical revue by Abe
Goldsmith, Jerry Goldman, Martin Charnin, David Panich. *Score:* Charnin,
Robert Kessler, Paul Nassau (music and lyrics). *Cast:* Charles Nelson
Reilly, Virginia Vestoff, Margaret Hall, Joe Ross, Grover Dale, Paul Dooley,
Judy Guyll, Joy Lynn Sica, Jack Kauflin.

During the peak years of the Cold War you wouldn't find too many jokes
about nuclear fallout on television and in the movies, and even Broadway
was a bit nervous about having fun with fallout shelters and civil defense. Yet
this sassy little Off-Broadway revue put the subject right in the title. Oddly,
most of the songs and sketches were about music, not the bomb, and the
title intrigued more than it delivered, and audiences were not turned off. In
fact, word of mouth was strong enough to let the show run through most of
the summer. A variety of young talent contributed to the sketches and score,
and the cast was similarly made up of unknowns, though Charles Nelson
Reilly, Virginia Vestoff, and Paul Dooley would not remain unknown for
long. Reilly was the most praised of the nine performers, his nervous sense of

comic timing and thin but resonating tenor singing voice allowing him to steal just about everything he was in. Some of the material was brainy (Einstein's theory of relativity, beat poets, classical music, Shakespeare, and so on) and some was more farcical and broad, including those references to Russia and the dreaded nuclear attack. There were even a few love ballads to round out the evening. *Fallout* was typical Off-Broadway fare and the kind of entertainment that would not be possible a decade later.

THE BILLY BARNES REVUE

[9 June 1959, York Playhouse, 64 performances; John Golden Theatre, 87 performances; Carnegie Hall Playhouse, 48 performances] a musical revue by Billy Barnes, Bob Rodgers. *Score:* Barnes (music and lyrics). *Cast:* Rodgers, Bert Convy, Ann Guilbert, Ken Berry, Joyce Jameson, Jackie Joseph, Len Weinrib, Patti Regan.

While Julius Monk and Ben Bagley were finding modest fame with their revues in New York, Billy Barnes was doing the same on the West Coast. He and his college chum Bob Rodgers put together a series of *Billy Barnes Revues* in Los Angles that earned him the title "Revue Master of Hollywood." Barnes brought his favorite performers (including his wife Joyce Jameson) to New York in 1959 and did very well for himself with this revue. Coming from Tinsel Town, the show had more than its fair share of material dealing with the movies, both current and past. Celebrity couple Arthur Miller and Marilyn Monroe went on safari with Ernest Hemingway and the recent film of *Cat on a Hot Tin Roof* was skewered as "Home in Mississippi." The first act finale was a clever sequence titled "The Thirties" which spoofed and paid homage to Shirley Temple, Fred Astaire, Ginger Rogers, Nelson Eddy, and Jeanette MacDonald, as well as the Warner Brothers' *Gold Digger* musicals with Dick Powell and Ruby Keeler. These films would be rediscovered and lampooned later in the 1960s, but Barnes was ahead of the game with his comic nostalgia. The beat generation was ribbed, as was Las Vegas, hospital shows, and the revue's hometown, with the daffy trio "City of the Angels." The two best songs in the revue were the childlike ditty "Where Are Your Children?" about youth gone wild with sex and drugs, and the tender ballad "(Have I Stayed) Too Long at the Fair?" beautifully sung by Jameson. (The song would later find wider recognition with a Barbra Streisand recording.) There seemed to be little of the usual snobbery by the press about the California-bred show, and *The Billy Barnes Revue* found success on the East Coast as it moved from theatre to theatre. After doing brisk business Off Broadway for eight weeks, it transferred to Broadway's John Golden Theatre where it ran another eleven weeks. When that theatre was booked, the revue went back to Off Broadway and played at the Carnegie Hall Playhouse for six weeks more. Barnes came back to New York in 1961 with his *The Billy Barnes People*, but it only lasted a week on Broadway. By that time Barnes was starting to work in television and he left the theatre to write songs and comic material for television specials for Carol Burnett, Danny Kaye, and others, eventually providing material on a regular basis for *Laugh-In* and *The Sonny and Cher Show*. Television had been luring talent away from the theatre since the early 1950s, and by the 1960s one was more likely to see sketches and spoofs on the tube than on stage.

Pieces of Eight

[24 September 1959, Upstairs at the Downstairs] a musical revue by Julius Monk, various. *Score:* various. *Cast:* Jane Connell, Estelle Parsons, Gerry Matthews, Ceil Cabot, Del Close, Gordon Connell.

The upcoming presidential election, the controversy of banning *Lady Chatterley's Lover*, and the usual New York City topics provided the material for Julius Monk's eighth revue. Regular performers Jane Connell, Cecil Cabot, and Gerry Matthews were joined by three others, most memorably the multitalented Estelle Parsons whose devastating comic timing and throaty singing voice were a fun contrast to Connell's high-flying chirping. Both women joined Cabot for the delicious "Radio City Music Hall" while all six performers had fun with the wacky "Steel Guitars and Barking Seals." Parsons was able to reveal a more serious side in "Everybody Wants to Be Loved," but the best ballad in the show was the beguiling "Season's Greetings" sung by Cabot that later became a staple in Mabel Mercer's nightclub act. Claibe Richardson, Martin Charnin, Rod Warren, and Bud McCreery were among the many contributors to the songs and sketches, all under Monk's astute supervision and his welcoming presence on stage as host. By this time a new Julius Monk revue was anticipated and expected as part of every Off-Broadway season, and the returning patrons considered the shows an annual necessity or an unofficial holiday.

LITTLE MARY SUNSHINE

[18 November 1959, Orpheum Theatre, 1,143 performances] a musical comedy by Rick Besoyan. *Score:* Besoyan (music and lyrics). *Cast:* Eileen Brennan, William Graham, John McMartin, Elizabeth Parrish, Elmarie Wendel, John Aniston, Mario Siletti, Ray James.

During the 1958–1959 Off-Broadway season, two old-style musicals were revived and both were smash hits. The 1920s pastiche musical comedy *The Boy Friend*, which had first played on Broadway only four years before, returned to New York and ran 763 performances. The 1917 collegiate musical *Leave It to Jane* was revived at the Sheridan Square Playhouse and surprised everyone by running 928 performances. These are big numbers for Off Broadway, but they were both bested by a new musical, *Little Mary Sunshine*, which poked fun at such old shows and managed to be highly entertaining. Rick Besoyan wrote the libretto, music, and lyrics and, while at first glance he seemed to be lampooning the 1924 hit *Rose-Marie*, the show took in a wide range of early musicals, from early twentieth-century Victor Herbert operettas to the 1920s Jerome Kern and Sigmund Romberg works. Yet the tone throughout was consistently light, tongue-in-cheek, and delightful. Little Mary Sunshine (Eileen Brennan) is the proprietress of the Colorado Inn in the Rocky Mountains where she sings chipper, optimistic songs to the guests and the locals. When she is threatened with eviction, Captain "Big Jim" Warington (William Graham) and the Colorado Rangers come to her rescue, and not only is the inn saved but Jim wins the heart of Mary. There were two charming subplots: Mary's saucy maid Nancy Twinkle (Elmarie Wendel) is romanced by the comic forest ranger Corporal Billy Jester (John McMartin); and the visiting opera singer Madame Ernestine Von Liebedich (Elizabeth Parrish) is wooed and won by the Washington diplomat General Oscar Fairfax (Mario Siletti). There was the friendly Chief Brown Bear (John Aniston) of the local Kadota Indians and his less-friendly son Yellow Feather (Ray James) who caused difficulties for everyone, and there were five young ladies from the Eastchester Finishing School back East to flirt with and end up married to the amiable forest rangers. The plotting was solid, the dialogue merrily stilted, and the characters happily recognized types.

Yet it was Besoyan's pastiche score that made *Little Mary Sunshine* sparkle. Like *The Boy Friend*, the songs were patterned after certain types but were very enjoyable for themselves. The title number, sung by the adoring rangers about their favorite female, recalled the title song of *Rose-Marie*, and the men's chorale "The Forest Rangers" echoed the same operetta's march "The Mounties." Both songs were as pleasing as the originals. Mary's optimistic "Look for a Sky of Blue" had the same quality as Kern's "Look for the Silver Lining" from *Sally* (1920), and there was no mistaking the operatic air "In Izzenschnooken on the Lovely Essenzook Zee" as Besoyan's homage to Kern and Hammerstein's "In Egern on the Tegern See" from *Music in the Air* (1932). Not all the songs were so specific, and often a number was more nimble or lyrical that one didn't worry about the reference. Billy and Nancy's breezy duet "Once in a Blue Moon"; Mary and Jim's fervent duet "Colorado Love Call"; and Ernestine and the General's rhapsodic duet "Do You Ever Dream of Vienna?" were richer than mere parody. Nancy got two sprightly numbers, the teasing "Naughty, Naughty Nancy" (recalling Herbert's title song for *Naughty Marietta*) and the sly "Mata Hari" (which had the same sass as Kern and P. G. Wodehouse's "Cleopatra" from *Leave It to Jane*). Even the small chorus got to sing some tuneful gems, such as the coy "How Do You Do?"; the rollicking "Such a Merry Party"; and the empty-headed frolic "Swinging and Playing Croquet." *Little Mary Sunshine* opened to exemplary reviews for both Besoyan's efforts and for the sharp and funny production. Eileen Brennan, who said she modeled her character after Disney's animated Snow White, was particularly commended for her sweet soprano singing voice and her ability to almost subliminally suggest the cockeyed nature of the operetta genre. John McMartin, who was deemed a funny and engaging Billy Jester, began his long and distinguished stage career with this show. *Little Mary Sunshine* ran three years and was then very popular with summer stock and amateur theatre groups for decades, enjoyed by audiences often too young to be familiar with the show's musical targets.

Chapter Three

───────────○───────────

Too Loud Not to Notice:
The 1960s

WHILE THE FIRST FEW YEARS OF THE 1960s in America were not all that different from the 1950s, it was clear from the start that change was in the air.
By the end of the decade the country would be a very different place than it
was in 1960. For a decade that opened with youthful vigor and optimism, as
personified in the new president John F. Kennedy, it ended in chaos, disillusionment, and hostility. During this time Off Broadway splintered off in as
many directions as the American psyche had. The generation gap was getting
wider every day, and the battle between young and old (and left and right)
was more obvious, particularly in the areas of politics and music. These two
topics of contention were represented by the war in Vietnam and rock music.
Both had been around for years, but by the mid-1960s the lines of distinction
were clearly drawn. America was being divided and, although this division
was not so obvious on Broadway, it was showing up on Off Broadway. The
playful and satiric revue survived, but it was getting less lighthearted and
more sarcastic. The traditional book musical continued but was deemed too
conventional by some, and loosely structured stories filled with angst took
precedence. And, most noticeably, the sound of the scores changed. Rock
music, which had only been hinted at in conventional Broadway musicals
such as *Bye Bye Birdie* and *Do Re Mi* (both in 1960), arrived on center stage
in the late 1960s. Yet Off Broadway remained remarkably diverse. Where else
could such different musicals like *You're a Good Man, Charlie Brown* and
Hair open within six months of each other and both become hits?

Even Broadway was not immune to the changes occurring across the
land. The 1960s produced such conventional, feel-good musical hits in
Camelot; Carnival; How to Succeed in Business without Really Trying; A

57

Funny Thing Happened on the Way to the Forum; *She Loves Me*; *Hello, Dolly!*; *Funny Girl*; *I Do! I Do!*; *Sweet Charity*; *Mame*; *George M!*; *Promises, Promises*; and *1776*, but there was no shortage of shows that had real substance, such as the popular *Fiddler on the Roof* and *Man of La Mancha*, and a handful of failures, *Hallelujah, Baby!*; *Kwamina*; *I Can Get It for You Wholesale*; and *Anyone Can Whistle*. More encouragingly, the decade's two most innovative Broadway shows, *Cabaret* and *Hair*, were hits; though the second came from Off Broadway.

The full spectrum of the changes the country was undergoing was best illustrated by the variety found in Off-Broadway musicals. It was here that the protests about the war were joined by the shouts of the civil rights movement, the recognition of the generation gap, and the antiestablishment fervor. Alongside such restless shows were comic revues, musical tributes to composers as diverse as Cole Porter and Kurt Weill, movie spoofs, revivals of old musicals, feel-good romances, literary musicals, and even shows that mocked the rebellious youth of the time. No matter what your politics or cultural orientation, Off Broadway had a musical for you. This was possible because there were more offerings than in any other previous decade and there were more venues. No longer was Off Broadway geographically restricted to Greenwich Village. Little playhouses sprung up in places far from downtown or Times Square, even finding a home in the boroughs. A good number of these productions were still commercial, and costs, while escalating each year, were still low enough that these productions made a profit Off Broadway. In fact, the overhead costs on Broadway had become too prohibitive that Off-Broadway producers sometimes found it more profitable *not* to transfer a hit to Broadway. The country may have been going to rack and ruin, but Off Broadway did very well in the 1960s.

During this time, Broadway's alternative venue was perceived by the New York playgoers (very few tourists attended Off-Broadway shows) as a fundamental part of the theatre scene. Of course the majority of the audience still preferred Broadway with its stars and big musicals, but Off Broadway was not thought of as so offbeat anymore. While it was considered slumming in earlier decades to see an Off-Broadway production, in the 1960s it was regarded as a healthy cultural diet. One went off the Street as one went to a foreign movie or an unusual art exhibit; not a mainstream event but one that a lot of people took seriously enough to want to include in their social lives. Also, the informality of Off Broadway was no longer such a contrast. In an earlier age one went to Broadway in formal attire but in more relaxed clothing to a Greenwich Village production. As the 1960s got more and more casual, Off Broadway did not seem so strange or forbidding. It was no longer slumming; it was as natural as going to a movie. This attitude change allowed Off Broadway to blossom during a turbulent decade. Whether you wanted to be challenged, confronted, or entertained, Off Broadway was able to provide a musical to satisfy.

By the end of the decade this pleasant situation would start to corrode. Off-Broadway musicals were more expensive to produce and to attend, and the sense of experimentation was waning. The truly radical and cutting edge theatre was springing up in tiny spaces that fell below the Off-Broadway radar. Halfway through the decade the term Off Off Broadway was being used on occasion, though it was unclear what distinguished the difference between the two venues. This would become more solidified in the 1970s, but the handwriting was on the wall: Off Broadway was threatened by its very success.

PARADE

[20 January 1960, Players Theatre, 95 performances] a musical revue. *Score:* Jerry Herman (music and lyrics). *Cast:* Dody Goodman, Charles Nelson Reilly, Lester James, Fia Karin, Richard Tone.

Six years after Jerry Herman's songs were first heard Off Broadway, this merry revue opened and his work was again noticed and applauded. It may have seemed to Herman that his career was going nowhere, but *Parade* would open up doors and he would soon be on Broadway where he would remain for decades. Much of the material in *Parade* came from a late-night cabaret show Herman had written in 1958 titled *Nightcap*, which played at the Showplace for several months. The topics covered in *Parade* were routine: urban living, love and sex, the opera world, the theatre season, television, Hollywood, and the Rockettes. It was clear that Herman's worldview was a showbiz one, as evidenced in the signature song "Show Tune." (He would later use the title for his autobiography and the melody for "It's Today" in *Mame*.) But if there were few surprises in the subject matter, *Parade* boasted a tuneful score and some vibrant performances. Dody Goodman and Charles Nelson Reilly handled the comic songs, and the other three performers did the ballads and up-tempo numbers. The temperamental Maria Callas was ribbed in "Maria in Spats"; uptown and downtown differences got in the way of romance in "Confession to a Park Avenue Mother"; the ageless high kickers at Radio City were diced in "The Last Rockette"; lesbian sex in the Woman's House of Detention was more than hinted at in "Save the Village"; and recent theatrical dramas and musicals of the depressing sort were chronicled in the waltzing comic duet "Jolly Theatrical Season." Another duet "Your Hand in Mine" and the ballads "Another Candle" and "The Next Time I Love" revealed Herman's ability to be as tender as he was funny. An unlikely but impressive number in the revue was "Two a Day," an amusing and fond tribute to the bygone days of vaudeville. It seemed even the young Herman was incurably nostalgic and didn't seem to care if his songs were considered old-fashioned. *Parade* was a modest production with a limited budget (Herman also served as director, musical director, and pianist), but its rewards were considerable. The revue ran twelve weeks before Herman, Goodman, and Reilly went on to bigger and better things.

FOUR BELOW STRIKES BACK

[28 January 1960, Downstairs at the Upstairs] a musical revue by Julius Monk, various. *Score:* various. *Cast:* Nancy Dussault, George Furth, Cy Young, Jenny Lou Law.

Julius Monk's series of numerically titled revues continued with *Four Below Strikes Back*, perhaps the oddest title of the group but one of the best collections of talent on- and back stage. Ronny Graham led a gang of writers and composers who came up with some witty sketches and sparkling songs. (One of the team, Tom Jones, would find himself four months later with the biggest hit in Off-Broadway history with *The Fantasticks*.) The quartet of performers was top-notch, comic actor George Furth getting the most laughs and singer Nancy Dussault carrying the ballads and the comedy equally well. Topical subjects included the revolution in Cuba ("The Castro Tango!"), the Cold War stateside ("The Family Fallout Shelter"), dirty books like *Lolita* ("The Constant Nymphet"), and corruption in the radio business ("Payola"). "Love, Here I Am" was a delectable ballad; "Merry-Go, Merry-Go-Round" was a contagious romp; "It's a Wonderful Day to Be Seventeen" was a joyous character song; and bittersweet nostalgia was conjured up in "Jefferson Davis Tyler's General Store." No one seems to know exactly how long *Four Below Strikes Back* ran, but one performance was recorded, so we do know how good it was.

THE FANTASTICKS

[3 May 1960, Sullivan Street Playhouse, 17,162 performances] a musical fable by Tom Jones based on Edmond Rostand's play *Les Romanesques*.

Score: Harvey Schmidt (music), Jones (lyrics). *Cast:* Jerry Orbach, Rita Gardner, Kenneth Nelson, William Larsen, Hugh Thomas, Thomas Bruce (aka Tom Jones), George Curley.

So much has been written about this little wonder of a musical that it might be best to get the superlatives out of the way at the start. *The Fantasticks* is still the finest of all Off-Broadway musicals. It ran longer than any other American musical (forty-two years), has been produced regionally more than any other Off-Broadway musical (over twelve thousand productions to date), has been produced around the world more than any other Off-Broadway musical (more than six hundred productions in at least seventy countries), and is still very much with us showcasing its many professional and amateur productions across the country and a long-running revival in New York. Yet numbers don't do justice to *The Fantasticks* because it is so small, so seemingly inconsequential that superlatives seem vulgar. Better to say it is the quintessential Off-Broadway musical.

The story, adapted from Edmond Rostand's 1895 French comedy *Les Romanesques*, is simplicity itself. The young lovers Matt (Kenneth Nelson) and Luisa (Rita Gardner) are neighbors, separated by a wall that their fathers, Hucklebee (William Larsen) and Bellamy (Hugh Thomas), have put up because they want their children to think they are enemies. In fact, they are using reverse psychology hoping that the two will fall in love. They do, and when the fathers have to call off the pretend feud, they hire the bandit El Gallo (Jerry Orbach) to try to abduct Luisa, knowing that Matt will save her and the two families can then become friends. El Gallo hires a rustic old actor (Tom Jones using the stage name Thomas Bruce) and his hammy assistant Mortimer (George Curley) to assist him in the attempted abduction, convincing the fathers that a first-class "rape" is called for in matters like these. All goes according to plan, but once the happy ending comes, the lovers find they are disenchanted with each other in the harsh sunlight and they part. Matt goes off to see the world and is cruelly treated, while Luisa makes plans for a romantic future with El Gallo, only to be abandoned by him. With the two lovers hurt and more mature, they realize they have a more genuine love for each other, and there is a second, more honest, happy ending. The time and location of the story is not specified, and even the characters are identified as Boy, Girl, Boy's Father, Girl's Father, Actor, and Man Who Dies, giving the tale a folk quality that helps make *The Fantasticks* universal. Yet there is something distinctly American about the piece although some songs are in the Latin mode and the bandit El Gallo is definitely a foreign figure. The

character of the Mute (Richard Stauffer) assists El Gallo and even represents
the wall between the two families, just as in Shakespeare's farcical "Pyramus
and Thisby" skit in *A Midsummer Night's Dream*. Tom Jones's libretto sometimes departs from prose, and sections of the script are in verse with musical
accompaniment. It is simple, narrative poetry that reminds one of a primitive
narrative ballad.

The music Harvey Schmidt composed for Jones's lyrics varies in style, yet
the whole score seems similarly nonspecific. The flamenco-like "It Depends
On What You Pay" and the tango "Never Say No" have a Spanish flavor; the
beatnik sounding "This Plum Is Too Ripe" is cool jazz; the expansive "I Can
See It" comes close to hot jazz; the farcical "Metaphor" is mock operetta;
the furious waltz "Round and Round" has a tarantella pattern; and the unembellished ballad "Try to Remember" is a folk song. These are not simple
pastiches as much as evocative songs that keep the story from identifying its
time and place. Other numbers in the sterling score can only be described as
"Off-Broadway" sounding. Luisa's eager "I am" song "Much More" is purely a
theatre number, coming across like her audition for the real world. The lovers' naive duet "Soon It's Gonna Rain" is innocence itself, both in its tinkling
music and dreamy lyric. Matt and Luisa's more mature duet "They Were You"
is a potent contrast to their earlier "Metaphor"; love is not a list song but a
plain and obvious realization. Even the overture for the show, unique in that
it uses none of the songs in the score, is a vivacious piece of music that suggests everything from a sexual dance of death to a circus. Jones's lyrics are
character driven but, like his script, there are few specifics. The examples
used in "Metaphor" and "Plant a Radish" are generic, the visions in "Round
and Round" are poetically distant, and the literary images used in "Try to
Remember" are eternal. No wonder this show went around the globe. *The
Fantasticks* has an outstanding score that never strives to stand apart; it has
that amazing quality of seeming easy and unassuming.

Jones and Schmidt began working on the musical as college students,
and it was originally planned as an elaborate *Romeo and Juliet* romance set in
their native Texas with the unfortunate title of *Joy Comes to Dead Horse*. The
arrival of *West Side Story* on Broadway scotched their plans, but when they
were requested to submit a one-act musical for a summer season at Barnard
College, they simplified their story to a brief parable about young love. Producer Loto Nore saw the one-act and urged the authors to write a full-length
version for Off Broadway. When they expanded the piece, they wisely kept
it in the form of a romantic fable and avoided any connection to the retired
Southwest setting (though some songs still conjured up the Spanish locale).
Nore was barely able to raise the $16,500 to open in the 144-seat Sullivan
Street Theatre, which encouraged designer Ed Wittstein to keep the setting

and costumes to a minimum. The Off-Broadway production was staged with imaginative economy by Word Baker using only a wooden platform and a trunkful of props and a cast of mostly newcomers. Jerry Orbach was particularly effective as El Gallo, commenting on the action and characters with a mixture of wry humor and somber reflection. Orbach's rendition of "Try to Remember" not only set the tone for the musical but was a chilling, understated act of hypnotism. Former child actor Kenneth Nelson was thirty years old in 1960 yet passed admirably as the teenager Matt, and Rita Garner was convincingly naive and enthusiastic as Luisa. Hugh Thomas and William Larson were a whimsical pair of fathers, yet both were careful not to be reduced to vaudeville clowns. Nore could not have had a better cast even if he had the money to hire more seasoned performers.

The Fantasticks opened without fanfare, and the few reviewers who came were modest in their praise. After the show won the Vernon Rice Award, business picked up and soon word of mouth did the rest, helped by the popularity of the song "Try to Remember." The cast recording also helped and, without ever being a hot ticket, The Fantasticks slowly but surely became a hit. In 1964, Hallmark Hall of Fame broadcast an abridged version of the musical with an impressive cast that included Ricardo Montalban as El Gallo, John Davidson and Susan Watson as the lovers, and Bert Lahr and Stanley Holloway as the fathers. It was the first time a television version had been shown of a musical still running in New York. George Schaefer directed the studio production, which resembled the Off-Broadway version in its simplicity. Within a decade of its opening in New York, productions were done all around the world, many where an American musical had never been seen before. The piece also remained a favorite with all kinds of theatre groups in the States, chalking up hundreds of revivals each year. All this time the show continued on in its original Off-Broadway home. For decades there had been talk of a film version of The Fantasticks, but no one really expected it to happen since it seemed to be such an obviously bad idea. A television studio could capture the intimacy of the piece, but what possibly could film have to offer? In 1995, United Artists thought otherwise: Jones wrote the screenplay, and Michael Ritchie directed. The result is probably the worst film version of a musical ever made. Conceptually, acting-wise, cinematically, and visually it was beyond anyone's most fearsome nightmare of what could be done to this charming little musical. The studio must have had similar feelings since they kept the film on the shelf for five years, only then giving it a limited release in 2000 before putting it out on video. By the millennium, New Yorkers had accepted the Off-Broadway production of The Fantasticks as a local landmark, something that would always be there. But it was not to be. In 2002, the building housing the Sullivan Street Playhouse was sold, the income from the small theatre was deemed insignificant in a real estate boom, and the show was forced to close on January 13, 2002. It was greatly missed, and few were surprised when *The Fantasticks* was revived in 2006 in another intimate space—this time uptown in the Theatre District. The production recreated the original (though the "rape" song "It Depends on What You Pay" had been rewritten years before so as not to offend those in a more sensitive sociological climate) and was welcomed back by the press and the public. The little theatre on 50th Street, where the revival continues to play, was later named the Jerry Orbach Theatre.

Aside from all the numbers and statistics, *The Fantasticks* holds an important place in the history of the American musical. The Off-Broadway musical revue had reshaped that genre in the 1950s, and unusual book musicals like *The Threepenny Opera* and *The Golden Apple* had demonstrated that an alternative musical could also be popular. But it was *The Fantasticks* that defined the Off-Broadway book musical: small, intimate, inventive, literate, and slightly unconventional. It made no apologies for its size and scope. *Once Upon a Mattress*, *Little Mary Sunshine*, and other successful book musicals had been scaled down for Off Broadway; *The Fantasticks* was created with its modest elements in place. There was never talk of transferring it to Broadway. The musical represented the essence of an Off-Broadway musical, and it still does. Not Broadway nor television nor the movies can do what this little musical does. The show doesn't even work in all theatres. The first London production was in a West End theatre and only ran forty-four performances. Years later an American national tour, featuring Robert Goulet as El Gallo, played in large houses and was a quick flop. One can go so far as to say that Off Broadway still exists because this is what it does best. Of course, many have tried to copy *The Fantasticks* over the decades. The formula seemed simple enough, yet no one has ever succeeded. Even Jones and Schmidt couldn't do it, although, like many others, they tried often enough. With its cardboard moon and sun, its timeless plot and basic character types, and its fragile sense of whimsy and romance, *The Fantasticks* proves to be as elusive as it is unforgettable.

ERNEST IN LOVE

[4 May 1960, Gramercy Arts Theatre, 111 performances] a musical comedy by Anne Croswell based on Oscar Wilde's play *The Importance of Being Earnest*. *Score:* Lee Pockriss (music), Croswell (lyrics). *Cast:* Sara Seegar, John Irving, Louis Edmonds, Leila Martin, Gerrianne Raphael, George Hall.

The unique aspect of this musical comedy of manners is not that it was based on Oscar Wilde's classic *The Importance of Being Earnest* but that it came from television. The English classic appeared as a musical on Broadway in 1927 as *Oh, Ernest!* and there were other attempts to musicalize Wilde in regional theatre and in Europe. Anne Croswell turned the three-act comedy into the sixty-minute musical *Who's Earnest?* for CBS's *U.S. Steel Hour* in 1957, also providing the lyrics for Lee Pockriss's handful of songs. While the witty Irishman may have been shortchanged in the greatly abridged teleplay, the delightful Wildean score helps to compensate him. The songs were literate and tuneful, echoing the wit of the original without ever competing with it. The telecast also boasted a superior cast who handled the Wilde dialogue (what was left of it) with aplomb. The broadcast went well enough that Croswell and Pockriss expanded the piece into a full-length stage musical, and it was produced Off Broadway three years later under the title *Ernest in Love*. The plot remained faithful to Wilde. Both Jack Worthing (John Irving) and Algernon Moncrief (Louis Edmonds) claim their names to be Earnest hoping to woo the ladies Gwendolyn (Leila Martin) and Cecily (Gerrianne Raphael). The pompous Lady Bracknell (Sara Seegar) is not about to allow either relationship to proceed to the altar until the forgetful Miss Prism (Lucy Landau) reveals that Jack is actually of aristocratic birth and was named Earnest. Several new songs were written and the drawing room comedy was opened up a bit for the musical stage, a number of different locations added, and some songs given to the servants and tradesmen. Yet *Ernest in Love* remained intimate, and dialogue and songs overrode any spectacle. Some of the numbers, such as "Perfection" and "A Handbag Is Not a Proper Mother," were delicious extensions of the play's wordy and ridiculous sense of humor. Yet the operetta duet "Lost" and some other numbers were blandly serious and not at all in keeping with the spirit of the play. "A Wicked Man" possessed a droll lyric worthy of Wilde, whereas "How Do You Find the Words?" was more like a Shavian number that was cut from *My Fair Lady*. (It was talk-song by Irving who seemed to have an even less musical pitch than Rex Harrison.) The only substantial disappointment with *Ernest in Love* was the cast; those who could act couldn't sing, and those with the pipes could not grasp the Wildean style. This was particularly obvious if one recalled the excellent television cast: David Atkinson (Jack), Edward Mulhare (Algernon), Edith King (Lady Bracknell), Dorothy Collins (Cecily), and Louise Troy (Gwendolen). Nevertheless, *Ernest in Love* was favorably reviewed and ran for fourteen weeks. A 2009 Off-Broadway revival by the Irish Repertory Theatre, featuring Beth Fowler as Lady Bracknell, was well enough received that it extended its limited engagement to seven weeks.

GREENWICH VILLAGE, U.S.A.

[28 September 1960, One Sheridan Square, 87 performances] a musical revue by Frank Gehrecke. *Score:* Jeanne Gargy (music and lyrics), Gehrecke, Herb Corey (lyrics). *Cast:* Jane A. Johnston, Saralou Cooper, Jack Betts, Dawn Hampton, James Pompeii, Pat Finley, James Harwood, Burke McHugh.

Making fun of Bohemian life in the Village was pretty old hat by the 1960s, but enough playgoers still liked that sort of thing, allowing *Greenwich Village, U.S.A.* to run eleven weeks. Beatniks, literary types, students from New York University, artists, jazz musicians, advocates of free love, and other denizens of the neighborhood were satirized with broad sketches and a score that moved from cool jazz to old-time honky-tonk. The title song was a frenzied salute to the Bohemian Village; in the rhythm piece "Sunday Brunch" the gossipy guests sounded like the salesmen in *The Music Man*'s "Rock Island"; "How About Us Last Night" was a bouncy jazz duet about the morning after; and an old apartment building was recalled nostalgically when the "Brownstone" was slated for demolition. As in the earlier revue *Parade*, there was a number about the neighborhood's Ladies House of Detention; "N.Y.U." was a jaunty song about the local university; "Shopkeepers Trio" was an old-fashioned harmonizing number; and there was even a satiric narrative ballet titled "Birth of a Beatnik." Some numbers fell flat, such as the mawkish ballad "Love Me"; a double entendre number about new Hi-Fidelity records called "Miss Hi-Fie"; and an empty march "Save the Village" that went nowhere. Producer and codirector Burke McHugh joined the cast, most of whom were pleasing enough without being exceptional. The ballad singer Dawn Hampton was a cut above the rest, particularly when she delivered the swinging "We Got Love." *Greenwich Village, U.S.A.* was not nearly as sharp-witted nor as polished as the Julius Monk revues and some other series which continued into the 1960s. The golden age of the Off-Broadway musical revue was waning, and by the mid-1960s it would move in new directions. In the meantime, shows like *Greenwich Village U.S.A.* seemed to have lost their purpose and proved mildly entertaining at best.

DRESSED TO THE NINES

[29 September 1960, Upstairs at the Downstairs] a musical revue by Julius Monk. *Score:* various (music and lyrics). *Cast:* Gerry Matthews, Gordon Connell, Bill Hinnant, Mary Louise Wilson, Ceil Calbot, Pat Ruhl.

As with some other Julius Monk revues, no record of how long *Dressed to the Nines* ran survived, but again a performance was recorded, and one can enjoy a taste of Monk's special way with satire and song. Although the term Off Off Broadway was not yet in general use, there were tiny theatres springing up around Manhattan that made Off Broadway look large and elegant. These small performance spaces were wryly ribbed in the song "The Theatre's in the Dining Room." There was also a mock blues number called "Billy's Blues," Florida was kidded in "Ft. Lauderdale," and "Sociable Amoeba" spoofed highbrow society. There was usually a nostalgic number in each Monk revue, and this one had the fervent "Bring Back the Roxy to Me" about the recently leveled movie palace. The showstopper of the evening was the politically incorrect "The Hate Song." (Interestingly, a different song with the same title was the high point in the revue *The Mad Show* six years later.) The sketches took on the electric company, pollution, television commercials, and "unexpurgated" dirty books. *Dressed to the Nines* had a uniformly excellent cast, but one could not help but single out the sharp voice and comic timing of Mary Louise Wilson.

VALMOUTH

[6 October 1960, York Playhouse, 14 performances] a musical play by Sandy Wilson based on the novel by Ronald Firbank. *Score:* Wilson (music and lyrics). *Cast:* Bertice Reading, Constance Carpenter, Alfred Toigo, Anne Francine, Elly Stone, Beatrice Pons, Gail Jones, Ralston Hill, Franklin Kiser.

It is odd to describe a musical based on a 1919 novel as being ahead of its time, but *Valmouth* was such a curiosity. The British import was truly unique, definitely strange, and clearly unsuccessful, closing in two weeks. Yet the score is notable and cannot be overlooked. Ronald Firbank's novel concerned the elderly patrons of a fictional Edwardian spa called Valmouth. The major characters were aged Roman Catholic women who were still physically active and sexually frustrated. The book was in the form of a fantasy of sorts—its sordid details were not to be taken literally. Firbank followed the novel with other books set in the same locale. Sandy Wilson, mostly known in America for writing the book, music, and lyrics for the pastiche musical *The Boy Friend*, took different events and characters from Firbank's novels and fashioned them into a bizarre musical that cannot be compared to any other. The ancient Lady Parvula de Panzoust (Constance

Carpenter) is chasing a young shepherd David Tooke (Franklin Kiser); the reformed courtesan Mrs. Hurstpierpoint (Anne Francine), who once had a brief dalliance with a British king, is trying to baptize the infant of the young unmarried Niri-Esther (Gail Jones) whose lover has left her for the sea; and the worldly Cardinal Pirelli (Ralston Hill) shows up and is willing to do the christening, but they learn he has been excommunicated for baptizing a dog. Holding sway over all of these eccentric people is the exotic masseur Mrs. Yajinavalkya (Bertice Reading) from India whose magical powers keep the old folks randy and spry. As for Mrs. Yaj herself, she is content with the 102-year-old Grannie Tooke (Beatrice Pons) as her "companion." Captain Dick Thoroughfare (Alfred Tiogo) returns to marry Niri-Esther, then fire descends on Valmouth, and the wicked are swept away while the innocent set off to find a better life on a South Seas island. Add to all this Sister Ecclesia (Elly Stone), a singing nun who only speaks one day each year, and you know *Valmouth* is not going to be another *The Boy Friend*.

Although many British critics called the musical depraved and smutty, others thought it audacious and oddly touching. English playgoers were curious enough to give the musical a healthy run in Hammersmith and then in London. Because of the popularity of *The Boy Friend* in New York in 1954, Sandy Wilson was someone Broadway producers courted. But none would risk doing *Valmouth* on the Street, yet some daring producers presented it Off Broadway where they spent an unprecedented $40,000 on the elaborate production. (Tony Walton did the lush sets and costumes as he had in London.) The press was more confused than outraged. Several did praise the score, and the cast was roundly applauded, but just explaining the show in the reviews was enough to frighten audiences away.

What kind of score comes from such an unorthodox musical? It had a 1920s flavor but was filtered through a 1950s cool jazz sound at times. The title song was a waltzing welcome number; "All the Girls Were Pretty (And All the Men Were Strong)" fondly looked back to past escapades; "Niri-Esther" was a dandy soft-shoe about the charms of the heroine; Mrs Yaj listed the fine qualities of her "Magic Fingers" and cut loose with the swinging "Big Best Shoes" about a night on the town; and "Where the Trees Are Green with Parrots" was a warm ballad about an exotic place in the tropics. There were a handful of songs about sex, filled with double entendres and clever word play, as in "Just Once More" and "Only a Passing Phase." Then there were some definitely offbeat numbers that grew out of the offbeat libretto: the Cardinal's wordy list song in which he compared (unfavorably) every other church to his "Cathedral of Clemenza"; the nun's furious "My Talking Day" with everything she wanted to say all year spilling out; an odd lullaby "Little Baby Girl" urging an infant to sleep now because as an adult she will be up nights worrying about her man; and Mrs. Yaj's recollection of her late husband "Mustapha," the song moving back and forth from a romantic fox-trot to a jazzy two-step. It was a glittering score but not enough to save the problematic subject matter and unconventional characters. *Valmouth* has found a small but determined following over the years, helped by the London cast recording starring Cleo Laine as Mrs. Yaj. A successful 1982 revival at Chichester (with several original cast members) was also recorded, and productions in England pop up on occasion. Stateside, you're not likely to see a revival in your neighborhood no matter where you live.

SMILING THE BOY FELL DEAD

[19 April 1961, Cherry Lane Theatre, 22 performances] a musical play by Ira Wallach. *Score:* David Baker (music), Sheldon Harnick (lyrics). *Cast:* Danny Meehan, Phil Leeds, Claiborne Cary, Joseph Macaulay, Warren Wade, Louise Larabee, Justine Johnson.

Though not as unusual as *Valmouth*, the similarly unique *Smiling the Boy Fell Dead* also was notable, and it didn't run much longer than Sandy Wilson's musical. Ira Wallach's libretto was a satiric take on the old Horatio Alger theme. The sly entrepreneur Simeon Moodis (Phil Leeds) believes that the days of the pioneer are over and the country will grow rich not by the farm but by staying far away from the farm. He makes deals, buys and sells things he never sees, and is always on the lookout for new opportunities. By contrast, the young and naive climber Waldo Templeton (Danny Meehan) is as honest as the day is long and often falls prey to sharks like Moodis. Yet fate is kind, and Waldo's mishaps eventually bring him a fortune and the heart of Dorothea Gatsby (Claiborne Cary). The tone of the story was light and sarcastic, the characters broad and likable, and the score pleasant and engaging. Sheldon Harnick, who had recently found success on Broadway with *Fiorello!*, returned to Off Broadway for *Smiling the Boy Fell Dead* and wrote the radiant lyrics for David Baker's music. The lovely ballad "If I Felt Any Younger Today" was the closest the show got to a hit song, but there was much to recommend in Waldo's eager "The ABCs of Success" and optimistic "I've Got a Wonderful Future," Moodis' cynical "Heredity-Environment," the merry "The Gatsby Bridge March," the arch "Dear Old Dad," and the lively "Temperance Polka." Both Leeds and Meehan were praised by the critics, but notices for the musical itself were mixed, and the venture closed in three weeks. Unlike the character of Waldo, *Smiling the Boy Fell Dead* seems to have had no future, and the show is now a footnote in Harnick's career.

THE SAP OF LIFE

[2 October 1961, One Sheridan Square, 49 performances] a musical play by Richard Maltby Jr. *Score:* David Shire (music), Maltby (lyrics). *Cast:* Kenneth Nelson, Jerry Dodge, Dina Paisner, Jack Bittner, Lilian Fields, Patricia Bruder, Lee Powell.

An unpretentious domestic musical, it is only remembered today as the first Off-Broadway appearance of the songwriting team of Richard Maltby Jr. and David Shire. Maltby's libretto was simple and workable. Country dwellers Oscar (Jack Bittner) and Jessie (Dina Paisner) are the parents of two sons, the elder Andrew (Kenneth Nelson) and the younger Horatio (Jerry Dodge), both of whom are grown up but avoiding the real world. The parents push Andrew out of the house, demanding he make his own way while discovering life and himself. Andrew goes to the big city, fumbles a bit at first, but ends up learning more about the world than his parents bargained for. Nelson, fresh from his stint as the Boy in *The Fantasticks*, was effective in another juvenile role, and there were compliments for Dodge who would soon be on Broadway. If *The Sap of Life* had any claim to fame, it was for its felicitous score filled with incisive character songs and ballads. The contagious march "Watching the Big Parade Go By" and the wry trio "She Loves Me Not" that the brothers sang with the pretty neighbor Sally Ann (Lee Powell) were perhaps the best two numbers, and both were later revived in Maltby-Shire revues. Also enjoyable were the charming duet "Children Have It Easy" sung by Andrew and his elderly Aunt Dot (Lilian Fields), the wistful ballad "Time and Time Again," and the brothers' catchy duet "Charmed Life." *The Sap of Life* managed to run six weeks, far from a smash hit but good enough to launch the songwriters' careers.

SEVEN COMES ELEVEN

[5 October 1961, Upstairs at the Downstairs] a musical revue by Julius Monk. *Score:* various. *Cast:* Mary Louise Wilson, Rex Robbins, Philip Bruns, Ceil Cabot, Donna Sanders, Steve Roland.

A song satirizing the controversial right-wing "John Birch Society" showed that even the lighthearted Julius Monk revues were getting a bit edgy in the

1960s. Other topical subjects that provided fodder for sketches and songs included the new First Lady ("The Jackie Look"), Cuba's Fidel Castro ("I Flew to Havana Last Wednesday"), and newfangled education theories ("School Daze"). The city was celebrated with tongue in cheek in "This Is New York!" and "New York Has a New Hotel"; the proliferation of Gilbert and Sullivan operettas in town was ribbed in "Captain of the Pinafores"; and the cast had fun with the tongue-twisting "Alma What's a Mater." The expected nostalgic offering was "Christmas Long Ago," and there was a frantic song of feminine triumph titled "I Found Him." (This last, by Jack Urbont and Bruce Geller, was heard again Off Broadway a month later in the team's *All in Love*.) Mary Louise Wilson was again the standout in an exceptional cast, and *Seven Comes Eleven* was a popular attraction at the intimate Upstairs at the Downstairs. The score was recorded but never released to stores, making the cast recording, which was only sold at the theatre during the run, the rarest and most sought after of all the Julius Monk revues.

O MARRY ME!

[27 October 1961, Gate Theatre, 21 performances] a musical comedy by Lola Pergament based on Oliver Goldsmith's play *She Stoops to Conquer*. *Score*: Pergament (lyrics), Robert Kessler (music). *Cast*: Chevi Colton, Muriel Greenspon, Ted Van Griethuysen, Elly Stone, James Harwood, Joe Silver, Leonard Drum.

ALL IN LOVE

[10 November 1961, Martinique Theatre, 141 performances] a musical comedy by Bruce Geller based on Sheridan's play *The Rivals*. *Score*: Jacques Urbont (music), Geller (lyrics). *Cast*: David Atkinson, Mimi Randolph, Gaylea Byrne, Lee Cass, Christina Gillespie, Dom DeLuise, Michael Davis.

Two British comedy classics of the eighteenth-century stage were musicalized and opened Off Broadway within two weeks of each other. Oliver Goldsmith's *She Stoops to Conquer* (1773) seems an ideal source for a musical with its larger-than-life characters, farcical plot, and possibilities for song. The resulting musical, *O Marry Me!*, was competent but uninspired, and not much was gained by adding a score and some dance to Goldsmith's original. The libretto was a faithful adaptation, pushing the time ahead to 1806 and retaining the English country setting. The eligible bachelor Marlow (Ted Van Griethuysen) is all tongue-tied when in the presence of proper young ladies but a charming rake when with servant girls. So Marlow's intended, the upper-class Kate Hardcastle (Chevi Colton), finds she must disguise herself and masquerade as a maidservant to discover what her fiancé is really like. The delightful subplots were also included, namely the misadventures of the pleasant rascal Tony Lumpkin (James Harwood), who tricks Marlow into believing his future father-in-law's country house is an inn, and the romance between Marlow's friend George Hastings (Leonard Drum) and Constance Neville (Elly Stone). Kate's parents' Squire (Joe Silver) and Mrs. Hardcastle (Muriel Greenspon) were more fun than the lovers, and they sang the whimsical duet "Time and Tide" and individually such merry numbers as "I Love Everything That's Old," "Motherly Love," and "Morality, or A Child's Worst Friend Is His Mother." Marlow cut up with Kate in "The Braggart Song," and Kate sang the wishful title number as a solo. Everything was in place for *O Marry Me!*, but its charms were limited. Weak notices and playgoers' lack of interest forced the musical to close in less than three weeks.

All in Love, inspired by Richard Brinsley Sheridan's *The Rivals* (1775), was not all that much better than *O Marry Me!*, but it was received with kinder notices and managed to find an audience for nearly five months. Bruce Geller's adaptation of the complicated original included many minor changes, dropping the secondary pair of lovers, and tweaking the ending a bit. In the eighteenth-century spa town of Bath, the aristocratic Lydia Languish (Gaylea Byrne) is in love with the dashing Captain Jack Absolute (David Atkinson) because she thinks he is a penniless poet. Jack's father Sir Anthony (Lee Cass) and Lydia's guardian aunt, the verbose language-butchering Mrs. Malaprop (Mimi Randolph), plot to unite their two charges not knowing that they are already in love. Jack, in essence, becomes his own rival as well as competition for his friend, the hayseed gentleman Bob Acres (Dom DeLuise), who also loves Lydia. The belligerent Irishman Sir Lucius O'Trigger (Michael Davis) and the saucy maidservant Lucy (Christina Gillespie) also get involved in the intrigues and end up together. The truth gets out, Lydia accepts Jack even though he is rich, and Bob inexplicably proposes to Mrs. Malaprop. (In Sheridan's play, it is Sir Anthony who ends up with the old crone.) The score was by Geller (lyrics) and Jacques Urbont (music), and the lyrics were mostly routine and by-the-numbers, but the music was frequently sprightly and melodic. Lucy performed two of the most vivacious numbers, the fast waltz "What Can It Be" and the giddy "I Found Him"; Jack sang the flowing ballads "I Love a Fool" and "The Lady Was Made to Be Loved"; and the men caroused to the musically complex "Why Wives." Other numbers fell flat and slowed down the comic plot. "Poor" was a tiresome operetta duet, Mrs. Malaprop's "A More Than Ordinary Glorious Vocabulary" sported feeble malapropisms, and even the colorful Bob Acres and Lucius O'Trigger each got only one number, the sterile comic song about elegant swearing called "Odds" and the repetitive march "Honour." *All in Love* boasted a stronger cast than *O Marry Me!*, and the production was more polished as well. Even with weak material, comic actor DeLuise made quite an impact, and full-voiced leading man Atkinson was in fine form. One of the less obvious treats of the show was the resplendent orchestrations by newcomer Jonathan Tunick who would go on to become the best in his field.

TIME, GENTLEMEN PLEASE

[4 November 1961, Strollers Theatre-Club, 351 performances] a musical revue. *Score:* various. *Cast:* Fred Stone, Margaret Burton, Tony Bateman, Joan Sterndale Bennett, Archie Harradine, Geoffrey Webb.

A British import that pleased New Yorkers for nearly a year (in two different engagements) was this very old-fashioned English music hall revue from the Players Theatre of London. With a single pianist and a "chairman" (Fred Stone) acting as emcee and host, *Time, Gentlemen Please* offered old variety favorites, most of which were not familiar to Americans. "Daddy Wouldn't Buy Me a Bow-Wow," "At the Seaside," "Jane, Jane From Maiden Lane," and "Little Yellow Bird" may have sounded slightly familiar, but few patrons had been exposed to such fun ditties as "Good Luck to the Girl Who Loves a Sailor," "Just Like the Ivy I'll Cling to You," and "Miss Julia, Whose Behavior Was Very Peculiar!" The cast of ten dazzled with their traditional musical hall style, even though it was more foreign than one might have suspected. The Chairman banged his gavel and announced each act with terrible jokes, hoofers pounded away at old-time dance steps, and singers fluttered and posed as they delivered songs as innocent as "The Girl I Kissed on the Stair" and as saucy as "Who Were You With Last Night?" *Time, Gentlemen Please* (the title came from the standard pub announcement at closing time) ran two months and then reopened on January 16 with some new material. Some patrons returned for another dose, and soon word of mouth was strong enough that the revue played another nine months.

SING MUSE!

[6 December 1961, Van Dam Theatre, 39 performances] a musical comedy by Erich Segal loosely based on Homer's *The Iliad*. *Score:* Segal (lyrics), Joseph Raposo (music). *Cast:* Karen Morrow, Brandon Maggart, Bob Spencer, Paul Michael, Ralph Stantley, William Pierson.

Just as the cult favorite *The Golden Apple* took episodes from Homer and musicalized them in an anachronistic way, *Sing Muse!* turned to *The Iliad* for inspiration for its circa 1920 musical comedy. The Grecian *femme fatale* Helen (Karen Morrow) was the focal character and the libretto by Erich Segal dealt with the romantic triangle involving her, her husband Menelaus (Ralph Stantley), and the Trojan interloper Paris (Bob Spencer). Adding to the complications were the brawny Greek Achilles (Paul Michael) and his young protégé Patroklos (Brandon Maggart). It was a thin and silly plot which climaxed with Helen and Paris stealing away to Asia Minor and starting the Trojan War. The musical is notable for some of the talents involved. Morrow made a smashing debut as Helen and composer Joe Raposo, who would soon move on to television and *Sesame Street*, provided some bubbly music for the score. Segal, who was to become better known for his books and screenplays, provided the lyrics which were occasionally cunning if often falling into cute gimmickry. The song titles "Helen Quit Your Yellin'" and "Out to Launch" give one an idea of the kind of humor that ran through the show. "You're in Love" and "Your Name May Be Paris" were among the pleasant duets for Helen and Paris; "The Wrath of Achilles" was a playful character number; Morrow shone in the wistful "In Our Little Salon'" and the title song was a tuneful salute to poetry and love. The charms of *Sing Muse!* were outweighed by its weaknesses and in five weeks it was gone, rarely if ever to be heard of again.

BLACK NATIVITY

[11 December 1961, 41st Street Theatre, 57 performances] a musical play by Langston Hughes. *Score:* Hughes, various. *Cast:* Alex Bradford, Marion Williams, Clive Thompson, Cleo Quitman, Carl Ford, Howard Sanders.

The renowned poet Langston Hughes turned to musical theatre during the last decades of his life and struggled to put the African American experience on the musical stages of Broadway and Off Broadway. His dramas and poems were not reaching as many Americans as he had hoped, and he believed the popular form of the musical was the road to take. For *Black Nativity* he told the Christmas story through an urban, contemporary point of view and used both traditional hymns and gospel numbers as well as a modern kind of gospel song to bring it to life. The first part of the musical was the traditional Nativity story but enacted by African Americans who use their own everyday language. The second part was about spreading the news of the savior and was mostly a celebration, showing how the nativity is still alive today. It was thrilling to hear favorites such as "Go Tell It on the Mountain" and "Come All Ye Faithful" alongside such modern, slangy numbers as "What You Gonna Name Your Baby?" and "Leak in the Building." The effect was far from irreverent and audiences immediately connected with the lively, involving show. Vinnette Carroll directed *Black Nativity*, which used actors as well as a gospel chorus. A few critics cheered the musical as refreshing and more moving than most Christmas programs; others thought the production amateurish and the new songs untheatrical. Business was good through the holiday season; then the show moved to another theatre and played through the month of January. It took a few years, but *Black Nativity* eventually caught on with African American theatre groups across the nation. Today it is often done during the holidays by all kinds of theatres. A production in Seattle returned for eleven Christmases, and a theatre in Boston has revived it every year for more than forty years. *Black Nativity* returned to Off Broadway when the Classic Theatre of Harlem revived it for a month in 2007.

MADAME APHRODITE

[29 December 1961, Orpheum Theatre, 13 performances] a musical comedy by Tad Mosel. *Score:* Jerry Herman (music and lyrics). *Cast:* Nancy Andrews, Jack Drummond, Cherry Davis, Rod Coblin, June Hyer, Harry Stanton, Lou Cutell, Ray Tudor.

After receiving some high compliments for his first Broadway show *Milk and Honey*, songwriter Jerry Herman returned to Off Broadway to score this rather daffy, unconventional musical. The haggard but crafty Madame Aphrodite (Nancy Andrews) creates fake beauty creams on her kitchen stove and promises her customers that true love will result when using her products.

She hires Barney (Jack Drummond) to sell her products, and he gives some
to the plain and shy Rosemary (Cherry Davis), who believes that the products are making her beautiful. When Barney and Rosemary end up together,
Madame Aphrodite explains that it was love that made her more lovely, not
the beauty creams. Nancy Andrews was deemed quite lively and cunning
as the title character, but the critics found little else to endorse. Even Herman's score was not favored, and the quirky book turned both reviewers and
playgoers off. *Madame Aphrodite* was a bit ahead of its time; this kind of
offbeat character would be embraced later in the decade. Highly respected
playwright Tad Mosel could not build a satisfying story around his central
character, and the opportunities for song did not flow naturally. "And a Drop
of Lavender Oil" was Madame's recipe number that supposedly paralleled
her character. "You I Like" and "I Don't Mind" were straightforward but did
not develop. More pleasing were the touching "The Girls Who Sit and Wait"
about love waiting to blossom, the optimistic "There Comes a Time" about
finding the strength to act on your convictions, and the revealing "Beautiful"
about self-discovery. (The music from this last number was later reused by
Herman for "A Little More Mascara" in *La Cage aux Folles*.) The oddball
musical closed inside of two weeks, and Herman returned to Broadway where
his next show was *Hello, Dolly!* Neither Herman nor *Madame Aphrodite* is a
lost gem; nor has anyone else ever tried to revise or revive it. Yet it is noteworthy in looking at Herman's career and the way Off Broadway was developing.

THE BANKER'S DAUGHTER

[21 January 1962, Jan Hus Playhouse, 68 performances] a musical play by
Edward Eliscu based on Dion Boucicault's play *The Streets of New York*.
Score: Sol Kaplan (music), Eliscu (lyrics). *Cast:* David Daniels, Joelle Jons,
Phil Leeds, Lloyd Gough, Helena Scott, Tony Kraber, Karen Morley.

A very popular melodrama of the nineteenth century was turned into a musical drama that was not played for laughs and managed to hold the attention of audiences for two months. In 1837 New York, Captain Fairweather
(Tony Kraber) distrusts the greedy banker Gideon Bloodgood (Lloyd Gough)
and the security of his bank and wants to withdraw the family fortune of
$100,000. A scuffle breaks out, the captain is killed, and the unscrupulous
bank clerk Oliver Badger (Phil Leeds) pockets the receipt for the money.
Twenty years later, the Fairweather family is destitute, while Bloodgood and

his snooty daughter Alida (Helena Scott) are living in a Brownstone mansion. When Badger tries to blackmail Bloodgood with the receipt, the tenement where the clerk lives is consumed in a mysterious fire. The handsome but unsuspecting Mark Livingston (David Daniels) is courting Alida, but when he discovers some incriminating papers and gets hold of the receipt, he confronts Bloodgood and spurns Alida. The Fairweather fortune is restored, and Mark marries the Captain's daughter Lucy (Joelle Jons). The story had a long history of popularity with audiences on two continents. The French play *Les Pauvres de Paris* was translated and adapted by Dion Boucicault as *The Poor of New York* in 1857. Later retitled *The Sidewalks of New York* and then *The Streets of New York*, the melodrama was a favorite in Manhattan and on the road. It was also a hit in England as *The Streets of London* and was altered over the years to each new locale it played, such as *The Streets of Liverpool, The Streets of Pittsburgh*, etc. Veteran songwriter Edward Eliscu wrote the libretto for *The Banker's Daughter* and provided the lyrics for Sol Kaplan's pastiche music. Critics found the score pleasantly old-fashioned, fitting its period, and two of the songs, "Unexpectedly" and "Say No More," enjoyed modest popularity. But playgoers in the 1960s had limited interest in nineteenth-century drama unless it was played for laughs. Ironically, a year later an Off-Broadway musical version of the same Boucicault play was turned into a comic piece and, under the title *The Streets of New York*, was a hit. As for *The Banker's Daughter,* it was not recorded or published and has all but disappeared. It's important to note that this musical had no connection to a different and also popular nineteenth-century melodrama by Bronson Howard titled *The Banker's Daughter* (1878).

FLY BLACKBIRD

[5 February 1962, Mayfair Theatre, 127 performances] a musical play by C. Jackson, James Hatch. *Score:* Jackson, Hatch (music and lyrics). *Cast:* Avon Long, Robert Guillaume, Mary Louise, Thelma Oliver, Micki Grant, Gilbert Price, Chele Abel, Michael Kermoyan.

This spirited African American musical was neither a political screed nor an escapist song and dance show. Coming as it did in the earlier years of the civil rights movement, it shed light on an issue that was very important to black Americans, and not much thought of by whites: how fast can change come and still be effective? The contemporary Southerner William Piper (Avon

Long) believes racial equality eventually will come but doesn't think his people should be too aggressive. He and the men of his generation sing "Everything Comes to Those Who Wait." His daughter Josie (Mary Louise), her beau Carl (Robert Guillaume), and other African American college students sing "Now" and want change to happen immediately. These two philosophies and the battle between two generations provided the musical its plot and substance. No one side wins, but by the end of the show William questions "Who's the Fool?" and the ensemble cries for its people to "Wake Up." Both the script and score by C. Jackson and James Hatch avoided preaching up to a point, but it was clear where *Fly Blackbird* stood. The songs were often effective, ranging from comic numbers like "The Housing Cha-Cha" and "Big Betty's Song" to the lyrical "Rivers to the South" and "Lilac Tree." *Fly Blackbird* also boasted a superior cast headed by the veteran performer Long and filled with future favorites such as Guillaume, Gilbert Price, Micki Grant, and Thelma Oliver. The musical debate was appealing enough to New Yorkers to run sixteen weeks.

HALF-PAST WEDNESDAY

[6 April 1962, Orpheum Theatre, 6 performances] a musical play by Anna Marie Barlow based on the Rumpelstiltskin story. *Score:* Robert Colby (music and lyrics), Nita Jonas (lyrics). *Cast:* David Winters, Dom DeLuise, Audre Johnston, Sean Garrison, Charles Welch, Holly Sherwood.

A musical that hoped to appeal to adults as well as children, *Half-Past Wednesday* had neither the charm of an adult musical fairy tale, such as *Once Upon a Mattress*, nor the humor or intrigue to appeal to kids. The Brothers Grimm tale of Rumplestiltskin was told without embellishment and innovation, the songs being the only different aspect of the German fairy tale. The dwarf (David Winters) helps the maiden Erelda (Audre Johnston) spin straw into gold so that she can keep the promise her father (Charles Welch) made to the King (Dom DeLuise). In this version Erelda marries a prince (Sean Garrison) rather than the king, and when they have a child, Rumplestiltskin returns demanding the baby, as Erelda had vowed to do. The only way the couple can keep their child is to recall Rumplestiltskin's name, which they do through trickery, and the dwarf is defeated. The clowning by DeLuise as a bumbling King was the closest the musical came to farce, and the dull love songs between Erelda and the prince pleased neither the adults nor the children. *Half-Past Wednesday* was scheduled for two performances at the Orpheum Theatre and families seemed to enjoy it enough that the producers brought the show back a few weeks later and it ran four more performances. The score was recorded with bits of dialogue to fill in the story in the hopes that it might sell as a children's record, but it never caught on, even after it was reissued as *Rumplestiltskin*.

KING OF THE WHOLE DAMN WORLD

[12 April 1962, Jan Hus Theatre, 43 performances] a musical play by George Panetta based on his play *Comic Strip*. *Score:* Robert Larimer (music and lyrics). *Cast:* Boris Aplon, Alan Howard, Tom Pedi, Francine Beers, Brendan Fay, Sheldon Golomb, Charlotte Whaley, Jerry Brent, Jackie Perkuhn.

The era of Fiorello LaGuardia's New York City of the 1940s was conjured up in this slight but atmospheric musical that was rarely exciting but often charming. George Panetta adapted his 1958 play *Comic Strip* about a Greenwich Village neighborhood peopled with colorful New Yorkers, and Robert Larimer wrote a pleasing score that was similarly atmospheric. The thin story for the show meandered along, much as the residents did, stopping for a philosophical song or comic number. The only thread of a plot concerned five-year-old Jimmy Potts (Sheldon Golomb) who has the word "cat" written on his head by some of the bored neighborhood kids who were looking for something to do. The residents panic and believe there is a "cat fiend" on the loose; therefore two incompetent cops, Sarge (Brendan Fay) and Hippo (Tom Pedi), are called in and bumble their way through the case. Much of the playing time was taken up with various New Yorkese types, such as the Italian barber Enrico Romani (Boris Aplon) and the lovelorn Jew Hannah Klein (Francine Beers). Just as the plot went nowhere fast, the songs were leisurely and often lazy. The kids expressed their boredom in "What to Do?"; Hannah sang the hopeful ballad "Who's Perfect for You?"; Hippo delivered the narrative ditty "Little Blue Dog" as if he were addressing LaGuardia; and Romani had the childlike number "Grasshopper Song." A bit more lively were the breezy "March You Off in Style (To Heaven or Hell)" and the sunny title song about feeling good about yourself. *King of the Whole Damn World* was like one long charm song, and playgoers were only charmed enough to let the show run a little over five weeks.

No Shoestrings

[11 October 1962, Upstairs at the Downstairs, 66 performances] a musical revue by Ben Bagley. *Score:* various. *Cast:* Jane Connell, Danny Carroll, Bill McCutcheon, Larry Holofcener, Jane Squibb, Patty Regan.

With his title gently mocking Richard Rodgers's current Broadway musical *No Strings* and his own series of *Shoestring Revues*, producer Ben Bagley was his usual pixie self even in this less-than-stellar show that ran two months in Julius Monk's favorite venue, Upstairs at the Downstairs. The cast was not to blame, especially the gnome-like Bill McCutcheon and the sharp-featured, shrill-voiced Jane Connell, but their material wavered from slightly clever to barely amusing. Many of the songwriters that Bagley had discovered in previous shows were now working on Broadway, and their absence was noticed in this revue. Still, every Bagley show came up with some delights, and this one had them in the opening "It's a Great Little World," an operetta spoof titled "The Student Vagabond," a travesty of Tchaikovsky called "Lac Des Scenes," and the closing number "Time to Say Goodnight." Topics ripe for satire included the Kennedys ("1600 Pennsylvania Avenue"), the arms race ("A Pawn for Wernher von Braun"), and urban flight ("Suburban Lullaby"). Too many songs never went much beyond their punning titles, such as "The Dark Lady of the Senates," "This Year of Disgrace," and "Hoffa Love Is Better Than None." Bagley's golden days in theatre were waning, and he would soon move on to producing a series of "revisited" recordings featuring little known songs by famous songwriters.

Dime a Dozen

[18 October 1962, Plaza 9 Theatre, 728 performances] a musical revue by Julius Monk. *Score:* various. *Cast:* Gerry Matthews, Mary Louise Wilson, Rex Robbins, Susan Browning, Jack Fletcher, Cecil Cabot.

Another master of the Off-Broadway musical revue, Julius Monk, was also coming to the end of his theatre career, but you wouldn't know it judging by this giant hit. *Dime a Dozen* ran longer than any of the other Monk revues, a whopping two years, and a double LP recording included most of the songs and even some of the sketches, so the show is well preserved. The song that stood out from the others was the jocular "Barry's Boys" which made fun of the conservative senator Barry Goldwater. Other satiric numbers about the city and local newsmakers included "Ode to an Eminent Daily," "Slow Down Moses" (about developer Robert Moses), "Lincoln Center," "The Minnows and the Sharks" (about Federal Communications Commission chair Newton Minow), and "The Plaza Waltz-Waltz." Other topics involving daily life in the early 1960s were spoofed in song, such as "Cholesterol Love Song," "Marching for Peace," "Ten Percent Banlon," and "Bless This School." The more straightforward ballads, such as "Something Good Like You" and "Johnny Come Lately," were also pleasing. The state of the theatre was addressed in the prankish "Battle Hymn of the Rialto," and the title number was a lively and catchy list song. The cast, as was usual for a Monk revue, was top notch, and because the show ran so long, some performers were replaced during the run.

RIVERWIND

[12 December 1962, Actors Playhouse, 433 performances] a musical play by John Jennings. *Score:* Jennings (music and lyrics). *Cast:* Lawrence Brooks, Elizabeth Parrish, Dawn Nickerson, Helon Blount, Martin J. Cassidy, Brooks Morton, Lovelady Powell.

An Off-Broadway hit that is rarely revived any more, *Riverwind* still boasts one of the best scores of the 1960s. Riverwind is a rustic tourist colony on the banks of the Wabash River in Indiana and is run by the philosophical widow Farrell (Helon Blount). Her employee John (Martin Cassidy) has fallen in love with the widow's daughter Jenny (Dawn Nickerson) but is too tentative to tell her. Dr. Fred Sumner (Lawrence Brooks) and his wife Louise (Elizabeth Parrish), who had honeymooned at Riverwind seventeen years ago, return to revive their failing marriage, but instead Fred has a dalliance with the impressionable Jenny. Also staying at the colony are Virginia (Lovelady Powell) and Burt (Brooks Morton), an unmarried couple living in sin and finding the romance fading. The plot was mostly the interaction between the characters and a slow realization that Fred still loves Louise,

Virginia and Burt are made for each other, and John finding the courage to woo the willing Jenny. It was far from a page turner of a tale, but all six characters were interesting and the songs were much more than that. John's "I Cannot Tell Her So" was aching with youthful misery, but his "I Love Your Laughing Face" was filled with unbridled love. Jenny's "I Want a Surprise" was innocence itself, and her duet with Fred titled "Pardon Me While I Dance" overflowed with joy. Fred and Louise sang the wistful and enticing title song, while the acerbic Virginia and Burt sang about their unconventional "American Family Plan" and viewed their relationship wryly in "Almost, But Not Quite." Other highlights in this remarkable score included the philosophical numbers "Sew the Buttons On," about avoiding too much contemplation in life, the practical "A Woman Must Never Grow Old," the tender "I'd Forgotten How Beautiful She Could Be," and the witty quartet "Wishing Song." John Jennings wrote both book and score, inspired by his growing up in Indiana, and it was quite clear he was very promising if not already quite accomplished. The cast did justice to the score and the characters, helped, no doubt, by the young but gifted director Adrian Hall. *Riverwind* opened during a newspaper strike in New York, taking more time for word of mouth to spread, but the show eventually caught on and enjoyed a successful run of over a year. The economical little musical received some regional productions, but it was too atmospheric, too subtle, and perhaps too Chekhovian to become a mainstream favorite. As for Jennings, he seemed to vanish from the theatre, with no further word about him until his death in 1988. Judging by his effervescent score for *Riverwind*, the American musical theatre was robbed.

GRAHAM CRACKERS

[23 January 1963, Upstairs at the Downstairs, 286 performances] a musical revue by Ronny Graham, various. *Score:* Graham, David Shire, Richard Maltby Jr., various. *Cast:* Bill McCutcheon, McLean Stevenson, Anita Darian, Pat Stanley, Bob Kaliban, Mona Abboud.

Performer and songwriter Ronny Graham had contributed so much material to various revues over the years (in particular the *New Faces* series on Broadway) that many felt it was apt that his name appeared in the title of one of his shows. Graham did not appear in *Graham Crackers*, but he directed it and wrote portions of the score with several contributions by the team of Richard Maltby Jr., David Shire, and others. The sketches were by Graham and others (a young Woody Allen provided one skit about psychoanalysis) and were typically timely and irreverent. The best musical numbers were by Maltby and Shire, including the comic songs "The Sound of Muzak" and "Crossword Puzzle," and the rousing finale "Come Join the Party." "Summer in New York" was an enticing ballad, "Lovely Light" set some verses by Edna St. Vincent Millay to music effectively, and "A Doodlin' Song" was a merry contribution by the established songwriters Cy Coleman and Carolyn Leigh. Even when the material disappointed, the skillful cast of comic performers did not. Pat Stanley was perhaps the most impressive with her ability to move from comedy to pathos effortlessly, Anita Darian was the most accomplished singer, and character actor Bill McCutcheon stole every scene or song he was in. *Graham Crackers* was not as sophisticated and polished as some of the other revues Graham had worked on in the past, but it was appealing enough to run over nine months.

THE WORLD OF KURT WEILL IN SONG

[6 June 1963, One Sheridan Square, 228 performances] a musical revue by Will Holt. *Score:* Kurt Weill (music), various (lyrics). *Cast:* Holt, Martha Schlamme.

Because of the long-running *The Threepenny Opera*, Kurt Weill and Off Broadway seemed ideal for each other, and over the decades there would be many revues of Weill's work in cabarets and other intimate spaces away from the Street. This two-person show offered samplings from Weill's theatre career, from his early German works to his final Broadway musical *Lost in the Stars*. Hit songs such as "Mack the Knife," "September Song," and "Speak Low" were included alongside less familiar numbers from his musicals and even obscure songs from the forgotten *Marie Galante* and *The Silver Lake*. Performer-songwriter Will Holt conceived, compiled, directed, and performed in the revue with Martha Schlamme, the two of them also offering commentary about Weill, his life, and the songs. Although the selections were limited to solos and duets, *The World of Kurt Weill in Song* was thorough and satisfying. Neither Holt nor Schlamme were conventional leading man–leading lady types, so they were very effective in delivering the less romanticized songs that called for a gritty flavor. Yet critics and audiences also applauded their renditions of the song standards and the revue was popular. After doing brisk business for seven months, the musical cabaret reopened in May 1964 and ran another two months. During the long run, Holt was replaced by Scott Merrill, the original MacHeath from the famous 1954 production of *The Threepenny Opera*. As a note, the original cast recording of the show was titled *A Kurt Weill Cabaret*.

BALLAD FOR BIMSHIRE

[15 October 1963, Mayfair Theatre, 74 performances] a musical play by Irving Burgie, Loften Mitchell. *Score*: Burgie (music and lyrics). *Cast*: Christine Spencer, Jimmy Randolph, Frederick O'Neal, Ossie Davis, Alyce Webb, Robert Hooks, Eugene Edwards.

The music of the Caribbean had rarely been incorporated into musicals, and when they were, as in *Jamaica* and *House of Flowers*, it was Broadway songwriters imitating the island sound. Irving Burgie, better known in the music business as Lord Burgess, was the real thing, having written many calypso hits including "Day O" for Harry Belafonte. Burgie provided the scintillating music for *Ballad for Bimshire*, and it was the show's greatest, if only, asset. On an island in the Barbados, the native girl Daphne Byfield (Christine Spencer) is loved by the honest islander Johnny Williams (Jimmy Randolph), but she is attracted to the dashing "Captain" Neddie Boyce (Frederick O'Neal) from New York City. The triangle was merely an excuse for some stimulating singing and dancing in the calypso style. Although there were some character numbers and romantic duets, the score rarely was dramatic in a musical theatre manner, and the show's ensemble numbers, such as "Belle Plain—I'm a Dandy," "Welcome Song," "'Fore Day Noon in the Mornin'," and "We Gon' Jump Up," were the most exciting. The three principals were first-class performers and were able to put over some of the other songs, such as Daphne's soaring "Deep in My Heart"; her sassy duet with the Captain titled "Have You Got Charm?"; and Johnny's pop-sounding "Silver Earring." The wonderful character actor Ossie Davis was underused in the role of the island dandy Sir Radio, as were such accomplished African American performers as Robert Hooks, Sylvia Moon, and Alyce Webb. *Ballad for Bimshire* produced no new hits for Lord Burgess, but audiences enjoyed the calypso musical for nine weeks.

THE STREETS OF NEW YORK

[29 October 1963, Maidman Playhouse, 318 performances] a musical play
by Barry Alan Grael based on the play by Dion Boucicault. *Score:* Richard
B. Chodosh (music), Grael (lyrics). *Cast:* Grael, Ralston Hill, Barbara Williams, David Cryer, Gail Johnson, Don Phelps.

Since Dion Boucicault's 1857 melodrama had made for a lackluster musical
titled *The Banker's Daughter* a year earlier, it was all the more surprising that
this version was both a critical and popular hit, running over ten months. Barry
Alan Grael adapted the play, taking few liberties in plot but several in tone.
He didn't turn the piece into a "mellerdramer," but he had fun with the characters all the same and was even able to draw parallels between the New York
of the 1880s and the 1960s. (A very funny number titled "Tourist Madrigal"
concerned the rudeness of New Yorkers.) The original play took place in 1837
and then again twenty years later. Grael handled the early part of the story
with a clever prologue, showing how the villainous banker Gideon Bloodgood
(Ralston Hill) cheated old Captain Fairweather (Ian Brown) out of the family
fortune. Years later Bloodgood's conniving daughter Alida (Barbara Williams)
tries to ensnare the honest Mark Livingston (David Cryer) into marriage even
though he loves the late Captain's sweet daughter Lucy (Gail Johnston). With
the help of the formerly corrupt bank clerk Badger (Grael), an important
document is uncovered that destroys Bloodgood and restores the fortune of the
penniless Fairweathers. Grael's script and lyrics treaded the fine line between
comic melodrama and camp. The astute direction by Joseph Hardy kept the
tone consistently light without sinking into total silliness. It certainly helped
that the songs were so splendid that one accepted the melodramatic stereotypes as living, breathing people worth rooting for. Mark and Lucy's lovely
duet "Aren't You Warm?" was sung as they viewed stereopticon slides of exotic
locales, and their triumphant "Love Wins Again" was so sincere it validated the
coincidences leading up to the happy ending. Badger joined three Mexicans
for the farcical "California" foreshadowing that this was one crook who was
going to turn good. Even the villains had a dash of real character, as when
Bloodgood sings about his ill-gotten gains from the dispossessed citizens, who
join him in a countermelody in "Where Can the Rich and Poor Be Friends?"
The evil Alida had two juicy numbers, the smug "He'll Come to Me Crawling"
and the vengeful "Laugh after Laugh." Richard B. Chodosh wrote the nimble
music that was far from simple, especially in the complex finales to each act.
The reviews were almost unanimously favorable, and audiences were equally

appreciative. Why *The Streets of New York* never quite caught on with theatres outside New York is unclear. It is far from overly sophisticated or elitist and does not have difficult production demands. Perhaps it sounds too much like a musical "mellerdramer" and does not interest regional theatre producers. The original cast recording was recently rereleased on CD, so perhaps this timeless little wonder will find a life in the hinterlands after all.

TRUMPETS OF THE LORD

[21 December 1963, Astor Place Playhouse, 160 performances] a musical play by Vinnette Carroll based on James Weldon Johnson's *God's Trombones*. *Score:* various. *Cast:* Al Freeman Jr., Theresa Merritt, Cicely Tyson, Lex Monson.

Vinnette Carroll, who would become the leading figure in African American Off-Off-Broadway musicals with shows transferring to Off Broadway and Broadway, first gained recognition with this gospel musical. The Reverend James Weldon Johnson had written a series of sermons in which he retold Bible stories in the "Negro" idiom. Carroll took a handful of these and put them into the format of three preachers and a soloist telling the stories using gospel song standards. Al Freeman Jr., Cicely Tyson, and Lex Monson played the three reverends, and Theresa Merritt did most of the singing, raising her voice full throttle in celebration while tales of Adam and Eve, Abraham, and Moses were told. It was a fairly static program with more narration than action, but the quartet of performers were so accomplished and the gospel songs so exhilarating that *Trumpets of the Lord* was far from dull or pedantic. Director Donald McKayle staged the sparse little musical with care, and critics were favorable in their reactions. Audiences kept the program on the boards for over five months, and Carroll's career was launched. Theodore Mann, one of the original producers of *Trumpets of the Lord*, revived the musical on Broadway in 1969 for a week at his Circle in the Square Theatre.

BAKER'S DOZEN

[9 January 1964, Plaza 9 Theatre, 469 performances] a musical revue by Julius Monk, various. *Score:* various. *Cast:* Jamie Ross, Ruth Buzzi, Barbara Carson, Nagle Jackson, Gerry Matthews, Richard Blair.

The song "Barry's Boys" from Julius Monk's previous revue *Dime a Dozen* had enjoyed further popularity when Barry Goldwater became the Republican candidate for president, and there was even a best-selling Kingston Trio recording of the number, so it was not surprising that Monk reprised the song in this show. Other news items making it into the revue were the New York World's Fair ("That Wonderful World-Wide Fair"), "Water Pollution," Mary McCarthy's popular novel *The Group* ("The Gripe of the Group"), and "National Service Corps." In addition to the up-tempo title number, the songs included the international pastiches "A New Italian Folk Song" and "Mescaline Hat Dance," the cosmetics spoof "Avon Garde," and the urban lament "Megalopolis." Among the show's many authors to find later success were William F. Brown (*The Wiz*), Clark Gesner (*You're a Good Man, Charlie Brown*), and Rod Warren who would start his own series of satiric revues. The cast of *Baker's Dozen* was as sharp as ever, this time newcomer Ruth Buzzi excelling at the comedy and Jamie Ross and Barbara Carson as the best vocalists. With the assassination of John F. Kennedy less than two months past, some wondered if topical musical revues would still appeal to playgoers, but *Baker's Dozen* had no trouble finding an audience for over a year.

JERICHO-JIM CROW

[12 January 1964, Sanctuary Theatre, 32 performances] a musical history by Langston Hughes. *Score:* Langston Hughes, Paul Campbell (music and lyrics), various. *Cast:* Gilbert Price, Micki Grant, Rosalie King, Joseph Attles, Dorothy Drake, William Cain, Hilda Harris.

Langston Hughes returned to his innovative idea of urban contemporary gospel that had used in *Black Nativity* three years earlier and this time applied it to the history of segregation in America. The characters were called Young Man, Young Girl, Old Man, Jim Crow, and so on, the same types facing prejudice throughout the years. The score was a mixture of new songs by Hughes and familiar gospel numbers that were delivered by a choir on stage. Such stirring ensemble pieces as "Go Down, Moses," "The Battle Hymn of the Republic," and "John Brown's Body" contrasted sharply with the solos and duets like "Where Will I Lie Down?," "Freedom Land," "Better Leave Segregation Alone," and "Is Massa Gwine to Sell Us Tomorrow?" The effect was both educational and moving. Alvin Ailey and William Hairston co-directed the gifted cast, Gilbert Price as Young Man being the most outstanding. *Jericho-Jim Crow* was produced by the Greenwich Players, National

Association for the Advancement of Colored People (NAACP), and others with the intention of instructing and entertaining. After running a month Off Broadway, the troupe took to the road and played in several cities. *Jericho-Jim Crow* was the last musical Hughes worked on. He died three years later, never seeing the changes that he had written about and hoped for all his life.

. . . AND IN THIS CORNER

[12 February 1964, Downstairs at the Upstairs, 410 performances] a musical revue by Rod Warren, Michael McWhinney. *Score:* Warren, McWhinney, various. *Cast:* Marian Mercer, Carol Morley, Bill Brown, Virgil Curry.

Writer Rod Warren, who had contributed material to Julius Monk's recent *Baker's Dozen*, began producing, with Michael McWhinney, his own series of revues with this successful musical that ran over a year. Such punning song titles as "Tristan and Isolated" and "The Dying Schwann" were typical of the kind of comedy that was served, and the movie, theatre, newspaper, and celebrity targets were very specific, as seen in "Dear Abbey," "Ads Infinitum," "The Judy Garland National Anthem," "Tokyo, Mon Amour," and "Subways Are for Skiing." The stock market song "Where the Bulls Are" was a crying ballad spoofing the popular "Where the Boys Are"; "Our New Best Friends" was a tuneful number about the phony elite; and the title song was a merry list song. Warren would recycle his songs and sketches in later revues and some became favorites that returning audiences looked forward to. Out of the capable cast, newcomer Marian Mercer was the most impressive. . . . *And in This Corner* played at Monk's old venue, Downstairs at the Upstairs, but this show and its sequels never seemed to capture the class and polish of the Monk revues.

Jo

[12 February 1964, Orpheum Theatre, 63 performances] a musical play by Don Parks, William Dyer based on Louisa May Alcott's novel *Little Women*. *Score:* Dyer (music), Parks (lyrics). *Cast:* Karin Wolfe, Joy Hodges, Jodi Williams, Keith Prentice, Kitty Sullivan, Susan Browning, Keith Prentice, Lowell Harris, Alice Yourman, Bernard F. Wurger.

There were few surprises in this musical version of Louisa May Alcott's *Little Women* since it was faithful to the book and retained all the major characters and episodes. The adaptation was solid but the songs rather routine, hence *Jo* ended up being a competent musical but far from an exceptional one. The tomboy Jo March (Karin Wolfe), her steadfast mother Marmee (Joy Hodges), and her three sisters endure genteel poverty during the Civil War while they await word from their father who is serving in the Union army. Jo's friendship with the rich neighbor Laurie (Keith Prentice) turns to romance on his part; but Jo wants to be a writer, and eventually she goes to New York City where she befriends the older German Professor Bhaer (Bernard F. Wurger). Laurie turns to Jo's youngest sister Amy (Jodi Williams) and they wed, causing Jo to doubt her decision until the professor comes back into her life. The various subplots were included in the musical, including the romance between the tutor John Brooke (Lowell Harris) and Jo's sensible sister Meg (Susan Browning), the role their rich Aunt March (Alice Yourman) played in the story, and even the death of the frail sister Beth (Kitty Sullivan). It was a lot of plot for one musical, and sometimes events seemed to rush by. The novel has its sentimental moments and these were somewhat exaggerated in the musical. (And was it really necessary to change the location from Concord to Harmony, Massachusetts?) The by-the-numbers songs arrived exactly where you expected them. The March women wailed "Hurry Home"; Jo worried that she was "Afraid to Fall in Love"; Laurie and Jo quarreled in the duet "Moods"; John's farewell song to Meg was "Time Will Be"; the professor reflected "If You Find a True Love"; Jo thought him "As Nice As Any Man"; and Jo and Laurie came to the conclusion that they were "More Than Friends." The performances were solid without sparkling, and the production was simple but sufficient. The notices were mixed, and *Jo* ran two months. Over the years it has been produced by theatre groups looking for a musical version of the popular story. The 2004 Broadway musical *Little Women* was not a success in New York, but that version has become a favorite with schools and community theatres. Ironically, the 2004 adaption was slap shot and the songs inferior, so, in comparison, *Jo* looks better and better.

THE AMOROUS FLEA

[17 February 1964, East 78th Street Playhouse, 93 performances] a musical comedy by Jerry Devine based on Moliere's *School for Wives*. Score: Bruce Montgomery (music and lyrics). Cast: Lew Parker, Imelda De Martin,

Philip Proctor, Ted Tiller, David C. Jones, Jack Fletcher, Ann Mitchell, Bryce Holman.

Moliere would seem a natural for the musical stage because of his clever plots, colorful characters, and piquant scenes that practically break down into solos, duets, and trios. Yet there have been few attempts and even fewer successes. This lively musical version of the 1662 comedy *School for Wives* was kept in the French neoclassic period and used songs to continue the story rather than delay it. The vain Arnolphe (Lew Parker) has raised his ward Agnes (Imelda De Martin) since childhood in a strict and secluded manner, keeping her far away from the evils of the world until she is old enough to marry him. Of course she falls in love with the young and handsome Horace (Philip Proctor) who is the son of Arnolphe's best friend Oronte (Ted Tiller), and before Arnolphe can wed Agnes, she plans to elope with Horace. In the typical Moliere way of securing a happy ending, Agnes's father Enrique (Bryce Holman) arrives and says she has long been betrothed to none other than Horace. Jerry Devine wrote the efficient and funny libretto, and Bruce Montgomery provided the songs, which the critics found amusing and catchy. The major characters were introduced through variations of the same song: "All About Me" for Arnolphe, "All About He" for Agnes, and "All About Him" for Arnolphe's friends. Agnes dreamed about the world on "The Other Side of the Wall"; Horace sang the soaring ballad "Learning Love"; Arnolphe prepared his ward for marriage with "Lessons on Life"; and the lovers had the lilting duet "Closeness Begets Closeness." The title song, oddly enough, was a sincere lament by Arnolphe after he loses her. The production and cast were well reviewed, particularly the full-voiced Proctor, and *The Amorous Flea* pleased audiences for three months. The score was never recorded, but theatre groups discovered the lucid little musical all the same, and productions still surface on occasion.

CINDY

[19 March 1964, Gate Theatre, 318 performances] musical play by Joe Sauter, Mike Sawyer. *Score:* Johnny Brandon (music and lyrics). *Cast:* Sawyer, Jacqueline Mayro, Johnny Harmon, Joe Masiell, Thelma Oliver, Tommy Karaty, Mark Stone, Sylvia Mann, Frank Nastasi.

A musical version of *Cinderella* reset in contemporary New York, *Cindy* managed to please adults more than kids although it still had a magical, fairy tale flavor at times. Papa (Frank Nastasi) and Mama Kreller (Sylvia Mann) run a delicatessen on the Lower East Side. Their daughter Cindy (Jacqueline Mayo) is tormented by her vain sisters, but she finds her Prince Charming in the personage of the rich bachelor Chuck Rosenthal (Joe Masiell) from the Upper West Side. There were two interesting aspects to Joe Sauter and Mike Sawyer's adaptation: three hip Storytellers (Thelma Oliver, Tommy Karaty, and Mark Stone) acted as a Greek chorus of sorts; and Cindy had a comic companion Lucky (Johnny Harmon) with whom she sang and confided in. In the traditional *Cinderella* pantomimes in Great Britain, this character was named Buttons and was an audience favorite. Lucky served the same purpose here, and it opened up the musical and comic possibilities. Johnny Brandon's songs had the gleeful bounce of a pantomime yet were strictly in the Broadway style. Cindy reflected on being "A Genuine Feminine Girl" and with Lucky sang "Let's Pretend." Cindy's parents had the comic duet "Papa, Let's Do It Again," while the spoiled sisters only wanted to "Think Mink!" Lucky's two solos, "Cindy" and "Call Me Lucky," suggested the British music hall style, and the Storytellers provided commentary in numbers like "Once Upon a Time" and "Tonight's the Night." Cindy and her "prince" had two felicitous duets, the tentative "Who Am I?" and the gushing "If It's Love." The score for *Cindy*, like that for *Once Upon a Mattress*, was light enough for a fairy tale yet solid enough for a full-fledged musical. Notices for *Cindy* were mostly favorable, and the show slowly caught on, running over ten months. The musical is not to be confused with a 1978 television musical with the same title which reset the *Cinderella* tale in 1943 Harlem.

THE GAME IS UP

[29 September 1964, Upstairs at the Downstairs, 620 performances] a musical revue by Rod Warren. *Score:* Warren, various. *Cast:* Marian Mercer, Richard Blair, Judy Knaiz, R. G. Brown, Carol Morley, Virgil Curry.

The attractive and funny Marian Mercer returned for Rod Warren's second revue and was joined by the nasal-voiced comedienne Judy Knaiz for the comic numbers. Again Warren wrote most of the songs and sketches (there was one sketch coauthored by beginner Joan Rivers and a song by the young composer Marvin Hamlisch), and the satire was again very specifically aimed. As indicated from the titles, "Adam Clayton Powell," "Discotheque," "Radio City Music Hall," and "Sunday Television" were about familiar topics. Lyndon Johnson's administration was ribbed in "The Great Society Waltz," and the Japanese film spoof "Tokyo, Mon Amour" was reprised from . . . *And in This Corner*. Some numbers eschewed satire and were pleasurable for their own sake, such as "Hip Hooray," "Loves Labours Lost," "Forgotten Words," and the list song "76 Foolish Things." Of the sketches, the funniest were "Ding Dong Cocktail Party," satirizing the popular children's show *Ding Dong School*, and "Hello, Columbus," a takeoff on Philip Roth's popular novella *Goodbye, Columbus*. *The Game Is Up* was even more successful than Warren's first venture, running eight months, closing down for a week to add new material, then reopening to run another year.

BITS AND PIECES, XIV

[6 October 1964, Plaza 9 Theatre, 426 performances] a musical revue by Julius Monk. *Score:* Michael Brown, various. *Cast:* Gerry Matthews, Barbara Carson, Nagle Jackson, Jamie Ross, Barbara Minkus, Nancy Myers.

A week after Rod Warren's *The Game Is Up* opened, he had competition from his old boss Julius Monk whose *Bits and Pieces, XIV* also had a long run (though not as long as Warren's). Monk had always placed a number in the titles of his revues, and this one was no exception with "XIV" added to keep tradition and indicate that this was his fourteenth production of some sort. Many of his regular performers from the past three or four shows returned, and his faithful songwriter Michael Brown still provided songs. Some favorites from earlier editions were reprised, but *Bits and Pieces, XIV* was not a retrospective and had plenty of new material. "New York on Five Dollars a Day" made fun of the popular guide book; "Alexander's Discount Rag" took on retail stores; "Stand Up and Flex" was about the physical fitness trend; and "The Gathering of the Clan" roasted the Ku Klux Klan. The nostalgic offering this time, "Don't Let Them Take the Paramount," was about old movie palaces being torn down. The sketches spoofed the New York World's Fair, television news anchormen, conference calls, and controversial plays. *Bits and Pieces, XIV* ran over a year.

THE SECRET LIFE OF WALTER MITTY

[6 October 1964, Players Theatre, 96 performances] a musical play by Joe Manchester based on the story by James Thurber. *Score:* Leon Carr (music), Earl Shuman (lyrics). *Cast:* Marc London, Lorraine Serabian, Charles Rydell, Cathryn Damon, Christopher Norris, Rudy Tronto, Eugene Roche, Rue McClanahan, Lette Rehnolds.

James Thurber's short story "The Secret Life of Walter Mitty" first appeared in *The New Yorker* in 1939 and eventually became the humorist's most famous story. A 1947 film version of the tale was merely an excuse for Danny Kaye's clowning in different costumes and voices, but the original story was dramatized more faithfully in the 1960 Broadway comic revue *A Thurber Carnival*. The author died in 1961, so one cannot say what Thurber would have thought of this musical adaptation which opened the story up even as it remained true to the spirit of the original. On his fortieth birthday, the mild-mannered and slightly forgetful Walter Mitty (Marc London) looks at his ordinary life with quiet regret. His bossy wife Agnes (Lorraine Serabian), his dead-end job, and his dull and everyday responsibilities cause him to daydream. In this secret life he is always the hero, saving lives on the operating table, working as a dashing secret agent, and facing a firing squad. At his favorite bar Walter meets the ambitious singer Willa de Wisp (Cathryn Damon) and is smitten with her. She is not interested in marriage and wants excitement in her life. Walter decides to run away with Willa and spend his days promoting her career. He plans to quit his job, sell his house, and cancel his life insurance, but at the last minute he is reminded of his sweet daughter Peninnah (Christopher Norris) and realizes that a typical suburban life is the only one for him. Yet it is clear that Walter will still dip into his secret life on occasion. Most of the characters and episodes in Joe Manchester's libretto were suggested in Thurber's story, and many of the songs also came from lines or ideas in the original. Leon Carr and Earl Shulman wrote the commendable score, which sounded contemporary yet had a dreamy, circus-like feel to it as well. From the hymnlike opening "Secret Life" to the rousing "The Walter Mitty March," the songs were marvelous set pieces that captured the Thurber tone. The hospital scene, for instance, was musicalized with "Drip, Drop, Tapoketa," a number that used voices to recreate the dripping of an IV and the ticktock of a heart monitor. "Don't Forget" set Agnes's nagging instructions to Walter to the tempo of traffic horns. When Walter decided to break loose from his dreary past in "Now That I Am Forty," the song had a frantic flamenco flavor. Willa's belief that "Marriage Is for Old Folks" was a cool jazz number, while her fantasy nightclub act, "Fan the Flame," was a hilarious mock *Folies de Bergere* number which descended into a silly French torch song. In one fantasy, two jilted women (Rue McClanahan and Lette Rehnolds) sang the beatnik-like "Two Little Pussycats," while in the real world Walter sang wistfully of his faded marriage in "Aggie" and enjoyed his daughter's company in "Walking with Peninnah." Even the minor characters had some choice songs, such as Walter's pal Fred Gorman (Eugene Roche) whose three stages of romance were described in "Hello, I Love You, Goodbye," and Willa's patient boyfriend Irving (Charles Rydell) sang the bucolic ballad "Willa." The first act finale was the optimistic march "Confidence," which was still being played by marching bands and for sports broadcasts long after the musical had disappeared. *The Secret Life of Walter Mitty* was superior Off-Broadway fare, and most of the critics said so, but audiences were cautious, and the show only managed a three-month run. (Perhaps the audiences recalled the 1947 movie from the late show on TV and were turned off.) There were some regional productions, but the musical is little known today, which is unfortunate because the script and score still hold up very well.

BABES IN THE WOOD

[28 December 1964, Orpheum Theatre, 45 performances] a musical comedy by Rick Besoyan based on Shakespeare's *A Midsummer Night Dream*. *Score:* Besoyan (music and lyrics). *Cast:* Kenneth McMillan, Elmarie Wendel, Don Stewart, Ruth Buzzi, Danny Carroll, Joleen Fodor, Richard Charles Hoh, Carol Glade, Edward Miller.

Rick Besoyan, who had provided book, music, and lyrics for the successful musical spoof *Little Mary Sunshine* in 1959, had moved on to Broadway for his next operetta pastiche, *The Student Gypsy*, in 1963, but it failed to run. So he returned to Off Broadway for his musical adaptation of *A Midsummer Night's Dream*, which he titled *Babes in the Wood*. (There were three different Broadway musicals with that title in the late nineteenth century, but none were about Shakespeare's comedy.) Although Besoyan kept the story in a forest outside of Athens in 300 BC, he cut several characters and famous scenes and just concentrated on the fairies, the two sets of young lovers, and Bottom (Kenneth McMillan), the weaver. It was an awkward and unsatisfying libretto and, forsaking Shakespeare's dialogue for lame jokes and physical humor, the musical was often an unnecessary annoyance. There were some inspired comics in the cast, but they were directed by Besoyan to overact ferociously. Robin Goodfellow (Elmarie Wendel) was played by a woman, Bottom had no fellow rude mechanicals to play off of, and the fairy king (Richard Charles Hoh) and queen (Carol Glade) were as dull as the lovers were hyperactive. Besoyan had shown a talent for satire, but it was not clear in *Babes in the Wood* just what he was satirizing. It certainly wasn't Shakespeare. Critics thought the score pleasant but forgettable. With no particular style to pastiche, Besoyan seemed lost, and the songs were not funny enough to be farce nor sincere enough to be involving. Poorly reviewed, *Babes in the Wood* struggled for six weeks then faded away. It was Besoyan's last produced musical before his premature death in 1970.

THE DECLINE AND FALL OF THE ENTIRE WORLD AS SEEN THROUGH THE EYES OF COLE PORTER REVISITED

[30 March 1965, Square East, 273 performances] a musical revue by Ben Bagley. *Score:* Cole Porter. *Cast:* Kaye Ballard, Harold Lang, William Hickey, Carmen Alvarez, Elmarie Wendel.

Producer Ben Bagley moved from original musical revues to a new career revisiting America's great songwriters with this show that looked at Cole Porter's lesser-known gems. One has to remember that a renewed interest in Porter, the Gershwins, Irving Berlin, Vincent Youmans, and other Broadway songwriters did not come about until the late 1960s. Because most of the shows these men scored were no longer produced, only their standards remained in the public ear. Bagley set out to rescue the many worthwhile songs that he felt deserved attention, and he started with the prolific Porter, compiling numbers from his 1916 to 1950 musicals. Over the decades several of these shows have been pieced together and recorded as full scores, but in 1965 it was virtually impossible to find a recording of such obscure but delightful songs as "Find Me a Primitive Man," "By the Mississinewah," "Ridin' High," and "Tale of the Oyster." *The Decline and Fall* offered thirty-three songs, and even the critics admitted that they only recognized a handful. They also admitted that there wasn't a dud in the whole evening and that unknown Porter was as delicious as "Hit Parade" Porter. Mostly forgotten musicals such as *Paris, You Never Know, Fifty Million Frenchmen, Leave It to Me, Wake Up and Dream,* and *Red, Hot and Blue* provided such masterful songs as "Don't Look at Me That Way," "What Shall I Do?" "I Worship You," "Most Gentlemen Don't Like Love," "Gigolo," and "Down in the Depths." There were no selections from *Anything Goes, Kiss Me, Kate,* or the 1950s musicals; they were too famous or recent to have hidden secrets. Yet Bagley must have worried that his audience might be disappointed not hearing the Porter hits, so the evening closed with a medley of standards and near-standards. He need not have worried because the notices for the revue were enthusiastic as were the comments on the nimble cast headed by the well-known comic actress Kaye Ballard and song-and-dance man Harold Lang. *The Decline and Fall* ran nine months and encouraged Bagley to "revisit" other songwriters. Unfortunately for Off Broadway, he did this through a series of records and not in stage revues. Bagley did a new edition of *The Decline and Fall* in December 1965 (which he titled *New Cole Porter Revue*), and it ran eight weeks; then he left the theatre. What Off Broadway lost, the song archives gained. The man who had shaken up the revue format with his *The Shoestring Revue* back in 1955 ended his career looking back at the past.

PICK A NUMBER, XV

[14 October 1965, Plaza 9 Theatre, 400 performances] a musical revue by Julius Monk, various. *Score:* various. *Cast:* Rex Robbins, Elizabeth Wilson, Bill Hinnant, Lee Beery, Liz Sheridan, John Svar, Nancy Parell, John Keatts.

Julius Monk's fifteenth and last revue was no less successful than his other shows; thus his swan song was a joyous entertainment. Several of the songs were by Clark Gesner, who would soon turn to book musicals and pen *You're a Good Man, Charlie Brown,* and the team of Tom Jones and Harvey Schmidt returned to write the sprightly "New York Is a Summer Festival." Other numbers about the city included "Coney Island" and "The Plaza's Gone Native," and there was a wry song about nostalgia titled "The Good Old Days." "Love, Here I Am" and "Almost a Love Song" were the ballads, and the evening ended with the classical pastiche "Societus Magnificat: An Oratorio." The sketches spoofed television's *Peyton Place* and other shows of the day. The cast of eight was a bit larger than in the past, lessening the opportunities to shine in solos. Character actress Elizabeth Wilson was a new face in a Monk revue, and she would soon be one of New York's busiest actors, though rarely in musicals. Monk directed the revue himself, and it was still in the sophisticated, tuxedoed style that he had introduced more than a decade earlier. *Pick a Number, XV* ran over a year, but it was Monk's last hurrah. He retired a few years later, and a special era in the Off-Broadway musical revue came to an end.

JUST FOR OPENERS

[3 November 1965, Upstairs at the Downstairs, 395 performances] a musical revue by Rod Warren, various. *Score:* Warren, various. *Cast:* Richard Blair, Madeline Kahn, Fannie Flagg, Stockton Brigel, R. G. Brown, Betty Aberlin.

Julius Monk's former protégé and present rival Rod Warren rarely presented material as smart as Monk's, but he was often blessed with superior casts. The unknown comic actresses Fannie Flagg and Madeline Kahn shone in *Just for Openers* (the former also contributed two sketches) and, like their fellow performers, they were often much better than their material. Still, there were some lively numbers, such as "Mr. Know-It-All," "Anyone Who's Anyone," "Where Did We Go Wrong?" and the title ditty. The current Broadway hit *Hello, Dolly!* was spoofed in "The 'Dolly' Sisters," and theatre audiences were ribbed in "The Matinee." Although the glory days of the Off-Broadway revue seemed to be over, *Just for Openers* had little difficulty finding an audience for a year.

GREAT SCOT!

[10 November 1965, Theatre Four, 38 performances] a musical play by Mark Conradt, Gregory Dawson. *Score:* Don McAfee (music), Nancy Leeds (lyrics). *Cast:* Allan Bruce, Joleen Fodor, Arthur Whitfield, Jack Eddleman, Charles Hudson.

For those who thought a musical about Robert Burns would feature the Scottish poet's works set to lilting music, *Great Scot!* was a big disappointment. The authors instead offered a raucous musical about young Robbie Burns the lover who was much too busy to write any poetry. In 1783 the country lad Robbie (Allan Bruce) is so successful with the girls that he is the envy of all the boys and the gossip of the village. He finds true love (and better sex) with the lass Jean Armour (Joleen Fodor), but her righteous father (Charles Hudson) is out to horsewhip him. Jean nobly sends Robbie off to become a poet. In Edinburgh Robbie is soon getting well known for his lusty lifestyle, his liberal politics, and his poetry. When he offends the Tories once too often, his career seems in jeopardy. Then Robbie hears that Jean has given birth to twins, so he returns home, marries the girl, and settles down to write more poetry. The libretto attempted to create a Tom Jones-like figure, but on stage it all came down to a lot of noisemaking and drinking. Burns's verses were replaced by such unpoetic song titles as "What a Shame," "That Special Day," and "We're Gonna Have a Wedding." When the score aimed to get lyrical, the best it could come up with was such drivel as "I'll Find a Dream Somewhere" and "Where Is That Rainbow?" The critics found little to recommend in *Great Scot!* except the music, which was described as spirited and melodic. The score was not recorded and revivals are extremely scarce, so one has to trust the reviews in this case. Joe Raposo was musical director and co-orchestrator, and it is likely the music sounded pretty good. *Great Scot!* struggled to run five weeks.

THE MAD SHOW

[5 January 1966, Actors Playhouse, 871 performances] a musical revue by Larry Siegel, Stan Hart based on *Mad Magazine*. *Score:* Mary Rodgers (music), Siegel, Marshall Barer, Steven Vinaver (lyrics). *Cast:* Linda Lavin, Dick Libertini, Jo Anne Worley, Paul Sand, MacIntyre Dixon.

The popular *Mad Magazine* was quite the rage in the 1960s for teens and adults who liked their satire broad and happily sophomoric. Off Broadway was the ideal venue for the musical revue based on the magazine, and the superb cast, cartoonish in their own unique way, often made the material seem better than it was. The generation gap provided much of the material for the revue as the adult cast frequently played disgruntled youths, as when they listed their woes in the caustic number "Misery Is . . ." (ribbing the current catch phrase "Happiness Is . . ." from the comic strip *Peanuts*) and when they became sadistic as they promised to stamp out hate in "The Hate Song." Mary Rodgers provided the sprightly music, and her *Once Upon a Mattress* lyricist Marshall Baer wrote several of the lyrics in the score; the songs (and sketches) have dated poorly, but the *Mad Magazine* sass is still there. "Well It Ain't" was a savage spoof of Bob Dylan, and the Christmas carol lampoon "The Gift of Maggie" was delightfully subversive, the later sung with panache by Jo Anne Worley. Linda Lavin shone in two numbers: the ditzy "Looking for Someone" in which her multiple personalities did a frenzied musical round; and in the hilarious Latin pastiche "The Boy from . . ." (a lambast of the current song hit "The Girl from Ipanema") in which a vapid female sings of her frustration with her obvious (but not to her) gay boyfriend. Rodgers's longtime friend Stephen Sondheim, using the nom de plume Esteban Ria Nido, wrote the sly lyric for the comic number, and it still entertains when heard in revues and in concert. *The Mad Show* never achieved the more intelligent wit of the 1950s Off-Broadway revues, but it was distinctly 1960s in attitude and revealed more about the era than better-written shows.

BELOW THE BELT

[21 June 1966, Upstairs at the Downstairs, 186 performances] a cabaret revue conceived by Rod Warren. *Score:* various. *Cast:* Madeline Kahn, Richard Blair, Lily Tomlin, Genna Carter, Robert Rovin.

MIXED DOUBLES

[19 October 1966, Upstairs at the Downstairs, 428 performances] a cabaret revue conceived by Rod Warren. *Score:* Warren, John Meyer, Steven Lawrence, Jerry Powell, James Rusk, Gene Bissell, various. *Cast:* Madeline Kahn, Judy Graubert, Robert Rovin, Janie Sell, Gary Sneed, Larry Moss.

Producer and writer Rod Warren managed a run of twenty-three weeks when he put the best sketches and songs from his previous revues into a program slyly titled *Below the Belt*. The targets of the show were sometimes personal attacks, as the title suggested, but most of it was just fun. A series of authors joined Warren in providing the songs and skits, and they were certainly helped by the presence of the unknown comedienne Lily Tomlin joining Madeline Kahn and the rest of the cast. Ten days after the revue closed,

Warren opened an even more successful venture, *Mixed Doubles*, which ran over a year. Kahn was on hand again when the six-actor revue took on familiar topics such as living in New York City, theatre critics (Walter Kerr was particularly roasted), and Kurt Weill musicals (Kahn delivered the funny "Das Chicago Song"). The actor-turned-politician Ronald Reagan was a timely target, and there were even spoofs of *Catcher in the Rye*, the recent shift toward liberalism, and the growing physical fitness mania. *Mixed Doubles* sometimes had the verve of a 1950s revue, but there was also something very "sexual revolution" about it. Warren and his shows are long forgotten now, and all that survives is a two-record, live recording of *Mixed Doubles* on vinyl, a hard-to-find item with a hefty price tag.

MAN WITH A LOAD OF MISCHIEF

[6 November 1966, Jan Hus Playhouse, 241 performances] a musical play by Ben Tarver adapted from the Ashley Dukes play. *Score:* Tarver (lyrics), John Clifton (music and lyrics). *Cast:* Virginia Vestoff, Reid Shelton, Alice Cannon, Raymond Thorne, Tom Noel, Lesslie Nicol.

An unlikely offering for the mid-1960s was the period musical *Man with a Load of Mischief*, which found an audience for eight months without a familiar name in the cast or creative team. If it seemed old-fashioned and quaint, it was because the intimate musical was based on a forgotten 1925 play of the same name by Ashley Dukes which had only lasted sixteen performances on Broadway. Ben Tarver adapted the old script with skill and provided lyrics that seemed comfortable in its early nineteenth-century setting. An aristocratic Lady (Virginia Vestoff) runs away from the Prince Regent and is pursued by a Lord (Raymond Thorne) who wishes to marry her. She finds refuge in the wayside inn called Man with a Load of Mischief run by the Innkeeper (Tom Noel) and his Wife (Lesslie Nicol). The Lord and his Manservant (Reid Shelton) arrive in hot pursuit, but soon the Lord is more entranced by the saucy Maid (Alice Cannon), while the Lady finds herself falling in love with the Manservant. The plot was far from a nail-biter, but there was a rustic charm to the familiarity of the piece, and the Ben Tarver–John Clifton score was exceptional. The haunting "(Come to the) Masquerade," the flippant "Goodbye, My Sweet," the wistful "Little Rag Doll," the music hall turn "Once You've Had a Little Taste," the lyrical "Make Way for My Lady," and the expansive folk ballad "Hulla-Baloo-Balay" were highlights in a score that would later develop a cult following, though revivals of the musical have been infrequent. What an atmospheric, romantic chamber musical without an agenda was doing Off Broadway as the 1960s started to sizzle is a curious phenomenon. In fact, *Man with a Load of Mischief* was closer in spirit to the decade's earlier *The Fantasticks* than other shows of its era.

VIET ROCK

[10 November 1966, Martinique Theatre, 62 performances] a play with songs by Megan Terry. *Score:* Marianne de Pury (music), Terry, various (lyrics). *Cast:* Marcia Kean Kurtz, Gerome Ragni, Seth Allen, Shami Chaikin, Paul Giovanni, Sharon Gans.

Although it barely qualifies as a musical, Megan Terry's antiwar play with songs, *Viet Rock,* was the prophetic footnote of its season. Opening a full year before *Hair*, it introduced a truly "rock" musical to the New York theatre and can be seen as an embryonic version of the more famous *Hair. Viet Rock* is perhaps the first rock musical, and for that reason some comments about rock music and the theatre might be helpful. The definition of rock music is controversial, and one man's rock is another man's pop or folk or country. What is clear is that the theatre was the last entertainment media to give in to rock. The music business first recognized the rock song, and it was through records in the 1950s that the sound was introduced to Americans. Very soon it was on the radio (though many stations refused to broadcast the "vulgar" sound for some years) and other media. The films *The Blackboard Jungle* (1955) and *Rock Around the Clock* (1956) helped spread the new sound, and it was even showing up on television, most famously with Elvis Presley's partially censored appearance on *The Ed Sullivan Show* in 1956. When the Beatles appeared on the same show eight years later, rock was everywhere. Except in the theatre. Cafe La Mama and other early Off-Off-Broadway troupes used rock as one of the elements in their anti-whatever productions, but even that was years after rock was heard everywhere else. Theatre, one of the most ancient of all art forms, has often been sluggish in accepting newfangled inventions, be it electric lights or television advertising. This cautiousness extended into the 1970s when Broadway finally broke down and accepted credit cards! Naturally, when the rock musical first appeared, it was not an easy birth. And even after it was born, it struggled for survival. To this day, rock and theatre have an irregular and uncomfortable relationship.

Avant-gardist playwright Terry was the only credited author of *Viet Rock*, but the vignettes and songs were the collaboration of the cast with Terry and composer Marianne de Pury. The thin plot, about a group of draftees who are sent to Vietnam where they are killed, was an excuse for a collage approach to the subject. The six songs may have been incidental to the action and characters, but they were definitely in the rock-folk mode rather than Broadway style. The piece had been kicking around Off Off Broadway since 1963 when an early version of *Viet Rock* was presented at Cafe La Mama. The production at the Martinique Theatre in the fall of 1966 was dismissed as a strident rant by the few critics who saw it, but the volatile little show found an audience for two months. One of the writer-performers in the cast was Gerome Ragni, who was exhilarated by the experience and began working on the script and lyrics for *Hair* with actor James Rado. *Viet Rock* was quickly forgotten, but the impact the ambitious piece had on the American musical should not be overlooked.

YOU'RE A GOOD MAN, CHARLIE BROWN

[7 March 1967, Theatre 80 at St. Marks, 1,597 performances] a musical play based on Charles Schulz's comic strip "Peanuts" by Clark Gesner. *Score:* Clark Gesner. *Cast:* Gary Burghoff, Bob Balaban, Reva Rose, Skip Hinnant, Bill Hinnant, Karen Johnson.

One of the longest-running and most revived of all Off-Broadway musicals, *You're a Good Man, Charlie Brown* was an unusual project. The musical began as a "concept album" of ten songs by Clark Gesner and featured Orson Bean as the title character, Barbara Minkus as Lucy, Bill Hinnant as Snoopy, and Gesner himself singing Linus's songs. The 1966 recording was not widely distributed, but it prompted producers to go ahead with the Off-Broadway production. Charles Schulz's comic strip *Peanuts* was more popular than ever, fueled by *A Charlie Brown Christmas* (1965), the first of many television specials featuring the gang of kids who had the anxieties of adults. Schulz had little to do with the creation of the musical, which had a libretto by Gesner. Yet the show felt like a Schulz original, and some of the familiar routines (Lucy as a psychiatrist, Snoopy as a flying ace, Linus's obsession with his blanket, and so on) seemed to be enhanced when musicalized. There is a childlike simplicity to the score but, like the comic strip, it suggests the restlessness and neuroses that hide inside these adultlike kids. The hymnlike "Happiness" that concluded the show is a conventional ballad, but all the other numbers are character-driven. The soft-shoe "My Blanket and Me" for Linus (Bob Balaban), the wry duet "Dr. Lucy (The Doctor Is In)" for Charlie Brown (Gary Burghoff) and Lucy (Reva Rose), and the razzle-dazzle strut "Suppertime" for Snoopy (Bill Hinnant) allow the characters to break out of the newspaper panels without vulgarizing themselves. Gesner's book is little more than a string of vignettes, spoken and sung, during a typical day in the life of the title hero. Joseph Hardy staged the little show without panache, and Alan Kimmel's sets and costumes, as well as Jules Fisher's lighting, were simplicity itself. Colorful geometric shapes projected behind the actors kept the picture as clean and uncluttered as the comic strip.

Musicals for kids were rare on Broadway and just about unheard of Off Broadway, but *You're a Good Man, Charlie Brown* had wide audience appeal, and the intimate Theatre 80 at St. Marks did brisk business for nearly four years. This was followed by a live-action television version, an animated television version, and hundreds of professional and amateur productions that found a gold mine in the economical musical. Yet the show still works best in an Off Broadway atmosphere and, like *The Fantasticks*, it suffers from inflated productions that try to work on a larger scale. When the musical closed in 1971, a production was presented on Broadway in the small Golden Theatre but, despite the fact that it had the same director and designers of the original, the show's intimacy was missing; the revival closed in a month. The musical was again revived on Broadway in 1999, the cast size was kept the same, but the kinetic projections and high-tech approach to the visuals worked against the piece; it ran an unprofitable 250 performances, thanks only to some outstanding performances. *You're a Good Man, Charlie Brown* is not a 1960s musical. It defies specific locale and time and seems oblivious to the real world. Yet what is more familiar than the tribulations of these pint-sized characters? The musical is also an archetypal Off-Broadway show: intimate, simple, and refreshing. Broadway cannot make this type of small-scale magic.

NOW IS THE TIME FOR ALL GOOD MEN

[26 September 1967, Theatre de Lys, 112 performances] a musical play by Gretchen Cryer. *Score:* Cryer (lyrics), Nancy Ford (music). *Cast:* David Cryer, Donna Curtis, Judy Frank, Sally Niven (pseudonym for Gretchen Cryer).

The ambitious antiwar piece *Now Is the Time for All Good Men* is most re-membered today as the first New York appearance of the songwriting team of Nancy Ford (music) and Gretchen Cryer (book and lyrics), American theatre's first female songwriting team. The high school English teacher Mike Butler (David Cryer) is a conscientious objector during the escalating Vietnam War and has served a prison sentence for his beliefs. When his unpatriotic past is revealed in the small Indiana town where he now works, both students and the community turn against him. Despite all this, Mike manages to open the eyes of the repressed teacher Sarah (Gretchen Cryer) and finds love. The score was a congenial blending of pop, light rock, folk, and some Broadway brass, a combination to be heard in the team's later (and better) scores as well. The antiestablishment tone of the piece was heard in two mock patriotic marches, "Good Enough for Grandpa" and "A Star on the Monument," and the traditional approach to education was lampooned in the clever "Keep 'em Busy." Less satisfying were the love songs, though there was charm and wit in the revealing character duet "Tea in the Rain." There was even a touch of bubblegum rock in the bouncy "Stuck-Up." Cryer's book was also typical of her later work, placing a character in crisis while exploring uncomfortable issues. As melodramatic as the show was, it turned preachy only on occasion, and there was plenty of humor, even if it was sometimes the acid kind. *Now Is the Time for All Good Men* found an audience for fourteen weeks, and the score was recorded; not a bad start for the intriguing young songwriting team.

*H*AIR

[29 October 1967, Public Theatre, 49 performances; Cheetah Theatre, 45 performances; Biltmore Theatre, 1,750 performances] a rock musical by Gerome Ragni, James Rado. *Score:* Rado, Ragni (lyrics), Galt MacDermot (music). *Cast:* Ragni, Walker Daniels, Jill O'Hara, Steve Dean, Sally Eaton, Arnold Wilkerson, Shelley Plimpton.

One of the most influential of all musicals, *Hair* is remembered as the first major rock musical of the American theatre, yet its Off-Broadway origins are less known. Hoping to get a lot of attention for his new venture, the Public Theatre, pioneering producer Joseph Papp presented the disjointed and promising show as its inaugural production, and it ran six weeks with author-lyricist Gerome Ragni as the hippie Berger and Walker Daniels as his friend Claude. Gerald Freedman directed the piece on a simple skeletal set and had his performers use handheld mikes and deliver their songs in rock concert style. The result was a lively, irreverent experiment that was typical of the open-minded Papp. It was commercial producer Michael Butler who saw the wider possibilities in the musical. When he couldn't get a Broadway house to take the musical, he reopened the show at the nightclub-like venue, the Cheetah Theatre Off Broadway, where word of mouth allowed it to run another six weeks. Butler then closed the show and brought in avant-garde director Tom O'Horgan to spice it up for Broadway. Coauthor James Rado now played Claude, there were some other cast changes, both score and script were revised ("Aquarius," for example, was moved from the second act to become the opening number), the piece was restaged with a more brazen flourish, and the much-talked-about nude scene was added. Three months later *Hair* opened on Broadway, received mostly favorable notices, and ran over four years. Some theatregoers preferred the Off-Broadway production, finding much of O'Horgan's theatrics artificial and overdone. Yet the show was always "in your face" from the start, and Butler knew what he was doing as he promoted his "tribal rock musical" on Broadway and on tour for several years. Interestingly, the London production of *Hair* ran even longer than the first Broadway production: a surprising 1,998 performances. It was also a hit in other cities around the world and was filmed in 1978. The rock musical returned to Broadway in 1977 for a misguided revival that ran only forty-three performances, in 2004 for a famous one-night benefit performance, and was a giant hit all over again with the exceptional 2009 revival which ran 519 performances.

The Rado-Ragni script for *Hair* is nearly plotless, made up of vignettes not unlike *You're a Good Man, Charlie Brown* in structure. The story might be described as an ordinary day in the life of a radical flower child with all the right topics conveniently covered: the war, sex, drugs, the establishment, race, and the destruction of the planet. Charlie Brown finds a bit of happiness at the end of his day; the hippie Claude dies in Vietnam at the end of *Hair*. The musical is more a celebration of ideas than a linear tale, and none of the characters are developed much beyond types. Yet *Hair* had no intention of working like a traditional musical. It wanted to be one of those spontaneous "happenings" that took place in the 1960s whenever a group of people and a collage of ideas took flight. It was also a rock concert but much more inventive and visual than most such concerts were at the time. The songs were central, as in a concert, and *Hair* survives today because of the vibrant score by Rado, Ragni, and composer Galt MacDermot. It was still possible in the 1960s for a Broadway song to climb the pop charts, but never before had they found fame on the rock charts. "Good Morning Starshine," "Easy to

Be Hard," "Hair," and "Let the Sun Shine In" were the runaway hits, but just as accomplished were such unique numbers as the simple torch song "Frank Mills," the pounding declaration "Ain't Got No," the exuberant "I Got Life," the wry "Black/White Boys," and the questioning ballad "Where Do I Go?" Just about any character could sing any song, they were that nonspecific. Yet every number revealed the sly, cocky voice of the "tribe." The score for *Hair* may not have been your everyday cast album, but it sure was theatrical.

The aftereffects of *Hair* have been misunderstood. The musical theatre did not turn to rock because of the show, and the Rodgers and Hammerstein model was not pushed aside for loose and carefree antimusicals. Off Broadway saw a rush of rock musicals for the next few years (most of them inferior), and Broadway offered a handful as well. The British-authored *Jesus Christ Superstar* was a success on the Street, as was *Two Gentlemen of Verona* (which originated Off Broadway) and, years later, *The Who's Tommy*; but there would not be another rock musical on Broadway to run longer than *Hair* until *Rent* twenty-five years later. Yet *Hair* was indeed influential and in ways that were not so obvious at the time. It was a protest musical and, beyond the obvious targets, the show was also antimusical theatre. Its attitude of mocking what audiences had held so dear for so many years was a new point of view. Broadway and Off-Broadway revues, we have seen, loved to lampoon the theatre, but it was all very affectionate. *Hair* was not affectionate. It was bold and unloving and questioned all the elements of the American musical. Theatre artists to follow would pick up on this, and musicals would not be afraid to defy the rules of the art form. Musicals as diverse as *Company*, *Evita*, *Dreamgirls*, *Assassins*, *Jelly's Last Jam*, *Tommy*, *Urinetown*, and *Passing Strange* owe something to *Hair*. They either mock or alter traditional storytelling to fit their purposes; each in its own way is a protest musical.

The other (and more practical) influence of *Hair* is the way it changed the sound of a theatre score. Because a rock band replaced the traditional pit orchestra in *Hair*, the performers were obviously miked, and there was no pretense that they weren't. Although only a small percentage of theatre musicals that followed used rock bands, all eventually amplified musicians and, consequently, actors. A revival of such a traditional piece as *The King and I* today has as much artificial sound as any rock concert. *Hair* signaled the end of natural sound in the stage musical. This is a legacy that is not appreciated by many theatregoers, but the economics of the business dictate it. Fewer musicians and sophisticated keyboards that can manufacture the sounds of various instruments have replaced the traditional theatre orchestra. The miking of actors had occurred on special occasions long before *Hair*, but it wouldn't be long after the first rock musical that shows were fully miked. *Hair* looked like a concert, and the microphones were visual symbols of this. But most subsequent shows took great pains to hide the mikes on the actors' bodies and pretend that electronics were not in use. It took a rock musical such as *Rent* to put the mikes back in view, and today amplification is a known and clearly observed activity. The effects of amplification go far beyond the simple sound of a musical. In the 1980s, Broadway producers decided that all orchestra seats and most of the upper part of the house could demand a top price. Why? With amplified sound, they argued, everyone can hear equally well, so there were no longer any "bad" seats. This is cockeyed logic, but it quickly became the norm. The protests of *Hair* have wrought more discontent than its creators ever imagined.

In Circles

[5 November 1967, Cherry Lane Theatre, 222 performances] a musical revue by Al Carmines. *Score:* Carmines (music), Gertrude Stein (lyrics). *Cast:* Carmines, Elaine Summers, Arlene Rothlein, David Vaughn, Julie Kurnitz, Theo Barnes.

If Joe Papp was the King of Off Broadway, the composer-producer Al Carmines was some sort of Prince of Off Off Broadway. For several seasons Carmines had operated his Judson Poets Theatre at the Judson Memorial Church, presenting new works that ranged from "plays with music" to "operas." Often based on well-known figures or literary works, these musical pieces were challenging, unconventional, obscure, and sometimes surprisingly enjoyable. *In Circles* was developed at the church then brought to Off Broadway where it received scattered and mixed notices. Yet the odd and uneven piece appealed enough to audiences to run over seven months then return in 1968 for another fifty-six performances. The literary figure this time was Gertrude Stein, the Queen of the Obscure, and while the title fragment was the centerpiece of the musical, other Stein pieces were incorporated into the foggy collage. The young cast, which included Carmines, played a group of contemplative students who gather on the porch of a château and engage in a dance of words, ideas, songs, and even dance itself. No efforts were made to explain or even thematically tie the various pieces together (which was true to Stein), though the audience was told that each of us lives in a separate circle. The most pleasing aspect of *In Circles* was Carmines's music which was set to Stein's words. Even those critics not intrigued with Stein's hodgepodge admitted to liking the music. The songs were not listed but it was hard to forget such pieces as the folklike "Can You See the Moon?"; the soothing "Do Not Despair"; and the quixotic "Papa Dozes, Mama Blows Her Noses." Carmines would never become as familiar a name Off Broadway as he was Off Off, but once in a while his work was welcomed there.

CURLY MCDIMPLE

[22 November 1967, Bert Wheeler Theatre, 931 performances] a musical spoof by Mary Boylan, Robert Dahdah. *Score:* Dahdah (music and lyrics). *Cast:* Bayn Johnson, George Hillman, Joyce Nolen, Paul Cahill, Helen Blount, Gene Gavin, Norma Bigtree.

Old movies from the 1930s were very popular in film revival houses in New York during the 1960s. Young audiences rediscovered the black-and-white Warner Brothers and Fox musicals and found them as enjoyable as they were ridiculous. Spoofing the Shirley Temple movies was appealing to both those with a nostalgic or a satirical frame of mind. Carol Burnett had done an outrageous version of Shirley tapping with the African American Bill "Bojangles" Robinson (Tiger Haynes) in the Broadway musical *Fade Out—Fade In* in 1964, and it was so memorable she returned to the character later in her television show. That was just a sketch, but Off Broadway's *Curly McDimple* was a full-length book musical that took the form of a standard Temple feature film. In the depths of the Depression, the moppet Curly (eight-year-old Bayn Johnson) comes to live at the boarding house run by Sarah (Helen Blount) where she cheers everyone up with her endlessly perky singing and dancing. She also manages to bring together the unemployed hoofer Jimmy (Paul Cahill) and the chorus girl Alice (Joyce Nolen). Bojangles (George Hillman) was also on hand to join Curly in the contagious "Dancing in the Rain" number. Although it may have become too campy or even cruel, *Curly McDimple* was actually quite nostalgic and even affectionate. The laughs were plentiful as the clichés were paraded across the stage, but audiences were giggling at the same thing in the revival houses. The economic little musical became a surprise hit, running two and a half years. It is more surprising that there was no cast recording. A few songs exist on demos, and the lyrics alone tell you that this was a delicious pastiche score with such Depression chasers as "Something Nice Is Going to Happen," "Hi de hi de hi, Hi de hi de ho," and "Swing-a-Ding-a-Ling." The playful nonsense reached a peak with the insipidly charming "Love Is the Loveliest Love Song." During the run, the unique film personality Butterfly McQueen was added to the cast with a new character written just for her to play. But *Curly McDimple* didn't need stars and can still be revived by groups who have an understanding and affection for the iconoclastic Temple films.

YOUR OWN THING

[13 January 1968, Orpheum Theatre, 933 performances] a rock musical by Donald Driver based on Shakespeare's *Twelfth Night*. *Score:* Hal Hester, Danny Apolinar (music and lyrics). *Cast:* Leland Palmer, Tom Ligon, Marcia Rodd, Rusty Thacker, Danny Apolinar, John Kuhner, Michael Valenti, Igors Gavon, Imogene Bliss.

The Elizabethan comedy *Twelfth Night* has more songs in it than any other Shakespeare play, so it is no wonder the piece is frequently being turned into a musical. On January 3, 1968, an Off-Broadway attempt titled *Love and Let Love* opened at the Sheridan Square Theatre and folded in two weeks. The day before it closed, another version, going under the title *Your Own Thing*, opened in Greenwich Village and was a hit. The earlier production was closer to Shakespeare than *Your Own Thing* which was a rock musical. In fact, it was a spoof of a rock musical, the first such satire of any note. *Hair* was just off and running, and already Off Broadway was lampooning the rock musical. Long hair is a symbol of antiestablishment in the Ragni-Rado-McDermott musical; in *Your Own Thing* it is a plot device. The boys in rock bands are wearing their locks so long that Viola (Leland Palmer) is able to get a job with the four-man rock group Apocalypse, and soon she is in love with the talent agent Orson (Tom Ligon) and chased by the record producer Olivia (Marcia Rodd, who was actually in the cast of *Love and Let Love* and left it to replace Marian Mercer during rehearsals for the second *Twelfth Night* musical). As cockeyed as the adaptation was, with Shakespeare's Illyria now a gleaming steel Manhattan, the unpretentious show was a delight from start to finish. *Your Own Thing* was also a visually vibrant production with its all-white setting on which tie-dye projections whirled and slides of famous faces, from Queen Elizabeth I to Humphrey Bogart to Shirley Temple, popped up and made pithy comments on the action. Such inspired silliness might have survived with a mediocre score, but the songs provided by Hal Hester and Danny Apolinar (who appeared onstage as members of the Apocalypse) were quite engaging, whether they were tender ballads using Shakespeare's poetry, as with "Come Away Death" and "She Never Told Her Love," or simple-minded rock numbers proclaiming "Baby! Baby!" and "The Now Generation," and the title song about being yourself. There was even a funky dance song called the "Hunca Muncha" that was so enjoyably awful it might have served as the theme song for a 1960s television series. One number, "The Middle Years," stood out from the others because it was a knowing character song and, as delivered by Rodd and Rusty Thacker (as Viola's twin Sebastian), it was a little marvel of a ballad. The characters in *Your Own Thing* may have been one-dimensional, but the cast was outstanding and seemed like lively extensions of the cartoon world on stage. Donald Driver wrote the clever book and directed with panache, and notices were enthusiastic. Critics were probably surprised that a rock musical could be such fun. (It was the first Off-Broadway musical to ever win the New York Drama Critics Circle Award.) Audience reaction was just as enthusiastic and *Your Own Thing* ran over two years. The musical is revived on occasion, but modern audiences have trouble with it, just as they would watching the television show *Laugh-In*. You had to be there.

JACQUES BREL IS ALIVE AND WELL AND LIVING IN PARIS

[22 January 1968, Village Gate, 1,847 performances] a cabaret revue by Eric Blau, Mort Shuman. *Score:* Blau, Shuman (English lyrics), Jacques Brel (music and French lyrics). *Cast:* Shuman, Elly Stone, Shawn Elliott, Alice Whitfield.

Here is an unlikely prospect for success: create a revue of unknown (in the States) French songs by an unknown (in the States) Belgian pop songwriter translated by unknown lyricists and have it performed by four unknown singers staged by an unknown director. To say that the show was a surprise hit is gross understatement. Jacques Brel was a well-known figure across Europe, but none of his songs had found wide popularity in America. Eric Blau and Mort Shuman had discovered the songs, translated them, and put them into a revue that briefly played Off Broadway in 1961 with the unfortunate title *O, Oysters!* Their translations took a lot of liberty with the French lyrics, and they used Americanisms on occasion but retained the Gallic tone of the originals. (Years later, once the revue made Brel famous in English-speaking countries, other translations were made, and Brel purists preferred them over those by Shuman and Blau.) Moni Yakim directed the revised, retitled revue as an intimate cabaret piece, using no narration or specific locations in the staging, letting the songs provide the theatrics. Since Brel's work was character driven, the revue was indeed theatrical; each song became an enthralling one-act play. Elly Stone, who had been in *O, Oysters!* and was Blau's wife, had a growing reputation from nightclub performances, but this show made her a cabaret star. The other cast members—Shawn Elliott, Alice Whitfield, and adaptor Shuman— also shone, and each had memorable solos. Among the songs to enjoy some popularity because of the revue were the haunting "Old Folks," the frenzied "Carousel," the beguiling "Timid Frieda," the merry torch song "Madeleine," the rapid-fire "Marathon," and the hopeful ballad "If We Only Had Love." *Jacques Brel Is Alive and Well and Living in Paris* received appreciative notices, but business was slow until word of mouth turned the little revue into one of the longest-running Off-Broadway musicals, lasting five years in its original production. (Brel himself did not see the show until 1970 because he refused to visit the States as a protest against the Vietnam War; he died in 1978 before reaching the age of fifty.) A Broadway version in 1972 featured Stone in a limited engagement, and critics felt the intimacy was lost, so subsequent revivals were Off Broadway, such as the twenty-fifth anniversary revival in 1992 which Stone directed. There was also a 2006 mounting Off Broadway which ran a profitable 384 performances. The show also toured and received hundreds of productions in cabarets, summer stock, and regional theatres. There was even a noisy and ineffective film version in 1974 which Brel appeared in. Revivals today still occur but, more importantly, the Jacques Brel revue had left a legacy we are still experiencing. It was the first widely successful revue dedicated to the work of one artist, and it was followed by many copies with varying quality and success. Bob Dylan, Rodgers and Hammerstein, the Beach Boys, Tammy Wynette, Leonard Cohen, Johnny Cash, Irving Berlin, Billie Holiday, the Beatles, Jerry Herman, and many other artists have been celebrated in stage revues, but only a few of the results have found success, such as the Thomas "Fats" Waller show *Ain't Misbehavin'* (1977), the Duke Ellington revue *Sophisticated Ladies* (1981), and the Leiber and Stoller musical *Smokey Joe's Cafe* (1995). (Some later shows using popular songs would be termed "jukebox" musicals, but those were book musicals, not revues.)

THE BELIEVERS

[9 May 1968, Garrick Theatre, 300 performances] a musical play by Josephine Jackson, Joseph A. Walker. *Score:* Jackson, Walker, Benjamin

Carter, various (music and lyrics). *Cast:* Jackson, Walker, Barry Hemphill, Anje Ray, Ron Steward, Benjamin Carter, Veronica Redd, Ladji Camara, Don Oliver.

Throughout the decade, African Americans were rediscovering and celebrating their history even when that history was filled with sorrow and injustice. A musical panorama of sorts titled *The Believers* was such a show, and it struck a nerve with playgoers, running thirty-eight weeks. The history piece went back to before the slave trade was established and continued up to the present day with race riots in different American cities. The title referred to the Africans who never lost hope even as they were enslaved and brought to the Americas. Much of the music was religious, ranging from Negro spirituals to blues to modern revival numbers. Coauthor Joseph A. Walker, who would find fame as the author of African American dramas in the 1970s, acted as narrator, and Josephine Jackson, who contributed to the script and the score, was also in the company which was called Voices Inc. With plenty of dance and African drumming included, the musical chronology was a lively affair filled with choral chanting, powerful solos, and spoke-sung numbers filled sometimes with bitterness, other times with joy. "This Old Ship," "Early One Morning Blues," "Where Do I Go From Here," and "Learn to Love" were perhaps the standout numbers, but the whole score, though the work of many, felt unified in spirit. More radical black musicals would follow, but the quality was rarely as consistent as that of *The Believers*.

Now

[5 June 1968, Cherry Lane Theatre, 22 performances] a musical revue by Marvin Gordon, George Haimsohn, et al. *Score:* Haimsohn (lyrics), John Aman (music). *Cast:* Aman, Sue Lawless, Rosalind Harris, Frank André, Lauree Berger, Ted Pugh.

One of the pitfalls of topical revues is that they are indeed topical and at the mercy of the current headlines. What provides fodder for songs and sketches may also invalidate those same songs and sketches. This was surely the case with the up-to-date show *Now*, which was a little too much in the present for some tastes. George Haimsohn, who would find more success later in the season with the musical *Dames at Sea*, cowrote the book and lyrics. Drugs, sex, hippies, and religion were fair game, as well as particular people in the news. Robert F. Kennedy's bid for the presidency was satirized in the song "Bobby Baby," and the day the show opened Kennedy won the California primary. It was also the day he was shot and killed. The song was cut, and yet a skit making fun of the recent shooting attempt on Andy Warhol was retained. Audiences were uncomfortable but only for three weeks.

WALK DOWN MAH STREET!

[12 June 1968, Players Theatre, 135 performances] a musical revue by Patricia Taylor Curtis. *Score:* P. T. Curtis (lyrics), Norman Curtis (music). *Cast:* Freddy Diaz, Gene Rounds, Denise Delapenha, Lorraine Feather, Vaughn Martinez, Kenneth Frett.

Another topical revue, this one concentrating on racial subjects for its sketches and songs, managed to run seventeen weeks, possibly because there were no political references to remind audiences of the death of Robert F. Kennedy the week before the show opened. The jaunty title number was both carefree and satiric, and the prejudices against African Americans were looked at in a wry rather than bitter manner. There was both pride and satire in "Basic Black," and even that much-revered African American staple, gospel music, was spoofed in "Walk, Lordy, Walk." On the other hand, there was honest emotion in "Don't Have to Take It Any More" and "For Four Hundred Years." The sketches looked at crime-ridden neighborhoods, jobs closed to black Americans, and the efforts of some African Americans to behave like white people. Perhaps white audiences felt a bit uncomfortable as they laughed. It was a volatile time, with urban race riots and the assassination of Martin Luther King two months earlier, thus a show that made light of racial inequality was treading dangerous ground. Yet *Walk Down Mah Street!* tread it successfully enough to make playgoers laugh without escaping the touchy subject matter.

HOW TO STEAL AN ELECTION

[13 October 1968, Pocket Theatre, 89 performances] a musical satire by William F. Brown. *Score:* Oscar Brand (music and lyrics). *Cast:* Bill

McCutcheon, Carole Demas, D. R. Allen, Clifton Davis, Del Hinkley, Beverly Ballard, Ed Crowley, Barbara Anson, Thom Koutsoukos.

How to Steal an Election might sound like a musical about the Watergate scandal, but this show predates that event and, ironically, is no longer producible because of the Nixon affair. The sassy little political revue looked at the ways in which all presidents (yes, even George Washington and John F. Kennedy) have twisted justice and legality in order to attain the highest office in the land. The show not only illustrated the fact in song and skits but actually came to the conclusion that such misbehavior is all part of the American way. This was all amusing enough in 1968 to run eleven weeks. The revue was held together by commentary by Calvin Coolidge (D. R. Allen) who comes back from the dead to enlighten an African American man (Clifton Davis) and a white woman (Carole Demas) who have just come from the recent riot-filled Democratic Convention in Chicago. The score consisted of actual campaign songs and period pieces, such as "Lucky Lindy," "Get on the Raft with Taft," and "Tippecanoe and Tyler Too," as well as new numbers that reflected Coolidge's observations. A touching lament about Kennedy titled "Mr. Might've Been" must have brought a tear to audience members, but Coolidge even deflates that idol by making references to the ways the Kennedy fortune was used to buy political success. Talking about a crooked Taft and Grant was easy; tackling Kennedy in the 1960s was trickier. The show ended with the cast singing the prophetic "More of the Same." They didn't know the half of it.

BALLAD FOR A FIRING SQUAD

[13 December 1968, Theatre de Lys, 7 performances] a musical play by Jerome Coopersmith. *Score:* Edward Thomas (music), Martin Charnin (lyrics). *Cast:* Renata Vaselle, James Hurst, Liz Sheridan, Neva Small, Stanley Church, Dominic Chianese, Joseph Corby.

Some musicals refuse to die, which is not always a good thing. The Broadway-bound *Mata Hari*, which closed out of town in 1967, was one of the most notorious flops of its era. An expensive, overwrought musical about the infamous World War I spy, the David Merrick production had such a disastrous opening night in Washington, D.C., that it provided merriment for theatre wags for years. Scenery got stuck, wigs refused to stick, lights did not cooperate, and the audience witnessed over three hours of tedium climaxed by the leading lady who, having been executed by a firing squad and lay dead on stage, decided to scratch her itchy nose to the delight of the weary playgoers. Merrick closed the fiasco out of town, but some thought a potentially potent show was lost. Composer Edward Thomas was among those convinced that a revival was called for; therefore he produced a new version Off Broadway the next year and retitled it *Ballad for a Firing Squad*. Reviewers conceded that the score was better on second hearing and that the book had its moments, but audiences were not interested. The production closed in a week and, although Thomas promised to reopen after the holidays, the show died a second death. Still *Mata Hari* refused to give up the ghost. An Off-Off-Broadway mounting by the York Theatre in 1996 ran twelve performances and, more importantly, much of the cast reassembled in 2001 to record the score. Now theatre lovers can judge for themselves.

Is *Mata Hari* an overlooked gem or the proverbial bad penny that keeps turning up? Jerome Coopersmith's book downplays the *femme fatale* aspect of the story and focuses on the complicated relationship between the sultry dancer Mata Hari and the upstanding French Captain LaFarge who sets out to prove she is a spy, only to fall in love with her. The musical never makes it clear if Mata is guilty or not, just as history has never proven the case one way or the other. Paralleling the love story are scenes with a young French soldier who is experiencing the horrors of war. The two tracks seem disjointed at times, but the antiwar scenes and songs give the musical some weight which can be viewed as thought-provoking or just pretentious. Thomas's music is quite accomplished, but the lyrics by Martin Charnin, an uneven wordsmith at the best of times, are frequently banal or lamely trying to be clever. The only song to receive any recognition is the antiwar ballad "Maman" in which the young Frenchman writes to his mother about the battle and his killing a young German soldier. The unadorned lyric and the slowly pulsating music turn the number into a powerful piece of music drama. There is also a sense of loss in the plaintive "Gone" which opens and closes the show. But little else in the score rings true as every French cliché is dragged out to try to create a Gallic atmosphere. *Mata Hari* may resurface on occasion, but it never manages to float for long.

DAMES AT SEA

[20 December 1968, Bouwerie Lane Theatre, 575 performances] a musical spoof by George Haimsohn, Robin Miller. *Score:* Haimsohn, Miller (lyrics), Jim Wise (music). *Cast:* Bernadette Peters, David Christmas, Tamara Long, Steve Elmore, Sally Stark, Joseph R. Sicari.

Moviegoers discovering (or rediscovering) the Ruby Keeler–Dick Powell–Joan Blondell film musicals of the 1930s in revival houses saw the stars gently spoofed on stage in *Dames at Sea*, a tuneful and accurate musical that cleverly recreated the Warner Brothers look with only five actors and two simple sets. Want-to-be-chorine Ruby (Bernadette Peters) travels from Centerville, U.S.A, to Manhattan to be on Broadway. She finds a sweetheart in songwriter-juvenile lead Dick (David Christmas) and becomes a stage star when she replaces the temperamental Mona Kent (Tamara Long) at the last minute. Bernadette Peters had played Ruby in 1966 in a one-act version of the pastiche musical Off-Off Broadway (where the piece carried the wry subtitle *Golddiggers Afloat*), but the long-running Off-Broadway version gave the baby-faced performer her first recognition. The script by George Haimsohn and Robin Miller managed to cram in a trunk load of Warner musical clichés, but it was the delectable score they wrote with composer Jim Wise that made the show sparkle. Each song recalled the dizzy, optimistic ditties from the Depression, from the bluesy torch song "That Mister Man of Mine" to the cheeky train number "Choo Choo Honeymoon" to the toe-tapping title song. "Raining in My Heart" was perfectly insipid, and "The Beguine" managed to spoof Cole Porter and *Rose-Marie* at the same time. The Busby Berkeley extravaganza "Shadow Waltz" from the screen became the simple but silly "Echo Waltz" on the small stage. By the time the whole cast was chirping the finale "Let's Have a Simple Wedding," the audience was in celluloid pastiche heaven. *Dames at Sea* ran two and a half years then went on to enjoy productions in Great Britain, France, Australia, Denmark, Germany—well, wherever theatregoers knew the old movies. In addition to hundreds of stock and school productions, the musical was revived Off Broadway in 1970, running 170 performances, and again in 1985 when it stayed for 278 performances. There was even a television version with Ann-Margaret, Dick Shawn, Anne Meara, Fred Gwynne, and Hollywood veteran Ann Miller in 1971. Young audiences today don't know the old films, so revivals are not frequent, but *Dames at Sea* can still entertain in a timeless and slaphappy manner.

PEACE

[27 January 1969, Astor Place Theatre, 192 performances] a musical version of Aristophanes' comedy by Tim Reynolds. *Score:* Reynolds (lyrics), Al Carmines (music). *Cast:* Reathel Bean, Judy Kurnitz, George McGrath, Arlene Rothlein, Lee Crespi, David Pursley, David Tice, David Vaughan.

PROMENADE

[4 June 1969, Promenade Theatre, 259 performances] a musical play by Maria Irene Fornes. *Score:* Fornes (lyrics), Al Carmines (music). *Cast:* Gilbert Price, Ty McConnell, Alice Playten, Madeline Kahn, Carrie Wilson, Margot Albert, Shannon Bolin, Sandra Schaeffer, Marc Allen III, Edmund Gaynes, George S. Irving, Pierre Epstein.

Composer-producer-performer Al Carmines continued to find success as he brought his offbeat musicals from Off-Off Broadway to slightly larger venues. The ancient Greek antiwar comedy *Peace*, perhaps Aristophanes' most obscure play, was turned into a minstrel show of sorts, and the parallels to the current war in Vietnam made the 421 BC work come to life. Weary of war, the Athenian nobleman Trygaeus (Reathel Bean) goes to Mt. Olympus where Peace (Arlene Rothlein) has been imprisoned by War (David Pursley) and General Disorder (David Tice). He rescues her and brings Peace to earth where all those who profit from war seek to restart the hostilities. Trygaeus outsmarts them and wins the beautiful Lisa (Julie Kurnitz) as his bride. The score by Carmines and lyricist Tim Reynolds was agreeably contemporary, and the numbers often broke down into effective sextets and ensemble numbers. "All the Dark Is Changed to Sunshine," "Things Are Starting to Grow Again," and "Summer's Nice" were the more optimistic numbers while Aristophanes' wit was hinted at in such ribald numbers as "Don't Do It, Mr. Hermes" and "Just Let Me Get My Hands on Peace." The cast was filled with Carmines regulars (though he himself did not appear in the show), who had developed a following by this time. The production was also more elaborate than Carmines's usual Off Off-Broadway offerings as the sets and costumes looked less budget minded. Trygaeus arrived in Paradise riding a giant dung beetle, which was as impressive as it was odd.

The minstrel show format didn't seem to offend audiences, and they kept *Peace* on the boards for nearly six months.

Even more successful was Carmines's *Promenade* which opened six months later in a new theatre named after the show (or was the show named after the theatre?). The black convict Number 106 (Gilbert Price) and the white convict Number 105 (Ty McConnell) dig themselves out of prison and set off on a *Candide*-like adventure in which they encounter the wickedness of Big Business and War and the lamentations of the common man. The large and varied cast of characters included neurotic women and love-starved men who spilled their troubles out to the two convicts before the hapless duo ended up back in jail. Avant-garde playwright Maria Irene Fornes wrote the repetitive lyrics and the grab bag of a book, which was overtly Brechtian, but often Carmines's music, echoing Kurt Weill, and the expert cast allowed the messy little show to soar. "The Cigarette Song" was the most obviously similar to Brecht-Weill numbers, but there was a *Threepenny Opera* feel also to the propulsive "Unrequited Love," the looney lament "Two Little Angels," and the ironic anthem "All Is Well in the City." The high point of the score is the devilish character number "Capricious and Fickle" in which Alice Playten belted out her disgust for a man who was as unfeeling as herself. *Promenade* attracted all the first-string critics, and most had very complimentary things to say, allowing the show to run seven and a half months. Audiences might not sit still for it today, but *Promenade* still has something to offer. It is shrill, in your face, and self-indulgent; for an antiestablishment musical in the 1960s these were qualities worth seeking out.

OH! CALCUTTA!

[17 June 1969, Eden Theatre, 704 performances; Belasco Theatre, 1,314 performances] a musical revue by Jules Feiffer, Samuel Beckett, Jacques Levy, John Lennon, Dan Greenburg, Leonard Melfi, Sam Shepard, et al. *Score:* The Open Window (Robert Dennis, Peter Schickele, Stanley Walden). *Cast:* Bill Macy, Margo Sappington, Mark Dempsey, Raina Barrett, George Welbes, Leon Russom, Alan Rachins, Boni Enten.

Although many people heard about the "nude revue," few realized *Oh! Calcutta!* was a musical. Not that anyone went to see the show for the singing and dancing. The notorious revue explored humankind's sexual hang-ups through the ages and did so with the cast naked for long sections of the evening. British critic Kenneth Tynan put together the adult program of sketches by several respected authors and lyricists, and the group The Open Window wrote the songs, which were mostly sung as background music performed by the group on stage. Yet there were a few real theatre songs, the most interesting being the musical sequence "I Don't Have a Song to Sing" about the auditions for the revue itself. The nervous actors expressed their thoughts in words and song, worrying about their physical and talent deficiencies, questioning how much humiliation they can endure, and confessing "I Want It." The number is a miniversion of *A Chorus Line* a half dozen years before that landmark musical was produced. *Oh! Calcutta!* received mostly negative reviews but was controversial and sensational enough to run 704 performances before it transferred to the Broadway venue and stayed for more than three years. In 1976 a replica of the original production opened in the tiny Edison Theatre (considered a Broadway house) and ran an astounding 5,959 performances. (It should be pointed out that this production sometimes gave ten performances a week instead of the usual eight, so the number does not reflect the length of time it ran.) Many of the patrons for the revue were foreign tourists who were drawn by the provocative promotion campaign in different languages. There was even a video/film version in 1972, taped during a performance and showing the audience arriving at the theatre and the actors back stage applying makeup to their nude bodies before the show begins. It was broadcast on cable and had a limited run in movie theatres without causing much of a stir. *Oh! Calcutta!* prompted other sex revues in the 1970s featuring nude performers, but the novelty had passed by the 1980s. Theatre observers felt audiences would never again be so easily enticed by such obvious sensationalism. They didn't know *Naked Boys Singing!* was looming in the future.

SALVATION

[24 September 1969, Jan Hus Theatre, 239 performances] a musical revue by Peter Link, C. C. Courtney. *Score:* Link, Courtney (music and lyrics). *Cast:* Link, Courtney, Joe Morton, Yolande Bavan, Boni Enten, Marta Heflin, Annie Rachel, Chapman Roberts.

One of the most interesting of the many offsprings of *Hair* was the rock musical *Salvation*, which used the premise of a mock religious revival meeting to explore the topical issues of the day. The preacher Monday (C. C. Courtney) runs the revival, which often gets out of hand as religious texts are turned inside out and the fervent members of the congregation stop the meeting to express themselves in song. The show never went anywhere, but the ride was exhilarating all the same, thanks to the dynamite cast and a noteworthy score. Courtney and Peter Link wrote the piece (Link performed in it too) and came up with one of the few rock scores of the time in which the lyrics were as accomplished as the music. Like the *Hair* songs, the numbers in *Salvation* used repetition and a pounding beat yet still managed to go places, develop an idea, and even display a bit of wit along the way. In other words, these were theatre songs. In "Daedalus," Ranee (Yolande Bavan) describes to her leering doctor the details in which her lover "melted her wings" and then left her to fall. A guilt-ridden LeRoy (Chapman Roberts) is haunted by his obsession for masturbation in "1001." Dierdre (Annie Rachel) regrets that she "Let the Moment Slip By" when she didn't sleep with her boyfriend before he went off to be killed in Vietnam. Sometimes the score veered away from rock and took up gospel, as with the wry "There Ain't No Flies on Jesus," or hymns, as with "For Ever." While some of the titles sound like 1960s bumper stickers, such as "If You Let Me Make Love to You Then Why Can't I Touch You?" and "Tomorrow Is the First Day of the Rest of My Life," even these numbers are propelled forward with some vivid writing. Most beguiling of all is the list song "Back to Genesis" in which the cast laments the present state of the world and longs for the days before Freud, IBM, the Sears and Roebuck catalogue, and the Bible itself. *Salvation* was well received by both the press and the public and ran over seven months. During the run there were changes in the cast, and unknown talents such as Barry Bostwick and Bette Midler got to shine. With material this flashy, it was a great way to get noticed.

GERTRUDE STEIN'S FIRST READER

[15 December 1969, Astor Place Theatre, 40 performances] a musical revue by Herbert Machiz. *Score:* Ann Sternberg (music), Gertrude Stein (lyrics). *Cast:* Sternberg, Joy Garrett, Frank Giordano, Michael Anthony, Sandra Thornton.

Gertrude Stein, the most unlyrical of poets, continued to attract composers who put her words to music. *The Gertrude Stein Reader* was Herbert Machiz's idea: evoke the simplicity of the poet's work by having them presented by children. Ann Sternberg wrote the music and was on stage as a pianist who encourages the kids to play games, recite passages, and generally romp about the stage just as Stein's poetry bounced about the page. It was an idea that was more interesting than practical because the children needed to be played by experienced adult performers who, no matter how talented, looked rather silly if not totally annoying. But many continue to find Stein's work just as annoying, yet in an odd way the evening was true to the poet. Some numbers turned out better than others. The carefree murder mystery song "The Three Sisters Who Are Not Sisters" had a childlike glee, and there was fun in the mini-opera "In a Garden." Each act ended with the simple song "Be Very Careful," which certainly carried a child's point of view. Stein is usually a tough sell, and the production only managed to run five weeks. Still, it was the sort of thing that only Off Broadway could do and find an audience for that long.

Chapter Four

○

Threat of Extinction: The 1970s

THE TURMOIL OF THE 1960s CONTINUED on for the first few years of the 1970s, and then, around the time Richard Nixon resigned from the presidency in 1974, things seemed to come to a breathless and uncomfortable halt. The rest of the decade was not lacking for issues. The women's movement was in full force, the civil rights battles of the 1960s were unresolved, and the recognition of gay and lesbian lifestyles were among the subjects prevalent in Off-Broadway musicals. Many of these shows were commendable, but there was a derelict feeling in the New York theatre during the 1970s, and Off Broadway was not immune to it. The city itself was at its lowest point. Crime, strikes, financial woes, loss of tourism, and other urban nightmares plagued New York City more, it seemed, than other major metropolises. No city in America received such bad press as New York did during this decade. The newspaper headline "Ford to NY: Drop Dead" was the blunt way of saying the president was not going to allow the federal government to bail out the bankrupt city. Jokes on television about muggers, corrupt cab drivers, cops on the take, garbage piling up on the streets, and 42nd Street as the capital of sleaze turned New York into an uncomfortable chuckle.

Certainly no one in the theatre was laughing. Broadway had fewer shows, more empty theatres, and less business than any time during the twentieth century. Times Square was far from glamorous, and theatregoers rushed through it going to and coming out of playhouses offering big musicals and Neil Simon comedies. Producers encouraged the city to provide more police in the Theatre District during performance times, and they even fiddled with curtain times, moving the standard 8:30 PM curtain to 7:30 PM so that theatregoers could get away from Times Square at an earlier hour. (The agreed-upon time of 8:00

PM was a later compromise.) Greenwich Village and the other neighborhoods where the Off-Broadway playhouses were located were deemed equally as dangerous because they were out of the way. Going Off Broadway had once meant slumming; now it meant taking your life in your hands. The drastic drop in New York City tourism did not affect Off Broadway as harshly as it did the Street, but even New Yorkers were getting nervous about seeking out the little theatre spaces scattered throughout the city.

All this considered, some very successful or important theatre productions managed to find life on and Off Broadway in the 1970s. Escapist hits on Broadway included *Applause, Two By Two, Grease, Pippin, The Magic Show, Shenandoah, Chicago, I Love My Wife, Annie, Dancin', and They're Playing Our Song*. Sometimes escapist, other times more demanding, was the flood of African American musicals on the Street. *Purlie; Ain't Supposed to Die a Natural Death; Don't Bother Me, I Can't Cope; Raisin; The Wiz; Bubbling Brown Sugar; Your Arms Too Short to Box with God*; and *Ain't Misbehavin'* (the last originating Off Broadway) were often mainstream hits, appealing to both black and white audiences. Following in the footsteps of *Hair*'s success, a handful of rock musicals opened on Broadway, but the only one to find success there was *Jesus Christ Superstar*. Broadway in the 1970s is perhaps most fondly remembered for the treasure trove of Stephen Sondheim musicals that were introduced during the decade: *Company; Follies; A Little Night Music; Pacific Overtures;* and *Sweeney Todd, the Demon Barber of Fleet Street*. No other Broadway offering during the 1970s was as innovative and invigorating as these far-reaching works which, while meeting with variable success the first time out, have only grown in stature over the years.

Off Broadway may not have produced a Sondheim in the 1970s, but it did introduce such songwriters as Stephen Schwartz, Richard Maltby Jr., David Shire, Carol Hall, and William Finn. The decade offered many high points, both artistically and commercially. The rock musicals that opened Off Broadway were of considerable interest; the number of revues diminished, but they still offered wry commentary on the times; and there were plenty of shows with nostalgia for the musical past, celebrating artists as different as Thomas "Fats" Waller and Noël Coward. Nine Off-Broadway musicals of the 1970s transferred to Broadway, and most of them showed a profit there. The rise in production costs Off Broadway meant fewer commercial enterprises and more nonprofit productions. The Public Theatre, New York Shakespeare Festival, Playwrights Horizons, Manhattan Theatre Club, Lincoln Center, and other theatre organizations offered some of the decade's best musicals and, in the case of *A Chorus Line* and some other shows, helped fund those nonprofit theatres through their success on the Street. Despite this, Off Broadway was in trouble. Like Broadway, the number of productions was down, the odds of making money were unfavorable, and the ambiance of going Off Broadway was slight. Perhaps the heyday of this alternative to Broadway was over and only extinction lay in the future.

THE LAST SWEET DAYS OF ISAAC

[26 January 1970, East Side Playhouse, 485 performances] a musical play by Gretchen Cryer. *Score:* Cryer (lyrics), Nancy Ford (music). *Cast:* Austin Pendleton, Fredricka Weber, John Long, Charles Collins, Louise Heath, C. David Colson.

The first Off-Broadway rock musical of the decade was indicative of many 1970s musicals: intriguing, fresh, and often exhilarating; but also confused, disjointed and not totally satisfying. Yet *The Last Sweet Days of Isaac* also suggested that strong characterization, adept songs, and even humor could be found in the rock show. The promise that Nancy Ford and Gretchen Cryer had shown in *Now Is the Time for All Good Men* was somewhat fulfilled with this pair of one-act musicals about the loss of opportunity and the lack of communication in the modern world. In the first act, the neurotic, hypertense Isaac (Austin Pendleton) and the frustrated poet-secretary Ingrid (Fredricka Weber) are trapped in an elevator and slowly learn to shed their inhibitions. Both characters are beautifully drawn in words and song, and the musical playlet is a tight, pleasing little gem. In the second act, which somehow takes place years earlier, Isaac is in jail and tries to communicate with the blonde inmate Alice (Weber) by way of television screens. At the end of the act she learns on the news that he has died in a protest demonstration. Or did he? Not only was the audience confused, but they didn't care. The incoherent second half just about buried all the joy of the first. Yet there were excellent songs in both of the playlets. The incisive character songs "A Transparent Crystal Moment," "Love You Came to Me," and "My Most Important Moments Go By" in the elevator were first rate. The less specific folk-rock numbers "Somebody Died Today," "I Want to Walk to San Francisco," and "Touching Your Hand Is Like Touching Your Mind" were not even sung by the characters but by the band and backup singers, yet they still pleased. Word Baker, who had staged *The Fantasticks* a decade earlier, used a similar kind of creative simplicity in directing the two playlets, but even he could not save the second act. Austin Pendleton was outstanding as Isaac, and his manic, heart-warming performance alone made the show worth seeing.

Prompted by many enthusiastic reviews and some Off-Broadway awards, *The Last Sweet Days of Isaac* ran more than a year. It is very rarely revived today. Is it hopelessly dated, or is it that second act? Probably both.

Joy

[27 January 1970, New Theatre, 208 performances] a musical revue by Oscar Brown Jr. *Score:* Brown (music and lyrics). *Cast:* Brown, Jean Pace, Sivuca.

A different sound for Off Broadway, and a sound that was welcomed for twenty-six weeks, was the enthralling folk and pop songs in the Brazilian style, as celebrated in the cabaret-like revue *Joy*. It featured the work of one man, Oscar Brown Jr., and required no narrative or characters. (To be accurate, the French songwriter-singer Charles Aznavour and some others collaborated with Brown on a few of the numbers.) Brown also performed in the revue with Jean Pace, the two of them accompanied by the Brazilian musician Sivuca who played a variety of instruments. African Americans Brown and Pace had done earlier versions of the revue in Chicago and San Francisco with success, and there was even a short gig in Central Park in the late 1960s. So what New Yorkers saw Off Broadway was a well-honed musical journey that felt as comfortable as a warm glove. Many themes were explored, from friendship and celebrations of nature to the heartbreak of love and the ache of prejudice. The erotic "Funny Feeling" explored women's sensuality, "Brown Baby" was an indelible lullaby, "Afro Blues" was an enticing lament, and the rhythmic "Mother Africa's Day" was a hopeful chant. The sound was very Brazilian in the chanting "Sky and Sea" then sometimes turned to traditional blues as with "Funky World." The title did not disappoint; there was indeed joy in this intimate show that seemed like an oasis from the rock and pop music all over town.

Billy Noname

[2 March 1970, Truck and Warehouse Theatre, 48 performances] a musical play by William Wellington Mackey. *Score:* Johnny Brandon (music and lyrics). *Cast:* Donny Burks, Alan Weeks, Hattie Winston, Andrea Saunders, Charles Moore, Gory Van Scott, Roger Lawson, Thommie Bush, Urylee Leonardos.

The Broadway musical *Hallelujah, Baby!* (1967) was an ambitious attempt to look at African Americans over a period of time by having a heroine (played by Leslie Uggams) go through the decades without aging very much. That intriguing if uneven show ran an unprofitable 293 performances. The same concept was attempted with *Billy Noname* and, as accomplished as it was at times, it fared poorly, closing after six weeks. The black Everyman appropriately called Billy Noname (Donny Burks) is the result of a street rape in a grim ghetto neighborhood in Bay Alley, U.S.A., in the Depression and the youth grows up without a father and without a strong self-identity. While America is enduring World War II, the bitter yet needy Billy fights his own war and decides to be a playwright and create fictional characters that seem more real to him than himself. During the civil rights movement he starts to find an identity as other African Americans demand to be recognized. But the assassination of Martin Luther King is a crushing blow, and the play ends with the urban race riots that followed. Billy still has no name. Johnny Brandon's score reflected the music of the different periods in the story, from swing in the 1940s to rhythm and blues in the 1950s to rock and soul in the 1960s. It was an exhilarating score, ranging from the plaintive character song "A Different Drummer" and the heartfelt "I Want to Live" to the snide "Color Me White" and the eruptive "Burn Baby Burn." The cast was top-notch (Alan Weeks, who was featured in *Hallelujah, Baby!* played the supporting role of Tiny Shannon in *Billy Noname*), and reviewers were also complimentary about the production standards. *Billy Noname* was a good idea for a musical, but one that failed to fully satisfy.

THE DRUNKARD

[13 April 1970, 13th Street Theatre, 48 performances] a musical comedy by W. H. S. Smith, Bro Herrod. *Score:* Barry Manilow (music), et al. *Cast:* Marie Santell, Clay Johns, Christopher Cable, Donna Saunders, Lou Vitacco, Joy Garrett, Drew Murphy, Susan Rush.

The most famous of all temperance plays, W. H. S. Smith's *The Drunkard* was first performed in Boston in 1844 and was followed by hundreds of productions during the rest of the century. By the 1930s the melodrama was a dated morality play filled with clichés that made an audience laugh rather than cringe with guilt. (In 1933 a small Los Angeles theatre produced the piece for laughs, and it ran over seven thousand performances!) Bro Herrod adapted the old script into an Off-Broadway musical. He also produced and directed the musical for which Barry Manilow adapted old songs (only a few of which were from the period) and wrote a handful of new ones. The result was a delightful musical comedy that allowed the audience to cheer the hero, hiss the villain, and sing along to the tuneful numbers. The plot is a familiar one because many of the elements were later used in silent films and satirical "mellerdramers." The two-faced, city-slicker lawyer Cribbs (Christopher Cable) owns the mortgage on the humble homestead of pretty Mary Wilson (Marie Santell) and her aged mother (Donna Sanders). Mary is loved and protected by the good-hearted, upstanding Edward Middleton (Clay Johns) who has only one weakness: alcohol. Cribbs uses this to his advantage, and soon Edward is a penniless souse in the Five Points district of New York City and framed as a forger by the evil Cribbs. It takes a temperance lecture by Edward's foster brother William (Drew Murphy) to save Edward who then saves the farm. Herrod was true to the period in his adaption by having the action interrupted by musical acts performed in front of a classic olio curtain. Other songs were sung by the characters in character, though there was almost a Brechtian flavor to the way the numbers were delivered directly to the audience. Among the vintage songs used were "Strolling Through the Park," "The Curse of the Aching Heart," and "Don't Swat Your Mother, Boys." Manilow's original ditties were not precise pastiches of nineteenth-century songs but more in the musical comedy mode. "Something Good Will Happen Soon" was a hopeful duet for mother and daughter (and later reprised by others), "For When You're Dead" was a dandy musical soliloquy for the villain, and the merry "Have Another Drink" was so contagious that it just about wiped out the temperance lesson of the piece. Manilow had just graduated from Juilliard, and the Off-Broadway assignment was his first job. Unfortunately the musical melodrama ran only six weeks, and both Manilow and the show would have to wait for recognition. By the end of the 1970s, Manilow was a famous arranger, songwriter, and performer, and *The Drunkard* was occasionally revived regionally, using his name as a selling point. The show is still too little known and proves to be a happy surprise when audiences discover it.

MAHAGONNY

[28 April 1970, Anderson Theatre, 8 performances] a musical play by Bertolt Brecht, Arnold Weinstein. *Score:* Brecht, Weinstein (lyrics), Kurt Weill (music). *Cast:* Frank Porretta, Alan Criofoot, Estelle Parsons, Barbara Harris, Bill Copeland, Don Crabtree, Jack De Lon, Val Pringle.

The German opera *Aufstieg und Fall der Stadt Mahagonny* (*The Rise and Fall of the City of Mahagonny*) premiered in Berlin in 1930 and took forty years to reach American shores as simply *Mahagonny*. Arnold Weinstein translated Bertolt Brecht's book and lyrics, and Kurt Weill's music was rearranged into a smaller music-theatre piece suitable for Off Broadway. Despite the wide popularity of Brecht and Weill's other early German work *The Threepenny Opera*, there was little interest in this opera, and it shuttered after a week. Two years later there was a resurgence of public interest in Weill because of a long-running Off-Broadway revue of his work; but it was too late for this production, and it would be left to opera houses to give *Mahagonny* the attention it deserved. All the same, Brecht and Weill saw their attack against materialism as a theatre piece, and it ought to have found a home Off Broadway as *The Threepenny Opera* had. The plot of *Mahagonny* is much darker and the satire on good and evil less fun than the earlier work. Some greedy crooks create the American metropolis of Mahagonny as a "city a gold" to attract the men who are returning to the States after having made their fortunes in Alaska. The ploy works, and Mahagonny is soon a paradise of saloons, whorehouses, and gambling joints. At the peak of the business frenzy it looks like this Sodom will be destroyed by an approaching hurricane, but the storm shifts and the city is spared, a sign that even nature blesses such greed and sin. When the innocent lumberjack Jimmy Mallory is unjustly accused and convicted of murder, the kangaroo court becomes a circus attraction, and only some of Jimmy's favorite whores are left to mourn his unjust execution. It was grim storytelling, and the different characters seemed more like variations of evil than people. Yet the musical is never dull or indifferent with such a marvelous score. "The Alabama Song," "As You Make Your Bed," and "Mandalay Song" have since become justly famous in cabarets and Weill revues, but the whole score is invigorating in its defiance and musical boldness. Perhaps the 1970 Off-Broadway mounting was lacking. It was a very elaborate production, needing weeks of previews and costing $350,000, a record for an Off-Broadway musical at this time. Notices were not encouraging, though one suspects the cast was not at fault. (The multitalented Estelle Parsons and Barbara Harris played the principal female characters.) Maybe it wasn't the right time for a diatribe against a fictional city of sin when there was enough in the real world to protest about. Regardless, *Mahagonny* survived to become a favorite in grand opera around the world. One wonders if Brecht and Weill would rather it come to life in an intimate Off-Broadway theatre.

COLETTE

[6 May 1970, Ellen Stewart Theatre, 101 performances] a musical play by Elinor Jones based on Colette's autobiographical writings. *Score:* Harvey Schmidt (music), Tom Jones (lyrics). *Cast:* Zoe Caldwell, Mildred Dunnock, Barry Bostwick, Keene Curtis, Charles Siebert, Holland Taylor.

Songwriters Tom Jones and Harvey Schmidt have a history of working on projects for years, often returning to their musicals with new songs and new titles. For example, their musicalization of *Our Town* has percolated for decades without ever getting a New York production. *Colette* is another of their undying devotions. Although its initial Off-Broadway mounting ran three months, Jones and Schmidt thought it deserved better and revised the musical for a 1982 Broadway production starring Diana Rigg which closed out of town. Further rewrites were made in 1983 and 1991, and then in 1994 the most recent version was recorded. What is it about *Colette* that they refuse to let go of it? Probably it is the character of the French authoress herself. The more you learn about her, the more fascinating she becomes. Yet on stage her life and career fail to impress. The original production survived because of Zoe Caldwell's luminous performance rather than for Colette herself; the actress was more interesting than the character. The first act of the script by Elinor Jones (Tom Jones's wife at the time) concerned the young Colette who marries the dashing Willy (Charles Siebert) only to see him pass off her writings as his own. It takes Colette a whole act to walk out on him. The second act jumped to the 1920s when Colette was a famous writer and she began a long affair with a much younger man (Barry Bostwick). In later versions of the musical, he was called Maurice and the two wed after several years as lovers. Many songs have been written and rewritten for *Colette* over the years, so the final score seems disjointed. No wonder the 1994 recording was retitled *Colette Collage*; it seems more like a collection rather than a unified score. That doesn't mean that there are no worthwhile songs to come out of this long-labored musical. Jones and Schmidt are top songwriters, and there is much here to savor. The theme for the show is the expansive "Joy," which might be the number closest to Colette's writing style. "The Music Hall" sequence is daffy and colorful, the knowing duet "Ooh-La-La" is engaging, and "La Vagabonde" is a spirited song and dance. Colette's mother Sido (Mildred Dunnock) sings the lyrical yet blunt "Love Is Not a Sentiment Worthy of Respect," and Colette's sarcastic "Decorate the Human Face" is first-rate, though it sure doesn't feel like it belongs in this show. Perhaps the subject matter of *Colette* is too European for American songwriters like Jones and Schmidt. Alan Jay Lerner and Frederick Loewe pulled it off with *Gigi*, which was based on a Colette story. Perhaps in its next reincarnation, *Colette* will star someone like Leslie Caron and all will be well.

THE ME NOBODY KNOWS

[18 May 1970, Orpheum Theatre, 208 performances; Helen Hayes Theatre, 586 performances] a musical revue by Stephen M. Joseph. *Score:* Gary William Friedman (music), Will Holt (lyrics). *Cast:* Irene Cara, Northern J. Calloway, Hattie Winston, Jose Fernandez, Gerri Dean, Laura Michaels, Melanie Henderson, Douglas Grant, Beverly Ann Bremers, Paul Mace, Kevin Lindsay, Carl Thomas.

Stage documentaries have always been rare; musical theatre documentaries are even rarer. An exception is this uncommonly poignant revue that voiced the concerns and dreams of children and young adults in contemporary inner-city society. Stephen M. Joseph and Herb Shapiro fashioned the script based on Robert H. Livingston's book, a collection of writings from kids between the ages of seven and eighteen attending public schools in New York City's tougher neighborhoods. Gary William Friedman composed the contemporary yet theatrical songs which sometimes used the actual words from the kids, other times expressed their thoughts in verse written by Will Holt. The result was an engrossing collage of voices and songs that expressed the young people's feeling about a variety of subjects and revealed an undaunted optimism in spite of their environment. The young cast included some performers who would go on to noteworthy adult careers, such as Irene Cara, Northern J. Calloway, and Hattie Winston. For a revue score, the songs are surprisingly connected in tone and point of view. Among the memorable numbers were the lullaby-like "Dream Babies," the echoing duet "Sounds," the breezy "If I Had a Million Dollars," the jaunty "Light Sings," and the yearning "Let Me Come In." The musical may have seemed like a hard sell to adult theatregoers, but some rave notices and strong word of mouth turned *The Me Nobody Knows* into a hit first Off Broadway and then on the Street. The revue needs to be performed by a very young cast, so professional revivals are problematic, but over the years many schools (with the required ethnic student body) have presented the show with success. Livingston directed the original, and Patricia Birch choreographed it, both of them keeping the staging simple. This was not a showcase for talented teens, an early kind of *Fame*, but a collection of voices expressing potent ideas. Consequently amateur productions have often been very effective.

SENSATIONS

[8 November 1970, Theatre Four, 16 performances] a rock musical by Paul Zakrzweski based on Shakespeare's *Romeo and Juliet*. *Score:* Zakrzweski (lyrics), Wally Haper (music). *Cast:* John Savage, Judy Gibson, Paulette Attie, Arthur Bartow, Joe Masiell, Ron Martin, James Ray.

Everyone knows that *Romeo and Juliet* has its fair share of love and violence, and so did *West Side Story*. But did it need drugs too? Evidently in the early 1970s it did. This rock version of Shakespeare's tale was set in contemporary times in which the plight of lovers Romeo (John Savage) and Juliet (Judy Gibson) was only one of the conflicts in a drug-infested, violence-prone modern city. While Shakespeare's original was reimagined for *West Side Story*, it seems the Bard just got in the way in *Sensations*. Not only was it not very good, it was blatantly unnecessary. Cast member Savage and Joe Masiell would go on to better things, and composer Wally Harper would later become one of the best musical arrangers in the business. There was also considerable talent back stage, such as Broadway designers William and Jean Eckart and actor-turned-director Jerry Dodge. *Sensations* is just a footnote in their careers and in the history of Off-Broadway musicals but one worth mentioning. Rock was thought to be the new sound of musical theatre, and any idea, old or new, was game for the pop treatment. *Sensations* disappeared in two weeks, as did many others that followed the same path. In this case Off Broadway was not experimenting; it seemed to be trying to cash in.

TOUCH

[8 November 1970, Village Arena Theatre, 422 performances] a musical play by Kenn Long. Amy Saltz. *Score:* Long (music and lyrics), Jim Crozier (music). *Cast:* Long, Ava Rosenblum, Phyllis Gibbs, Barbara Ellis, Susan Rosenblum, Gerald S. Doff.

The rock music was softer and the tone more mellow in this supposedly "feel good" musical. The characters were mostly young people who were trying to find themselves, which they did when they joined a commune. Once there, they found others who were searching, so soon everyone is connecting, sex and drugs being the most common ice breakers. Although it portrayed a radically different kind of lifestyle, there wasn't much else that was radical about the show. Maybe that is why the critics were gently approving and audiences came and enjoyed it for more than a year. The cast was capable, and the songs were adequate, so there wasn't much to complain about. Some playgoers were possibly a little frustrated with such touchy-feely numbers as "Susan's Song" and "Reaching, Touching," others might have found "Tripping" a bit naive, and the cynical ones would have found the characters' "Declaration" hollow and the "Confrontation Song" anticlimactic. But this was a show difficult to hate; how can you hate a cipher? None of the talent onstage and backstage went on to do anything of note, but for a year or so they were able to please theatregoers of the early 1970s in a simple and nonconfrontational way.

STAG MOVIE

[3 January 1971, Gate Theatre, 88 performances. musical comedy by David Newburge. *Score:* Newburge (lyrics), Jacques Urbont (music). *Cast:* Hy Anzell, Brad Sullivan, Tod Miller, Adrienne Barbeau, Stan Wiest, Renata Mannhardt, Moose Matthews, Shirl Bernheim.

With so much onstage nudity during the 1970–1971 season, the critics were hard pressed to agree on the worst of the bunch; but when it came to musicals, *Stag Movie* got the most votes. There was something dishonest about this labored show that was one of many that hoped to follow in the footsteps of *Oh! Calcutta!* That revue made no excuses; it was about sexuality. *Stag Movie* was dishonest because it felt it needed to justify all its nudity and simulated sex. In a motel room near JFK airport, the porn filmmaker Mike Rosenthal (Hy Anzell) is shooting a stag film with a low budget and even lower aspirations. His three porn stars—Rip Cord (Brad Sullivan), Cookie Kovac (Adrienne Barbeau), and Tommy Tucker (Tod Miller)—may lament the state of things with songs like "I Want More Out of Life Than This" and "Grocery Boy," but they spend more time singing about sex in such unsubtle numbers as "Get Your Rocks Off Rock," "It's So Good," and the inevitable "Try a Trio." It would be naive to say *Stag Movie* lasted eleven weeks because of the talented cast, though the actors were quite accomplished and some went on to notable careers. (What the fine veteran comic actor Anzell was doing in this show is as puzzling as it is disturbing.) When a musical concludes with the principals proclaiming in song "We Came Together," you know the term "dramatic climax" has been abused forever.

GODSPELL

[17 May 1971, Cherry Lane Theatre, 2,124 performances] a musical play by John-Michael Tebelak based on *St. Matthew's Gospel*. *Score:* Stephen Schwartz (music and lyrics). *Cast:* Stephen Nathan, David Haskell, Lamar Alford, Robin Lamont, Sonia Manzano, Herb Simon, Joanne Jonas, Peggy Gordon, Jeffrey Mylett, Gilmer McCormick.

In the Middle Ages, they would call this a "mystery play" (because it is based on the Bible), but today it is considered a sort of theatre miracle: a small, economic musical with endless appeal. *Godspell* was not only the biggest hit of its season, it went on to become one of the most famous and familiar of all Off-Broadway musicals. The intimate, exhilarating musical version of *St. Matthew's Gospel* ("Godspell" is the ancient version of the word "gospel") employed a loose, playful style that has often been copied but rarely equaled. Many theatre pieces in the 1960s and 1970s claimed to be "happenings," those spontaneous celebrations that are supposed to magically happen when actors, audience, and ideas come together. Although it is rehearsed and well structured, *Godspell* actually feels like a happening. It has the sensibility of a religious revival and, at the same time, suggests the circus antics of the Marx Brothers. Church groups love to produce it, but the success of the piece is that it is not at all like a religious ceremony. Jesus wearing a Superman T-shirt may have raised some eyebrows, but playgoers like Him all the better for it.

Godspell introduced songwriter Stephen Schwartz to theatregoers, and much of the success of the musical can be attributed to his score. But it was John-Michael Tebelak who conceived and developed the show, writing it as a college production when he was a student at Carnegie-Mellon University and tweaking it until the seeming chaos on stage was rock solid. His libretto chronicled the life of Jesus from his baptism to his death, enacted by an ensemble of circuslike performers using jokes, mime, vaudeville bits, and songs. St. Matthew's version has several parables, with Tebelak turning them into skits, puppet shows, games, charades, and sweet fables. The simple setting, comprised mostly of props and a chain-link fence, contrasted nicely with the colorful costumes. In Tebelak's concept, the playing area was a children's playground of sorts. Since he also staged the Off-Broadway production, it was hard to tell where writer left off and director took over.

The musical had been produced with a different score before Schwartz was brought into the project. His new songs pick up on Tebelak's quirky storytelling style, giving the score an incredible range. Folk, blues, jazz, gospel, rock, and whatnot all find their way into the songs; yet many people still think of the show as a rock musical. The steady, folklike "Day By Day" was the most popular number in the score, but other favorites included the vaudeville number "All for the Best"; the rousing "Bless the Lord"; the sultry "Turn Back, O Man"; the revival-like "We Beseech Thee"; the rhythmic "Save the People"; the rocking "Light of the World"; and the fervent "All Good Gifts." Filled with so much variety, the *Godspell* score still sounds like a whole. (One number, the touching folk song "By My Side," was written by composer Peggy Gordon and lyricist Jay Hamburger for the earlier version and, as beautiful and haunting as it is, the song does stand out as being less theatrical than the others.) The free-spirited, tuneful musical quickly found an audience for over five years Off Broadway. There was a film version in 1973, and a 1976 Broadway revival, also directed by Tebelak, retained the staging and spirit of the original, and it ran 527 performances. A 1988 Off-Broadway revival, which ran 225 performances, was directed by Don Scardino, the Jesus from the Broadway company. An Off-Off-Broadway production in 2000 later transferred to Off Broadway and was recorded. The show continues to be one of the most frequently produced musicals in school, community, regional, and summer stock theatres, not to mention churches. It may not be presented in synagogues, but I'll bet you they all know the songs.

Two Gentlemen of Verona

[22 July 1971, Delacorte Theatre, 14 performances; St. James Theatre, 627 performances] a musical comedy by Mel Shapiro, John Guare based on Shakespeare's *The Two Gentlemen of Verona*. *Score:* Guare (lyrics), Galt MacDermot (music). *Cast:* Raul Julia, Clifton Davis, Jonelle Allen, Carla Pinza, Alix Elias, Jerry Stiller, Frank O'Brien, Norman Matlock.

A clever if substandard musical version of the dark Shakespearean comedy, the show is most remembered today as the musical that beat out *Follies* for the Tony Award that season. That recognition is something of a gift because, as enjoyable as the musical can be, it is one that is difficult to remember. Come to think of it, Shakespeare's *The Two Gentlemen of Verona* is fairly forgettable too. The project garnered a lot of interest before it opened because the production featured composer Galt MacDermot's first score since *Hair* and it was produced by Joseph Papp at the Delacorte Theatre in Central Park, a place that had rarely seen musicals. John Guare wrote the lyrics and adapted Shakespeare's text with Mel Shapiro, who also directed. They reset the tale in urban America with a Latino and African American flavor added to the plot, characters, and songs. African American Clifton Davis (Valentine) and Hispanic Raul Julia (Proteus) were the two friends of the title, Jonelle Allen (Silvia) and Diana Davilla (Julia) their sweethearts, and Norman Matlock was the Duke of Milan. The script used little of Shakespeare's dialogue and was filled instead with modern slang, ethnic humor, and many topical references, including antiwar sentiments regarding the Vietnam War. Guare's lyrics are weak (in one song he even runs out of rhymes for "fuck"), but MacDermot's music is jubilant and a worthy follow-up to *Hair*. Rock blends with Latin rhythms, and the result is delicious. Highlights include the propulsive "I Love My Father"; the political march "Bring All the Boys Back Home"; the spirited duet "Night Letter"; the contagious "Summer, Summer"; and the lovely "Who Is Sylvia?"—one of the few numbers to employ Shakespeare's words. The New York Shakespeare Festival mounting was so well received that Papp brought it to Broadway where after a slow start it caught on and ran a year and a half. There was a tour, but the double-album cast recording never caught on, and there were very few revivals. The show seemed to disappear from memory. Then a 2006 revival of the musical, also staged in Central Park, was a critical and popular success. Kathleen Marshall was the clever director and choreographer, and the young cast was highly praised. There was no Broadway transfer this time, and soon *Two Gentlemen of Verona* disappeared again, doomed perhaps to forever be a footnote.

LOOK ME UP

[6 October 1971, Plaza 9 Music Hall, 406 performances] a musical revue by Laurence Taylor. *Score:* various. *Cast:* Jeff Richards, Zan Charisse, Ted Agress, Kevin Christopher, Robin Field, Linda Kurtz, Connie Day, Geoffrey Webb, Don Liberto, Mary Kay Kolas, Linda Gerard, Murphy Cross.

One must remember that the rocking, radical 1970s was also a time of great nostalgia. One of the biggest Broadway hits of the era was the revival of the 1925 musical *No, No, Nanette*. The popular movie documentary *That's Entertainment!* (1974) was letting audiences rediscover the great film musicals of the past. Contemporary Broadway and Hollywood were not coming up with escapist products, so audiences turned to the past for refuge from the modern. This perhaps explains why the modest little cabaret show *Look Me Up* managed to run nearly a year. The revue celebrated the songs and dances of the 1920s, and there were plenty of theatregoers old enough to remember that decade with affection. There was nothing exceptional about the concept or the presentation, but the songs were glorious. Familiar and forgotten gems by the Gershwins, Kern, Hammerstein, DeSylva, Brown and Henderson, Rodgers and Hart, Youmans, and many others came tumbling forth, and nostalgia ran high. The cast was personable, talented, and full of energy (they even performed during the intermission), and the older playgoers were reassured that the youth of America had not all gone bad. The title of the revue is puzzling; no song entitled *Look Me Up* was sung in the show, and the phrase doesn't tell one anything about what kind of entertainment this will be. Nevertheless, word of mouth did its job, and a lot of people did indeed look up the show.

WANTED

[19 January 1972, Cherry Lane Theatre, 79 performances] a musical revue by David Epstein. *Score:* Al Carmines (music and lyrics). *Cast:* Merwin

Goldsmith, June Gable, Lee Guilliatt, Peter Lombard, Reathel Bean, Frank Coppola.

The outlaws turned out to be the good guys in this revue that deconstructed history and poked fun at the establishment. Billy the Kid, John Dillinger, Jesse James, Ma Barker, and other "wanted" criminals tell their side of the story in a series of songs and sketches that made light of moral questions of good and bad. Yet there was an undercurrent of truth in the show as the forces of law were seen as equally greedy, power hungry, and dishonest. The villains sang "Who's On Our Side?" as they managed to endear themselves to the audience despite years of bad publicity. Al Carmines had presented the revue at his Off-Off-Broadway home at the Judson Memorial Church and wrote the lively score which found room for some love songs and tender character numbers as well as such explosive rants as "I Want to Blow Up the World." "Jailhouse Blues" and "The Lord Is My Light" were surprisingly affecting numbers as well. David Epstein penned the script and contributed lyrics for a handful of the songs, and the revue was more mainstream than much of Carmines's work. Yet the commercial venture failed to catch on, closing after ten weeks, though critics said it deserved to run. In hindsight, the revue is somewhat reminiscent of the later musical *Assassins*, which did a similar about-face with history. *Wanted* was funnier than the darkly comic *Assassins*, and it wasn't as well written or scored as the Stephen Sondheim–John Weidman work, but it was a unique musical all the same.

HARK!

[22 May 1972, Mercer O'Casey Theatre, 152 performances] a musical revue. *Score:* Dan Goggin, Marvin Solley (music), Robert Lorick (lyrics). *Cast:* Goggin, Solley, Sharron Miller, Jack Blackton, Danny Guerrero, Elaine Petricoff.

A slight but likable musical revue with the exuberant title *Hark!* opened late in its season and was so well reviewed it ran through the summer. The cast was young, the writers were young, and the theme was youth. Theme might be too strong a word for this agreeable hodgepodge of a show that looked at the contemporary world through youthful eyes. Sometimes naive, often sentimental, occasionally irreverent, the revue covered such familiar topics as young love, living in the suburbs, getting a job, dealing with parents, and worrying about the future. The cast may have been somewhat sarcastic when they sang "Hip Hooray for America" and got a bit trying in the title number, but there were also moments of off-guard sincerity, as with the loaded question "What D'Ya Wanna Be?" and the starry "I See the People." Composer Dan Goggin would go on to considerable success with *Nunsense* Off Broadway (and everywhere else), and lyricist Robert Lorick would later write expert lyrics for the Broadway musical *The Tap Dance Kid* (1983). Their young talent was nurtured in the invigorating little musical, and *Hark!* demonstrated that growing pains did not have to be painful to watch.

JOAN

[19 June 1972, Circle in the Square Theatre, 64 performances] a musical play by Al Carmines. *Score:* Carmines (music and lyrics). *Cast:* Lee Guilliatt, Essie Borden, Tracy Moore, Ira Siff, Julie Kurnitz, Emily Adams.

Another Al Carmines Off-Off-Broadway production from his Judson Poet's Theatre that transferred to a commercial run Off Broadway was *Joan*, a very modern-looking and modern-sounding version of the story of St. Joan of Arc. The warrior-saint had been the subject of plays, films, and operas making the tale of her accomplishment on the battlefield and her persecution and execution because of religious beliefs familiar. But Carmines, this time writing script, music, and lyrics (as well as serving as onstage pianist), saw Joan (Lee Guilliatt) as a contemporary figure and used rock music and modern anachronisms to turn her into a twentieth-century heroine, feminist, activist, and (still) saint. Joan's war record had to be rethought a bit because war victors were not popular heroes in the 1970s. Some were surprised that the radical Carmines took religion very seriously in this musical and, while the church was seen as corrupt and self-serving, devotion to God was not belittled. After all, Carmines was an ordained minister; he just didn't behave like one. There were fervent prayers in the score, but there were also some satirical numbers, such as "The Religious Establishment" and "I'm Madame Margaret the Therapist"; some disarming moments, as when the Virgin Mary sings "I Live a Little"; and Joan realizes "Faith Is Such a Simple Thing." Despite some favorable notices, *Joan* was not as popular as some of Carmines's earlier musicals. It managed to run eight weeks and was recorded, making it possible to hear and understand what the prodigious Carmines was all about.

BERLIN TO BROADWAY WITH KURT WEILL

[1 October 1972, Theatre de Lys, 152 performances] a musical revue. *Score:* Kurt Weill (music), various (lyrics). *Cast:* Ken Kercheval, Jerry Lanning, Margery Cohen, Judy Lander, Hal Watters.

Some forty theatre songs with music by Kurt Weill were heard in this "musical voyage" which celebrated the German-born American's life, career, and work. The voyage covered his early years in Germany, his brief time in Paris, then his American years on Broadway. (Weill's short Hollywood career was not mentioned, neither were his many opera and orchestral credits.) Except for a few numbers, the songs appeared in the scenario in chronological order, letting the audience see and hear Weill's amazing ability to move from European music to American idioms. The narration (delivered by cast member Ken Kercheval) was brief and to the point, and some songs were only heard in abbreviated versions, but this was no *Reader's Digest* look at Weill. The revue captured the tone and atmosphere for each of Weill's musicals using no scenery and the simplest of costume pieces. The cast was outstanding, both as vocalists and as interpreters of the piercing lyrics, and the staging by veteran choreographer Donald Saddler was unobtrusively effective. (Interestingly, the show played at the famous Theatre de Lys where *The Threepenny Opera* had run for so many years.) The reviews were favorable, but New York had seen several cabaret revues of Weill's work (and would see more in the future), so the revue managed only a modest run of nineteen weeks. It deserved much better for this show remains the best of all the Weill compilations. Happily, regional theatres and colleges picked up the revue, and there were many productions. (A 2000 Off-Broadway revival ran 121 performances.) Another fortunate outcome of the original production was the two-record cast recording which sold very well and was a superb introduction to Weill's work for those not familiar with him except for the hit song "Mack the Knife." (I am happy to report that the wonderful Marc Blitzstein translation was used for all the songs from *The Threepenny Opera* section of the revue.) *Berlin to Broadway with Kurt Weill* is considered one of the best of its genre: the biographical revue about a songwriter. Other shows have tried to copy its format and expertise, but only occasionally has this revue been matched.

OH COWARD!

[4 October 1972, New Theatre, 294 performances] a musical revue by Roderick Cook. *Score:* Noël Coward (music and lyrics). *Cast:* Cook, Barbara Carson, Jamie Ross.

Three days after Kurt Weill was celebrated Off Broadway, a very different songwriter was brought to life in another expert revue. Noël Coward the playwright and songwriter was brought to life not so much by biography (though the narration occasionally provided some history) but by capturing the light, sophisticated spirit of the man and his work. Roderick Cook devised and directed *Oh Coward!*, which did not take a chronological approach but a thematic one. Sections of the show looked at Coward's family, his music hall years, and his comments on travel, England, love, and women. In addition to the songs, brief excerpts from some of the plays were performed, and Coward quotes from his autobiographies and short stories were sprinkled throughout. Cook was joined by cabaret veterans Jamie Ross and Barbara Carson, and the threesome were as charming as they were talented. The whole evening seemed as breezy as, well, a Noël Coward play. Yet as effortless as it appeared to audiences, the show had a long and discouraging history. Cook had appeared in Coward's unsuccessful Broadway musical *The Girl Who Came to Supper* (1969) and, like many, was fascinated by the man and his talent. He put together a Coward revue titled *Noël Coward's Sweet Potato* in 1968, and it struggled to run five and a half weeks. Cook reworked the material, developing it in different regional theatres, then returned to New York with this smaller, sparer version. Although Coward was popular on Broadway and the West End, his unique talent for words seemed better served in an intimate Off-Broadway venue. Critics and audiences must have agreed because the revue was well reviewed and audiences came for nine months. The economical little show was ideal for cabarets, summer stock, and regional theatre, turning out many revivals. Other Coward revues preceded and followed *Oh Coward!*, but this one is still considered the best.

DOCTOR SELAVY'S MAGIC THEATRE

[23 November 1972, Mercer O'Casey Theatre, 144 performances] a musical play by Richard Foreman. *Score:* Stanley Silverman (music), Tom

Hendry (lyrics). *Cast:* George McGrath, Ron Farber, Denise Delapenha, Jessica Harper, Amy Taubin, Mary Delson, Steve Menken.

The age-old paradox of sanity being only a matter of perspective was revived and musicalized in a comic piece that surprised and pleased the critics. The man behind the concept was avant-gardist Richard Foreman whose puzzling, defiant theatre works were often fascinating but rarely what you would call enjoyable. Yet he wrote and directed *Doctor Selavy's Magic Theatre* in a freewheeling, satirical manner, and for once a Foreman show was a lot of fun. The peculiar Dr. Selavy (George McGrath) runs an asylum where the Patient (Ron Farber) is being treated for insanity. Of course what was happening in the world seems insane to the Patient—it's really the doctor who should be treated. What could have been ponderous or preachy ended up being entertaining; this was no musical *One Flew Over the Cuckoo's Nest*. The rock score by Stanley Silverman and Tom Hendry was also playful as it turned the sane world into a series of pastiche numbers: "Swinging at the Stock Exchange," "Bankrupt Blues," "Where You Been Hiding Till Now," and "Money in the Bank." The plaintive "I Live By My Wits" and the knowing "Life on the Inside" were among the other notable songs in a score that never took itself too seriously. There was even a Rock Singer (Jessica Harper) and a Female Pirate (Mary Delson) in the looney bin to help move things along. *Doctor Selavy's Magic Theatre* ran a profitable three and a half months and was nominated for several awards. It is unfortunate that Foreman did not return to this kind of theatre more often.

THE CONTRAST

[28 November 1972, Eastside Playhouse, 24 performances] a musical comedy by Anthony Stimac based on Royall Tyler's play. *Score:* Don Pippin (music), Steve Brown (lyrics). *Cast:* Philip MacKenzie, Ty McConnell, Elaine Kerr, Robert G. Denison, Grady Clarkson, Pamela Adams, Connie Danese.

Royall Tyler's 1787 comedy *The Contrast* is the first successful comedy written by an American. The contrast of the title refers to the difference between the American way and the British manner. The play is still funny today, can still be performed (though it rarely is), and is ideal musical comedy material. The foppish Brit Dimple (Ty McConnell) tries to woo an American girl (*any* rich American girl) for her money. His snobby servant Jessamy (Grady Clarkson) is likewise courting the servant girl Jenny (Pamela Adams) downstairs. Dimple is discovered to be a cad, and Colonel Manly (Robert G. Denison) gets the society girl. Jessamy is refused by Jenny, and she goes to Jonathan (Philip MacKenzie), the most famous character in the play. Dubbed Jonathan the Yankee, he is the archetypal rugged, honest American and the inspiration for two centuries of favorite characters in Westerns and other genres. Anthony Stimac made no major plot or character changes in his musical libretto, therefore the production was much like a revival with songs added. The score by Don Pippin and Steve Brown does not try to sound eighteenth century, but neither is it too contemporary. It is a pleasant and charming set of songs that range from Dimple and Jessamy's haughty "Dear Lord Chesterfield" to the simple, unaffected duet "A Sort of Counting Song" for Jonathan and Jenny. The contrast of cultures and character is best seen in the competitive "A Hundred Thousand Ways" in which Jonathan and Jessamy square off in song. The musical had first been produced earlier in the year Off Off Broadway at the Greenwich Village Mews, and it was promising enough that it was given a commercial run Off Broadway, only to be met with indifference, and it closed in three weeks. There have been subsequent productions regionally, but *The Contrast* remains a little-known curiosity that deserves an audience.

RAINBOW

[18 December 1972, Orpheum Theatre, 48 performances] a rock musical by James and Ted Rado. *Score:* James Rado (music and lyrics). *Cast:* Gregory V. Karliss, Kay Cole, Philip A. D., Michael D. Arian, Camille, Meat Loaf, Bobby C. Ferguson.

The three creators of *Hair* went their separate ways in 1972 and met with failure on and Off Broadway. Galt MacDermot reteamed with Gerome Ragni and came up with the Broadway flop *Dude*. Working with others, MacDermott had an even bigger fiasco on the Street with *Via Galactica*. James Rado fared only slightly better with *Rainbow*, an Off-Broadway antiwar musical that he cowrote with his brother Ted and scored by himself. After the hero Man (Gregory V. Karliss) is killed fighting in Vietnam, he travels the universe looking for answers but only finds evidence of an unloving world filled with frightened, uncaring, or corrupt people. (Interestingly, both *Dude* and *Via Galactia* were also about a disgruntled man's journey.) The musical fantasy made no effort to be logical or coherent as over forty songs gushed from the stage and characters came and went as in Oz. "Over the rainbow" in this show meant a different kind of nightmare. There was even a chorus of Rainbeams to help guide or distract Man at every turn. Most of the songs were in the rock mode, but there were also some devilish pastiche numbers that added different musical styles to the potpourri. Critics found some vivid imagery and arresting moments along the way but agreed that the collage was too messy to be totally effective. Six weeks was enough for curious playgoers to see what this unofficial sequel to *Hair* was like. Sadly, New York would never again see a new work by James Rado.

NATIONAL LAMPOON'S LEMMINGS

[25 January, 1973, Village Gate, 350 performances] a musical revue by Tony Hendra, David Axelrod, Anne Beatts, Sean Kelly, Henry Beard, et al. *Score:* Paul Jacobs, Christopher Guest (music), Axelrod, Beatts, Beard, et al. (lyrics). *Cast:* John Belushi, Alice Playten, Chevy Chase, Christopher Guest, Garry Goodrow, Mary-Jenifer Mitchell, Paul Jacobs.

First there was the college parody magazine *Harvard Lampoon*. It was literate, irreverent, and very funny. In 1970 it left academia and was published as *National Lampoon* with its college-satire now even more wicked but not as highbrow. The circulation of the comic publication was at its peak in 1973 when the musical revue *National Lampoon's Lemmings* opened Off Broadway. While anything and everything from politics to sex to movies were ripe targets for the magazine, the theatre version leveled most its guns on the music scene, in particular rock music. The revue was structured around a music event called the "Woodchuck Festival of Peace, Love and Death" during which the cast of seven portrayed various characters performing, attending, or commenting on the Woodstock festival travesty. The songs were not listed in the program, and the sketches changed throughout the run, making it difficult to say exactly what happened during each performance. (Unfortunately, there was no cast album and, looking at the original cast, what a recording it would have made!) Tony Hendra, a veteran writer from the topical television show *That Was the Week That Was*, was the head writer, but several artists onstage and backstage contributed to the material, much as with an improv group. Also, during the nearly-one-year run the revue added current items as they appeared in the news. Hendra directed the show, and it brought early recognition for future stars Christopher Guest, John Belushi, and Chevy Chase. Although interest in the magazine waned by the 1980s and it ceased publication in 1998, the *National Lampoon* name lived on in a series of movies that bore it in the title, as well as in two other stage revues in the future.

EL GRANDE DE COCA-COLA

[13 February 1973, Mercer Arts Center, 1,114 performances] a musical revue by Ron House, Diz White, et al. *Score:* House, White, et al. *Cast:* House, White, Sally Willis, Alan Shearman, John Neville-Andrews.

New York's first long-running musical in Spanish was so physical, so silly, and so over-the-top that audiences didn't need to know a word of Español to follow the thin plot and enjoy the shenanigans. In the small Honduras town of Trujillo, the overly ambitious impresario Don Pepe Hernandez (Ron House) books some international stars and promises the locals and the tourists a night of stellar entertainment called "Parade of Stars." When none of the performers show up, Hernandez borrows money from his uncle Miguel (Alan Shearman) who runs the nearby Coca-Cola bottling plant, rents a dilapidated nightclub, and tries to pass his relatives off as the performers. Of course the show is dreadful, and rarely has bad entertainment been so much fun. As expected, the jugglers drop everything, the chorines bump into each other, and the singers are painfully untalented. There is a blind blues chanteuse who sounds pretty good, but she sings with her back to the audience then falls off the stage when trying to exit. It was that kind of show. Much of the lines were in a kind of pidgin Spanish with doses of mispronounced French and German thrown in for good measure. The five-member cast were gifted clowns and expert enough to make nontalent seem like gold. They also created the script and the songs (which were not listed in the program) as an improv troupe might. The production began as a touring piece developed by the American House and cast member Diz White. They called themselves the Moan Low Spectacular and performed the multilingual program throughout Europe before finding success Off Broadway, where they remained for nearly three years. Although *El Grande de Coca-Cola* was not recorded, the dizzy script and songs were written down and licensed for production, and there have been a considerable number of regional mountings over the years.

WHAT'S A NICE COUNTRY LIKE YOU DOING IN A STATE LIKE THIS?

[19 April 1973, Upstage at Jimmy's, 543 performances] a musical revue by Ira Gasman, Cary Hoffman, Bernie Travis. *Score:* Hoffman (music), Gasman (lyrics). *Cast:* Priscilla Lopez, Sam Freed, Betty Lynn Buckley, Barry Michlin, Bill La Vallee.

Crime, pornography, and corrupt politicians seemed to be everywhere in 1973. As New York City prepared for a mayoral primary, this topical revue was at the right place at the right time. The five-character piece was seen Off Off Broadway and in a cabaret before the American Place Theatre gave it a home in its new venue not far from the Theatre District. The songs and sketches were aimed at various targets, but much of the evening focused on politics, from Nixon's White House dealing with the growing embarrassment known as Watergate, to local politicos promising to save New York from bankruptcy and muggers. Critics praised the revue for its spot-on satire and wicked sense of humor. There were also plaudits for the gifted cast which included future stars Betty Buckley and Priscilla Lopez. Enough New Yorkers decided to laugh at their woes and keep the show running for seventeen months. As elections passed and politicians tumbled off of their pedestals, the little musical continued to update its references and remained timely. There was a sequel in 1984 by the same authors titled *What's a Nice Country Like You Still Doing in a State Like This?* which also played at the American Place, but it ran only a month. The original revue was licensed for regional productions, and you can still do a "revised" version if you want. One wonders how out-of-date that revision must be by now!

THE FAGGOT

[18 June 1973, Truck and Warehouse Theatre, 182 performances] a musical revue by Al Carmines. *Score:* Carmines (music and lyrics). *Cast:* Carmines, Julie Kurnitz, Essie Borden, Ira Siff, Lee Guilliatt, Frank Coppola.

Off-Off-Broadway impresario Al Carmines had presented cutting-edge works about a variety of uncomfortable subjects in the past, and it only made sense that he would be one of the first to write a musical exploring homosexuality. Gay characters had started to become familiar on the stage since the mid-1960s, and the play *The Boys in the Band* (1968) was the first mainstream hit to examine homosexual lifestyles. But musicals had only used gay characters gingerly, such as the star's overt hairdresser Duane Fox in the Broadway hit *Applause* (1970). The blunt, somewhat offensive title of Carmine's musical made it quite clear this would be a direct and fearless treatment of the subject, and it was. Yet rather than a sociopolitical sermon or a campy spoof, *The Faggot* was surprisingly engaging in both its songs and spoken words. Sometimes the revue looked at the past, conjuring up Oscar Wilde, Gertrude Stein, Alice B. Toklas, and even Catherine the Great. Other times it poked fun at current homosexual obsessions, from porn stars to gay bars. The most moving sections of the program were those in which modern attitudes toward "faggots" were expressed; sometimes chilling, other times humbling. Some critics felt the show contained Carmines's best score yet. (Otis L. Guernsey Jr. in the *Best Plays* edition thought *The Faggot* the very best musical of the season, both on and Off Broadway.) The songs are indeed rich with compassion, humor, and understanding. The opening "Women with Women—Men with Men" was unapologetic and matter of fact. A group of bar patrons revealed the complexity of gay relationships in "A Gay Bar Cantata," and the encounter between a hustler and a pickup was musicalized as a five-minute opera. "Ordinary Things" was a bittersweet list song, while "What Is a Queen" was a sincere cry for understanding. The company concluded the revue with the knowledge that "Everyone Is Different," a song of both defiance and resolve. Like Carmines's other musicals, *The Faggot* was first developed at his Off-Off-Broadway venue at the Judson Memorial Church. Commercial producers brought it to Off Broadway, where it ran five and a half months. It would be Carmines's last notable production; not a bad finale to an always intriguing career.

CANDIDE

[11 December 1973, Brooklyn Academy of Music, 48 performances; Broadway Theatre, 740 performances] a musical satire by Hugh Wheeler. *Score:* Leonard Bernstein (music), Richard Wilbur, Stephen Sondheim, John Latouche (lyrics). *Cast:* Lewis J. Stadlen, Mark Baker, Maureen Brennan, June Gable, Sam Freed, Deborah St. Darr.

Although it contains one of the musical theatre's greatest scores, the 1956 Broadway musical *Candide* suffered from book problems and closed after only seventy-three performances. The overture became a staple with symphony orchestras around the world, the aria "Glitter and Be Gay" became an opera solo favorite, and the cast recording was a big seller. Revivals were rare, and it seemed that the musical was never to be anything but a glorious failure. There are very few second chances in the world of musical theatre, but *Candide* got one when the Chelsea Theatre Center of Brooklyn commissioned a new libretto by Hugh Wheeler and asked Harold Prince to stage the piece, not as a grand opera or lavish Broadway show but as an intimate, irreverent Off-Broadway lark. Wheeler's book used little of the original libretto written by Lillian Hellman and was not afraid to take liberties with Voltaire's classic novella. What was an elaborate French satire became a lively American cartoon with Voltaire (Lewis J. Stadlen) himself providing the wry narration. The score was reorchestrated for a smaller ensemble, and Stephen Sondheim provided some new lyrics for new songs that were needed for the altered story. Leonard Bernstein's marvelous music was retained, and some of his discarded melodies from the original were utilized. The result was not a revival but a fresh new work that pleased the press and the public, though music aficionados bemoaned the loss of the opera qualities of the original. Much of the freshness came from Prince, who staged the itinerant tale on a series of platforms spread throughout the theatre with audience members sitting in clumps amidst the action. As Voltaire's characters traveled across continents in the story, actors traipsed from platform to platform by way of bridges and pathways through the spectators. At one point when the characters were aboard a ship, all the platforms swayed, and it seemed the entire theatre was rocking back and forth on the waves. The six-week engagement quickly sold out, and Prince agreed to restage the piece for Broadway if he could recreate the same theatrical environment. The Broadway Theatre was gutted of seats, scaffolding was built everywhere, parts of the audience sat on what used to be the stage, and the musical was just as raucous and delightful in the big space as it had been in Brooklyn. The new *Candide* met with another round of raves and ran two years on Broadway. More importantly, the new version put *Candide* into the repertory of producible musicals. Regional theatres, schools, and summer stock productions used the new version, as did opera companies who restored the more complicated orchestrations but kept the new libretto. Prince restaged the piece for some of these opera companies, and then in 1997 directed a Broadway revival that managed a run of only 103 performances. Wheeler, Prince, and the others involved in the Off-Broadway rethinking performed one of the greatest rescue jobs in the history of the American theatre. Now *Candide* is a produced classic and not just a disembodied score of genius.

LET MY PEOPLE COME

[8 January 1974, Village Gate, 1,327 performances] a musical revue. *Score:* Earl Wilson Jr. (music and lyrics). *Cast:* Ian Naylor, Tobie Columbus, Christine Anderson, Lorraine Davidson, Alan Evans.

It seemed nobody liked the sex revue *Let My People Come*. Not the critics, not the theatre community, not the Building Commission, not the State Liquor Authority, and eventually not even the author. But audiences flocked to the little "sexual musical" in which patrons sat at tables and drank while skits and songs about variations on sexual intercourse were performed. Much of the show's wit was on the level of the smirking title, which also served as the musical number that ended the show. Other such subtle song titles included "Give It to Me," "Felatio 101," "Poontang," and "Come in My Mouth." For those hoping for some musical cleverness, there was the Andrews Sisters-like swing number "The Cunnilingus Champion of Co. C." This was sophomoric humor at its most unappealing form. Yet audiences laughed, enjoyed the occasional nudity, and drank alcohol until there was some dispute over the liquor license and the show was nearly closed down by the City. The shrewd producer Phil Osterman knew this was not a show for the press, never holding an opening night. The revue just began running, and no critics were invited. A few went on their own and dismissed the whole undertaking as crude and amateurish, but *Let My People Come* was not an entertainment that relied on critical acclaim. After doing brisk business for two years, Osterman decided to bring his show to Broadway. The League of Broadway Theatres—currently battling the infiltration of porn shops, massage parlors, and blue movies into the Theatre District—fought to keep Osterman's grimy little musical away, but they lost. Even Earl Wilson Jr. (son of the famed newspaper columnist of the day), who wrote the revue's songs and sketches, objected to Osterman's rewriting and (get this) sullying his work and tried to block the Broadway transfer. He also lost the battle, and *Let My People Come* opened on Broadway in 1976. Again no critics were invited, and again the public came, though for only three months.

THE GREAT MACDADDY

[12 February 1974, St. Marks Playhouse, 72 performances] a musical play by Paul Carter Harrison. *Score:* Harrison (lyrics), Coleridge-Taylor

Perinson (music). *Cast:* Al Freeman Jr., David Downing, Adolph Caesar, Hattie Winston, Charles Weldon, Graham Brown, Martha Short-Goldsen, Sati Jamal.

The Negro Ensemble Company (NEC) was one of the most influential and long-lasting African American troupes in New York theatre. It was founded in 1967 and for the next three decades introduced many of the finest black plays of its era. Yet rarely did it attempt musicals; therefore *The Great Macdaddy* was both atypical and refreshing. During the years of Prohibition, the African American drifter Macdaddy (David Downing) sets off on an odyssey looking for his old friend Wine (Graham Brown), and as he travels across America he encounters surreal and symbolic foes and forces that illustrate the black man's lack of belonging. Many of Macdaddy's antagonists come in the form of the villain Scag (Al Freeman Jr.), an African American who represented Macdaddy's inner enemies. The story was an original one, but author Paul Carter Harrison stated the style of the storytelling was inspired by Amos Tutuola's novel *The Palm Wine Drinkard*. Critics felt the fantasy-morality piece was endlessly imaginative and the cast, made up of NEC regulars, were just as effective in a musical as they had been in the company's dramas. Renowned playwright-actor Douglas Turner Ward, a cofounder of NEC, directed *The Great Macdaddy*, and much of the success of the show could be credited to him. Little was said by the critics about the songs which Harrison wrote with Coleridge-Taylor Perkinson. While the NEC usually kept each entry on the boards for a month, *The Great Macdaddy* ran nine weeks. In 1977 the company brought the musical back for another fifty-six performances.

FASHION

[18 February 1974, McAlpin Rooftop Theatre, 94 performances] a musical comedy by Anna Cora Mowatt, Anthony Stimac. *Score:* Don Pippin (music), Steve Brown (lyrics). *Cast:* Mary Jo Catlett, Ty McConnell, Henrietta Valor, Rhoda Butler, Holland Taylor, Jan Buttram, Susan Romann.

Playwright Anthony Stimac, composer Don Pippin, and lyricist Steve Brown had turned the early American comedy *The Contrast* into a pleasing (but short-lived) musical in 1972. When they musicalized another early American classic, Anna Cora Mowatt's 1845 comedy of manners *Fashion*, they came up with a modest success. The nineteenth-century hit concerned the newly wealthy New Yorker Mrs. Tiffany, who considers her ways those of high society and foolishly falls prey to every scoundrel who hopes to make a buck on her snobbery. It remains a very funny piece and has enjoyed many revivals over the years. Stimac's version turns the old comedy into a play-within-a-play. The Long Island Masque and Wig Society, an amateur troupe made up entirely of women, is performing a musical version of Mowatt's play and are struggling through their dress rehearsal. Women play all the roles except for the male director (Ty McConnell) who portrays the phony French Count Jolimaitre in the community theatre production. The double musical entertained on both levels, for the original script was still fun and the antics of the local ladies were equally humorous. The songs were spirited and captured the wit of the old comedy of manners. Mrs. Tiffany (Mary Jo Catlett) boasted to her family "You See Before You What Fashion Can Do" and was thrilled at the thought of "My Daughter the Countess." Other numbers ranged from the romantic, such as "A Life without Her," to the farcical with "Why Should They Know about Paris?" The hero of the piece, the solid American Adam Trueman (Henrietta Valor), celebrated "The Good Old American Way" with the frustrated Mr. Tiffany (Jan Buttram), and the masculine duet was deliciously ludicrous when sung by two society ladies. The reviewers applauded the clever concept, and the gifted cast and the musical ran nearly three months. Community groups, including the kind spoofed in *Fashion*, found the musical an appealing property because of its all-female cast. A production in California in 1974 featured Catlett and Valor from the Off-Broadway cast and was recorded. *Fashion* may be a bit gimmicky, but it holds together thematically (the show onstage and backstage are both about social pretense) and can still be produced effectively.

I'LL DIE IF I CAN'T LIVE FOREVER

[31 October 1974, The Improvisation, 81 performances] musical revue by Karen Johnson. *Score:* Joyce Stoner (music and lyrics). *Cast:* Gail Johnston, Mark T. Long, Michael David Laibson, Nancy Reddon, Don Bradford, Tom Hastings, Maureen Maloney.

An idea for a musical: a group of young performers desperate for their big break in show business express in songs and flashbacks their hopes, disappointments, and even their past that led them to become stagestruck. Is this *A Chorus Line?* Not yet. This little musical opened Off Broadway while Michael Bennett was still interviewing dancers for his concept show that opened five months later. Is this *Fame?* It also predates that 1980 film in which the ambitious youngsters echo this title when they sing "I wanna live forever." Exactly what was *I'll Die If I Can't Live Forever?* It was a satirical musical revue that made fun of shows like *A Chorus Line* and *Fame.* The six aspiring performers are neurotic, driven, unfulfilled, and targets for showbiz clichés. Some lament that "My Life's a Musical Comedy," while others acknowledge the fact that "There's Always Someone Who'll Tell You 'No.'" Their lives as Broadway wannabes makes them reflect about the "Joys of Manhattan Life" with sarcasm and bemoan the necessity of living frugally with "The Roommate Beguine" and "We're Strangers Who Sleep Side By Side." It seems their sex lives are not satisfactory either, as with the desperate "Let's Have a Rodgers and Hammerstein Affair" and the observation "Where Would We Be without Perverts?" There were plenty of things going on in this musical which was structured around the auditions for a show. The big difference from the upcoming *A Chorus Line* is that the revue made fun of the pains and dreams that were treated with such reverence in the Bennett musical. One would think that it was a conscious spoof of *A Chorus Line* if it had opened after that famous show. As it was, *I'll Die If I Can't Live Forever* received appreciative notices and found an audience for ten weeks, closing before Bennett's dancers offered their lives and hopes at the Public Theatre. The revue is now a footnote in theatre history, but you've got to smile at a show in which the earnest aspirants sing the self-confused "Less Is More and More."

DIAMOND STUDS

[14 January 1975, Westside Theatre, 232 performances] a musical play by Jim Wann. *Score:* Wann, Bland Simpson (music and lyrics). *Cast:* Wann, Simpson, Jim Watson, Jan Davidson, Mike Sheehan, Rick Simpson, John Foley, Tommy Thompson, Madelyn Smoak.

The Chelsea Theatre Center of Brooklyn was introducing countless new plays and adaptations of foreign works, and they found themselves performing in a couple of boroughs at the same time. In Manhattan they had a hit with *Diamond Studs*, which opened Off Broadway to laudatory notices and stayed for seven months. The story of outlaw Jesse James (Jim Wann) was told as a "saloon musical" complete with an onstage band, plenty of rough-housing, and foot-stomping songs both old and new. Most of the cast played musical instruments as well as historical and fictional characters—for example, Jesse played guitar while he confronted detective Allen Pinkerton (Mike Sheehan), who was beating away on the drums. Belle Starr (Madelyn Smoak) and other famous names dropped in for a song or two, and the audience was encouraged to sing along as if they were indeed in a saloon. There was no hidden agenda or subtle antiestablishment subtext to the program; the show simply sought to entertain, and it did so without apology. Half of the score were adaptations of traditional songs such as "When I Was a Cowboy," "Bright Morning Star," and "The Year of Jubilo." The new numbers were expert pastiches, sometimes with a modern smirk, as with "Jesse James Robbed This Train" and "Put It Where the Moon Don't Shine." The jubilant "Cakewalk into Kansas City" concluded both acts, and it was difficult for the audience to not get up and dance along with the cast. An added bonus was the instrumental proficiency of the quartet called The Red Clay Ramblers who also played characters. *Diamond Studs* was far from the more demanding fare that the Chelsea Theatre usually offered; but that was the beauty of this vital troupe that saw no limits on theatre.

LOVERS

[27 January 1975, Players Theatre, 118 performances] musical play by Peter del Valle. *Score:* Del Valle (lyrics), Steve Sterner (music). *Cast:* Michael Cascone, John Ingle, Martin Rivera, Robert Sevra, Reathel Bean, Gary Sneed.

An innocuous musical with the innocuous title *Lovers* found an audience for fifteen weeks because the subject matter was new enough to the musical theatre to attract audiences looking for something beyond heterosexual romance. The musical *The Faggot* (1973) had centered on homosexuality with honesty and verve; *Lovers* relied more on pathos and sentimentality. Six gay men connect, break up, find happiness, experience rejection, and somehow come to the conclusion that love has made them stronger. If this hadn't been about gay lifestyle, it might have been dismissed as cliché-ridden drivel. But there was still something refreshing about the alternate kind of love that kept *Lovers* intriguing enough for both straight and gay playgoers. While some distinctly homosexual topics were covered in such songs as "Belt & Leather" and "Role-Playing," many of the numbers were generic love songs with all the traditional emotions expressed. There was humor and a kind of healthy bitchiness at times, but usually the tone was solemn, even reverent. "Somebody, Somebody Hold Me," "There Is Always You," "Don't Betray His Love," and the title song were more familiar than one expected in a musical about alternate love. There was even a number titled "Hymn" which, despite its double meaning, was simply a hymn. *Lovers* was such an earnest affirmation of homosexual love that it was hard not to like, even if it said very little.

THE NATIONAL LAMPOON SHOW

[2 March 1975, New Palladium, 180 performances] a musical revue by Sean Kelly, the cast. *Score:* Paul Jacobs (music), the cast (lyrics). *Cast:* John Belushi, Gilda Radner, Harold Ramis, Bill Murray, Brian Doyle-Murray.

A sequel of sorts to the popular revue *National Lampoon's Lemmings* (1973), the new edition shared only two writers (Sean Kelly and Paul Jacobs) and one cast member (John Belushi) with the earlier work, but it was similar in tone and content. Again no songs were listed, and the material changed to reflect what was happening in the news during the five and a half months the revue ran. Martin Charnin was listed as director but, like any talented improv group, much of the show grew out of the ensemble work of the cast. And what a cast this edition boasted! Belushi was joined by a nimble and sparkling quartet of young performers who would later find fame with him on the television show *Saturday Night Live* which premiered in October 1975, a few months after this revue closed. Belushi, Gilda Radner, and Bill Murray in particular would be instrumental in giving that live television program its golden years, and some of the classic routines and characters that became nationwide favorites were first developed during this Off-Broadway run. Interestingly, only Radner ever returned to the New York stage. It seemed that television was the ideal venue for sharp, topical satire, not the stage. This new development probably began all the way back in the 1950s when the impact of television was first felt. By 1975 a brilliant cast like this could not stay in the theatre very long when a wider audience was to be found on the airwaves.

BE KIND TO PEOPLE WEEK

[23 March 1975, Belmont Theatre, 100 performances] a musical comedy by Jack Bussins, Ellsworth Olin. *Score:* Bussins, Olin (music and lyrics). *Cast:* Naura Hayden, Kenneth Cory, Bobby Lee, Nell Carter, Kevin Cory, Maureen Moore, Alan Kass, Grenoldo Frazier.

An odd but likable little musical with a rosy complexion, *Be Kind to People Week* was a gentle satire about doing good in the world. The young and optimistic Hope Healy (Naura Hayden) decides that if all the pressure groups and militant organizations got together, there would be love and understanding in the world. Here she attempts to band together the feminists and the antiwar protesters with the blue collar workers and the black power groups. Of course Hope learns that they all hate each other as much as they hate the establishment they are all protesting against, but she is undeterred, and the fable ends with a sweetly naive but feel-good conclusion. Many of the songs were variations of love or friendship songs with titles like "All I Got Is You," "I Need You," "To Love Is to Live," and the coy "I'm in Like with You." Some numbers were wide-eyed tributes, such as "Black Is Beautiful" and "Mad about You Manhattan." Others sounded like bumper stickers, as in "A Smile Is Up" and the title song. The tone was slightly mocking without being sour. Except for Hayden, the rest of the cast used their own names for their characters, and some critics pointed out that the big-voiced Nell Carter was a real find. *Be Kind to People Week* was appealing enough to find an audience for thirteen weeks.

PHILEMON

[8 April 1975, Portfolio Studio, 48 performances] a musical play by Tom Jones. *Score:* Jones (lyrics), Harvey Schmidt (music). *Cast:* Dick Latessa, Leila Martin, Michael Glenn-Smith, Virginia Gregory, Howard Ross, Drew Katzman, Kathrin King Segal.

After finding varying success scoring the 1970s Broadway musicals *110 in the Shade, I Do! I Do!,* and *Celebration,* Tom Jones and Harvey Schmidt returned to Off Broadway and founded the Portofino Theatre Workshop, a place where they (and others) could experiment with small, innovative musicals. In other words, they left the Street and went looking and hoping for something along the lines of their *The Fantasticks. Philemon* was certainly like that earlier show in scope and presentation. On a simple stage some players enact the true story of a clown in ancient Greece with a small band and a cast of seven. From that point on, the new work is not at all like *The Fantasticks*, for the plot is that of a morality play and there is no sweetness, young love, or a happy ending. When the clown Cockian (Dick Latessa) is arrested on the streets of Antioch in 287 AD, the Roman Commander (Howard Ross) offers to spare Cockian's life if he will impersonate the Christian bishop Philemon whom the Romans have captured and killed in Egypt. Joining the other Christians in jail, Cockian, as Philemon, is to find out who is the leader of the Antioch Christian movement. Cockian agrees, and in the process of being Philemon and befriending the Christians, he converts and ends up dying a martyr's death. This somber tale is given some relief by the arguments Cockian has with his performing partner Kiki (Kathrin King Segal) and his abandoned wife Marsyas (Virginia Gregory), but things get serious indeed when Cockian encounters the real Philemon's wife (Leila Martin) and betrays the young Christian prisoner Andos (Michael Glenn-Smith). Cockian finds redemption in his death, but it is not in a "happy ending" way. Much of *Philemon* was very moving, and the cast was exceptional, particularly character actor Latessa who moved believably from comic to martyr. The songs are sometimes accomplished but lack variety. The engaging opening number "Within This Empty Space" sets the scene and brings the audience into the piece much like "Try to Remember" did in *The Fantasticks*. But what follows is so grim and somber that the score never seems to come to life. Songs that described torture, despair, hunger, poverty, and senseless death; when there were finally some songs about hope and love, one was too numb to believe them. Perhaps Jones and Schmidt did their job too well; this religious morality musical is so fervent it feels more like a sermon than a drama. In keeping with the experimental nature of the Portofino Studio, the musical was developed over a long rehearsal period and was scheduled for only six weeks. *Philemon* was later produced regionally, and there was a fine television version in 1976 which featured the Portofino cast. Jones and Schmidt left the glitter of Broadway far behind with *Philemon*, but what they accomplished must be classified as a minor work.

A Chorus Line

[15 April 1975, Public Theatre, 101 performances; Shubert Theatre, 6,137 performances] a musical play by James Kirkwood, Nicholas Dante. *Score:*

Marvin Hamlisch (music), Edward Kleban (lyrics). *Cast:* Donna McKech-
nie, Robert LuPone, Wayne Cilento, Priscilla Lopez, Pamela Blair, Carole
Bishop, Sammy Williams, Renee Baughman, Baayork Lee, Thomas J.
Walsh.

A musical theatre phenomenon that few could foresee as a Broadway blockbuster, the Off-Broadway production of *A Chorus Line* was a small-scale
experiment at the Public Theatre not unlike what Tom Jones and Harvey
Schmidt were attempting at the Portofino Theatre Workshop. In fact, creator Michael Bennett told producer Joe Papp that the experiment might not
even result in a production. Papp agreed, and with no pressure to present a
finished product, Bennett and his dancers and collaborators had the freedom
to make something personal and, at the same time, far reaching. What little
plot there is is more a frame than a complete picture. As eighteen dancers
audition for a chorus of eight in a new Broadway musical, the director Zach
(Robert LuPone) interviews them and asks each to reveal something about
themselves. This leads to reminiscences, confessions, and expressions of
both joy and despair, particularly for Cassie (Donna McKechnie) who used
to be Zach's lover. By the end of the audition, eight fortunate dancers are
chosen, but everyone returns in a musical salute to chorus dancers everywhere. Director-choreographer Bennett used taped interviews with actual
Broadway dancers, focusing on their shared emotions about performing.
James Kirkwood and Nicholas Dante shaped the material into a libretto using the framework of an audition, and Marvin Hamlisch and Edward Kleban
wrote songs that built on the ideas expressed in the interviews. A good deal
of the material was created and refined during the rehearsal period, and Bennett was pleased enough to let audiences see what they had come up with.
A Chorus Line opened at the Public's Newman Theatre and was rapturously
received by audiences and critics. After running thirteen weeks, the show
transferred to Broadway where it broke the record for the longest-running
musical: fourteen years. Although book, score, and dancers were all praised,
A Chorus Line was mostly a triumph for Bennett, who rose to the top ranks
of director-choreographers because of the musical.

The debate continues whether *A Chorus Line* was more effective in its
Off-Broadway venue or at the large and elaborate Shubert Theatre on Broadway. There was certainly something special about discovering this exciting new
work in the intimate Newman Theatre, and many felt that the musical, being
a character-driven show, lost something on Broadway. Others argue that *A
Chorus Line* is about Broadway and Broadway dancers with Broadway dreams
and that it belonged in a Broadway house. In some ways, the dancing became

more important in the Schubert, while the characters dominated at the New-man. The score, many believe, was more potent Off Broadway. Since much of the show is dancing, A Chorus Line has fewer songs than most stage musicals. In many ways the songs are extensions or alternatives to the confessional monologues that the dancers deliver. "Nothing," "I Can Do That," "Dance: Ten; Looks: Three," and "Sing!" are very specific, each exploring one person's dilemma, while other numbers, such as "Hello Twelve, Hello Thirteen, Hello Love" and "At the Ballet," echo the thoughts and feelings of several of those who auditioned. Kleban's lyrics are incisive and personal, and Hamlisch's music never strays far from the Broadway idiom, as if these dancers can only express themselves with theatre music. "What I Did for Love" and "One" were the only songs to find wide popularity because they can work outside of the context of the musical. Yet for many musical theatre lovers, the entire score is potent and memorable.

When A Chorus Line closed in 1990, emptiness was felt on Broadway. Not only because the show had been running so long but because its presence on Broadway symbolized something permanent to its many fans. Although A Chorus Line was distinctly an American musical, it found popularity outside the States, particularly in London where it ran 903 performances. Sixteen years after the original had closed in New York, the musical was revived on Broadway, and a new generation experienced what many older theatregoers fondly remembered. Bob Avian, who had served as assistant director on the original, restaged the musical in 2006 exactly as Bennett had first presented it leaving few surprises in this production, which also used the original set and costume designs. Critics welcomed the show back to Broadway, and audiences responded as if it were a new hit. (There was a film version in 1985 that was roundly panned by the press and lovers of the original show.) Summer stock and college revivals of A Chorus Line continue to keep the musical alive. From its first performance at the Public Theatre, the show had such wide appeal and struck a nerve with audiences that it remains an emotional favorite for many.

BOY MEETS BOY

[17 September 1975, Actors Playhouse, 463 performances] musical play by Billy Solly, Donald Ward. Score: Solly (music and lyrics). Cast: Joe Barrett, David Gallegly, Raymond Wood, Rita Gordon.

Broadway didn't get its first "gay musical" until *La Cage aux Folles* in 1983, but the new genre was popping up Off Broadway by the mid-1970s. Before AIDS, a gay show could be slaphappy and carefree without any dark subtext. Such was the case with *Boy Meets Boy*, a pastiche of a 1930s escapist musical comedy with a slight but oh-so-important switch in the cast of characters. The English aristocrat Guy Rose (David Gallegly) wishes to escape from the pressure of being a widely recognized nobleman and goes incognito in Paris. There he meets and falls in love with the American journalist Casey O'Brien, (Joe Barrett) but he continues to conceal his true identity. The usual complications follow, and after some light love songs, Guy and Casey are together for good. Structurally and musically the show followed the formulaic pattern of a light romance of the past. The songs pastiched the 1930s with varying success. "Does Anybody Love?" had a touch of Nöel Coward, and "What Do I Care?" sometimes sounded like a Cole Porter torch song. Some of the numbers for the small chorus (made up of men and women) were also agreeable, but too often a contemporary sound could be detected in words and music; sometimes *Boy Meets Boy* sounded more 1970s than Depression era. All the same, the tone of the production was accurate enough to be tuneful and enjoyable, and audiences responded for more than a year. A long run in Los Angeles was followed by several regional productions. The work is still stageworthy, but a different kind of nostalgia sets in when viewed today. *Boy Meets Boy* reminds one of the 1970s, before the AIDS epidemic, when there was nothing threatening or foreboding about a gay musical.

CHRISTY

[14 October 1975, Bert Wheeler Theatre, 40 performances] a musical play by Bernie Spiro based on John M. Synge's play *The Playboy of the Western World*. *Score:* Lawrence J. Blank (music), Spiro (lyrics). *Cast:* Jimi Elmer, Betty Forsyth, Bea Swanson, John Canary, Alexander Sokoloff, Bruce Levitt.

There is such lilting music in the Irish dialogue of John Millington Synge's masterpiece *The Playboy of the Western World* that a musical version was inevitable. This one was faithful to the play and utilized Synge's words as lyrics as much as possible. The classic plot was largely unaltered. The weakling Christy Mahon (Jimi Elmer) finds himself a local hero in a secluded Irish village when he boasts of having killed his "da" with a shovel. When it is learned that Christy's father (Bruce Levitt) is very much alive, the town turns against the boy, and he again attempts to clobber the old man to death. The villagers are appalled by his actions, but Old Mahon is impressed, and father and son are reconciled to each other. The most effective songs were the two duets between the phony hero and the passionate barkeeper's daughter Pegeen (Betty Forsyth): "Until the Likes of You" and "The Heart's a Wonder." The expected Irish jig music was heard in the male group numbers "Down the Hatch" and "Grain of the Salt of the Earth," while the women of the town expressed themselves with "To Please the Woman in Me" and the lively "Rumors." Christy's solos, "Picture Me" and the title song, were matched by Pegeen's lovely "The Morning After." A solid cast and first-rate production values added to the enjoyment, but the musical had trouble finding an audience and had to close after five weeks. Some critics argued that there was enough music in the poetic language of the original, but *Christy* had its own merits and ought to have been seen by more playgoers.

TUSCALOOSA'S CALLING ME . . . BUT I'M NOT GOING!

[1 December 1975, Top of the Gate, 429 performances] a musical revue by Bill Heyer, Hank Beebe, Sam Dann. *Score:* Heyer (lyrics), Beebe (music). *Cast:* Len Gochman, Patti Perkins, Renny Temple.

Although it was sassy and a bit ribald at times, this oddly titled revue was, underneath all the jokes, a love song to New York City. It was not about the attractions that tourists visit but about the day-by-day living in the city. New York was in its darkest days in the mid-1970s with crime rates high and financial foundations crumbling. Denied federal bailout money, the city was considered unlivable to outsiders and to many residents as well. Yet this little revue celebrated the little things that made New York wonderful, such as the great institution called the "Delicatessen." The opening number, "Only Right Here in New York City," unabashedly praised its uniqueness, and the dreamy "New York from the Air" extolled its beauty. The title song, about refusing to move away from New York, was as lyrical and fervent as a hymn. The trials of surviving in the city were listed with glee in "Everything You Hate Is Right Here," and in the sketches the show lampooned the tourists who complain and sneer but never know what New York is really like. There was even a comic song about the recent flood of nudity in the theatre, deftly titled

"(Their) Things Were Out." The trio of performers had the New York edge in their delivery, and James Hammerstein directed with precision. Whether tourists enjoyed the revue as much as New Yorkers did is questionable, but the demand for tickets was great enough that *Tuscaloosa's Calling Me . . . But I'm Not Going!* ran for over a year. Could the musical play outside of New York? Well, those wishing they lived in Manhattan would like it.

LOVESONG

[5 October 1976, Village Gate Theatre, 23 performances] a musical revue by Henry Comor. *Score:* Michael Valenti (music), various (lyrics). *Cast:* Jess Richards, Melanie Chartoff, Sigrid Heath, Ty McConnell.

What could be more unimaginative as a revue of songs about love? Yet how original this little show seemed when the subject was handled by such "lyricists" as Lord Byron, Sir Walter Raleigh, A. E. Houseman, Dorothy Parker, Richard Brinsley Sheridan, Leigh Hunt, and Christina Rossetti. Henry Comor collected the words from great writers over the centuries, and Michael Valenti set them to music that was as varied as the authors themselves, though he never tried to sound antique or period. Some texts were familiar, others obscure, and several were surprisingly effective as songs. The twenty-seven numbers followed a pattern, starting with courtship songs, proceeding to numbers about the married state, then concluding with old lovers parting only in death. It was all very engaging, especially when sung by the gifted cast of four. But *Lovesong* was difficult to sell because no matter how you described it, the revue sounded a bit too academic to be enjoyable. After all, when was the last time poet Robert Herrick had a hit song? Despite a few glowing notices, the musical could barely hold on for three weeks, but the score was recorded and later licensed and was produced in cabarets and other smaller spaces.

THE CLUB

[14 October 1976, Circle in the Square, 674 performances] a musical revue by Eve Merriam. *Score:* various. *Cast:* C. Monferdini, J. Beretta, T. White, M. Dell, G. Hodes, M. Innerarity, J. J. Hafner.

A feminist musical with a wicked twist, *The Club* was entertaining and fascinating to watch. At first the male chauvinism that it attacked was handled lightly and with winking sarcasm, but by the conclusion of this period revue the audience was quite disarmed. In an exclusive men's club in 1905, the pompous members (and a male servant) drink, trade quips about the frailties of the weaker sex, and sing authentic Victorian songs that are surprising in their narrow-mindedness. Eve Merriam wrote the bits of dialogue and selected the fourteen songs written between 1894 and 1905, the only famous one being "A Woman Is Only a Woman (But a Good Cigar Is a Smoke)." It was an intriguing idea, but the show took on a whole new level of meaning because the men were played by women, their first names reduced in the program to initials. It could have been an easy gimmick, but Tommy Tune, in his directing debut, handled the piece with both delicacy and flair. The female performers did not present an exaggerated parody of male pomposity but instead were so believable that the audience was enthralled by the accuracy and naturalness of their portrayals. At the end of the performance, the ladies removed their disguises, and audience reacted with delight even though the deception was well-known from the beginning of the evening. The whole cast was splendid, but the standouts were Carole Monferdini as the young rake Freddie and Gloria Hodes as the silly-ass Bertie. *The Club* had been workshopped and developed Off Off Broadway and then at the Lenox Arts Center in Stockbridge, Massachusetts. When it opened Off Broadway, the critics applauded both the concept and the performances, and audiences kept the revue running a year and a half. Professional and amateur theatre groups were attracted to the all-female show, but most found out it was a much more difficult feat to pull off than anticipated. Tune had made it all look so natural and easy that his wizardry was not obvious. All the same, his directing career was launched with *The Club*.

JOSEPH AND THE AMAZING TECHNICOLOR DREAMCOAT

[30 December 1976, Brooklyn Academy of Music, 23 performances] musical play by Andrew Lloyd Webber, Tim Rice. *Score:* Rice (lyrics), Webber (music). *Cast:* David-James Carroll, Cleavon Little, Terry Eno, Jess Pearson, Stuart Pankin, Leonard John Crofoot, Tony Hoty.

Much simpler and lighter in tone than Andrew Lloyd Webber and Tim Rice's *Jesus Christ Superstar* and *Evita*, this popular musical was actually written before those hit shows and saw many productions before New York first saw

it Off Broadway. Biblical Joseph (David-James Carroll), the favorite son of
Jacob (Tony Hoty), is sold by his jealous brothers into slavery and is taken
to Egypt. Imprisoned for being falsely accused of seducing the wife of the
pyramid builder Potiphar (Terry Eno), Joseph reveals a talent for interpret-
ing dreams, and when he explains a puzzling dream that the Pharaoh (Jess
Pearson) has been having, Joseph rises in stature and becomes Pharaoh's
right-hand man. A famine torments the land, and Joseph's brothers come to
Egypt where he tests them, then forgives them. The piece began as a twenty-
minute cantata which was performed by a London boys school in 1967. A
British producer saw commercial possibilities in the piece, and Webber and
Rice added songs, and it was seen on the concert stage, as a concept album,
and regionally in the States before the Brooklyn Academy of Music brought
over London director Frank Dunlop to stage the limited-engagement Off
Broadway. The musical did not begin to catch on in New York until a 1981
Off-Broadway mounting which transferred to Broadway and stayed for 747
performances. By that time many Americans knew the musical well from
the many amateur productions across the country. Over the years even more
songs had been added to fill out the story and make it a full (if still short)
evening's entertainment. The tuneful score consists of serious ballads, such
as the pleasing "Any Dream Will Do" and the heartfelt "Close Every Door,"
and clever pastiche numbers, like the French café song "Those Canaan Days"
and the country-western spoof "One More Angel in Heaven." Some numbers,
such as "Jacob and Sons" and "Potiphar," simply told the story and were led
by the Narrator (Cleavon Little) who would subsequently be played by a
female in most productions because the cast of characters remains almost
entirely male. *Joseph and the Amazing Technicolor Dreamcoat* returned to
Broadway in 1993, and there were television versions in 1991, 1999, and
2000. The musical remains a favorite in schools and summer stock.

NIGHTCLUB CANTATA

[9 January 1977, Top of the Gate, 145 performances] a musical revue by
Elizabeth Swados. *Score:* Swados (music and lyrics), various (lyrics). *Cast:*
Swados, Paul Kandel, JoAnna Peled, Karen Evans, David Schechter, Shel-
ley Plimpton, Mark Zagaeski, Rocky Greenburg.

The career of songwriter-director Elizabeth Swados was set in motion
with this popular Off-Broadway revue that was contemporary in subject

and sound. Swados had composed incidental music for some avant-garde nonmusical productions, but her songs were first heard here. Many of the lyrics in the piece were taken from the words of such contemporary authors as Sylvia Plath, Carson McCullers, Frank O'Hara, and Muriel Rukseyer. Swados wrote several other lyrics, fashioned the piece together, and wrote the sketches, directed it, and appeared in the cast. Many critics thought Swados a talent to be reckoned with, though she would always have a limited popularity throughout her career on and Off Broadway. There was more variety in *Nightclub Cantata* than in her later works, and the range of the songs was quite impressive, from such tender numbers as "Things I Didn't Know I Loved" and "Ballad of a Sad Cafe" to the farcical "Dibarti" in which a married couple have a fight using Hebrew chanting. Delmore Schwartz's celebrated short story "In Dreams Begin Responsibilities" was dramatized and children's writings were set to music in "Adolescents," a foreshadowing of Swados's later musical *Runaways*. The music bordered on rock but often relied heavily on folk and blues; it was different but accessible. *Nightclub Cantata* had been workshopped Off Off Broadway and at the Lenox Arts Center in Massachusetts before coming to Off Broadway for a run of four and a half months. The musical revue was later produced by college theatres and cabarets with success.

STARTING HERE, STARTING NOW

[7 March 1977, Barbarann Theatre Restaurant, 120 performances] a musical revue. *Score:* Richard Maltby Jr. (lyrics), David Shire (music). *Cast:* Loni Ackerman, Margery Cohen, George Lee Andrews.

For ten years songwriters Richard Maltby Jr. and David Shire had been scoring little musicals that folded before opening or played in such remote Off-Off-Broadway venues that nobody noticed them. Out of desperation (and a bit of inspiration) they decided to collect the best songs and put them into a plotless, characterless revue. After a short run at the Manhattan Theatre Club, *Starting Here, Starting Now* opened Off Broadway, got appreciative notices, and ran over four months, but it was the cast recording and the many subsequent productions regionally that made this a much-loved musical revue. Most of the songs dealt with living in New York City and young love and marriage, yet the variety was considerable, and it was clear that here was a masterful songwriting team. The trio of performers was also expert and, under Maltby's direction, the little cabaret act sparkled. The title song was already well known because Barbra Streisand had recorded it. Its long musical phrases and enticing lyrics were ideal for the long-breathed singer but "Starting Here, Starting Now" was equally effective when sung by Loni Ackerman, George Lee Andrews, and Margery Cohen Off Broadway. Other highlights include the hyperlament "Sunday Times Crossword Puzzle," the belligerent "I Don't Remember Christmas," the ironic "We Can Talk to Each Other," the bittersweet "Watching the Parade Go By," the debonair "Flair," the wry duet "I Think I May Want to Remember Today," and the demanding "What About Today?" All in all, the show boasts one of finest revue scores of its era. Maltby and Shire would have a roller-coaster career of hits and flops, but to many the songs from *Starting Here, Starting Now* remain their best.

HAPPY END

[8 March 1977, Academy of Music, 56 performances; Martin Beck Theatre, 75 performances] a musical play by Elisabeth Hauptman. *Score:* Kurt Weill (music), Bertolt Brecht, Michael Feingold (lyrics). *Cast:* Christopher Lloyd, Shirley Knight, Donna Emmanuel, Grayson Hall, Benjamin Rayson, Tony Azito.

As with *Mahagonny*, this was a decades-old German music-theatre piece by Bertolt Brecht and Kurt Weill which finally had its New York premiere Off Broadway. The 1929 musical is somewhat similar to *Guys and Dolls*, yet the tone is much darker and cynical. In Chicago during the Roaring Twenties, gunman Billy Cracker (Christopher Lloyd) is the top man in a gang run by an elusive female gangster known as "The Fly" (Grayson Hall). Billy falls for the Salvation Army lass Lt. Lillian Holiday (Shirley Knight) who is seemingly naive but knows how to cut loose with a bawdy song when asked to. The Fly tries to frame Billy because she thinks he is trying to take over the operation but, like Mack the Knife, Billy survives without reforming. Instead of the lovable gangsters of *Guys and Dolls*, *Happy End* boasts such unsavory cohorts as the Oriental menace "Governor" Nakamura (Tony Azito) and the killer "Baby Face" Flint (Raymond J. Barry). The script was filled with left-wing propaganda, and the cartoon-like characters seemed out of a dark comic book. But the songs were glorious, including the rousing "The Bilbao Song," the heartbreaking torch song "Surabaya Johnny," the lusty "The Sailors' Tango," the hymnlike "Don't Be Afraid," and the fast and furious "The Mandalay Song." Some of these were already familiar to audiences from Weill revues and recordings by Weill's widow Lotte Lenya. The new adaptation by Michael Feingold had been produced at the Yale Repertory Theatre before the Chelsea Theatre Center offered it as part of their season. It was well enough received that it transferred to Broadway with Meryl Streep and Bob Gunton as Lillian and Billy; Streep was not yet a movie star, and interest in the dark musical was limited, shutting down after nine weeks. Yet *Happy End* enjoyed a healthy afterlife in regional theatres and has joined the ranks of Weill's producible works.

AIN'T MISBEHAVIN'

[8 February 1978, Manhattan Theatre Club, 28 performances; Longacre Theatre, 1,604 performances] a musical revue by Murray Horwitz, Richard Maltby Jr. *Score:* Thomas "Fats" Waller (music), various (lyrics). *Cast:* Nell Carter, Andre De Shields, Irene Cara, Ken Page, Armelia McQueen.

One of Broadway's favorite and most successful musical revues, the beloved musical tribute to Thomas "Fats" Waller started Off Broadway as a month-long cabaret act at the Manhattan Theatre Club. Glowing reviews allowed it to quickly move to Broadway (with Charlaine Woodard replacing Irene Cara in the five-member cast), where it set the standard for revues celebrating a single artist. *Ain't Misbehavin'* has rarely been equaled, though dozens of clones have followed in its footsteps over the years. What makes this musical so special? Very few of the songs were written for the theatre, there are no specific characters or situations, there is no narration or any information given about Waller, and only a handful of the numbers are familiar to contemporary audiences. Yet *Ain't Misbehavin'* soars on stages everywhere. Perhaps it is the way the revue captures the spirit of Waller so well: sassy, irreverent, sexy, sardonic, joyful, even despondent. Each musical number feels like a theatrical event, conjuring up a time and place as well as an attitude. From the celebratory "Spreadin' Rhythm Around" and the sexy "Honeysuckle Rose" to the caustic "Your Feet's Too Big" and the chilling "Black and Blue," the songs come to life in the theatre. It helped that the musical direction by Luther Henderson, the direction by Richard Maltby Jr., and the performances by an astounding quintet of singer-actors were all superior. The intimate show lost none of its luster when it transferred to a bigger Broadway house because Waller and his music are bigger than life. *Ain't Misbehavin'* also succeeds with theatre groups all over because it is one of the great ensemble musicals.

After Nell Carter became a television star, the original cast was reassembled in 1988 for a Broadway revival, and she was top-billed and given an extra song to justify her star stature. It offset the balance. *Ain't Misbehavin'* is about Fats Waller; it needs no other star.

RUNAWAYS

[21 February 1978, Public Theatre, 80 performances; Plymouth Theatre, 267 performances] a musical play by Elizabeth Swados. *Score:* Swados (music and lyrics). *Cast:* Evan Miranda, Diane Lane, Josie De Guzman, Anthony Imperato, David Schechter, Karen Evans, Trini Alvarado.

A grim subject matter—young people who have run away from abusive families and eke out a living on the streets through their wits or by prostitution—became a surprisingly uplifting musical because it was so honest and unapologetic. These kids were funny, heartbreaking, sarcastic, and resilient, but rarely bitter or defeatist. Elizabeth Swados fashioned the revue from interviews with real runaways, then used their words to create songs and soliloquies about the different things on the kids' minds. It was even announced that some of the cast members were actual runaways. Yet *Runaways* didn't feel like a documentary. Swados called it a "collage," and there was variety in both song and speeches. The tone was light and carefree with "Find Me a Hero," pounding in "Every Now and Then," comic in "The Revenge Song," hopeful in "The Undiscovered Son," and mocking in "Where Are the People Who Did *Hair*?" Swados's music ranged from Latin, as in "No Lullabies for Luis," to an early form of rap in "Enterprise," but much of the rest of the score was heavily influenced by the 1970s disco sound and seems somewhat dated today. Joe Papp presented *Runaways* at his Public Theatre, and critical and popular reactions were so favorable that after ten weeks he moved it to Broadway where it ran eight months.

THE BEST LITTLE WHOREHOUSE IN TEXAS

[17 April 1978, Entermedia Theatre, 64 performances; 46th Street Theatre, 1,639 performances] a musical comedy by Larry L. King, Peter Masterson. *Score:* Carol Hall (music and lyrics). *Cast:* Henderson Forsythe,

Carlin Glynn, Jay Garner, Clint Allmon, Delores Hall, Pamela Blair, Susan Mansur.

This popular musical spoof of Texas morals and politics was first show-cased Off Off Broadway then moved to Off Broadway for eight weeks. Even there it seemed like a big Broadway hit, so it quickly transferred to a Broadway house and remained for four years. Larry L. King and Peter Masterson wrote the politically incorrect libretto about the infamous brothel known as the Chicken Ranch, which had been a Texas landmark since the 1840s. Its days are numbered when television evangelist Melvin P. Thorpe (Clint Allmon) uses it as a platform for his patriotic, right-wing self-promotion. The local sheriff Ed Earl Dodd (Henderson Forsythe) tries to protect the Ranch's proprietress Mona Stangley (Carlin Glynn) and her girls, but once Thorpe's crusade gets underway, not even the Governor (Jay Garner) can stop it. It was all harmless fun, playing off Southern stereotypes and, despite its title, not very provocative. Carol Hall wrote the commendable songs that were country-flavored yet had a Broadway feel to them as well. Among the most memorable numbers were the rhythmic "20 Fans" that introduced the characters and the situation, the incisive character song "Bus From Amarillo," the plaintive "Hard Candy Christmas," the foot-stomping "The Aggie Song," the mock-gospel number "Twenty-four Hours of Lovin'," and the wry soft-shoe "The Sidestep." Reviewers particularly lauded co-director/choreographer Tommy Tune's inventive dances and the estimable cast headed by Glynn and Forsythe, two veteran supporting players who finally stood out in leading roles on Broadway. Off Broadway, *The Best Little Whorehouse in Texas* had a simple set and used simple and economic devices to create an effect, such as the blow-up dummy cheerleaders during the football half-time entertainment. The set was enlarged for the bigger Broadway house, but the band remained small and was on stage as originally played. Yet this show never felt like an Off-Broadway musical. Perhaps the creators had their eyes on Broadway from the very start. The musical is revived in both large and small venues and seems to work equally well. All the same, *The Best Little Whorehouse in Texas* always seems like a big Broadway hit. The musical was turned into an unsatisfying film in 1982. Most of the creative staff from the stage production reassembled for the unnecessary sequel *The Best Little Whorehouse Goes Public* in 1994, which was denounced by the critics and closed after fifteen performances.

I'M GETTING MY ACT TOGETHER AND
TAKING IT ON THE ROAD

[16 May 1978, Public Theatre/Circle in the Square, 1,165 performances] a musical play by Gretchen Cryer. *Score:* Cryer (lyrics), Nancy Ford (music). *Cast:* Cryer, Joel Fabiani, Margot Rose, Betty Aberlin, Don Scardino.

The finest of the handful of contemporary musicals by Nancy Ford and Gretchen Cryer, this long-titled, long-running Off-Broadway show was one of the few works of the decade that dealt effectively with women's issues, yet it was far more than a feminist musical. The thirty-nine-year-old singer-actress Heather (Cryer) auditions her new nightclub act for her manager Joe (Joel Fabiani), hoping to convince him that she should present a more honest portrayal of herself rather than the glossy, fanciful persona that she has faked in the past. Joe believes the false image is more lucrative but, in a series of songs she wrote, Heather expresses the frustration of trying to please men throughout her life: her father, her ex-husband, and now Joe. By the end of her rehearsal, Heather has liberated herself from her past doubts and faces the future with a more confident and self-fulfilled attitude. The intimate musical was alternately funny and sobering, and Cryer's autobiographical tale and powerful performance were both exhilarating. The pop score was not very integrated since all the numbers were part of Heather's nightclub act, yet the songs were unified thematically, and one can feel Heather's self-awareness growing just by listening to the cast recording. The lullaby-like "Dear Tom" is quietly disarming, the jubilant "Natural High" avoids cliché through its ro-bustness, the comic "Strong Woman Number" has a very frustrating subtext, the lyrical "Miss America" has a disturbing lyric, and the vapid but appealing "In a Simple Way I Love You" is an accurate pastiche of the kinds of num-bers Heather has been forced to sing all her life. Perhaps the finest song in the score is the straightforward "Old Friend" that resonates with honesty. Word Baker directed the show with a delicate touch, though it still struck some male audience members as preachy and one-sided. Actually, watching how uncomfortable the musical made some playgoers was as interesting as the show itself. In both her libretto and lyrics, Cryer was exploring touchy subjects, and it was clear she struck a nerve on occasion. *I'm Getting My Act Together and Taking It on the Road* ran six months at the Public Theatre, then producer Joseph Papp moved it to the Circle in the Square downtown where it stayed for nearly three years. The knowing little musical is rarely revived today. Being a product of the 1970s women's movement, it strikes many as dated. Possibly, though, the issues remain, and Cryer's observations about male-female relationships are still accurate.

PIANO BAR

[8 June 1978, Westside Theatre, 125 performances] a musical revue by Doris Willens, Rob Fremont. *Score:* Willens (lyrics), Fremont (music). *Cast:* Kelly Bishop, Steve Elmore, Karen De Vito, Richard Ryder, Joel Silberman, Jim McMahon.

The modest little revue *Piano Bar* had weak material, but the performers seemed to triumph because this less-than-satisfying musical managed a run of sixteen weeks. On a rainy Tuesday, four strangers find refuge from the weather in Sweet Sue's pub where Prince (Joel Silberman) plays at the piano bar. For no apparent reason, each of the patrons delves into their pasts and sings about lost love, lost dreams, parents, and well, life. It is not terribly exciting because the characters, their feelings, and the songs used to express them lack any spark of life. The expected numbers about dating, breakups, and past regrets seemed to come and go without creating much of an effect on the characters or the audience. When the songwriters tried to get clever in a number about different kinds of "New York Cliché," it was a bland list and not very thought-provoking. Kelly Bishop and Steve Elmore had impressive Broadway credits, but the entire cast was more than competent. The revue had been workshopped Off Off Broadway five months earlier with a mostly different cast. The transfer to a commercial run Off Broadway received mixed notices for the show but some praise for the cast, getting audiences to check it out. The show was recorded and licensed for regional theatres, and there were some productions by groups looking for an economical cabaret-like entertainment.

A BROADWAY MUSICAL

[10 October 1978, Theatre of the Riverside Church, 26 performances; Lunt-Fontanne Theatre, 1 performance] a musical play by William F.

Brown. *Score:* Charles Strouse (music), Lee Adams (lyrics). *Cast:* Helen Gallagher, Julius LaRosa, Alan Weeks, Larry Marshall, Anne Francine, Larry Riley, Dan Strayhorn, Ron Ferrell, Gwyda Donhowe.

Songwriters Charles Strouse and Lee Adams had Broadway hits together with *Bye Bye Birdie, Applause,* and *Golden Boy.* For the last they wrote songs for Sammy Davis Jr., and the experience was so bizarre that they thought it might make a musical in itself. William F. Brown, the author of the current Broadway hit *The Wiz,* wrote the script about a bunch of white producers and songwriters trying to put together a show starring an African American singing star. The intent was to satirize Broadway, the recent craze for black musicals, and the discordant results when people with very different mindsets try to work together. It was an idea not without possibilities, but Brown's libretto was filled with unfunny caricatures, and the fine line between satire and poor taste dissolved quickly. Strouse and Lee worked with African American director-choreographer George Faison (also from *The Wiz*) to solve many problems. Instead of taking the troubled musical on the road for polishing, it was produced Off Broadway with the idea of fixing it up during the three-week run. But the producers, who seemed as crass and wrong-headed as the ones in the plot, decided to fire Faison, bring in celebrated director-choreographer Gower Champion, and open on Broadway as soon as possible. Champion increased the size and glitz of the production while destroying the sense of the piece. Stars Julius LaRosa and Helen Gallagher fled, and *A Broadway Musical* was a one-night flop on Broadway. Perhaps a promising musical satire was destroyed, or maybe the show never had a chance. All that is certain is that Strouse's music was commendable; he recycled some of the melodies for later shows, and they are splendid. In a way, what *A Broadway Musical* tried to do was what Mel Brooks did nearly two dozen years later on Broadway with *The Producers:* lampoon Broadway by being gleefully and politically incorrect.

IN TROUSERS

[8 December 1978, Playwrights Horizons, 28 performances] a musical play by William Finn. *Score:* Finn (music and lyrics). *Cast:* Chip Zien, Alison Fraser, Mary Testa, Joanna Green.

This little musical introduced the bisexual character of Marvin, the song-writer William Finn, and a distinctive new voice to the American theatre. Not that *In Trousers* is a great musical or even a good one; but the hints of a superior talent are there all the same. Jumping back and forth through time, we see Marvin (Chip Zien) about to leave his wife for his gay lover Whizzer, then we see him in high school with an absurd crush on his teacher Miss Goldberg, then he is wooing his wife Trina, then he is a kid making demands on his parents to be noticed and loved. It was a bit confusing and often messy, but the sung-through score was so tuneful and exhilarating and the lyrics so manic and refreshing that *In Trousers* was a magical journey from start to finish. Finn burst on the scene with this little-noticed show (it was just a one-month run as part of a new musicals workshop at Playwrights Horizons), and immediately it was clear that he sounded like no other composer or lyricist. Over the years Finn's work has been compared to that of Stephen Sondheim, but that is just a way of saying he is difficult to pinpoint. The music is contemporary but not rock nor folk nor pop. It can be flowing and lyrical one moment then quickly turn dissonant and harsh. Similarly, the lyrics are sometimes a manic jumble of words, other times simple and pointed. The opening number "Marvin's Giddy Seizures" is more raucous and crazed than any musical ever started with. Marvin's angst is explored in such aggressive numbers as the desperate "My Chance to Survive the Night" and the sexual fantasy "The Rape of Miss Goldberg by Marvin." Real sex is recalled in "Whizzer Going Down," while the traditional love song is given quite a spin in numbers like "Love Me for What I Am (Not for What I Try to Be)" and "Your Lips and Me." The melodic trios "High School Ladies at Five O'Clock" and "Set Those Sails" are more conventional but enthralling all the same, and there has never been a musical theatre song quite like the no-holds-barred "How Marvin Eats His Breakfast." The whole score is one surprise after another. Few saw the original production, but thankfully it was recorded and one can hear what was so exciting about *In Trousers*. The recording also makes it possible to appreciate the thrilling performances by Zien as Marvin and by Alison Fraser, Mary Testa, and Joanna Green as the women in his life. (Whizzer is sung about but never appears.) The short engagement did not bring much recognition to Finn or the musical, and when *In Trousers* was given an inept commercial production Off Broadway in 1985, it ran only two weeks. The story of Marvin would be continued in the later, more cohesive, musicals *March of the Falsettos* and *Falsettoland*, which are frequently revived while this first installment receives far fewer productions. Yet there is still something startling and exciting about *In Trousers*, like remembering the first time you saw your favorite movie star.

MY OLD FRIENDS

[12 January 1979, Orpheum Theatre, 100 performances; 22 Steps Theatre, 53 performances] a musical play by Mel Mandel, Norman Sachs. *Score:* Mandel, Sachs (music and lyrics). *Cast:* Peter Walker, Sylvia Davis, Maxine Sullivan, Allen Swift.

The John Kander and Fred Ebb musical *70, Girls, 70,* about the spry residents of an old folks' home, was a quick flop on Broadway in 1971 despite an outstanding score and an elderly cast of veteran performers. For some reason audiences didn't want to see senior citizens singing and dancing with more energy than folks half their age. *My Old Friends* had a similar subject but was quieter, less exciting, and playgoers liked it. It seems, on stage at any rate, old people should act their age. At the Golden Age Retirement Hotel, the residents have their expected complaints, reminisce a lot, and generally keep up a sunny disposition. There is even a budding romance between the widower and retired carpenter Peter Schermann (Peter Walker) and the level-headed widow Heloise Michaud (Sylvia Davis). They make for a nice, if dull, couple, and they fit into the atmosphere of the place where not much ever happens. *My Old Friends* avoided the obvious stereotypes but didn't replace them with much else so the evening, both book and score, was bland. Audiences didn't mind bland, and the little musical ran nearly three months before transferring to a tiny Broadway house. Broadway playgoers were not as welcoming to bland, and despite some appreciative reviews and nods of approval by bus groups, the show struggled to run past six weeks. The songs in *My Old Friends* were pleasant but forgettable. Peter sang "What We Need around Here" to liven up things, but the list song was as lifeless as the residents he was trying to wake up. One old timer came in and proclaimed in song "I Bought a Bicycle," and that sufficed for an up-tempo number. Even when two ladies recalled "Mambo '52," the Latin number sounded like it was on slow speed. Among the cast members was the great jazz singer Maxine Sullivan, and she brought a lot of class to "A Little Starch Left," but the song itself was stiff and contrived. *My Old Friends* was not recorded, but it was licensed for amateur theatre groups and found some takers. After all, what other senior citizen musical is there except *70, Girls, 70?* At least *My Old Friends* requires no vigorous tap dancing.

THE UMBRELLAS OF CHERBOURG

[1 February 1979, Public Theatre/Theatre Cabaret, 36 performances] a musical play by Charles Burr. *Score:* Michel Legrand (music and French lyrics), Sheldon Harnick, Charles Burr (English lyrics). *Cast:* Stefanianne Christopherson, Dean Pitchford, Judith Roberts, Maureen Silliman, Laurence Guittard, Lizabeth Pritchett, Marc Jordan, Stephen Bogardus.

Jacques Demy's 1964 film *Les Parapluies de Cherbourg* is a one-of-a-kind wonder, a sung-through modern opera filled with unforgettable color images and boasting a superb score by Michel Legrand. A stage version sounded like a good idea; a stage version with American lyricist Sheldon Harnick handling the adaptation sounded like a great idea. Joe Papp commissioned the piece and gave it a home in his Public Theatre for a one-month booking. What didn't sound like a good idea was hiring avant-gardist Andrei Serban to direct. He had been tampering with classics by Brecht, Chekhov, and others for years, and the result was always controversial (which Papp loved). *The Umbrellas of Cherbourg* has a realistic story that took the form of an opera. It was an already challenging project without being deconstructed by Serban. The romantic tale concerned the young French girl Genevieve Emery (Stefanianne Christopherson) who is in love with the garage mechanic Guy (Dean Pitchford), much to the displeasure of her mother (Judith Roberts). Madame Emery is relieved when Guy is drafted and is stationed in Algeria, but soon Genevieve learns that she is pregnant. The wealthy Frenchman Cassard (Laurence Guittard) has fallen in love with Genevieve, and he and Madame Emery convince the girl to marry him. Guy is wounded in Africa and is sent home only to find Genevieve married and slowly falling in love with her husband. He weds the quiet Madeleine (Maureen Silliman), who has long loved Guy and cared for his ailing aunt. After a time, Guy has opened his own filling station, and one day he and Genevieve meet once again when she is driving with her daughter on a trip. The two still love each other but are practical and part ways as the sound of their old love song fills the air. This is not the kind of story that needs a surreal approach, which is what Serban gave it. Plastic panels flew in and out, characters were directed to behave like stylistic puppets, and the romantic music was practically mocked by the staging. As with all Serban productions, the critics were divided in their opinions about every aspect of the musical. The lack of consensus discouraged Papp from moving the show into a Broadway house, and it closed at the end of the month. Even more unfortunate, the score was never recorded. One can still listen to Legrand's marvelous film soundtrack, but not to hear Harnick's English lyrics is a shame.

DISPATCHES

[18 April 1979, Public Theatre/Theatre Cabaret, 63 performances], a musical play by Michael Herr, Elizabeth Swados. *Score:* Swados (music and lyrics). *Cast:* Karen Evans, Paul McCrane, Roger Lawson, William Parry, David Schechter, Gedde Watanabe, Rodney Hudson.

The Vietnam War had sputtered to a close by 1975, but plays and musicals dealing with the conflict and its aftermath were still prevalent at the end of the decade. News reporter Michael Herr collected his writings about the war and published them in a book titled *Dispatches*. Songwriter-director Elizabeth Swados turned the dispatches into a revue which she labeled a "rock-war musical." She had done this kind of documentary musical in the past with *Runaways*, but in the case of *Dispatches* Swados's creativity seemed to be drying up. Of course the stories were powerful and some of the stark images memorable, but little seemed to be gained by the rock songs. Some critics even felt the score detracted and weakened the potent subject matter. Others applauded the songs, which were mostly about the soldiers' reaction to what was happening around them. Sometimes the numbers were about military specifics, as in "Song of the LURP (Long Range Reconnaissance Patrol)" and "Helicopter, Helicopter," and other times were about the more personal side of war, as with "Thou Shalt Not Be Afraid" and "I See a Road." "Stoned in Saigon" was about the drug aspect of the war, and the finale "Burning and Freezing" summed up the conflicting feelings the GIs had about Vietnam. Joe Papp presented the uncompromising work at the Public Theatre, and it was well attended for eight weeks.

SCRAMBLED FEET

[11 June 1979, Village Gate Upstairs, 831 performances] a musical revue by John Driver, Jeffrey Haddow. *Score:* Driver, Haddow (music and lyrics). *Cast:* Driver, Haddow, Evalyn Baron, Roger Neil, Hermione.

Before *Forbidden Broadway* there was *Scrambled Feet*, an irreverent little revue that poked fun at the current theatre season in New York. The idea was
a throwback to the turn of the century when Weber and Fields made fun of
the current dramas by musicalizing them and giving them such silly names as
Hoity Toity and *Cyranose de Bric-a-Brac*. We've seen how 1950s revues often
took aim at fellow showbiz folk and had a field day spoofing Tennessee Williams and other serious playwrights. The New York theatre had not seen for a
long time such specific lampooning of itself when *Scrambled Feet* opened at
the end of the decade, and it was considered refreshingly new by both critics
and playgoers, running over two years. College pals John Driver and Jeffrey
Haddow workshopped the idea Off Off Broadway then put together a satirical
revue in Chicago in which the current productions in the Windy City were
ribbed. It was well received; thus Driver and Haddow rewrote the material for
New York, added some songs, and appeared in the show with Evalyn Baron
and Roger Neil. The humor was timely, far from subtle, but engaging all the
same. Actors were seen "Makin' the Rounds," songwriters were involved in the
"Composer Tango," there was wry "Advice to Producers," and matinee audience members who coughed and noisily opened candy wrappers were taken
to task in "Theatre Party Ladies" (sung by the three men in drag). Two current
Broadway dramas, *The Elephant Man* about an abused deformed freak and
Whose Life Is It Anyway? about a paralyzed artist, were ridiculed by a wrestling
match between the two physically challenged leads. The musical hit *Annie*
was used to scoff at the use of audience-loving animals on stage, though this
time it was a duck named Hermione who was rescued from the butcher to
become a Broadway star. Unlike the later *Forbidden Broadway* series, the music in *Scrambled Feet* was original and did not try to echo actual songs. Yet the
musical commentary was often as funny as the sketches. During the long run
the material had to be revised as the theatrical targets changed. Also, being so
topical and local, productions elsewhere and at a later time were problematic.
All the same, a revised version of the revue was broadcast on cable television
in 1984 with Madeline Kahn joining some of the original cast members. While
it ran in New York, *Scrambled Feet* was a very "with it" show and proved that
theatre mocking theatre was still a good idea.

Big Bad Burlesque

[14 August 1979, Orpheum Theatre, 112 performances] a musical revue
by Don Brockett. *Score:* Brockett (music and lyrics). *Cast:* Steve Lieb-

man, Tina Kay, Jim Walton, Mitchell Steven Tebo, Danny Herman, Roy Doliner, Susan Orem.

It is difficult to spoof American burlesque because the genre mocks itself, reducing comedy to leering jokes and performing to stripping. This revue, which originated in Pittsburgh, sometimes was a lampoon of the old burlesque days but more often than not was just a recreation of the onstage and backstage world of the grind houses. Although there was no plot, the revue featured a cast of traditional burlesque types, from the Top Banana (Steve Liebman) and Straight Man (Roy Doliner) to the Soubrette (Susan Orem) and the headlining stripper, euphemistically known as an Ecdysiast (Tina Kay). There were some original songs by creator-director Don Brockett and some far-from-original skits that covered familiar burlesque territory. The one thing the show did not emphasize was nudity, otherwise it might have run far longer than fourteen weeks. Instead the tone was more comic and even affectionate for the long-gone genre. The title of the revue was ironic; it was a small production, and there was nothing very naughty about it in terms of what else was going on on the New York stage at the time. *Big Bad Burlesque* suffered from an unlucky coincidence. Three months into its run, *Sugar Babies* opened on Broadway and was a smash hit, running over two years. It was similar, but the Broadway production *was* big, had stars Mickey Rooney and Ann Miller, and great songs from the golden years of burlesque. When *Sugar Babies* appeared, business for the Off-Broadway revue plummeted. It was unfortunate because *Big Bad Burlesque* had its merits and managed to capture the genre in a modest way.

THE KING OF SCHNORRERS

[9 October 1979, Harold Clurman Theatre, 30 performances; Playhouse Theatre, 63 performances] a musical play by Judd Woldin based on Israel Zangwill's *The King of Schnorres*. *Score:* Woldin (music and lyrics). *Cast:* Lloyd Battista, Sophie Schwab, Philip Casnoff, Ralph Bruneau, Jerry Meyer, Ed Dixon.

An offbeat yet engaging musical with limited audience appeal, *The King of Schnorrers* had a unique look and sound to it. In 1791, the Jewish beggars (or "schnorres") in the East End of London are ruled by the egotistical Da Costa (Lloyd Battista). When his daughter Deborah (Sophie Schwab) falls in love with the poor but clever artist David Ben Yonkel (Philip Casnoff), the "King of Schnorrers" uses all his wily powers to break up the romance. But David outwits Da Costa and wins the girl and the day. Based on a Jewish folk tale, the story was novelized by Israel Zangwill with a lot of gritty atmosphere and characters full of bravado. As a musical, it came off as an unwholesome *Fiddler on the Roof.* The songs by Judd Woldin, who also adapted Zangwill's book, were filled with period flavor including some vivacious klezmer sounds. Da Costa boasted about his thieving ways in "The Fine Art of Schnorring," Deborah sang the beguiling "Guided by Love," there was a lovely "Sephardic Lullaby," and everyone claimed to have plenty of "Chutzpah." The Off-Broadway production, directed and choreographed by Grover Dale, was colorful, rambunctious, and pleasantly rough-and-tumble. The show had originated at the George Street Playhouse in New Jersey, and its Off-Broadway producers were pleased enough with the reception the musical received that after a month it transferred to Broadway, where it could not find an audience and struggled to run two months. Such a scruffy and ragged musical did not belong on Broadway, and *The King of Schnorrers* might have found a following if it had stayed at the intimate Harold Clurman Theatre. Composer Woldin had found some success writing a very different sound for the Broadway musical *Raisin* in 1973; some critics thought his work on the Jewish period musical was better. After the Broadway run, the authors revised the show and, under the new title *Petticoat Lane,* it was produced in a regional theatre in New Jersey. With yet another title change, this time with the off-putting title *Tatterdemalion,* the musical attempted Off Broadway again in 1985 but only lasted three weeks.

God Bless You, Mr. Rosewater

[14 October 1979, Entermedia Theatre, 49 performances] a musical play by Howard Ashman based on Kurt Vonnegut Jr.'s book. *Score:* Ashman, Dennis Green (lyrics), Alan Menken (music). *Cast:* Frederick Coffin, Jonathan Hadary, Janie Sell, Pierre Epstein, Ed Vannuys, Will Hussung.

The quixotic fiction of Kurt Vonnegut Jr. seems to be ideal for the musical stage. The characters are theatrically over the top, the plots are outrageous, and the themes broad and stimulating. Vonnegut's antiestablishment views may be a little too offbeat for Broadway, but surely Off Broadway would find the material palatable. Evidently not. The musicalization of Vonnegut's *God Bless You, Mr. Rosewater* received mixed notices and folded after six weeks. The newcomers Howard Ashman (book and lyrics) and Alan Menken (music) were not even deemed "promising." What went wrong? The 1965 novel is really a series of short stories that are episodes in the adventures of Eliot Rosewater, a millionaire philanthropist who goes around the country joining volunteer fire departments, getting happily drunk, and generally acting odd. When he settles in Rosewater, Indiana, Eliot starts to give away his millions to the deserving citizens instead of letting the greedy Rosewater Foundation in New York City distribute it. The foundation lawyer Norman Mushari attempts to have Eliot declared insane so he can claim the money in the name of a Rosewater relative who is under his thumb. It is a delightful fable on the page with the good and the bad guys clearly marked and the unique Vonnegut style moving the episodes in a breezy manner. Ashman's libretto was faithful to the original; so faithful that some critics found little reason to musicalize the story. Since the score was not recorded, the effectiveness of the songs is up to debate. (The musical is licensed for production, and there have been some mountings across the country.) What the press agreed on was the polish and talent of the production. After being workshopped Off Off Broadway, the show was given a commercial production directed by Ashman. The cast, led by Frederick Coffin (Eliot) and Jonathan Hadary (Mushari), was lauded as well. But these were not money notices and, despite Vonnegut's popularity, audiences did not seem to be interested. Ashman and Menken would prove to be more than promising with their break-out hit *Little Shop of Horrors* three years later, and *God Bless You, Mr. Rosewater* ended up being a footnote in their careers. Another footnote: Vonnegut fans will be pleased to know that the author's alter ego Kilgore Trout (Pierre Epstein) shows up in the musical, but he didn't get a song to sing.

ONE MO' TIME

[22 October 1979, Village Gate Downstairs, 1,372 performances] a musical revue by Vernel Bagneris. *Score:* various. *Cast:* Bagneris, Topsy Chapman, Sylvia "Kuumba" Williams, Thais Clark, John Stell.

The last Off-Broadway musical of the 1970s was also one of its longest-running. *One Mo' Time* quietly opened in the secondary space of the Village

Gate with no advance or much publicity, but it slowly caught on, critics eventually found it and highly recommended it, and the little show ran over three years. Actually, to say it opened quietly is misleading because this was a rowdy, raucous revue from the start, and both critics and playgoers used "hot" to describe the evening. The setting is the Lyric Theatre in New Orleans in 1926 in which four African American performers tear up the place as part of the black vaudeville circuit. The songs were all authentic period numbers ranging from the familiar, such as "Tiger Rag," "Everybody Loves My Baby," "After You're Gone," and "There'll Be a Hot Time in the Old Town Tonight," to some less-known gems, such as "Kiss Me Sweet" and "You've Got the Right Key But the Wrong Key Hole." In addition to the great songs, the show featured a thin plot, about the plight of African American performers working in the South under Jim Crow laws and a white theatre owner who is withholding the actors' pay, and a lot of dancing, particularly the Charleston, the Black Bottom, and the Cakewalk. Performer-director Vernel Bagneris put together the revue in New Orleans, where it was successful enough to interest some Off-Broadway producers. The tiny space added to the contagious spirit of the show, and *One Mo' Time* became the Off-Broadway revue to see. Comparisons were made to *Ain't Misbehavin'*, which was then playing in a Broadway house. The Fats Waller musical was also hot, but in a classy, high-style manner. *One Mo' Time* was down and dirty fun, more sizzling than sophisticated. Bagneris took his revue on tour and also performed it in London; a decade later he offered the sequel *Further Mo'*.

Pins and Needles (1937). During the long run of the topical Harold Rome revue, the songs and sketches had to be revised to keep up to date with the headlines. By 1939 the world leaders who sang the sarcastic "Four Little Angels of Peace" were (left to right) Neville Chamberlain, Benito Mussolini, Tojo, and Adolph Hitler. Is that the shadow of Rome's head in the orchestra pit? *Photofest*

The Cradle Will Rock (1937). Actress Olive Stanton poses outside the Maxine Elliott Theatre for a publicity shot for the upcoming Marc Blitzstein musical on Broadway. The wistful look on Stanton's face suggests that she knows it will not happen. The day of the announced opening, the show was canceled by the Federal Theatre Project, and Blitzstein and company had to find a new venue, this time off Broadway. *Photofest*

The Threepenny Opera (1954). The dark and sinister mood of the Bertolt Brecht–Kurt Weill "music drama" is captured in this photo. The passion and the hatred the whore Jenny (Lotte Lenya) feels toward the womanizing Macheath (Scott Merrill) is all too clear in Lenya's face. *Photofest*

The Golden Apple (1954). There are not many chandeliers or helicopters Off Broadway, but there was a hot air balloon in this unique musical which set Homer's epic poems in the American Northwest. Paris (Jonathan Lucas) and Helen (Kaye Ballard) elope together via balloon, thereby starting a war between two rival towns in the state of Washington. *Photofest*

The Littlest Revue (1956). Like the 1929 Broadway hit *The Little Show*, Ben Bagley's saucy musical revue proudly proclaimed its small size in the title. Both revues were loaded with young and promising talent backstage and onstage. Pictured from the Bagley show are Dorothy Jarnac and Joel Grey. *Photofest*

Little Mary Sunshine (1959). You didn't have to know much about American operettas of the 1920s and 1930s to enjoy this lovable spoof of the genre, but some of the parallels to old shows and songs were especially delicious to those in the know. Little Mary Sunshine (Eileen Brennan) confides in the Indian guide Fleet Foot (Robert Chambers) while her beau Captain "Big Jim" Warington (William Graham) looks a little perplexed. *Photofest*

The Fantasticks (1960). Who would have thought that such a small-cast musical could provide employment Off Broadway for hundreds of actors over the years? Jerry Orbach (top center) and members of the original cast strike a now-famous pose. They are (left to right) George Curley, Hugh Thomas, Kenneth Nelson, Rita Gardner, William Larson, and Thomas Bruce (aka author Tom Jones). *Photofest*

You're a Good Man, Charlie Brown (1967). Lucy (Reva Rose) contemplates the power of five separate fingers when combined into a fist, all part of her method of dominating her younger brother Linus (Bob Balaban). Since the characters in the *Peanuts* comic strip often spoke like adults, it made sense that they be played by adult actors on stage. *Photofest*

Promenade (1969). Two convicts (Ty McConnell, left, and Gilbert Price) dig themselves out of jail only to find that the world outside is another form of prison. Madeline Kahn (left) and Shannon Bolin were among the ensemble cast members who played the various characters the two men encountered in this very 1960s musical. *Promenade* was perhaps the most accessible of the many musicals scored and directed by Al Carmines, the Joe Papp of the Off-Off-Broadway scene. *Photofest*

I'm Getting My Act Together and Taking It on the Road (1978). The longest-running of all "feminist" musicals, this potent little show alternated between glib satire and heartfelt sobriety, all in the form of a rehearsal for a nightclub act. Author Gretchen Cryer (center) played the pop singer Heather who is weary of vapid ballads and failed relationships with men. Her backup singers are Margot Rose (left) and Betty Aberlin. *Photofest*

Little Shop of Horrors (1982). The plant Audrey II, having devoured four major characters in the musical, threatens to eat the audience next. The finale of this sci-fi spoof offers spectacle in the Off-Broadway mode: clever, campy, and oddly thrilling. The faces of (left to right) Mushnik (Hy Anzell), Orin (Franc Luz), Seymour (Lee Wilkof), and Audrey (Ellen Greene) can be seen in the plant singing the cautionary "Don't Feed the Plants." *Photofest*

Hello Again (1994). Michael John LaChiusa, who wrote the book, music, and lyrics for this merry and revealing musical about sex and love throughout the twentieth century, remains one of Off Broadway's most exciting artists even though he never finds a wide audience. In this scene, the Husband (Dennis Parlato) seduces The Young Thing (John Cameron Mitchell) in his cabin on the *Titanic*; both the voyage and the relationship will end badly. *Joan Marcus/ Marc Bryan-Brown/Photofest*

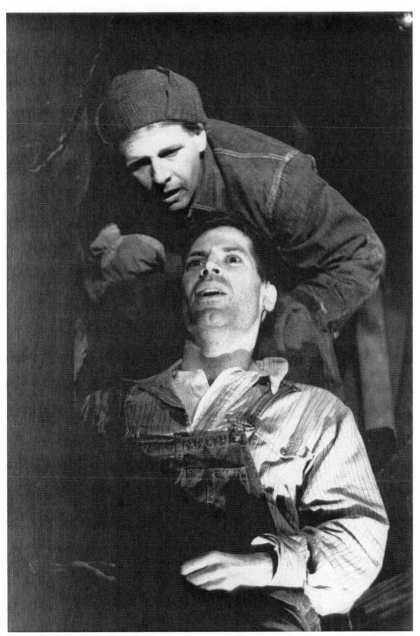

Floyd Collins (1996). Songwriter Adam Guettel made a notable debut with this challenging musical that defied many storytelling and musical conventions. The Kentucky farmer Floyd Collins (Christopher Innvar) is trapped in a cave far below the surface, yet the newspaper reporter Skeets Miller (Martin Moran) appears to be right next to him with words of encouragement. *Joan Marcus/Photofest*

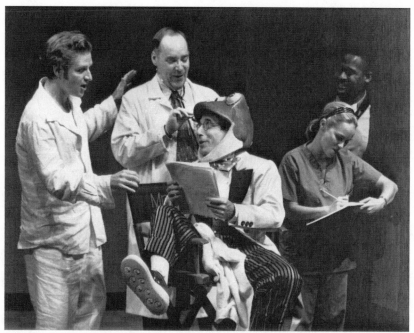

A New Brain (1998). Songwriter Gordon Schwinn (Malcolm Gets, far left) cannot escape from his boss and nemesis Mr. Bungee (Chip Zien, seated) even in the hospital where the children's TV show frog still haunts him in his imagination. Also crowding Gordon's psyche are (left to right) a doctor (John Jellison), a nurse (Kristin Chenoweth), and a minister (Keith Byron Kirk). *Joan Marcus/Photofest*

Chapter Five

━━━━━━━━━━━━━━━◯━━━━━━━━━━━━━━━

A New Face:
The 1980s

AMERICA GOT DOWN TO BUSINESS IN THE 1980s, and big business was the word in the corporate sector, particularly in New York City. Tourism flourished, much of the city seemed cleaner and safer, the Theatre District became people-friendly, and live theatre left the doldrums of the past decade behind. Broadway shows were costing more than ever to produce, and the ticket prices escalated in a way that was not proportional to these costs. Most theatres on the Street eliminated multipricing, and venues that had five or more differently priced seats were offering two: the entire house and the rear (or second) balcony. There was no such thing as "cheap" seats any more. Fortunately there were more discounts than in the past, in particular the TKTS booth in Times Square whose reduced-priced ticket sales accounted for a good portion of Broadway's box office. Musicals ran longer than anyone ever thought a show could run and earned more than Ziegfeld himself could have imagined. But the hit-flop ratio was steeper than ever, and it seemed that one could either make a killing on Broadway or end up in the poor house. The day of most shows being "modest" successes was gone.

On Broadway, the most obvious change came in the form of a British musical invasion. Andrew Lloyd Webber and Tim Rice's *Jesus Christ Superstar* had been the only profitable rock musical of the 1970s, and their *Evita* opened in 1979 and made it clear this was not a one-show phenomenon. The 1980s saw Webber return with such crowd pleasers as *Cats, Starlight Express,* and *Phantom of the Opera,* joined by other British imports such as *Chess, Me and My Girl,* and *Les Misérables.* This invasion was not welcomed by American artists, but the American public had no qualms about embracing such shows, and most of the British musicals were runaway hits. The list of

181

homegrown musicals to have long runs in the 1980s was also impressive: *Barnum*, *42nd Street*, *Woman of the Year*, *Nine*, *My One and Only*, *La Cage aux Folles*, *Big River*, *Jerome Robbins' Broadway*, *Grand Hotel*, and *City of Angels*. There were fewer African American musicals on Broadway, but *Sophisticated Ladies*, *Dreamgirls*, and *The Tap Dance Kid* were critical and box office successes. Again Stephen Sondheim came up with the decade's most intriguing musicals: *Sunday in the Park with George*, *Into the Woods*, and the short-lived *Merrily We Roll Along*. It seemed that even some of the Broadway flops were to be admired, as with *Baby*, *The Rink*, *Rags*, and *Is There Life After High School?* Even though costs and prices continued to rise, so did the number of productions and audience attendance. All in all, Broadway was recovering from the nadir of the 1970s.

Off Broadway there was little concern about the British invasion. These giant shows were identified by their dazzling spectacle, and the small musicals away from the Street were not competing with that kind of entertainment. Instead Off Broadway offered a wide variety of shows that included ethnic works, quirky contemporary musicals, nostalgic and satiric revues, campy musicals, pop operas, dark and atmospheric pieces, and silly, mindless entertainments (e.g., *Nunsense*) that were surprisingly popular. In no other previous decade had the offerings Off Broadway been as diverse as those of the 1980s. It was getting more and more difficult to describe just what an Off-Broadway musical was like. Yet it was clear that there were plenty of them to choose from, be it demanding nonprofit theatre faire or television-like commercial entertainment. Such a spread may have taken the edginess away from Off Broadway, but it still allowed exceptional musicals to be written, to be performed, and to find an audience.

SHAKESPEARE'S CABARET

[1 February 1980, Colonnades Theatre Lab, 40 performances] a musical revue by Lance Mulcahy. *Score:* Mulcahy (music), William Shakespeare (lyrics). *Cast:* Maureen Brennan, Patti Perkins, Mel Johnson Jr., Peter Van Norden, Roxanne Reese, Keith R. Rice, Alan Brasington.

The Bard of Avon continued to provide words for Off-Broadway musicals with this straightforward revue with the straightforward title. Not only lyrics from the plays but the sonnets and other nontheatre poetry were set to agreeable music composed by Lance Mulcahy, who also assembled the revue. One of the pleasant surprises was the variety of songs that the concept allowed. The expected love ballads and the bawdy drinking songs were plentiful, but there were also entrancing numbers taken from lesser-known plays such as *Pericles*, *The Winter's Tale*, and *All's Well That Ends Well*. The poem "The Passionate Pilgrim" provided lyrics for four songs, and even the blunt, nonromantic *King Lear* offered a haunting ditty called "Fathers That Wear Rags." Romeo and Juliet's first exchange "If I Profane" made for such a lovely duet that one could forget that this tale had already been musicalized as *West Side Story*. Mulcahy wisely avoided setting famous quotable quotes to music (thankfully, there was no song about "To be or not to be"), yet *Hamlet* provided a handful of songs, most memorably "How Should I Your True Love Know?" Even Shakespeare's mysterious epitaph ("Curse be he who moves these bones") was set to music, and it made a touching finale. Critics found the young cast versatile and engaging, and the five-week engagement at the Colonnades Lab Theatre was well attended. In 1986 Mulcahy offered a sequel, *Sweet Will*, which also boasted some impressive music and offered some new and unlikely songs from Shakespeare's plays and sonnets. The Off-Broadway revue failed to catch on and closed in a week.

THE HOUSEWIVES' CANTATA

[18 February 1980, Theatre Four, 24 performances] a musical play by William Holtzman. *Score:* Mira J. Spektor (music), June Siegel (lyrics). *Cast:* Sharon Talbot, Patti Karr, Forbesy Russell, William Perley.

A book musical with a promising concept, *The Housewives' Cantata* disappointed the critics and closed in three weeks, not allowing audiences time to discover it. It is questionable if the little musical would have run, but audiences deserved to hear a commendable score and enjoy a refreshing story. Sisters Flora (Patti Karr), Lily (Sharon Talbot), and Heather (Forbesy Russell) are first seen in 1962 as they deal with the sexual revolution, men, and their own sisterhood. Subsequent scenes show the trio in 1972 embroiled in precarious marriages and, finally, in 1980, as mature women discovering their own identity. As several critics pointed out, the plot was similar to the long-running Off-Broadway play *Vanities* (1976) about three female friends in three different points in their lives. But *The Housewives' Cantata* offered more substance than that earlier work, and the songs allowed the characters to develop beyond simple types. Passing fads and trends were satirized in

"Song of the Bourgeois Beatnik," domestic boredom was musicalized as the "Dirty Dish Rag," marital troubles were revealed in "Adultery Waltz" and "Divorce Lament," and housing situations were sung of in "Suburban Rose" and "Apartment Lament." Yet the most satisfying numbers were those in which the expansive spirit of the sisters was captured, as in "Little Women," "Song of the Open Road," and "A New Song."

The three actresses played off each other beautifully, as they did with William Perley who portrayed all the men in the piece. Legendary producer Cheryl Crawford copresented the smart little musical for a commercial run, but times had changed, and even the veteran show person could not turn *The Housewives' Cantata* into a hit. Luckily, the score was recorded but mostly by different performers than the ones Off Broadway.

BLUES IN THE NIGHT

[26 March 1980, Playhouse 46, 51 performances] a musical revue by Sheldon Epps. *Score:* various. *Cast:* Suzanne M. Henry, David Brunetti, Rise Collins, Gwen Sheperd.

For some critics, the most satisfying of the many musicals using old standards was this small but potent revue filled with wonderful blues numbers. There was no plot, yet it had characters and atmosphere and felt like a book musical at times. In a rundown Chicago saloon during the Depression, three women try to get through the night by singing of failed love and lost dreams to the accompaniment of a male pianist. There was no dialogue, but each song seemed to tell a part of a story that suggested all three women were pining over the same male heel. What sounds like one long dirge was actually very lively and included plenty of humor and bite along with all the blues. Expected standards such as "Am I Blue?," "Sophisticated Lady," "Lush Life," "Willow Weep for Me," "I Gotta Right to Sing the Blues," and the title song were joined by some delectable numbers that widened the spectrum, from "Stompin' at the Savoy" and "Baby Doll" to "Take It Right Back" and "Take Me for a Buggy Ride." Sheldon Epps put the revue together and directed expertly, and the racially mixed cast did more than justice to the marvelous material. (Even pianist David Burnetti sang solo and with the women.) *Blues in the Night* was the season closer for the nonprofit The Production Company and was only slated for five weeks. The run was extended for another week, then Epps pushed for a Broadway transfer. That did not happen until 1982, when the revue opened on Broadway with Broadway favorite Leslie Uggams joined by Debbie Shapiro and Jean Du Shon. Epps again directed, and the production met with favorable notices. After *Ain't Misbehavin'*, *Bubbling Brown Sugar*, *Sophisticated Ladies*, and other shows using African American song favorites, *Blues in the Night* was one revue too many, and the Broadway version lasted only fifty-three performances. A 1987 London version was well received (and recorded), and in 1988 Epps again brought the show to Off Broadway, this time with Leilani Jones, Carol Woods (who was in the London production), and Brenda Pressley in the cast. It ran only forty-five performances. *Blues in the Night* lives on in regional productions and continues to entertain with its timeless song standards.

THE HAGGADAH, A PASSOVER CANTATA

[31 March 1980, Public Theatre/LuEsther Hall, 64 performances] a musical play by Elizabeth Swados adapted from Elie Wiesel's *Moses: A Portrait of a Leader*, the Haggadah, and the Old Testament. *Score:* Swados (music and lyrics). *Cast:* David Schechter, Esther Levy, Keith David, Zvee Scooler, Martha Plimpton, Aisha Kahlil, Craig Chang.

The story of Exodus, from the birth of Moses to the deliverance from Egypt to the death of Moses, was given a reverent yet lively retelling in this musical piece that used a variety of theatrics such as masks and puppets in its presentation. Elizabeth Swados wrote the book, using several sources, and provided the songs, which ranged from hymns and chants to light rock and blues. The evening began with two children asking "The Four Questions" about the meaning of Passover, and the famous story was retold using narration and songs. "By the Waters of Babylon" and "God of Faithful" were among the inspirational numbers, the lamentations of the Hebrews were musicalized with such songs as "Slave Chant," "We Are All Dead Men," and "Why Hast Thou Done Evil to These People?" Familiar events were turned into musical scenes, as with "The Burning Bush," "Death of the Firstborn," "Crossing the Red Sea," and "The Golden Calf." The Ten Commandments themselves became a song as did "The Death of Moses." Critics and playgoers used to Swados's more outspoken and in-your-face approach found *The Haggadah* tamer and less exhilarating. Yet as a "Passover Cantata" it was very satisfying for many and pleased audiences for two months. Some critics pointed out the talented young girl Martha Plimpton, who was featured in several numbers, and complimented her on the sincerity of her performance. Plimpton was not in the company when Joe Papp brought the musical back to the Public Theatre a year later with an all-black cast. This time it ran seventy-two performances.

TINTYPES

[17 April 1980, Theatre of St. Peter's Church, 134 performances; John Golden Theatre, 93 performances] a musical revue by Mary Kyle, Mel Marvin, Gary Pearle. *Score:* various. *Cast:* Jerry Zaks, Lynne Thigpen, Carolyn Mignini, Trey Wilson, Mary Catherine Wright.

While it broke no records Off and later on Broadway, *Tintypes* would become a favorite with summer stock and regional theatres looking for an economical little musical that offered both nostalgia and insight. Using songs from the 1890s through World War I, the show was much more than a revue of old standards. Coauthor and director Gary Pearle staged the five-person musical like a collage of potent images about the American experience using some letters and speeches but mostly depending on the songs to recreate the era thematically. The wave of immigrants was represented by a thick-accented rendition of "The Yankee Doodle Boy," a saucy delivery of "I Don't Care," and an ethnically charged version of "A Hot Time in the Old Town Tonight." The new inventions and wonders of the period were celebrated in a section titled "Wheels" that included "Meet Me in St. Louis," "Daisy Bell (A Bicycle Built for Two)," and "Wabash Cannonball." The dark side of progress was explored in a section titled "The Factory" where songs of woe, like "Wayfaring Stranger" and "Sometimes I Feel Like a Motherless Child," were balanced by bittersweet numbers such as "I'll Take You Home Again, Kathleen" and a hopeful "America the Beautiful." Colorful personalities of the day, particularly Teddy Roosevelt and Anna Held, were represented by songs sung by and about them. The wide gap between rich and poor, black and white, was musicalized with "When It's All Goin' Out and Nothin' Comin' In," "Nobody," "Jonah Man," and other long-forgotten songs that were surprisingly still tuneful and potent. A salute to the vaudeville of the period included some of the show's most familiar numbers, from "You're a Grand Old Flag" to "Bill Bailey, Won't You Please Come Home?," and the evening ended with a lovely medley of "Toyland," "Bethena," and "Smiles," the effect being like a farewell to a dreamlike past. All five performers had plenty of chances to shine in the song-packed revue, and none disappointed, though Jerry Zaks and Lynn Thigpen received the greatest praise. The American National Theatre and Academy (ANTA) production had been developed in regional theatre and was welcomed Off Broadway with complimentary reviews and strong word of mouth. After running through the summer, the producers unwisely transferred *Tintypes* to Broadway, where it also received favorable if not enthusiastic notices. The same cast of talented unknowns was retained, as was the staging from the Off-Broadway production. But this was not a Broadway blockbuster, and the musical struggled to run three months. Not until it returned to regional theatre with dozens of productions each year did *Tintypes* become the hit it deserved to be.

REALLY ROSIE

[14 October 1980, Chelsea Theatre Center Upstairs Theatre, 274 performances] a musical comedy by Maurice Sendak. *Score:* Sendak (lyrics), Carole King (music). *Cast:* Tisha Campbell, April Lerman, Wade Raley, Jermaine Campbell, B. J. Barie, Matthew Kolmes, Joe LaBenz IV.

Two of Maurice Sendak's illustrated children's books, *The Sign on Rosie's Door* and *Nutshell Library*, provided the characters and verse for this delightful little musical about kids played by kids acting like adults. The precocious Rosie (Tisha Campbell) lives on Avenue P in Brooklyn and fantasizes that she is a movie director and star and that the neighborhood kids are her cast and crew. Their charade is often interrupted by whatever comes their way, from interfering adults to quirky tangents about stubborn "Pierre" (B. J. Barie) or the joys of "Chicken Soup with Rice." In addition to those familiar Sendak poems were the merry alphabet song "Alligators All Around" and the joyous counting ditty "One Was Johnny." Carole King provided the exuberant music for the poems, and the songs were first heard in an animated television special in 1975 in which King provided the voice of Rosie. *Really Rosie* was adapted for the stage and first produced at the Musical Theatre Lab in Washington, D.C., before the Chelsea Theatre Center presented it Off Broadway. Reviews were mixed, but audiences wanted to see the popular children's books on stage, so the playful production, directed and choreographed by Patricia Birch, ran nearly nine months. Sendak himself designed the sets and costumes, and fans of the books enjoyed the look of the show as well. Subsequent productions have been done regionally with adults cast as the

Nutshell kids, but the musical seems to make more sense performed by kids in school productions.

KA-BOOM!

[20 November 1980, Carter Theatre, 71 performances] a musical play by Bruce Kluger. *Score:* Joe Ercole (music), Kluger (lyrics). *Cast:* John Hall, Andrea Wright, Judith Bro, Ken Ward, Terry Barnes, Fannie Whitehead.

John-Michael Tebelak, who had conceived and directed *Godspell*, used similar theatrics in a musical play in which the characters enacted a parable. Although the tale was biblical in tone, the premise was less substantial. A nuclear war has destroyed most of the inhabitants of the planet, but the six survivors are not so downhearted that they don't have the energy to put on a show for themselves about new beginnings entitled *Creation, Part II*. Like *Godspell*, the songs were sometimes hymns, other times vaudeville, but none were very impressive. This second creation story offered new original parents in "The Ballad of Adam and Evie"; God was honored with numbers as diverse as "Oh, Lord"; "Believe Us/Receive Us"; "Gimme a G"; and "Bump and Grind for God"; and the future was embraced with "Let the Show Go On." The material was problematic, but Tebelak showed endless resources in the staging, helping *Ka-Boom!* seem better than it actually was. Critics were not thrilled, but enough playgoers were interested to let the musical run nearly nine weeks.

TRIXIE TRUE, TEEN DETECTIVE

[4 December 1980, Theatre de Lys, 86 performances] a musical comedy by Kelly Hamilton. *Score:* Hamilton (music and lyrics). *Cast:* Kathy Andrini, Gene Lindsay, Marilyn Sokol, Alison Bevan, Marianna Allen, Keith Rice, Kith Caldwell, Marianna Allen, Jay Lowman.

Nineteen-forties adolescent fiction, in particular the teenage detectives like the Hardy Boys and Nancy Drew, were gently satirized in this spirited musical that worked on more than one level. Writer Joe Sneed (Gene Lindsay) is the pride and joy of Snood Publishing because of his series of popular books featuring the teen detective Trixie True (Kathy Andrini). But Joe is tired of turning out new and contrived adventures for the spunky heroine, and as he embarks on a new book, he toys with the possibility of killing off the annoying Trixie. Scenes at the publishing office alternated with those featuring Trixie in her hometown of Cherry Hill, New Jersey, and songs were used for both stories. While Trixie had such optimistic numbers as "This Is Indeed My Lucky Day" and "Trixie's on the Case!," and the publisher Mrs. Snood (Marilyn Sokol) offered a more sardonic view with "Teen Fiction." Trixie and her boyfriend Dick Dickerson (Keith Rice) sang the cautious puppy love duet "You Haven't Got Time for Love" yet found time to fantasize about being "Mr. and Mrs. Dick Dickerson." The most enjoyable numbers were those pastiching the 1940s sound, such as "Rita from Argentina" and "A Katzenjammer Kinda Song." A very similar premise would be used years later on Broadway in another pulp fiction spoof *City of Angels* (1989), which was wittier than *Trixie True, Teen Detective*, but there was much to recommend in the earlier musical. Some appreciative notices helped the show run eleven weeks, followed by the occasional regional production.

ALICE IN CONCERT

[29 December 1980, Public Theatre/Anspacher Theatre, 32 performances] a musical comedy by Elizabeth Swados based on Lewis Carroll's *Alice in Wonderland* and *Through the Looking Glass*. *Score:* Swados (music and lyrics), Carroll (lyrics). *Cast:* Meryl Streep, Mark Linn-Baker, Amanda Plummer, Michael Jeter, Sheila Dabney, Deborah Rush, Richard Cox.

The ongoing collaboration between composer-author Elizabeth Swados and producer Joe Papp continued with *Alice in Concert*, perhaps the most enjoyable of her many entries presented at the Public Theatre. Swados gave Lewis Carroll's *Alice in Wonderland* and *Through the Looking Glass* a contemporary retelling that used modern anachronisms and current slang while remaining faithful to the original characters and events. Carroll's "Jabberwocky" and other verses were musicalized with a slightly rocking sound, and the score included many short numbers with original lyrics sung by and about the many characters in the two books. Although all this was familiar territory, *Alice in Concert* seemed fresh and different enough to garner enthusiastic reviews and full houses for its one-month engagement. Granted, much of the critical praise was for the production itself, directed by Papp and choreographed by Graciela Daniele. It also helped that it had an outstanding cast led by Meryl Streep who was a funny, quixotic Alice. Among her colleagues to go on to notable careers were Deborah Rush, Mark Linn-Baker, Michael Jeter, and Amanda Plummer. The show's title was misleading. It was not a concert but a fully staged production with suggested costumes and scenery. The piece had originally been presented in a concert version entitled *Wonderland in Concert*. The staged presentation was not a concert, and it is likely that subsequent productions of *Alice in Concert* have been limited because of the inaccurate title.

MARRY ME A LITTLE

[12 March 1981, Actors Playhouse, 96 performances] a musical play by Craig Lucas. *Score*: Stephen Sondheim (music and lyrics). *Cast*: Lucas, Suzanne Henry.

A treasure chest of unheard Stephen Sondheim songs was the reason this two-person musical was worth seeing, the thought being that second-rate Sondheim was better than first-rate anybody else. Yet these songs, mostly cut from Sondheim productions before opening, were not all second tier works. In fact, some numbers, such as the title song removed from *Company* and replaced by "Being Alive," went on to become oft-performed and oft-recorded Sondheim favorites because of this Off-Broadway showcase. ("Marry Me a Little," for example, was effectively added to the 1995 Broadway revival of *Company*.) "There Won't Be Trumpets," cut from *Anyone Can Whistle*, was similarly given new life, and the *Follies* reject "Can That Boy Foxtrot!" was so funny it was difficult to believe it nearly disappeared until heard in the Broadway revue *Side By Side by Sondheim* (1977). There were other numbers, such as "Bang!," "Silly People," and "Two Fairy Tales" from *A Little Night Music*, that were more interesting than satisfying and it was not hard to see why they were cut. A bonus for Sondheim fans was the inclusion of some songs from his first show *Saturday Night*, a musical that never got to rehearsals because the producer died. The infectious title song from that aborted project was used to set up the premise for *Marry Me a Little*. Two lonely New Yorkers (Craig Lucas and Suzanne Henry) each sit in their Manhattan apartments on a Saturday night and, in a stream of consciousness cycle of songs, express past and present regrets and joys. The two sometimes performed duets together, though they remained in separate spaces as their musical thoughts joined together. Director René Norman staged the piece in a single apartment, showcasing two strangers who were often physically close, yet they lived apart. It may have been a bit contrived, but as the musical progressed, a relationship was developed through the songs, for no dialogue was used in the show. *Marry Me a Little* was the idea of performer Lucas, who requested that Sondheim allow the unused songs to be performed as a mini book musical rather than a revue. The concept mostly worked, and how much better it was to hear these character-driven numbers sung in the context of a story, even if it was a slight story at that. *Marry Me a Little* played to Sondheim fans and others for three months, followed by productions by many regional theatres looking for an economical two-person musical. A York Theatre revival Off Off Broadway, featuring Liz Callaway and John Jillison, ran twenty performances in 1987. The original Off-Broadway recording allowed many musical theatre lovers far from New York City to discover a new set of Sondheim songs; not a bad legacy for the little show.

I Can't Keep Running in Place

[14 May 1981, Westside Arts Theatre, 208 performances] a musical play by Barbara Schottenfeld. *Score:* Schottenfeld (music and lyrics). *Cast:* Helen Gallagher, Marcia Rodd, Joy Franz, Bev Larson, Evalyn Baron, Jennie Ventriss, Mary Donnet.

A lot of feminine angst as well as womanly bonding was covered in this uneven but often fascinating musical that intrigued audiences for half a year. Psychiatrist Michelle (Marcia Rodd) runs a six-week assertiveness training session for six very troubled, very different women who meet weekly in a Soho loft. Since Michelle herself is greatly conflicted, there is no shortage of wounded personas to fill the time. Topics ranged from romantic relationships and penis envy to job hunting and facing a future living alone. The six participants represented a cross section of modern women, but that meant they sometimes fell into stereotypes. The songs allowed the characters to open up, both individually and as a group, and the characters often made more sense singing than in the dialogue. The nervous ladies first meet trying to convince each other "I'm Glad I'm Here," then grow in confidence so that by the last session they can wonder "Where Will I Be Next Wednesday?" Michelle teaches them "Don't Say Yes If You Want to Say No" and eventually becomes reconciled to the fact that "I'm on My Own." Two overweight characters argue that there is "More of Me to Love," but the most telling number was when Eileen (Joy Franz) breaks down and sings the title song. Barbara Schottenfeld wrote both book and score and, if nothing else, provided fertile material for the superb cast. In addition to Marcia Rodd, the other standout was Helen Gallagher as Beth, an older woman who contemplated her situation in the song "I Live Alone" and finally confronts the "Almosts, Maybes and Perhaps" in her life. *I Can't Keep Running in Place* may seem dated and a bit simplistic today, but performed in the furor of the 1980s women's movement, it struck a nerve in many audience members.

MARCH OF THE FALSETTOS

[20 May 1981, Playwrights Horizons, 268 performances] a musical play by William Finn. *Score:* Finn (music and lyrics). *Cast:* Michael Rupert, Alison Fraser, Stephen Bogardus, Chip Zien, James Kushner.

The promise that songwriter William Finn showed in *In Trousers* (1979) was more than fulfilled with the marvelous musical sequel *March of the Falsettos*. Director James Lapine guided Finn and helped him shape the messy, exciting material into a coherent musical without sacrificing any of Finn's quirky talent for high-flying theatrics and musical hijinks. The sung-through one-act show was both exhilarating and disarmingly moving without ever becoming quite conventional. The neurotic New Yorker Marvin (Michael Rupert) leaves his wife Trina (Alison Fraser) and teenage son Jason (James Kushner) to be with his male lover Whizzer (Stephen Bogardus). This drives Trina to her ex-husband's psychiatrist Mendel (Chip Zien), and the two fall in love and marry. When Whizzer finds Marvin as impossible to live with as Trina did, he leaves Marvin who only finds solace by watching his son begin to put together his own ideas about happiness.

Characters and ideas that were cleverly kicked around in *In Trousers* were more grounded in *March of the Falsettos*, yet there was still a frantic, sometimes surreal, tone to the whole show, most brazenly seen in the oddball title song sung by the four males in falsetto voices. The hilarious "Four Jews in a Room Bitching" was perhaps the most rapid, furious song that ever opened an American musical; yet the closing number "Father to Son" was one of the quietest. Some scenes took the form of mini-operas filled with exaggerated emotions, other songs were combative duets, and the five-member cast often found itself commenting on the private thoughts of a particular character. The musical roller coaster of a show did stop for some telling moments. "Trina's Song" was a sarcastic but painful solo for a woman who is weary of living for the men in her life, Jason contemplated his future sexual preference in "My Father's a Homo," and Whizzer faced his own superficiality in "The Games I Play." From start to finish, it was the most exciting new score to hit Off Broadway since *Hair*. The production itself was as highly praised as the script/score with outstanding performances by all five players. (Some would return to the same characters in subsequent productions of *March of the Falsettos* and its sequel *Falsettoland*.) Lapine's staging was simple yet ingenious, letting the action flow from place to place without the blinking of an eye or the dropping of a note. The show was a whirlwind of a musical, and often Lapine's direction was as chaotic, but it never lost focus. Like *In Trousers*, *March of the Falsettos* was workshopped Off Off Broadway at Playwrights Horizons before the same company offered an extended run Off Broadway. Propitious reviews and a growing interest in Finn allowed the musical to run nearly nine months, followed by many regional productions.

March of the Falsettos established Finn as a major figure in American musical theatre. Not only were his music and lyrics invigorating and fresh, but his subject matter was also innovative. Musicals about homosexuals had been labeled gay musicals and limited themselves to a special worldview. In Finn's works, the gay characters were just a given circumstance. His musicals were not about being gay but about people who happened to be homosexual. Marvin is a crazed, self-centered, yet likable man whose need for attention is insatiable. His sexual identity is somewhat confused because sex is just one small part of his driven personality. The other characters are defined by how they react to this firecracker of a man. The plotting is determined by interpersonal relationships, not outside forces, so everyone is responsible for their fate in *March of the Falsettos*. This will change later when the AIDS epidemic becomes a deadly outside force in *Falsettoland*. Finn's musicals are so character-driven that all the issues, from sex to religion to love to death, become personal. Not until you consider how rarely this occurs in American musicals does one realize that Finn is as unique as he is dazzling.

EL BRAVO

[16 June 1981, Entermedia Theatre, 48 performances] a musical play by José Fernandez and Thom Schiera based on a story by Fernandez and

Kenneth Waissman. *Score:* John Clifton (music and lyrics). *Cast:* Aurelio
Padron, Ray De Mattis, Michael Jeter, Yamil Borges, Keith Jochim, Lenka
Peterson, Dennis Daniels.

A true Hispanic musical hit was decades away, but some early efforts revealed the possibilities of a flavorful show utilizing the Spanish culture in
America. Composer-lyricist John Clifton, who had written the glorious score
for *Man with a Load of Mischief*, was not Hispanic, but his music served as
a theatrical version of the real thing in the musical fable *El Bravo*. The book
by José Fernandez and Thom Schiera placed the legend of Robin Hood in
one of New York City's El Bario neighborhoods with the put-upon resident
Pepe DeMarco (Aurelio Patron) taking on the guise of El Bravo and stealing
from the corrupt wealthy to give to his poor neighbors. Friar Tuck became
Father Tucker (Ray De Mattis), Maid Marion was turned into Chiquita
Bonita (Yamil Borges) but everyone called her Mariana, and the Sheriff of
Nottingham was the grasping Cruikshank (Michael Jeter). There were few
surprises in the story, but the transition to modern times offered some playful opportunities for sassy dialogue peppered with Spanish phrases. Since
the score was not recorded, one can only rely on the reviews, which seemed
as indifferent to the songs as they were to *El Bravo* in general. Patricia Birch
directed and choreographed the somewhat elaborate production, which was
a commercial venture, so it lost a bundle when it closed in six weeks. With
The Capeman and *In the Heights* far in the future, Hispanic musical theatre
would be limited to revivals of *West Side Story* and *El Grande de Coca-Cola*
for some time yet.

PUMP BOYS AND DINETTES

[1 October 1981, Colonnades Theatre, 112 performances; Princess Theatre, 573 performances] a musical revue by Jim Wann. *Score:* Wann, the
cast (music and lyrics). *Cast:* Wann, Debra Monk, Mark Hardwick, Cass
Morgan, John Schimmel, John Foley.

Country-pop music filled this clever little revue that pleased audiences who
liked the genre and also those who disliked such tunes. This was possible
because the musical spoofed rural life even as it held a kind of affection

for it. A gas station on Highway 57 sits across the road from a diner where sisters Prudie (Debra Monk) and Rhetta Cupp (Cass Morgan) are the flirty waitresses. Four of the pump boys, the type proud of their "Farmer Tans," join the Cupp sisters in the diner for an improvised concert just for their own amusement, playing musical instruments as well as singing with the waitresses. There was no plot, and topics close to the characters were turned into song. The Cupp sisters sang about tips with a lot of sexy innuendo, one gas jockey recalled "The Night Dolly Parton Was Almost Mine," and the men encouraged the girls to put on their "Drinkin' Shoes" and go out and party. "Serve Yourself" was the bitter lament about an unfaithful sweetheart using gas station lingo to express romantic feelings, "Taking It Slow" was a rapid ditty in praise of idleness, and "Be Good or Be Gone" was a torch number with Grand Ole Opry grit. Sometimes the spoofing was so slight the audience didn't know whether to laugh or to take it all seriously, as during the maudlin tribute to motherhood called "Mawaw" and the teary "Sisters," and two songs about the glory of fishing may be two too many for any musical. The cast, who contributed to the score that Jim Wann wrote, was outstanding, most of them accomplished musicians as well as performers. Reviewers highly recommended the unpretentious little show, and after running three and a half months Off Broadway, the producers moved it to the intimate Princess Theatre on Broadway where it stayed for a year and a half. *Pump Boys and Dinettes* also enjoyed a productive life in regional and summer theatre, but often the satire was lost in these productions far from New York, and audiences just enjoyed the musical as a straightforward country music show. Some of the original writer-performers of *Pump Boys and Dinettes* would take their spoofing in another direction in the later musical *Oil City Symphony*.

Cotton Patch Gospel

[21 October 1981, Lamb's Theatre, 193 performances] a musical fable by Tom Key, Russell Treyz based on Clarence Jordan's *The Cotton Patch Version of Matthew and John. Score:* Harry Chapin (music and lyrics). *Cast:* Key, Scott Ainslie, Pete Corum, Jim Lauderdale, Michael Mark.

Just before his premature death in July 1981, songwriter-humanitarian Harry Chapin wrote the folk songs for this musical version of Clarence Jordan's books in which some New Testament stories were set in rural Georgia. The musical concentrated on St. Matthew's gospel, the same source material for

Godspell, yet the two shows were very different. *Cotton Patch Gospel* had a gentle humor, a folksy language, and an easygoing tone, all of which were captured in Chapin's songs. Tom Key played the narrator Matthew and many other characters while he was given vocal and instrumental support by four folk singers-musicians. "Something Is Brewing in Gainesville" set the stage for the birth of Jesus with its narrative ballad style. Later the disciples of the Lord proclaim "We're Going to Atlanta" as they follow him to a cotton patch in Jerusalem where the tragic events are viewed with hop in "One More Tomorrow" and "Jubilation." The songs rarely turned into theatre or character numbers but instead commented on the action which was left to the audience's imagination. The cast sang "I Wonder" at the end of the narrative, concluding the show like a sermon disguised as a folk concert. Notices were complimentary, and Chapin admirers helped keep *Cotton Patch Gospel* on the boards for six months. The video version released in 1988 was not a recreation of the stage work but featured Key and was close in spirit to the Off-Broadway production.

TOMFOOLERY

[14 December 1981, Top of the Gate, 120 performances] a musical revue by Cameron Mackintosh, Robin Ray. *Score*: Tom Lehrer (music and lyrics). *Cast*: Joy Franz, MacIntyre Dixon, Donald Corren, Jonathan Hadary.

Humorist Tom Lehrer had been very popular in the 1960s with his comedy albums in which he sang original songs satirizing the topical events of the day. The compilation of his work in an Off-Broadway revue was problematic, for not only was Lehrer no longer a familiar name but some of his targets were no longer familiar. British producer Cameron Mackintosh was a fan of Lehrer and coauthored *Tomfoolery*, which he presented in London. He also produced the Off-Broadway version in which four diverse and talented performers did justice to the satiric material and appealed to older audiences who remembered Lehrer and his songs. Headlines from the 1950s provided musical spoofs of the Cold War and the threat of nuclear destruction with "So Long Mom (I'm Off to Drop the Bomb)" and "We Will All Go Together," while the nation's involvement in foreign wars in Korea and Vietnam was lampooned with "Send the Marines." In the 1960s the Second Vatican Council prompted the hilarious "Vatican Rag," foreign inventors in America were mockingly saluted with "Wernher von Braun," and the Domino Theory about the spread of Communism was ribbed with "Who's Next?" Other songs were less time-centered, such as the wicked view of racism "I Wanna to Go Back to Dixie" and the numbers finding humor in such taboo subjects as incest ("Oedipus Rex") and necrophilia ("I Hold Your Hand in Mine"). Both audiences and critics were delighted to see how well some of Lehrer's satire still held up. All the same, *Tomfoolery* was a tough sell in the 1980s and the commercial venture closed inside of four months, followed by some regional productions. It is fair to say that the revue must have created some new fans of Tom Lehrer and perhaps his old albums sold a little better because of the show. More likely, Lehrer fans remained fans, and the passage of time had made the cultist humorist a fond memory from a past era.

FORBIDDEN BROADWAY

[4 May 1982, Palsson's Supper Club, 2,332 performances] a musical revue by Gerard Alessandrini. *Score:* Alessandrini (lyrics), various (music). *Cast:* Alessandrini, Fred Barton, Bill Carmichael, Nora Mae Lyng, Chloé Webb.

The most successful musical series in the history of Off Broadway, *Forbidden Broadway* is not so much a long-run but a series of editions of the same premise: spoofing Broadway shows, songwriters, and stars by rewriting the lyrics to familiar songs and performing them in the distinct style of stage celebrities. The clever lyricist and conceiver of the revue is Gerald Alessandrini who put together a small-scale *Forbidden Broadway* Off Off Broadway in 1981 with Nora Mae Lyng and himself as the performers. The next year he reopened an expanded version of the revue at Palsson's Supper Club, which was technically Off Off Broadway as well. As the show caught on with the theatre community (even stars enjoyed coming to see themselves parodied) and then the public, it ran and ran, moving from theatre to theatre over the years, never officially closing but taking a hiatus while new material and casts were assembled. Later in its history, the show took on subtitles to assure audiences that this was indeed a new production, though often favorite numbers from past editions were repeated. Under such silly titles as *Forbidden Broadway Strikes Back, Forbidden Broadway in Rehab,* and *Forbidden Broadway: Rude Awakening*, the revue continues on; new Broadway shows and revivals continue to supply fodder for new editions.

Alessandrini writes and directs each new edition, which usually uses the original music from the stage musicals but is reset with satirical lyrics. The shows mock all of the Broadway entries democratically, and most songwriters are pleased to allow their music to be used in the revues. When Andrew Lloyd Webber refused permission to use his music, Alessandrini composed a very Webber-like melody for his *Phantom of the Opera* spoof. The cast members are usually unknowns but with a talent for impersonation or mimicry and sometimes when the material is weak the performances make the show still worthwhile. Some critics and playgoers find the *Forbidden Broadway* humor sophomoric, and sometimes a song lampoon runs out of ideas and keeps harping on the same joke. But usually the revues are unpretentious fun, and the series continues to have a considerable following. A parallel program called *Forbidden Hollywood* was attempted in 1995, but it failed to catch on.

HERRINGBONE

[30 June 1982, Playwrights Horizons, 46 performances] a play with songs by Tom Cone. *Score:* Skip Kennon (music), Ellen Fitzhugh (lyrics). *Cast:* David Rounds, Kennon.

With only a handful of songs, the solo play *Herringbone* barely qualified as a musical. Yet as a fascinating theatre piece and a showcase for a brilliant performer, the show was more than satisfying for those willing to accept its bewildering premise and the exceptional talent of character actor David Rounds. In a small Alabama town during the Depression, the Nookin family is hoping for an inheritance from a deceased uncle who had money. Instead, the dead man only offers advice and a magical wish that the eight-year-old George Nookin will succeed in life. Suddenly George is possessed by the ghost of an aged vaudeville song-and-dance man named Lou, and the young George is proclaimed a child prodigy performer. His parents buy him a new herringbone suit and whisk him off to Hollywood where he is exploited by both the studios and his family. It was an odd, disturbing tale, made all the more unusual by having Rounds play all the characters, from young George to his parents to old Lou. (He was joined on stage only by a pianist named Thumbs DuBlois, played by the show's composer Skip Kennon.) Because Rounds was magnificent and the songs were expert pastiches of vaudeville numbers from the 1920s and 1930s, *Herringbone* felt like a full-fledged musical. Rounds had appeared in an earlier production in Chicago, and in New York the limited engagement at Playwrights Horizons was extended. Reviews for the piece were mixed, but everyone adulated Rounds, and audiences wanted to see his remarkable performance. Rounds might have continued playing *Herringbone* for years in theatres across the country, but his death from AIDS in 1983 cut short the career of the actor and the musical. Eventually regional theatres attempted the difficult little piece and found success when an extraordinary actor could be found to play it. B. D. Wong, for example, triumphed in the role at the McCarter Theatre in Princeton.

LITTLE SHOP OF HORRORS

[27 July 1982, Orpheum Theatre, 2,209 performances], a musical satire by Howard Ashman based on the 1960 film. *Score:* Ashman (lyrics), Alan Menken (music). *Cast:* Lee Wilkof, Ellen Greene, Hy Anzell, Franc Luc, Leilani Jones, Jennifer Leigh Warren, Sheila Kay Davis, Ron Taylor.

A science fiction spoof that was offbeat enough to be different and yet engaging enough to be appealing to a wide audience, *Little Shop of Horrors* created a new genre of Off-Broadway musical: the camp pulp musical. Shows had satirized movies and cheap fiction before, but never had a musical walked the line between satire and homage as this one did. The 1960 cult film on which the show is closely based was a low-budget feature with cheesy effects, amateurish acting, and an illogical but interesting premise. Howard Ashman, who wrote the stage adaptation as well as the lyrics, improved the movie plot, fleshed out the characters, and gave the dialogue a stilted yet sincere style that was refreshing. The film was enjoyable because it was bad; the stage version was delightful because it was well done. Alan Menken's early 1960s pastiche music established the time period, and the songs enhanced the cockeyed story in a way that made *Little Shop of Horrors* a tightly integrated musical treat.

The nerdy botanist Seymour Krelbourn (Lee Wilkof), who works in the floundering flower shop of Mr. Mushnik (Hy Anzell) and silently loves the sensual salesgirl Audrey (Ellen Greene), comes upon a mysterious plant that brings him fame and fortune as long as he feeds it human blood. As the plant continues to grow, its demands do too until Seymour is feeding it body parts from Audrey's sadistic dentist boyfriend Orin (Franc Luc). Eventually the plant devours Seymour, Audrey, and everyone on planet Earth, even threatening the audience. Such a cartoonish plot could only sustain itself for so long, but the characters were developed to the point that one was caught up in the people, something that rarely happens in science fiction. Seymour is an awkward klutz yet, like Audrey, we like him and find ourselves willing to accept him. Audrey is not just a blonde birdbrain but a weak-willed child who has vivid hopes for the future despite her dreary and abusive present. The Jewish caricature Mr. Mushnik finds a spark of self-worth when he grows to think of Seymour as his son, and even the one-joke sadomasochist Orin sees his abnormal behavior as a healthy zest for life. The three Urchins (Leilani Jones, Jennifer Leigh Warren, and Sheila Kay Davis) act as a Motown-flavored Greek chorus who not only comment on the action but often take the viewpoint of a specific character for whom they become backup singers. One only has to see how little of all this cohesiveness is in the original B movie to appreciate Ashman's brilliant libretto.

Yet any musical stands on its score, and the songs for *Little Shop of Horrors* are, each and every one of them, a marvel. "Skid Row (Downtown)" sets the scene by being both complaining and uplifting. Audrey's heartbreakingly funny solo "Somewhere That's Green" is one of the American theatre's finest "I am" songs. "Mushnik and Son" is a dandy vaudeville turn, the kind of number Mushnik would fondly remember, while the numbers by the three Urchins have the sound and attitude of the "girl group" songs of the early 1960s. The voice of the Plant (Ron Taylor) provides the sinister, sci-fi tone of the genre, yet its songs, such as "Feed Me" and "Suppertime," are so rhythmically intoxicating that the Plant sometimes comes across like a revival preacher. Orin's proud solo "Dentist!" is a comic treasure with an Elvis-like flair. Seymour gets to sing the most telling numbers, from his pathetic plea "Grow for Me" to his resolve in "Now (It's Just the Gas)." The score climaxes with the oddball but very affecting love duet "Suddenly Seymour," which soars in such a way that the cartoon facade of the characters falls away. By the time the cast is singing the propulsive finale "Don't Feed the Plants," the audience has come full circle and feel like it has become part of the circus itself. Ashman directed the small but ingenious production which used cleverness rather than special effects to convey the science fiction aspect of the piece. The plant was portrayed at various stages by a series of puppets; not quite high tech but neither were they the cheap effects in the film. Ellen Greene became a star of sorts, at least when it came to playing Audrey. She reprised the role in the London production and in the film version.

Little Shop of Horrors was first performed as a showcase Off Off Broadway at the WPA Theatre. A group of notable Broadway producers (including Cameron Mackintosh and the Shuberts) were shrewd enough to give it a commercial run Off Broadway. Reviews were propitious, and *Little Shop of Horrors* soon developed a following, allowing it to run nearly six years, followed by hundreds of productions in regional theatre, summer stock, and schools. The musical continues to be a favorite across the country. The London production ran 813 performances, and the 1986 movie version, with Rick Moranis as Seymour, was fairly faithful to the Off-Broadway mounting and was also successful. A 2003 Broadway revival directed by Jerry Zaks may not have been as vivid as the original, but it boasted a fine cast, headed by Hunter Foster and Kerry Butler as Seymour and Audrey, and a high-tech plant that was more spectacular than the Off-Broadway version. Despite lackluster notices, the production was popular enough to run 372 performances.

If *Little Shop of Horrors* originated today Off Broadway, producers would rush it to Broadway where more money and greater notoriety awaited. But the 1982 production stayed Off Broadway where it really belonged and found fame in its own way. It also opened the door for many later campy sci-fi–pulp fiction musicals, few of which matched *Little Shop of Horrors* in quality. *Bat Boy*, *The Evil Dead*, and *The Toxic Avenger* are just a few of the Off-Broadway shows that clearly followed the path carved out by the Ashman-Menken original.

CHARLOTTE SWEET

[12 August 1982, Westside Arts Center, 102 performances] a musical comedy by Michael Colby. *Score:* Colby (lyrics), Gerald Jay Markoe (music). *Cast:* Mara Beckerman, Christopher Seppe, Alan Brasington, Merle Louise, Sandra Wheeler, Polly Pen, Nicholas Wyman, Michael McCormick.

The British music hall and French Grand Guignol melodrama, two genres not particularly favored by Americans, were both spoofed in this sung-through musical that was unique if not always satisfying. In Victorian England, the innocent coloratura Charlotte Sweet (Mara Beckerman) is taken from her Liverpool sweetheart Ludlow Ladd Grimble (Christopher Seppe) and sold into the Circus of Voices, a touring music hall troupe full of eccentric-voiced singers and run by the villainous couple Barnaby (Alan Brasington) and Katinka Bugaboo (Sandra Wheeler). When Charlotte's high singing voice is destroyed with overuse, Barnaby pumps her full of helium before each performance so she can still hit the high notes. Ludlow finally catches up with the troupe, gets past the Bugaloos' defenses by disguising himself as Queen Victoria, several characters get shot only to find they are not hurt, and the contrived plot comes to a contrived happy end. The musical was exaggerated nonsense and very lively, though the satire was perhaps too subtle because little of the show was as enjoyable as it was interesting. The score was expert with accurately pastiched turn-of-the-century songs, from sing-along ditties to sentimental ballads. Charlotte's arias "A-Weaving" and "Lonely Canary" were the most pleasing of the many musical numbers. The lyrics were a collection of rhymed couplets and triplets and whatever-lets and often were dazzling, but the craftsmanship outshone the sense of fun. The vocal demands of the cast were considerable, with performers who had to sing high, low, fast, with echoes, and (in one schizophrenic character) in solo duets. Again, the resulting performances were more impressive than delightful, and *Charlotte Sweet* became a show that many admired more than they liked. Still, enough playgoers were intrigued to let the musical run thirteen weeks, followed by some regional productions when the right cast could be found.

UPSTAIRS AT O'NEALS'

[29 October 1982, O'Neals' Theatre, 308 performances] a cabaret revue by Martin Charnin. *Score:* various. *Cast:* Bebe Neuwirth, Sarah Weeks, Douglas Bernstein, Richard Ryder, Randall Edwards, Michon Peacock.

A smart little cabaret show without an agenda, *Upstairs at O'Neals'* recalled the intimate revues of the 1950s and early 1960s. There was no theme or premise that ran through the songs and sketches (though several numbers were about the New York theatre world), and the topics ranged from current fashion models to fairy tales. Yet this grab bag of a show was highly appealing on several levels. The songs, by a variety of songwriters, were sometimes parodies with vaguely familiar tunes, other times were wholly original numbers with a fresh outlook on a subject. The revue was also refreshing in the way it did not take itself very seriously, sometimes poking fun at the revue format itself, as in the droll number "Stools" and in the vamping title song. Perhaps the best of the parody numbers was "Soap Operetta," which captured the daytime serial language even as it broke into accurate Gilbert and Sullivan pastiches. "Talkin' Morosco Blues" was a folk protest song that found the hypocrisy in its own principles, and there was a touch of Yiddish temperament in "Momma's Turn" in which the mothers of the leading critics of the day lamented the embarrassing jobs their sons held. But *Upstairs at O'Neals'* was just as enjoyable in its quieter songs that did not rely on pastiche, such as the beguiling "I Furnished My One Room Apartment" and the painfully nostalgic "Boy, Do We Need It Now." There were some misfires, such as an unfunny number about fashion designer food titled "Signed, Peeled, Delivered" and the Irish folk song spoof "The Soldier and the Washerworker," which bent over backward not to be gender specific. Yet on the whole the show bounced along happily, thanks in no small part to the funny and vocally pleasing cast members. Only Bebe Neuwirth would go on to substantial popularity, but all six performers were loaded with talent and shone individually and as an ensemble. Critical reaction to the unpretentious musical was highly favorable, and the cabaret revue found an audience for ten months.

SNOOPY

[20 December 1982, Lamb's Theatre, 152 performances] a musical by Warren Lockhart, Arthur Whitelaw, Michael L. Grace based on Charles Schulz's comic strip *Peanuts*. *Score:* Larry Grossman (music), Hal Hackady (lyric). *Cast:* David Garrison, Terry Kirwin, Kay Cole, Stephen Fenning, Vicki Lewis, Cathy Cahn, Deborah Graham.

Neither a sequel nor a whole new animal, *Snoopy* often seemed like an unnecessary continuation of the *Peanuts* saga, but much of it was so entertaining that all was forgiven. Although the beagle Snoopy (David Garrison) was featured, much of the musical dealt with the familiar humans Charlie (Terry Kirwin), Lucy (Kay Cole), and Linus (Stephen Fenning) from *You're a Good Man, Charlie Brown*. Added were the straight-talking Peppermint Patty (Vicki Lewis), Charlie's sister Sally (Deborah Brown), and the silent bird Woodstock (Cathy Cahn). Although the new musical avoided repeating such classic *Peanuts* episodes as Lucy as a psychiatrist and Charlie trying to fly a kite, some scenes and musical numbers were obviously patterned after the earlier show, such as the brazen "The Big Bow-Wow," trying to stop the show like "Suppertime" did, and an ensemble number at school called "Edgar Allen Poe" that reminded one of the much better "Book Report." Several hands contributed to the episodic libretto, and the score was written by accomplished tunesmiths Larry Grossman and Hal Hackady, two Broadway songwriters who had provided good songs for bad musicals such as *Minnie's Boys* (1970), *Goodtime Charley* (1975), and *A Doll's Life* (1982). Grossman's music for *Snoopy* was melodic and fun, utilizing ragtime in "Dime a Dozen," spirited marching music for "Don't Be Anything Less Than Everything You Can Be," and vaudeville "Mammy" song style for the sportive "Mother's Day." "I Know Now" captured the child's point of view beautifully, there was pathos and humor in the engaging lullaby "Poor Sweet Baby," and "Clouds" was a delightful ensemble number in which the characters described what the cloud formations looked like in their imagination. The show ended with "Just One Person," a tender ballad meant to be inspiring but came off rather preachy and a poor substitute for the original's "Happiness." *Snoopy* had premiered in San Francisco in 1975 and was recorded. When it arrived on Off Broadway, the musical met with mixed notices but many compliments for the cast. Audiences were interested enough to let the show run nineteen weeks, followed by a London version the next year and some regional productions. But *Snoopy* never caught on like *You're a Good Man, Charlie Brown*, and revivals of the earlier work continued on as *Snoopy* seemed to fade away.

TAKING MY TURN

[9 June 1983, Entermedia Theatre, 345 performances] a musical play by Robert H. Livingston. *Score:* Gary William Friedman (music), Will Holt (lyrics). *Cast:* Margaret Whiting, Marni Nixon, Tiger Haynes, Sheila Smith, Cissy Houston, Mace Barrett, Victor Griffin, Ted Thurston.

Songwriters Gary William Friedman and Will Holt joined up with their *The Me Nobody Knows* librettist Robert H. Livingston and came up with another thought-provoking and lyrical musical which found an audience for nearly a year. Their earlier show was about urban kids; *Taking My Turn* was about senior citizens. Yet both had the same tone of voice: sincere, frank, funny, and touching. Both musicals were also inspired by the writings and comments of actual people. Although the characters had names, *Taking My Turn* was barely a book musical. It followed an octet of "people in their prime" over the course of a year, and a series of songs and monologues covered different subjects, from retirement and health complaints to sex and death. The title song was the ensemble's boastful plea to be heard and not counted out of society, the optimistic "Pick More Daisies" was actually youthful in temperament, and the aches and pains of old age were ribbed in "Fine for the Shape I'm In." Two of the most heartfelt numbers recalled the past: one woman remembered concerts in the park in "Vivaldi," while another was still haunted by the memory of her deceased son in "In April." As good as the material was, it was the cast that shone brightest and was responsible for the season-long run. Popular singers Margaret Whiting and

Marni Nixon were joined by lesser known but equally talented character actors of a certain age. Unlike the bland seniors in *My Old Friends* or the razzle-dazzle ones in the Broadway flop *70, Girls, 70*, these were characters you could identify with and believe even as they entertained you. The original cast recreated their performances the next year for a videotaping of the musical, and some regional theatres have revived *Taking My Turn*, though it is not an easy show to cast.

PREPPIES

[18 August 1983, Promenade Theatre, 52 performances] a musical comedy by David Taylor, Carlos Davis. *Score:* Gary Portnoy, Judy Hart Angelo (music and lyrics). *Cast:* Beth Fowler, Bob Walton, Kathleen Rowe McAllen, Dennis Bailey, David Sabin, Michael Ingram, Susan Dow, John Scherer.

Making fun of people with too much money and not enough brains has been a theatrical staple in New York City since the comedy of manners of the mid-1800s. Lampooning rich prep-school kids goes back almost as far. More recent was the labeling of such well-off adolescents as "preppies," and they were popping up quite frequently in films and television. A musical satire about such types seemed natural, but *Preppies* was far from inspired and only worked as the broadest and most simple-minded of farces. This is a world where the young heroes are named Parker Richardson Endicott IV (Bob Walton) and Angelica Livermore Atwater (Kathleen Rowe McAllen) but are called Cotty and Muffy by their class. Two shrewd outsiders, Marie (Beth Fowler) and Joe Pantry (Michael Ingram), discover that a huge fortune, with land that includes Central Park and most of Wyoming, is just waiting for someone to inherit it. They set out to find the ideal preppie to pose as the lucky heir, leading them into a lifestyle in which kids are primed for kindergarten interviews, getting into the right country club and Ivy League school is paramount, and love is allowed only with the right vapid heiress. The characters were more cartoonish than satirical, and the songs were lightweight in melody and ideas. The production, which had originated at the Goodspeed Opera House in Connecticut, boasted a quality cast and was slickly directed and choreographed by Tony Tanner, but critics found the material labored, and playgoers were not as interested in preppies as the producers had hoped.

TALLULAH

[30 October 1983, West Side Arts Center/Cheryl Crawford Theatre, 42 performances] a musical play by Tony Lang. *Score:* Arthur Siegel (music), Mae Richard (lyrics). *Cast:* Helen Gallagher, Russell Nype, Joel Craig.

Helen Gallagher never became a major Broadway star because her vehicles failed to run, but she was never less than stellar in her many stage performances. *Tallulah* was another Gallagher vehicle not worth seeing except for its leading lady who received glowing notices but still couldn't keep this show open for six weeks. The musical's subject matter was not without possibilities. Tallulah Bankhead was a unique, bizarre, fascinating star of stage, screen, radio, and television. A Southern debutante, daughter of a powerful senator (Russell Nype), Bankhead had a checkered career in the States and in Europe with plenty of fiascos and comebacks. The musical *Tallulah* attempted to tell her story in the format of a revue with a lot of gay innuendo and raised eyebrows passing as wit. One of the most frequently imitated of all stars, the gravel-voiced Bankhead was a magnet for camp. Opening *Tallulah* with a chorus of boys singing "Darling" to and with Gallagher was campy without being particularly clever. What followed was a dreary parade of anecdotes and easily forgettable songs that even Gallagher couldn't spin into gold. Also wasted was the wonderful character actor Russell Nype who, in his last New York stage appearance, vainly tried to turn Senator Bankhead into something beyond a one-joke caricature. Long after *Tallulah* closed, Tovah Feldshuh had a bit more success playing Bankhead in the nonmusicals *Tallulah's Party* (1998) and *Tallulah Hallelujah!* (2001).

SUNSET

[7 November 1983, Village Gate Theatre, 1 performance] a musical play by Gary William Friedman (music), Will Holt (lyrics). *Cast:* Tammy Grimes, Ronee Blakley, Walt Hunter, Kim Milford.

Not quite a revival and not an original either, *Sunset* was a rewritten, reimagined version of the 1978 Broadway flop *Platinum*, which was a star vehicle for Alexis Smith. The 1940s singing star Lila is passé by the 1970s, so she goes into a recording studio to try to cut a record in the contemporary style. The rock star Dan Danger is also on the skids and, needing to make a splash at his next concert, he asks Lila if he can borrow one of her glitzy beaded dresses to wear on a television special and stimulate some talk. Lila and Dan hit it off, he promises to write her a hit song, and it looks like romance for the cross-generational relationship, the two even blending the nostalgic 1940s sound and the rock beat in their songs. What was meant to be an involving character study was so artificial that even the sometimes-commendable score by Gary William Friedman and Will Holt proved to be ineffective. But Friedman and Holt, who had scored *The Me Nobody Knows* and *Taking My Turn*, were still able to write some agreeable numbers in the old style, such as "Nothing But," and in the rock idiom, as with "Rock Is My Way of Life." Lila sang some juicy solos with "Destiny" and "Moments," and there was even an early rap number called "Dan's Rap." *Sunset* was originally produced in Buffalo with Smith glowing as Lila and Tommy Tune directing with a flourish. A new book was written for the Broadway version, the title was changed to *Platinum*, but only Smith received good notices. The elaborate production, directed by Joe Layton, was one of the most expensive of the season, and when *Platinum* closed in a month, it lost a bundle. With no book writer credited, *Platinum* was turned into the four-person Off-Broadway musical *Sunset* with the songs telling the thin story. Tammy Grimes played Lila and did an admirable job, but with no book to support her Lila made little sense, and what was originally a character musical was left characterless. Critics felt that what was bad about *Platinum* was all that was left in *Sunset*, with the producer pulling the plug after opening night. Somewhere in the premise and the score for *Sunset* was an interesting musical, but it never surfaced in any of the three versions.

THE HUMAN COMEDY

[28 December 1983, Public Theatre/Anspacher Theatre, 79 performances; Royale Theatre, 13 performances] a musical play by William Dumaresq based on William Saroyan's novel. *Score*: Galt MacDermot (music), Dumaresq (lyrics). *Cast*: Rex Smith, Bonnie Koloc, Mary Elizabeth Mastrantonio, Stephen Geoffreys, Delores Hall, Caroline Peyton, Laurie Franks, Josh Blake, Anne Marie Bobby.

Perhaps the saddest casualty of the 1983–1984 New York theatre season was the failure of this ambitious and often enthralling musical play. *The Human*

Comedy offered Galt MacDermot's best score since *Hair*, the book based on a William Saroyan novel and film was rich with engaging characters, and the sung-through piece was given a splendid production both Off and then on Broadway. Yet *The Human Comedy* was not a success and, even sadder, it still has not received the recognition it deserves.

In the small California town of Ithaca during World War II, the residents go through their everyday lives with dread and hope. For the widowed Kate MacCauley (Bonnie Koloc), all her concerns are for her children, who are either in the war or at home dealing with the pains of growing up. The death of her son Marcus (Don Kehr) brings momentary tragedy, then life struggles on, particularly when Marcus's army friend Tobey (Joseph Kolinski) comes to town looking for the family that he's heard so much about. The large cast of characters also included featured performances by Rex Smith, Mary Elizabeth Mastrantonio, Stephen Geoffreys, Josh Blake, Gordon Connell, Caroline Peyton, and Debra Byrd, all directed expertly by Wilford Leach. The entire cast remained on stage during the performance and served as a Greek chorus commenting on the action and joining the other characters in song. It was an episodic tale and one that might have been bathed in sentimentality (as it had in the film) had the creators not handled the material so well. Some called *The Human Comedy* an opera because it was filled with music (over eighty separate musical numbers) and all dialogue was sung or delivered in a recitative style. Yet the show did not sound or feel like an opera with its wonderful blending of swing, jazz, folk, and gospel music. William Dumaresq adapted Saroyan's words into lyrics that were more conversational than poetic, often avoiding rhymes and traditional song structure. MacDermot's music provided the poetry, and the resulting score was frequently intoxicating. The different musical styles were revealing expressions of everyday emotions, sometimes as simple as a hymn, as in "Everlasting" and "When I Am Lost," other times complicated, as with the bitter "I Don't Know Who to Hate" or the questioning "Everything Is Changed." "Long Past Sunset" and "Somewhere, Someone" were engaging folk songs, while "Beautiful Music" was a rousing gospel number which took its energy from the sounds of the telegraph office bringing dreaded news of the war dead. MacDermot also composed music to convey the rushing of the passing train as well as a musical theme for the teenager's bicycle as he delivers the telegrams. *The Human Comedy* was flooded with music, and all of it was superior. The musical was so well received by the press Off Broadway at the Public Theatre that producer Joe Papp moved it to Broadway; probably a major mistake. It was an intimate show, and few thought it played as well in the larger venue. Off-Broadway audiences were just beginning to discover the musical downtown but *The Human Comedy* was very atmospheric and too low-key for Broadway.

The second round of reviews was not as enthusiastic and, with no stars or splashy productions values (slide projections were added for the production at the Royale Theatre), playgoers seemed to ignore the musical, and it was forced to close after thirteen performances. The cast recorded the score, but the double album was not released for several years. By then *The Human Comedy* was all but forgotten, and so it remains. Its unusual casting and music demands do not encourage revivals, but mostly it is not done because no one knows it. Opera companies have not picked up on the show because it is not the kind of music that demands opera voices. One can only hope that a major revival somewhere someday will bring *The Human Comedy* back to life.

A . . . My Name Is Alice

[24 February 1984, American Place Theatre, 353 performances] a musical revue by Joan Micklin Silver, Julianne Boyd, various. *Score:* various. *Cast:* Randy Graff, Charlaine Woodard, Alaina Reed, Mary Gordon Murray, Roo Brown.

The 1980s being the decade of the women's movement, there were many plays and musicals that were labeled "feminist," when in reality they were personal about women's issues and not political. Few of these shows were more fun and yet as moving as the revue *A . . . My Name Is Alice.* Joan Micklin Silver and Julianne Boyd commissioned songs and sketches from twenty-eight male and female writers, assembled them into a five-woman revue format, and codirected the show. Without being preachy or bitter, the musical found both joy and pathos in the plight of the American woman in the 1980s. Male-female relationships were touched upon, but much of the show was about the rivalry and bonding between sisters, friends, and coworkers. Highlights from the score included the friction between a modern parent and a traditional teacher in "Welcome to Kindergarten," the sardonic "Good Thing I Learned to Dance," the cliché-ridden parody "The French Song," and the disturbing "At My Age" in which a teenager and a mature woman each wait for their date to arrive and express similarly vulnerable emotions. The sketch that received the most laughs involved the all-female basketball team called the Detroit Persons. The mostly excellent material was beautifully performed by the five actresses who played a variety of characters, each song or sketch often feeling like a complete one-act play. *A . . . My Name Is Alice* was developed Off Off Broadway at the American Place Theatre as part of its Women's Project, then moved to Off Broadway in a commercial run that was applauded by the press. Word of mouth soon secured the musical a reputation for being enjoyable as well as revealing, helping the show run nearly a year. *A . . . My Name Is Alice* enjoyed several regional productions, and in 1995 Silver and Boyd assembled a sequel entitled *A . . . My Name Is Still Alice*.

HEY, MA . . . KAYE BALLARD

[27 February 1984, Promenade Theatre, 62 performances] a musical play by Kaye Ballard. *Score:* David Levy, Leslie Eberhard, Ballard (music and lyrics), various. *Cast:* Ballard.

The 1990s were filled with one-person shows on and Off Broadway in which well-known or even obscure performers played themselves. Character actress Kaye Ballard got a jump start on this trend with her one-person autobiographical musical *Hey, Ma . . . Kaye Ballard*, which was unique in its day. The veteran of stage, nightclubs, and television chronicled her life and career, sometimes using song standards of the time to set up the period, and other times singing new songs that filled in the story. These original numbers, some of which Ballard helped write, looked pretty feeble next to such beloved songs of the past such as "You Made Me Love You," "Without a Song," "Down in the Depths," and "Cookin' Breakfast for the One I Love." Perhaps the musical highlight of the musical was hearing Ballad reprise two numbers she introduced on stage, the sultry "Lazy Afternoon" from *The Golden Apple* and "Always, Always You" from *Carnival*. Just how satisfying a show *Hey, Ma . . . Kaye Ballard* was depended on one's taste for the funny, mannered talents of the performer, yet the critics had to hand it to her for coming up with an actual musical play and not just a rehashed nightclub act.

LOVE

[15 April 1984, Audrey Wood Theatre, 17 performances] a musical comedy by Jeffrey Sweet based on Murray Schisgal's comedy *Luv*. *Score:* Howard Marren (music), Susan Birkenhead (lyrics). *Cast:* Nathan Lane, Stephen Vinovich, Judy Kaye.

Although Murray Schisgal's offbeat comedy *Luv* was one of the longest-running nonmusicals of the 1960s, revivals were rare by the 1980s, and the three-character piece was labeled a curiosity that was "of its time." A musical version of the 1964 play that was extremely faithful to the original was probably as unnecessary as it was unwanted. The unhappily married Milt (Stephen Vinovich) gets rid of his wife Ellen (Judy Kaye) by encouraging her to fall in love with the perennial loser Harry (Nathan Lane). The scheme works, but Ellen and Harry make an even more dreadful pairing than the original couple. Milt grows disenchanted with his new girlfriend, and he and Ellen unsuccessfully try to murder Harry so that they can get back together. It was an odd, satirical play that satirized both the theatre of the absurd and conventional plays, and its single setting on a bridge forced all the action to come to the locale in a classical manner. The musical version, lamely retitled *Love*, slowed the action down with routine songs, softened the characters, and eliminated the weirdness in the piece. In fact, the only bit of absurdism about the project was that the Outer Critics Circle gave *Love* an award. The three performers could not be faulted, and it was telling that such outstanding talents as Lane and Kaye (yet to become stage stars) could not rescue this material. *Love* folded in two weeks but returned to Off Broadway in 1991 again with Kaye, supported by David Green and Austin Pendleton, under the better title *What about Luv?* The revival lasted five weeks this time, and there were some regional productions as well.

NITE CLUB CONFIDENTIAL

[10 May 1984, Ballroom Theatre, 156 performances] a musical cabaret by Dennis Deal. *Score:* Deal, Albert Evans, various (music and lyrics). *Cast:* Stephen Berger, Fay DeWitt, Steve Gideon, Denise Nolin, Tom Spiroff.

Like *Hey Ma . . . Kaye Ballard*, this cabaret revue mixed old standards among its new songs to give an authentic feeling for the period, in this case, the 1950s. In a smoky nightclub not of the best quality, five desperate performers entertain the patrons while their backstage relationships are revealed in bits and pieces. The little plot there was concerned an eager young stud using a fading chanteuse as a stepping-stone to further his career. The languid, decadent tone of the tale was reflected in the songs. Dennis Deal and Albert Evans rearranged the music for such favorites as "That Old Black Magic," "Something's Gotta Give," "Love Isn't Born, It's Made," and "Goody, Goody," and wrote several new numbers that sometimes pastiched other standards, such as "The Long Goodbye" which echoed "The Man That Got Away." Of the new numbers, the most satisfying were the brazen "The Canarsie Diner," the fatalistic "Dead End Street," and the droll "Put the Blame on Mamie," which was not the sultry Rita Hayworth number "Put the Blame on Mame" but a new concoction about Mamie Eisenhower. All the songs were delivered with a polish and weary professionalism by the commendable cast, the veteran Fay DeWitt often stealing the show as the Kay Thompson-like singer Kay Goodman. *Nite Club Confidential* was first presented Off Off Broadway at the Riverwest Theatre and was popular enough to be held over for forty-eight performances. The commercial transfer to Off Broadway was also popular, treading the boards for twenty weeks.

SHADES OF HARLEM

[21 August 1984, Village Gate Downstairs, 258 performances] a cabaret revue by Jeree Palmer. *Score:* various. *Cast:* Palmer, Branice McKenzie, Ty Stephens, Frank Owens.

Once again, a handful of new songs were mixed with old favorites in a revue that was heavy on nostalgia and atmosphere. *Shades of Harlem* sought to recreate an evening at the Cotton Club during its heyday in the 1920s, and it came close enough to the mark to please playgoers for more than eight months. Cast members Jeree Palmer and Ty Stephens joined musical director-pianist Frank Owens in writing a few new songs in the Harlem Renaissance manner, but they seemed like pleasant diversions in between the performance of golden classics such as "Take the A Train," "I Got Rhythm," "Satin Doll," "It Don't Mean a Thing (If It Ain't Got That Swing)," "I Got It Bad and That Ain't Good," "Body and Soul," and (currently also heard in *Nite Club Confidential*) "That Old Black Magic." Some of these numbers could not have been heard at the Cotton Club in the 1920s, but they all captured the spirit of the famous club which was the birthplace of many important songs and performers. The three featured performers in *Shades of Harlem* (Palmer, Stephens, and Branice McKenzie) were backed up by a line of seven chorines, and the musical arrangements were as expert as the singers. There was nothing unique or innovative about the cabaret revue, but that didn't keep it from being highly entertaining and offering a glimpse into what the Cotton Club might have been like.

Rap Master Ronnie

[3 October 1984, Top of the Gate, 49 performances] a musical revue by Garry Trudeau, Elizabeth Swados. *Score:* Trudeau (lyrics), Swados (music and lyrics). *Cast:* Reathel Bean, Catherine Cox, Richard Ryder, Mel Johnson Jr., Ernestine Jackson.

Songwriter Elizabeth Swados teamed up with the popular comic strip artist and author Garry Trudeau on the Broadway musical *Doonesbury* the previous year, and it struggled to run three months. Swados and Trudeau had even less success with this musical revue spoofing the current president, Ronald Reagan (Reathel Bean). Like most U.S. presidents, Reagan was ripe for satire, and caricatures of a senile, smiling, ineffectual movie star in the White House were commonplace after the first three years of his term in office. Trudeau was a brilliant political satirist in the newspaper comics but, as *Doonesbury* had shown, his style did not adapt well to the stage. *Rap Master Ronnie* was often enjoyable, sometimes wickedly accurate, but rarely very satisfying. Perhaps Reagan was such a bland public figure that even a satire of him turned routine and predictable. The songs sometimes had punch, such as Reagan's cowboy mentality in "The Round Up" and the musical plea of an African American woman to "Take That Smile Off Your Face," but too much of the score was merely pleasant and mildly satiric. The show opened a month before Election Day and, when Reagan was reelected, *Rap Master Ronnie* seemed even less potent—it closed a week later.

Kuni-Leml

[9 October 1984, Audrey Wood Theatre, 298 performances] a musical farce by Nahma Sandrow based on Avrom Goldfadn's Yiddish play *The Fanatic*. *Score:* Raphael Crystal (music), Richard Engquist (lyrics). *Cast:* Stuart Zagnit, Barbara McCulloh, Mark Zeller, Scott Wentworth, Susan Friedman, Adam Heller, Steve Sterner, Gene Varrone.

The subtitle for Avrom Goldfadn's Yiddish farce *The Fanatic* is *The Two Kuni-Lemls,* and that pretty much tells the plot of this silly but likable musical. In Odessa in 1880, Reb Pinkhos (Mark Zeller) hopes to marry his daughter

Caroline (Barbara McCulloh) to the devout and unappealing rabbinical student Kuni-Leml (Stuart Zagnit), but she's in love with her penniless tutor Max (Scott Wentworth). Max disguises himself as Kuni-Leml to woo Caroline, and a series of complications follow until the confusion concludes with a double wedding: Max and Caroline, Kuni-Leml and the matchmaker's daughter Libe (Susan Friedman). It was all predicable nonsense, and it had entertained audiences in the Yiddish theatre for decades. The musical version was faithful to its source and managed to keep the farce moving even when the songs slowed down the plot. Raphael Crystal's music was a pleasing pastiche of Eastern European folk, klezmer, and Broadway. Richard Engquist's lyrics were often forced and awkward but retained the farcical tone of Nahma Sandrow's libretto. One dutifully listened with a smile to the list song "The Boy Is Perfect" sung by the matchmaker Kalmen (Gene Varrone) even though it was a one-joke number. The lovers sang a silly love duet ("Cuckoo") and an earnest one ("Nothing Counts But Love"), but more fun were the character songs for Kuni-Leml and Libe. Her "Don't Worry Darling" was a delightful soliloquy about being unmarried, and Kuni-Leml's "What's My Name?" nicely portrayed a weakling unsure of his own confusion. When Kuni-Leml and Libe united for the funny philosophical duet "Do Horses Talk to Horses?," the score reached an impressive level of musical farce. *Kuni-Leml* was first presented Off Off Broadway by the Jewish Repertory Theatre who moved it to Off Broadway then coproduced it on Broadway, where it received enthusiastic notices and ran nearly ten months. The Jewish Rep revised the musical in 1998 for a one-month run, and the score was finally recorded. Although the show is very Jewish in its names, terminology, and traditions, it has been enjoyed by all kinds of audiences over the years. The eight-character musical is economical because of its simple production demands. It is surprising it is not done more often. Perhaps it's the title.

DIAMONDS

[16 December 1984, Circle in the Square, 122 performances] a musical revue. *Score:* various. *Cast:* Scott Holmes, Loni Ackerman, Chip Zien, Dick Latessa, Jackee Harry, Susan Bigelow, Larry Riley, Nestor Serrano, Wade Raley, Dwayne Markee.

Broadway producer-director Harold Prince took his first foray into Off Broadway when he asked some forty songwriters and authors to contribute to this musical revue about baseball. With contributions by such celebrated artists as Kander and Ebb, Comden and Green, Cy Coleman, Alan Menken, Howard Ashman, and others, some of the material was first-rate. Prince also solicited work from some emerging Off-Broadway writers as well, such as Jim Wann, Gerald Alessandrini, Ellen Fitzhugh, and Craig Carnelia, and their contributions were also impressive. The score was never recorded, but individual numbers have been picked up by singers over the years and performed in concert or recorded. The wistful "The Boys of Summer" (by Larry Grossman and Ellen Fitzhugh), the expansive "Diamonds Are Forever," and the evocative "Winter in New York" (both by Kander and Ebb) were among the praised numbers, yet the magic of America's favorite pastime was probably best captured in the simple ballad "What You'd Call a Dream" (by Craig Carnelia) in which a man looks back with pride at the day he batted a home run and it seemed the sky was full of diamonds. Other notable songs included "In the Cards" about baseball card collections and "Hundreds of Hats" in which baseball caps took on a mythic quality. The revue avoided using the standard "Take Me Out to the Ball Game," but they did include the famous Bud Abbott–Lou Costello sketch "Who's on First." Another fun skit was an ethnic version of "Casey at the Bat" called "Kasi Atta Bat" and a burlesque-like sketch called "The Dodger Game" complete with a baggy-pants comic, a straight man, and a well-endowed female. Prince directed the superior cast, who displayed a wide range of talent, and the press generally endorsed *Diamonds*. Yet, except for *Damn Yankees*, musicals and baseball didn't seem to mix, and the revue was not a major hit. All the same, it ran four months and was licensed for amateur productions, allowing some theatregoers across the country to have been able to see this little gem of a show.

3 GUYS NAKED FROM THE WAIST DOWN

[5 February 1985, Minetta Lane Theatre, 160 performances], a musical play by Jerry Colker. *Score:* Colker (lyrics), Michael Rupert (music). *Cast:* Colker, Scott Bakula, John Kassir.

Despite its seemingly provocative title (which audience members soon found out was showbiz slang for stand-up comedians), there was nothing very bold or daring about this shallow musical that preached that life in big time entertainment was shallow. The contrived plot followed three eager comics in New York City who have dreams of fame, so they band together and soon become famous doing a mindless television series. One of the threesome cannot deal with the hypocrisy, and he commits suicide. The surviving two set off on their own careers. One stays in California, but the other returns to New York and opens his own comedy club where he encourages young talent to find fame and avoid the same mistakes he did. Not only were the three characters superficial and empty, they weren't even funny. The jokes were often bitter without being clever, and the songs that attempted comedy were loud and feeble. The score bent over backward to sound contemporary and hip but was mostly recycled rock and jazz with pretentious lyrics. The only time the musical numbers seemed to come to life was when the songwriters parodied Elvis Presley, Bob Dylan, and Gilbert and Sullivan. (The fact that the trio appeared on Johnny Carson's TV show because of their spoof of Gilbert and Sullivan was one of the many plot points that was hard to swallow.) The three performers were earnest and not without talent, and sometimes audiences were more interested in them than in the characters they were playing. Reviews were mixed, but playgoers were not so picky and kept *3 Guys Naked from the Waist Down* on the boards for five months. Maybe it was that title.

LIES & LEGENDS: THE MUSICAL STORIES OF HARRY CHAPIN

[24 April 1985, Village Gate, 79 performances] a musical revue by Joseph Stern. *Score:* Harry Chapin (music and lyrics). *Cast:* Terri Klausner, Martin Vidnovic, John Herrera, Joanna Glushak, Ron Orbach.

The late Harry Chapin's folk songs had often been described as "story songs" because of their narrative nature and the way they depicted characters. After the modest success of his *Cotton Patch Gospel*, these ballads were collected and presented in a revue called *Lies and Legends: The Musical Stories of Harry Chapin*. Unlike the earlier show, *Lies and Legends* resembled a concert more than a revue even though the capable cast found the theatrics in each piece. The musical was also more somber than the biblical show, many of the songs with unhappy or even tragic tales to tell. The program started and ended with the optimistic "Circle" about the passing of time and the belief that people from your past will return again. But the first act ended with the disconcerting "Sniper," which viewed a mass killer from inside his head and the memories others had of him. All the most popular Chapin songs were included, such as "Taxi," about a cab driver in San Francisco who picks up an ex-lover one night in the rain, and "Cat's in the Cradle," about a father who was too busy to watch his son grow up. Troubled relationships were explored in "Shooting Star" and "Tangled Up Puppet," and a musician recalled when he played for a "Dance Band on the Titanic." A bit lighter in tone was "30,000 Pounds of Bananas" about the wreck of a truckload of fruit. It was questionable if fans of Chapin found the evening very satisfying, being used to hearing the songs in concert and on records by the singer-songwriter. Did they really want to hear these pieces performed as duets and ensemble numbers? In some ways the musical was more effective for playgoers first discovering Chapin's work; though why anyone unfamiliar with Chapin would be drawn to the show is questionable. Critical reaction was mixed, and *Lies and Legends* managed to run ten weeks.

Mayor

[13 May 1985, Top of the Gate, 185 performances] a musical revue by Warren Leight based on Edward I. Koch's memoir. *Score:* Charles Strouse (music and lyrics). *Cast:* Lenny Wolpe, Ken Jennings, Kathryn McAteer, Ilene Kristen, Keith Curran, Nancy Giles, Douglas Bernstein, Marion J. Caffey.

Ed Koch, mayor of New York City during the 1980s, may not have won all his political battles during his eleven years in office, but his many books were popular, and his 1984 memoir *Mayor* was a best seller. Within a year it was turned into an Off-Broadway musical that was a cross between a revue and a book show. Warren Leight's libretto showed a typical day in the life of the outspoken, scrappy mayor (Lenny Wolpe) as he dealt with city issues, celebrities, and upholding his image as an optimistic champion for "My City." Broadway veteran composer Charles Strouse wrote the tuneful music as well as the lyrics, which were predictable but enjoyable. "You Can Be a New Yorker Too!" and "Hootspa" had the eager quality of Strouse's *Annie* songs, and some of Koch's signature phrases were musicalized with glee, as in "What You See Is What You Get" and "How'm I Doin'?" Aspects of New York provided fodder for the show, as with "Out-of-Towner," "Staten Island B. P.," "Guardian Angel," and "The Last 'I Love New York' Song." There was a merry "March of the Yuppies" and a rousing call for "Good Times." None of the songs were particularly memorable, but they felt part of a whole and fit in nicely with the episodic nature of the show. Wolpe bore an uncanny resemblance to the real Koch, flashing the familiar smile and capturing Koch's

Jewish–New York character, and the rest of cast had fun playing celebrities ranging from Cardinal John O'Connor to hotel empress Leona Helmsley. Theatre critics were more approving of the musical than Koch's political critics were of his policies, and *Mayor* ran six months, then reopened for another seventy performances at the Latin Quarter, a small venue that was technically a Broadway house. *Mayor* was obviously a show mainly for New Yorkers, yet the musical enjoyed some regional productions, particularly while Koch remained in office until 1989.

THE MYSTERY OF EDWIN DROOD

[4 August 1985, Delacorte Theatre, 24 performances; Imperial Theatre, 608 performances] a musical mystery by Rupert Holmes based on Charles Dickens's book. *Score:* Holmes (music and lyrics). *Cast:* George Rose, Betty Buckley, Howard McGillin, Patti Cohenour, Cleo Laine, Jana Schneider, Larry Shue, John Herrera, Joe Grifasi.

The tireless producer Joe Papp is remembered as outspoken, controversial, and stubbornly dedicated to his projects. What is sometimes forgotten is how unpredictable he could be, often surprising audiences and critics with his choices of material to produce. The Shakespeare series in Central Park had often gone in directions away from conventional Bard productions, but few offerings were as unlikely as *The Mystery of Edwin Drood*. What other New York producer would present a British music hall version of an unfinished Charles Dickens novel with book, music, lyrics, and even the orchestrations by a theatre newcomer? Not that Rupert Holmes was an untried beginner, having written some pop hits that climbed the charts, but he was not someone to whom you entrusted a giant period musical. The project was also unlikely because there was nothing American in the characters, story, locale, or score. Even *My Fair Lady* sounded like a Broadway musical; *The Mystery of Edwin Drood* never did. Victorian parlor songs, British vaudeville ditties, London music hall sing-alongs, and love duets sung by two women (one in a trouser role) was not what you expected in Central Park.

In the Victorian England cathedral town of Cloisterham, the arrogant young Edwin Drood (Betty Buckley in the trouser role) quarrels with a variety of characters and then mysteriously disappears, throwing suspicion on a handful of people. The suspects are a delightfully varied group of Dickens characters: the virginal Rosa Bud (Patti Cohenour), the sinister John Jasper (Howard McGillin), the dope peddler Princess Puffer (Cleo Laine), the vengeful Neville Landless (John Herrera) from Ceylon, his quixotic sister Helena (Jana Schneider), and even the seemly benign Rev. Mr. Crisparkle (Larry Shue). Since Dickens never finished the novel, the solution to who murdered Drood was posed to the audience, and they voted on the likely culprit. The tale was then completed accordingly, a different musical ending for each outcome. The music hall Chairman (George Rose) acted as host and narrated the story, and the Victorian actors often broke character to comment on the action or sing a song out of context. These musical interruptions were often delicious, such as the vivacious "Off to the Races," the rapid patter song "Both Sides of the Coin," and the catchy "Don't Quit While You're Ahead." "Moon Fall" was the recurring ballad, very stiff and formal yet exotic and mysterious as well, and "Perfect Strangers" was the entrancing female duet. Jasper's character song "A Man Could Go Quite Mad" was as manic as the Princess Puffer's lament "The Wages of Sin" was languid, both numbers suggesting the drugged condition of the characters. Gilbert and Sullivan were never far away in Holmes's score, such as in the complex act finale "The Name of Love," the multipart "No Good Can Come from Bad," and the expository "Out on a Limerick." Regardless of who turned out to be the culprit, Drood returned for the finale with the rousing "The Writing on the Wall."

Wilfred Leach directed with ingenious touches, and Graciela Daniele devised the raucous choreography. *The Mystery of Edwin Drood* was a musical whodunit, an infrequent genre if there ever was one, and was presented in the format of a British music hall performance. It was a show-within-a-show like *Kiss Me, Kate,* though the backstage story here was not nearly as interesting. The result was a very foreign product which some audience members did not warm up to. Yet the critics loved the musical, and enough playgoers found it so enjoyable that they got past its strangeness and made it a hit. After its three-week run in the park, Papp moved the show to a Broadway house where it found an audience for twenty months. As idyllic as the Central Park atmosphere was, many felt *The Mystery of Edwin Drood* actually played better in a traditional house with a proscenium and boxes. The unlikely musical continued to surprise when it was later produced by many regional theatres, summer stock, and college groups. Yet in London, where they have musicalized many Dickens novels, the show only survived sixty-eight performances.

YOURS, ANNE

[13 October 1985, Playhouse 91, 57 performances] a musical play by Enid Flutterman based on Anne Frank's *Diary of a Young Girl.* Score: Flutterman (lyrics), Michael Cohen (music). *Cast:* Trini Alvarado, George Guidall, David Cady, Betty Aberlin, Ann Talman, Dana Zeller-Alexis, Hal Robinson, Merwin Goldsmith.

Is it possible to musicalize the story of Anne Frank without trivializing the material? This chamber piece was earnest in intent and faithful in execution but, despite its merits, most critics agreed that nothing new was brought to the story by adding songs. In fact, the voice of the Jewish teenager found in her diary is so potently unembellished that turning her entries into songs, no matter how delicately done, seemed jarring. Enid Flutterman's libretto was based on the popular 1955 play version *The Diary of Anne Frank* by Frances Goodrich and Albert Hackett as well as the published diary, yet the result was a static piece filled more with reflections than theatrical action. Anne (Trini Alvarado) served as both narrator and main character who often came alive on stage. The other characters suffered, remaining cloudy figures even when given a song, such as "For the Children" sung by Anne's parents (George Guidall and Dana Zeller-Alexis). The score mostly consisted of Anne's numbers, either musical entries in her diary or singing about her fascination with "Hollywood." Her duets with the fellow teen Peter Van Daan (David Cady) were problematic. No one expected (or wanted) love songs for this pair, but their numbers "I Am Not a Jew" and "I Think Myself Out" were less than satisfying. The few numbers sung by all the characters, such as the exposition piece "An Ordinary Day" or the expected "The First Chanukah Night," were even harder to accept; singing aloud together seemed awkward for these people in hiding. Interest in Anne Frank has never waned, and a 1978 revival of the Goodrich-Hackett play ran ten weeks. Enough playgoers were interested in *Yours, Anne* to keep it on the boards for six weeks, an unprofitable number for a commercial mounting.

THE GOLDEN LAND

[11 November 1985, Second Avenue Theatre, 277 performances] a musical revue in Yiddish and English by Zalmen Mlotek, Moise Rosenfeld. *Score:* various. *Cast:* Bruce Adler, Neva Small, Avi Hoffman, Marc Krause, Phylis Berk, Joanne Borts.

For older Jewish New Yorkers, nostalgia ran high in this musical revue of ethnic songs that were performed in both English and Yiddish. The immigrant experience from the turn of the century to the 1940s was told in musical numbers, many of them familiar to the survivors and offspring of those generations. Love songs, lullabies, dance songs, comic numbers, wedding songs, hymns, and even a few mainstream standards such as "Brother, Can You Spare a Dime?" filled the program which was directed with panache by Jacques Levy and choreographed with zest by Donald Saddler. The six cast members were similarly talented, though Bruce Adler got the best notices. Some numbers were in broken English, such as the opener "Amerike, Hurrah far Uncle Sem!" and the ensemble number "Vatch Your Step!" Others needed no translation, such as the fervent "Gebentsht Iz Amerike" (Blessed Is America) and the catchy "Yidl Mitn Fidl" (Yidl with His Fiddle). The dark side of immigrant life was not ignored, as with "Ballad of the Triangle Fire," and the plight of "Arbeter Froyen" (Working Women), but much of *The Golden Land* was uplifting and spirited. Similar to the earlier *Tintypes* but focusing specifically on the Jewish immigrants, the musical, which had been developed Off Off Broadway and regionally, was well received by the press and playgoers in New York and ran into the summer.

PERSONALS

[24 November 1985, Minetta Lane Theatre, 265 performances] a musical revue by David Crane, Seth Friedman, Marta Kauffman. *Score:* Crane, Friedman, Kaufman, William Dreskin, Joel Phillip Friedman, Alan Menken, Stephen Schwartz, Michael Skloff. *Cast:* Jason Alexander, Dee Hoty, Trey Wilson, Jeff Keller, Laura Dean, Nancy Opel.

Questionable material performed by unquestionable talent resulted in a eight-and-a-half-month run for this contrived but entertaining revue that was supposedly about New Yorkers seeking romance through the personal ads in newspapers and magazines, but it was just another show about relationships. The sly opening number, "Nothing to Do with Love," showed singles composing an ad that would come across more attractive than sincere. A virginal high school senior advertises for a "teacher" to help him enter manhood, and he gets hundreds of responses in the funny "After School Special." But few of the numbers after those two had anything to do with personal ads, and the show trod familiar territory filled with personal problems. After a series of bad relationships, some singles decide "I'd Rather Dance Alone," while some women gripe about the dates their mothers arrange for them in "Mama's Boys." An oddball *ménage à trois* involving a bisexual dwarf was the subject of "A Little Happiness," and in "I Could Always Go to You" two female friends, who always turn to the other after a failed romance, decide to become lovers only to be left without a confidant when that relationship fails. The best musical number, "Moving in with Linda," showed a man embarking on a more permanent arrangement with his girlfriend only to find old lovers popping out of his luggage on the day he moves in. Some songs were misfires and did not seem to fit in with the rest of the show, such as three men wishing they were still in "Second Grade." Pleasing but also out of place was the hopeful finale "Some Things Don't End," one of three numbers with music by Stephen Schwartz. Often the music in *Personals* was better than the lyrics, utilizing everything from 1950s rock and roll to tender contemporary melodies in the pop manner. The sketches were deemed by the press to be less interesting than the songs, often using repetition or off-color jokes to pound away at being funny. They were written by David Crane, Marta Kaufman, and Seth Friedman, fellow students at Brandeis University where they first wrote *Personals* and had it produced. Over the years the material was much changed, but there was still something sophomoric about the comedy in the Off-Broadway production. Some reviewers labeled it television sitcom humor and, indeed, the three writers would find plenty of success penning hit television shows such as *Friends* in the 1990s. How come the mediocre *Personals* ran as long as it did? The six cast members rose above their material and often made the revue seem like gold. Jason Alexander, Dee Hoty, and Nancy Opel would soon become Broadway favorites, but just as accomplished were Laura Dean, Trey Wilson, and Jeff Keller. Alexander would also find success on television, often turning weak writing into palatable comedy. Perhaps one can point to *Personals* and see the effect television was having on Off-Broadway humor. The dumbing down of comedy for the mass media would spread to little New York theatres, and sharp, intelligent musical revues would just about disappear.

NUNSENSE

[12 December 1985, Cherry Lane Theatre, 3,672 performances] a musical comedy by Dan Goggin. *Score:* Goggin (music and lyrics). *Cast:* Christine

Anderson, Vicki Belmonte, Marilyn Farina, Semina De Laurentis, Suzi Winson.

If *Personals* could run 265 performances on sophomoric material, imagine how long a musical could run that was both juvenile and nonsensical. Nine years, in fact. And that was only the beginning. *Nunsense* would receive hundreds of productions each year, break records for many theatres, and save several theatre companies from bankruptcy. Not bad for a one-joke show with a forgettable score. *Nunsense* began not as a theatre piece but a series of greeting cards designed by Dan Goggin that showed a nun in traditional habit photographed in unlikely situations. Goggin arranged for the actress Marilyn Farina, dressed as Sister Mary Cordelia, to appear at card stores, and the patrons enjoyed seeing a nun doing anything un-nun-like. Goggin then put together a fifteen-minute cabaret act with nuns and monks pulling off similar shenanigans. Called *The Nunsense Story*, it played more than nine months at a Greenwich Village club. Audiences found the monks unfunny but loved the nuns. Goggin then created the musical that took the boards by storm first Off Broadway, then on tour, in theatres across the nation, and even in dozens of foreign countries. The premise for *Nunsense* is silly and slight. The Order of the Little Sisters of Hoboken needs to raise some money in a hurry. When Sister Julia made a bad batch of vichyssoise, most of the nuns at the convent died of food poisoning. The five surviving nuns put on a musical revue to raise funds to bury the deceased, who are still waiting in the freezer. "We've Got to Clean Out the Freezer" they sing, and the audience falls on the floor with laughter. It was that kind of evening. The songs Goggin wrote were pastiches of different musical genres, the lyrics often stating the obvious and going nowhere. The gospel number "Holier Than Thou," the country western "I Could've Gone to Nashville," and the vaudeville turn "Just a Coupla Sisters" would land with a thud if they were not sung by ladies in habits. Bad puns abound, as with "Nunsense Is Habit Forming," and anything recalling Catholic doctrine or teaching was sure to get a laugh, as in "So You Want to Be a Nun" and "Growing Up Catholic." If nuns singing pop songs wasn't funny enough for you, nuns dancing was a surefire gimmick. "Tackle the Temptation with a Time Step" was the big tap number that brought down the house, though it was sometimes upstaged by Sr. Mary Amnesia's ventriloquist act with a puppet nun. Some critics dismissed *Nunsense* as tired satire without a bite; others found it a slight but harmless romp. Audiences disagreed, and the show became a franchise. There were the inevitable sequels, including *Nunsense II: The Second Coming*, a country

music version, a Jewish version, and even an all-drag variation lamely titled
A-Men! They were only curiosities. Audiences wanted to see the original, and
they did. Over and over again.

TO WHOM IT MAY CONCERN

[16 December 1985, St. Stephen's Church, 106 performances] a musical
play by Carol Hall. *Score:* Hall (music and lyrics). *Cast:* Hall, Gretchen
Cryer, Tamara Tunie, George Gerdes, Al DeCristo, William Hardy, Guy
Stroman, Kecia Lewis-Evans, Dylan Baker, Michael Hirsch.

Carol Hall, who wrote the sparkling songs for *The Best Little Whorehouse
in Texas*, provided the book and score and also played a major role in this
ninety-minute musical set in a church. During a nondescript religious
service, the thoughts of the celebrants and participants were vocalized in
songs, monologues, and poetry. Critics felt the nonmusical sections uneven
but cheered the score, which was filled with gospel, country, pop, and contemporary sounds. While much of this reflection was on the role of religion
in modern times, each number was personal rather than preachy, theatrical
rather than solemn. While the ensemble sang of "When I Consider the
Heavens" and addressed God in the title song, one female member of the
congregation thought of "My Sort of Ex-Boyfriend," and a male participant
was haunted by "Jenny Rebecca." A couple optimistically thought "Ain't
Love Easy," while a stranger to the group led the ensemble in the more blunt
"Ain't Nobody Got a Bed of Roses." The superb musical arrangements and
direction by Michael O'Flaherty were most appreciated during the soaring
ensemble numbers such as "Make a Joyful Noise," "Truly My Soul," and
"Walk in Love." The strong cast, under the direction of Geraldine Fitzgerald,
was filled with variety and talent, and the musical was wisely presented in a
church, letting the audience feel like one of the congregation. The location
may have put off some playgoers who feared that this was just a gospel program, but enough patrons were drawn by the encouraging notices and word
of mouth to let *To Whom It May Concern* run thirteen weeks. It deserved
better, just as it deserved to be recorded but wasn't. The musical had first
been presented at the summer theatre festival in Williamstown, Massachusetts, and after the New York run, it was produced by some theatre and/or
church groups across the country.

BEEHIVE

[30 March 1986, Top of the Gate, 600 performances] musical revue by Larry Gallagher. *Score:* various. *Cast:* Alison Fraser, Gina Taylor, Jasmine Guy, Pattie Darcy, Adriane Lenox, Laura Theodore.

It wasn't too early for nostalgia for the 1960s, as evidenced by the popularity of this musical revue filled with hit songs from that decade. There was no throbbing rock or protest folk songs in *Beehive*, though, for it celebrated the pop songs of female singers and girl groups who popularized such light-hearted ditties as "To Sir with Love," "Downtown," and "It's My Party (And I'll Cry If I Want To)." While the six-member cast made no effort to impersonate Lulu, Petula Clark, Lesley Gore, and the other American and British pop singers, neither did they deviate from the bubblegum sound of those feminist songs that true feminists later abhorred. There was a bit more bite in "R-E-S-P-E-C-T" and "You Don't Own Me," but much of *Beehive* consisted of girls crying about their man. The revue's title came from the puffed-up beehive hairdos that were popular in that decade, and the show looked as 1960s as it sounded. The musical, directed by creator Larry Gallagher, boasted fifty costumes and thirty-five wigs for its small cast, and the producers pointed out that the company went through fifteen cans of hairspray each week. In many ways, *Beehive* was a guilty pleasure. One looked back at these often empty-headed hits and shuddered to think that one sang and danced and fell in love to the sound of them. Yet their appeal was still unmistakable. Audiences loved hearing "The Name Game," "Where the Boys Are," "Don't Sleep in the Subway," "My Boyfriend's Back," "The Beat Goes On," "Make Your Own Kind of Music," and other tunes that stubbornly stuck in their heads. For nineteen months the naive and innocent aspects of the 1960s were alive Off Broadway.

GOBLIN MARKET

[13 April 1986, Circle in the Square, 89 performances] a musical play by Peggy Harmon, Polly Pen based on Christina Rossetti's poem. *Score:* Pen, various (music), Rossetti, various (lyrics). *Cast:* Terri Klausner, Ann Morrison.

One of the most unusual and hypnotic musicals of the decade was this one based on an 1862 poem by Christina Rossetti, a work that feminists were rediscovering and citing as a seminal work in women's literature. Sisters Lizzie (Ann Morrison) and Laura (Terri Klausner) live together in a cottage near a forest where male goblins dwell. They know enough to keep out of the woods after dark, but one day Laura encounters one of the creatures near a stream, and he offers her some magical fruit for the price of one of her tears. Eating the fruit allows Laura to blossom into womanhood in a way that both fascinates and terrorizes the two sisters. For lack of the fruit, Laura starts to weaken and die, and Lizzie is only able to revive her by offering the goblins money for more of the magical fruit. The goblins are angered, and they symbolically rape Lizzie and smear the pulp of the fruit all over her body. Laura tastes the pulp from Lizzie's body, and the two sisters return to normal. The sexual suggestions in the narrative poem had baffled and delighted critics over the century, and even the illustrations in the printed edition, drawn by the poet's brother Dante Gabriel Rossetti, have been seen as everything from an ideal of Victorian sisterhood to an erotic view of feminine enslavement. As adapted by Polly Pen and Peggy Harmon, the musical *Goblin Market* portrayed the sisters as adults who remembered the past when they were young girls in their family nursery. They relived the events of the poem, though no goblins or other actors appeared, and the long one-act musical became a series of solo reflections and duets that revealed the shifting moods of the two women as they were affected by the goblins. Much of the score featured music by Pen, but passages by Brahams, John Gay, and Charles Ives were also used, just as various lyricists contributed to Rossetti's verses. The result was a curious mixture of Victorian parlor songs, haunting contemporary melodies, British folk songs, and modern opera. Highlights of the score included the hypnotic "Come Buy, Come Buy," the languid lullaby "Sleep, Laura, Sleep," and the entrancing duet "Passing Away." *Goblin Market* had been developed Off Off Broadway at the Vineyard Theatre before moving to the Circle in the Square. Andre Ernotte directed the moody production, set in a somewhat surreal nursery, and Klausner and Morrison gave poignant performances filled with youthful giddiness and erotic subtext. The critics thought more highly of *Goblin Market* than playgoers, who kept it on the boards for only eleven weeks despite reviews citing it the best musical of the season. Such an esoteric and offbeat show would never have become a mainstream hit, yet it reflects the impact that *Goblin Market* had on its selective audiences to run as long as it did.

NATIONAL LAMPOON'S CLASS OF '86

[22 May 1986, Village Gate Downstairs, 53 performances] a satiric musical revue by Andrew Simmons, John Belushi, Chevy Chase, Stephen Collins, Christopher Guest, various. *Score:* various. *Cast:* Veanne Cox, Tommy Koenig, John Michael Higgins, Annie Golden, Roger Bumpass, Brian Brucker O'Connor.

Just as the glory days of the television show *Saturday Night Live* had passed with the departure of the original cast members and writers, so too the Off-Broadway *National Lampoon* series seemed lackluster by the mid-1980s. A few of the originals contributed to the sketches, but the results were uneven, ranging from skits about restaurants and apartment living to the expected spoofs of Ronald Reagan and test-tube babies. The songs were even less impressive, with tired jokes about Yuppies, cocaine, and the religious Right. Even an edgy number about Apartheid seemed to lack punch. The young and spirited cast was not without talent, but they were expected to fill mighty big shoes and, with second-class material, they were not able to. While the earlier *National Lampoon* revues ran and ran, this version survived only six and a half weeks.

OLYMPUS ON MY MIND

[15 July 1986, Lamb's Theatre, 207 performances] a musical comedy by Barry Harman based on Heinrich Von Kleist's *Amphitryon*. *Score:* Harman (lyrics), Grant Sturiale (music). *Cast:* Martin Vidnovic, Emily Zacharias, Lewis J. Stadlen, Jason Graae, Peggy Hewitt, Elizabeth Austin.

The mythological legend of Amphitryon, about Jupiter taking the form of the mortal Amphitryon to seduce his wife Alcmene, had been dramatized so many times that French playwright Jean Giraudoux called his 1937 stage version *Amphitryon 38*. In 1950, the tale was turned into the Cole Porter musical *Out of This World*, a lesser work with an outstanding (but mostly forgotten) score. Barry Harman based this musical variation on an 1807 German stage work by Von Kleist, but it was closer to vaudeville and Rodgers and Hart than a Teutonic or mythological piece. The premise of *Olympus on My Mind* is that the musical is being produced by Murray the Furrier and that he insisted that his girlfriend, the chorine Delores (Elizabeth Austin), appear throughout the show. She first joins the three-man chorus then later pops up in unrelated production numbers wearing Murray's furs. The concept was funny, if a bit repetitive, and gave the mythological story a subplot of sorts. Harman's script was filled with vaudeville panache with lots of jokes (particularly puns), and his lyrics were equally spry. Grant Sturiale's music was also zesty, and the score was an eclectic mix of splendid ballads, rousing tap numbers, clever character songs, and pint-sized production showstoppers. In fact, sometimes the songs seemed too good for such a silly script, especially in the touching advice song "Don't Bring Her Flowers," the lilting love duet "Heaven on Earth," and the bluesy lament "Olympus Is a Lonely Town." More raucous were the vivacious "The Gods on Tap," the carefree "At Liberty in Thebes," and Delores' Las Vegas-like number "A Star Is Born." A sparkling cast, ably directed by Harmon and choreographed by Pamela Sousa, was so much fun that some critics compared the experience to an expert revival of *The Boys from Syracuse*. Audiences also enjoyed themselves, allowing the musical to run over six months, followed by some regional productions. *Olympus on My Mind* boasts one of the best musical comedy scores of the 1980s (though it sounds more like the 1930s or 1940s), but the book is too inconsequential for most theatre groups, and it hasn't been revived as often as it should.

LADY DAY AT EMERSON'S BAR AND GRILL

[3 September 1986, Westside Arts Theatre, 281 performances] a musical play by Lanie Robertson. *Score:* various. *Cast:* Lonette McKee, Bambi Herrera.

The great blues singer Billie Holiday would become the subject of several cabaret shows, but the most popular, in New York and across the country, was this intimate program that began as a nightclub act then gradually turned into an autobiography of sorts. Emerson's is a South Philadelphia club, and in

1959 Holiday (Lonette McKee), four months before her death, is performing her act, singing song favorites and providing some innocuous chatter between numbers. Soon the segues become personal, and by the end of the show she has told her story and purged some of her demons. It was a familiar story to audience members because of the 1972 film *Lady Sings the Blues*, but McKee's indelible performance, both in singing the songs and chronicling her life, was so masterful that it seemed like it had never been told before. "'Taint Nobody's Bizness If I Do," "Good Morning Heartache," "Lover Man," "Strange Fruit," and all the Holiday classic songs were performed and, sung in between episodes of her story, they took on even greater potency. While some critics quibbled about the format, all extolled McKee and highly recommended the musical. Audiences took their advice, and the cabaret show ran nine months. *Lady Day at Emerson's Bar and Grill* became a favorite of summer stock and regional theatres looking for an economical little musical with a memorable score of standards.

ANGRY HOUSEWIVES

[7 September 1986, Minetta Lane Theatre, 137 performances] a musical play by A. M. Collins. *Score:* Chad Henry (music and lyrics). *Cast:* Lee Wilkof, Vicki Lewis, Michael Manasseri, Camille Saviola, Nicholas Wyman, Michael Lemback, Lorna Patterson, Carolyn Casanave.

After long runs in Seattle and Chicago, this mock-feminist musical managed to run Off-Broadway seventeen weeks despite lackluster notices by the press. Four discontented wives are fed up with their domestic lives and emotional problems, therefore they form a punk rock band called Angry Housewives and audition at a local club called the Lewd Fingers. There they win a talent contest and reach some sort of understanding of their lives. Both the women and their problems were contrived and stereotypic, and the pounding, smug songs they sang did little to enlighten matters. "It's Gonna Be Fun" they agree when the band forms, and by opening night the only thing they have to offer is "Eat Your @*!#@*!#! (Fucking) Cornflakes." The musical numbers off stage involving the wives' family members were equally obtuse. Yet many saw this as a satire of punk rock and feminist problems and, helped by a first-class cast, *Angry Housewives* developed a following of sorts. Perhaps seeing a widow and a schoolteacher getting down and dirty as punk musicians struck audiences just as funny as the nuns tap dancing in *Nunsense*.

SEX TIPS FOR MODERN GIRLS

[5 October 1986, Susan Bloch Theatre, 198 performances] a musical revue by Edward Astley, Susan Astley, Kim Seary, et al. *Score:* E. Astley, S. Astley, Seary, various (music and lyrics). *Cast:* Seary, E. Astley, Hilary Strang, Christine Willes.

A less angry feminist musical was *Sex Tips for Modern Girls*, which had originated in Vancouver, Canada, and covered familiar ground: men, mother-hood, sex, and self-fulfillment. Three women gave their thoughts in songs and monologues on these topics and more while co-author Edward Astley played all the men in their troubled lives. There was an honest sense of humor in the show, and the score ranged from smutty, as with "Oh! K-Y Chorale (or, Beyond the Labia Majora)," to the tender, as in "Who Will Be There." Some-times the songwriters strained too hard, as in "Penis Envoy" and "Up to My Tits in Water," but much of *Sex Tips for Modern Girls* seemed on target and engaging. The Canadian cast performed the revue for five weeks, and the show closed when they returned home. But business had been good, so *Sex Tips for Modern Girls* was recast with Americans, and it reopened at the Ac-tors' Playhouse where it ran another five months.

GROUCHO: A LIFE IN REVUE

[8 October 1986, Lucille Lortel Theatre, 254 performances] a musical play by Arthur Marx, Robert Fisher. *Score:* Harry Ruby, various (music), Bert Kalmar, various (lyrics). *Cast:* Frank Ferrante, Les Marsden, Faith Prince, Rusty Magee.

Fans of comic Groucho Marx got to hear some of their favorite lines and songs in this play with music written by Marx's son Arthur with Robert Fisher. Frank Ferrante's impersonation of Groucho was accomplished all around, playing the young, energetic comic in his vaudeville days to the aged, wry celebrity performing his one-man show at Carnegie Hall. This celebrated concert served as the starting point for the program, followed by flashbacks which included brothers Chico and Harpo (both played by Les Marsden) as well as their wives, sweethearts, and colleague Margaret Dumont (all played by Faith Prince). It was not a terribly original concept, but it worked well enough to feature the versatile performers and recreate the essence of the Marx Brothers. Ferrante and company sang such favorites as "Hello, I Must Be Going," "Hooray for Captain Spaulding," and "Lydia, the Tattooed Lady," as well as such period numbers as "Ma Blushin' Rosie" and "Mr. Gallagher and Mr. Shean." (Al Shean was the brothers' uncle.) There were enough Groucho admirers to keep *Groucho: A Life in Revue* on the boards for eight months, then the musical found success regionally and in London.

BROWNSTONE

[8 October 1986, Christian C. Yegen Theatre, 69 performances] a musical play by Josh Rubins, Andrew Cadiff. *Score:* Peter Larson, Rubins (music and lyrics). *Cast:* Liz Callaway, Rex Smith, Ernestine Jackson, Kimberly Farr, Ben Harney.

In the 1980s the Roundabout Theatre Company was known for its play revivals. In the 1990s it would become even more popular because of its musical revivals. So the original musical *Brownstone* was very atypical for the organization in 1986 and did not get the attention it deserved. A young couple and three single New Yorkers live in the same brownstone apartment building, and over the course of a year, their lives are changed in many ways, although there is little interaction among the different dwellers. Stuart (Rex Smith) is the newcomer to the city, and his dream of success in Manhattan is gradually modified during the time from one autumn to another. The would-be writer Howard (Ben Harney) struggles with his novel while his wife Mary (Ernestine Jackson) dreams of having a child to fulfill her life. The two single women in the building have a different agenda. Joan (Kimberly Farr) is an aggressive lawyer whose out-of-town boyfriend only enters her consciousness intermittently, while the fragile Claudia (Liz Callaway) is trying to pick up the pieces after a failed relationship. Not much happened plot-wise, and *Brownstone* often felt more like a modern oratorio than a book musical, but the score was often exhilarating. The ensemble numbers "Someone's Moving In" and "Someone's Moving Out" framed the piece that was mostly musicalized with solos and duets. The anxious ballad "Not Today," the glowing fantasy number "Fiction Writer," the revealing duet "We Should Talk," the wistful "We Came Along Too Late," and the heart-wrenching "Since You Stayed Here" were high points in a score that was often lyrical and sincere.

Brownstone had originated Off Off Broadway at the Hudson Theatre Guild, and the Roundabout opened its season with the chamber piece, allowing it to run eight and a half weeks. The musical pretty much disappeared until a revival at the Berkshire Theatre Festival fifteen years later, prompting a studio recording of the score in 2003.

HAVE I GOT A GIRL FOR YOU!

[29 October 1986, Second Avenue Theatre, 78 performances] a musical spoof by Joel Greenhouse, Penny Rockwell. *Score:* Dick Gallagher (music and lyrics). *Cast:* Gregory Jbara, J. P. Dougherty, Walter Hudson, Semina De Laurentis, Dennis Parlato, Ritamarie Kelly.

Musical parodies of Hollywood movies took a step backward with this noisy, annoying show that spoofed horror films, in particular the camp classic *The Bride of Frankenstein*. Baron John Von Frankenstein (Walter Hudson) and Dr. Pretorius (J. P. Dougherty) created a bride for the Monster (Gregory Jbara), and the predictable tale was interrupted by lame jokes and unnecessary songs. There was an empty-headed romance between Frankenstein and the nurse Mary Phillips (Semina De Laurentis), and there were the expected musical numbers with the local peasants serving as a mini-chorus. Much of the show reminded critics of Mel Brooks's film satire *Young Frankenstein* (which would be musicalized two decades later), and the comparisons were not favorable. Yet maybe just mentioning the movie was enough to interest audiences, for they kept *Have I Got a Girl for You!* running for nearly ten weeks.

THE KNIFE

[10 March 1987, Public Theatre/Estelle Newman Theatre, 32 performances] a musical play by David Hare. *Score:* Nick Bicat (music), Tim Rose Price (lyrics). *Cast:* Mandy Patinkin, Cass Morgan, Mary Elizabeth Mastrantonio, Mary Gordon Murray, Dennis Parlato, Mary Testa, William Parry.

Esteemed British playwright David Hare attempted a musical for the first and only time in his busy career, and the result was anything but predictable. Peter (Mandy Patinkin), a husband and a father, is a chef at a hotel in Winchester, England, who befriends Jenny (Mary Elizabeth Mastrantonio) whom he has accidentally stumbled on in her room when she was naked. Seeing an attractive female in the altogether does not arouse lust in Peter, but instead he realizes that he wishes to become a woman. The two become soul mates of sorts, and Jenny encourages Peter to go to Morocco and have a sex change operation so that they can become female best friends. The night before the operation Jenny argues with Peter and walks out on him, but he goes through with the operation anyway. Renaming himself Liz after the transformation, Peter gradually learns that his change of sex has not solved his problems dealing with life. At a social function, Jenny and Liz/Peter meet again (they are wearing the same dress!) and reach some kind of understanding. The improbable tale was told in earnest, and the rock score never stopped, the piece being sung through. The lyrics were not by Hare, so it was assumed he provided the story and characters rather than the actual text for this modern opera. Much of *The Knife* was awkward and improbable, yet both critics and playgoers found it intermittently fascinating. Many liked the score, and praise for the cast was enthusiastic, particularly for Patinkin. Hare directed (as he did many of his works), and reviewers found the staging as uneven as the writing. Yet there was something admirable about such a bold undertaking. *The Knife* found no producers in England, but Joe Papp was not afraid to present it for a month at the Public Theatre where it contributed to his reputation for being unpredictable and controversial.

STAGGERLEE

[18 March 1987, Second Avenue Theatre, 118 performances] a musical play by Vernel Bagneris. *Score*: Allen Toussaint (music and lyrics). *Cast*: Adam Wade, Reginald Veljohnson, Juanita Brooks, Ruth Brown, Carol Sutton.

Vernel Bagneris, the creator of *One Mo' Time*, went back to his African American past again for his folk tale musical *Staggerlee*, but the musical was problematic at best, and only its vivacious score found approval. The legend of Staggerlee goes back to 1895 when the pimp "Stag" Lee Shelton shot a man to death on the streets of St. Louis, and stories started circulating about his adventures as he ran from the law. By the 1920s there was a popular song about Staggerlee, which over the years has been recorded by many folk, country western, and rhythm and blues singers, as well as published stories and later a graphic novel. Bagneris's version was episodic and somewhat disjointed as the story was told in the late 1950s by some patrons in a bar in the South. To give the tale a love interest, Bagneris concentrated on the attempts of the fugitive Staggerlee (Adam Wade) to woo the innocent Zelita (Juanita Brooks) despite the machinations of her sly mother Elenora (Ruth Brown). Since Staggerlee was a not very likable antihero, the story never quite grabbed the audience, but the spirited songs by Allen Toussaint certainly did. Without using the famous song from the past, Toussaint conjured up the folklike nature of the tale, and the rhythm and blues score occasionally brought the show to life. It helped that the cast was first rate and that Bagneris's staging sparkled. Mixed notices led to a run of fifteen weeks, but unfortunately the score was not recorded.

THREE POSTCARDS

[14 May 1987, Playwrights Horizons, 22 performances] a musical play by Craig Lucas. *Score:* Craig Carnelia (music and lyrics). *Cast:* Carnelia, Jane Galloway, Maureen Silliman, Karen Trott, Brad O'Hare.

Songwriter Craig Carnelia had written expert songs for short-lived revues and a superior score for the Broadway failure *Is There Life After High School?* (1982), but he was (and still is) largely unknown. His full powers for incisive character songs were best revealed in this little musical that Playwrights Horizons presented for a three-week run at the end of its season. Notices were appreciative, but there was no demand for a longer run, so it closed. The editors of *Best Plays* later named it the finest musical of the season, Broadway and Off, but the score was not recorded, and the musical has pretty much disappeared. There were productions in Chicago, Los Angeles, and elsewhere, and Carnelia later recorded some of the songs himself, but *Three Postcards* is still an unknown gem.

In a swank little Greenwich Village restaurant on an off night, the only patrons are three girlfriends who have known each other since childhood. Big Jane (Jane Galloway) has gone through more boyfriends, money, and jobs than she cares to remember, but she is still hopeful. Little Jane (Maureen Silliman) is blunt and not afraid to criticize Big Jane even though her own marriage is on the rocks. The third friend, K. C. (Karen Trott), has recently lost her mother and is still dealing with the loss and her own sense of mortality. While the three women engage in small talk, reminiscences, and even accusations, their private thoughts are musicalized, often overlapping with humorous and sobering results. At one point Big Jane imagines that the waiter Walter (Brad O'Hare) is her shrink, and their session keeps getting interrupted by contributions from the other two women. Craig Lucas's script was filled with details that eventually combined to create a full picture of these three complex, likable women. His dialogue consisted of slangy small talk, vivid recollections, and funny arguments. When one first met the three friends, one wanted to categorize them into types, but with each new story or turn of the conversation the characters refused such simplification. Had Wendy Wasserstein ever written a musical libretto, it would sound something like this.

As potent as the script was, it was in the score that *Three Postcards* reaches its most emotional and entrancing heights. Carnelia's songs are brainy and witty but never artificial. The music is contemporary without a trace of pop or rock. He is also very economical, expressing many ideas in a few words and musical phrases. The three women separately consider "What the Song Should Say," listing what they hope to get out of such a reunion. As her two friends chatter on about different topics, Little Jane fantasizes that the waiter and the pianist (Carnelia) are sexually aroused by her and woo her with "I've Been Watching You." K. C. recalls her mother by thinking about "The Picture in the Hall," and a whole past generation comes alive in her recollection of details. The title song is a tricky and farcical trio in which postcards Big Jane sent from the Caribbean are read by Little Jane, who forwards them on to K. C., the three voices becoming a montage of ridiculousness and desperation. Perhaps the finest number in *Three Postcards* is the waiter's musical soliloquy "Cast of Thousands," in which he chronicles a handful of details about his life and a full picture emerges between the lines. Lucas would go on to write many plays (as well as the musical *The Light in the Piazza*), and Carnelia would continue to write good songs and be denied recognition (he later did the lyrics for the Broadway almost-ran *Sweet Smell of Success*), but both men were in top form in *Three Postcards*.

No Way to Treat a Lady

[27 May 1987, Hudson Guild Theatre, 28 performances] a musical play by Douglas J. Cohen based on William Goldman's novel. *Score:* Cohen (music and lyrics). *Cast:* Stephen Bogardus, Peter Slutsker, Liz Callaway, June Gable.

Because it ran only three and a half weeks Off Off Broadway at the Hudson Guild Theatre, it took quite a while for the clever musical thriller *No Way to Treat a Lady* to get any recognition. But a 1996 Off-Broadway revival and a cast recording have since made the little musical a cult favorite. The unemployed actor Kit Gill (Peter Slutsker) is haunted by the ghost of his mother, a famous actress, and sets out to impress her by becoming a serial killer who plays different roles as he murders middle-aged women. The restless detective Morris Brummell (Stephen Bogardus) is henpecked by his mother (who is very much alive) but sees hope when he gets the case of the serial killer and hopes to find fame by solving it. The two very different men have something in common, and once Kit starts telephoning Morris with clues and hints about his crimes, an odd rivalry develops, made more acute by Morris's girlfriend Sarah (Liz Callaway) who feels she is competing for her sweetheart's attention. Kit tries to defeat Morris by strangling Sarah, but Morris rescues her in time and shoots Kit who dies to the strains of his dead mother singing of her affection for him. The story was somewhat familiar to audiences because of William Goldman's book and a 1968 film version. Douglas J. Cohen adapted the story for four actors (June Gable played both mothers and some of Kit's murder victims) and wrote a score that often moved the plot along in a suspenseful way. The funny, revealing "I Need a Life" introduced the two male characters effectively, the waltzing "What Shall I Sing for You?" showed both the tender and obsessive side of mother love, and the eager "Once More from the Top" illustrated the desperate side of the villain. There were two dandy duets: the wry "So Far, So Good" when Morris and Sarah first met and sized each other up in their thoughts, and the sexy "First Move" in which Morris's plan to seduce Sarah overlapped with Kit's preparation for a new murder. Cohan's music sometimes employed ethnic melodies, such as the Irish ditty "Only a Heartbeat Away" and the Italian fandango "Safer in My Arms." Often the songs were able to create tension and then quickly relieve it through music, as with "Front Page News" and Mrs. Brummell's hilarious "I Hear Humming." *No Way to Treat a Lady* was very much a performer's showcase too, with Gable playing a series of daffy women and Slutsker playing broad character types, from an Irish priest to a fearful matron to a fey dancing instructor. When the York Theatre Company revived the musical in 1996, it also boasted a superb cast—Adam Grupper as Morris, Paul Schoeffler as Kit, Marguerite McIntyre as Sarah, and Alix Korey as all the matrons—whose performances were preserved on CD. But the real star of the show remains Cohen, whose script and score are a little masterwork of comic suspense.

BITTERSUITE

[5 October 1987, Palsson's Supper Club, 211 performances] a musical revue. *Score:* Elliot Weiss (music), Michael Champagne (lyrics). *Cast:* Suzanne Blakeslee, David Edwards, Byron Nease, Barbara Marineau.

Critics had trouble describing this musical revue about contemporary life, some calling it eclectic, others writing that the authors tossed anything and everything into the soup. Yet several admitted it was an entertaining and sometimes insightful hodgepodge and recommended it. Two men and two women played a variety of roles in sketches and songs that covered everything from dating and parenthood to getting older and reviewing past mistakes. The score embraced old-time Tin Pan Alley, smoky nightclub numbers, farcical waltzes, nonsense songs, and mock operetta. The tone was mostly satirical, though the revue had its touching moments, as in the ballad "I'll Be There" and the reflective "Fathers and Sons." *Bittersuite*, subtitled "songs of experience," ran twenty-six weeks, then soon after it closed a new edition titled *Bittersuite—One More Time* opened at the same venue and ran eighteen performances. The new version featured a different cast and a handful of new songs by the same songwriters. *Bittersuite* later found life in regional theatres, including a well-received production in San Francisco.

SARAFINA!

[25 October 1987, Mitzi E. Newhouse Theatre, 81 performances; Cort Theatre, 597 performances] a musical play by Mbongeni Ngema. *Score:* Ngema, Hugh Masekela (music and lyrics). *Cast:* Leleti Khumalo, Pat Mlaba, Mhlathi Khuzwayo, Nhlanhla Ngema, Congo Hadebe.

An import from South Africa, this rousing musical was about the triumph of the human spirit, even though it took place under the shadow of Apartheid.

In a Johannesburg high school for blacks, the students put on a play about
Nelson Mandela who was imprisoned at the time. The crushing oppression of
Apartheid was evident, but the musical centered on the vivacious Soweto girl
Sarafina (Leleti Khumalo) as she and her classmates celebrated their youth,
their tribal culture, and their belief in a better world. What the show lacked
in plot and character development it had in vitality and musical power. The
songs were all in the pulsating African flavor, a style known as Mbaqanga,
which was heard in the black neighborhoods of Johannesburg. Yet many
of the songs were sung in English, and the score was easily accessible to
all audiences. "Give Us Power" and "Freedom Is Coming Tomorrow" were
straightforward and demanding, while other numbers such as "Africa Burning
in the Sun" and "Yes! Mistress It's a Pity" were poignant and understated. The
score climaxed with "Bring Back Nelson Mandela" in which Sarafina portrayed the human rights leader and expressed what she believed he would say
if he were freed. The score also included some traditional African songs, and
there were a few in the native Xosa (or clicking) language which Apartheid
had outlawed. Author Mbongeni Ngema directed the fiery production which
also featured vigorous choreography by Ndaba Mhlongo. The young cast from
Johannesburg thrilled the press and the playgoers, and *Sarafina!* overrode its
weaknesses to become a hit. It quickly sold out its ten-week engagement in
Lincoln Center's Off-Broadway venue and then transferred to the intimate
Cort Theatre on Broadway and pleased audiences for nineteen months. A
film version in 1992 added adult characters and spent much footage showing
the oppression of Apartheid, but Leleti Khumalo reprised her Sarafina, and
the movie intermittently came to life when the students were featured.

BIRDS OF PARADISE

[26 October 1987, Promenade Theatre, 24 performances] a musical play
by Winnie Holzman, David Evans. *Score:* Holzman (lyrics), Evans (music). *Cast:* Todd Graff, John Cunningham, Crista Moore, Barbara Walsh,
Donna Murphy, Mary Beth Peil, Andrew Hill Newman, J. K. Simmons.

With its triple-level plot, intricate songs, and complex characters, *Birds of
Paradise* was invigorating theatregoing even though it didn't quite come off.
Yet there was so much talent and good ideas present that the musical has
developed a cult following and has found some life regionally after its disappointing three-week run Off Broadway. The first plot concerns the members

of the Harbour Island Players, a community theatre filled with eager and not untalented artists. The celebrated actor Lawrence Wood (John Cunningham) hails from the area and returns to direct a new musical by local writer Homer (Todd Graff). All are very impressed by him, including Homer's girlfriend Julia (Crista Moore), who falls for the stage star, but all are disillusioned when Wood suddenly picks up and leaves before opening night for a Broadway job. The second plot concerns Homer's play, a surreal version of Chekhov's *The Seagull* set in Antarctica with singing penguins. The third plot is Chekhov's play itself, which is paralleled in all the backstage proceedings. The script by Winnie Holzman and David Evans was intelligent and funny if a bit contrived at times, but their score rarely fumbled. From the intriguing opening "So Many Nights," in which each member of the Harbour Players expressed his or her excitement about the upcoming project, to the reflective closing "Something New," when the company accepts and rejoices in Homer's new ending for the musical, the score is filled with varied delights. The love duet "Coming True," the bittersweet lament "Things I Can't Forget," Wood's smug and pathetic character song "Somebody," the entrancing ballad "Imagining You," and the raucous title number were highlights in a superb score. The cast, which included future Broadway leads Donna Murphy, Mary Beth Peil, and Barbara Walsh, was first class, as was the direction by Arthur Laurents. *Birds of Paradise* had begun as a project at New York University and, with Laurents's name recognition, it found a producer for Off Broadway. The show's short run was a cruel disappointment, but *Birds of Paradise* lives on because of its cast recording.

OIL CITY SYMPHONY

[5 November 1987, Circle in the Square, 626 performances] a musical revue by Mike Craver, Debra Monk, Mary Murfitt, Mark Hardwick. *Score:* Craver, Monk, Murfitt, Hardwick. *Cast:* Craver, Monk, Murfitt, Hardwick.

Some of the talent behind the popular *Pump Boys and Dinettes* reteamed for this funnier, more musically satisfying revue, and it tickled the audience's funny bone for twenty months. Four singer-musicians who liked to play middle-of-the-road hits while in high school in Oil City, Ohio, join together in the school gym and perform a show to honor their old music teacher Miss Reves. The foursome play a variety of instruments and sing songs (some oldies, others originals) in a determined and earnest manner, and the "concert" they performed was hilarious. These bright-eyed adults were not untalented, but they obviously had always been out of touch and continued to not see how ridiculous they are. Calling themselves the Oil City Symphony, the quartet introduced themselves and elaborated on their uninteresting lives between songs. At one point they even insisted on the whole audience standing up and doing "The Hokey Pokey." To hear their off-kilter renditions of standards like "Baby, It's Cold Outside" and witness the theme from the movie *Exodus* performed as a drum tour de force were silly enough, but it was in their original songs that *Oil City Symphony* reached its zany peak. The desperate-to-be-hip "My Old Kentucky Rock and Roll Home," the perky "Beehive Polka," the nostalgic "Bus Ride," the naive ballad "Iris," and the idiotically idyllic "Ohio Afternoon" were among the most incongruously amusing numbers. The cast, who wrote the new songs as well as provided all instrumental accompaniment for the show, were splendid, attacking their material straightfaced and without the least hint of self-awareness. The musical had started as a Christmas program Off Off Broadway, was expanded and polished in Dallas, then opened at the Circle in The Square Downtown, which was converted to look like a high school gym. Reviews were encouraging, and word of mouth was even stronger, so *Oil City Symphony* soon caught on. The only mistake the creators made was the show's title. It confused potential audiences, some who came were disappointed it was not a concert, and there was no symphony. The producers changed the title to simply *Oil City*, but by that time the musical had found its stride. What is unfortunate is that regional productions used the original title and the confusion in the hinterlands was even greater; many a fine production was not seen by as many people as it might have with a better title.

THE NO-FRILLS REVUE

[25 November 1987, Cherry Lane Theatre, 207 performances] a musical revue by Martin Charnin, Douglas Bernstein, Denis Markell. *Score:* various. *Cast:* Bob Stillman, Lynn Paynter, Andre Montgomery, Adinah Alexander, Sarah Knapp, Stephani Hardy, Sasha Charnin, Clare Fields.

Director-writer Martin Charnin and other talent from the witty revue *Upstairs at O'Neals'* joined forces with a multitude of different artists and came up with this musical which patterned itself on the smart and sassy Off-Broadway revues of the past. Even its title was homage to Ben Bagley's *The Shoestring*

Revue. Ronny Graham, who wrote some of those past glories, wrote some of the sketches and lyrics, and the other contributors included such talents as Craig Carnelia, Marvin Hamlisch, Douglas Bernstein, Sally Weeks, and Thomas Meehan. While the subjects for the songs and sketches covered many fields, from high school reunions to supermarket mishaps, the most entertaining items had to do with show business, particularly the theatre. Musical fans most enjoyed the mini-musical spoofs: *West Side Story* as written by Jerry Herman, *Annie* as done by Stephen Sondheim, and *Fiddler on the Roof* as penned by Noël Coward. The old Abbott and Costello routine "Who's on First" was merrily updated in the number "Bud, Lou, and Who?" The revues themselves were lampooned in the title song and the funny "Stools," a holdover from *Upstairs at O'Neals'*. The nine-member cast was perhaps a few too many, for only a handful had solos, and the chances to shine individually were limited. Once again Charnin directed, and the revue breezed along nicely, bringing enjoyment that was satisfying if not memorable. *The No-Frills Revue* ran twenty-six weeks and, with some updating and revisions, was produced regionally on occasion.

TEN PERCENT REVUE

[13 April 1988, Susan Bloch Theatre, 239 performances] a musical revue by Tom Wilson Weinberg. *Score*: Weinberg (music and lyrics). *Cast*: Valerie Hill, Timothy Williams, Robert Tate, Trish Kane, Lisa Bernstein.

A musical revue that ran slightly longer was Tom Wilson Weinberg's *Ten Percent Revue*. The title referred to the percentage of the population who were not heterosexual, and the show was notable for the way it gave equal time to lesbians and gays. Much of the material was predictable, but both gay and straight audiences found the musical appealing enough to run nearly eight months. *Ten Percent Revue* was performed in a handful of different American cities, then in 1987 Weinberg made a cast recording. The Off-Broadway production opened a year later and received appreciative if not glowing notices. Most of the numbers were list songs which chronicled examples of an idea rather than develop it. "Not Allowed" listed legal and social rules gays should not break. In "Wedding Song" couples lamented all the marriage ceremony customs, from photo albums to toasts, that were denied to them. "We're Everywhere" rattled off all the different places on earth where gays could be found, while "Flaunting It" was a series of examples of gay behavior judged by others to be too overt. More interesting was "If I Were/I'd Like to Be" in which a gay man lists the attributes (and clichés) about lesbians that he wishes he had while a gay woman fantasizes about being a male homosexual. A song about three-way sex called "Threesome" was witless and went nowhere, but a sketch about high-minded personal ads with crass subtexts was funny. When the revue shifted its tone in the later half and offered songs, statistics, and quotes about the AIDS epidemic, the effect was jarring because much of what preceded it wallowed in broad stereotypes. Only in "Before Stonewall," a knowing ballad about hidden gay love, did the score offer something memorable.

LUCKY STIFF

[25 April 1988, Playwrights Horizons, 15 performances] a musical farce by Lynn Ahrens based on Michael Butterworth's book *The Man Who Broke the Bank at Monte Carlo*. *Score*: Ahrens (lyrics), Stephen Flaherty (music). *Cast*: Stephen Stout, Mary Testa, Julie White, Stuart Zagnit, Paul Kandel, Ron Farber.

This bubbly musical farce would be noteworthy, if for no other reason, because it introduced Lynn Ahrens and Stephen Flaherty, the busiest and best new songwriting team during the final decades of the century. Yet *Lucky Stiff* is a superior piece of musical nonsense and would still be regularly revived today no matter whose names were attached to it. To call it promising is an understatement; it delivers and does not need to be viewed as an early work by up-and-coming artists. Ahrens adapted the little known novel *The Man Who Broke the Bank at Monte Carlo* about a weird last will and testament that requires a dead body to be transported across Europe. It was not very encouraging material, and most writers would dismiss the premise as too silly and too complicated to put on stage. But Ahrens's version is swift, funny, very physical and, hardest of all, it uses songs to continue the shenanigans rather than slow them down. Here is a musical that knows when to speed up and when to quiet down for a touching character moment and never stops being a farce. It ranks with *The Boys from Syracuse* and *A Funny Thing Happened on the Way to the Forum* when it comes to plotting and scoring and the way in which the two can coexist.

The mild-mannered, frustrated Brit Harry Witherspoon (Stephen Stout), trapped in a dull job in London inventorying shoes, sees his life change when a will from his late Uncle Anthony leaves him $6 million if he will take the stuffed corpse of his deceased relative on a holiday to Monte Carlo. Harry reluctantly agrees, but when the oddball twosome arrive in France, two others are there who are also trying to get the inheritance: the late Anthony's nearsighted mistress Rita La Porta (Mary Testa), who needs cash before her gangster husband finds out she stole it from him, and the naive animal lover Annabel Glick (Julie White), who knows the money will go to the Universal Dog Home of Brooklyn if Harry does not fulfill the requirements of the will. Rita's brother, the henpecked optometrist Vinnie DiRuzzio (Stuart Zagnit), who has been forced to aid the scatterbrained Rita, and the suspicious Luigi Gaudi (Paul Kandel), who seems to pop up everywhere Harry goes, are also involved in the chaos, which climaxes with the discovery that Anthony is not dead but substituted the body of his friend to find out who tried to kill him. Like all good farces, much of *Lucky Stiff* was surprisingly logical. Even rarer, some of the characters actually had more than one layer to them, and the unlikely romance between the dog-hating Harry and the reticent Annabel was touching and believable. Although the action traveled from Atlantic City to England to the French Riviera, it all seemed like a concise door-slamming bedroom farce. The physical humor, such as marvelous bits with the wheelchair-laden corpse, was matched by character humor and breezy dialogue. Even if the script had been in shambles, the score for *Lucky Stiff* would still deserve attention. Stephen Flaherty would prove to be one of the most musically versatile composers over the next few decades, and *Lucky Stiff* is filled with Broadway brass, pseudo-French numbers, light operetta, and contemporary music that avoids rock and pop. His music can be as oddball as the situation, as with the opening "Something Funny's Going On" and the chaotic "Him, Them, It, Her." The recurring "Good to Be Alive" is a vigorous theme song that changes meaning with Ahrens's sly lyrics. The musical monologues "Mr. Witherspoon's Friday Night," "Rita's Confession," and "The Phone Call" are hilarious pieces of mock recitative, while the conversational "Fancy Meeting You Here" and the nightmare sequence "Welcome Back, Mr. Witherspoon" are musical storytelling at its best. Just as resplendent are the score's two quietest moments: Annabel's wry lament "Times Like This," in which she longs for the comfort of an animal over human company, and the funny-sad duet "Nice," in which Harry and Annabel admit they will miss their rivalry. In the soft-shoe number "Lucky," Harry dances with his dead uncle, turning the wheelchair into a willing dancing partner. This is sublime silliness as only *Lucky Stiff* could imagine it.

Playwrights Horizons sandwiched in the new musical for two weeks between other offerings, and it received little attention by the press or the public. Much of the cast of unknowns were highly praised, as was the direction by Thommie Walsh. *Lucky Stiff* might have faded from memory had it not been recorded in 1994 with an excellent cast, some of whom were in the original Off-Broadway production. An Off-Off-Broadway mounting in 2003 by the York Theatre Company resulted in a second recording, and these two CDs are what brought the show to the attention of regional, college, and summer theatres. Of course, Ahrens and Flaherty were quite well known by the 1990s, and interest in their work also lead theatres to discover the early joys of *Lucky Stiff*. The little musical was lucky after all; it is a theatre story with a happy ending.

URBAN BLIGHT

[19 June 1988, City Center Stage I, 48 performances] a musical revue by Christopher Durang, Terrence McNally, Wendy Wasserstein, Jules Feiffer, Shel Silverstein, George C. Wolfe, various. *Score:* Richard Maltby Jr. (lyrics), David Shire (music). *Cast:* Faith Prince, John Rubenstein, Larry Fishburne, Oliver Platt, E. Katherine Kerr, Rex Robbins, Nancy Giles.

When the Manhattan Theatre Club was putting together a musical revue about contemporary life in New York City, artistic director Lynn Meadow commissioned sketches from a wide range of American playwrights, and she received material from everyone from Christopher Durang to Arthur Miller. The plan was to solicit songs from various songwriters as well, but when she and John Tillinger, the show's director, asked Richard Maltby Jr. and David Shire to contribute, the team handed them a file full of songs about urban living that had been accumulating over the years. Six were chosen for the revue (Edward Kleban provided the only other song) and, ironically, it was the songs that were mostly praised by the press, not the skits by the celebrated playwrights. Several aspects of Manhattan living were covered in the revue, and the sketches varied in tone and temperament, yet it was in the songs that the show came alive. A married couple accidentally reveals to the audience (and each other) how their relationship failed, all done in the format of a carefree lounge ballad. A woman no longer young insists that she's not complaining while she sings her "Life Story" about trying to start over after a divorce. The 1980s health kick was satirized in "Aerobicantata," and the revue opened and closed with the cautionary "Don't Fall for the Lights" about the lure of the city. Most lauded was the effervescent character song "Miss Byrd," in which a repressed secretary breaks out of her shell and into the sexual revolution without ever leaving her swivel chair. The cast, a mixture of musical comedy talent and actors known for their work in nonmusicals, was uniformly terrific, but it was the singers, such as Faith Prince and Nancy Giles, who shone the most. The six-week engagement of *Urban Blight* was well received by the critics and the public, but the score was not recorded. Some of Maltby and Shire's songs would later reappear in their revue *Closer Than Ever* and be recorded then.

Suds

[25 September 1988, Criterion Center, 81 performances] a musical play by Melinda Gilb, Steve Gunderson, Bryan Scott. *Score:* various. *Cast:* Gilb, Gunderson, Christine Sevec, Susan Mosher.

Audiences were treated to fifty-one song hits from the 1960s in this musical revue, subtitled *The Rocking '60s Musical Soap Opera*, which had an uninspired but workable premise. Heartbroken Cindy (Christine Sevec) sits in a laundromat in the early 1960s and is so depressed over her failed love life that she considers ending it all until three guardian angels in flashy attire and big hairdos come to cheer her up with song favorites of the era. The numbers ranged from bubblegum "girl group" songs such as "It's My Party" to the Beatles' "Do You Want to Know a Secret," with plenty of Burt Bacharach, Hal David, Ellie Greenwich, Neil Sedaka, and James Brown in between. Except for the presence of a male angel (coauthor Steve Gunderson), the show often resembled the all-girl revue *Beehive* and, like that show, it was an agreeable nonevent. *Suds* was more bare bones than *Beehive* without the parade of costumes and wigs, and it did not prove to be as popular. All the same, the revue, which had originated at the Old Globe Playhouse in San Diego, found an audience for eight weeks.

The Taffetas

[12 October 1988, Cherry Lane Theatre, 165 performances] a musical revue by Rick Lewis. *Score:* various. *Cast:* Jody Abrahams, Tia Speros, Melanie Mitchell, Karen Curlee.

While audiences were enjoying Sixties lite rock and easy listening in *Suds*, a revue opened that celebrated the Fifties, a decade a bit further removed and deeper into nostalgia. On the now-defunct Dumont network, a girl group from Muncie, Indiana, called The Taffetas make their television debut in a musical cavalcade of the decade's hit songs. It was an even slimmer premise than *Suds*, but all that counted were the songs. The program was organized into different musical sequences, such as "For Lovers and Dreamers," "Juke Box Heart Throb," "Medley for Broken Hearts," and "Swinging and Ringing with the Taffetas." Most of the songs were delivered in four-part harmony by the quartet of taffeta-clad girls, but there were some solos as well, which provided a relief from all the girlish crooning. Very little 1950s rock and roll made it into the program, the emphasis being on middle-of-the-road hits like "Mr. Sandman," "You Belong to Me," "Tennessee Waltz," "Where the Boys Are," and "Music! Music! Music!" Simple or nonsense ditties like "Doggy in the Window" and "Rag Mop" provided the show's lighter moments, and even the singing commercial "See the U.S.A. in Your Chevrolet" was tossed in for good measure. By the end of the evening, forty-five songs had been delivered by the four performers who were applauded for their singing prowess and ability to mimic some of the stars who made the songs famous. Critics thought the evening harmless fun but, weary from *Beehive* and *Suds*, could not work up much enthusiasm for the piece. *The Taffetas* had been developed Off Off Broadway as a cabaret program, and it pretty much stayed small and intimate Off Broadway, where it ran twenty-one weeks. A few years later, after the success of the four-man revue *Forever Plaid*, regional and summer theatres looking for a female version of that hit revived *The Taffetas* and treated audiences to similar songs from the same time period.

THE MIDDLE OF NOWHERE

[20 November 1988, Astor Place Theatre, 24 performances] a musical play by Tracy Friedman. *Score:* Randy Newman (music and lyrics). *Cast:* Roger Robinson, Vondie Curtis-Hall, Diana Castle, Michael Arlen, Tony Hoylen.

The parade of musicals using already-familiar songs continued with *The Middle of Nowhere*, which attempted to go beyond a predictable catalogue of hits and be about something. In a Louisiana bus depot far off the main road, four travelers (a redneck, a young girl, a salesman, and a GI) are stranded for a while. It is 1969, a time of racial tension, and the four white passengers feel uncomfortable about the African American station attendant Joe (Roger Robinson), who is their only link to the outside world. The awkwardness is broken by a flash of lightning which turns the depot into a fantasy vaudeville stage, and the five characters perform a surreal minstrel show that is both satiric and disturbing. The numbers they sang were all songs popularized by songwriter-singer Randy Newman, and they contained enough variety and character to become theatrical showpieces. The evocative "I Think It's Going to Rain Today," the wry "Short People," the breezy "Sail Away," the abrasive "Rednecks," and the ballad "Louisiana 1927" were among the Newman songs that found considerable potency when placed into the context of the five characters. Author Tracy Friedman also directed and choreographed the little musical and managed to make the unusual premise work most of the time. Reviews were supportive but audiences were sparse, and *The Middle of Nowhere* folded after three weeks.

SWEETHEARTS

[7 December, 1988, Actors Playhouse, 54 performances] a musical revue. *Score:* various. *Cast:* Antoinette Mille, Walter Adkins.

For playgoers yearning for nostalgia of the 1930s, there was this two-character show which was subtitled *Nostalgic Musical Memories of Jeanette MacDonald and Nelson Eddy*. The operatic duets by the famous movie couple had become fodder for satire and even camp by the 1960s, but this musical salute to the singing team was done straight. The careers of MacDonald and Eddy were chronicled between selections from such film operettas as *Rose-Marie*, *New Moon*, *Naughty Marietta*, and *Sweethearts*. Songs sung on the screen by just one of the duo were also included, but it was the duets that were highlighted, the voices of Antoinette Mille and Walter Adkins rising together in joyous abandon. No one was listed as author of the narration or as director, so it was assumed that pianist-conductor David Wolfson was behind the project which had originated in Tacoma, Washington. The audience appeal of *Sweethearts* was limited, to say the least, but operetta fans (or was it MacDonald-Eddy fans?) came for seven weeks.

GENESIS

[17 January 1989, Public Theatre/LuEsther Hall, 8 performances] a musical play by A. J. Antoon, Robert Montgomery based on medieval mystery plays. *Score:* Antoon, Montgomery (lyrics), Michael Ward (music). *Cast:* Russ Thacker, Stephen Bogardus, Mary Munger, David Patrick Kelly, Christine Toy, Braden Danner.

SONGS OF PARADISE

[23 January 1989, Public Theatre/Susan Stein Sheva Theatre, 136 performances] a musical in Yiddish by Miriam Hoffman, Rena Berkowicz Borow, based on biblical poetry by Itsik Manger. *Score:* Hoffman, Borow (lyrics), Rosalie Gerut (music). *Cast:* Gerut, Avi Hoffman, Adrienne Cooper, David Kener, Eleanor Reissa.

Producer Joseph Papp offered two biblical musicals opening within a week in two different venues at the Public Theatre, and both were of interest even though they dealt with the same stories from the Old Testament. Director and coauthor A. J. Antoon's *Genesis* was subtitled *Music and Miracles for a New Age* and went back to a handful of mystery plays from the Middle Ages for its text. The creation, the fall of Adam and Eve, the murder of Cain, Noah's flood, and the test of Abraham's faith by his willingness to sacrifice his son Isaac were the familiar tales which were pretty much sung through. Michael Ward's music was not strictly medieval but suggested the flavor of such music even as it had a modern "new wave" sound. Lynn Taylor-Corbett choreographed the superior cast, and designer John Conklin provided some stunning visuals. The one-week presentation was deemed quite impressive, yet Papp did not extend the run. He did let the second musical, *Songs of Paradise*, continue on, and audiences came for seventeen weeks. The Bible was again the source, this time as seen through the Yiddish poetry of Itsik Manger. A cast of five portrayed Adam and Eve (Odem and Khave in Yiddish) and their sons and offspring through to Abraham (Avrum), Jacob (Yankev), and Joseph (Yosef), and the musical was performed in both English and Yiddish. First developed at the YIVO Institute for Jewish Research, the musical was presented under the title of the Joseph Papp Yiddish Theatre in Riverdale, New York, before transferring to Off Broadway. The tone of the show varied considerably throughout the program, ranging from reverent passages of grief and lamentation to Yiddish vaudeville schtick. Rosalie Gerut's music was praised for its variety and tuneful quality, and the cast members, under the direction of fellow performer Avi Hoffman, were also commended for their versatility. Some critics preferred *Genesis* over *Songs of Paradise*, but Papp had more invested in the latter, so it was held over. The Yiddish-English production also had a greater appeal to New Yorkers, and it ran to the end of the season, and Papp brought it back the following season for thirty-two performances.

LAUGHING MATTERS

[18 May 1989, St. Peter's Church, 85 performances] a musical revue by Linda Wallem, Peter Tolan. *Score:* Tolan (music and lyrics). *Cast:* Wallem, Tolan.

With its wickedly funny parody of Stephen Sondheim (the Dick and Jane early reader books were presented in the songwriter's complex style), this revue was reminiscent of an edition of *Forbidden Broadway*. Yet most of the revue *Laughing Matters* consisted of two-person sketches about urban life, and show business was only on the periphery. Linda Wallem and Peter Tolan wrote and performed all the skits, under the direction of Martin Charnin, and often the two comic actors were better than their material. All the same, the handful of songs by Tolan was right on the money. In addition to the Sondheim spoof, there was "When You Live in New York" that took Lenny Bruce's point of view about non-Jews acting like Jews, and an oddball song about a dog named "Max" who has peculiar food appetites. Some critics described Wallem and Tolan as a 1980s version of Elaine May and Mike Nichols, though more in performance than in the script. Word of mouth for *Laughing Matters* was strong, helping the economic little show run over ten weeks.

SHOWING OFF

[18 May 1989, Steve McGraw's, 172 performances] a musical cabaret by Douglas Bernstein, Denis Markell. *Score:* Bernstein, Markell (music and lyrics). *Cast:* Bernstein, Donna Murphy, Veanne Cox, Mark Sawyer.

Performers also outshone their material in the cabaret revue *Showing Off*, which found a following and ran five and a half months. Douglas Bernstein, a veteran of several topical revues, cowrote and led a superb cast in this wry look at life in New York City in 1989. The sketches covered native New Yorkers versus transplanted ones, Gotham newspapers, and of course urban romance. The songs were more character oriented, though there was a splendid parody of the children's singing favorite Raffi in concert. The title song celebrated New York cockiness, and apartment living was sung about in "Rental Cruelty," but the best songs were more personal, as in the quixotic "Joshua Noveck," the lilting "Michele," and the reflective "How Things Change." The production, directed and choreographed by Michael Leeds, was minimal, but with Bernstein, Veanne Cox, Mark Sawyer, and Donna Murphy all in top form, *Showing Off* didn't need much else.

PRIVATES ON PARADE

[22 August 1989, Christian C. Yegen Theatre, 64 performances] a play with songs by Peter Nichols. *Score:* Nichols (lyrics), Denis King (music). *Cast:* Jim Dale, Simon Jones, Donna Murphy, Jim Fyfe, Edward Hibbert, Gregory Jbara, Ross Bickell, John Curry, Stephen Lee, Tom Matsusaka, Donald Burton.

Donna Murphy went from an American revue to the British semi-musical *Privates on Parade*. She was one of few American actors to join Brit Jim Dale when he played the civilian female impersonator Terri Dennis who entertains British troops stationed in Singapore and Malaysia in 1947. Under the questionable leadership of Major Giles Flack (Simon Jones), the entertainment unit, titled Song and Dance Unit South East Asia (S.A.D.U.S.E.A.), is third rate, but the desperate soldiers are eager for any diversion, and they cheer the tawdry music hall numbers and the ribald jokes. The naive Pvt. Steven Flowers (Jim Fyfe) is new to the outfit, while the hardened Sylvia Morgan (Murphy), the only female in the gang, has no illusions left. When Flack stupidly leads his outfit into a zone where Communists are battling the locals, some members of the unit die, and the trivial nature of the enterprise turns very sobering. Playwright Peter Nichols wrote the lyrics for the hopelessly cheery songs, which had music by Denis King, that accurately pastiched the variety numbers of the era. While some songs had a phony international flavor, such as "Danke Schön," "The Latin American Way," and "Les Girls," most were very British and nicely contrasted stiff upper lip with bawdy humor. The old-time sing-along "Sunnyside Lane," the vampy "Could You Please Inform Us," and the smirking title number were not your usual musical theatre fare but were closer to an adult-rated pantomime. All the songs in *Privates on Parade* were part of the shows being performed, and some might hesitate to call the production a musical, but there were a dozen musical numbers, and sometimes they even commented on the action as in the Broadway musical *Cabaret*, particularly with the double-edged "The Price of Peace." *Privates on Parade* was not a new work, having premiered in London in 1977 (with Dale as Terri) and filmed in 1982. It had its American premiere at the Long Wharf Theatre in New Haven, and it was that production, directed by Larry Carpenter and choreographed by Daniel Pelzig, that was presented by the Roundabout Theatre Off Broadway. Critical reaction was decidedly mixed, some commentators finding the show potent and disturbing, others dismissing it as a toothless antiwar piece. Most agreed that Dale's performance, from his campy impersonations of Carmen Miranda and Marlene Dietrich to his heartbreaking moments of lucidity, was compelling. Audiences had only two months to see for themselves, then it was gone. Being cited as the Best Foreign Play by the New York Drama Critics Circle at the end of the season came too late since *Privates on Parade* was gone before November. Ambitious theatre companies have revived it on occasion, but the show still seems too British for most American audiences.

Closer Than Ever

[6 November 1989, Cherry Lane Theatre, 288 performances] a musical revue. *Score:* David Shire (music), Richard Maltby Jr. (lyrics). *Cast:* Sally Mayes, Lynne Wintersteller, Richard Muenz, Brent Barrett, Patrick Scott Brady.

The songs for this impressive musical revue came from a variety of sources, from unproduced musicals to produced flops and private numbers written for family members, and the quality of the material varied as well, but there was no mistaking that the songwriting team of Richard Maltby Jr. and David Shire were at the peak of their powers. One of innumerable shows about coping with the tribulations of contemporary urban life, *Closer Than Ever* distinguished itself by focusing on early and late middle-aged people giving a maturity and wider scope of understanding in the songs. Sometimes wisdom came from experience, but usually the characters singing were only beginning to put the pieces together, and there were some who were still clueless. Nearly all the songs were incisive character numbers, even those in which the character was annoying or the sentiments expressed were labored. Some numbers, such as "Patterns," "One of the Good Guys," "Life Story," and "Three Friends," told a story that stretched over years. Others were more immediate reactions to the present situation, such as the upwardly mobile couple juggling their lives and their baby in "Fandango" or the frantic man going berserk over unrequited love in "What Am I Doin'?" The score included some dandy list songs as well, such as "The Bear, the Tiger, the Hamster and the Mole" in which a self-sufficient woman names all the species in which the female does not need a male, or the rejected female who bitterly describes to her ex-lover all the kinds of friends she already has when he asks "You Want to Be My Friend?" "She Loves Me Not" was a simple, straightforward ballad about not having your affections returned, sung by a man about a woman, a woman about a man, and a man about a man. The four cast members had only a few ensemble numbers, though the opening "Doors" was a bright and busy song about life's unknown qualities, and the merry "March of Time" ruefully acknowledged those little signs of aging. Less satisfying were numbers that seemed to be put into the revue for personal reasons and felt out of place, such as a salute to the two songwriters' fathers in "If I Sing" and the musical kvetching about needed exercise in "There's Nothing Like It." Since all the numbers were personal rather than satirical commentaries on the times, the funny "The Sound of Muzak," a wry look at mass-produced public music written by the team back in 1965 and updated, surely felt like it came from another revue. The score included pieces from the team's Broadway entry *Baby* and their Off-Broadway revues *The Sap of Life* and *Urban Blight*, as well as several trunk tunes going back to the 1960s. In fact, only a handful of the twenty-five songs performed were written for the new show. Regardless of the resulting unevenness, *Closer Than Ever* played beautifully on stage, and each cast member, under the direction of Maltby, had opportunities to shine individually. The critics applauded the intelligent, character-driven revue, and audiences responded favorably, keeping the show on the boards for nine months. Regional theatres also welcomed the thought-provoking musical, encouraged by the well-produced, complete recording of the score by the original cast. Two of those cast members, Sally Mayes and Lynne Wintersteller, also appeared two decades later in the 2010 Off-Broadway revival which Maltby again directed. Some lyrics were altered to keep the show contemporary, and a new song, "Dating Again," was added.

Up Against It

[4 December 1989, Public Theatre/LuEsther Hall, 16 performances] a musical by Tom Ross based on a screenplay by Joe Orton. *Score:* Todd Rundgren (music and lyrics). *Cast:* Roger Bart, Philip Casnoff, Alison Fraser, Dan Tubb, Tony Dibuono, Mari Nelson.

A curious footnote in the careers of British playwright Joe Orton and the Beatles is the screenplay *Up Against It* which Orton wrote for the Fab Four in the 1960s. The project never materialized, but the script was published and in 1989 was turned into a musical by Tom Ross. Since the Beatles had penned no songs for the unmade film, rock songwriter Todd Rundgren provided the score which turned out to be less rock and more a pastiche of theatre songs, from Gilbert and Sullivan airs and British music hall turns to bright Broadway ditties and Bertolt Brecht–Kurt Weill spoofs. In the stage version, three Brit friends, Ian McTurk (Philip Casnoff), Christopher Low (Roger Bart), and Jack Ramsay (Dan Tubb), have little interest in women yet are besieged by them at every turn, making the boys antifeminists and setting them on a plot to assassinate the first female Prime Minister. (It was the suggestion that the Liverpool friends are gay that caused the Beatles to pass on *Up Against It*.) Like the screenplay, the tale is told as an absurdist fantasy with the songs rarely having much to do with the outlandish story or characters. The cartoon-like scenery and erratic staging may have been aiming for a *Yellow Submarine* look, but critics thought the Public Theatre production a hopeless and toothless jumble. Despite the continuing interest in the Beatles and the recent interest in Orton, the two-week engagement passed without notoriety.

Romance in Hard Times

[28 December 1989, Public Theatre/Newman Theatre, 6 performances] a musical play by William Finn. *Score:* Finn (music and lyrics). *Cast:* Lillias White, Cleavon Derricks, Alix Korey, Lawrence Clayton, Victor Trent Cook, Peggy Hewett, Michael Mandell, J. P. Dougherty, Amanda Naughton, Stacey Lynn Brass.

Even in such a muddled musical as *Romance in Hard Times*, it was clear that William Finn was still worth paying attention to. Playgoers only had a week to pay attention and few took the opportunity, so the Public Theatre production disappeared without a cast recording. A few of the songs were later recorded and heard in Finn revues; it was not a complete loss. But one look at the cast list, one can see that there was something special going on here. Finn wrote the book as well as the score, and the piece was first workshopped under the title of *America Kicks Up Its Heels*. By the time the show opened at the Public, all the old songs but one was dropped, the cast of predominantly white characters had become mostly African American, and the script was a mess. In a soup kitchen in New York City during the Depression, First Lady Eleanor Roosevelt (Peggy Hewett) makes an unscheduled appearance, and the workers and patrons of the place express their opinions about America and describe the problems they face in their lives. The story took the form of a fable, but the issues were real enough, and the characters, at least when they were singing, had more depth than mere types, pulling the musical in two directions. Soup distributor Hennie (Lillias White), a very determined and very pregnant African American woman, served as the spokesperson of the group, and she found her full voice in the lullaby "That's Enough for Me," singing to her unborn child to stay in the womb until the world is a better place. The character of Hennie was balanced by the wealthy white socialite Zoe (Alix Korey), who sings about how she and all her friends saw their world collapse in 1929 in "All Fall Down." White and Korey were outstanding, as were many of the fine cast members, but they labored in vain. *Romance in Hard Times* is hardly worth saving, but surely the entire score deserves to be heard some day.

Chapter Six

—◯—

Battling the Big Bucks: The 1990s

CORPORATE MERGERS PROLIFERATED in the entertainment business world in the 1990s, and for the first time live theatre in New York was drawn into the corporate whirl. With Broadway musicals costing up to $14 million to produce, the days of the lone producer and a handful of backers were over. It took major corporations to come up with that kind of money, and such companies saw to it that theatre paid back the favor. Musical hits were no longer just stage successes but financial enterprises that included long sit-down runs in major cities, international deals, and merchandising gold mines. Corporations invested in the playhouses as well as the shows; their names started showing up on marquees, and with deep pockets they could afford to tryout, fix, and market a property until it was almost guaranteed to sell on a grand scale. This trend was started by the Disney Company, but other corporations soon followed. The business of Broadway changed dramatically, and for the most part, audiences responded favorably to the big corporate shows.

The most obvious perk from this corporate invasion was the revitalization of 42nd Street, once a showplace of the legitimate theatre but for years an embarrassment to the city. Not only were theatres restored or rebuilt, the street itself and its entertainment offerings were reimagined. Some decried the turning of 42nd Street into a clean and wholesome mall, but unquestionably the transition worked, and New York City, not to mention theatre, benefited. Once again the New Amsterdam Theatre was the most beautiful playhouse in the city, movie theatres and restaurants filled the street, and Times Square was more popular than ever. No matter what one thought of the mammoth shows that thrived in the new Theatre District, the place had the smell of success everywhere.

255

The so-called British musical invasion of the 1980s waned during the next decade. The London hit *Miss Saigon* was equally popular in New York, but the imports *Aspects of Love* and *Sunset Boulevard* failed to make box office gold. Broadway had its own homegrown hits with such mainstream successes as *The Secret Garden*, *The Will Rogers Follies*, *Crazy for You*, *Smokey Joe's Cafe*, *Titanic*, *Jekyll and Hyde*, and *Fosse*. More demanding but also popular were *Jelly's Last Jam*, *The Who's Tommy*, *The Kiss of the Spider Woman*, *Ragtime*, *Bring in 'da Noise Bring in 'da Funk*, and *Rent* (the last two originating Off Broadway). The newcomer on the live theatre scene was the Disney Company, which scored two mega-hits in a row with *Beauty and the Beast* and *The Lion King*.

Off Broadway did not go corporate, but the costs of presenting a musical off the Street had gotten so prohibitive that most entries came from the nonprofit theatre companies. There were a handful of commercial musicals that ran, but it seemed the best work was to be found in limited runs at Playwrights Horizons, the Public Theatre, the WPA Theatre, Lincoln Center, and the New York Theatre Workshop. Off Broadway sent five musicals to Broadway, and all but one were financial successes there. The musical variety offered during the 1990s can be illustrated by the diversity of the songwriters who were represented Off Broadway. Veterans such as Stephen Sondheim, Bob Merrill, Charles Strouse, John Kander, and Fred Ebb were joined by such impressive young talents as Jeanine Tesori, Adam Guettel, Robert Jason Brown, Michael John LaChiusa, Jonathan Larson, Stephen Flaherty, and Lynn Ahrens. Few of these new and old songwriters found themselves with long-run hits, but they managed to make a noticeable mark on the New York theatre all the same.

HANNAH . . . 1939

[4 May 1990, Vineyard Theatre, 46 performances] a musical play by Bob Merrill. *Score:* Merrill (music and lyrics). *Cast:* Julie Wilson, Neva Small, Tony Carlin, Yusef Bulos, Leigh Berry, Lori Wilner.

Late in his career, the Broadway songwriter Bob Merrill turned to Off Broadway for this very serious musical for which he wrote the book as well as the score. When the Nazis overrun Prague in 1939, they take over the clothing business owned by Hannah Schuler (Julie Wilson), an internationally recognized fashion designer and an aristocratic Jew, and force the laborers in her shops to manufacture German uniforms. Hannah protects her workers by befriending her enemy, Lt. Kurt Wald (Tony Carlin), who supervises the business. Some uniforms are reported stolen, and a handful of Jews, disguised as Germans, are caught fleeing the country. Three of Hannah's dearest seamstresses are arrested and, despite Hannah's pleading, Wald can do nothing to help them. Hannah agrees to design and make a beautiful gown for the wife of the German Commandant (Richard Thomsen) to free her workers, but when she learns they have died in a concentration camp, she takes her revenge. At the unveiling of the gown before the German high command, Hannah drenches the dress in blood and declares it is "Jewish blood." She is arrested, and Wald is ordered to take her to the train station, where she will be sent to a concentration camp. This grim tale was somewhat relieved by some flashbacks to past and happier times, but there was no escaping the fatalistic direction the story was taking. The score recalled the early music of Kurt Weill with some Viennese waltzes and Jewish klezmer tunes surfacing on occasion. "Ah, Our Germans" was a Teutonic march; "Gentle Afternoon" was a guarded duet between Hannah and her German customer Gerte (Leigh Beery); "Someday" was a hopeful anthem; "Martina" was an unadorned love ballad; and "The Pearl We Called Prague" was a sorrowful waltz. In most cases the music was more satisfying than the lyrics which sometimes attacked the serious subject matter with determined angst. Although Julie Wilson had appeared in a few Broadway musicals, she was mostly known as a cabaret performer. Her Hannah sounded a lot like Lotte Lenya at times because of the Weill-like music, yet it was an exhilarating performance that found the humor within the tragic character. The Vineyard Theatre production was scheduled for a month but interest was such that *Hannah . . . 1939* was extended for six weeks. It was a modest triumph for Merrill who had gone through a long dry spell. But it was also his last musical. Three years later he used a pen name when he contributed lyrics to the short-lived Broadway musical *The Red Shoes*, and five years after that he committed suicide.

ONCE ON THIS ISLAND

[6 May 1990, Playwrights Horizons, 24 performances; Booth Theatre, 469 performances] a musical play by Lynn Ahrens based on Rosa Guy's novel *My Love, My Love. Score:* Ahrens (lyrics), Stephen Flaherty (music). *Cast:* La Chanze, Jerry Dixon, Sheila Gibbs, Gerry McIntyre, Kecia Lewis-Evans, Afi McClendon, Milton Craig Nealy, Andrea Frierson, Eric Riley.

The musical farce *Lucky Stiff* may have prepared audiences for a series of expertly scored musicals by Lynn Ahrens and Stephen Flaherty, yet few musicals could be further in sound and temperament than *Lucky Stiff* and *Once on This Island*. The Caribbean-set show resounded with the music of the islands yet still remained within the frame of a Broadway score. The variety of Flaherty's music within the calypso framework was matched by Ahren's folklike lyrics that eschewed the clever rhymes or urban turn of phrase that made *Lucky Stiff* so distinctive. The storytelling and the score were one, the musical virtually sung through, and the result was a captivating piece of theatre narrative dance and song. Ahrens adapted Rosa Guy's novel *My Love, My Love* as a story within a story, the inhabitants of an Antilles island telling the tale of Ti Moune to calm a frightened child during a tropical storm. The story was a bittersweet fairy tale about the orphaned child Ti Moune (La Chanze) who is raised by a childless couple and grows up to fall in love with the wealthy, light-skinned Daniel (Jerry Dixon) from the other side of the island. Even though she saved his life after a car accident and offered her life for his to the god of death, he cannot marry Ti Moune. The family insists on a wedding with a light-skinned aristocrat. Ti Moune dies and magically blossoms into a tree that looks over Daniel's children in the garden. The ensemble played various inhabitants of the island, gods and goddesses, and nature itself. As staged by director-choreographer Graciela Daniele, *Once on This Island* was a celebration of bodies and voices and was thrillingly theatrical without becoming arty or pretentious. The rhythms of the music dictated the tempo of the storytelling, yet the musical easily moved from swift and energetic numbers to quiet and intimate ones. Ensemble pieces such as the opening "We Dance," the ingenious exposition number "Some Say," and the joyous acclamation of nature "Mama Will Provide" were balanced by the lovely ballads "Forever Yours," "The Human Heart," and "Some Girls." Ti Moune's eager "I am" song "Waiting for Life" was a showstopper, and it launched the career of African American leading lady La Chanze. *Once on This Island* was so deceptively simple and roundly accessible to all kinds of audiences that it was easy to watch and enjoy. Despite the many American musicals of the past that have been set in the island tropics, this was one of the few times it sounded authentic. *House of Flowers* and *Jamaica*, for example, offered little of the sound of the locale in their scores; *Once on This Island* overflowed with local flavor without sacrificing any of the appeal of a Broadway musical. The intimate Off-Broadway production at Playwrights Horizons quickly sold out its three-week engagement and then moved to a small Broadway house where it ran fifteen months. Although it calls for an all-black company, *Once on This Island* would later receive many school productions with racially mixed casts. It would also become popular in regional and summer theatres, particularly after Ahrens and Flaherty became better known.

FURTHER MO'

[17 May 1990, Village Gate Downstairs, 174 performances] a musical revue by Vernel Bagneris. *Score:* various. *Cast:* Bagneris, Topsy Chapman, James "Red" Wilcher, Frozine Thomas, Sandra Reaves-Phillips.

Writer-performer-director Vernel Bagneris returned to the same vaudeville Lyric Theatre in 1927 New Orleans that was the setting for his popular *One Mo' Time* (1979) for this sequel which offered the same characters performing different songs of the period. Because so many standards made up the first show, *Further Mo'* relied on less known but often equally pleasing numbers. "Here Comes the Hot Tamale Man," "One Hour Mama," "West Indies Blues," and "Don't Advertise Your Man" may not have had the ring of familiarity, but they stopped the show nonetheless. Even the recognized "Mississippi Mud," "Alabama Bound," and "Home Sweet Home" were given distinctive renditions, and the riotous evening ended with a pulsating ensemble version of "A Hot Time in the Old Town Tonight." Of the five cast members, Bagneris and Topsy Chapman were from the 1979 edition, Bagneris again directed, and Pepsi Bethel did the raucous choreography. *One Mo' Time* had run nearly four years, but *Further Mo'* had to settle for six months.

FOREVER PLAID

[20 May 1990, Steve McGraw's, 1,811 performances] a musical revue by Stuart Ross. *Score:* various. *Cast:* Jason Graae, Guy Stroman, David Engel, Stan Chandler.

Nostalgia was twisted, spoofed, and embraced in this delightful homage to the guy groups of the 1950s and early 1960s when The Four Freshmen, The Four Lads, the Hi-Lows, and other harmonizing quartets were popular. Rather than just present a revue of pop hits as in *The Taffetas* and *Beehive*, *Forever Plaid* had a quirky and surprisingly workable premise to hold the show together. An amateur foursome calling themselves the Plaids were just about to get their professional break in 1964 when the car they were traveling in was hit by a bus full of teens on their way to New York to see the Beatles on *The Ed Sullivan Show*. The four tuxedoed singers died in the wreck but decades later get a chance to return to earth and give the show they had rehearsed so diligently. They may have been rank amateurs in their poise and performing mannerisms, but their singing was first rate, and the songs sparkled. Stuart Ross conceived the idea and directed the revue with the right amount of farce and sincerity, but the bottom line was the singing, and few musicals Off Broadway sounded so good. Four-part harmony versions of "Three Coins in the Fountain," "No Not Much," and "Love Is a Many Splendored Thing" were as thrilling as they were corny, and solo versions of "Rags to Riches" and "Cry" were equally effective even though most playgoers could not recall them as hits by Tony Bennett and Johnnie Ray. Musical arranger James Raitt created some ingenious medleys, such as a handful of Caribbean songs, an unlikely pairing of "Undecided" with "Gonna Be This or That," and a mix of "Chain Gang" and "Sixteen Tons" that made the two numbers seem destined to be paired. There was even a hilarious medley of different holiday songs sung in the Plaid style and a Plaid version of some Beatles songs showing that the four nerds wanted to be hip. The dialogue patter between numbers, in which the four young men made silly revelations about themselves, was strained and sometimes fell flat, but there was always a song that soon came to the rescue. All four performers were excellent comics as well as singers, which certainly helped. Ross first presented *Forever Plaid* in Teaneck, New Jersey, then Off Off Broadway. Producer Gene Wolsk saw the possibilities in the show and turned the nightclub act at Steve McGraw's into a full-fledged Off-Broadway commercial run. Word of mouth was strong, and the little venue had a hit on its hands, running nearly five years. After Ross presented versions in different cities, *Forever Plaid* became a favorite of regional, summer, and even school theatres. (The cast was greatly expanded and used women in the school version.) Why is the revue so popular with audiences of all ages? The songs are still potent. Playgoers may laugh at the clumsy, virginal Plaids and find their old-time crooning style rather dated, but deep down everyone finds the songs highly appealing. Maybe *Forever Plaid* allows one to lower your guard and enjoy the guilty pleasure of old but still satisfying popular music.

FALSETTOLAND

[28 June 1990, Playwrights Horizons, 215 performances] a musical play by William Finn, James Lapine. *Score:* Finn (music and lyrics). *Cast:* Michael Rupert, Faith Prince, Stephen Bogardus, Chip Zien, Danny Gerard, Heather MacRae, Janet Metz.

After his Broadway failure *Dangerous Games* and his Off-Broadway flop *Romance in Hard Times*, William Finn was back in top form with this sequel to *March of the Falsettos*. Sequels in any media tend to disappoint, but *Falsettoland* was deemed even richer, more involving, and more accomplished than the original. The sung-through musical concerned the family arguments over young Jason (Danny Gerard) and his upcoming bar mitzvah and the return of Whizzer (Stephen Bogardus) into the chaotic life of Marvin (Michael Rupert). The two plotlines converge when Whizzer contracts AIDS and Jason insists on waiting for him to get well before he will go through with the Jewish coming-of-age ceremony. When it is clear Whizzer will not recover, the bar mitzvah is held in his hospital room, and there is a complete sense of family once again. A pair of lesbians (Heather MacRae and Janet Metz) were added for the sequel and, one of them being a doctor, audiences saw the beginnings of the AIDS epidemic from a physician's point of view. Faith Prince played the frustrated wife Trina this time around, but Chip Zien reprised his psychiatrist Mendel who has married her. Director James Lapine was so instrumental in the structuring of the one-act musical that he was listed as coauthor by the time it opened. *Falsettoland* is better structured than *March of the Falsettos*, and the tricks of the first musical are somewhat tamer in the second, but Finn's music and lyrics are still wildly imaginative and far from conventional. Musical highlights include Trina's aria "Holding to the Ground," the vaudeville turn "Everyone Hates His Parents" delivered by Mendel and Jason, the multicharacter numbers "The Baseball Game" and "Days Like This," which look into the thoughts of several characters at once, and the heartbreaking duet "What Would I Do?" in which Marvin and Whizzer finally resolve their inflammatory love-hate relationship. Most critics extolled the small, tight production and placed Finn near the top of American theatre songwriters. The seven-week engagement at Playwrights Horizons was well attended, and then the musical moved to the larger Off-Broadway house the Lucille Lortel Theatre, where it stayed for another twenty weeks. Regional productions of *Falsettoland* followed, but eventually the musical would be more often produced as part of an evening titled *Falsettos*, which included a song from *In Trousers* and the complete text of *March of the Falsettos* and *Falsettoland*. The only downside to the success of *Falsettoland* was the way it pegged Finn as the author of the "Marvin" musicals, incapable of coming up with a hit when he moved away from these now-familiar characters. It would take several years before this misconception would be destroyed.

BROADWAY JUKEBOX

[19 July 1990, John Houseman Theatre, 50 performances] a musical revue by Ed Linderman. *Score:* various. *Cast:* Beth Leavel, Gerry McIntyre, Amelia Prentice, Sal Viviano, Robert Michael Baker, Susan Flynn.

Musical theatre geeks were in heaven with *Broadway Jukebox*, a revue that had no intention of pleasing the mainstream playgoer. Instead, lovers of obscure musicals were treated to songs from mostly forgotten shows, proving that flop musicals sometimes have terrific songs. When audience members arrived at the John Houseman Theatre, they were handed a list of ninety songs from these lovable losers and asked to select the musical numbers they wanted to hear. Some of the revue was set in stone, but several of the thirty songs performed each night were taken from the audience's tally. True musical fans, of course, knew all the songs and were thrilled to hear them performed on stage. Yet even the less informed were charmed by the quality of the numbers, and there was much to be said about the talented young cast who performed them. Ed Linderman conceived the revue, selected the song possibilities, and accompanied the cast on the piano. It was a grand idea and well executed; musicals fans kept the show running for six weeks. The title was misleading: only a few of these songs were ever jukebox hits. The title should have indicated that these songs were lost gems and that the show was not just another parade of standards.

SMOKE ON THE MOUNTAIN

[14 August 1990, Lamb's Theatre, 368 performances] a musical comedy by Alan Bailey, Connie Ray. *Score:* Mike Carver, Mark Hardwick, various. *Cast:* Ray, Kevin Chamberlin, Robert Olsen, Linda Kerns, Reathel Bean, Dan Manning, Jane Potter.

Mike Carver and Mark Hardwick, two veterans of the tongue-in-cheek musicals *Pump Boys and Dinettes* and *Oil City Symphony*, provided much of the music for another gentle spoof, this one poking fun at gospel singers and Christian America. Alan Bailey and Connie Ray wrote the script which was set in 1938 in Mount Pleasant, North Carolina. The Rev. Marvin Oglethorpe (Kevin Chamberlin) books the traveling Sanders Family Singers into his church to lift the spirits of his Depression-weary parishioners. The show they perform consists of pop hymns, corny jokes, homespun parables, and a lot of audience participation. The musical did not lampoon religion as much as it illustrated the cracker-barrel mentality of rural churchgoing. The score included gospel standards and new pastiche numbers, both often funny in their innocence and folksy manner. In fact, it was hard to tell the new songs from the real McCoys. "I'll Never Die (I'll Just Change My Address)," "I'm Using My Bible for a Roadmap," "No Tears in Heaven," and "I'll Walk Every Step of the Way" were so sincere that one couldn't help buying into the whole silly charade. The cast, many of whom played instruments as well as singing the numbers, had just the right tone and the piece, as directed by coauthor Bailey, was surprisingly contagious. *Smoke on the Mountain* played at the Lamb's Theatre as an Off-Off-Broadway production then, with rewritten contracts, continued on for nearly a year as an Off-Broadway entry. There was no original cast recording of the musical never receiving as many regional productions as it deserves, but a 1998 Off-Broadway revival ran ten weeks.

THE GIFTS OF THE MAGI

[4 December 1990, Lamb's Theatre, 32 performances] a musical play by Mark St. Germain based on O. Henry's Christmas tales. *Score:* Germain (lyrics), Randy Courts (music and lyrics). *Cast:* Paul Jackel, Lyn Vaux, Sarah Knapp, Gordon Stanley, Ron Lee Savin, Richard Blake.

O. Henry's classic short story "The Gift of the Magi," about an impoverished couple (Paul Jackel and Lyn Vaux) who each give up their dearest possession to buy the other a Christmas gift, and "The Cop and the Anthem," about the tramp Soapy Smith (Ron Lee Savin) who tries desperately to get arrested so that he will have a warm place to sleep on Christmas Eve, were awkwardly combined in this seasonal musical that pleased audiences during the holidays. The show was held together by the newsboy Willie (Richard Blake) who acted as narrator as he worked the streets of 1908 New York City. Two characters named City Him (Gordon Stanley) and City Her (Sarah Kemp) played all the other New Yorkers needed to fill out the two tales. The songs, with their Christmas card-like lyrics and predictable music, added little to the show, which stood on the power of the original stories rather than the bland adaptation. *The Gifts of the Magi* had first been presented Off Off Broadway at the Lamb's Theatre during the 1984 holiday season and had become an annual event. It was not contracted as an Off-Broadway entry until 1990 when it played a month at the same theatre. The musical would return for some subsequent Christmases and was later picked up by regional and amateur theatres looking for a small-cast, low-budget show for the holidays.

ASSASSINS

[27 January 1991, Playwrights Horizons, 25 performances] a musical play by John Weidman. *Score:* Stephen Sondheim (music and lyrics). *Cast:* Victor Gerber, Jonathan Hadary, Terrence Mann, Debra Monk, Jace Alexander, Patrick Cassidy, Annie Golden, Greg Germann, William Parry, Eddie Korbich, Lee Wilkof.

At an age and time in his career when most Broadway songwriters found themselves repeating patterns from their past, Stephen Sondheim continued to experiment and premiered one of his most daring works Off Broadway. *Assassins* was a darkly comic piece of music theatre that looked at the various men and women who have killed or attempted to assassinate U.S. presidents over the years. In a series of scenes and songs, the historical characters come forward and express themselves, all their distorted dreams and twisted minds revealed with pathos, humor, and anger. Leading the group is John Wilkes Booth (Victor Garber) who sees Lincoln as the curse of humanity. He is joined by the angry immigrant Leon Czolgosz (Terrence Mann), the publicity-hungry Charles Guiteau (Jonathan Hadary), the fumbling Sara Jane Moore (Debra Monk), the love-smitten John Hinckley (Greg Germann), the cultist Lynne "Squeaky" Fromme (Annie Golden), and others. The musical climaxes in a Dallas warehouse with Booth encouraging Lee Harvey Oswald (Jace Alexander) to find fame and glory by shooting John F. Kennedy.

John Weidman wrote the disturbing and yet oddly entertaining libretto. Although historically accurate, the script did not use a conventional approach to dramatize the many events. Time was bent or ignored as assassins from different centuries spoke to each other in a bar or joined together in song. The narrating Balladeer (Patrick Cassidy) commented on the characters in song using Brechtian manner. Some scenes were farcical, such as Moore's attempts in vain to shoot Gerald Ford, others were surreal, as with Guiteau's cakewalking up the scaffold to his death, and others were fervent, such as

Booth's final hours alive. The climactic scene with Oswald was chilling in its logic and development. Weidman, who had written a similarly conceptual approach to history years earlier with his libretto for Sondheim's *Pacific Overtures* (1976), proved himself again an exciting author of musical scripts with *Assassins*. It is one of the finest of all Sondheim librettos.

Sondheim wrote a score that sounded unlike any of his many previous efforts. Pastiching American music from past eras, he came up with song types rarely heard on a musical theatre stage: the cakewalking "Ballad of Guitau," the 1960s pop ballad "Unworthy of Your Love," the nineteenth-century narrative "Ballad of Booth," and the disarming march "Another National Anthem." Other songs were timeless commentaries, such as the bouncy "Everybody's Got the Right" and the seething "Gun Song." One recognized touches of the familiar Sondheim here and there, but for the most part these songs revealed an exciting new aspect of the esteemed songwriter's career. The Playwrights Horizons production, directed by Jerry Zaks, featured a sterling cast, and the limited run quickly sold out. Yet the reviews were mixed, some critics misinterpreting the show as a commendation of assassins and, with patriotism running high because of the Gulf War, it was deemed unwise to transfer the musical to Broadway. After dozens of productions regionally and in London, the disturbing and revealing musical was finally seen on Broadway in 2004 in a Roundabout Theatre mounting directed with verve and style by Joe Mantello. The reviews were exemplary, and the limited run was extended for 101 performances. Despite its uncomfortable subject matter and the demands it makes on audiences, *Assassins* is frequently revived by regional and college theatres.

AND THE WORLD GOES 'ROUND

[18 March 1991, Westside Theatre, 408 performances] a musical revue by Scott Ellis, Susan Stroman, David Thompson. *Score:* John Kander (music), Fred Ebb (lyrics). *Cast:* Bob Cuccioli, Karen Mason, Jim Walton, Karen Ziemba, Brenda Pressley.

What might have been just another revue saluting the work of Broadway songwriters turned into a sparkling musical treat presented and performed with wit and care. *And the World Goes 'Round* took songs that John Kander and Fred Ebb had written for the stage, movies, and recording artists and put them into a lively revue that was performed with zest by five up-and-coming talents. There was no chronological or thematic format to the show, and it used no narration. The songs spoke for themselves, and given the variety of material, the revue was a buoyant musical journey. Broadway and film hits and losers were represented, as well as numbers the team had written for such stars as Liza Minnelli and Barbra Streisand. No attempt was made to recreate the original sources; the theatricality of each song was enough. Critics and audiences discovered how wide a range of songs Kander and Ebb had written and found a new appreciation for their thirty-year career. *And the World Goes 'Round* launched the careers of director Scott Ellis and choreographer Susan Stroman. With hardly any production values to work with, these two artists created musical theatre magic in the small Off-Broadway space. Stroman's clever use of props (a trademark of her work in the years to come) was particularly noticed by the press. Rave notices kept the little revue on the boards for more than a year. *And the World Goes 'Round* had premiered at the Whole Theatre in Montclair, New Jersey, and after its success in New York the revue was presented in many other regional theatres as well as in summer stock, usually under the revised title *The World Goes 'Round*.

PAGEANT

[2 May 1991, Blue Angel, 462 performances] a musical comedy by Robert Longbottom. *Score:* Bill Russell, Frank Kelly (music and lyrics). *Cast:* Dick Scanlan, J. T. Cromwell, Joe Joyce, David Drake, Randl Ash, Russell Garrett, John Salvatore.

High camp and low satire met in this musical spoof of beauty contests that was also a drag show. The Glamouresse Cosmetic Company's annual beauty pageant pits six beauty queens against each other for the title of Miss Glamouresse, and the contestants go through the usual pageant rituals: evening gown competition, bathing suit displays, and talent show. The girls also do commercials for Glamouresse products throughout the evening. The fact that the sextet of females was played by males added a new level to the satire, making the musical almost surreal at times. The songs were the expected hymns to beauty, cheery numbers about "Girl Power," and the "Something Extra" each gal has to make her special. The contestants represented America's different regions and sported such titles as Miss Bible Belt, Miss Great Plains, and Miss Industrial Northeast. The smiling host Frankie

Cavalier (J. T. Cromwell) and a former winner (John Salvatore) were added to the fun. Even better, the new Miss Glamouresse was chosen by a group of judges selected from the audience each night. Spoofing beauty pageants had been a stable of musical revues for decades, but *Pageant* put a ridiculous new spin on the old premise. Robert Longbottom directed and provided the cheesy choreography, yet often it was Gregg Barnes's costumes that stole the show. *Pageant* was a healthy hit Off Broadway, running fifteen months, and was just as successful when recreated in major cities across the country.

SONG OF SINGAPORE

[23 May 1991, Singapore Theatre, 459 performances] a musical spoof by Allan Katz, Erik Frandsen, Michael Garin, Robert Hipkens, Paula Lockheart. *Score:* Frandsen, Garin, Hipkens, Lockheart (music and lyrics). *Cast:* Frandsen, Hipkens, Garin, Donna Murphy, Cathy Foy, Francis Kane.

Most of the fun in this spoof of *Casablanca* and other films filled with pre–Pearl Harbor intrigue was the performance space. A cabaret on Irving Place was dubbed the Singapore Theatre and turned into a smoky Singapore waterfront dive with the audience sitting at tables and served drinks with paper umbrellas in them. The locale is Harry S. Lime's Singapore Cafe in which the band, the Malayan Melody Makers, sing and the entertainment includes the amnesiac singer Rose (Donna Murphy) who just might be the lost Amelia Earhart. The convoluted plot involved some stolen jewels, a murdered customer, corrupt police, the sinister dragon lady Chah Li (Cathy Foy), and the approaching Japanese armies. Yet atmosphere counted for more than story, and much of that ambiance came in the expert pastiche songs which ranged from 1940s swing and cool jazz to comic ditties and South Seas ballads. Rose sang the best of the score, such as the steamy "You Gotta Do What You Gotta Do," the evocative ballad "Sunrise," the boogie-woogie "Serve It Up," and the bluesy "I Can't Remember." The police chief sang a silly number about the lovemaking of sea creatures in "Harbour of Love"; Chah Li delivered the pseudo-Oriental folk song "Foolish Geese"; and the band cut loose with the conga number "Shake, Shake, Shake" with audience members joining the conga line. The production brought the first wide recognition to Donna Murphy who had been giving excellent performances in small roles for years. The show also marked the final credit for the gifted director A. J. Antoon who died soon after the production opened. *Song of Singapore* was developed Off Off Broadway and in Cleveland before finding a home Off Broadway. Critical praise and positive word of mouth helped the show eventually develop an audience, and it ran fifteen months. Regional productions have been sporadic because the show doesn't work unless the nightclub aura is recreated.

PROM QUEENS UNCHAINED

[30 June 1991, Village Gate, 57 performances] a musical spoof by Stephen Witkin. *Score:* Keith Herrmann (music). Larry Goodsight (lyrics). *Cast:* Dana Ertischek, Don Crosby, Mark Traxler, Susan Levine, Pamela Lloyd.

What *Song of Singapore* did for the 1940s, the loopy musical spoof *Prom Queens Unchained* did for the 1950s. Filled with iconic clichés of the decade, the musical most resembled a cheap sci-fi movie in which an extraterrestrial alien infiltrates the world of some all-American kids in a small all-American town. The plot was so complicated with new subplots popping up every few minutes that the show made *Song of Singapore*'s storyline seem simple. The setting is Robert Underwood High School in 1959, and while the girls plot and plan over who will be the queen of the upcoming prom, a series of murders has both students and school officials in a frenzy. In one of the more bizarre sequences, a nerdy science student experiments in the school lab and instead of turning himself into a superpowered monster his right arm turns to hamburger. It was that kind of show. The tuneful score pastiched the Fifties sound nicely but often had crude or racy lyrics filled with too-obvious double entendres. The contenders for the prom queen crown vowed to do anything to win, including "Going All the Way," Communist propaganda had some students "Seeing Red," and couples crooned "Squeeze Me in the Rain." More satisfying were the cheery ensemble numbers that captured the innocent glee of the era, such as "That Special Night," "Sherry's Theme," and "Give Your Love." Yet even these came across as sinister because of the grisly events surrounding each number. *Prom Queens Unchained* was far from clever or subtle, but its entertainment value could not be denied. Watching a dated drive-in movie in the form of an Off-Broadway musical had a limited appeal in New York, and the show only lasted seven weeks, though some regional productions have had fun with it on occasion.

RETURN TO THE FORBIDDEN PLANET

[13 October 1991, Variety Arts Theatre, 245 performances] a musical comedy by Bob Carlton. *Score:* various. *Cast:* Steve Steiner, Gabriel Barre, Erin Hill, Louis Tucci, Robert McCormick, James Doohan, Julee Cruise.

This British import has the dubious distinction of being one of the first "jukebox musicals," those later-popular hybrids in which nontheatre pop songs were forced into a plot so the show could claim a lot of hit songs. The songs in this case were rock and roll favorites from the 1950s and early 1960s, and the plot came from Shakespeare's *The Tempest*. The 1956 sci-fi film *Forbidden Planet* had cleverly reset the Shakespeare play in outer space with the Prospero character as a sinister scientist marooned on a desert planet with his daughter. With no other humans on the planet (Ariel became Robby the Robot), the daughter fell in love with the first man to land there. Many of Shakespeare's themes were retained in the film, and it became one of the few thought-provoking science fiction movies of the decade. The British musical version may have been suggested by the film but the characters were renamed, the situations trivialized, and the camp dialogue filled with quotations from various Shakespeare works. The setting was the planet D'Illyria in 2024, and much of the action revolved around the Caliban creature, a monster with tentacles that attacks the spaceship. Some of the songs had sci-fi connections, such as "(Hey) Mr. Spaceman," "Robot Man," "Monster Mash," "Telstar," and "Great Balls of Fire" (which then referred to heavenly bodies in space), and others were more forced. The rocket ship blasted off to the sounds of "Wipeout," Captain Tempest (Robert McCormick) fell in love with Miranda (Erin Hill) at first sight with "Good Vibrations," and the mad scientist Dr. Prospero (Steve Steiner) sang "I'm Gonna Change the World." Other pop hits thrown into the mix turned rock and roll into metaphors for scientific jargon, as with "Shake, Rattle and Roll"; "All Shook Up"; and "Shakin' All Over." Love songs and ballads, such as "Young Girl"; "(Why Must I Be a) Teenager in Love"; and "Oh, Pretty Woman" were easy to insert, but one had to suspend a lot of logic to accept "Good Golly Miss Molly" and "The Shoop Shoop Song." *Return to the Forbidden Planet* had been a huge success in London, winning major awards and becoming a cult musical favorite. Broadway producers must have been wary because the show opened Off Broadway where it camped for eight months. Although the musical left little impact (regional and school productions have been few), it did foreshadow a trend for jukebox musicals, both hits and flops.

GROUNDHOG

[14 April 1992, City Center Stage II, 40 performances] a musical play by Elizabeth Swados. *Score:* Swados (music and lyrics). *Cast:* David Schechter, Anne Bobby, Bill Buell, Anne Marie Milazzo, Lauren Mufson, Michael Sottile.

An autobiographical musical with strong sociopolitical subject matter, *Groundhog* impressed some critics but was too disturbing to find much of an audience during its five-week run at the Manhattan Theatre Club. In New York City in the mid-1980s, a brilliant but mentally disabled man nicknamed Groundhog (David Schechter) becomes a celebrity of sorts when the media uses him to illustrate the state of the homeless and the ineffectual ways the city is dealing with the problem. Groundhog's sister Gila (Anne Bobby) is torn between having him institutionalized and letting him keep his independence, knowing he will be destroyed if he loses his freedom. Various doctors, politicians, social workers, and even meteorologists are involved in Groundhog's case, and he ends up dying on the streets. Author Elizabeth Swados drew from her personal experiences with her brother, a victim of homelessness and an early death. Gila was the only fully developed character in the musical and served as the conscience of the people, while the administrators were portrayed as callous stereotypes. Swados wrote over forty musical numbers for *Groundhog*, many of them short and in the Brechtian commentary style, and few of them were very melodic. Only in personal songs such as "Danilo's Rap," "Just Trust Me," and "Who Will It Be?" did the score veer away from musical proclamations and recitative speeches. All the same, much of *Groundhog* was powerful theatre and with true sincerity that helped the musical make its points effectively.

RUTHLESS!

[6 May 1992, Players Theatre, 302 performances] a musical spoof by Joel Paley. *Score:* Paley (lyrics), Marvin Laird (music). *Cast:* Laura Bundy, Donna English, Joel Vig, Susan Mansur, Denise Lor, Joanne Baum.

The parade of musical spoofs Off Broadway continued with *Ruthless!* Diabolical children, delusional stage mothers, clawing contenders, greedy agents, and jaded theatre critics who hate musicals were the subjects of the campy satire, and before the evening was complete *Gypsy*, *The Bad Seed*, and *All About Eve* were echoed and mocked. Suburban grade school moppet Tina Denmark (Laura Bundy) is so eager for the lead in her school's musical production of *Pippi Longstocking* that when she doesn't get the role, she murders her competition. This only mildly distresses her mother Judy (Donna English) who has show business frustrations of her own. She turns the kid into the police and, when Tina is sent to the Daisy Clover School for Psychotic Ingénues, Judy goes to Broadway and becomes a musical star. The grasping talent agent Sylvia St. Croix (Joel Vig in drag) gets Tina out of reform school and brings her to New York where she is in competition with the wannabe actress Eave (Joann Baum) to displace Judy. After a lot of backstabbing left and right, Judy returns to suburbia to be a housewife, and Tina heads for Hollywood. It was not the cleverest of plots, and many of the scenes seemed labored, but the campy and cliché-ridden dialogue was frequently funny, and the songs were brazen and amusing. Marvin Laird's music was in the slick, showbiz style and provided plenty of opportunities for belting and mimicking Broadway stars like Ethel Merman. Joel Paley's lyrics, like his libretto, were fearlessly campy with obvious rhymes and dozens of clichés sandwiched in. Both music and lyrics flew by so rapidly that even the weakest songs were turned into brash showstoppers by the gifted cast. Particularly impressive was Laura Bundy who had the talent and the sense of mockery to make Tina both delightful and freakish. Her claim that she was "Born to Entertain," and her determination "To Play This Part" displayed a monstrous ego that verged on the surreal. Donna English's ditzy then determined Judy was also a psychotic treat, her self-effacing claim to be nothing more than "Tina's Mother" turning into the risible "It Will Never Be That Way Again" in which the housewife within her battles the Broadway star. Judy's mother was the sour theatre critic Lita Encore (Denise Lor) who sang the Merman-like ditty "I Hate Musicals," and the ambitious Eave lusted after the star's career in "A Penthouse Apartment." *Ruthless!* was loud and witless but enjoyable all the same. Critical reaction was positive, and audiences responded for more than nine months. A 1994 production in Los Angeles was also a success and was recorded. Needing a grotesquely talented moppet to play Tina has kept *Ruthless!* from getting numerous productions, but it is still done on occasion.

EATING RAOUL

[13 May 1992, Union Square Theatre, 47 performances] a musical satire by Paul Bartel. *Score:* Jed Feuer (music), Boyd Graham (lyrics). *Cast:* Eddie

Korbich, Courtenay Collins, Adrian Zmed, Susan Wood, M. W. Reid, Jonathan Brody, David Masenheimer, Cindy Benson, Lovette George.

One of the first, but certainly not the last, musicals to attempt the success of *Little Shop of Horrors* by musicalizing a cheap horror flick, *Eating Raoul* had much to recommend even though it did not catch on with the public. Paul Bartel's 1982 independent flick had become a cult favorite and, with its similarities to *Little Shop of Horrors* and *Sweeney Todd*, had great musical potential. Bartel adapted his screenplay for the stage, and a surprisingly potent score by Jed Feuer and Boyd Graham matched the wacky tone of the script. As in the film, the plot centered on the sexless, dreary couple Paul (Eddie Korbich) and Mary Bland (Courtenay Collins) who abhor the swinging sexy 1960s in Los Angeles and only dream of opening a gourmet restaurant. When an oversexed intruder attacks Mary in her apartment and she kills him with her frying pan, the couple discovers a wad of cash in his wallet. The Blands then start luring swingers to their apartment, bumping them off with the frying pan, and soon have enough money to open their restaurant. The Mexican burglar Raoul (Adrian Zmed), who has pretensions to becoming a lounge lizard, catches on to their scheme and goes into business with the couple, disposing of the bodies for them. But soon Raoul is after Mary, and she has to decide between the two men. Raoul gets the frying pan treatment and becomes the main entry for their celebratory gourmet dinner. The film was cheesy and uneven, funny scenes separated by dull sequences. Bartel condensed and tightened up the plot for the stage, leaving room for some farcical musical numbers. The cast set the scene with such funny songs as "La La Land" and "Swing, Swing, Swing"; the Blands naively sang of "A Small Restaurant"; the lusty Raoul and his backup singers delivered the slimy "A Tool for You"; the cockeyed trio celebrated their partnership with the risible "Think About Tomorrow"; and everyone joined Mary and stopped the show in the eleven o'clock spot with "One Last Bop." Critical reaction was surprisingly harsh for *Eating Raoul*, but fans of the movie sought out the little show long enough to keep it running six weeks. Theatre groups not afraid of cannibalism had fun with it, but the show has never found a wide audience. Was *Eating Raoul* more off-putting than *Little Shop of Horrors*? It was certainly less gory since death by frying pan was a relatively bloodless form of murder. But like the many *Little Shop of Horrors* copies to follow, this show never transcended the original to become something more substantial when turned into a musical. *Eating Raoul* was simply an offbeat musical of an offbeat film.

BALANCING ACT

[15 June 1992, Westside Theatre, 56 performances] a musical play by Dan Goggin. *Score*: Goggin (music and lyrics). *Cast*: Craig Wells, Diane Fratantoni, Christine Toy, J. B. Adams, Suzanne Hevner, Nancy E. Carroll.

Dan Goggin, who had created the still-running *Nunsense*, tackled a more substantial idea in *Balancing Act* and came up with one of the dreariest musicals of its season. The audience never saw the Main Character all evening, but they were left with different "sides" to the character, as personified by five actors stuck with names like Ambitious Side, Humorous Side, Sensitive Side, and you get the idea. The Main Character leaves Hometown, U.S.A., to become an actor, his journey taking him to New York and then to Hollywood. Along the way, he meets various characters (all played by Nancy E. Carroll) who figure in his search for a job, a meaningful relationship, and happiness. There were dramatic possibilities in this modern morality play, and theatrically it had some good ideas, such as all five "sides" singing in unison for the Main Character and having the different "sides" react differently to the various characters he meets. Yet the issues at stake were bland, the dialogue pedestrian, and the songs rather routine. The score sometimes pastiched different musical styles, as with the smoky "Play Away the Blues" and the brassy "The Kid's Gonna Make It," but there was a sameness about the songs that added to the numbness. *Balancing Act* originated in Waterbury, Connecticut, then had no trouble finding a producer Off Broadway because of Goggin's track record with *Nunsense*. Reviewers, aching to bring the successful author down a notch, were unnecessarily dismissive about *Balancing Act*, but word of mouth wasn't much better. After a forced run of seven weeks, the musical moved to the Douglas Fairbanks Theatre and played on Sunday nights when *Nunsense* wasn't performing.

WEIRD ROMANCE

[21 June 1992, WPA Theatre, 50 performances] a musical play by Alan Brennert, David Spencer. *Score*: Alan Menken (music), Spencer (lyrics). *Cast*: Ellen Greene, Jonathan Hadary, Danny Burstein, Jessica Molaskey, Valerie Pettiford, Sal Viviano, Eric Riley, Marguerite MacIntyre, William Youmans.

A program with the unfortunate title *Weird Romance* billed itself as "Two One-Act Musicals of Speculative Fiction" which was another way of saying "science fiction with songs." But this was no campy space adventure or gory alien encounter. *Weird Romance* was serious musical theatre; one might even say humorless because it was so earnest and tackled such somber topics. "The Girl Who Was Plugged In," based on a story by James Tiptree Jr. (pen name for Alice Sheldon), told the bittersweet tale of a sickly bag lady P. Burke (Ellen Greene) whose soul is put into the body of Delphi (Marguerite MacIntyre), a beautiful android manufactured by T. S. Isham (Jonathan Hadary) and his company GTX. When Isham's son Paul (Sal Viviano) falls in love with Delphi, he discovers the true P. Burke inside, but the romance is destroyed by the callous Isham who only wanted Delphi to sell various products to her adoring public. Alan Brennart adapted his own story "Her Pilgrim Soul" for the second act plot. The scientist Kevin Drayton (Hadary) creates amazingly realistic holographic images, but he is discontented with his marriage to Carol (Jessica Molaskey) and with life in general. When the holographic image of a woman (Greene) appears on its own, Kevin and his assistant Daniel (Danny Burstein) discover that she is Nola Granville, a woman who lived a hundred years ago. Each day Nola ages quickly, and before she dies a second time, she teaches Kevin not to be afraid of life, and he returns to his wife. Although both tales were romantic and very emotional, it was sometimes difficult to connect to the robots and light images. These romances were not so weird as distant. Much of the dialogue was artificial and full of pretty speeches, but when the characters, human or otherwise, sang, they did come to life. Alan Menken, Hollywood's most successful composer because of the recent series of Disney film musicals, wrote a first-rate score, and David Spencer provided the delicate and involving lyrics. Rarely has such a fine set of songs jumped out of such a flat script. "Stop and See Me," the entrancing "I am" song for the homeless P. Burke, was touching without being sentimental. The scientist Kevin's "I am" song, "My Orderly World," was analytical and revealing. "That's Where We Come In" and "You Remember" were two very different kinds of waltzes, the pastiche number "I Can Show You a Thing or Two" effectively echoed a 1940s crooning ballad, and the love song "Eyes That Never Lie" ranked among Menken's best. The science nerd Daniel sang the dandy list song "Need to Know" about his obsessive curiosity, and there was a glittering duet titled "Worth It" sung by the android and the woman whose soul was within her. The cast was splendid, particularly Greene who had become famous for her Audrey in Menken's *Little Shop of Horrors*. Despite Menken's popularity, *Weird Romance* did not go anywhere after its six-week engagement at the WPA Theatre. It is an oddly unsatisfying musical, but its score justifies a second look.

HELLO MUDDAH, HELLO FADDUH

[5 December 1992, Circle in the Square, 235 performances] a musical comedy by Douglas Bernstein, Rob Krausz. *Score:* Allan Sherman (music and lyrics), various (music). *Cast:* Tovah Feldshuh, Jason Graae, Mary Testa, Stephen Berger, Paul Kreppel.

In the 1960s, the comic Allan Sherman recorded six popular comedy albums in which he sang songs about suburban Jewish life, the lyrics usually set to famous classical or popular standards. These silly ditties were so memorable that to this day a generation of Americans cannot hear "On Top of Old Smokey" or "Frere Jacques" without thinking of Sherman's parody versions. Douglas Bernstein and Rob Krausz collected two dozen of these farcical numbers and used them to tell the story of a typical Jewish male from his childhood to his marriage and to his retirement days in Florida. A nimble cast of five played the main character at different ages and all the people in his life. The authors titled the musical "Hello Muddah, Hello Fadduh" after one of the best remembered Sherman songs: a letter home from a Jewish kid at summer camp. Other popular numbers from the albums included "Sarah Jackman," "I Can't Dance," "Shake Hands with Your Uncle Max," and "Here's to the Crabgrass." Evidently enough playgoers remembered Sherman (or enough wanted to find out about his songs) because the revue did brisk business for seven and a half months. When it was revived Off Broadway in 2001, it was again popular enough to run 124 performances.

WINGS

[9 March 1993, Public Theatre/Estelle R. Newman Theatre, 47 performances] a musical play by Arthur Perlman based on Arthur Kopit's play. *Score:* Perlman (lyrics), Jeffrey Lunden (music). *Cast:* Linda Stephens, Rita Gardner, William Brown, Hollis Resnik, Ross Lehman, Ora Jones.

Turning Arthur Kopit's 1978 drama *Wings* into a musical was a daunting task since the original had little plot and concerned the psychological state of a woman who has suffered a stroke. The chamber opera that Arthur Perlman and Jeffrey Lunden created was done with taste and talent, but it was a work more admired than embraced. The musical adaptation was so faithful to the original play that some reviewers questioned why musicalize the piece at all. Yet the beauty of some of the score was a justification in itself, and the American musical theatre is richer having such a quality product as *Wings*. The aged Emily Stilson (Linda Stephens alternating with Rita Gardner), who had been a stunt pilot in her youth, is listening to a record player when the music goes berserk. It is not the player but her perception of it that has gone haywire as we experience her stroke from Emily's point of view. What followed was a series of encounters with doctors and therapists over the next two years as Emily fights to regain her senses, her memory, and her power of speech. The music was often atonal and repetitive, reflecting Emily's confused state, and since everything was as Emily heard it, the effect was at times disturbing, annoying, and frustrating. The score consisted of thirty musical numbers punctuated with bits of dialogue creating an effect that of an avant-garde opera, yet some individual numbers stood out as set pieces. In "Out on the Wing," Emily recalled her days as a wing walker in her family's air show, the Nurse (Ora Jones) sang a nonsense march about food called "Yum, Yummy, Yum" which was how Emily interpreted the woman bringing her dinner tray in the hospital, and "I Wonder What's Inside" was the number in which both Emily grasps for understanding while the staff tries to imagine what is going on in her mind. Emily and her therapist Amy (Hollis Resnick) sang a rhapsodic song about "Snow"; the stroke victim Billy (Ross Hehman), who used to be a cook, had one of the evening's lighter moments with "Recipe for Cheesecake," which he sang using the wrong word on occasion; and the musical concluded with Emily's regaining more of her memory in the soaring title song. As with the play, *Wings* depended on a strong performance by the actress playing Emily, and Linda Stephens was enthusiastically lauded for her penetrating portrayal that never sank into self-pity or sentiment. *Wings* originated at the Goodman Theatre in Chicago; then was given a six-week run at the Public Theatre Off Broadway. As propitious as the reviews were, it was a difficult musical to sell to the public, and productions since then have been rare. Was *Wings* too highbrow for theatre audiences? Possibly, yet opera audiences have yet to embrace it, and that is the more likely venue for the musical. Perhaps some musicals are so uncompromising in their intent that they defy general acceptance. If so, *Wings* is a good example.

Putting It Together

[1 April 1993, City Center Theatre Stage I, 96 performances] a musical revue by Julia McKenzie. *Score:* Stephen Sondheim (music and lyrics).

Cast: Julie Andrews, Stephen Collins, Rachel York, Christopher Durang, Michael Rupert.

A revue of Stephen Sondheim songs titled Side By Side by Sondheim had been a hit on Broadway in 1977 with no stars in the cast. That show had originated in London, as had this new Sondheim revue, which producer Cameron Mackintosh had presented in Oxford in 1992. This time the American version was Off Broadway, and it indeed had a star. Julie Andrews returned to the New York legitimate stage for the first time in thirty-three years in the Manhattan Theatre Club production of Putting It Together. It was, to put it mildly, an event, and the twelve-week run was very popular. To hear Andrews sing such delectable Sondheim showstoppers as "Could I Leave You?" and "Like It Was" was musical theatre heaven, yet the star was not featured any more than the other four cast members, with many of her numbers being duets and ensemble pieces. Andrews and Rachel York sang the beguiling duet "Every Day a Little Death," Stephen Collins partnered with the star for the acerbic "Country House," and she joined Michael Rupert and Christopher Durang in such group numbers as "What Would We Do Without You?" and "Back in Business," as well as the title number. Sondheim and director Julia McKenzie (who had appeared in Side By Side by Sondheim) put together the show which had little dialogue but told a story of sorts through the songs. The five characters gathered at a swank cocktail party where light banter and snide insinuations soon turned to recriminations and outward hostility. Such a premise meant that none of the characters were very likable but the performers sure were, so audiences overlooked the concept's faults. The delivery of the Sondheim numbers, both popular and obscure, was first rate and, despite the presence of a superstar in the cast, the musical ended up being an ensemble piece. Critics carped about the details but applauded the entire cast, welcoming Andrews back to the stage with sincere appreciation. Regional theatres found success with the economic revue even without the benefit of names in the cast. Putting It Together ended up on Broadway in 1999 with Carol Burnett playing Andrews's character with her own distinctive panache, and the production ran 101 performances.

HOWARD CRABTREE'S WHOOP-DEE-DOO!

[29 June 1993, Actors Playhouse, 258 performances] a musical revue by Charles Catanese, Howard Crabtree, Dick Gallagher, Phillip George,

Peter Morris, Mark Waldrop. *Score:* Gallagher, Morris, Waldrop (music and lyrics). *Cast:* Crabtree, Morris, Keith Cromwell, Alan Tulin, Richard Stegman, Ron Skobel, Tommy Femia, David Lowenstein, Jay Rogers.

If you didn't know that the Howard Crabtree of the title was a costume designer, it became very clear after the first number in this revue that the costumes were the stars. Crabtree's outfits were not elaborate or expensive but rather ingenious, over the top, and very witty. Oversized wigs and hats, clashing colors, and costumes as props seemed to be the philosophy. At the same time the fancy duds looked handmade and on the cheap; a wonderful combination of frugality and excess. The show itself was a sort of *Follies* in which eight males played both sexes in sketches and songs as the producer (Crabtree himself) is heckled by one of the boys (Jay Rogers) about the questionable taste of the whole project. *Howard Crabtree's Whoop-Dee-Doo!* was very gay but not exclusively so, and both the skits and the musical numbers were enjoyable for anyone who loved outrageous theatrics. In the show some writers performed a backers' audition for a musical about Nancy Reagan, magic fairies threw down their wands and went on strike, and an army of potatoes was upset when a banana joined its ranks. The merry musical numbers mocked (and envied) the much married Liz Taylor in "Elizabeth"; the Invisible Dance Company performed even though "you could see right through them"; and the finale "Less Is More" was a fabulous salute to excess. The highlight of the revue was "You Are My Idol" in which a plane flying over a jungle accidentally dropped Broadway cast albums and other theatre memorabilia down onto a tribe that embraced the offering from the gods. Soon the natives were musical theatre fans and were idolizing and imitating Ethel Merman and other gay icons. Critics accepted the musical as unpretentious fun and highly recommended it. Gay and straight audiences thought likewise and kept it on the boards for more than eight months. Under the abridged title *Whoop-Dee-Doo!* the revue also enjoyed many regional productions in large cities.

ANNIE WARBUCKS

[9 August 1993, Variety Arts Theatre, 200 performances] a musical comedy by Thomas Meehan based on the comic strip *Little Orphan Annie. Score:* Charles Strouse (music), Martin Charnin (lyrics). *Cast:* Harve

Presnell, Donna McKechnie, Kathryn Zaremba, Arlene Robertson, Marguerite MacIntyre, Harvey Evans, Raymond Thorne.

When the sequel *Annie 2: Miss Hannigan's Revenge* closed out of town in 1990, the authors went back to the drawing board and came up with this very pleasing musical that in some respects was as proficient as the original *Annie* (1977). Not only was Miss Hannigan's revenge dropped, the character herself was eliminated and replaced by the sly Child Welfare Commissioner Harriet Doyle (Arlene Robertson) who insists that zillionaire Daddy Warbucks (Harve Presnell) marry within sixty days so that the adopted Annie (Kathryn Zaremba) will have a mother. Doyle plots to have Warbucks marry her ex-con daughter Florence (Donna McKechnie) then bump him off after the wedding. But Warbucks travels the country looking for an appropriate mate while all the time it is clear that his assistant Grace Farrell (Marguerite MacIntyre) is the ideal wife and mother. With the help of FDR (Raymond Thorne), Doyle is exposed and Warbucks ends up with Grace. It was a charming and useful plot which served the sprightly characters well. The score did not have a runaway hit like "Tomorrow," but it was very accomplished, sometimes superior to the original. Annie got such spunky numbers as "I Got Me" and "Annie Isn't Just Annie Any More"; Warbucks joined her in the touching "Changes" and the merry "When You Smile"; the orphans warned Annie in the sassy "The Other Woman"; Harriet and Florence cut loose with the sinister "Leave It to the Girls"; Florence revealed her dual nature in "But You Go On"; Grace sang the engaging torch song "It Would Have Been Wonderful"; and Warbucks had a reflective moment with the gentle "A Younger Man." Again Martin Charnin directed and Peter Genaro choreographed, and the production, though on a smaller scale in an Off-Broadway venue, was as polished and as well-performed as the original. But what was *Annie Warbucks* doing Off Broadway? In its conception and execution, it was meant to be a big and bright Broadway musical. *Annie 2: Miss Hannigan's Revenge* had lost a bundle, and the producers must have been wary of the costs of mounting *Annie Warbucks* on the Street. But turning a Broadway show into an Off-Broadway entry to save money seems like a lack of confidence. Audiences must have sensed this because they kept the musical running for only six months. The lackluster reviews certainly didn't help; the press was particularly nasty with what they considered a retitled version of a well-known flop. Curiously, *Annie Warbucks* never caught on regionally either. Amateur groups who had embraced *Annie* went on reviving the original and pretty much ignored the sequel. *Annie Warbucks* is still an orphan.

FIRST LADY SUITE

[15 December 1993, Public Theatre/Susan Stine Shiva Theatre, 15 performances] a musical play by Michael John LaChiusa. *Score:* LaChiusa (music and lyrics). *Cast:* Carol Woods, Maureen Moore, Carolann Page, Debra Stricklin, Alice Playten, Priscilla Baskerville, David Wasson.

HELLO AGAIN

[30 January 1994, Mitzi E. Newhouse Theatre, 101 performances] a musical play by Michael John LaChiusa based on Arthur Schnitzer's *La Ronde.* *Score:* LaChiusa (music and lyrics). *Cast:* Donna Murphy, Judy Blazer. John Dossett, Malcolm Gets, John Cameron Mitchell, Carolee Carmello, Dennis Parlato, Michele Pawk, Michael Park, David A. White.

Michael John LaChiusa, the most uncompromising composer-lyricist working in the American theatre at the end of the century, came on the New York scene during the 1993–1994 season. He made his Off-Broadway debut with the elegant, revealing chamber piece *First Lady Suite* about four wives of U.S. presidents. In the first section, Eleanor Roosevelt (Carolann Page) is flying with her assistant and companion Lorena Hickok (Carol Woods) and Amelia Earhart (Maureen Moore) in Earhart's Lockheed Electra. It is 1936, and Eleanor is coming into her own as a woman and as a public figure. As the three soar through the night joyfully, Amelia lets Eleanor take the controls for a bit, and "Hicks" soliloquizes about the deep affection she and Eleanor share. The second section was the most farcical. President Truman's daughter Margaret (Debra Stricklin) tries to sing at a 1950 luncheon for the Christian Mothers and Daughters, but all the time she is being upstaged by her mother, Bess (David Wasson). In the third part of the musical, it is 1957, and Maimie Eisenhower (Alice Playten) is alone in her bedroom at the White House on her birthday. She fantasizes that African American singer Marian Anderson (Priscilla Baskerville) appears to her and then whisks her off to North Africa where Mamie confronts Ike (Wasson) about his affair with Kay Summersby (Stricklin). The musical concluded in November 1963 when Air Force One was heading toward Dallas. Jacqueline Kennedy (Moore) has a premonition of disaster, her assistant Mary Gallagher (Stricklin) muses about the difficulties of tending to the First Lady, and JFK's aide Evelyn Lincoln (Page) takes pride in the small part she is playing in the administration. Like LaChiusa's later works, the premise was unconventional, and the score was difficult. While the characters sometimes spoke to each other, most of the piece consisted of musical soliloquies by the various women. Because the songs sometimes eschewed clear melodic patterns and the lyrics did not rely on rhymes, LaChiusa's work was described as an atonal opera or art song cycle. Such observations would be made about much of LaChiusa's later work as well. He usually writes his own librettos, but the musicals are mostly sung through, and the songs tell the story. Yet his dialogue that pops up amidst the musical numbers is stinging and vibrant. Few songwriters in the theatre today are such potent playwrights as LaChiusa. *First Lady Suite* was given only a two-week engagement at the Public Theatre, but it garnered some attention from the press. LaChiusa rewrote the musical, changing the order of the sequences, cutting the Trumans' scene, and adding an opening and closing number in which the First Ladies sing together. The revised version was performed in several cities, the 2002 Los Angeles production being the one that was recorded. By that time LaChiusa was a well-known artist, and *First Lady Suite* would be labeled an early and minor work.

A month after *First Lady Suite* closed at the Public Theatre, another Michael John LaChiusa musical opened at Lincoln Center. *Hello Again* was an arresting little musical that captured the musical sounds and sexual mores of different decades in the twentieth century. Critical and popular reception this time was more favorable, and the musical was held over for thirteen weeks. *Hello Again* is considered by some to be LaChiusa's best musical. It is certainly his most accessible. Loosely based on Arthur Schnitzler's 1903 comedy of amoral manners *La Ronde,* the libretto follows ten sexual encounters in which one partner in each coupling appears in the next episode, each segment taking place in a different era. The Whore (Donna Murphy) beds the circa 1900 Soldier (David A. White) who then seduces the Nurse (Judy Blazer) before he ships out for World War II; the Nurse then sleeps with the 1960s College Boy (Michael Park) who then seduces the Young Wife (Carolee Carmello) during the Depression, and on and on. In the last scene the 1990s Senator (John Dossett) has a confrontation with the Whore, and the plotting has come full circle. LaChiusa's songs pastiched each period accurately and effectively; full melodic lines and traditional rhymes were used this time. The sound of 1940s jump-and-jive was heard in "I Gotta Little Time," disco infiltrated "Safe," old-time Viennese waltzing filled "Listen to the Music," 1960s pop flavored "In Some Other Life," and jazz was heard in "Silent Movie." Other numbers were thrilling even as they transcended time, such as the soaring duet "The One I Love," the plaintive ballad "Tom," the heartbreaking confession "The Bed Was Not My Own," and the tentative and mysterious title song. Once again the bits of dialogue within the mostly sung musical sparkled with wit and honesty, and the balance between song and prose was ingeniously done. Graciela Daniele directed and choreographed the outstanding cast, which also featured John Cameron Mitchell, Malcolm Gets, Dennis Parlato, and Michele Pawk, most of whom would soon be major players on Broadway. *Hello Again* has enjoyed continued life in regional and college theatres; in fact, it remains LaChiusa's most-performed work.

THAT'S LIFE!

[1 August 1994, Playhouse 91, 292 performances] a musical revue by Helen Butleroff. *Score:* Rick Cummins, Dick Gallagher, various (music), Susan DiLallo, Dan Kael, Stacey Luftig, various (lyrics). *Cast:* Lisa Rochelle, Steve Sterner, Cheryl Stern, David Beach, Robert Michael Baker.

To be Jewish or not to be Jewish, that was the question bantered about in this waggish contemporary revue with a comfortably old-fashioned temperament. Some of the numbers were about holding on to one's Jewish heritage in the modern world, celebrating "More Than 5700 Years" of Judaism, aching for "A Share of Paradise," and cutting loose with "The Gerhrunken Meshuggena Rag." Other songs covered the ways Jews hide or downplay their culture, as in "I Can Pass," "Endangered Species," and "It's Beyond Me." Nose jobs were lampooned in "Rhinoplasty," loss of traditions were lamented in "It's Hard to Be a Patriarch Today," and past prejudices were recalled in "In a Schoolyard in Brooklyn." One memorable number titled "Gorgeous Kay" looked at Jews having to celebrate Christmas with gentile in-laws. Yet the revue never got too somber or disturbing; it was all pleasant kvetching, as summarized by the happy-go-lucky "We All Could Be Jewish If We Tried a Little Harder." *That's Life!* originated Off Off Broadway at the Jewish Repertory Theatre and was so well received it moved to Off Broadway where it entertained audiences for more than nine months.

JELLY ROLL!

[9 August 1994, 47th Street Theatre, 319 performances] a musical revue by Vernel Bagneris. *Score:* Jelly Roll Morton, various (music and lyrics). *Cast:* Bagneris.

Gregory Hines had received a round of plaudits for his portrayal of pioneer jazz composer Jelly Roll Morton in the Broadway musical *Jelly's Last Jam* in 1992, so this one-man musical subtitled "The Music and the Man" was setting itself up for some difficult comparisons. But writer-performer Vernel Bagneris, who had put together the popular *One Mo' Time*, rose to the occasion and critics praised his script and performance. Bagneris's Morton was considered more sophisticated and sly than Hines's energetic portrayal, and the moody but elegant character came through in Bagneris's wry commentary, smooth singing, and lyrical dancing. Morton was not a likable character, being something of a snob and racist, and he came across as a very sad and lonely soul in *Jelly Roll!* While *Jelly's Last Jam* featured songs that set original lyrics to Morton's music, Bagneris's version depended on actual songs from the period, including numbers not by Morton. Verdi's "Le Miserere" from *Il Trovatore* was jazzed up to show Morton's French roots; standards such as "Ballin' the Jack," "Didn't He Ramble," and "Tiger Rag" were performed as part of Morton's repertoire; and Morton classics like "Jelly Roll Blues," "Wolverines," "Animale Ball," and "Sweet Substitute" revealed Morton in his element. Accompanied only by pianist Morten Gunnar Larsen, Bagneris had no trouble holding the stage with his mesmerizing performance. *Jelly Roll!* ran nearly a year and won a handful of Off-Broadway awards at season's end.

NUNSENSE 2: THE SEQUEL

[31 October 1994, Douglas Fairbanks Theatre, 149 performances] a musical revue by Dan Goggin. *Score:* Goggin (music and lyrics). *Cast:* Nancy E. Carroll, Terri White, Semina De Laurentis, Carolyn Droscoski, Susan Emerson.

Nunsense found success belaboring a thin premise for two silly acts. The inevitable sequel could not even come up with an original thin premise. The same nuns decide to put on another benefit six weeks after their first, still raising money by singing and dancing to the delight of indiscriminating audiences. Creator Dan Goggin recycled some tunes from *Nunsense* and gave them new lyrics. Sister Mary Amnesia (Semina De Laurentis) again pulled out her puppet for a number, and Sister Mary Hubert (Terri White) again delivered a raucous gospel number. Instead of a big tap number, this time around the five Little Sisters of Hoboken did a furious can-can sophomorically titled "Yes, We Can." They also considered going into the funeral business and advertised "We're the Nuns to Come To." Once again the performers were more interesting than their material, and once again *Nunsense 2* went on far too long to support its cute idea. Audiences were curious enough to keep the sequel running for four months. When business waned, the original *Nunsense* was performed in repertory with the sequel, but after a few weeks the nuns went back to the convent. When the sequel was recorded, it was given the title *Nunsense II: The Second Coming*. It was an ominous sign; further comings were still to come.

DAS BARBECÜ

[10 November 1994, Minetta Lane Theatre, 30 performances] a musical spoof by Jim Luigs. *Score:* Luigs (lyrics), Scott Warrender (music). *Cast:* J. K. Simmons, Sally Mayes, Carolee Carmello, Julie Johnson, Jerry McGarity.

Another musical that stretched a thin premise longer than it was willing to work was this silly version of Wagner's mammoth opera cycle *Der Ring dea Nibelungen* set in Texas and using country and western tunes. Opera spoofs were plentiful in musical revues in the 1950s when theatre audiences were more familiar with the masterworks of the genre. But those lampoons were usually just one extended sketch within the show. *Das Barbecü* was a full-length musical and was most fun if you knew the Wagner works. Others had to be content enjoying the sprightly hootenanny score. Opera lovers were amused to find Wagner's mythic lovers, gods, giants, dwarves, and Rhine maidens all played by five energetic hillbillies who are caught up in backwoods family feuds, a shotgun wedding, a musical salute to guacamole, and even a synchronized swimming show. The score was tuneful and likable in a giddy way, most of the songs being country and western knockoffs with titles like "Hog-Tie Your Man," "Rodeo Romeo," and "After the Gold Is Gone." There were some appealing cowboy ballads, such as "Wanderin' Man" and "County Fair," and some jubilant numbers like "A Ring of Gold in Texas" and "Turn the Tide." Director Christopher Ashley and choreographer Stephen Terrell kept the farcical musical moving and threw in everything from lassos and lariat tricks to steel guitars and a rousing two-step number. It also helped that the five cast members were as prankish as they were versatile. *Das Barbecü* had found success in Seattle, Baltimore, and at the Goodspeed Opera House in Connecticut, but New Yorkers were not interested and the commercial enterprise closed within a month. Subsequent productions regionally have done better, and the buffoonish musical still resurfaces once in a while.

THE PETRIFIED PRINCE

[18 December 1994, Public Theatre/Martison Hall, 32 performances] a musical by Edward Gallardo based on a screenplay by Ingmar Bergman. *Score*: Michael John LaChiusa (music and lyrics). *Cast*: Alexander Gaberman, Candy Buckley, Daisy Prince, Mal Z. Lawrence, Timothy Jerome, Jane White, Marilyn Cooper, Loni Ackerman.

One of the most anticipated events of the New York theatre season was a musical version of an unfilmed Ingmar Bergman screenplay titled *The Petrified Prince*. The interest was not so much in Bergman but in the show's director, Harold Prince in one of his rare Off-Broadway projects, and in the new score by the gifted Michael John LaChiusa. When the Public Theatre offering proved to be a major disappointment, *The Petrified Prince* disappeared after its month-long engagement, never recorded or published. The project was not without possibilities. Bergman's political fairy tale was set in 1807 in the mythical country of Slavonia where the death of King Maximilian (Mal Z. Lawrence) puts his son Prince Samson (Alexander Baberman) on the throne. Samson is "petrified" in that he is somewhat autistic and has a psychological block that renders him mute on occasion. With such a feeble leader, Slavonia is threatened by everyone from Napoleon to the Pope, but the prince perseveres and, with the love of the gentle prostitute Elise (Daisy Prince), Samson overcomes his handicaps and his political rivals and survives to rule the Ruritanian country effectively. Critics thought the fable implausible and unbelievable, yet how many fables are? The score was dismissed as ineffective, though one wonders how a listener can judge something as difficult as a LaChiusa song on one hearing. The reviews applauded Prince's imaginative, direction which was visually exciting and included constructivist sets, biomechanic movement by the actors, theatrical tableaus, and a chorus of puppets who played singing animals. There were also compliments for some of the cast, which was filled with both new and veteran talent. Was *The Petrified Prince* the misguided mess the press reported, a daring Harold Prince experiment that failed, or a neglected gem? Unless it is revived or recorded some day, we'll never know for sure.

JACK'S HOLIDAY

[5 March 1995, Playwrights Horizons, 25 performances] a musical play by Mark St. Germain. *Score:* Randy Courts (music), Germain (lyrics). *Cast:* Allen Fitzpatrick, Judy Blazer, Greg Naughton, Alix Korey, Henry Stram, Dennis Parlato, Mark Lotito, Herb Foster, Michael X. Martin, Lauren Ward, Ann Runolfsson, Nicolas Coster, Michael Mulheren.

A talented cast and a pleasing score were done in by a problematic script in this period musical filled with intriguing ideas. In 1891, the theatrical troupe Swan's Players from England arrives in New York City on tour, among them the general utility man Jack (Allen Fitzpatrick), who is really the infamous Jack the Ripper. He hopes to capture the attention of the local police and captivate the public as he had in London, but Jack finds Manhattan so filled with evil and corruption that his murders do not get the kind of publicity he expects. The young newspaper reporter Will Bolger (Greg Naughton) tries to make his name covering the murders, as does Inspector Thomas Byrnes (Dennis Parlato), but even when Jack is after the prostitute Mary Healey (Judy Blazer), with whom Will is in love, events fail to make Jack as big a celebrity as in London. Mark St. Germain's libretto drew many parallels between yellow journalism at the end of the nineteenth century and in the present day, and raised many questions about sensationalism and truth. What the script did not offer was fully developed characters or much suspense. Critics compared the piece unfavorably to *Sweeney Todd*, which Susan H. Schulman, the director of *Jack's Holiday*, had staged effectively at the Circle in the Square in 1989. There were plenty of compliments for her direction of the new work, as there were for Jerome Sirlin's evocative sets and projections, but most reviewers found the musical more interesting than involving. Judy Blazer got the best notices, but generally the cast was applauded by the press, as were the songs they sang. The score by Germain (lyrics) and Randy Courts (music) was not recorded but, judging by the reviews, there was much to admire in the wry "Tricks of the Trade," the tentative duet "What I Almost Said," the ballad "If You Will Dream of Me," and the ambitious song thirsting for fame "All You Want Is Always." The Playwrights Horizons' production of *Jack's Holiday* ran its three-week engagement, followed over the years by some regional productions.

SWINGTIME CANTEEN

[14 March 1995, Blue Angel, 294 performances] a musical revue by Linda Thorsen Bond, William Repicci, Charles Busch. *Score:* various. *Cast:* Alison Fraser, Emily Loesser, Debra Barsha, Jackie Sanders, Marcy McGuigan.

Vintage songs from the World War II era were given a slick and nostalgic presentation in this revue featuring women singers and female musicians. The setting is the U.S. Eighth Air Force hangar in London in 1944, and movie star Marian Ames (Alison Fraser) is entertaining the troops with her singers and all-girl band from the Hollywood Canteen. The USO show includes some patriotic patter and some sexy jokes for the troops, while backstage rivalries fester and nerves are on edge. This performance is the first stop on a tour of the front lines, and the last section of the show is to be broadcast on the radio. After some setbacks (the brass are thinking of canceling the tour fearing it is too dangerous for women) and an air raid that cuts off the electricity for a while, everyone pulls together for the big finish. It was all amusing filler, but what mattered were the songs, over thirty of them heard individually or in expertly arranged medleys. British favorites such as "A Nightingale Sang in Berkeley Square" and "Pack Up Your Troubles in Your Old Kit Bag" were performed alongside American favorites like "Ac-cent-tchu-ate the Positive," "I'm Old Fashioned," "You'll Never Know," "Don't Fence Me In," and "Sing Sing Sing." Of course patriotic numbers were included, and songs such as "Praise the Lord and Pass the Ammunition," "Thank Your Lucky Stars and Stripes," and "Bugle Call Rag" were delivered with panache and not a touch of camp. Amidst the familiar songs were some less-known delights such as "Daddy," "His Rocking Horse Ran Away," "Love Isn't Born," and "How High the Moon." Fraser was outstanding, pulling off both comic and sentimental songs with equal verve, and the rest of the female cast and band also shone, in particular the chorine Katie Gammersflugel played by Emily Loesser (whose father wrote several of the featured numbers). *Swingtime Canteen* originated as a community theatre project in Midland, Texas, put together by Linda Thorsen Bond. Producer William Repicci brought in playwright

Charles Busch, and the two of them revised the script and presented it at the Bay Street Theatre in Sag Harbor, New York. Repicci then coproduced the Off-Broadway production which was well received by both the press and the public. During its ten-month run, Busch took over the role of Marian Ames and gave a bizarre but heartfelt drag performance. At one point in the run, the lone surviving Andrews Sister Maxene joined the company, and when the girls did a medley of the Sisters' wartime hits, nostalgia ruled supreme.

JOHN & JEN

[1 June 1995, Lamb's Little Theatre, 114 performances] a musical play by Andrew Lippa, Tom Greenwald. *Score:* Lippa (music), Greenwald (lyrics). *Cast:* James Ludwig, Carolee Carmello.

A musical soap opera on a very small scale, *john & jen* was intimate to the point of being embarrassing. Two actors played the musical's three characters, and the plot was a series of sensitive duets and duologues that were of limited interest to anyone besides the title characters. Jen (Carolee Carmello) does all she can to protect her younger brother John (James Ludwig) from their abusive father. When Jen goes off to become a hippie, John enlists in the army and is killed in Vietnam. Years later, Jen is a single mother whose desperate affections for her son John (Ludwig) are smothering him to death. After a lot of serious talk and musical lamenting, Jen learns to start to let go. As the title suggests, this was definitely a "lower case" musical with big issues tackled by little people who were not particularly unique or interesting. Audiences were able to stick with this dreary trio thanks to the luminous performances by Carmello and Ludwig. The supersensitive score was sometimes engaging, often annoying. So many sincere and revealing numbers in one musical did not leave much room for variety, and numbness set in, yet a few songs found their voice, such as the determined "The Road Ends Here" and the confessional "That Was My Way." Other numbers, like "Smile of Your Dreams" and "Every Goodbye Is Hello," were as awful as their titles suggested. *john & jen* originated at the Goodspeed Opera House in Connecticut and was picked up by the Lamb's Theatre Off Off Broadway. The producers were encouraged by audience reactions, rewrote the contracts, and continued on as an Off-Broadway entry for fourteen weeks. The two-actor musical is sometimes revived by theatres looking for a small, bare-bones musical.

ZOMBIES FROM BEYOND

[23 October 1995, Players Theatre, 72 performances] a musical spoof by James Valcq. *Score:* Valcq (music and lyrics). *Cast:* Matt McClanahan, Claire Morkin, Susan Gottschalk, Michael Shelle, Jeremy Czarniak, Robert Boles, Suzanne Graff.

Some appreciative reviews helped this sci-fi musical spoof run nine weeks Off Broadway, but it has pretty much faded from the stratosphere since then. The musical send-up of 1950s alien invader movies was broadly played and tunefully pleasing, but it lacked the inventiveness of a musical parody like *Little Shop of Horrors*. In 1955, Major Malone (Michael Shelle) and the staff at the Milwaukee Space Center are worried about the Cold War and the space race but have bigger problems when a flying saucer lands nearby, piloted by the comely alien Zombina (Susan Gottschalk) who is looking for men to repopulate her planet. The Major's daughter Mary (Claire Morkin) must fight to keep her sweetheart, the rocket scientist Trenton Corbett (Matt McClanahan), and the other men from being brainwashed by Zombina and whisked away to become intergalactic breeders. The silly script was filled with cartoonish characters, smirking references to the Eisenhower era, and slaphappy musical numbers. Mary and Trenton sang the inanely romantic "Second Planet on the Right," Zombina vamped her way through "The Last Man on Earth," delivery boy Billy Krutzik (Jeremy Czarniak) furiously tap danced with his "Atomic Feet," the Major led the cast in the vigilant "Keep Watching the Skies," and Zombina and her Zombettes brought down the house with the rocking title number. If *Zombies from Beyond* was mindless, it was also unpretentious and tongue in cheek enough not to be annoying.

SONGS FOR A NEW WORLD

[26 October 1995, WPA Theatre, 27 performances] a musical revue by Jason Robert Brown (music and lyrics). *Cast:* Jessica Molaskey, Brooks Ashmanskas, Billy Porter, Andrea Burns.

This revue comprised of fascinating "story songs" was the New York professional debut for Jason Robert Brown, a busy orchestrator, pianist, and arranger who finally was recognized as a theatre songwriter with this show. Brown, of course, had been writing songs for years. It was when he approached performer Daisy Prince about directing an evening of these very individual story songs that the original revue started to enfold. There was no theme or "concept" for *Songs for a New World*, yet these disparate little musical dramas were highly theatrical, and the revue felt like a planned, cohesive program. There was also a lot of variety, the numbers as different as the romantic duet "I'd Give It All for You" and the Brechtian spoof "Surabaya-Santa." If there was a constant in the score, it was the sense of something ending in each song, be it a life, a relationship, or a job. Among the many highlights of the revue were: "The Stars and the Moon," in which a wealthy woman sees all her wishes come true and it is leading her to suicide; "Steam Train," with a poor boy dreaming of breaking out of poverty by becoming a sports star; "On the Deck of a Spanish Sailing Ship, 1492," which was not about Columbus but a group of Jews being deported from Spain to the New World; "I'm Not Afraid of Anything," sung by a girl on a swing whose ache for adventure is not understood by her family, friends, or boyfriend; and "The World Was Dancing," in which a father sinks the family fortune into a store then lets it burn to the ground. The revue opened with the complex "The New World" in which various characters consider a momentous change about to happen in their lives even as disaster seems to be waiting around the corner. The musical ended with the personal "Hear My Song" which Brown sang with the company of four, offering all the evening's stories as comfort during times of trial. *Songs for a New World* took three years for Brown and Prince to compile as new numbers were written and existing songs tried out. The show was workshopped in Toronto then played at the WPA Theatre which was technically an Off Off-Broadway venue. The short run of three and a half weeks passed quickly, and few reviewers or playgoers were even aware of it. It was not until an original cast recording of the score was released in 1996 that the revue started to catch on. Also, interest in Brown multiplied after his first Broadway show *Parade* (1998) in which his score was much lauded. Soon *Songs for a New World* was receiving dozens of regional productions, and it continues to be a favorite in colleges and with more ambitious theatre groups. Many of Brown's advocates consider this early work to be his finest because it is what Brown does best: telling a multileveled story in a single song.

Bring in 'da Noise Bring in 'da Funk

[15 November 1995, Public Theatre/Estelle R. Newman Theatre, 85 performances; Ambassador Theatre, 1,135 performances] a musical revue by

Reg E. Gaines. *Score:* Gaines (lyrics), Ann Duquesnay, Zane Mark, Daryl Waters (music). *Cast:* Duquesnay, Gaines, Savion Glover, Jared Crawford, Jimmy Tate, Dule Hill, Raymond King, Baakari Wilder, Vincent Bingham.

Difficult to describe and impossible to categorize, this vibrant musical revue followed the evolution of American dance, in particular tap, as illustrated through the history of African Americans, from slaves using primitive drums to the hip-hop street dancers of the day. It was primarily a dance show, yet the theatrical nature of the staging, narration, and songs made the musical unique and enthralling. Reg E. Gaines wrote the book that consisted mostly of poetic narration delivered by the author. Aside from the piercing instrumental dance music, there were songs mostly sung by Ann Duquesnay who composed the music. But the star of the show was the propulsive young choreographer-dancer Savion Glover, who helped develop the show with director George C. Wolfe. Glover's tap dancing looked like no other tapping. He called it "hitting," and that partially described the way Glover's feet and the floor became partners in an exhilarating explosion of passion. The history in *Bring in 'da Noise Bring in 'da Funk* was often harsh as the action traveled from slave ships to farms to city slums. Yet the musical was not preachy or heavy-handed; the African American experience was celebrated with all its joy and bitterness. The score ranged from ragtime, jazz, and blues to contemporary rock, gospel, and hip-hop. Some numbers, such as "The Chicago Riot Rag," "The Whirligig Stomp," and "The Lost Beat Swing," were accurate pastiches of past styles. Other songs, such as "Hot Fun," "Hittin'," and the title number, were right up-to-the-minute and seemed to defy traditional song structure. Rhythm ruled the entire musical, and the dancing did more than keep to the beat; it challenged one's very idea of theatre choreography. *Bring in 'da Noise Bring in 'da Funk* was so popular that, after selling out at the Public's largest venue for ten weeks, the show transferred to Broadway. The only change, Jeffrey Wright taking Gaines's place as narrator, was deemed for the better. Audiences responded as enthusiastically as the critics, and the musical ran for more than three years.

RENT

[26 January 1996, New York Theatre Workshop, 56 performances; Nederlander Theatre, 5,012 performances] a musical play by Jonathan Larson.

Score: Larson (music and lyrics). *Cast:* Adam Pascal, Anthony Rapp, Daphne Rubin-Vega, Idina Menzel, Wilson Jermaine Heredia, Fredi Walker, Taye Diggs.

A popular rock musical loosely based on the Puccini opera *La Boheme*, this thrilling show was both the Off-Broadway debut and swan song for the gifted author-composer-lyricist Jonathan Larson. *Rent* was also the most popular rock musical in the American theatre since *Hair* nearly thirty years earlier.

Struggling composer Roger Davis (Adam Pascal) and video artist Mark Cohen (Anthony Rapp) live in the East Village of Manhattan in the 1990s with other bohemian artists who try to be true to their artistic visions while struggling with sour love affairs, poverty, and AIDS. Roger reluctantly falls in love with the dancer Mimi Marquez (Daphne Rubin-Vega); Mark's ex-girlfriend, performance artist Maureen Johnson (Idina Menzel), takes up with legal aid worker Joanne Jefferson (Fredi Walker); and ex-professor Tom Collins (Jesse L. Martin) finds true love with drag queen Angel Schunard (Wilson Jermaine Heredia). Over the course of a year, these relationships are threatened by jealousy, infidelity, and death. In the end, the survivors find hope with each other and discover from Mimi, who was close to death but returned, that the deceased Angel urges them to love and live on. The sung-through rock musical used a variety of musical styles, from the tango to blues to folk, but at heart it was a very contemporary sounding score that was not afraid of using rock to do what theatre songs were supposed to do. The show was character driven, and the songs often were specific to certain people in the drama. Most of the characters were struggling artists, yet they could not be lumped together as simple types. Larson's lyrics are poignant but rarely sentimental, romantic but far from gushing. He was not afraid to show his characters' weaknesses and built an empathy with the audience by sometimes showing them at their worst. While most rock musicals of the past concentrated on protest or celebration, *Rent* was more incisive, looking at youth and youthful ideas with humor, sadness, and honesty.

Within the framework of rock, Larson was still able to find a great deal of variety in his score. The recurring complaint that all the numbers in a rock score tend to blend together into one continuous blur could not be said about *Rent*. "One Song Glory" was a lyrical yet painful cry for acknowledgment. "I'll Cover You" and "Light My Candle" were two very different kinds of romantic duets, and "Today for You" told a brash story with a feverish Latin rhythm. "Seasons of Love" was a quiet ballad, while the title song was a shout of defiance. Also rare for a rock musical, the lyrics were often witty, and the words sometimes took precedence over the beat, as in "Tango: Maureen," "Sante Fe," and "Without You." *Rent* boasted the finest rock score since *Hair* and, as that 1960s show still can pack a wallop, so too will *Rent* for many years to come.

The musical was developed and first produced by the New York Theatre Workshop, directed by Michael Greif, and featuring a young and unforgettable cast. Has any one musical, Off Broadway or on, ever produced so many future stars? The drama on stage was matched by the backstage tragedy when the night before the first preview performance the young Larson died suddenly of an undetected brain disorder. The first performances were drenched in emotion, but both critics and audiences could tell that there was much more to *Rent* than a sentimental reaction to the circumstances surrounding its birth. The seven-week engagement sold out, then the show transferred to Broadway without losing any of its intimacy and power. The producers wisely moved *Rent* into the dilapidated Nederlander Theatre, a bit removed from the Theatre District. Instead of fixing up the theatre, they tarted it up with garish and funky fixtures and carpeting and recreated the East Village on Broadway. *Rent* still felt like an Off-Broadway experience. After many tours, a film version, a taping of the final performance, and now regional and school productions, *Rent* is still a potent stage piece. Set in the 1990s and a product of that era, it is already becoming a period piece like *Hair*. The show made history and now is part of history.

COWGIRLS

[1 April 1996, Minetta Lane Theatre, 319 performances] a musical comedy by Betsy Howie. *Score*: Mary Murfitt (music and lyrics). *Cast*: Murfitt, Howie, Jackie Sanders, Rhonda Coullet, Mary Ehrlinger, Lori Fischer.

Those seemingly polar extremes, country music and classical music, combined and made an odd but enjoyable concoction in *Cowgirls*, an all-female revue that featured performers who were also musicians. Mary Murfitt, a veteran of that other singer-musician show *Oil City Symphony*, wrote the country and western pastiche numbers which were performed alongside pieces from Chopin, Brahms, Beethoven, and Gilbert and Sullivan. The premise that brought such disparate sounds together was far-fetched but logical in a cockeyed way. Jo Carlson (Rhonda Coulett) is desperate to save her late father's Hiram Hall, a country and western saloon in Rexford, Texas.

She books into the theatre the touring Cowgirl Trio (Mary Ehrlinger, Lori Fischer, and Muffit), but when they arrive, they are a female classical group called the Coghill Trio. Meanwhile, Jo's friends Mo (Betsy Howie) and Mickey (Jackie Sanders) have not-so-hidden ambitions to become country singing stars (something Jo aspires to as well) and the two insist that they perform the kind of songs that the patrons of Hiram Hall expect. The compromise is a mixture of both trios on stage with incongruous musical and comic results. The song "From Chopin to Country" summed up the evening pretty well as classical favorites such as "Brahms' Lullaby" and "Three Little Maids from School" started to sound a bit countrified, and strains of Mozart were heard in country entries like "Looking for a Miracle." By the end of the show the two kinds of music were overlapping, and the two trios were starting to perform each other's material. All six of the characters were going through some kind of crisis, from dashed illusions to pregnancy. Audiences got to know each of the sextet by the end of the musical, but they were rarely as interesting as the music they produced. By the second act, numbers like "We're a Travelin' Trio," "Saddle Tramp Blues," "They're All Cowgirls to Me," and the title song sounded like old favorites. *Cowgirls* had found success in theatres in Florida, the Berkshire Festival in Massachusetts, and the Old Globe in California before the Off-Broadway production. In New York, critical reaction to the revue, the multitalented performers, and the score was mostly supportive allowing *Cowgirls* to tread the boards for ten months. The casting demands for singer-musicians make the musical difficult to produce, but there have been successful regional productions since the Manhattan run.

FLOYD COLLINS

[3 March 1996, Playwrights Horizons, 25 performances] a musical play by Tina Landau. *Score:* Landau (lyrics), Adam Guettel (music and lyrics). *Cast:* Christopher Innvar, Jason Danieley, Theresa McCarthy, Martin Moran, Cass Morgan, Don Chastain, Brian d'Arcy James.

This engrossing, tragic musical with an unusual subject introduced song-writer Adam Guettel to the press and theatregoing public, and during its short run at Playwrights Horizons, the musical made quite an impact, mostly because of its stunning score. In the winter of 1925, the Kentucky farmer

Floyd Collins (Christopher Innvar) is exploring a cave on the family property when he gets trapped 150 feet below the surface. The efforts to rescue him make national news, and the site soon turns into a media circus as journalists and thousands of curious onlookers arrive. By the time the rescuers reach Collins, he has died of exposure, and the circus disbands. Tina Landau's libretto, based on a true event, eschewed conventional storytelling and used dreams, flashbacks, and other theatrical devices to explore the mind-set of Floyd and his family. The score was an eclectic mix of country, ragtime, and folk music; yet the resulting sound was so unique that even familiar genres sounded different in Guettel's hands. Also, many of the songs took a stream of consciousness approach, meaning traditional song structure was abandoned, rhymes were infrequent, and melodic lines went in patterns that could only be described as avant garde. For example, Floyd's first number "The Call" runs more than twelve minutes and is broken into different sections as he runs through the emotions of eagerness to jubilation to panic and then despair. At one point he is so exhilarated by the echo that his voice makes in the cave that he performs a celebratory duet with himself. Another duet, "The Riddle Song," is sung by Floyd and his brother Homer (Jason Danieley) as they quiz each other with riddles that conjure up scenes from their childhood. It is a thrilling and yet pathetic tribute to brotherly love sung by two rough but poetic men. Once the press descends on the Collins farm, the city newspapermen bring a honky-tonk quality to the rural setting with the funny and callous "Is That Remarkable?" in which headlines and sensational news writing take on a carnival quality. The Collins family is uneducated, but a homespun dignity is manifest in such numbers as "Lucky" sung by sister Nellie (Theresa McCarthy) and her stepmother Miss Jane (Cass Morgan), in the parents' tender "Heart an' Hand," and in the Collins' "Family Hymn." "Through the Mountain" is a heartfelt folk ballad, while "Tween a Rock and a Hard Place" is a raucous song of hillbilly pride. The most devastating musical number is "The Dream," in which Floyd hallucinates and sees his family successful and happy as crowds flock to the site because the cave is a major tourist attraction. Few theatre scores hit on so many different kinds of emotion as *Floyd Collins* did.

A good deal of publicity was generated over the fact that Guettel was the grandson of Richard Rodgers. Although this score was very different from Rodgers's strong melody line and conventional structure, the passion in the music in *Floyd Collins* was just as potent. The musical was first produced at the American Music Theatre Festival in Philadelphia in 1994, then after some revisions was presented Off Broadway for a three-week run at Playwrights Horizons. Landau directed the ingenious production which used space unrealistically, the cave and the world outside it all staged as if in some dream. Possibly because of Guettel's theatrical lineage, most of the major critics sought out the show, and their reaction was enthusiastic for the score even if some found the subject too morbid or dreary. The original cast recording was embraced by musical theatre lovers, and soon there were numerous productions in regional, community, and college theatres. *Floyd Collins* immediately placed Guettel among the most promising and exciting new songwriters in the American theatre.

ZOMBIE PROM

[9 April 1996, Variety Arts Theatre, 28 performances] a musical satire by John Dempsey. *Score:* Dana P. Rowe (music), Dempsey (lyrics). *Cast:* Richard Roland, Jessica-Snow Wilson, Karen Murphy, Stephen Bienski, Richard Muenz, Marc Lovci, Rebecca Rich.

The parade of *Little Shop of Horrors* knockoffs continued, but didn't end, with *Zombie Prom*, a sci-fi spoof that also hoped to latch on to the popularity of *Grease*. To add to the stew, bits of *Bye Bye Birdie* and *The Rocky Horror Picture Show* were also thrown in. One would think borrowing from so many successful sources that the results should have been better than what played Off Broadway for three and a half weeks. Enrico Fermi High School sits in the shadow of an atomic power plant in the 1950s and is ruled with a heavy hand by Principal Deliah Strict (Karen Murphy). Pretty coed Toffee (Jessica-Snow Wilson) loves the troublemaking orphan Jonny (Richard Roland), and when Toffee's parents put an end to the romance, Jonny runs his motorcycle into the power plant and dies. They bury the radioactive Jonny in a lead coffin at the bottom of the sea, but he returns as a zombie to regain Toffee's love and take her to the prom. The script was a series of movie clichés, and the characters were simpleminded, but there was much to admire in the 1950s pastiche score by Dana P. Rowe and John Dempsey. Principal Strict sang the hilarious character number "Rules, Regulations and Respect"; the lovers crooned "How Can I Say Goodbye" and "Forbidden Love"; early rock and roll was satirized in "That's the Beat for Me"; and everyone danced to the title tune. The music may have been routine at times, but the lyrics were often better than one expected in such a sophomoric enterprise. *Zombie Prom* enjoyed some community and school productions when those groups were not busy doing *Grease* or *Little Shop of Horrors*.

I LOVE YOU, YOU'RE PERFECT, NOW CHANGE

[1 August 1996, Westside Theatre Upstairs, 5,003 performances] a musical revue by Joe DiPietro. *Score:* DiPietro (lyrics), Jimmy Roberts (music). *Cast:* Jennifer Simard, Jordan Leeds, Robert Roznowski, Melissa Weil.

Those who found the lengthy title of this musical revue to be witty and philosophical were mostly likely to have a good time because, like its title, the show was cliché-ridden and familiar. It was also truthful at times because clichés are often true. For the more discriminating playgoers, *I Love You, You're Perfect, Now Change* was a labored evening, something that would barely hold your attention on television. But it seems this group was in the minority because the show ran more than thirteen years Off Broadway and has received hundreds of productions regionally, proving nothing breeds familiarity like the familiar. The musical was unique in that it was all about heterosexual relationships, something frequently ignored over the past few decades. Joe DiPietro wrote the sketches and lyrics for Jimmy Roberts's music, and both the scenes and the songs were routine at best but struck a nerve with audiences who recognized the clichés about dating, marriage, parenthood, and aging. Blind dates, nerdy or macho men, mousy or overachieving single women, the lack of straight men, nightmare weddings and honeymoons, parents who resort to baby talk and are too tired for sex, and practical geriatric romance were all paraded before the audience with a tired sense of predictability. The songs were toothless pastiches of pop, country, Gregorian chant, tangos, and cantatas with lyrics that never developed an idea but resorted to lists and examples. The challenge for the performers was to not slip into easy caricature but often that's all there was to work with. The few sincere songs in the show bordered on mawkishness, yet even that seemed to be expected. Like *Nunsense*, this economical little musical has saved many a financially strapped theatre group by providing a cheap and easy hit. It's something to be thankful for, especially if you don't have to sit through *I Love You, You're Perfect, Now Change.*

WHEN PIGS FLY

[14 August 1996, Douglas Fairbanks Theatre, 840 performances] a musical revue by Mark Waldrop. *Score:* Waldrop (lyrics), Dick Gallagher (music).

Most of the artistic staff from the riotous *Whoop-Dee-Doo!* returned for this equally wacky revue that again sported outrageously funny costumes by the production's creator Howard Crabtree. The harried producer Howard (Michael West) is putting on a topical revue with the usual backstage temperaments flaring up. But the real fireworks were on stage with the gay-oriented sketches and the slapstick musical numbers. In the show a Midwest community theatre producer announced his upcoming season to the board arguing that they can't keep doing *Paint Your Wagon*. A deluded Bette Davis dressed as Baby Jane took her frustration out on a life-size Joan Crawford doll. A conservative matron, dressed like Dolly Levi, fought to bring old-time musical comedy to her small-town theatre with such projects as *Lord of the Fries*, *Annie 3*, and *Quasimodo*. The songs, again by Dick Gallagher and Mark Waldrop, were even better this time around. Right-wingers Newt Gingrich, Strom Thurmond, and Rush Limbaugh were evoked in a tortured "Torch Song," a gay nuptial was imagined in "Hawaiian Wedding Day," and the sincere "Laughing Matters" looked at the cruelties in the real world and wondered how one can keep a sense of humor. The most memorable numbers were those that utilized Crabtree's zany costumes. A fey pair of song-and-dance men danced to "Light in the Loafers" as their shoes lit up; the four queens from a deck of cards performed "You've Got to Stay in the Game"; a centaur wearing a feathery half-man, half-horse costume sang "Not All Man"; and some beauty queens obsessed with their looks proudly recommended "Wear Your Vanity with Pride" as they paraded in *Follies*-like costumes in the form of vanity cabinets. Some critics found *When Pigs Fly* more accomplished than *Whoop-Dee-Doo!*, and most of the notices were laudatory, allowing it to run nearly three times as long as the earlier revue.

RADIO GALS

The very early days of radio, when anyone who could find an open frequency could transmit sound through the airwaves, was conjured up in this clever if not totally satisfying musical comedy by the creators of *Oil City Symphony*, *Smoke on the Mountain*, and other satirical musicals. The setting is 1927 in Cedar Ridge, Arkansas, where the retired music teacher Hazel C. Hunt (Carole Cook) gathers her former students (she calls them her Hazelnuts) in her living room to broadcast music on the 100-watt Western Electric radio transmitter that she was given as a retirement gift. The Hazelnuts sing and play musical instruments, their repertoire consisting of hillbilly ballads, gospel-flavored numbers, and novelty songs. O. B. Abbott (Matthew Bennett), an inspector from the Department of Commerce, catches the frequency on his radio and traces down Hazel and her illegal operation, but the crafty old woman discovers that beneath the bureaucrat is an accordion player with a fine tenor voice, and soon O. B. is one of her Hazelnuts. It was a silly but useful premise that allowed for some wacky original songs by Mike Craver and Mark Hardwick and ridiculous on-the-air banter that included merry advertisements for the cure-all tonic Horehound Compound. Some of the numbers, such as "Buster, He's a Hot Dog Now" and "When It's Sweetpea Time in Georgia," were so obvious that the corn was forced. Yet much of the score was quite proficient, and songs like "Dear Mr. Gershwin," "Edna Jones, The Elephant Girl," and "Why Did You Make Me Love You?" caught the simple, rural charm of those old time hits. *Radio Gals* was first presented in Little Rock, Arkansas, and Pasadena, California, then only lasted five weeks Off Broadway despite some glowing notices. Regional theatres looking for a good vehicle for a mostly female cast have had success with it.

A BRIEF HISTORY OF WHITE MUSIC

[19 November 1996, Village Gate, 308 performances] a musical spoof by DeeDee Thomas, David Tweedy. *Score:* various. *Cast:* Deborah Keeling, Wendy Edmead, James Alexander.

The risible title of this revue did not warn audiences that there was a political agenda here, but the show was so enjoyable that even surprised playgoers walked away with a bubbly feeling. The premise used a cockeyed kind of sociopolitical logic. When rhythm and blues went mainstream in the late 1940s and grew in popularity in the 1950s and early 1960s, the genre was often represented by white singers performing in the hip style of the African

Americans who had originated the sound. It was felt that such "race music" would be more palatable to most Americans if they were sung by artists (from Buddy Holly to Elvis Presley to the Beatles) who were not black. With this idea in mind, DeeDee Thomas and David Tweedy concocted *A Brief History of White Music* in which white-bread jukebox favorites were performed by three African American performers. Black entertainers mimicking white singers who had tried to sound black was not only thought-provoking but also highly entertaining. Such 1950s and 1960s hits as "Who Put the Bomp," "That'll Be the Day," "Where the Boys Are," "Leader of the Pack," "Blue Suede Shoes," "California Dreaming," "These Boots Are Made for Walking," and "Do Wah Diddy Diddy" sounded slightly different when sung by African Americans James Alexander, Wendy Edmead, and Deborah Keeling, but the songs were no less fun. The press found the premise interesting and the performers first rate, so, with the help of strong word of mouth, *A Brief History of White Music* ran for more than nine months.

VIOLET

[11 March 1997, Playwrights Horizons, 32 performances] a musical play by Brian Crawley based on Doris Betts's *The Ugliest Pilgrim*. *Score:* Crawley (lyrics), Jeanine Tesori (music). *Cast:* Lauren Ward, Michael McElroy, Michael Park, Cass Morgan, Robert Westenberg.

An intimate, oddly poignant Off-Broadway musical, the chamber piece brought the first recognition to promising composer Jeanine Tesori. The Southern girl Violet (Lauren Ward) is marked with a facial scar she's had since her father had an accident with his ax. In 1964 she sets out from Spruce Pine, North Carolina, by bus to attend a revivalist meeting held by a televangelist in Oklahoma with the hopes of getting cured. On the journey she befriends two servicemen, good ol' boy Monty (Michael Park) and the African American Flick (Michael McElroy). The faith healing at the revival does not remove the scar, but Violet does find the strength to overcome her prejudices and return the love of Flick. Based on Doris Betts's novel *The Ugliest Pilgrim*, the libretto by Brian Crawley was efficient and understated with natural dialogue that had music of its own. Crawley also wrote the lyrics for Tesori's country-flavored music, and the score was compelling. The folk number "Water in the Well" which opened the show sounded so authentic that one mistook it for a standard. The soaring numbers "On My Way" and "Let It Sing" were stirring without being Broadwayized. Violet was a complex, bitter character who was scarred inside and out, yet some of her songs revealed an aching tenderness, as in "Lay Down Your Head" and "Look at Me" which she sang with her younger self (Amanda Posner). Other highlights in this delectable score included the snappy "Luck of the Draw," the rousing "Bring Me to Light," the gospel pastiche "Raise Me Up," and the poignant duet "Hard to Say Goodbye." *Violet* had been developed at the O'Neill Music Theatre Conference in Connecticut then was produced by Playwrights Horizons for a one-month run. Susan Schulman staged the itinerant musical beautifully on the small stage, and the performances were expert all around, particularly Ward's fierce and fascinating Violet. The reviews were auspicious, the show won a handful of prestigious awards, and plans were made to move the production to a commercial venue for an open run; but an unfavorable notice in the all-powerful *New York Times* scuttled the transfer. Because of the original cast recording, *Violet* has since been slowly but steadily finding recognition in regional theatres and colleges.

ALWAYS . . . PATSY CLINE

[24 June 1997, Variety Arts Theatre, 192 performances] a musical play by Ted Swindley. *Score*: various. *Cast*: Tori Lynn Palazola, Margo Martindale.

Rather than just a tribute concert with someone impersonating the country music star, *Always . . . Patsy Cline* was a two-character musical play that avoided many of the clichés of showbiz biographies. The story of Cline (Tori Lynn Palazola) was told from the point of view of the Texan Louise (Margo Martindale), an ardent fan of the star who befriended Cline in the late 1950s. Patsy and Louise reminisce together, relate episodes in Cline's life, and even sing some numbers together. Louise tells the story after Cline's death in an airplane crash in 1963, but the script by Ted Swindley is not a sentimental eulogy. Of course, the reason for the show was to hear such Cline favorites as "Faded Love," "Sweet Dreams," "Lovesick Blues," and "Crazy." Critics disagreed on how effective Palazola was in capturing Cline's sound and mannerisms, but many thought the biomusical to be quite proficient. *Always . . . Patsy Cline* was first produced in Nashville in 1994 and was recorded. The Off-Broadway run was a modest success at twenty-four weeks, but the economic little show became a favorite in regional and summer theatres, receiving hundreds of productions and drawing country music fans who were rarely interested in musical theatre.

THE LAST SESSION

[17 October 1997, 47th Street Theatre, 154 performances] a musical play by Jim Brochu. *Score:* Steve Schalchlin (music and lyrics), various. *Cast:* Bob Stillman, Grace Garland, Amy Coleman, Dean Bradshaw, Stephen Bienskie.

Of the various musicals about the AIDS epidemic that surfaced in the 1990s, this one may not have gotten much attention but many consider it one of the best. The notable rock musician-composer-singer Gideon (Bob Stillman) is dying of AIDS and wishes to commit suicide. But first he wants to record one last album of songs about the various aspects of the disease and how it affects the people close to the afflicted ones. He tells only the sardonic recording studio engineer Jim (Dean Bradshaw) about his plan to kill himself right after the session, but Gideon's ex-wife Vicki (Amy Coleman), his African American friend Tryshia (Grace Garland), and the Christian songwriter Buddy (Stephen Bienskie) join Gideon for the session and suspect something is up. Buddy tries to save Gideon's soul while the others offer so much love and understanding that the suicide never happens. The songs by Steve Schalchlin were incisive, potent, and avoided sentimentality, the driving rock music keeping any of them from becoming maudlin laments or angry diatribes. Gideon argued "At Least I Know What's Killing Me," Tryshia praised "The Singer and the Song," Buddy offered the ballad "Going It Alone," and Gideon and his friends reflected on AIDS support groups in "The Group." Perhaps the most disturbing number was "Somebody's Friend" about all the false rumors circulating about a cure for the disease. *The Last Session* began when Schalchlin gave Jim Brochu a set of songs about AIDS, and the latter wrote the libretto abound them. After a successful run Off Off Broadway, the musical moved to Off Broadway and ran five months. Musicals about AIDS do not do well outside of large cities, and *The Last Session* was no exception. Yet the quality of the score is unmistakable.

SECRETS EVERY SMART TRAVELER SHOULD KNOW

[30 October 1997, Triad Theatre, 953 performances] a musical revue by Douglas Bernstein, Francesca Blumenthal, Stan Freeman, various. *Score:*

Bernstein, Blumenthal, Freeman, et al. (music and lyrics). *Cast:* Freeman, Jay Lenohart, Kathy Fitzgerald, James Darrah, Liz McConahay, Michael McGrath.

A musical revue that exhausted its feeble subject matter well before the finale was the annoying but embarrassingly popular *Secrets Every Smart Traveler Should Know.* The title was misleading, for this did not offer tips about traveling but instead was filled with uninspired kvetching about bad travel experiences. Not only were the songs and sketches predictable, most audience members probably had more interesting travel stories than the ones which they were bombarded with all evening. Lost luggage, Montezuma's revenge, overpriced car rentals, delays in airports, overeating at the cruise ship buffet, unfriendly customs officials, and other expected topics were acted out or sung without a shred of wit or insight. Some ideas didn't even make sense, such as complaining about too much classical music at Salzburg or talent shows on cruises; as if anyone is forced to attend such things. The revue was based on Wendy Perrin's nonfiction book that collected favorite stories she had uncovered as a writer for *Condé Nast Traveler.* A variety of authors provided the songs and sketches, which were consistently unimpressive. A sketch parodying *Private Lives* and a song about coming home from Acapulco with a guide as a souvenir, for example, were so sophomoric that one suspected the show came from some wretched dinner theatre. Most critics were politely dismissive, but audiences were not deterred; *Secrets Every Smart Traveler Should Know* ran two and a half years. Had they offered a buffet, it would have run a decade.

THE SHOW GOES ON

[17 December 1997, Theatre at St. Peter's Church, 88 performances] a musical revue by Tom Jones, Harvey Schmidt. *Score:* Jones (lyrics), Schmidt (music). *Cast:* Jones, Schmidt, JoAnn Cunningham, J. Mark McVey, Emma Lampert.

Over the decades Broadway had seen Betty Comden, Adolph Green, Sammy Cahn, and other songwriters perform in revues of their works. It was appropriate that a retrospective by Tom Jones and Harvey Schmidt should be seen

Off Broadway where their *The Fantasticks* was in its thirty-seventh year. Subtitled "A Portfolio of Theatre Songs," the revue avoided a chronological "and
then we wrote" format but skipped through the career of the two songwriters
telling stories and presenting songs from both hits and flops. Jones wrote the
wry narration, and he delivered it in a self-deprecating style while Schmidt
accompanied three singers on the piano. The anecdotes were honest, funny,
and revealing, and the musical numbers chosen revealed the wide variety of
songs the team had written over the years. Selections from *The Fantasticks*,
110 in the Shade, *Celebration*, *I Do! I Do!*, and other shows were sometimes
familiar, but the evening was most interesting when songs cut from these
shows were performed with sardonic commentary by Jones. What made *The
Show Goes On* so enjoyable was the lack of pretension even as first-class
material was being delivered. It seemed Jones and Schmidt didn't take things
too seriously, and playgoers seem to like them all the more because of it. The
limited run by the York Theatre Company was so well received by the press
that the revue was held over for eleven weeks.

HEDWIG AND THE ANGRY INCH

[14 February 1998, Jane Street Theatre, 857 performances] a musical play
by John Cameron Mitchell. *Score:* Stephen Trask (music and lyrics). *Cast:*
Mitchell, Miriam Shor.

An Off-Broadway cult hit along the lines of *The Rocky Horror Show*, this dazzling little rock musical was the most audacious, most daring, most in-your-
face show New York had seen in a long time. The offbeat musical took the
form of a concert with Hedwig (John Cameron Mitchell) narrating his/her tale
between songs. Young Hansel was born in East Berlin the year the Wall went
up and grows into a confused transsexual. He marries an American GI to get
to the States but has to have a sex change operation to qualify. The operation
is botched, and Hedwig is left with an inch of undetermined sexual embarrassment. Once in America, she is dumped by the GI and has an affair with a
military brat named Tommy Gnosis who becomes a rock star using Hedwig's
songs, then he too abandons her. Left singing rock and roll dirges in third-class
dives, Hedwig continues on, searching for a personal and sexual identity. The
bewigged, heavily made up Mitchell, who also wrote the script, was mesmerizing, singing the rock score by Stephen Trask, telling his/her story with a
phony German accent, and exuding a strange sensuality that was sexy without

knowing which sex it was. Songs such as "Origin of Love," "Angry Inch," "Wicked Little Town," and "Tear Me Down" made no pretense of sounding like theatre numbers; they were undiluted rock and fierce in their sound and ideas. *Hedwig and the Angry Inch* originated Off Off Broadway and was too outrageous to be ignored. The contracts were rewritten as an Off-Broadway entry, and the musical rocked Greenwich Village for more than two years. The 2001 film version, directed by and featuring Mitchell, gave the musical further recognition, and regional productions by adventurous theatre groups followed.

SATURN RETURNS: A CONCERT

[31 March 1998, Public Theatre/LuEsther Hall, 16 performances] a musical revue by Adam Guettel (music and lyrics), Ellen Fitzhugh (lyrics). *Cast:* Bob Stillman, Annie Golden, Jose Llana, Vivian Cherry, Lawrence Clayton, Theresa McCarthy.

Because of *Floyd Collins*, there was a good deal of interest in songwriter Adam Guettel's next project: a song cycle that looked at ancient myths with a contemporary temperament. Calling the program a concert was inaccurate, for Tina Landau staged the musical, and it was far from an inert recital. But there were no recurring characters or plot; each song was a minidrama that centered on emotional reactions to events rather than a story as in Jason Robert Brown's *Songs for a New World*. Guettel's music was sometimes difficult, always fascinating, and the lyrics (by Ellen Fitzhugh and Guettel) were frequently more intriguing than engaging. Yet the cycle provided for an extraordinary musical ride filled with everything from complex, atonal numbers like "Icarus" and "Sisyphus" to simple, straightforward ballads such as "Hero and Leander" and "How Can I Lose You?" Other notable numbers included the rhythmic duet "Pegasus," the madrigal-like march "At the Sounding," the haunting lullaby "Children of the Heavenly King," the rousing gospel number "There's a Shout," the odd lament "Awaiting You," and the yearning title song. Being a series of disparate songs, *Saturn Returns* never approached the emotional impact of *Floyd Collins*, and critical reaction to the show was mixed. The program played at the Public Theatre for only two weeks, but much of the score was later recorded with other Guettel songs and titled *Myths & Hymns*. It was clear that Guettel was still a remarkable talent, but *Saturn Returns* did little to further his career. It was not until his Broadway musical *Light in the Piazza* in 2005 that it was clear that this was one brilliant songwriter.

DINAH WAS

[28 May 1998, Gramercy Theatre, 242 performances] a musical play by Oliver Goldstick. *Score:* various. *Cast:* Yvette Freeman, Adriane Lenox, Darryl Alan Reed, Vince Viverito.

Musicals about Billie Holiday, Bessie Smith, Ella Fitzgerald, and other African American singers had found their way to the stage and screen, so it was not surprising when the tragic life of the "Queen of the Blues" Dinah Washington showed up Off Broadway. Oliver Goldstick's libretto took place in the lobby of the Sahara Hotel in Las Vegas in 1959. Dinah (Yvette Freeman) is the first black singer ever booked into the venue, and she is given top billing but not allowed to stay at the whites-only establishment. Dinah dresses up in her furs, parades through the front doors of the hotel, and vows to sit in the lobby until they let her register as a guest. Friends, family, and an ex-husband join her for the sit-in, and flashbacks tell her sad story: Born poor in Tuscaloosa, Alabama, raised in the ghetto in Chicago, touring with gospel singing groups, and finally seeing her jazz and blues records climb the charts, Dinah is strong and defiant throughout. Also recounted were her six failed marriages and trouble with drugs, which led to her death of an overdose four years later at the age of thirty-nine. It was a grim tale that was dramatically numbing, but the songs brought the musical to life and made it exhilarating at times. "Sometimes I'm Happy," "I Won't Cry Anymore," "What a Difference a Day Makes," "Long John Blues," "I Don't Hurt Anymore," and other hits were performed with proficiency and heart by Freeman, and sometimes she was joined by other characters, most effectively the African American hotel maid Violet (Adriane Lenox), who sang some entrancing duets with Dinah. *Dinah Was* was first produced at the Williamstown Theatre Festival in Massachusetts, and then was seen Off Off Broadway before transferring to the larger Off-Broadway theatre for a run of eight months. Freeman reprised her performance in various cities, and her Los Angeles production was recorded in 2005.

A NEW BRAIN

[18 June 1998, Mitzi E. Newhouse Theatre, 78 performances] a musical play by William Finn, James Lapine. *Score:* Finn (music and lyrics). *Cast:*

Malcolm Gets, Chip Zien, Christopher Innvar, Penny Fuller, Mary Testa, Liz Larsen, Michael Mandell, Kristin Chenoweth.

For those who thought songwriter William Finn could only write an effective musical if it concerned his neurotic Marvin character, this inventive and deeply moving work dispelled such thoughts. A New Brain had nothing to do with Marvin and was not only as accomplished as the Falsettos musicals but revealed a quieter, more introspective aspect to Finn's talent. The sung-through piece was autobiographical, based on a medical crisis in Finn's life, yet there was no self-pity or moroseness about the piece. Gordon Schwinn (Malcolm Gets) writes songs for a children's television show character, the frog Mr. Bungee (Chip Zien), but dreams of creating a body of songs that say something worthwhile. When Gordon collapses in a restaurant and is hospitalized, his friends gather around him, including his ex-lover Roger (Christopher Innvar) and Gordon's fretful mother Mimi (Penny Fuller). A brain tumor is discovered, and treatments in the hospital bring on hallucinations of the present, such as a tormenting Mr. Bungee, and the past, as with memories of a gambling-addict father and Gordon's former happiness with Roger. The tumor is operated on successfully, and by the time Gordon comes back to life, his perspective has changed, deciding he will now live for "Time and Music." The Jewish and gay issues of the Falsettos musicals were far in the background in A New Brain. These characters and their problems were more mainstream, and the recognition factor was much more potent than in Finn's previous work. James Lapine again worked with Finn on the libretto and, while the structure was much more conventional than, say, In Trousers, the plot still took off in unusual and exciting ways. Also, the score was Finn's richest yet, hitting emotional extremes without ever going overboard. Gordon proclaimed his love for writing songs in "Heart and Music" and recalled his father gambling away the family fortune at the races with the sardonic yet heartfelt "They're Off." Mrs. Schwinn dealt with her son's illness with comic bitterness in "Throw It Out" and with mellow acceptance with "The Music Still Plays On." A bag lady (Mary Testa) barked the double-meaning number "Change," and Gordon's friends explained the family emotional baggage in the wry "Gordo's Law of Genetics." Roger sang the show's most entrancing ballad "Sailing," a lilting number that conjured up images of pure euphoria. From the children's ditty "I Feel So Much Spring" to the deeply troubled "A Really Lousy Day in the Universe," the score for A New Brian was a marvel. Graciela Daniele directed and choreographed the small-scale musical, and the Lincoln Center production boasted a superlative cast. The limited engagement of ten weeks did not garner the kind of praise and notoriety that one expected, though once the cast recording was released, *A New Brain* quickly received many productions across the country. It continues to be produced, and it continues to astound.

NUNSENSE A-MEN!

[23 June 1998, 47th Street Theatre, 231 performances] a musical revue by Dan Goggin. *Score:* Goggin (music and lyrics). *Cast:* Danny Vaccaro, Lothair Eaton, Tom Dwyer, Doan Mackenzie, Greg White, David Titus.

The wholesome and inane entertainment of *Nunsense* and its sequel became campy and off-color shenanigans in *Nunsense A-Men!*, a drag version of the original show. Casting men as the six Little Sisters of Hoboken gave the show a slightly subversive edge and, though revisions to the script and score were minor, the tone changed. This time around the revue seemed more mocking, and turning the happy singing nuns into drag stereotypes made the proceedings a bit grotesque. This was not necessarily a bad thing, and some playgoers who did not enjoy *Nunsense* the first time around found this travesty of the original more to their liking. The Off-Broadway entry certainly appealed to gay audiences more than the first one, but much of what pleased mainstream theatregoers continued to please them with guys as the nuns. The seven-month run was not so impressive when compared to the years that *Nunsense* ran, but for a one-joke musical with a second level added, it was a successful venture.

ROLLIN' ON THE T.O.B.A.

[28 January 1999, 47th Street Theatre, 45 performances; Henry Miller's Theatre, 14 performances] a musical play by Ronald "Smokey" Stevens, Jaye Stewart. *Score:* various. *Cast:* Stevens, Rudy Roberson, Sandra Reaves-Phillips.

IT AIN'T NOTHIN' BUT THE BLUES

[26 March 1999, New Victory Theatre, 16 performances; Vivian Beaumont Theatre, 276 performances] a musical revue by Charles Bevel, Ron Taylor, various. *Score:* various. *Cast:* Bevel, Taylor, Gretha Boston, Gregory Porter, Dan Wheetman, Eloise Laws, Carter Calvert.

Two musical revues celebrating African American music of the past opened Off Broadway early in 1999, and both moved to Broadway but with different results. *Rollin' on the T.O.B.A.* was about the end of the era of black vaudeville and was set in 1931 when the Theatre Owner's Booking Association (T.O.B.A.) was in decline. Because of its harsh treatment of African American performers, the T.O.B.A. became unofficially known in the business as Tough On Black Asses. The musical followed the plight of three such performers as they traveled the vaudeville circuit by train and tried to make ends meet between engagements. Most of the songs they performed onstage and backstage came from the repertoire of African American music, from renowned standards such as "St. Louis Blues," "Nobody," and "A Good Man Is Hard to Find" to lesser known gems like "One Hour Mama," "Hop Scop Blues," and "Ugly Chile." Ronald "Smokey" Stevens cowrote a handful of new numbers in the same style, including the jaunty "Travelin' Blues" and the catchy title song. Stevens also wrote the script, directed and choreographed the show, and played one of the trio of vaudevillians. For the sketches performed on the circuit, Steven adapted some comic tales from Langston Hughes's *The Simple Stories.* The musical was first produced Off Off Broadway by the AMAS Musical Theatre then transferred to Off Broadway where it gathered a following during its five-and-a-half-week run. The press felt *Rollin' on the T.O.B.A.* was uneven and lacked polish but applauded the sparkling score. The producers were encouraged enough to again transfer the show, this time to Broadway's dilapidated Henry Miller Theatre. The ambiance certainly helped recreate the feeling of dying vaudeville, but audiences were not interested, and the musical closed inside of two weeks.

It Ain't Nothin' But the Blues also played Off Broadway, but when it transferred to the Street, the musical found an audience for nine months. *It Ain't Nothin' But the Blues* took a historical rather than personal approach to its music and tended to be all-encompassing rather than specific. In fact, the term "blues" was used so freely in the show that some questioned if most of its forty or so songs were indeed real blues. Using slides and some narration, the history of the blues from slave chants to twentieth-century pop hits was covered by five African American and two white performers. This time there were no critical quibbles about the polish of the production and the slick showmanship of the cast. Gretha Boston and Ron Taylor got the lion's share of the applause, but the whole cast was masterful in the way it performed such diverse numbers as "Blood Done Signed My Name"; "Let the Good Times Roll"; "I've Been Living with the Blues"; "Fever"; "Wang Dang Doodle"; "Strange Fruit"; "I Can't Stop Lovin' You"; "Good Night, Irene"; and "Walkin' Blues." The Off-Broadway engagement was for only two weeks, but when Lincoln Center suddenly found itself with an empty theatre, they welcomed *It Ain't Nothin' But the Blues* into the Vivian Beaumont Theatre. When that season's Tony Awards ceremony was running overtime and the musical number from the Tony-nominated *It Ain't Nothin' But the Blues* was cut at the last minute, there were such loud complaints from the producers that the controversy gave the revue the publicity it needed to find an audience.

BRIGHT LIGHTS BIG CITY

[24 February 1999, New York Theatre Workshop, 31 performances] a musical play by Paul Scott Goodman based on the novel by Jay McInerney. *Score:* Goodman (music and lyrics). *Cast:* Goodman, Patrick Wilson, Napiera Daniele Groves, Natascia Diaz, Jerry Dixon, Kerry O'Malley, Annmarie Milazzo, Ken Marks, Carla Bianco, Liza Lapira, Jacqueline Arnold, John Link Graney.

Because of the popularity of Jay McInerney's 1984 "Yuppie novel" and the less successful 1988 movie version, the title *Bright Lights Big City* (taken from a 1961 song by Jimmy Reed) was a familiar one, and there was a lot of interest in the Off-Broadway musical adaptation. But this interest quickly waned after the mostly negative reviews came out and the one-month run at the New York Theatre Workshop was not extended. The unnamed central character in the book, a fact-checker at a Manhattan magazine who boozes and does cocaine each night as part of living in the fast lane in 1980s New York City, was called Jaime Conway in the film. The musical had two actors portray the character: the Writer (libretto writer Paul Scott Goodman), who acts as narrator and commentator, and Jaime (Patrick Wilson) who interacts with the other characters. The device allowed some of the novel's style to come through but, as in the film, the plot changes and additions often turned the tale into a hip, cautionary melodrama. Jaime's model-wife Amanda (Napiera Daniele Groves) leaves him, and he is left paling around with his witty but shallow best friend Tad (Jerry Dixon). Jaime's drug-induced hallucinations were very theatrical if not very revealing, and the hopeful ending (Jaime finally pulls himself together and starts to write his novel) seemed trite. There were compliments for the strong cast and the lively direction by Michael Greif, but too many reviewers felt the musical trivialized a hard-hitting book. Because the New York Theatre Workshop had recently struck gold with another rock musical directed by Greif, Jonathan Larson's *Rent*, expectations were high, and some felt the new show was not given a fair chance. When a studio recording of the score was released in 2005, there were many who felt *Bright Lights Big City* was better than it had first seemed. The score, also by Goodman, is rock-folk-pop that often recalls *Rent* but lacks an edge in both music and lyrics. The music pulsates predictably, and Goodman's lyrics are often too simplistic for the issues they attempt to address. The song "I Love Drugs" is as sterile as its title, "Beautiful Sunday" is an empty romantic ballad, "I Wanna Have Sex Tonight" is blunt and has no where to go, "So Many Little Things" aches to be poetic but comes across as banal, and the title song sounds more like a commercial ditty inviting one to buy a product so you can party. More accomplished are the sarcastic list song "I Hate the French," the breezy character number "To Model," and the recurring "Monstrous Events" which has a bit of verve. A London production of *Bright Lights Big City* did not fare any better than the New York run, but there have been the occasional regional mountings.

If Love Were All

[10 June 1999, Lucille Lortel Theatre, 101 performances] a musical revue by Sheridan Morley, Leigh Lawson. *Score:* Noël Coward (music and lyrics). *Cast:* Harry Groener, Twiggy.

First presented in London as *Noel & Gertie*, this two-character musical about Noël Coward and Gertrude Lawrence arrived in New York for the centenary of Coward's birth. The script by Sheridan Morley and Leigh Lawson (who had played Coward in the British production) traced the friendship between the two performers from when they were teenagers in variety together through their years as stage stars on two continents. Coward (Harry Groener) and Lawrence (Twiggy, who had played the role in London) reminisced together, read letters and recited anecdotes, and sang songs individually and together. It was not a terribly unique way to tell their story, but it worked, the whole evening coming off as a valentine from Coward to Lawrence. Groener wisely avoided doing a Coward impersonation and suggested the master's style and charm in an understated manner. Twiggy's thin but pleasant voice was actually close to that of Lawrence, who was never a belting musical star. The rapport between the two performers was quite engaging, and the Coward-Lawrence friendship was not difficult to understand. All of the songs were by Coward even though most of Lawrence's musical career was singing numbers by others. In fact, the only time the two appeared together in a musical was in a few one-acts that were part of his *Tonight at 8:30*. But an evening of Coward songs is a rich enough repertoire for any show, and numbers like "Someday I'll Find You," "I'll See You Again," "You Were There," and the title song seemed to be the essence of the couple's relationship. The humor may have been dry in the Coward manner, but the two performers cut loose with such farcical numbers as "Mad Dogs and Englishmen"; "Don't Put Your Daughter on the Stage, Mrs. Worthington"; and "Has Anybody Seen Our Ship?" Lawson made changes in Morley's script, rearranged some of the songs, and added some dance to *Noel & Gertie*, then directed *If Love Were All* when it was presented at the Bay Street Theatre in Sag Harbor, New York. The Off-Broadway production met with laudatory notices, but playgoers were reticent and kept the musical on the boards for only three months.

AFTER THE FAIR

[15 July 1999, Theatre at St. Peter's, 30 performances] a musical play by Stephen Cole based on Thomas Hardy's story *On the Western Circuit*. *Score:* Matthew Ward (music), Cole (lyrics). *Cast:* Michele Pawk, David Staller, James Ludwig, Jennifer Piech.

A four-character chamber piece intelligently written and scored with proficiency, *After the Fair* was curiously disappointing. Everything was in place, and there was little to find fault with, yet it was lifeless and ultimately uninvolving. Based on a story by Thomas Hardy, the musical took place in rural England in 1897 and focused on the childless Edith Harnham (Michele Pawk) caught in a dry and loveless marriage with stuffy Arthur (David Staller). When their maid Anna (Jennifer Piech) meets the dashing Londoner

Charles (James Ludwig) at a local fair, the two have a sexual tryst before he leaves for the city. Charles writes a letter to Anna who is thrilled but illiterate, so she asks Edith to write a love letter for her. A series of letters follows, Edith pouring her pent-up emotions into her writing, and she falls in love with Charles's equally passionate responses. Anna's pregnancy brings Charles back to town, and only after they are wed does he realize that Edith was the author of the letters and the one he loves. This *Cyrano*-like tale ended on a more positive note: Charles and Anna start married life in London, and Arthur starts to show more interest in his transformed wife. There was an intimate little musical in this story, and librettist-lyricist Stephen Cole and composer Matthew Ward found it and put it on the stage with efficiency and clarity. The songs, many of which continued the plot effectively, were admirable though rarely enthralling. The recurring letter theme "Beloved" grew on one, and there was a spark of life in "A Spot of Tea," the closest the show ever came to frivolity. But one listened to the score and followed the story dutifully rather than with interest. The notices were critical of some of the performers but agreed that Pawk's portrayal of the cautious and blossoming Edith was splendid. After productions in Irving, Texas, Chicago, and Seattle, *After the Fair* was presented by the York Theatre Company Off Broadway for a month. There was no demand for an extension, and the musical has been little heard of since.

NAKED BOYS SINGING!

[22 July 1999, Actors Playhouse, 3,000+ performances] a musical revue by Robert Schrock, various. *Score:* various. *Cast:* Sean McNally, Adam Michaels, Daniel C. Levine, Tim Burke, Jonathan Brody, Glenn Steven Allen, Tom Gualitieri, Trance Thompson.

If comely lads singing and dancing in the altogether does not embarrass you, then you might blush at the fact that this show has run more than ten years. Even creator Robert Schrock must be surprised that his naughty but harmless little revue has found a mainstream audience in New York and several other cities (not to mention other countries). The tone of the show was definitely gay (there was even a salute to beefy Robert Mitchum), yet audiences for *Naked Boys Singing!* include women who find the revue titillating and funny. And Schrock surely believed in truth in advertising because this musical was not a tease. The only surprise was that *Naked Boys Singing!* ended up being more campy and silly than crude. The sketches and songs by various authors looked at every angle of male nudity, from locker room scenes to making porn movies to house cleaning in the buff. The songs tended to be smirky with arch titles like "Members Only," "Perky Little Porn Star," and "Nothin' But the Radio On." The lyrics were often juvenile but never coarse, and the music was melodic and catchy without being very memorable. If the show had no inhibitions, it also had no pretensions to be anything but a celebration of "Gratuitous Nudity," as one song stated. The revue only got partially serious with the musical number "Window to Window" in which two strangers see each other from a distance and yearn to meet. *Naked Boys Singing!* originated in Los Angeles then went to the Actors Playhouse Off Broadway where the critic-proof show quickly found an audience.

THE DONKEY SHOW

[12 August 1999, Club El Flamingo, 1,488 performances] a musical comedy by Diane Paulus, Randy Weiner based on Shakespeare's *A Midsummer Night's Dream*. *Score*: various. *Cast*: Jordin Ruderman, Rachel Benbow Murdy, Anna Wilson, Dan Cryer, Emily Hellstrom, Orlando Santana, Oscar Estevez.

More male bodies could be found in this unusual musical that carried the subtitle "A Midsummer Night's Disco," though the boys were joined by some scantily clad women as they enacted the story of Shakespeare's comedy in song and dance. The setting was a 1970s discotheque with the audience drinking and dancing before and after the show. Shakespeare's verse was jettisoned, and the fantasy became a burlesque show, filled with ingenious staging and pulsating dancing. The score consisted of popular disco tunes such as "Car Wash," "Last Dance," "I Will Survive," "I Love the Nightlife," "I'm Your Boogie Man," and "We Are Family." None of the songs helped to tell the story, but they were fun to revisit in a campy way. Those unfamiliar with the Shakespeare original had trouble following the plot, but the story was just an excuse for a wild night in a nightclub. Audience members sat and stood right in the middle of the action, and it seemed the whole Club El Flamingo was jumping to the disco beat. Critics found *The Donkey Show* unique and scintillating and recommended it for those looking for an alternate night of theatregoing. There were plaudits particularly for creators Diane Paulus and Randy Weiner, who also staged the unconventional musical. The orgy-like atmosphere turned some playgoers off, but word of mouth soon turned the musical into a must see. *The Donkey Show* was particularly popular with bachelorette parties and other women's gatherings. The production was considered an Off-Off-Broadway entry when it opened, but soon contracts were rewritten as an Off-Broadway production, and it ran six years (though not the traditional eight performances a week). Versions in other cities followed, and some were also very popular.

CONTACT

[7 October 1999, Mitzi E. Newhouse Theatre, 101 performances; Vivian Beaumont Theatre, 1,010 performances] a dance musical by Jerome Weidman, Susan Stroman. *Score:* various. *Cast:* Boyd Gaines, Karen Ziemba, Deborah Yates, Stephanie Michels, Scott Taylor, Séan Martin Hingston, Jason Antoon.

Dance musicals have always been rare Off Broadway unless they started as experiments such as *A Chorus Line*. *Contact* was also an experiment of sorts, opening in the Off-Broadway venue of the Mitzi Newhouse Theatre at Lincoln Center and becoming so popular that after its three-month run it moved upstairs to the Broadway venue of the Vivian Beaumont Theatre where it ran nearly three years. Choreographer Susan Stroman conceived and staged the unusual entertainment written by John Weidman (though there was hardly any dialogue) that consisted of three tales told mostly in dance and using recordings of classical and pop standards as the score. An aristocrat (Séan Martin Hingston) disguises himself as his own servant (Scott Taylor) in order to frolic with a lady (Stephanie Michels) on a swing; the abused wife (Karen Ziemba) of a mobster escapes into a fantasy world while dining at an Italian restaurant; and a suicidal man (Boyd Gaines) chases an elusive girl (Deborah Yates) about town only to discover that she lives in the apartment above his. Each tale had an O. Henry-like twist at the end that struck many playgoers as feeble, to say the least; one expected more from the librettist of *Pacific Overtures* and *Assassins*. Although there was no singing and the characters were sketches at best, the dancing was sublime, and Stroman certainly knew how to tell a story through dance, even if the stories were hardly worth telling. Most critics heartily recommended the entertainment, and patrons took their advice, turning *Contact* into one of the biggest hits in the history of Lincoln Center.

SHOCKHEADED PETER

[14 October 1999, New Victory Theatre, 15 performances] a musical play by Julian Bleach, Anthony Cairns, Graeme Gilmour, Tamzin Griffin, Jo Pocock. *Score:* Tiger Lillies (music), Martyn Jacques (lyrics). *Cast:* Bleach, Cairns, Gilmour, Griffin, Pocock.

A British import that looked and sounded quite unlike anything currently in New York, this oddball musical used actors and puppets to tell grisly stories about the horrible things that happen to bad boys and girls. The inspiration for the bizarre "junk opera" was the 1845 German children's book *Der Struwwelpeter* (Shaggy Peter) by Heinrich Hoffmann, a series of tales in which misbehaving kids suffer terrible consequences. Using cartoonish scenery, various kinds of puppets, actors in grotesque makeup, and eleven narrative songs, the pantomime musical told of naughty tots who had their thumbs cut off, were boiled in hot coffee, starved to death, burnt up, or blown away in a storm. While body parts flew about the stage, tombstones popped out of the floor, humans and puppets engaged in a weird dance of death, and the carnival-like songs were sung in eerie falsetto voices. The total effect was mesmerizing, to say the least. Martyn Jacques and his two cohorts Adrian Huge and Adrian Stout, calling themselves the Tiger Lillies, wrote the bizarre music, and Jacques adapted Hoffmann's rhymed German verse into creepy lyrics. *Shockheaded Peter* won a handful of awards in London before the troupe toured the States, stopping at New York's New Victory Theatre for two weeks. Critics raved, audiences were puzzled (just *whom* was this show for?), and then the production continued on its tour. The British production returned to Manhattan in 2005 where it played the Little Shubert Theatre Off Broadway, receiving another round of critical plaudits and winning several awards. Audiences were again reticent, but word of mouth was strong enough that *Shockheaded Peter* developed a cult following. The English cast returned home after a few weeks, and the musical continued with an American cast for 112 performances.

JAMES JOYCE'S THE DEAD

[28 October 1999, Playwrights Horizons, 38 performances; Belasco Theatre, 112 performances] a musical play by Richard Nelson based on a James Joyce short story. *Score:* Nelson (lyrics), Shaun Davey (music and lyrics). *Cast:* Sally Ann Howes, Marni Nixon, Emily Skinner, Christopher Walken, Blair Brown, Brian Davies, Alice Ripley, Stephen Spinella, Daisy Eagan, John Kelly, Paddy Croft.

A quiet, atmospheric, but engrossing musical play, *James Joyce's The Dead* was so well received Off Broadway at Playwrights Horizons that after a month it transferred to Broadway, only to struggle for fourteen weeks. The Dublin spinster sisters Julia (Sally Ann Howes) and Kate Morkan (Marni Nixon) throw their annual Christmas gathering with their niece Mary Jane (Emily Skinner). The guests are a varied lot, some living in the past and others trying not to remember the past. Gabriel Conroy (Christopher Walken) narrates the story, and a confession by his wife Gretta (Blair Brown), that the only love of her life was a boy who died years ago, served as the main crisis of the piece. Richard Nelson wrote the libretto, based on one of Joyce's short stories in *The Dubliners*, and it had a Chekhovian feel to it with bits of conversation picked up here and there and a variety of interesting characters who seemed to drift in and out of focus. Nelson also provided the lyrics for Shaun Davey's music, and the songs did not sound like a Broadway score; given the unusual source material, they shouldn't have. Instead of character numbers and theatre music, the partygoers entertained each other with Irish ballads and dance songs. Some of them, such as "When Lovely Lady Stoops" and "Naughty Girls," had no connection to the plot or characters, while the lilting "Goldenhair" and operatic "D'Arcy's Aria" were integral to the story. The liveliest number was the thumping jig "Wake the Dead" which was filled with a robust and pagan temperament, even if it was too repetitive for the stage. The same rhymed couplets and recurring music was great if you were dancing but a bit numbing to listen to for as long as the partygoers insisted on singing it. The musical ended with two songs that were the thoughts of the central couple. Gretta recalled the boy she once loved in "Michael Furey," and Gabriel summed up his misgivings about the evening's activities in "The Living and the Dead." Both numbers were still Irish pastiches but seemed inconsistent after an evening of parlor songs and in a musical that had so far avoided the convention of traditional musical theatre songs. Nelson directed the musical, which boasted an outstanding cast from major players down to the onstage musician characters, and Sean Curran choreographed the Irish dancing, which was highly commended. *James Joyce's The Dead* was unlikely to become a mainstream hit, for its appeal was limited and its theatrics understated. Yet it was a unique and haunting musical that is fondly remembered by those who were on the same wavelength as its creators.

OUR SINATRA

[19 December 1999, Blue Angel Theatre, 1,096 performances] a musical revue by Eric Comstock, Christopher Gines, Hilary Kole. *Score:* various. *Cast:* Comstock, Gines, Kole.

The standard format to salute (or cash in on) a famous singer is to find someone with a slight physical resemblance and a strong vocal talent, place the character at some point in his or her life that allows for reminiscing, add some autobiographical material, then have the character perform hits from the singer's career. *Our Sinatra* ignored this formula and instead presented three performers (two men and a woman) who sang over sixty of Sinatra's songs with no attempt made to impersonate the late crooner. As pleasing as it all was, the revue said nothing about Sinatra's life (a tricky topic), career, style, or reasons for his longtime popularity. Instead the little patter between songs was about Sinatra's connection to the song, such as how he found it or in what manner he introduced it. One walked away with dozens of wonderful songs swimming in your head but only the knowledge that Sinatra sure had a lot of hits. Since most of these songs were sung and recorded by many other singers, the catalog didn't even tell you much about Sinatra's era. He recorded so many numbers from the decades before he became famous, such as standards by Rodgers and Hart, Hammerstein and Kern, and the Gerswhins, that *Our Sinatra* might just as well been titled the Great American Songbook. Eric Comstock, Christopher Gines, and Hilary Kole, who put the revue together, were deemed talented and engaging by the press, and some of the harmonizing trio versions of the songs were particularly praised. Since his death in 1998, Sinatra's popularity had grown and audiences were as anxious to hear his songs as they had for decades previously. So an Off-Broadway revue without a Sinatra clone but Sinatra's songs was very appealing, and the musical ran three years. *Our Sinatra* continues to be a favorite with theatre groups looking for an economical little revue with plenty of nostalgic pull.

Chapter Seven

Fodder for Broadway: The 2000s

THE FIRST DECADE OF THE NEW CENTURY was overshadowed by the events that occurred on September 11, 2001. America seemed to be a less secure, more vulnerable place after the two World Trade Towers fell, and this feeling of unease was felt more in New York City than anywhere else. As with the months following the attack on Pearl Harbor and those following the assassination of John F. Kennedy, theatregoing seemed a frivolous pastime in the weeks after 9/11. For the city, the immediate drop in tourism and the steep decline in theatre attendance were disasters akin to the attacks themselves. Since theatre brought more money into the city than all the museums and sports teams combined, it was not surprising that the campaign to revitalize New York focused on Broadway. Audiences gradually returned, but when they did they wanted to see *The Producers, Mamma Mia!,* and other escapist musicals rather than *Sweet Smell of Success, Amour,* and more cerebral shows. The list of other Broadway musical hits from the decade support this feeling: *Aida, The Full Monty, Thoroughly Modern Millie, Hairspray, Movin' Out, Wicked, Spamalot, Dirty Rotten Scoundrels, Jersey Boys, The Drowsy Chaperone, Mary Poppins, Contact* (which originated Off Broadway), *The Light in the Piazza,* and *The Color Purple.* Only the last two named could be considered nonescapist, though there are obviously some highly commendable musicals on the list.

Off Broadway recovered from the dire events of 9/11 in a different way. Never a tourist mecca, Off Broadway offered a rich variety of musicals, and local theatregoers responded favorably. Musicals based on movies and television shows, tributes to all kinds of nontheatre music ranging from country and western to salsa, campy outlooks on popular culture, tabloid-like musi-

319

cals, and stark operas were among the diverse offerings Off Broadway during the decade. Twelve Off-Broadway musicals made the transfer to Broadway, the most yet seen in any decade. But five of those transfers fumbled badly on the Street even though they all got excellent reviews. It was becoming evident that there was a distinct difference between an Off-Broadway musical hit and a Broadway moneymaker. Still producers were willing to take the risk, moving any musical with favorable press and/or box office to Broadway to become a bona fide theatre hit. Frankly, those five unsuccessful musical transfers did not belong on Broadway. That is obvious in hindsight. If Off Broadway was to provide fodder for Broadway, it took a lot of insight and luck to know when to send a musical into the Broadway arena.

SATURDAY NIGHT

[17 February 2000, Second Stage Theatre, 45 performances] a musical play by Julius J. Epstein. *Score:* Stephen Sondheim (music and lyrics). *Cast:* David Campbell, Michael Benjamin Washington, Kirk McDonald, Greg Zola, Andrea Burns, Lauren Ward, Joey Sorge, Christopher Fitzgerald, Natascia A. Diaz, Clarke Thorell.

A piece of Stephen Sondheim juvenilia is of more interest than the mature works of most other songwriters, as demonstrated by this musical Sondheim wrote music and lyrics for back in the early 1950s. A Broadway production was slated, but when the producer died, so did the project, and the twenty-four-year-old Sondheim had to wait a few more years before his name appeared on a marquee. *Saturday Night* had not totally disappeared, though. Several of the songs had been recorded by various artists over the decades, but the musical itself was not produced until 1997 when a London fringe theatre gave *Saturday Night* a full production and recorded it. The first American mounting was in Chicago in 1999, then the Second Stage offered this version Off Broadway. The plot, set in Brooklyn in 1929, concerns four young guys who are ambitious, oversexed, and a bit too brash for their own good. They move to Manhattan and hope to take Wall Street by storm, but egos, romance, a crooked bond scheme, and finally the longing for home all get in the way. It was a workable story filled with lively characters created by librettist Julius J. Epstein. Sondheim's score is the real surprise. It has a polish, a wonderful sense of melody, and lyric skill far beyond that of the novice. Critics have complained for decades that Sondheim's music is not hummable, a criticism that has often proved false. The songs in *Saturday Night* are more than hummable, they are melodically contagious. The title song echoes through one's head long after the show has ended, and the ensemble number "One Wonderful Day" is the kind of tune that follows you around for days. The jaunty "Love's a Bond" is a naive list song in which Wall Street terms are used as a metaphor for romance, the sly "Exhibit A" is one stockbroker's system for seducing women, and the Brooklynites wryly note that what is so glamourous "In the Movies" is rather mundane in real life. Other highlights in the score include the merry trio "A Moment with You," the warm duet "Too Many People," the complicated character number "Class," and the lilting ballad "All for You." The Second Stage production, directed and choreographed by the up-and-coming Kathleen Marshall, was top-notch, and the reviews were strong enough that after its five and a half weeks, Off-Broadway efforts were made to bring *Saturday Night* to Broadway. The plans fell through, but the musical has seen many productions regionally and has become much more than a mere curiosity for Sondheim fans.

THE WILD PARTY

[24 February 2000, City Center Stage I, 54 performances] a musical play by Andrew Lippa. *Score:* Lippa (music and lyrics). *Cast:* Julia Murney, Brian d'Arcy James, Idina Menzel, Taye Diggs, Kena Tangi Dorsey, Alix Korey, Lawrence Keigwin, Raymond Jaramillo McLeod, Jennifer Cody.

An unrelenting and nightmarish musical set in the Jazz Age, *The Wild Party* brought the first recognition to Andrew Lippa who wrote the book, music, and lyrics. The show was far from a hit, but it was an auspicious debut all the same. The 1920s vaudeville performers and lovers Queenie (Julia Murney) and Burrs (Brian d'Arcy James) throw a decadent, gin-soaked party for friends and their hangers-on. During the festivities, Queenie is attracted to the gangster Black (Taye Diggs), the kept man of her friend and rival Kate (Idina Menzel), which raises Burrs's jealousy, and the party ends in bloodshed. The songs were mostly pastiches of the jazzy Roaring Twenties, though incongruously pop-rock slipped in at times, as in the dance number "The Juggernaut." The opening "Queenie Was a Blonde/The Apartment" was a frenetic and exciting way to set the tone and introduce the characters. Much of what followed was sung through, but individual numbers stood out, such as the mocking and ominous ballad "Poor Child"; the samba-flavored "Raise the Roof"; the raucous "A Wild, Wild Party"; the suicidal "Let Me Drown"; and, most memorably, the ribald "An Old-Fashioned Love Story" sung by an oversexed lesbian (Alix Korey). Lippa proved to be a better composer than a lyricist, but it was clear this was a talent to be reckoned with. The plot, characters, and some of the verses came directly from Joseph Moncure March's 1928 narrative poem of the same title. The Manhattan Theatre Club production, directed by Gabriel Barre and choreographed by Mark Denby, boasted a sensational young cast coming into their own. *The Wild Party* impressed reviewers without really pleasing them, and so the notices were ambivalent. All the same, business for the seven-week engagement was brisk. Four days after the Off-Broadway production closed, another musical version of March's poem, also titled *The Wild Party*, opened on Broadway with a score by Michael John LaChiusa and with a starry cast that featured Toni Collette, Mandy Patinkin, Tonya Pinkins, and Eartha Kitt. It also received mixed notices and closed after sixty-eight performances. Both shows were faithful to the poem so they were very similar, though LaChiusa's score was pure pastiche and never veered from the period. Of the two musicals, Lippa's *The Wild Party* is more frequently done by regional and college theatres.

TAKING A CHANCE ON LOVE

[2 March 2000, Theatre at St. Peter's, 29 performances] a musical revue by Erik Haagensen. *Score:* John Latouche (lyrics), various (music). *Cast:* Jerry Dixon, Donna English, Eddie Korbich, Terry Burrell.

Although John Latouche is a lesser known Broadway lyricist, he wrote a considerable amount of material before his premature death. This York Theatre Company revue, assembled by Erik Haagensen, was subtitled "The Life and Lyrics of John Latouche" and it was an honest, loving portrayal of both. Latouche was considered the "bad boy of Broadway." He was temperamental, outrageous, and difficult to work with. He was also openly homosexual in an era that frowned on such behavior. (Latouche died in 1956 at the age of forty-one.) He was also a fearless, unsentimental lyricist with a caustic sense of humor. Some critics consider Latouche an antecedent to Stephen Sondheim because of his sardonic wit and pessimistic view of life. *Taking a Chance on Love* offered selections from Latouche's famous works, such as *Cabin in the Sky* and *The Golden Apple*, as well as such forgotten musicals as *The Vamp*,

Banjo Eyes, *Beggar's Holiday*, and *Ballet Ballads*. Even his opera *The Ballad of Baby Doe* was included, painting a complete picture of Latouche's range and versatility. Although he worked with such composers as Vernon Duke, Jerome Moross, Leonard Bernstein, and Duke Ellington, he had few successes in his career, so *Taking a Chance on Love* was not a series of hit songs. It was filled with both familiar numbers, such as "Lazy Afternoon," "Cabin in the Sky," and the title song, and wonderful surprises, such as the "Four Little Misfits," "Maybe I Should Change My Ways," and "Have You Met Delilah?" The splendid cast of four performed the songs with style and sass, and they also delivered the narration about Latouche with a warm and knowing sense of comradeship. The one-month engagement met with some excellent reviews, but Latouche was not a household name, hence no demand for an extension or transfer.

THE BUBBLY BLACK GIRL SHEDS HER CHAMELEON SKIN

[20 June 2000, Playwrights Horizons, 32 performances] a musical play by Kirsten Childs. *Score:* Childs (music and lyrics). *Cast:* La Chanze, Darius de Haas, Duane Boutte, Jerry Dixon, Cheryl Alexander, Jonathan Dokuchitz.

Playwrights Horizons introduced composer-lyricist-author Kirsten Childs with this musical that boasted a vivacious episodic tale, some sparkling performances, and a score that was, well, bubbly. The plot followed the spunky African American Viveca Stanton (La Chanze) over several decades as she searched for her ethnic identity. It was a familiar and humorless premise, but Childs told it as a modern odyssey. Born in Southern California with a dream of becoming a great dancer, Viveca learns as a child in the early 1960s that the world will accept her blackness if she is as sunny as the weather. African American children are being bombed in a church in Birmingham, but Viveca is too busy straightening her hair and trying to pass to realize the civil rights movement has started. In the 1970s the high schooler befriends Valley girls and others not of her race in her efforts to be accepted. By the 1980s she is in New York City and getting the attention of a famous choreographer by her ability to turn her ethnicity on and off. But Broadway is not ready for an African American leading lady in a mainstream show. Viveca gives up show business and opens a dance school in Harlem.

There were both white and black lovers along the journey, each of them bringing out a different side to the chameleon-like Viveca. Childs's libretto was sassy, smart, and filled with surprises. Viveca's talking white doll Sweet Chitty Chatty admitted she was a phony and was really a black doll in disguise. Viveca's straightened hair turned into a huge afro when she was hosed down at an antiwar rally. When one of her boyfriends told her that his grandmother taught him never to be a one-woman man, Viveca fantasized about committing granny-cide. This roguish kind of storytelling was continued in the score which captured the sound of the different decades even as it had its own cockeyed individual style. From the bouncy opening "Welcome to My L. A." to the reflective "There Was a Girl," the songs balanced the sincere with the sarcastic. "Sweet Chitty Chatty" was a rhythmic round of hand clapping, teenage angst was satirized in "Give It Up," and Viveca and her coworkers lamented the plight of those stuck in the "Secretarial Pool." "Director Bob" was a musical and visual parody of Bob Fosse and his style, the seductive "Come with Me" was so cool and breezy it was laughable, and even the love ballad "Beautiful Bright Blue Sky" was energetic and playful. The production was further powered by an effervescent performance by La Chanze as Viveca who, as she had at the same theatre with *Once on This Island*, lit up the stage with her emotive singing, but this time she was also allowed to show her considerable comic talents. *The Bubbly Black Girl Sheds Her Chameleon Skin* was given a month-long run and received some Off-Broadway awards at season's end. Some regional productions followed, but the musical is still being discovered.

4 GUYS NAMED JOSÉ . . . AND UNA MUJER NAMED MARIA!

[18 September 2000, Blue Angel Theatre, 191 performances] a musical revue by David Coffman, Dolores Prida. *Score:* various. *Cast:* Philip Anthony, Ricardo Puente, Lissette Gonzalez, Allen Hidalgo, Henry Gainza.

Making fun of the African American revue *Five Guys Named Moe* and striking a blow for Hispanics, this dandy little musical often moved beyond mockery to be rather romantic when the beguiling Latin standards were sung. Four strangers who hail from Mexico, Puerto Rico, Cuba, and the Dominican Republic chance to meet at Burrito World in Omaha, Nebraska. They find out they are all named José and all share a love for the traditional Hispanic songs taught to them by their parents. The four Josés decide to put on a revue that will fight Latin stereotypes by offering these beloved songs. They turn the local Veteran's Hall into a Caribbean paradise and hire a girl named Maria to join the act and provide a feminine touch. Maria doesn't show up on opening night but her roommate, also named Maria (Lissette Gonzalez), does, and she's worked into the show. The evening is touch and go, especially when each of the four Josés falls madly in love with Maria, but they get through it, and Maria ends up running off with a guy in the band. *4 Guys Named José* . . . was unpretentious fun that played off the stereotypes it hoped to refute, but if the plot was nonsense, the songs and the singing (both in Spanish and English) were heavenly. "Besame Mucho," "La Cumbancha," "Perfidia," and other Latin standards were mixed with lesser known numbers, and one soon understood why these songs were so endearing to the Josés. The Off-Broadway production was favorably reviewed, and the musical ran more than six months before going on tour.

A CLASS ACT

[9 November 2000, City Center Stage II, 29 performances; Ambassador Theatre, 105 performances] a musical play by Linda Kline, Lonny Price. *Score:* Edward Kleban (music and lyrics). *Cast:* Price, Randy Graff, Carolee Carmello, David Hibbard, Ray Wills, Jonathan Freeman, Nancy Anderson, Julia Murney.

The late composer-lyricist Edward Kleban was saluted in this very personal musical play about his life, written by and for his friends and often slipping into self-indulgence. Kleban, who penned the lyrics for *A Chorus Line*, was a talented if troubled artist, and the songs helped audiences get through the labored libretto. Kleban (Lonny Price) appears as a ghost at the tribute his friends are throwing in the Shubert Theatre after he dies from cancer in 1987. He insists he tell his own story with the plot jumping back to his college days when he suffered a nervous breakdown. Kleban pulls through with the support of his girlfriend Sophie (Randy Graff) who encourages him to pursue his dream of becoming a songwriter. Scenes of struggle, more nervous breakdowns, and the on-and-off relationship with Sophie follow until Kleban finally gets the *A Chorus Line* assignment and becomes rich. His career after such a success falters, and when he dies at the age of forty-eight, the money from *A Chorus Line* is used to nurture new talent. Such a sentimental tale might have been more potent had it been understated, but *A Class Act* was an outright valentine to Kleban, and some audience members felt like they were intruding on a family memorial service. Kleban's songs varied in quality, but the good ones were very good. Forcing them into a biographical musical was not always the best way to appreciate them, but the potency of the torchy "Next Best Thing to Love" or the pragmatic list song "Better" could not be denied. Other notable numbers included the wry samba "Mona," the jaunty "Charm Song," the joyous "Paris through the Window," the contrapuntal "Gauguin's Shoes," and the bittersweet "Under Separate Cover." The Manhattan Theatre Club production, directed by coauthor and performer Price, was suitably small and intimate, and the performers were commendable, particularly Graff. Notices for the one-month engagement were not enthusiastic, but the producers felt that their teary homage belonged on Broadway. The production was enlarged physically, but the story was still too small for any stage. *A Class Act* opened in a large Broadway house and got poorer reviews the second time around. Competition was tough (*The Producers* opened a month later), and the show struggled to run thirteen weeks.

AMERICAN RHAPSODY

[10 November 2000, 231 performances] a musical revue by Ruth Leon, KT Sullivan, Mark Nadler. *Score:* George Gershwin (music), Ira Gershwin (lyrics). *Cast:* Sullivan, Nadler.

Revues, new book musicals, and nightclub acts featuring the songs of George Gershwin were far from rare over the previous decades, and the 2000–2001 season saw two more. On Broadway the one-man show *George Gershwin Alone* struggled, but Off Broadway *American Rhapsody* had no trouble attracting an audience for more than seven months. Performers-creators KT Sullivan and Mark Nadler confined their repertoire to songs George Gershwin wrote with his brother Ira, which were no meager pickings to say the least. There was narration scripted by Ruth Leon, but by this late date there was little to say about the Gershwins that wasn't common knowledge, and audiences sat through the patter dutifully and waited for Sullivan and Nadler to launch into another duet, solo, or medley. Leon directed and Donald Saddler staged the little bit of dance there was with a flair that made two bodies in motion seem sublime. The press was appreciative of the gimmick-free revue and of the two pleasing performers who let the songs do their magic for them.

PETE 'N' KEELY

[14 December 2000, John Houseman Theatre, 96 performances] a musical comedy by James Hindman. *Score:* Patrick S. Brady, Mark Waldrop (music and lyrics). *Cast:* Sally Mayes, George Dvorsky.

Critics cheered this satiric look at showbiz phoniness, so it was surprising it ran only three months. Perhaps the targets of the musical were not familiar to younger audiences, for one had to understand a 1960s TV variety show to fully appreciate the proficiency (and accuracy) of *Pete 'n' Keely*. Peter Bartel (George Dvorsky) and his wife Keely Stevens (Sally Mayes) were a favorite singing couple on television and in nightclubs, but five years earlier they split up after a fight at Caesars Palace in Las Vegas. In 1968 they reteam for a live television special and, as much as they try to come across as a happily reunited couple, their hostility keeps surfacing during the show. James Hindman's libretto was hilariously two-faced with private and public personas clashing. The couple sang familiar songs, ranging from "Fever" and "But Beautiful" to "Daddy" and "The Battle Hymn of the Republic." Patrick S. Brady and Mark Waldrop wrote the new specialty numbers for *Pete 'n' Keely*, most memorably the ambivalent ballad "Wasn't It Fine?" and the comic duet "Too Fat to Fit" about Santa not being able to squeeze down the chimney on Christmas Eve. Mayes and Dvorsky were sublimely silly as the battling couple, and they were helped by a series of outlandish costumes designed by Bob Mackie (who had costumed some of the top variety shows on the tube). *Pete 'n' Keely* was not for all tastes, but for those who recalled the glitzy, hollow television variety shows of the Sixties, it was inspired buffoonery.

BAT BOY: THE MUSICAL

[21 March 2001, Union Square Theatre, 260 performances] a musical satire by Keythe Farley, Brian Flemming. *Score:* Laurence O'Keefe (music and lyrics). *Cast:* Deven May, Kerry Butler, Kaitlin Hopkins, Sean McCourt, Richard Pruitt, Dick Storm, Trent Armand Kendall.

If *Little Shop of Horrors* was reset in the backwoods of West Virginia and some of the sci-fi clichés were turned into supermarket tabloid clichés, the result would be *Bat Boy: The Musical*. Inspired from a sensational headline in the trashy *Weekly World News*, the tale concerned another creature that needs to drink blood to survive. In a cave near Hope Falls, West Virginia, some teenagers discover a boy with bat ears and fangs. The freakish fellow is taken in by the local veterinarian Dr. Parker (Sean McCourt), his wife Meredith (Kaitlin Hopkins), and their teenage daughter Shelley (Kerry Butler). The bigoted townsfolk learn about the creature and want to have "bat boy" destroyed, especially when many of the cows in the county are dying of a mysterious disease. All the same, the Parkers educate the boy, whom they name Edgar, and soon he is a genteel sophisticate who speaks with an Oxbridge accent (because he watched so much *Masterpiece Theatre* on PBS). The plot then goes haywire when sex-starved Dr. Parker, jealous of the affection his wife shows toward Edgar, starts killing some locals and tells the mob that the bat boy is responsible. Shelley and Edgar fall in love and even have sex in the woods (encouraged by the other animals), but the romance is doomed when it is discovered Shelley and Edgar are twins; Meredith had been raped by a flock of bats. Wishing to die, Edgar goads the vet into killing him, Meredith is knifed to death in the melee, and Shelley is left to mourn the loss of lover and family. Just as the plotting was uneven, so too was the writing, maudlin scenes mixed with clever, satiric ones. The score was equally schizophrenic, with dazzling numbers, like "Show You a Thing or Two" and "Three Bedroom House" filled with musical zip and splendid lyrics, and trite and unfunny songs that went nowhere, such as "Apology to a Cow" and "Ruthie's Lullaby." On the other hand, the direction by Scott Schwartz was consistently ingenious, and sometimes the staging of a number was far more entertaining than the content. Any musical that managed to spoof both *My Fair Lady* and *The Lion King* in its direction was worth taking a look at. Also, the performances throughout were top-notch, with Devon May balancing the odd and the endearing aspects of Edgar and newcomer Kerry Butler garnering a lot attention as the ditzy yet passionate Shelley. *Bat Boy: The Musical* was developed in Los Angeles and Off Off Broadway before opening for a commercial run Off Broadway. A majority of the critics applauded and recommended it, helping the show to run over eight months. The critical and popular reaction in London was less enthusiastic, but the musical later became a favorite of colleges in the States.

LOVE, JANIS

[22 April 2001, Village Gate, 713 performances] a musical play by Randall Myler. *Score:* various. *Cast:* Catherine Curtin, Andra Mitrovich, Cathy Richardson, Seth Jones.

One does not speak of musical theatre and the late rock singer Janis Joplin in the same breath, but the two were combined very well in this intimate show that was very popular, running nearly two years. The fiery, self-destructive star was viewed in a different light in *Love, Janis*. Joplin's tender, truthful letters that she wrote to her mother over the years were gathered and published in a book by Laura Joplin (Janis' sister), and Randall Myler used the letters to create an intimate portrait of the singer. While Catherine Curtain played Janis off stage and read the letters, Andra Motrovich (alternating with Cathy Richardson) sang the rock numbers associated with Joplin. The contrast between the spoken words and the blasting singing voice made the musical work; a whole evening of one or the other would have been numbing. Nineteen of Joplin's hits were sung, including "Me and Bobby McGee," "Piece of My Heart," "Mercedes Benz," "Get It While You Can," and "Let the Good Times Roll," and for those who thought the letters lacking in drama, the concert part of the show was quite satisfying. *Love, Janis* originated at the Denver Theatre Center and then played in Chicago before arriving Off Broadway, where it met with mixed notices. Audiences, particularly Joplin fans, were not deterred, and the musical was a hit.

THE IT GIRL

[3 May 2001, Theatre at St. Peter's, 29 performances] a musical comedy by Michael Small, B. T. McNicholl based on the 1927 movie *It*. *Score:* Paul McKibbins (music), McNicholl (lyrics). *Cast:* Jean Louise Kelly, Stephen DeRosa, Jessica Boevers, Jonathan Dokuchitz, Susan M. Haefner, Danette Holden, Monte Wheeler.

Some kinds of nostalgia went over well Off Broadway at the turn of the new century, and other kinds didn't. Shows about Frank Sinatra, Janis Joplin, and Dinah Washington each had their fans, but a musical spoofing silent movies and the Roaring Twenties had a smaller built-in audience, so *The IT Girl* only survived a month. Based on the 1927 silent film starring the provocative Clara Bow, the musical followed the screenplay fairly closely. Betty Lou Spenser (Jean Louisa Kelly) is a crafty flapper who works as a salesgirl in a large department store and sets her cap to win Jonathan Waltham (Jonathan Dokuchitz), the playboy son of the store's owner. Betty Lou is known for her sex appeal, referred to as "it" in the musical, but she can't get Jonathan's attention until she talks the dandy Monty Montgomery (Stephen DeRosa) into taking her to the Ritz where Jonathan likes to dine. The two finally meet, sparks fly, and marriage is in the works until a news reporter digs up some dirt about Betty Lou, and it takes a lot of explaining to get the couple together by the finale. The film was more famous for establishing Bow as a sexy film star than for its own merits; but it did coin the 1920s expression "it." *The IT Girl* was a lighthearted spoof of the film, never took itself seriously, and added zest to the predictable plot with a score of new songs that accurately pastiched the Jazz Age sound. When the characters took in "Coney Island," the song was as bubbly as a 1920s carefree standard; Betty Lou and the flappers sang the frivolous "Why Not?"; Betty Lou's rival Adela Van Norman (Jessica Boevers) recalled her tattered love life and vowed revenge with "A Perfect Plan'"; Betty Lou and Jonathan had the chipper duet "You're the Best Thing That Ever Happened to Me"; and Monty led the cast in the contagious frolic "It." It was a charming and catchy score, and the energetic cast did it justice, but *The IT Girl* was never exceptional musical theatre and received politely affirmative notices. A group of producers behind the York Theatre Company production had the idea of moving the show to Broadway or at least a larger house Off Broadway. But business was spotty, and *The IT Girl* closed, only to resurface in summer stock on occasion. Ironically, the very similar musical *Thoroughly Modern Millie* opened a year later on Broadway and did very well.

URINETOWN

[6 May 2001, American Theatre of Actors, 58 performances; Henry Miller's Theatre, 965 performances] a musical satire by Greg Kotis. *Score:* Kotis (lyrics), Mark Hollmann (music and lyrics). *Cast:* Hunter Foster, John Cullum, Jennifer Laura Thompson, Nancy Opel, Daniel Marcus, Jeff McCarthy.

From the first measures of the overture, it was clear that this musical with the off-putting title was going to be in the mode of the early Bertolt Brecht–Kurt Weill music dramas such as *The Threepenny Opera*. Yet you didn't need to recognize the connection or the slyly accurate way the score and the plot echoed those German musicals to enjoy *Urinetown* for the strange and appealing show that it was. As the ridiculous plot unfolded, its very absurdity was noticed and commented on by the authors and the characters. The musical ended up being not so much a satire of Brecht and Weill as a spoof on the very nature of the theatre musical itself. In a town devastated by a water shortage, the grasping Caldwell B. Cladwell (John Cullum) and his private enterprise Urine Good Company control all the public toilets, the only facilities available to the populace. Those caught breaking the law and not using these for-pay amenities are carted away to Urinetown, a mysterious place from which no one ever returns. The radical Bobby Strong (Hunter Foster) leads a revolution against the Cladwell regime, even though he is in love with Cladwell's daughter Hope (Jennifer Laura Thompson). Hope is held hostage by the rebels, and Bobby is captured by Cladwell's police and sent to Urinetown. It turns out there is no such place; Bobby is thrown from the top of a tall building and his remains secretly disposed of. Hope picks up the cause, topples her father's monopoly, and provides free water for all. But, like those dark German works, the happy ending is soured by the eventual loss of all water and the return of discontent. As the innocent Little Sally (Spencer Kayden) tells the show's narrator, police officer Lockstock (Jeff McCarthy), this is a terrible premise for a musical. *Urinetown* continually told its audience why such a show shouldn't work then went on to entertain them on different levels. The clumsy exposition at the top of the show was enjoyable for its clumsiness. The villain and the hero were equally one-dimensional and equally fun. The wry supporting characters were so artificial that they seemed to forget why they were there. Greg Kotis's libretto was an affectionate lampoon on all the elements that make a musical work; it was a loving antimusical. The score by Kotis and composer Mark Hollmann managed to find a lot of variety within the limitations it set for itself. "Run, Freedom, Run!" was a rousing yet humorously empty gospel number; "Mr. Cladwell," a bouncy Broadway soft shoe; and "I See a River," a mocking march. Much of the rest of the score was firmly in the Brecht-Weill tradition, such as the wordy "Cop Song," the diabolical "Don't Be the Bunny," the jazzy "Snuff That Girl," the teary lament "Tell Her I Love Her," and the very Weill-like title number. All of this in the wrong hands would have made for a dismal inside joke, but the production directed by John Rando and choreographed by John Carrafa was as ingenious as the writing, and the cast was masterful, finding the spark of truth in the cartoon characters. *Urinetown* was first produced at the New York International Fringe Festival Off Off Broadway. The Off-Broadway mounting was so well received that the show moved to the dilapidated but atmospheric Henry Miller's Theatre on Broadway where it was even more popular, running two and a half years. The musical is a bit too subversive for many mainstream regional theatres, but it has become very popular with colleges and more ambitious little theatres.

TICK, TICK . . . BOOM!

[13 June 2001, Jane Street Theatre, 215 performances] a musical play by
Jonathan Larson, David Auburn. *Score:* Larson (music and lyrics). *Cast:*
Raúl Esparza, Amy Spanger, Jerry Dixon.

Having died before his rock musical *Rent* became famous, Jonathan Larson
had no subsequent works; but he had been writing songs and workshopping
musicals for several years before *Rent*, making it no surprise that this material
was gathered and a "new" Jonathan Larson show was presented to the public.
Tick, Tick . . . Boom! took songs that Larson had written for these early efforts
and strung them together with a book by David Auburn that ended up being
a biography and a tribute to Larson. The seeds of *Rent* could be detected
throughout the score, yet there was something unique about the new show,
and in some ways it illustrated that the songwriter's talents had been considerable, even more than in his break-out hit musical. Because even Off-Off-
Broadway showcases were getting expensive in the late 1980s, Larson fashioned a show in 1990 which required only one character who also acted as
the show's only musician. He called it *Boho Days* then later retitled it *30/90*,
referring to the character (and Larson) turning thirty years old in the year
1990. Of course Larson played the actor-musician himself, and he performed
it in various small venues hoping to get his work noticed. When his "rock
monologue" was still being presented after the year 1990, Larson renamed it
Tick, Tick . . . Boom! Years later Auburn added some characters that Larson
only spoke about in the one-man show, and this allowed the main character
"Johnny" to leave his piano at times and interact with these people. The plot
is minimal. Johnny (Raúl Esparza) has wanted to write songs for the theatre
ever since he was a stagestruck teen appearing in his high school musicals.
He leaves his comfortable middle-class home in the suburbs and moves into
a cheap apartment in the East Village of Manhattan with his school friend
Michael (Jerry Dixon). Johnny works at a diner and writes songs, which he
plays for whoever will listen. His relationship with his girlfriend Susan (Amy
Spanger) is complicated, and his friendship with Michael is tested when the
later is diagnosed as HIV positive. Johnny's workshop of his musical *Suburbia*
gets some recognition, most memorably by a complimentary phone call from
Stephen Sondheim, and Johnny faces his thirtieth birthday with hope for the
future. Simply but effectively staged by Scott Schwartz, *Tick, Tick . . . Boom!*
was very engaging, and Esparza's portrayal of the sarcastic, sensitive Johnny
was free of sentiment yet very moving. The songs ranged in quality, but this

was clearly the work of a very gifted songwriter. The dreaded birthday song "30/90" was pure rock and roll, while "Therapy" was a rollicking hoedown duet with a mocking lyric. Sondheim's first act finale from *Sunday in the Park with George* was reset in the diner as the farcical "Sunday," "No More" was a pulsating double song about the squalor of the Village and the classy apartments Uptown, and "Green Green Dress" was an unabashed celebration of sexual excitement. The most autobiographical, and consequently the most haunting, song in the show was "Why?" in which Johnny chronicles his love of the theatre through the years and resolves that he will write songs for musicals every day for the rest of his life. Comparing *Tick, Tick . . . Boom!* to *Rent*, most critics dismissed the former as a curiosity and a minor work. Yet to fully realize and understand the breadth and depth of Larson's talent, this little musical was just as revealing as the more polished, more popular *Rent*.

THE SPITFIRE GRILL

[2 October 2001, Duke on 42nd Street, 15 performances] a musical play by James Valcq, Fred Alley based on the 1996 film. *Score:* Valcq (music), Alley (lyrics). *Cast:* Garrett Long, Phyllis Somerville, Liz Callaway, Armand Schultz, Steven Pasquale, Mary Gordon Murray, Stephen Sinclair.

Critical and popular reactions to this warmhearted musical about small-town life were decidedly mixed, yet after its short Off-Broadway run *The Spitfire Grill* has found new life elsewhere and continues to divide audiences regarding its merits. Based on the 1996 film of the same title, the musical version is set in the small Wisconsin town of Gilead, where Percy Talbot (Garrett Long), a young West Virginia woman just released from jail, goes to live because it sounds so idyllic. She gets a job at the local diner The Spitfire Grill owned and run by the sharp-tongued widow Hannah Ferguson (Phyllis Somerville). Percy quickly befriends the local citizen Shelby Thorpe (Liz Callaway), but most of the townspeople are suspicious of Percy and gossip about her behind her back. Hannah has been trying unsuccessfully to sell the diner for some time, and to help her out, Percy suggests a raffle. They advertise in out-of-town newspapers that those interested in owning The Spitfire Grill should send in $1,000 and an essay about why they want to run a diner. The winner will be given the diner for no extra cost. The plan works, and soon the money and the essays start rolling in. Percy also helps Hannah by reuniting her with her son Eli (Stephen Sinclair), a Vietnam War deserter who has been hiding in the woods outside of Gilead. Unlike the film, the musical ends with Hannah giving The Spitfire Grill to Percy and Shelby. James Valcq and Fred Alley adapted the screenplay for the stage, telling the story with only seven characters, and they also provided the homespun score that consisted of simple folk tunes and hymnlike numbers. The songs were far from sophisticated and sometimes even amateurish, but some numbers proved to be very effective, such as the wistful "A Ring around the Moon" and the beguiling love duet "This Wide Woods." *The Spitfire Grill* was developed and first produced at the George Street Playhouse in New Jersey and was brought to New York by the Playwrights Horizons. Most critics praised the musical for its simplicity and sincerity, others found it dull and old-fashioned. Audiences had little time to decide for themselves, for the musical was gone within two weeks. (Opening a few weeks after the World Trade Center tragedy on September 11 did not help matters.) Yet *The Spitfire Grill* proved to be very appealing to the rest of the country, for it received dozens of regional productions within a few years and continues to be done with success. There have also been versions in England, Germany, South Korea, and Japan. Just as the movie was dismissed as a "chick flick" by many, the musical's tender and sentimental nature makes it a show one either warmly embraces or coldly rejects.

REEFER MADNESS

[7 October 2001, Variety Arts Theatre, 25 performances] a musical spoof by Kevin Murphy, Dan Studney. *Score:* Studney (music), Murphy (lyrics). *Cast:* Christian Campbell, Kristen Bell, Gregg Edelman, Erin Matthews, Robert Torti, Michele Pawk, John Kassir.

The 1938 docudrama film *Reefer Madness* was rediscovered in the 1960s and became a favorite in revival houses in which patrons, stoned or sober, laughed at the preposterous cautionary movie about the evils of marijuana. This stage musical version of the film was first presented in Los Angeles in 1999 and was a popular hit, was recorded, then headed to New York with much the same cast. Clean-cut teenager Jimmy Harper (Christian Campbell) gets ensnared into pot smoking by the villainous Jack (Robert Torti), and soon Jimmy has his sweetheart Mary Lane (Kristen Bell) flying high, making the two flagrantly promiscuous and culminating in murder, dismembering, and Jimmy's execution. The libretto followed the film's plot but exaggerated the characters so that what was once unintentional camp was turned to unfunny farce. The songs were feeble pastiches of any kind of music that appealed to the songwriters at the time. "Down at the Ol' Five and Dime" was a thumping swing number, "Listen to Jesus, Jimmy" a hyped-up gospel song, "Lonely Pew" a mock hymn and torch number, "Mary Jane/Mary Lane" a pop love song with endless repetition, and the title number a lifeless march. The lyrics were facile and occasionally funny without ever being clever or witty. Critical reaction ranged from the mildly amused to the dismissive, and audiences weren't interested enough to keep the musical on the boards for a whole month. Yet *Showtime* turned the little musical into an overproduced movie (with several original cast members) for cable TV in 2005, and a few regional productions have sprung up over the years. *Reefer Madness* was probably a bad idea for a musical, even though it tried to recreate the success of *Little Shop of Horrors* by turning a camp-cult favorite into an Off-Broadway hit. The big difference was talent. Yet one wonders if even Howard Ashman and Alan Menken could have turned a pot-head classic into a satisfying musical spoof.

ROADSIDE

[29 November 2001, Theatre at St. Peter's, 29 performances] a musical play by Tom Jones based on Lynn Riggs's play. *Score:* Jones (lyric), Harvey Schmidt (music). *Cast:* Julie Johnson, Jonathan Beck Reed, G. W. Bailey, James Hindman, Tom Flagg, Steve Barcus, Ryan Appleby, Jennifer Allen, William Ryall.

A promising combination of material and songwriters turned to major disappointment in *Roadside*, a rural musical by the authors of *The Fantasticks* and *110 in the Shade*. The simple charm of those two shows was needed for this musical version of a 1930 play by Lynn Riggs (whose *Green Grow the Lilacs* was turned into *Oklahoma!*); the result was simple but rarely charming. Crusty old Pap Raider (G. W. Bailey) wanders the Oklahoma Territory in 1900 with his feisty daughter Hannie (Julie Johnson) in an old wagon. The milquetoast farmer Buzzey Hale (James Hindman) proposes to Hannie, but he is too tame for her since she longs for a wild, passionate man. She finds him in the rowdy, madcap cowboy Texas (Jonathan Beck Reed), who has just torn apart the town of Verdigree. The two are taken with each other immediately, and there is a wild night of celebration. But when the Marshall (William Ryall) comes looking for Texas, the cowboy is too hung over to fight and just throws up in a stew pot. The angry Hannie socks Texas on the jaw and says she's through with him. On the day she is to wed Buzzey, Texas stirs up another rampage and is just about hung before he convinces Hannie and the authorities that he is the spirit of the West and represents all the territory folk. It was a thin story, but then so was *Green Grows the Lilacs*. The characters in *Roadside* never felt like anything other than types, and Tom Jones's libretto took the form of a traveling show, complete with unconnected olio acts, leaving the whole venture to seem superficial. A marvelous score might have glossed over the plot and character weaknesses, but the songs Jones and Harvey Schmidt wrote were uneven, with some delightful numbers followed by routine ones. The opening "Uncle Billy's Travelin' Family Show" dutifully introduces the company actors and makes a pitch for buying Uncle Billy's Popcorn. The entrancing title song followed, and the musical quickly soared. "Roadside" was evocative and lilting, a country and western version of "Try to Remember" that conjured up the prairie and its mysterious allure. Unfortunately the story that followed was more brash than enchanting, and none of the subsequent songs came close to "Roadside" in quality or temperament. The olio numbers, such as "Lookin' at the Moon" and "My Little Prairie Flower," were fun and diverting in a cornpone way, "Personality Plus" was a dandy ragtime ditty, and "The Way It Should Be" was a pleasing ballad. Jones and Schmidt first attempted to musicalize Riggs's play in the 1950s and returned to it a half a century later. Their experience and polish was evident, but all the pieces failed to fall into place for *Roadside*. The York Theatre Company production met with negative notices and folded inside of a month. A few weeks before it opened, the producers of *The Fantasticks* announced that the long-running phenomenon would close in a few months. *Roadside* seemed to be a poor consolation for those who were saddened by the passing of an American landmark.

THE LAST FIVE YEARS

[3 March 2002, Minetta Lane Theatre, 73 performances] a musical play by Jason Robert Brown. *Score:* Brown (music and lyrics). *Cast:* Sherie René Scott, Norbert Leo Butz.

Alternately straightforward and complex, this intimate song cycle managed to be highly dramatic without a word of dialogue. Thirteen solos and one duet were all that was needed to tell you everything about two people and the sad journey their relationship traveled. The charming if self-absorbed writer Jamie Wellerstein (Norbert Leo Butz) and the loving but nonassertive actress

Cathy Hyatt (Sherie René Scott) meet, fall in love, wed, fall out of love, and divorce over the course of five years. Jamie tells the story through songs in chronological order while Cathy's songs start after the divorce and travel back through time. The only time the two sing together is in the middle of the tale when Jamie and Cathy wed. The premise sounded more confusing than it had to be, but somehow the two opposite song journeys made the musical more potent and allowed for a greater depth of character in both cases. Of course it wouldn't matter what direction the story went if the songs had not been powerful minidramas in themselves. As with songwriter Jason Robert Brown's earlier *Songs for a New World*, these numbers were story songs, but this time the stories were confined to two characters at different points in their relationship. The score for *The Last Five Years* was nothing less than a marvel. Instead of getting tired of these two people, they became more interesting with each number. Cathy's lament "Still Hurting" that opened the show was as direct and moving as her "Goodbye Until Tomorrow" at the close of the musical when she sang to Jamie at the end of their first date. In between were some lighter moments, such as Cathy's wry commentary on doing summer stock in "A Summer in Ohio" and Jamie's comic anticipation of his family's reaction to his dating a non-Jew in "Jamie's Song: Shiksa Goddess." Other highlights in the score included Jamie's fear of commitment in "Moving Too Fast," Cathy's pride in his writing success in "I'm a Part of That," Jamie entertaining Cathy on their first Christmas together with the ethnic "The Schmuel Song," and Cathy's hilarious stream of consciousness during an audition in "Climbing Uphill." The show's duet "The Next Ten Minutes," in which the two characters were not only together but on the same wavelength, took place on a boat in Central Park and during their wedding ceremony, their short-term and long-term vows blending in a beautiful love song. *The Last Five Years* was first produced in Chicago then was given a commercial mounting Off Broadway. Critics admired the score and the cast, but the musical itself received a mixed press, and it closed after nine weeks. Once the cast recording was released, praise for Brown's songs followed, as did many regional productions and versions in Canada, Mexico, and across Europe.

MENOPAUSE: THE MUSICAL

[4 April 2002, Theatre Four, 1,724 performances] a musical revue by Jeanie Linders. *Score:* Linders (lyrics), various (music). *Cast:* Mary Jo McConnell, Joy Lynn Matthews, Joyce A. Presutti, Carolann Page.

A gold mine that has saved cash-strapped theatres across the country when they couldn't do *Nunsense* a third time, *Menopause: The Musical* is a critic-proof, male-proof revue about the change of life that strikes a nerve with women over a certain age. Four middle-aged females, identified only as Power Woman, Iowa Housewife, Earth Mother, and Soap Star, are shopping for lingerie at a sale at Bloomingdale's department store and recognize in each other fellow spirits in menopausal crisis. They launch into twenty-five songs about mood swings, chocolate craving, hot flashes, midnight sweats, temporary memory lapses, and sexual confusion. Jeanie Linders wrote the score, which consisted of popular songs from the 1950s, 1960s, and 1970s with slightly altered lyrics. "Good Vibrations" and "Change, Change, Change" took on a new meaning in the show's context, and there were feeble but frequently funny rewrites such as "Stayin' Alive" becoming "Stayin' Awake"; "My Guy" into "My Thighs"; "Puff the Magic Dragon" to "Puff, My God I'm Draggin'"; and "The Lion Sleeps Tonight" into "My Husband Sleeps Tonight." If you weren't looking for wit, it was all harmless fun better enjoyed if you were not a young female or a male of any age. *Menopause: The Musical* originated in Orlando, Florida, then took Off Broadway by storm, running more than four years. But this was nothing compared to the popularity of the show across the country, where regional productions broke box office records and the musical was brought back more than once without losing any of its momentum. Some of the references were changed, and the musical was also a hit in England and other foreign countries. With the money rolling in, Linders created a research foundation for ovarian cancer and menopause-related ailments, and collections are made at each performance for this charity. So one can scoff at *Menopause: The Musical*, but the silly show has the last laugh. Besides, at what other musical can you purchase a souvenir "hot flash fan"?

THE PRINCE AND THE PAUPER

[16 June 2002, Lamb's Theatre, 194 performances] a musical play by Bernie Garzia, Ray Roderick based on Mark Twain's novel. *Score:* Neil Berg (music and lyrics), Garzia (lyrics). *Cast:* Dennis Michael Hall, Gerard Canonico, Michael McCormick, Sally Wilfert, Allison Fisher, Kathy Brier, Rob Evan, Stephen Zinnato.

That Off-Broadway rarity, a family musical, managed to overcome the odds and find an audience in two separate engagements. *The Prince and the Pau-*

per was an economic stage adaptation of Mark Twain's adventure tale performed by a cast of twelve and featuring a score of vigorous and hummable songs. Much of the show rested on the shoulders of the two boys playing the title roles, but Dennis Michael Hall as Prince Edward and Gerard Canonico as the pauper Tom Canty who takes his place were both deemed proficient and likable by the press. The songs came at the expected places and held few surprises but had spirit. The Prince's yearning for "The Thrill of Adventure," the boys' playful duet "If I Were You," the quizzical "Is This Love?" about puppy love, and the soaring ballad "Twilight" were the better numbers in the show. *The Prince and the Pauper* received respectable reviews and ran four months in the summer and fall. The Lamb's Theatre was encouraged enough to bring the musical back for the holidays, and it played for another five weeks. When the show was revived Off Broadway in 2003, it ran another 102 performances.

HARLEM SONG

[6 August 2002, Apollo Theatre, 146 performances] a musical revue by George C. Wolfe. *Score:* Wolfe (lyrics), Zane Mark, Daryl Waters (music). *Cast:* Queen Esther, B. J. Crosby, David St. Louis, Rosa Curry, Rosa Evangelina, Randy A. Davis.

LITTLE HAM

[26 September 2002, John Houseman Theatre, 77 performances] a musical play by Dan Owens based on Langston Hughes's play. *Score:* Judd Woldin (music and lyrics), Richard Engquist (lyrics). *Cast:* André Garner, Monica L. Patton, Richard Vida, Brenda Braxton, Joe Wilson Jr.

The Harlem of the past came alive in two Off-Broadway musicals that opened within six weeks of each other. The famed Apollo Theatre in Harlem was not considered Off Broadway by some, but the revue *Harlem Song* had Off-Broadway contracts, so it was treated like one. Creator George C. Wolfe put together the tribute to Harlem, its culture, and its music; curiously, half of the songs were new (by Zane Mark and Daryl Waters) and no match for standards like the breezy "Take the A Train," the sassy "Well Alright Then," and the vampy "For Sale." All the same, *Harlem Song* had many memorable musical moments, such as the swinging "Tarzan of Harlem," the rousing rag "Miss Linda Brown," and the bluesy "Drop Me Off in Harlem." Wolfe chose to concentrate on the history of the Apollo from the turn of the century into the 1940s, the era when Jimmie Lunceford, Count Basie, and Cab Calloway reigned there. This left out many songs and artists who flourished at the famed establishment in the 1950s and 1960s. But if the material and the scope were uneven, the cast was outstanding, particularly Queen Esther and B. J. Crosby, and the show never flagged under Wolfe's direction and the choreography by Ken Robertson. Some critics carped that *Harlem Song* was closer to an African American vaudeville show than an Off-Broadway revue, but audiences were not so concerned with labels and kept the show on the boards for eighteen weeks.

The Harlem Renaissance was conjured up again in *Little Ham* (subtitled a "Harlem jazzical"), a farcical musical comedy based on a play by Langston Hughes, one of the shining lights of that Renaissance. In 1936 the Harlem small-time hood Hamlet Hitchcock Jones (André Garner), known to his friends as Little Ham, is talked into working for Louie "The Nail" Mahoney (Richard Vida), a white mobster from Downtown. Ham is in love with the big-mouthed saloon owner Tiny Lee (Monica L. Patton) and hopes to impress her with his big-time underworld connections. When Ham discovers that Louie plans to take over the numbers racket in Harlem and put all of Ham's friends out of business, he sets out to outwit Louie, keep Harlem black, and win the heart of Tiny. The characters were broadly drawn cartoons and, despite the Depression setting, the outlook was sunny and carefree. The original score pastiched the era and, while it was questionable if the new songs were authentic jazz, they certainly were Broadway jazz. Ham sang a romantic tribute to his world with the moody "Harlem, You're My Girl"; Tiny instructed a gangster's moll to give up the racketeer with the swinging "No!"; Tiny and Ham saluted the easy life in the duet "Wastin' Time"; and the cast proclaimed the "Angels" were on their side in a throbbing gospel number. Because several of Hughes's characters were of the Damon Runyonesque variety, *Little Ham* was unfavorably compared to *Guys and Dolls*. It wasn't in that class, but it was a bright and tuneful musical in its own right. Producer Erik Krebs had spent years getting *Little Ham* to Off Broadway. The first productions were at the George Street Playhouse in New Jersey and the Westport Country Playhouse in Connecticut, followed by an Off-Off-Broadway mounting at the AMAS Musical Theatre in 2001. The commercial run at the John Houseman Theatre met with mixed notices, and *Little Ham* struggled to run two months.

JOLSON AND COMPANY

[29 September 2002, Century Center for the Performing Arts, 97 performances] a musical play by Stephen Mo Hanan, Jay Berkow. *Score:* various. *Cast:* Hanan, Robert Ari, Nancy Anderson.

There had been several attempts to build a musical around the life and songs of Al Jolson; some closed out of town, others staggered into Manhattan and quickly closed. This musical biography was more fortunate, garnering decent notices and running three months. Although it was packed with the Jolson standards "Swanee," "California, Here I Come," "Sonny Boy," "April Showers," "My Mammy," and many others, *Jolson and Company* was not a revue. It spent just as much playing time not singing but relating the life of the beloved performer. One should say beloved by his public, because the libretto by Stephen Mo Hanan (who played Jolson) and Jay Berkow made it clear that Jolson was not very lovable off stage and was one of the most temperamental and unhappy of showbiz giants. Taking the form of an interview Jolson gave in his later years, the plot followed the "jazz singer" from his youth in poverty and his early days in vaudeville through his glory days on Broadway and in the movies to his comeback in the 1940s. Nancy Anderson played his wives and other women in his life, while Robert Ari stood in for all the male friends and enemies. *Jolson and Company* did not set out to idolize or memorialize Jolson, but the greatness of the man still came through, warts and all. Much of the success of the evening was due to Hanan's vigorous performance that avoided clichéd mannerisms while accurately recreating the old Jolson magic. The actor also bore an uncanny resemblance to the great star, giving the show a documentary look. *Jolson and Company* was first presented Off Off Broadway by the York Theatre Company in 1999, and then was given a commercial run Off Broadway at the Century Center for the Performing Arts.

A MAN OF NO IMPORTANCE

[10 October 2002, Mitzi E. Newhouse Theatre, 93 performances] a musical play by Terrence McNally based on the screenplay by Barry Devlin. *Score:* Lynn Ahrens (lyrics), Stephen Flaherty (music). *Cast:* Roger Rees,

Faith Prince, Steven Pasquale, Charles Keating, Jessica Molaskey, Ronn Carroll, Katherine McGrath.

After three large Broadway musicals that met with variable success, song-writers Lynn Ahrens and Stephen Flaherty returned to Off Broadway with their *Ragtime* librettist Terrence McNally and offered this small-scale musical based on the 1994 film *A Man of No Importance*. In 1964 Dublin, the middle-aged bus conductor Alfie Byrne (Roger Rees) reads poetry to his riders and directs plays for the St. Imelda's Players, an amateur theatre group run through the local church. Alfie's sister Lily (Faith Prince) is still waiting for her younger brother to get married, but Alfie is a closeted homosexual and is quietly in love with the bus driver Robbie Fay (Steven Pasquale), who likes Alfie but is unaware of his feelings. Alfie's latest theatre venture, Oscar Wilde's *Salome*, has the amateur players all excited, but righteous members of the church board deem the play obscene and stop the rehearsals. Taking the advice from Oscar Wilde (Charles Keating), whose image appears to Alfie in a mirror, that he must face up to his homosexuality, Alfie dresses up like Wilde and goes into a local pub to confront the man who closed *Salome*. His boldness is rewarded with blows, and Alfie's secret is out, much to the distress of Lily who insists she still loves her brother. Alfie's crush on Robbie ends when he catches the driver making love to a married woman. Once they get over the shock, the St. Imelda's Players and other friends rally around Alfie and accept him for who he is, and they all anticipate working on the next theatrical venture. Flaherty, who had pastiched Caribbean and ragtime music so effectively in the past, composed a flowing Irish-flavored score, and Ahren's character driven lyrics were excellent. "Love Who You Love" and "Princess" sounded like ancient Irish ballads yet were still theatrical. "The Streets of Dublin" was a lusty number with the energy of an Irish jig, "Books" was a comic duet saturated with homespun Irish philosophy, and "Going Up" was a funny and feverish salute to community theatre, the different characters reading their program bios aloud between verses. The ensemble number "Art" was a hilarious musical scene in which different backstage members of St. Imalda's Players proudly demonstrated their artistic inspiration through outrageously bad production ideas. McNally's libretto was faithful to the film but reimagined the story in stage terms. The duet "Man in the Mirror" with Wilde and Aflie on opposite sides of a mirror and "Confession" in which Robbie comments in song on the sins that Alfie confesses to the priest were marvelous theatrical moments. Joe Mantello directed the first-class cast, staging the musical simply and effectively. The bus was just a series of chairs, and the action often took place in several places at once. Despite the presence of Broadway star Prince and London stage star Rees in the cast, *A Man of No Importance* felt like an ensemble piece. Some critics called it a small and modest musical and gave it faint approval; others complimented the authors for being able to scale themselves down to create an intimate Off-Broadway show. Because most of the songs were so integrated into the story, few of the numbers stood out as showcases, leaving most reviewers unimpressed with the score. Only after *A Man of No Importance* was recorded did compliments for the songs surface. The British film had not been very popular in the States, and audience interest in a musical version was not very strong. The Lincoln Center production played its three-month engagement then departed.

DEBBIE DOES DALLAS

[29 October 2002, Jane Street Theatre, 127 performances] a musical spoof by Erica Schmidt. *Score:* Schmidt, various. (lyrics), Andrew Sherman (music). *Cast:* Sherie René Scott, Jama Williamson, Caitlin Miller, John Patrick Walker, Paul Fitzgerald, Mary Catherine Garrison.

What do you get when you take a famous porno flick, remove the nudity and overt sex, and replace them with songs and a wicked sense of humor? *Debbie Does Dallas* was just another outlandish entry at the New York International Fringe Festival until some producers thought it could be worked into a mainstream Off-Broadway musical. The 1978 porn original went on to become one of the top-grossing movies in its field—*Debbie Does Dallas* had name recognition. It also had a thin and contrived plot that served as an excuse for a series of sexual encounters. The musical version did not worry about developing the characters or the story but instead lampooned the original and offered a lot of songs and innuendo. Debbie Benton (Sherie René Scott), from wholesome middle America, is captain of her school cheerleading team and dreams of becoming one of the Dallas Cowgirls. Out of the blue a letter arrives inviting her to come to Dallas to join the cheerleaders, but Debbie doesn't have money for bus fare. She and her fellow cheerleaders all get minimum-wage jobs to raise the money, but the cash doesn't start to roll in until the girls take a suggestion from Debbie's boss to bestow sexual favors for clients that he rounds up. Soon the cheerleaders have a thriving business, and there's enough dough for all of them to go to Dallas. The libretto was a series of inane conversations that satirized innocence and sex with the same broad strokes. The score consisted of tuneful numbers ranging from pop-rock to folk-country with lyrics that were overflowing with double (and single) entendres. The yearning ballads "Debbie Benton" and "Small Town Girl" gave way to the raunchier "The Dildo Rag," "I Wanna Do Debbie," and "Dallas . . . I'm Coming!" before the show ended with the mock-inspirational "Where I Need to Go." Scott was so effective as the vapid, clueless Debbie that *Debbie Does Dallas* was often funnier than its material. Still, most of the critics were not impressed, and word of mouth was needed to keep the musical on the boards for four months.

LITTLE FISH

[13 February 2003, Second Stage Theatre, 29 performances] a musical play by Michael John LaChiusa. *Score:* LaChiusa (music and lyrics). *Cast:* Jennifer Laura Thompson, Lea DeLaria, Eric Jordan Young, Hugh Panero, Marcy Harriell, Jesse Tyler Ferguson, Celia Keenan-Bolger, Ken Marks.

After writing the very serious Broadway musicals *Marie Christine* and *The Wild Party*, two period pieces with pastiche scores, songwriter Michael John LaChiusa returned to Off Broadway with this contemporary musical about living and dealing with life in Manhattan. Charlotte (Jennifer Laura Thompson) is a short story writer who decides to give up cigarettes, and the resulting trauma forces her to examine her life thus far. What followed was a series of scenes from the past and present involving her ex-lover Robert (Hugh Panaro), her crazy roommate Cinder (Lea DeLaria), and her friends Marco (Jesse Tyler Ferguson) and Kathy (Marcy Harriell). Charlotte takes up jogging and swimming at the local Y, but this is just another way of running away from her problems. Finally she has a breakdown, and as she is about to take up smoking again, Charlotte realizes that she has the power to change her life, becoming a little fish in a rushing current but an individual all the same. Adapted from two short stories by Deborah Eisenberg, *Little Fish* had a premise that was very ponderous, but the sung-through musical was lively, sometimes funny, and always perceptive. The songs had a driving, contemporary beat but veered away from rock or pop. The title song was a heartfelt plea for friendship in a cold world, "Flotsam" was a fantasy in which Charlotte meets Anne Frank (Celia Keenan-Bolger), who tells her what she thinks of Charlotte's short stories, "Simple Creature" was about confronting loneliness, and in "He" Charlotte meets and dances with an attractive man while her ex-lover's comments crowd her mind. As directed and choreographed by Graciela Daniele, the ninety-minute, intermissionless *Little Fish* was a surreal journey that floated along like a dream. Some critics saw the musical as a statement about life in post–9/11 New York, even comparing the work to Sondheim's *Company*. Other reviewers thought *Little Fish* more interesting than involving. Mainstream audiences were cautious about LaChiusa, and the month-long engagement at the Second Stage was not extended. The musical was more successful in Los Angeles (where it was recorded), and there have been some regional and international productions.

RADIANT BABY

[2 March 2003, Public Theatre/Newman Theatre, 25 performances] a musical play by Stuart Ross based on John Gruen's *Keith Haring: The Authorized Biography*. *Score:* Debra Barsha (music), Ross, Ira Gasman (lyrics). *Cast:* Daniel Reichard, Aaron Lohr, Remy Zaken, Kate Jennings Grant, Keong Sim, Gabriel Enrique Alvarez.

Few Off-Broadway musicals early in the new century were as visually exciting as *Radiant Baby*, a biomusical about pop artist Keith Haring. Its script and songs could not match its visuals, and it failed to catch on, but there was something exciting about the show all the same. Set mostly in Manhattan's Paradise Disco in 1988, Haring (Daniel Reichard) struggles with his art as he deals with an overabundance of sex and drugs. Nothing much new there. But Haring was a graffiti artist, and his explosive decoration of subway cars made him famous and took him from renegade to acclaimed artist before he died of AIDS at the age of thirty-one. Stuart Ross's libretto used a Greek chorus of young art students who praised, questioned, derided, and participated with Haring in prose and song. Some critics found it exhilarating, others irritating. Pop composer Debra Barsha wrote the propulsive music, and Ross and Ira Gasman provided the harsh lyrics. The score incorporated everything from rock and roll and soul to rhythm and blues and funk, with even a bit of rap thrown in for good measure. "Paradise" was the expected disco number, "Get Me to New York" was young Haring's rocking song of ambition, "Art Attack" and "Spirit of the Line" sought to musically explain what Haring was doing visually, "Faster Than the Speed of Light" was about his drug use, and the show ended with the sentimental but moving "Stay." There were a few weak spots in the score, such as when Haring's lover Carlos (Aaron Lohr) sang the vapid ballad "I Really Loved You," but for the most part it was a winning set of songs. As directed by George C. Wolfe and choreographed by Fatima Robinson, *Radiant Baby* moved and pounded as projections of Haring's work exploded onto Riccardo Hernández's eye-popping sets. But all the pyrotechnics were defeated by a weak script, one-dimensional characters, and a sense that there was more flash here than substance. Producer Wolfe must have had high hopes for *Radiant Baby* going to Broadway, for it was an expensive and elaborate production done in the Public Theatre's largest venue. Reviews were mostly tepid and audience interest limited, so it closed after its scheduled three weeks.

MY LIFE WITH ALBERTINE

[13 March 2003, Playwrights Horizons, 22 performances] a musical play by Richard Nelson based on sections of Marcel Proust's *Remembrance of Things Past*. *Score:* Nelson (lyrics), Ricky Ian Gordon (music). *Cast:* Brent Carver, Kelli O'Hara, Chad Kimball, Emily Skinner, Donna Lynne Champlin.

Richard Nelson, who had written the musical *James Joyce's The Dead,* turned to Marcel Proust and his mammoth epic *Remembrance of Times Past* for this intimate musical set in a *salle du théâtre*, a private theatre in a Paris home. The Narrator (Brent Carver) sets the scene by evoking the summer of 1898 when the young, would-be composer Marcel (Chad Kimball) first meets the beguiling orphan Albertine (Kelli O'Hara). Over the next ten years their relationship fluctuates from gentle teasing to passionate lovemaking to jealous rages. Albertine's close friendship with known lesbians, including the cabaret star Mlle. Lea (Emily Skinner), is often the source of the couple's battles, and on the day Marcel decides to push Albertine out of his life, he learns she has left him. The tale ends with a series of letters, the last one from Albertine arriving after her death and filled with love. The Narrator was the older Marcel who often joined in the story and songs, even comforting his younger self at times. The songs by Ricky Ian Gordon were mostly reflective ballads that suggested the art songs of the period with muted melody and rich resonance. "My Soul Weeps" was a mournful poem Albertine shared with Marcel, Marcel's Grandmother (Donna Lynne Champlin) sang a lilting "Lullabye," "Is It Too Late?" was Albertine's mellow request for forgiveness, "If It Is True" was a waltzing love song, and Marcel and the Narrator considered the quixotic nature of their lover with "The Different Albertines." There was a cabaret flavor to "Balbec-by-the-Sea," "Sometimes," and "I Need Me a Girl," but it was too little to break up the lulling nature of the score as a whole. Nelson directed the musical as a chamber piece, and the three principal performers were splendid even though the material never let any of them cut loose and sparkle. Proust's poetic ruminations had lost a great deal in film and television attempts, yet the quiet, atmospheric *My Life with Albertine* did not seem to get any closer to dramatizing the French author. The Playwrights Horizons production ran its scheduled three weeks without any demand for an extension.

AVENUE Q

[19 March 2003, Vineyard Theatre, 47 performances; John Golden Theatre, 2,534 performances] a musical comedy by Jeff Whitty. *Score:* Robert Lopez, Jeff Marx (music and lyrics). *Cast:* John Tartaglia, Stephanie D'Abruzzo, Jordan Gelber, Rick Lyon, Ann Harada, Natalie Venetia Belcon, Jennifer Barnhart.

If there was any question that the Off-Broadway musical was turning into television, the hugely popular *Avenue Q* seemed to settle the matter. A spoof of TV's *Sesame Street* using sit-com jokes and commercial ad songs, the sassy little musical was not only a child of television, it regarded the mass medium as its mentor. Even the unfunny appearance of "Gary Coleman," a sad piece of tube trivia, as he kept popping up in the musical was a desperate attempt to remind audiences that the only reality is television reality. On a set that resembled PBS's *Sesame Street*, the residents of an apartment building are mostly young and both sexually and professionally confused. Whereas the kids' show helped to provide answers and understanding for young America, the folks on Avenue Q are clueless. Princeton (John Tartaglia) has brains but no common sense, Kate Monster (Stephanie D'Abruzzo) is a love-starved kindergarten teacher, neurotic Brian (Jordan Gelber) is unemployed and engaged to the straight-talking Asian Christmas Eve (Ann Harada), Rod (Tartaglia) and Nicky (Rick Lyon) are roommates who insist they are not gay but Rod really is, Trekkie Monster (Lyon) is obsessed with the Internet, and Gary Coleman (Natalie Venetia Belcon) is the building's lay-about super. The episodic plot, scripted by Jeff Whitty, concerns Princeton's arrival on Avenue Q and his difficult romance with Kate, Rod's coming out of the closet, the wedding of Brian and Christmas Eve, and a happy ending with Rod finding a guy and Princeton returning to Kate as she gets to open her own school for overlooked monsters. As in *Sesame Street*, some of these characters were played by humans and others by puppets, and they were all one-dimensional but funny in a cartoonish way.

Also like the kids' show, *Avenue Q* used songs to explore an idea rather than develop character or continue the plot. A subject would be brought up, such as racism, pornography, or homosexuality, and the characters would merrily break into a tuneful ditty that often recalled the melodic songs from the television program. The big difference was in the lyrics, which were adult in nature and often crude. They also had the habit of going nowhere. Each song's title told you all you needed to know because the lyric rarely developed an idea or kept up any verbal energy. "Everyone's a Little Bit Racist" was a list of examples that all were pretty much the same. "The Internet Is for Porn" had nothing to say outside the title. "Schadenfreude" sought to explore the pleasure people feel at others' pain, but the examples lacked wit and faded away before the song ended. The soul number "You Can Be as Loud as the Hell You Want (When You're Makin' Love)" is a dead-end song from the start, and even the generic theme song that opens the show resorts to repetition because it's not even sure what it is trying to introduce. The musical ends with the list song "For Now," which thinks that just mentioning people and things is enough to make a song work. Songwriters Robert Lopez and Jeff Marx are more successful when they concentrate on character rather than jokes. The amusing "It Sucks to Be Me" is a fun way to introduce the various residents, there is more than a little heart in the ballad "There's a Fine, Fine Line," and the trio "Fantasies Come True" reveals some depth not found in the script.

Avenue Q opened at the Vineyard Theatre with a personable cast and some cunning puppet work by Rick Lyon. (How many shows can claim to have "full frontal puppet nudity" and cloth-character copulation?) Reviews were mostly enthusiastic, so the producers decided to brave Broadway. When it opened in the small John Golden Theatre, another round of good notices followed, and the musical was off and running. Word of mouth and winning some major awards kept the little venue crowded for nearly seven years. Even before the show closed, it was announced that *Avenue Q* would reopen Off Broadway on October 21, 2009, and it continues on at the New World Stages 3 at this writing. One of the most successful musicals ever to come from Off Broadway, *Avenue Q* cannot be dismissed as just another *Nunsense* or *I Love You, You're Perfect, Now Change*. This musical is pivotal in the direction Off Broadway is taking. Which brings us back to the idea of television and theatre. *Avenue Q* is very similar to a sketch one might experience on *Saturday Night Live*. (That show did a spoof of *Mister Rogers' Neighborhood* set in a violent ghetto.) An idea that might have sustained a five-minute comedy skit on the tube has been inflated into a full evening of theatre without adding anything very substantial. There are some songs, more jokes, and more characters, but essentially *Avenue Q* is still a television sketch. The popularity of the show demonstrates the distressing thought that theatre that is like television is most likely to succeed. *Avenue Q* certainly has brought in a younger audience everywhere it is performed, from Las Vegas to London. The show is definitely for the generations raised on *Sesame Street*, and those older have no reason to see it or criticize it. Yet when the older generation turned its back on *Hair* two dozen years earlier, it was because that rock musical was too loud, too irreverent, and too political. What is their complaint about *Avenue Q*? It is recycled television. The Off-Broadway musical, which once sought to be an alternative to other media, now wants to be like television. Some fear *Avenue Q* is only the tip of the iceberg and reality show musicals are not far away.

ZANNA, DON'T!

[20 March 2003, John Houseman Theatre, 112 performances] a musical fable by Tim Acito. *Score:* Acito, Alexander Dinelaris (music and lyrics). *Cast:* Jai Rodriguez, Jared Zeus, Anika Larsen, Shelley Thomas, Robb Sharp, Enrico Rodriguez, Amanda Ryan, Darius Nichols.

A silly but thought-provoking premise and a pleasing set of songs made this musical fable a delight from start to finish even though it lacked the polish of a better crafted show. The all-American town of Heartsville seems right out of a squeaky-clean television sit-com with young love blossoming at the local high school. The only difference in this upside-down world is that homosexuality is the norm and heterosexuality is considered deviant behavior. This topsy-turvy way of life makes for some interesting new clichés: the students on the chess team are the school heroes, while the footballers are considered nerds, the cheerleaders ride mechanical bulls, and the radical class play is about letting heteros into the military. All the romantic doings at Heartsville High seem to be under the magic influence of Zanna (Jai Rodriguez), a fairy (in both senses of the word) whose job is to see that love flourishes. Zanna arranges for the new guy in town, quarterback Steve (Jared Zeus), to meet the chess champ Mike (Enrico Rodriguez). Zanna also steers the brainy Roberta (Anika Larsen) away from her unfaithful girlfriend and into the arms of the bull-rider Kate (Shelley Thomas). This sweetly innocent way of life is threatened when Kate and Steve have to do a controversial love scene in the school play and the two find they have romantic feelings for each other. The two become outcasts and, in order to save the couple, Zanna works a spell that turns the town heterosexual. This of course makes Zanna the freak, and it takes a bit of soul searching before the town accepts Zanna into their hetero world. There were some serious holes in the plot, and some scenes didn't play, but most of *Zanna, Don't!* was clever, likable, and even touching. Similarly, the score was uneven with some awkward rhyming in the lyrics but the music was generally engaging. The male duet "I Think We Got Love" was goofy and charming at the same time; "Ride 'Em" was a sexy, ridiculous number for the mechanical bull riders; "Don't Ask, Don't Tell" was the mocking song from the school play; "I Could Write Books" was a heartfelt if slightly idiotic torch song; "Sometime, Do You Think We Could Fall in Love?" was a jaunty invitation for romance; and "Straight to Heaven" was a sock-hop dance number with an uncomfortable subtext. Perhaps the finest musical number was the delectable quartet "Do You Know What It's Like?" as the two couple's confused emotions overlapped in a lyrical way. *Zanna, Don't!* was developed Off Off Broadway at the AMAS Musical Theatre then transferred to Off Broadway where it met with mostly supportive reviews. After running three and a half months in New York and successful Los Angeles and Boston productions, there was talk of doing some rewriting (which it needed, including that cute title) and trying for Broadway in the future. But the plans never materialized and *Zanna, Don't!* became available for regional theatres, some of which have found it a potent little show with a conscience.

ELEGIES: A SONG CYCLE

[24 March 2003, Mitzi E. Newhouse Theatre, 9 performances] a musical revue by William Finn (music and lyrics). *Cast:* Betty Buckley, Michael Rupert, Carolee Carmello, Christian Borle, Keith Byron Kirk.

Songwriter William Finn had come very close to death and wrote about it in *A New Brain*. The subject of this plotless cycle of songs was death itself: recognizing it, dealing with it, embracing it, and remembering those who have passed on. Such a somber topic might have led to an evening of morbid reflection, but *Elegies* was full of life, and the variety of ways the songs considered death was masterful. There was no premise or format for the eighteen songs, though people mentioned in one number sometimes appeared in another. Highly autobiographical, *Elegies* chronicled Finn's memory of many personal friends (some famous, some not) whom he had lost. Yet his memories were filled with humor and affection, so few of them were typical songs of mourning. A veteran teacher with a fatal disease looks back at the hundreds of students she taught and finds comfort if "Only One" of them was transformed by her life's work. A woman recalls with comic insight the annual celebration of "Passover" with relatives, many of whom are no longer alive. "Mark's All-Male Thanksgiving" was a fond memory of gay gatherings that were decimated by the AIDS epidemic. The simple affection for pets was explored in the seriocomic "My Dogs." "Anytime (I Am There)" was the promise to always be present even after death. "Goodbye" was the farewell phone call to a loved one from someone in the World Trade Tower on that fateful day. "Infinite Joy" was a soaring acceptance of everything that makes life worth living. Each musical number was individual and told its own story, but there was a subtle pattern to *Elegies* that made it much more than a revue of songs. Graciela Daniele staged the simple production which featured a dynamite cast of established performers and very promising new ones. The producers at the Lincoln Center knew that the commercial possibilities for a show filled with elegies were limited, so they presented the cycle on Sunday nights when their downstairs venue, the Mitzi E. Newhouse Theatre, was dark. Once the theatre was available, *Elegies* returned and ran another week. As well-received as the cast recording was, productions of the show are infrequent (though a Boston and a Toronto production were praised). It remains a tough sell to audiences, but the rewards of the cycle are plentiful.

HANK WILLIAMS: LOST HIGHWAY

[26 March 2003, Little Shubert Theatre, 132 performances] a musical play by Randal Myler, Mark Harelik. *Score:* Hank Williams (music and lyrics). *Cast:* Jason Petty, Michael P. Moran, Margaret Bowman, Michael J. Howell.

A show that succeeded as both a concert and a biography, *Hank Williams: Lost Highway* dramatized the life and work of the legendary country music singer-songwriter who was so influential to later artists within and outside of the country and western genre. The script chronicled the short but significant life of Williams (Jason Petty) from his youth in the backwoods of Alabama, through his radio and then recording career which made him a star at the

Grand Ole Opry, to his tragic decline because of alcohol and morphine, leaving him dead at the age of twenty-nine. The story was told through scenes with the various people in his life, in particular his strong-willed mother Lilly (Margaret Bowman) and his first and difficult wife Audrey (Tertia Lynch). The songs were performed by Williams and a country band called the Drifting Cowboys, though his protégé Tee-To (Michael W. Howell) sang some memorable numbers as well. The score included songs from Williams's gospel and blues records, but much of the evening was comprised of the unique "honky-tonk" numbers that made Williams so unique. "Your Cheatin' Heart," "Jambalaya (On the Bayou)," "Hey, Good Lookin'," "Lovesick Blues," and the title tune were among the expected classics, but the two dozen musical numbers in *Hank Williams: Lost Highway* also included some lesser-known works that demonstrated Williams's variety and agility. Critics hailed Jason Petty's performance as an actor and singer, cheering his ability to capture the Williams sound but also to portray the innocent, inexperienced, gullible aspect of this man who did not live long enough to fully mature. *Hank Williams: Lost Highway* premiered at the Denver Theatre Center then played Off Off Broadway at the Manhattan Ensemble Theatre who moved it to Off Broadway. New York City was not considered the ideal town for a country and western musical, but audiences kept the show running for more than four months. Needless to say, the musical did much better in the hinterlands.

BOOBS! THE MUSICAL

[19 May 2003, Triad Theatre, 304 performances] a musical revue by Steve Mackes, Michael Whaley. *Score:* Ruth Wallis (music and lyrics). *Cast:* Robert Hunt, Jenny Lynn Suckling, Rebecca Young, Max Perlman, J. Brandon Savage.

In the 1950s and 1960s a handful of female cabaret singers cut out a niche for themselves singing risqué songs and offering adults concerts. One of the most durable of these naughty chanteuses was Ruth Wallis, dubbed the Queen of the Party Song, whose career stretched from the 1940s until the early 1970s. She wrote more than 150 novelty songs, all with blatantly double entendre lyrics, and recorded many albums which were a guilty pleasure for many. Wallis was alive and in her eighties when Steve Mackes and Michael Whaley assembled her songs in a revue titled *Boobs! The Musical*, a not very subtle eye-catcher of which Wallis would surely approve. The show's subtitle was more accurate: *The World According to Ruth Wallis*. It was a narrow and repetitive world, most of the songs coming down to body parts and sexual activity, but it was easy to see how these naughty numbers were so refreshingly bold in a more innocent era when they were banned from radio play in many cities. Song titles like "Johnny Has a Yo-Yo," "The Hawaiian Lei Song," "Hopalong Chastity," "The Dinghy Song," "Stay Out of My Pantry," and "Don't Bite Off More Than You Can Chew" pretty much describe the tone of the revue. It is difficult to say whether audiences remembered Wallis or they were just attracted by the show's title, but *Boobs!* managed to run nearly ten months.

THE THING ABOUT MEN

[27 August 2003, Promenade Theatre, 199 performances] a musical comedy by Joe DiPietro. *Score:* DiPietro (lyrics), Jimmy Roberts (music). *Cast:* Marc Kudisch, Leah Hocking, Ron Bohmer, Daniel Reichard, Jennifer Simard.

Jimmy Roberts and Joe DiPietro, who had wallowed in clichés in the long-running *I Love You, You're Perfect, Now Change*, had less commercial success but came up with this much better musical because they had specific characters to musicalize rather than generalities. The self-centered, high-achieving ad executive Tom Ambrose (Marc Kudisch) has money, power, and a mistress, but he is deflated when he finds out his wife Lucy (Leah Hocking) is having an affair with the bohemian artist Sebastian (Ron Bohmer). When the penniless Sebastian posts some flyers looking for a roommate to share his filthy downtown apartment, Tom moves in with revenge on his mind; instead the two egotistical men bond even though they are opposites in many ways. Tom realizes that Sebastian really loves Lucy, so he helps the scruffy artist to get a job as a creative director at his firm, turning the free-spirited slob into a slick Madison Avenue executive. Lucy is not thrilled with the transformation, and Tom and Lucy end up back together. The libretto, based on the 1985 German film *Männer* (*Men*), was filled with implausible plot twists and awkward shifts in character, but there was also something likable about this tale of unlikable people. Much of the credit was probably due to the sparkling performances by the three principals (and the felicitous work by Jennifer Simard and Daniel Reichard as all the supporting characters) who managed to make such self-absorbed people fun. The score for *The Thing about Men* was a mixed bag, the vibrant music often overshadowing the prosaic lyrics.

Still there was much to enjoy in such expositional numbers as the opening "Oh, What a Man!" and the first act finale "Downtown Bohemian Slum." The male duet "The Greatest Friend" revealed the vulnerable side to Tom and Sebastian, Lucy had a juicy tirade with "Because," and Tom's quiet torch song "The Better Man Won" was quite beguiling. *The Thing about Men* was first produced in Sacramento, California, then opened Off Broadway to some appreciative reviews. The musical ran seven months, and there were later productions in London and Australia.

LISTEN TO MY HEART: THE SONGS OF DAVID FRIEDMAN

[23 October 2003, Upstairs at Studio 54, 52 performances] a musical revue by David Friedman (music and lyrics), various (lyrics). *Cast:* Friedman, Alix Korey, Joe Cassidy, Michael Hunsaker, Allison Briner, Anne Runolfsson.

Songwriter David Friedman was far from a household name, but his legion of fans had been growing for some time, and this revue of his work pleased them and created new admirers. A noted Broadway conductor and music arranger of Disney animated musicals, Friedman had been writing songs for some time, and they were recorded by several notable singers, most memorably Nancy LaMott and Laurie Beechman, two beloved artists who died too young. Since many of Friedman's songs were optimistic ballads and messages of hope, the recordings by these two late singers made the songs resonate with emotion. The revue *Listen to My Heart* featured twenty-seven numbers, including such hopeful ballads as "Help Is on the Way," "We Can Be Kind," and the soaring title number. Yet Friedman's considerable range was also evident. There were the comic numbers "My Simple Wish," the selfish whining of an actress who wants to make it big without effort; "If You Love Me, Please Don't Feed Me," the hilarious lament of an overweight man to his kitchen-happy wife; and "I'm Not My Mother," the feisty complaint of a woman still trying to cut the apron strings. "He Comes Home Tired" was a beautiful picture of domestic serenity, "My White Knight" was a country-flavored salute to an ordinary man, "Two Different Worlds" was an entrancing love duet, and the heartbreaking "Catch Me" was the plea of a suicidal lost soul. The five performers who joined Friedman on stage were expert interpreters of character songs, and each one got to shine on several occasions. *Listen to*

My Heart: The Songs of David Friedman ran six and a half weeks, not nearly as long as his fans felt he deserved.

FAME ON 42ND STREET

[11 November 2003, Little Shubert Theatre, 264 performances] a musical play by José Fernandez based on the MGM film. *Score:* Steve Margoshes (music), Jacques Levy (lyrics). *Cast:* José Vegas, Christopher J. Hanke, Sara Schmidt, Nicole Leach, Q. Smith, Cheryl Freeman.

The 1980 film *Fame* has a long and troublesome history on the stage, and this retitled Off-Broadway version is probably not the end of the story. Set in Manhattan's High School of the Performing Arts over a four-year period, the popular movie wavered between a gritty, realistic look at show business and a romanticized "let's put on a show" musical. The young hopefuls struggle through auditions, classes, rehearsals, setbacks, family troubles, and sexual anxiety, every once in a while bursting into song and dance everywhere from the street to the cafeteria. The film was highly charged, joyfully noisy, and very engaging to younger moviegoers. Most of the songs were by Michael Gore (music) and Dean Pitchford (lyrics), the most memorable being "I Sing the Body Electric," "Red Light," and the explosive title number. *Fame* was one of the first films to employ digital audio on the soundtrack, and it was recorded onto a compact disc, two years before CDs were introduced. The long-running television series began in 1982, and *Fame* was hotter than ever. Broadway was the obvious next stop, but the creators of the stage version were only granted permission to use the title song, and the new score by Steve Margoshes and Jacques Levy paled in comparison to the earlier numbers. Broadway plans fell through, and *Fame* was not seen on a professional stage until the 1995 London production, which was poorly reviewed but was an audience favorite. With Broadway still not interested, a professional tour was launched in the States in 1999. Amateur rights had been available for some time, so it seemed like *Fame* was everywhere but New York City.

Fame on 42nd Street was basically the same show that Broadway had passed on. Over the years the trite songs and clumsy plotting stayed the same, and only a vibrant cast could bring the tired musical to life. The Off-Broadway mounting had some impressive individuals, most memorably Q. Smith, who belted "Mabel's Prayer" with verve, and veteran performer Cheryl Freeman who, as the teacher Ester Sherman, delivered the gospel number

"These Are My Children" with style. Much of the show was high energy and low quality, and notices were disapproving. Even with its confusing title, which led some to think the musical was a sequel, *Fame on 42nd Street* found an audience for eight and a half months.

CAROLINE, OR CHANGE

[30 November 2003, Public Theatre/Newman Theatre, 106 performances; Eugene O'Neill Theatre, 136 performances] a musical play by Tony Kushner. *Score:* Kushner (lyrics), Jeanine Tesori (music). *Cast:* Tonya Pinkins, Harrison Chad, Anika Noni Rose, Veanne Cox, David Costabile, Alice Playten, Reathel Bean, Larry Keith, Chuck Cooper.

The poetic, atmospheric, sung-through *Caroline, or Change* may have been lean on plot but was rich in characterization, and the bluesy score was sometimes intoxicating. Playwright Tony Kushner, who had penned *Angels in America* and other provocative plays, wrote the autobiographical libretto and the resplendent lyrics. Composer Jeanine Tesori, whose work ranged from the dark *Violet* to the sunny *Thoroughly Modern Millie*, wrote the masterful music which incorporated 1960s pop, classic blues, Jewish folk, and touches of gospel. Score, story, and characters blended together in a thrilling manner, making *Caroline, or Change* the finest musical to come from Off Broadway in quite some time.

The African American servant Caroline Thibodeaux (Tonya Pinkins) does the laundry in the basement of the Jewish Gellman family home in Louisiana in the early 1960s, finding companionship with her singing washing machine and with the young Noah Gellman (Harrison Chad) who idolizes her. The divorced Caroline has her own children to worry about, one in Vietnam, the teenage Emmie (Anika Noni Rose) running around with radical ideas, and the younger ones always needing something she cannot afford. On the day President Kennedy is assassinated, the Gellman family is in shock, but the Thibodeaux kids feel it has nothing to do with them. Noah's stepmother Rose (Veanne Cox), in her efforts to help the moody boy gain responsibility, tells Caroline she can keep any loose change he forgets to take out of his pockets, and soon Noah is helping the Thibodeaux family by purposely leaving money in clothes sent down to the laundry. But the relationship between Caroline and Noah is forever changed when he accidentally leaves a $20 bill given to him by his grandfather (Larry Keith) in his pocket, and she insists it is hers to keep. At the same time the friction between Caroline and Emmie explodes, and Caroline's frustration with her life pushes her to turn a corner and learn to live with sorrow. The musical numbers were more extended musical scenes than songs, yet there were many memorable moments that stood out, such as the lilting "Moon Change," the powerful soliloquy "Lot's Wife," the childlike ditty "Roosevelt Pertrucius Coleslaw," the weary plea "Gonna Pass Me a Law," the soulful "Underwater," the self-mocking "The Chanukah Party," the musical phone call "Long Distance," and the haunting duet "Noah Go to Sleep." Yet as proficient as each number was on its own, it was the way the whole show moved to the heartbeat of the score that made *Caroline, or Change* so scintillating. Some critics carped about the details, but the reviews were mostly enthusiastic and unanimously extolled Pinkins's unsentimental, compelling performance. She was given able support by a uniformly superb cast, even the demanding role of young Noah given a stinging, unsentimental portrayal by Harrison Chad. The George C. Wolfe–directed production did brisk business at the Public Theatre during its thirteen-week run, so the fateful decision to transfer to Broadway was made. In retrospect it was not a propitious move. *Caroline, or Change* had difficulty finding an audience and closed after seventeen weeks. The musical was better appreciated in Los Angeles and London with Pinkins reprising her fascinating Caroline, and later some ambitious regional theatres found success with it. Had the show remained Off Broadway, it is likely it would have run and run because it was the kind of musical that flourished on word of mouth, not critical acclaim. Regardless, *Caroline, or Change* was a marvel, and the American musical theatre is richer because of it.

THE MUSICAL OF MUSICALS—THE MUSICAL

[16 December 2003, Theatre at St. Peter's, 512 performances] a musical spoof by Eric Rockwell, Joanne Bogart. *Score:* Rockwell (music), Bogart (lyrics). *Cast:* Rockwell, Bogart, Lovette George, Craig Fols.

Along the lines of the *Forbidden Broadway* revues, this clever and prankish show went one step further by lampooning both the music and the lyrics of famous Broadway songwriters instead of just writing new words to familiar show tunes. *The Musical of Musicals—The Musical* also satirized the librettos of classic musicals by blending several works into one simple plot with dozens of variations. The evening consisted of five mini-musicals, each lampooning the style and subject matter of one artist or artistic team. The storyline was pretty much the same for all five entries: a heroine (Lovette George) is threatened by a villain (Eric Rockwell) but is supported by her matronly friend (Joanne Bogart) and saved by the hero (Craig Fols). The best spoof was the first one: *Corn!* a Rodgers and Hammerstein potpourri that mixed *Oklahoma!* and *Carousel* with tidbits from the team's other shows. With song titles like "Oh, What Beautiful Corn," "I Don't Love You," "So-Willy-Quey," and "Clam Dip," it was easy to pick out which songs were being ribbed. Yet each of these had original music that suggested Rodgers's style without actually copying it. Several of Stephen Sondheim's shows were jumbled together in *A Little Complex*, the villain being a Sweeney Todd-like George Seurat-like artist who murders people. Less satisfying were the Jerry Herman takeoff *Dear Abby!* and the Andrew Lloyd Webber spoof *Aspects of Juanita*. The former had the glitzy sound of *Mame* and *Hello, Dolly!* but such big, expressive shows were already over the top, and exaggerating them seemed repetitive. The Webber piece was more mean-spirited than the others, the jokes being more about the songwriter than the characters in his sung-through musicals. The evening ended with the more pleasing *Speakeasy*, a lampoon of Kander and Ebb's shows, mostly *Cabaret* and *Chicago*. Performer Rockwell composed the sly music, and co-actor Bogart wrote the slapstick lyrics. Both of them penned the silly librettos which were not afraid of musical theatre in-jokes and outrageous puns. All four performers, directed and choreographed by Pamela Hunt, had the vocal prowess to sing the songs with eager sincerity yet had a droll sense of farce. The York Theatre production, ran its scheduled five-week engagement, steadily building an audience along the way. Four months later the musical re-opened at the same venue and did brisk business for five more months. The space was needed for other productions, therefore *The Musical of Musicals–The Musical* transferred to a different Off-Broadway house and ran seven more months. Regional productions are not as frequent as one would expect for such a funny, economical revue. The weak title might be somewhat responsible for that. But the bigger problem is that the show assumes its audience knows these musicals, both famous and obscure, very well in order to fully appreciate the revue's incongruous sense of humor.

JOHNNY GUITAR

[23 March 2004, Century Center for the Performing Arts, 63 performances] a musical comedy by Nicholas van Hoogsstraten. *Score:* Joel Higgins (music and lyrics), Martin Silvestri (music). *Cast:* Steve Blanchard,

Ann Crumb, Judy McLane, Robert Evan, Ed Sala, Robb Sapp, Jason Edwards, David Sinkus, Grant Norman.

This musical version of the Joan Crawford cult film favorite *Johnny Guitar* (1954) turned the piece into a campy cowboy (and cowgirl) show, which was not much of a transition since the original movie was fairly ridiculous. What could have been a routine 1950s movie of Western romance went in strange directions and climaxed with a gunfight between Crawford and Mercedes McCambridge, a weird step forward for feminism on the prairie. The musical version didn't try to play it straight and, although it lacked the bizarre persona of Crawford, it was unpretentious fun. The former gunslinger Johnny Guitar (Steve Blanchard) returns to the Arizona cattle town where he once had a torrid affair with the sexy saloon keeper Vienna (Judy McLane). Johnny gets tangled up with the bandit The Dancin' Kid (Robert Evan), the sweetheart of the town's richest citizen, Emma Small (Ann Crumb). Soon the men take a backseat to the action, and Vienna and Emma fight it out in the grand tradition of the Old West. The score was a pleasant collection of cowboy ballads, hoedown numbers, and even a smattering of doo-woop thrown in to recreate the 1950s feel of the original. Vienna's "I am" song "Branded a Tramp" had a touch of rockabilly in it, Johnny's "A Smoke and a Good Cup of Coffee" was a philosophical folk song, and "Old Santa Fe" was a narrative ballad. The title song, sung by Vienna, had a Spanish feel to it, but the torchy cowboy lament "Tell Me a Lie" and the duet "We've Had Our Moments" were pure country. *Johnny Guitar* may have had limited appeal in New York, for even with some strong notices it lasted only eight weeks, but it has proven to be more popular outside of the city.

BARE

[19 April 2004, American Theatre of Actors, 43 performances] a musical play by Jon Hartmere Jr., Damon Intrabartolo. *Score:* Intrabartolo (music), Hartmere (lyrics). *Cast:* Michael Arden, John Hill, Jennifer Leigh Green, Aaron Lohr, Nadia Joy Johnson, Romelda Benjamin.

A musical about a teen coming of age, which proudly billed itself as "a pop opera," was dismissed as pretentious drivel by most of the critics, but *bare* refuses to fade away and has built quite a following with young audiences and young performers. At a Catholic boarding school, the class whiz Jason (Michael Arden) and fellow altar boy John (John Hill) have closeted feelings for each other, but both hide their love because of the homophobia at school. When the drama teacher Sister Chantelle (Romelda Benjamin) casts both boys in the drama club production of *Romeo and Juliet*, Jason is attracted to Ivy (Jennifer Leigh Green), the promiscuous teen playing Juliet. After a lot of soul searching, Jason sleeps with Ivy, and when she gets pregnant, he goes on a drug binge, actually dying on stage after delivering Mercutio's Queen Mab speech. This purple melodrama hit every adolescent pitfall from sexual identity to overeating; Jason's sister Nadia (Natalie Joy Johnson) is not cast as Juliet because she's too fat. The pop-rock songs were neither memorable nor awful, filled with meaningful lyrics and plenty of chances to do some *American Idol* belting. "Touch My Soul" was the routine love song for the heterosexual couple, "Are You There?" was the just as familiar duet for the gay couple, "One" was an anthem about individuality, the title song was the climactic number about baring your soul, and the show ended with the hymn "No Voice." The musical had first been presented in Los Angeles then ran five weeks Off Broadway. The producers announced that it was pursuing plans to present *bare* on Broadway, but they never materialized. Once the very similar and more powerful *Spring Awakening* opened a year later Off Broadway and *did* move to the Street, *bare* was made available to amateur groups. The score was recorded in 2007, and the show's fan base grew, resulting in many productions regionally.

NEWSICAL

[7 October 2004, Upstairs at Studio 54, 215 performances] a musical revue by Rick Crom. *Score:* Crom (music and lyrics). *Cast:* Todd Alan Johnson, Kim Cea, Stephanie Kurtzuba, Jeff Skowron.

A topical revue that remained topical by continually updating its material, *Newsical* was satiric and mildly outspoken without ever being too upsetting. The targets were familiar, including famous names from George W. Bush to Martha Stewart, and hitting on topics that were currently or recently in the news. Song titles "Dubya, We Love You," "Felt Up at the Airport," "Arnold and the Kennedys," "America Online," "Prozac, Ritalin, Trim Spa," and "Nobody Messes with Liza" give away the whole show. Rick Crom wrote (and rewrote) the songs as well as the sketches, and the cast was complimented for its ability to impersonate the celebrities as well as perform the farcical songs. Enough reviewers and playgoers enjoyed *Newsical* to keep it running seven months, some even returning to see the updated material. When the show closed Off Broadway, it toured for quite a while and was a success. In 2009 a new version of *Newsical* subtitled "We Distort, You Decide" opened Off Broadway with a different cast and mostly new material. (Both versions ended with the touching ballad "Denial.") President Barack Obama was spoofed in "Yes We Can (But Not Just Yet)," Celine Dion's singing was lampooned, and there were plenty of jokes about Hillary Clinton and Sarah Palin. "Flu Shot" and "The Boy in the Balloon" hit upon very recent news, as was computer dating and the television reality couple "John and Kate." Reviews again were supportive, and audiences returned.

THE 25TH ANNUAL PUTNAM COUNTY SPELLING BEE

[7 February 2005, Second Stage Theatre, 48 performances; Circle in the Square, 1,136 performances] a musical comedy by Rachel Sheinkin. *Score:* William Finn (music and lyrics). *Cast:* Dan Fogler, Celia Keenan-Bolger, Jose Llana, Sarah Saltzberg, Jesse Tyler Ferguson, Lisa Howard, Derrick Baskin, Deborah S. Craig, Jay Reiss.

An intimate, small-scale musical that played comfortably at the Second Stage Off Broadway, the clever and touching little show seemed unlikely to succeed on Broadway, but it became a surprise hit all the same. The six finalists in the local spelling bee are an awkward bunch of young adolescents, some neglected by parents and others suffering from too much family. As they go through the elimination rounds, the characters break away from the bee and reveal aspects of themselves others do not see, from sexual frustration to yearning to be accepted. The talented cast not only played the adolescents winningly but sometimes doubled as parents and other adults. Rachel Sheinkin wrote the humorous libretto, and William Finn contributed the songs which ranged from the incongruous to the heartfelt. The overweight, overconfident William Barfee (Dan Fogler) revealed his unique memorization technique in "Magic Foot"; the boy scout Tripp Barrington (Jose Llana) blamed his lack of concentration on "My Unfortunate Erection"; the Asian whiz kid Gramery Park (Deborah S. Craig) proclaimed "I Speak Six Languages" but admitted she was sick and tired of always being the best at everything; the oddball Leaf Coneybear (Jesse Tyler Ferguson) had been led to believe "I'm Not That Smart" by his unconventional family, so he was pleasantly surprised when he did something right; the neglected Olive Ostrovsky (Celia Keenan-Bolger) sought recognition from her absent dad and clung to "My Friend, the Dictionary"; and mousy Logan Schwarzengrubeniere (Sarah Saltzberg) relentlessly tried to please her two fathers and sang of the pressure in "Woe Is Me." Other numbers, involving the adults running the spelling bee and the kids together were also estimable, particularly the chaotic "Pandemonium," the heartfelt "The I Love You Song," and recurring motifs such as "My Favorite Moment of the Bee" and the "Goodbye" refrain each time a contestant was eliminated. Part of the charm of the musical was seeing adults play the teens with dead-on accuracy and the use of some volunteers from the audience as fellow contestants. James Lapine directed the musical which had originated at the Barrington Stage Company in Massachusetts then played Off Broadway for six weeks before making the transfer to Broadway. After the propitious reviews came out, the box office slowly picked up, and the show ran more than three years. A tour and regional productions followed. *The 25th Annual Putnam County Spelling Bee* had such a strong libretto, leaving room for improvisation with the audience volunteers each performance, that Finn's songs were mostly overlooked. It is not a powerful score on the level of *A New Brain*, but the songs added a level to the characters that raised them up from stereotypes. In its own quiet way, it is a splendid set of songs, none of which could survive outside of the context of the musical, so they do not cross over and get performed as many of Finn's songs are.

ALTAR BOYZ

[1 March 2005, Dodger Stages, 2,032 performances] a musical revue by Kevin Del Aguila. *Score:* Gary Adler, Michael Patrick Walker (music and lyrics). *Cast:* Scott Porter, David Josefsberg, Ryan Duncan, Tyler Maynard, Andy Karl.

Another one-joke revue on the order of *Nunsense* that found many fans was this slick and artificial musical with enjoyable songs that said little but still entertained. The gimmick was Christian music sung by a very hip "boy band," a variation on the idea of nuns singing and dancing in the aforementioned show. The Altar Boyz were four hunks by the names of Matthew, Mark, Luke, and Juan, with the Jewish kid Abraham added for a laugh. The musical recreated the last concert on their "Raise the Praise" tour, and there was a machine on stage that measured the burdened souls in the audience. By singing and opening their hearts to the Lord and the assembled ones, the boys hoped to decrease that number of discontented souls in the house. The patter between songs was arch and forced, but the singing was fun, the quintet performing all the expected moves and harmonies of a boy group. So that the audience understood that this was satiric, the lyrics were filled with double entendres that the innocent boys supposedly didn't understand. Matthew (Scott Porter) sang "Something about You" about a girl he loves but refuses to have sex with until after marriage, his horny subtext clear to everyone but himself. Abraham (David Josefsberg) believed "Everybody Fits" as he sang about universal acceptance by God, but the song was really about how sex is the great equalizer. Even "Church Rulz" got a bit raunchy as rapid standing, sitting, and genuflecting led to an orgasm of sorts. Some numbers were more farcical than others, such as "The Calling" about Jesus contacting the boys on their cell phones. Other songs were straightforward gospel numbers or hymns, but choreographed to come across as anything but reverent. There was a touch of disco in "Rhythm in Me" and some rap in "The Miracle Song," proving that Christian faith comes in all forms. *Altar Boyz* originated at the 2004 New York Theatre Festival then opened Off Broadway the following year for a commercial run. Critical reaction was mixed, but the show was an immediate hit with audiences. In addition to its five-year-plus run in New York, there was a successful tour, international productions, and many regional mountings. Unlike *Nunsense*, no *Altar Boyz* sequels have yet materialized; but with the right kind of faith, anything is possible.

DESSA ROSE

[21 March 2005, Mitzi E. Newhouse Theatre, 80 performances] a musical play by Lynn Ahrens based on the book by Sherley Anne Williams. *Score:* Ahrens (lyrics) and Stephen Flaherty (music). *Cast:* La Chanze, Rachel York, Michael Hayden, Norm Lewis, William Parry, Rebecca Eichenberger, Kecia Lewis, Eric Jordan Young, Tina Fabrique.

Lynn Ahrens and Stephen Flaherty's musical play about two strong women in the antebellum South had as many characters, songs, episodes, flashbacks, and drama as their epic Broadway musical *Ragtime*, but it was enacted by a cast of twelve and staged by Graciela Daniele on a simple stage of wooden planks. *Dessa Rose* was an ambitious undertaking, to say the least, and it was received with modest admiration by the press who thought it flawed. Audiences who saw it at Lincoln Center embraced the difficult musical during its ten-week run, but the future of the show was overshadowed by the arrival of *The Color Purple* on Broadway later that year. The name recognition of Alice Walker's book and the greater accessibility of *The Color Purple* made it a hit, and *Dessa Rose* was soon forgotten. (Ironically, the marvelous actress-singer La Chanze played the central character in both musicals.) *Dessa Rose* was also taken from a novel. Sherley Anne Williams based her book on two actual women and put their stories together to tell a long and complex tale. The young African American Dessa Rose is involved in a slave rebellion and is condemned to die, but because she is pregnant, she is jailed until the baby is born. With the help of friends, she escapes and finds refuge at the farm of the white woman Ruth (Rachel York), a Charleston belle who has been abandoned by her husband. Ruth, who has an infant of her own, has started to take in runaway slaves. She hides Dessa Rose and, after her baby is born, nurses it when the sickly Dessa Rose is unable to. The fugitive slaves plot a complicated scheme with Ruth to pretend to be sold by the white woman at various auctions, raising money for freedom. The plan works for a while until Dessa Rose's past catches up with her and she is arrested. Ruth helps Dessa Rose escape again, and Dessa Rose goes out West to freedom. This chronology was narrated by Dessa Rose and Ruth in their eighties and was broken up with flashbacks and subplots about various men who try to love and/or rape each woman at different times in the story. *Dessa Rose* was not sung through, but there were over thirty separate songs that were interwoven into the narrative in an operatic way. Folk, gospel, blues, country, hymns, and Broadway ballads were all used in the lengthy score. "Fly Away" was a rousing gospel number, "Twelve Children" told of the ancestry and heritage of Dessa Rose's family, "In the Bend of My Arm" was a sensual love song, "Something of My Own" was Dessa Rose's yearning "I am" song, "At the Glen" was Ruth's contemplation of loneliness, "Just Over the Line" was a lively montage about the auctions, and "We Are Descended" opened and closed the musical by celebrating the strong women in one's history. It was a glorious score that was not fully appreciated until the cast recording was released. *Dessa Rose* has an uncertain future, but that does not diminish the value of what Ahrens and Flaherty created.

CAPTAIN LOUIE

[8 May 2005, Theatre at St. Peter's, 46 performances] a musical play by Anthony Stein. *Score:* Stephen Schwartz (music and lyrics). *Cast:* Jimmy

Dieffenbach, Ronny Mercedes, Brandon Michael Arrington, Alexio Barboza, Sara Kapner, Kelsey Fatebene.

This new Stephen Schwartz work was actually a revised version of a thirty-five-minute musical he wrote over two decades earlier for a children's theatre festival in New York. Based on Ezra Jack Keats's 1978 picture book *The Trip*, the musical *Captain Louie* explored the imagination of a lonely boy. Louie (Jimmy Dieffenbach) is, as his song states, the "New Kid in the Neighborhood" with no friends on Halloween to trick or treat with. His toy airplane suggests they take a trip together, so in Louie's mind they fly back to his old neighborhood where he meets up with old friends in Halloween costumes. Dressed as Captain Louie, he leads the gang into a spooky neighborhood to collect candy. A new kid named Julio (Ronny Mercedes), who Louis doesn't know, joins them, and by the end of Halloween night Louie has the courage to return home and make new friends in his neighborhood. Like most picture books, the artwork was more enticing than the plot, and the stage version recreated Keats's paper cutout look. Schwartz's score was a melodic delight, the songs not talking down to kids with simplistic music and juvenile lyrics. "Trick or Treat" was a bouncy gospel number, "Big Red Plane" and "Looza on the Block" were lite-rock with a salsa flavor, "Home Again" was an unsentimental ballad, "Shadows" was a vigorous tango, and the title song was a soaring pop anthem. It was perhaps the Schwartz score that is closest to his *Godspell* because of its innocence and unbridled enthusiasm for simple emotions. The new hour-long version of *Captain Louie* was first presented at the Kennedy Center in Washington then was booked by the York Theatre Company for six weeks Off Broadway. It was so well received that the musical reopened late in 2005 at the Little Shubert Theatre Off Broadway for another two weeks. A tour followed; then amateur rights were made available. Theatres across the country are slowly discovering this sunny family musical which is several notches above most children's theatre.

THE GREAT AMERICAN TRAILER PARK MUSICAL

[27 September 2005, Dodger Stages, 80 performances] a musical comedy by Betsy Kelso. *Score:* David Nehls (music and lyrics). *Cast:* Linda Hart, Shuler Hensley, Orfeh, Wayne Wilcox, Leslie Kritzer, Kaitlin Hopkins, Marya Grandy.

This musical farce had fun trashing the trailer park trash who inhabit North Florida's Armadillo Acres, playing off their lack of brains but overabundance of heart. Toll booth collector Norbert Garstecki (Shuler Hensley) is about to celebrate his twentieth wedding anniversary with his agoraphobic wife Jeannie (Kaitlin Hopkins) who is afraid to leave her trailer ever since their child was kidnapped years ago. Frustrated sexually (and in every other way), Norbert falls into a passionate affair with a newcomer to the trailer park, the stripper Pippi (Orfeh) who shows off at the local Litter Box Show Palace. Pippi's glue-sniffing ex-beau Duke (Wayne Wilcox) travels from Oklahoma looking for Pippi, who ran out on him. Jeannine finds out about Norbert and Pippi and refuses to leave her trailer even though a hurricane is heading to North Florida. Just as Pippi and Jeannine have it out with a cat fight, Duke arrives and, after some gunshots, a few surprise revelations, and a couple of reconciliations, the play ends happily for all. The uninspired plot was spiced up with some ribald dialogue and three female residents of Armadillo Acres (Leslie Kritzer, Linda Hart, and Marya Grandy) who serve as salty narrators and maintain the trailer park milieu and philosophy. The songs were mostly in the rockabilly style, the lyrics very countrified and the music maintaining a pop beat even in some of the ballads. "It Doesn't Take a Genius" was a rocking love song about recognizing love, "Flushed Down the Pipes" was a crusty lament of lost love using household metaphors, "Owner of My Heart" was a simple-minded torch song, the contrapuntal songs "But He's Mine" and "It's Never Easy" were in the cry-in-your-beer mode, "That's Why I Love My Man" was a list of all the disreputable qualities that disappear once the lights go out, and "This Side of the Tracks" opened and closed the show proudly describing the joys of trailer park culture. The score had no pretensions to be anything more than a set of tuneful, foul-mouthed songs. After all, how many theatre scores devote a whole song to "Road Kill"? *The Great American Trailer Park Musical* originated at the New York Musical Theatre Festival the year before. The Off-Broadway production boasted an accomplished cast who doubled on occasion, such as the women becoming the lusty males at the strip club. The reviews were mixed, and the musical managed to run ten weeks before enjoying a second and more successful life in the hinterlands.

FIVE COURSE LOVE

[16 October 2005, Minetta Lane Theatre, 70 performances] a musical comedy by Gregg Coffin. *Score:* Coffin (music and lyrics) *Cast:* Heather Ayers, John Bolton, Jeff Gurner.

An interesting plot premise and some playful pastiche songs made this evening of five mini-musicals quite enjoyable even if parts of it lagged. Each of the five scenes took place in a different restaurant in which love was given a run for its money in the musical style suggested by the locale. The uptight bachelor Matt goes to a sushi eatery to meet a blind date but discovers the place has been turned into a Texas Bar-B-Q house and the girl is a red-hot cowgirl. Sparks immediately fly, and the two are almost in the sack until it is learned she is waiting for a burly race car driver named Ken and he is at another table. At an Italian eatery, the gangster Gino has a clandestine meeting with Sophia, the wife of his mobster boss Nicky. When Nicky shows up in the parking lot, Sophia realizes Gino used her just so he can wipe out Nicky, so she shoots Gino dead. The headwaiter Heimlich at a restaurant in Germany is nervous when his secret lover Gretchen enters the haus to meet with her lover Klaus, whom Heimlich has also had an affair with. The two men go off together and leave the oversexed Gretchen in a stew. At a cantina in Mexico, the bandit Guillermo woos the virginal Rosalinda away from the steadfast Ernesto whose honest love cannot compete with Guillermo's fiery passion. The last scene was in an American diner in the 1950s where the waitress Kitty is reading romance novels, including the evening's previous four stories. She loves the thick-headed Clutch who does not catch on even after Kitty writes him an unsigned letter telling him to come to the diner to meet his mystery love. The frustrated Kitty is given romantic advice from Gino, Heimlich, and Guillermo, then Matt (from the first story) enters and the two of them quickly see true love in the eyes of the other. The five plots were little more than skits peopled by stereotypes, and some overstayed their welcome, but the musical came together nicely at the end and was worth the journey. The score consisted of unsubtle spoofs of different kinds of music: the Texas roadhouse was filled with country and western ditties, the Italian scene was a feverish Puccini opera, the German triangle was set to polka tunes, the Mexican tale was full of flaming flamenco melodies, and the diner was bobbing to early rock and roll. Gregg Coffin, who wrote the book, music, and lyrics, had a habit of sometimes stooping to easy jokes and blatant double entendres, but there were some winning moments along the way. The cowboy ballad "Morning Light" went beyond cliché, the triple song tarantella "If Nicky Knew" was quite clever, the Mexican ballad "Come Be My Love" and the Elvis-like crying ballad "It's a Mystery" were silly soaring duets, and the final "Love Looking Back At Me" eschewed pastiche and went right for the heart. Much of the fun in *Five Course Love* was watching the three very proficient performers (Heather Ayers, John Bolton, and Jeff Gurner) play fifteen very different characters, giving full voice to everything from opera to Grand Ole Opry. The show had originated at the GeVa Theatre in Rochester, New York, and after its two-month run Off Broadway it was produced by several other regional theatres.

SEE WHAT I WANNA SEE

[30 October 2005, Public Theatre/Anspacher Theatre, 41 performances] two musical plays by Michael John LaChiusa based on two short stories by Ryunosuke Akutagawa. *Score:* LaChiusa (music and lyrics). *Cast:* Idina Menzel, Marc Kudisch, Aaron Lohr, Henry Stram, Mary Testa.

BERNARDA ALBA

[6 March 2006, Mitzi E. Newhouse Theatre, 40 performances] a musical play by Michael John LaChiusa based on Garcia Lorca's play *The House of Bernarda Alba. Score:* LaChiusa (music and lyrics). *Cast:* Phylicia Rashad, Sally Murphy, Daphne Rubin-Vega, Judith Blazer, Saundra Santiago, Nikki M. James.

The ever-productive, ever-challenging songwriter Michael John LaChiusa had two new works produced Off Broadway during the 2005–2006 season, both of them equally demanding and thought-provoking. They also had unlikely sources (Japanese short stories and a Spanish classic drama) for musicals, which was nothing new for this unlikely artist.

See What I Wanna See consisted of two musicals based on prose pieces by the acclaimed short story writer Ryunosuke Akutagawa, most remembered for *Rashomon*. That famous tale was musicalized as *R Shomon* by LaChiusa and reset in 1951 New York where a man has been found murdered in Central Park. The Janitor (Henry Stram) who discovered the body tells the police he knows nothing of what happened. The Thief (Aaron Lohr) tells the police he knocked out the Husband (Marc Kudisch), raped his Wife (Idina Menzel), then went back to kill the Husband. When the Wife is interrogated, she tells her version of the story: after she was raped, she found her husband alive, and they decided to commit suicide together. She stabbed him but hadn't the courage to kill herself. Using a Medium (Mary Testa), the dead Husband tells his version: the promiscuous Wife seduced the Thief in front of the Husband then they left him, so the Husband committed suicide. Which version was the truth is left to the audience to decide. (The title came from the movie marquee near the park that advertised *Rashomon*, but the "a" was missing.)

The second part of the evening, *Gloryday*, was set in a rectory in contemporary New York City where a Priest (Stram) confesses to his superior about a hoax he has instigated. Questioning his faith and the very existence of God, the Priest decided to disillusion people about their beliefs. He left a written message in Central Park saying that Christ would appear at a certain time on a named date and reveal himself to the people. To his surprise, the Priests find thousands of people gathered in the park, and it becomes a media event. Among those gathered were his atheistic Aunt Monica (Testa), an actress (Menzel) with a drug problem, and an accountant (Kudisch) who has escaped from the world by living in the park. When the time for the appearance came, a sudden thunderstorm rose up and sent everyone scattering for shelter. Only the Priest remained to see a bright light appear over the lake, but no one believed him when he tried to tell them later. A lie has become the truth. Before each of these mini-musicals were scenes from Medieval Japan. The mistress Kesa (Menzel) prepares to murder her lover Morito (Kudisch) with a knife as soon as they finish making love. When the two characters reappear before *Gloryday*, Morito strangles Kesa to death during their lovemaking. LaChiusa's score was nearly sung through, with only bits of prose between and within the many songs. The lyrics were harsh and direct, using repetition and overlapping voices that surrounded the action. The music was jazz-influenced yet not a pastiche of classic themes of the past. The melodic lines were short, and the music was often as abrupt as the frantic thought patterns of the characters. Few songs stood out on their own, though the Janitor's "Best Not to Get Involved," Aunt Monica's "The Greatest Practical Joke," and the title number were striking and memorable. *See What I Wanna to See* met with the wildly mixed notices that were by now expected with any LaChiusa work. After the five-week run at the Public Theatre the musical was picked up by only the most adventurous theatre companies elsewhere.

Two months after *See What I Wanna See* closed, *Bernarda Alba* opened at Lincoln Center's Off-Broadway venue. Federico Garcia Lorca's *The House of Bernarda Alba* (1936) was considered the Spanish masterpiece of the twentieth century, but revivals in English were not frequent. LaChiusa's libretto, again mostly sung, did not deviate too radically from Lorca's play, even retaining the three-act structure. The harsh widow Bernarda Alba (Phylicia Rashad) vows to keep her five unmarried daughters in mourning and away from men. The handsome Pepe el Romano, who has stolen the heart of all the girls in their little Spanish village, tries to court Bernarda's eldest daughter Angustias (Saundra Santiago), but the stern mother confines Angustias, much against the warnings of her mother, the aged Maria Jospha (Yolande Bavan), and her faithful servant Poncia (Candy Buckley). Over time, the youngest daughter Adela (Nikki M. James) has been sneaking out of the house to meet with Pepe. When Bernarda decides to allow Pepe to become engaged to Angustias, Adela's jealousy and passion ignite. Pepe and Adela are caught making love by Adela's sister Martirio (Daphne Rubin-Vega) who informs her mother. Bernarda goes off with a shotgun to kill Pepe, and Martirio returns and lies to Adela, saying Pepe is dead. In grief, Adela hangs herself in her room, and Bernarda finds bitter satisfaction in telling the world that her daughter died a virgin. As expected, the score was very Spanish with variations of pounding flamenco, folk dirges, and lyrical ballads adding to the repressive atmosphere and the seething sexual frustration. Among the memorable numbers were the zesty work song "I Will Dream of What I Saw"; the ancient grandmother's "Lullaby" sung to an imaginary baby; the lilting ballad "Love, Let Me Sing to You"; the lusty narrative song "The Mare and the Stallion"; and the seething "Open the Door" about lovemaking. Critics were again of vastly differing opinions about LaChiusa and *Bernarda Alda*, but most extolled the powerhouse cast, particularly Rashad's fierce, gritty performance as the unbending matriarch. There were also many compliments for Graciela Daniele, who directed and choreographed the musical with grace and a firm hand. The five-week engagement at the Mitzi E. Newhouse Theatre played mostly to subscribers, and there was no demand for an extension or a move upstairs to the Broadway venue. Even more demanding than *See What I Wanna See*, *Bernarda Alba* has received a very limited number of regional productions.

I Love You Because

[14 February 2006, Village Theatre, 111 performances] musical play by Ryan Cunningham based on Jane Austen's *Pride and Prejudice*. *Score:* Cunningham (lyrics), Joshua Salzman (music). *Cast:* Colin Hanlon, Farah Alvin, Stephanie D'Abruzzo, David A. Austin, Jordan Leeds, Courtney Balan.

Although this "Modern Day Musical Love Story" claimed to be inspired by *Pride and Prejudice*, it offered none of Austen's characters, insight, or even plot. Instead it was a tiresome tale of two couples who slip in and out of romance and at the end of the evening are supposed to have grown. The authors reversed the gender of Austen's two main characters and retained parts of their names; since these people had nothing in common with Austen's, it was a senseless change. Would-be poet Austin Bennett (Colin Hanlon) makes his living writing verse for greeting cards and is distraught when he finds his girlfriend unfaithful. His slob of a brother Jeff (David A. Austin) encourages him to play the field and sets up a double blind date. Austin and the flighty photographer Marcy Fitzwilliams (Farah Alvin) don't hit it off and spend two acts telling each other why they don't like each other before deciding they do. Jeff has a more sensual relationship with the insurance actuary Diana Bingsley (Stephanie D'Abruzzo), but they also quarrel on and off until they give in to a happy ending. The libretto was filled with empty dialogue and painfully familiar scenes. The songs were a bit better, using pop-rock most of the time and even slipping into doo-wop on occasion, which made it seem far from "modern." "The Actuary Song" was a fun list number, "Just Not Now" was a tearful ballad, "Because of You" was an up-tempo love song, and the title number listed their faults and reasons why Marcy and Austin should not be in love but they were. Mixed notices did not matter because *I Love You Because* soon got a reputation for being a nonthreatening date evening, so it ran fourteen weeks. Productions in Britain and Australia were followed by American regional theatres which were looking for another *I Love You, You're Perfect, Now Change.*

GREY GARDENS

[6 March 2006, Playwrights Horizons, 63 performances; Walter Kerr Theatre, 307 performances] a musical play by Doug Wright suggested by the documentary film. *Score:* Scott Frankel (music), Michael Korie (lyrics). *Cast:* Christine Ebersole, Mary Louise Wilson, Sara Gettelfinger, John McMartin, Matt Cavanaugh, Bob Stillman, Michael Potts.

Few musicals early in the new century met with such decidedly contrasting reviews as this intriguing show based on a cult documentary film. Audiences were similarly divided on the merits of *Grey Gardens* but on one point everyone agreed: Christine Ebersole gave a wacky, moving, indelible performance. The Maysles brothers' 1973 movie is a fascinating portrait of the formerly wealthy Edith Bouvier Beale and her oddball daughter Edie who lived in squalor in a decaying Long Island mansion named Grey Gardens. The two Beales seemed unphased by the camera as they recalled old times, philosophized about life, and quarreled with each other. It is a funny and pathetic film that once seen is not easily forgotten. It is also a very unlikely prospect for a play no less a musical since it has no plot. Doug Wright's libretto used the movie as a jumping off point for a story told at two points in the Beales' lives. In 1941, the society darling Edith (Ebersole) is throwing an elegant party at Grey Gardens to celebrate the engagement of her debutante daughter Edie (Sara Gettelfinger) to Joseph P. Kennedy Jr. (Matt Cavenaugh). Edith has planned to sing a repertoire of song favorites to entertain the guests, causing one of the many rifts between mother and daughter. The party is ruined when Edith's husband telegrams to say he is getting a divorce, the scandal quickly snuffing out the Kennedy engagement. The second act took place in the dilapidated mansion in 1973, the year the two women were captured on film. The aged Edith (Mary Louise Wilson) and the middle-aged, unmarried Edie (Ebersole) still have a love-hate relationship as they dig up the past, toss recriminations back and forth, and disagree on almost everything. Edie makes an effort to leave Grey Gardens, but she can get no farther than the garden gate, trapped like her mother in a private world that has left them separated from the real world. There was still little plot, but seeing the characters at two very different times had a dramatic pull. Some critics described the insightful character study as Chekhovian; others said *Grey Gardens* went nowhere. Notices were more favorable regarding the score by Scott Frankel and Michael Korie. The first act was filled with marvelous pastiche songs, some continuing the story and others part of Edith's repertoire. "The Five-Fifteen" was a clever exposition number, "Better Fall Out of Love" was a witty duet for Edie and Joe Kennedy, "Drift Away" was a flowing Cole Porter-like number sung by Edith's pianist George Gould Strong (Bob Stillman), and "Being Bouvier" was a merry march by Edie's grandfather J. V. "Major" Bouvier (John McMartin). The songwriters were equally adept at writing songs that might have been popular in the 1940s: the unintentionally racist "Hominy Grits," the chummy duet "Peas in a Pod," and the intoxicating operetta aria "Will You." The second act included some numbers that echoed the past, as the patriotic march "The House We Live In" and the gospel revival piece "Choose to Be Happy." But most of the 1973 songs were character numbers that, like the documentary, showed the sad as well as the farcical side of these two eccentric women. The oddly touching "Jerry Likes My Corn," the hilarious fashion lesson "The Revolutionary Costume for Today," the haunting "Around the World," and the piercing song of disillusionment "Another Winter in a Summer Town" were compelling theatre numbers, and Frankel and Korie were quickly regarded as songwriters to watch. Although the critical and popular reaction to the musical was not strong enough to warrant an extension after the two-month run at Playwrights Horizons, the cheers for Ebersole's dynamic double performance encouraged the producers to try and turn *Grey Gardens* into a Broadway hit. The authors reworked parts of the script and made some changes in the score, cutting five songs and adding three new ones. The relationship between Edie and Joe was strengthened as was the placement of the grandfather in the story. With the recasting of young Edie and larger and more elaborate sets, *Greg Gardens* opened six months later on Broadway where it still met with mixed notices except for further unanimous adulation for Ebersole. Her performance allowed the musical to survive on Broadway for a little over nine months. Commentators disagreed about whether the show was better Off or on Broadway. The intimacy of the Playwrights Horizons' venue was a plus, but the libretto and score were stronger on Broadway. (Since each production was recorded, it is possible for theatregoers to listen and decide for themselves.) *Grey Gardens* would receive several regional productions, usually in spaces that were not too large, and be very well received. So perhaps it remains an Off-Broadway show after all.

SPRING AWAKENING

[15 June 2006, Linda Gross Theatre, 54 performances; Eugene O'Neill Theatre, 595 performances] a musical play by Steven Sater based on the play by Frank Wedekind. *Score:* Sater (lyrics), Duncan Sheik (music). *Cast:* Jonathan Groff, John Gallagher Jr., Lea Michele, Frank Wood, Mary McCann, Lauren Pritchard, Jonathan B. Wright, Gideon Glick, Lilli Cooper.

An expressionistic musical about the perils of adolescence, the powerful piece was lauded as new and daring when both the story and the style were both over one hundred years old. The young teenagers in a nineteenth-century German town are sexually confused, sexually ignorant, or just sexually charged as their strict upbringing adds to the tension. It drives the academically weak student Moritz (John Gallagher Jr.) to suicide and leads the nonconformist Melchior (Jonathan Groff) and the too-innocent Wendla (Lea Michele) into a sexual liaison that leaves her pregnant and has him sent away to a reformatory. She dies during a botched abortion, and Melchior is left haunted and comforted by the ghosts of Moritz and Wendla. Steven Sater's libretto closely followed Frank Wedekind's 1891 expressionistic drama; so close it was nearly a word-for-word translation that stopped abruptly for songs. In the Brechtian manner, the songs did nothing to continue the plot and only rarely helped develop the characters. True to expressionism, everything was blunt, obvious, and unrealistic. What was most interesting in this musicalization of Wedekind was how the show retained a period look and feel in the book scenes but burst into rock with handheld microphones for the musical numbers. As directed by Michael Mayer, the contrast was far from confusing, but rather vivid and unique. Unfortunately the songs disappointed, and *Spring Awakening* was one of the few musicals to lose its power every time the score interrupted. Duncan Sheik's music found plenty of variety while sticking to a rock mode. The ballads were fluid and the more propulsive rock numbers had more than just beat to them. It was the lyrics (also by Sater) that embarrassed, filled as they were with clichés, repetition, and very unoriginal drivel. Just the song titles "The Word of Your Body," "The Mirror-Blue Night," "The Dark I Know Well," and "The Song of Purple Summer" were hints that this was lyric writing on a pretentious and hollow level. The repeated phrases in "The Bitch of Living," "Totally Fucked," and others were numbing, and only the vibrant music and staging kept the audience from concentrating on how empty the words were. But, as has often happened in the past, weak lyrics did not stop a musical from being a frequently exhilarating experience. Mayer's direction, having the cast, band, and some of the audience surround the action as it leaped from period drama to contemporary rock, and the few but memorable dances choreographed by Bill T. Jones were the true strengths behind the show. The Atlantic Theatre Company production also boasted a young but impressive cast who managed to pull off both the Wedekind scenes and the modern musical numbers. The Off-Broadway production was so well received by the press and the public that it was slightly retooled and sent to Broadway. The original set was enlarged, but the concept of the staging remained the same. The two actors who played all the adult characters were recast with Broadway veterans Stephen Spinella and Christine Estabrook, but the rest of the ensemble remained the same. Notices were again favorable, but box office business was sluggish at first. Yet as word of mouth spread, the musical gradually became very popular, especially with young audiences, and it ran a year and a half. Those critics who foolishly declared *Spring Awakening* to be an innovative breakthrough in musical theatre were uninformed of the past, but there was something so exciting about the show that it was easy to see how one might think this was so. Expressionism and musicals go way back together. *Peggy-Ann*, *Lady in the Dark*, *Company*, *Tommy*, *Jelly's Last Jam*, and many others successfully used expressionism. That does not detract from *Spring Awakening*, but it does put things in perspective.

[TITLE OF SHOW]

[20 July 2006, Vineyard Theatre, 84 performances; Lyceum Theatre, 102 performances] a musical comedy by Hunter Bell. *Score:* Jeff Bowen (music and lyrics). *Cast:* Bell, Bowen, Heidi Blickenstaff, Susan Blackwell.

Off-Broadway musicals based on bad ideas were nothing new, but the saucy little *[title of show]* earned the distinction of being the first musical based on no idea at all. To some theatregoers this was an exciting breakthrough in originality; for others it was a new low for Off Broadway. When Hunter Bell and Jeff Bowen wanted to come up with a new musical to submit to the New York Musical Theatre Festival in 2004, they decided to write about writing a new musical for the New York Musical Theatre Festival. They wrote about themselves and their dreams of having a hit on Broadway. With the help of two actresses, Susan Blackwell and Heidi Blickenstaff who played themselves, the four wrote and rehearsed a musical about them writing and rehearsing a musical. When they needed a title for it all, they just used the field [title of show] on the submission form as their title. This was all very clever or terribly irritating, depending on your point of view. The dialogue was so conversational that it bordered on the banal, both admirers and detractors comparing it to an unedited documentary. The songs stretched to come up with reasons to exist, but they were often enjoyable in an idle, meandering way. "What Kind of Girl Is She?" was a funny competitive female duet; "Die Vampire, Die" was a mocking view of self-doubts; "Secondary Characters" was the satiric lament of the two overlooked actresses who bonded together; and there was a touch of sincerity in the ballad "A Way Back to Then." Like the script, the lyrics often wallowed in theatre in-jokes and other showbiz references. Both "Two Nobodies in New York" and "Part of It All" listed all the things that fame could bring, both "An Original Musical" and "Monkeys and Playbills" were lists of flop musicals that rhymed, and "Nine People's Favorite Things" was an embarrassing plea to be loved just for being different. *[title of show]* was picked up by the New York Musical Theatre Festival Off Off Broadway for three weeks in 2004 then was produced two years later Off Broadway. Critics either loved it or loathed it, and audiences came to see for themselves. After doing healthy business for ten weeks, the producers made the audacious choice to move *[title of show]* to a Broadway house. Some critics who liked it before and saw it again were less impressed this time around (some had already reviewed it twice), and the show had a lot of trouble finding an audience. After playing to mostly empty houses for three months, *[title of show]* closed. Should it have stayed Off Broadway? Or even Off Off Broadway? Probably, because such a slim joke got less funny the more it moved up in the world.

SHOUT!

[27 July 2006, Julia Miles Theatre, 157 performances] a musical revue by Phillip George, David Lowenstein, Peter Charles Morris. *Score:* various.

Cast: Carole Shelley, Erin Crosby, Marie-France Arcilla, Casey Clark, Erica Schroeder.

A pleasing bit of nostalgic fluff from England, *Shout!* was subtitled "The Mod Musical" and celebrated the British pop songs of the 1960s. Six English "birds" in Swinging London act out the magazine *Shout!*, which covers the music and style of the day. The revue used a magazine format complete with letters asking for advice, true confessions, advertisements, fashion tips, and some twenty hit songs. The catalogue consisted mostly of songs introduced by female stars, such as "Downtown," "The Look of Love," "Goldfinger," "I Couldn't Live without Your Love," "Alfie," " Georgy Girl," and the title number. The songs were not only sung in the Sixties pop style, but the dancing, clothes, and hairstyles were also revived with panache. *Shout!* had been a hit in London, but it was rewritten and revised for Off Broadway, making sure the expressions were not too foreign and that the ads made sense. The press found the revue enjoyable if not exceptional, but word of mouth was strong enough to keep *Shout!* on the boards for twenty weeks. The musical has received some regional productions and is still being discovered by theatre groups in America.

EVIL DEAD: THE MUSICAL

[1 November 2006, New World Stages, 126 performances] a musical spoof by George Reinblatt based on the three *Evil Dead* movies. *Score:* Reinblatt (music and lyrics), Frank Cipolla, Christopher Bond, Melissa Morris (music). *Cast:* Ryan Ward, Jennifer Bryne, Darryl Winslow, Brandon Wardell, Jenna Coker, Renee Klapmeyer, Tom Walker, Ryan Williams.

A popular cult movie series became a modest Off-Broadway cult musical that, if nothing else, held the record for murders, dismemberment, and blood on the New York musical stage. The *Evil Dead* horror flicks first came upon the scene in 1981 and immediately became a favorite of moviegoers seeking plenty of gore, crude humor, and a bit of sex thrown in for good measure. The stage version combined the plots and characters from several films, so it was action packed to the point of ridiculous confusion. The first few rows of the theatre were labeled the "splatter zone," and patrons who sat there were guaranteed to be showered with stage blood. (Ponchos were sold as well as white T-shirts that read "I Survived the Splatter Zone" and were worn to pick up some souvenir blood.) The spirit of the three films was definitely alive in the musical. College student Ash (Ryan Ward), who works as a housewares salesman at S-Mart, and his girlfriend Linda (Jennifer Byrne) drive out into the Canadian wilderness with some oddball friends and hangers-on to break into a cabin for a weekend of booze and sex. They discover a Book of the Dead in an abandoned hut, and soon trees are attacking the girls, humans are turning into demons, guns and axes are employed, and body parts go flying. At one point in the action, Ash is the only nondemon left, so when his hand starts acting strangely, he cuts it off with a chain saw. Others arrive at the cabin, dead characters return to life, and the Book of the Dead is finally used to put the dead to rest. Back at S-Mart, Ash tells of his weekend adventures, but no one at the store believes him until a female demon attacks and Ash blows her away with a rifle from the sporting goods department. The rock score, filled with repetition and shouting, was just as subtle as the libretto, the lyrics blatant and obvious and the music pounding away unrelentlessly. Most of the songs were daffy reflections on what was going on, such as "What the Fuck Was That?" and "All the Men in My Life Keep Getting Killed by Canadian Demons." Other numbers were used to give voice to the "deadites" and other critters, such as "Do the Necronomicon," "Join Us," and "Look Who's Evil Now." All in all, it was a loud and silly score that served as a noisy soundtrack behind all the action. After early productions in Toronto and Montreal, *Evil Dead* opened Off Broadway and was immediately embraced by fans of the three movies. Unfortunately they only kept the musical alive for four months. But like the Canadian demons on stage and screen, *Evil Dead* lives on in little theatres across Canada and the States, not to mention Tokyo and Seoul.

GUTENBERG! THE MUSICAL!

[21 January 2007, Actors Playhouse, 126 performances] a musical comedy by Scott Brown, Anthony King. *Score:* Brown, King (music and lyrics). *Cast:* Christopher Fitzgerald, Jeremy Shamos.

A clever spoof of big empty Broadway musicals fraught with heavy themes, *Gutenberg! The Musical!* struck most critics and audiences as a wickedly funny musical that played on different levels. Unknown authors Bud Davenport (Christopher Fitzgerald) and Doug Simon (Jeremy Shamos) hold a backer's audition for their new megamusical *Gutenberg!*, hoping to interest a Broadway producer and investors. Since they have no money to pay actors and musicians, Bud and Doug play all thirty roles themselves, changing hats with the characters' names on them. The duo not only do all the dialogue for the ridiculous musical but also sing all the songs and make comments on how the piece was created. The plot of their show is ludicrous and pretentious. Winemaker Gutenberg turns his winepress into the first printing press, but he is opposed by an evil monk who wants to keep the people of fifteenth-century Germany illiterate. There was an incongruous love plot between Gutenberg and his faithful sweetheart Helvetica, as well as funny incidental characters, including a rabidly anti-Semitic little girl. (The authors explained that she foreshadowed the Holocaust, and her presence gave their musical the necessary "important issue" needed on Broadway.) As Bud and Doug presented their show with unabashed pride and enthusiasm, they also revealed aspects of their own lives that added to the merriment, including an unrequited love one has for the other. The songs in *Gutenberg!* were on the grand scale of Broadway pop operas with banal lyrics, catchy tunes that repeated endlessly, and theatrics ripe for spectacle and special effects. (At one point the two authors simulated a long chorus line with a series of hats on a clothesline.) Some of the numbers offered clichéd German music, as in the spooky "Haunted German Wood" and the idiotically happy "Festival." Others were in the form of heartbreaking character laments, as in Helvetica's "I Can't Read," and of course there were the stirring empty anthems such as "Tomorrow Is Tonight" and the "Finale," which encouraged everyone to "eat dreams." Observing a farcical performance of a delightfully dreadful musical was pleasure enough, but the ingenious staging by Alex Timber and the achingly sincere performances by Fitzgerald and Shamos were the icing on the cake. *Gutenberg! The Musical!* had quite a track record before it opened Off Broadway. It had begun as a forty-five minute piece presented Off Off Broadway in 2005 that found an audience for a whole year. A two-act version was seen in London and for two summers at the New York Musical Theatre Festival before the musical opened at the Actors' Playhouse to encouraging reviews. Its run of sixteen weeks has been followed by many regional productions across America and overseas.

IN THE HEIGHTS

[8 February 2007, 37 Arts Theatre, 181 performances; Richard Rodgers Theatre, 1,185 performances] a musical play by Quiara Alegría Hudes.

Score: Lin-Manuel Miranda (music and lyrics). *Cast:* Miranda, Mandy Gonzalez, Christopher Jackson, Karen Olivo, Olga Merediz, Priscilla Lopez, Andrea Burns, Robin De Jesus.

In the Heights was the first Hispanic musical to find success with mainstream audiences. It was not a radical or preachy show, but a sweetly gentle one that had loving characters (and no villains) and celebrated the close-knit Latino culture with story, song, and dance. In fact, it was a very old-fashioned musical in many ways, but its character and sound were unique. During a heat wave in a Hispanic neighborhood of Washington Heights, the bodega owner Usnavi (Lin-Manuel Miranda) and his friends all dream of a better life. Usnavi hopes to one day return to his native island of the Dominican Republic, his girlfriend Vanessa (Karen Olivo) wants to live in Manhattan, Nina (Mandy Gonzalez) wants to return to college even though she has lost her scholarship, Usnavi's African American friend Benny (Christopher Jackson) wants a promotion in his dead-end job, and the aged Abuela Claudia (Olga Merediz), a Cuban who raised Usnavi, buys lottery tickets thinking that money will cure all woes. During a power outage, Nina and Benny spend the night together, which infuriates her family because Benny is not Latino. Abuela Claudia wins the lottery, and she and Usnavi plan to sell the bodega and move to the Dominican Republic because he has broken up with Vanessa. But that night Abuela Claudia dies in her sleep, and Usnavi realizes that the Washington Heights neighborhood is his real home, and he decides to stay. Nina returns to college, Benny strikes out in his own business, and the local graffiti artist Pete (Seth Stewart) paints a mural of Abuela Claudia on Usnavi's bodega. It was a loose and uneventful plot, but it provided plenty of opportunity to develop the various characters and easily led to singing and dancing. The score for *In the Heights* was very contemporary Hispanic with a lot of rap, though not the angry or abrasive rap one might expect in a musical about a struggling people. The title number, which introduced the setting and major characters, provided exposition in a sly and merry manner, Vanessa's eager "I am" song "It Won't Be Long Now" had a florid Caribbean sound, "No Me Diga" was a sassy gossip number, "Breathe" was a lilting homecoming ballad, "Paciencia Y Fe (Patience and Faith)" was Abuela Claudia's restless memory of Cuba, "Sunrise" was a bilingual love duet, "Carnaval del Barrio" was a fiery ensemble number filled with sexual tension, and "When the Sun Goes Down" was a flowing farewell song. (The lyrics, like the libretto, used Spanish frequently, but there was never any question about the meaning.) The songs naturally led to dance, and the musical often moved like a carnival celebration. Yet the most impressive aspect of the show was its open-hearted humanity. It was about family, and the warmth of the people portrayed was contagious. Lin-Manuel Miranda, who wrote the score, had been working on the musical ever since he was in college, and it went through many revisions until Quiara Alegría Hudes was brought in to strengthen the libretto. His performance as Usnavi held the loosely plotted show together, but he received strong support from a gifted cast. Also of note was the vibrant choreography by Andy Blankenbuehler. Reviews for the Off-Broadway production were so exemplary that after six months *In the Heights* moved to Broadway without losing any of its power. Its long run is a testament to the wide appeal of the musical, playing to all kinds of audiences and charming all of them.

ADRIFT IN MACAO

[13 February 2007, 59E59 Theatre, 24 performances] a musical spoof by Christopher Durang. *Score:* Durang (lyrics), Peter Melnick (music). *Cast:* Will Swenson, Michele Ragusa, Alan Campbell, Orville Mendoza, Rachel De Benedet, Jonathan Rayson, Elisa Van Duyne.

This *film noir* send-up set in a smoky nightclub in the Orient was slyly written and performed, but the musical spoof had trouble sustaining itself over the course of a full evening. All the same, there was much to enjoy in *Adrift in Macao*, and it boasted an expert score. Rick Shaw (Will Swenson) is the proprietor of a nightclub in Macao, China, where various underworld figures mingle with tourists, and murder and intrigue are never far away. The ravishing American Lureena (Rachel de Benedet) is stuck in the foreign city with nothing but the slinky evening gown she is wearing, so she gets a job singing world-weary ballads at the club even though she doesn't know the lyrics. Another American, Mitch (Alan Campbell), is running away from a trumped-up murder charge and is involved with the club's other singer, the drug-addict Corinna (Michele Ragusa), but he is drawn to the alluring Lureena. Everyone in Macao is trying to contact the secret Mr. McGuffin, and the mysterious Chinaman Tempura (Orville Mendoza) promises Rick and Mitch to lead them to the powerful crime boss. After a double cross, a chase, and an ambush, it is revealed that Tempura is really the Irishman McGuffin, and he escapes. The two girls get jobs singing in a Bangkok and Manhattan club respectively, and everyone reappears for the finale, which is a daffy sing-along. The dialogue was ridiculously clichéd, and the meandering plot never went anywhere, but the score was a treat and helped audiences get to the incongruous ending. Comic playwright Christopher Durang wrote both book and lyrics, and they were consistently witty, employing far-fetched rhymes, silly lists, and tongue-twisting double talk. Peter Mednick composed the sprightly music which was much better than mere pastiche. Melnick is the grandson of Richard Rodgers (and cousin to Adam Guettel), and more than one review pointed out the Rodgers-like melodic line in some of the songs. "In a Foreign City (in a Slinky Dress)" and "Grumpy Mood" made up the hilarious opening number that introduced Lureen and Mitch; "Sparks" was a swinging number about sexual attraction; "Tempura's Song" was a snarling list song about how awful Americans were; "Pretty Moon Over Macao" was the atmospheric ballad that became a farce when Lureen tried to make up the lyrics she couldn't remember; "Mambo Malaysian" was a ludicrous mix of tango, mambo, and Asian sounds; and the title song was both languid and spirited. Best of all was the sing-along number "Ticky Ticky Tock" with its contagious rhythmic bounce and farcical lyric filled with ingeniously eccentric rhymes. But a sparkling score could not save *Adrift in Macao* with its thin sketchlike libretto. After early productions at Vassar College and in Philadelphia, the musical was given a three-week engagement by Primary Stages Off Broadway. There was no demand for an extension, but regional theatres have discovered *Adrift in Macao*, and its cunning score will not be forgotten.

PASSING STRANGE

[14 May 2007, Public Theatre/Anspacher Theatre, 56 performances; Belasco Theatre, 165 performances] a musical play by Stew. *Score:* Stew (music and lyrics), Heidi Rodewald (music). *Cast:* Stew, Daniel Breaker, De'Adre Aziza, Eisa Davis, Colman Domingo, Chad Goodridge, Rebecca Naomi Jones.

During its Off-Broadway and Broadway runs, *Passing Strange* got the reputation for being the musical for people who didn't like musicals. This was a dubious compliment, but it explained that *Passing Strange* was not going to do what musicals usually did. Yet it was very satisfying musical theatre in its way. The rock singer-songwriter Stew was the first to admit that he didn't write show tunes. He couldn't, and he didn't want to. *Passing Strange* began as *Stew's Travelogue (of Demonically Energized Souls)* with just Stew sitting in a club singing his songs and telling his own story without traditional scenes or supporting characters. As the piece developed, an actor called Youth (Daniel Breaker) played the younger Stew while the modern-day version remained on stage as musician, commentator, and singer. The story was a coming-of-age tale without any earthshaking innovations. Guitar musician Youth grows up in a middle-class neighborhood in Los Angeles loving rock music and not content to live within the confines of his mother's church-centered existence. In the 1970s he travels to Europe to explore the world and himself. In decadent Amsterdam he indulges in sex and drugs and has a life-changing relationship with the free-spirited Marianna (De'Adre Aziza). In Berlin, Youth finds his sociopolitical side stimulated. As he journeys, Youth's musical style changes, and when he realizes that his art is his life no matter where he lives, he returns home. Much of the show was sung, even the onstage band members joining in the vocals. Stew's commentary to the audience (and even to his younger self) kept the theatrics to a minimum, giving *Passing Strange* a Brechtian slant. The score, by Stew and Heidi Rodewald, was eclectic, using rock, gospel blues, punk, and jazz. As in a concert, some songs continued on without worrying about the story line or the characters. When characters did sing, they received vocal backup from other characters who remained on stage even though they were not in that part of the story. There was very little physical action, so *Passing Strange* often looked as well as sounded like an intimate concert. "We Might Play All Night" was the unapologetic opening number; "Keys" was a sensual trio; "Identity" was a searing look at one's own culture; Stew's impression of his mother's religion was sardonically related in "Baptist Fashion Show" and "Church Blues Revelation"; a street riot was recreated with the furious rock number "May Day (There's a Riot Goin' Down)"; "Sole Brother" was a mocking rap song; "Arlington Hill" was an evocative memory ballad; "The Black One" was a tuneful, sarcastic song about African American stereotypes; "Youth's Unfinished Song" was a torch song that could not be completed; and "Work the Wound" was an honest testament to why one creates.

Passing Strange was first presented at Joe's Pub at the Public Theatre, then was seen in two different versions at the Sundance Theatre Lab. After a run at the Berkeley Repertory Theatre, the musical returned to the Public and played in the larger Anspacher Theatre. Reviews were mostly raves, critics labeled the show a whole new musical theatre experience, and the seven-week run was well attended. Eight months after it closed, *Passing Strange* reopened on Broadway and received another round of auspicious notices. Then something went wrong. The musical for people who didn't like musicals was better liked by the critics than the public. Many of those who saw *Passing Strange* on Broadway found it electrifying but, even with positive word of mouth, it was hard to sell tickets to a Broadway show that wasn't

Broadway in spirit, attitude, score, or satisfaction. Also, Stew's intimate, personal journey, which had played so well at Joe's Pub, was now a large-scale concert just by the nature of the venue. It didn't look like a Broadway show and, more problematic, it didn't seem like an Off-Broadway show either. *Passing Strange* played to small houses for five months then folded. Its last three performances were filmed, edited together with backstage scenes and commentary, and released as a quasi-documentary film in 2009. Some felt the movie was more involving than the actual Broadway production it was about. Perhaps what was refreshingly different Off Broadway was just too different for Broadway audiences. Yet how different was *Passing Strange?* Its uniqueness came from Stew's disregard for the conventional musical. At one point in the show he told the audience that this was the point when "an upbeat gotta-leave-this-town kinda show tune" was needed. But, he assured them, he didn't know how to write such a song, so they would just continue on without one. This is not innovative and groundbreaking theatre; it is very personal theatre that makes its own choices. The critics who hailed a whole new direction in American musical theatre will be sadly disappointed. The future of *Passing Strange* is problematic as well. Does one want to see this musical with someone else playing Stew? Perhaps. It is too early to say. But in hindsight it is easy to say that *Passing Strange* belongs Off Broadway and might have run a few years if it had stayed there.

WALMARTOPIA

[3 September 2007, Minetta Lane Theatre, 136 performances] a musical satire by Catherine Capellaro, Andrew Rohn. *Score:* Capellaro, Rohn (music and lyrics), Steve Tyska (lyrics). *Cast:* Cheryl Freeman, Nikki M. James, Bradley Dean, Stephen DeRosa, Brennen Leath, Scotty Watson.

A toothless sociopolitical satire with an easy and predictable target, *Walmartopia* was an odd choice for New York City, one of the few places in the States that did not have a Wal-Mart store. Perhaps New Yorkers felt superior to the rest of the country for not having the corporate giant in their neighborhood, but even they had trouble warming up to so obvious and unclever a musical spoof. Vicki Latrell (Cheryl Freeman) and her teenage daughter Maia (Nikki M. James) work at a Wal-Mart in Wisconsin and ruffle the feathers of the bosses when they complain about their dead-end jobs. The mad scientist Dr. Normal (Stephen DeRosa) uses his time machine to whisk the Latrells to the year 2037 when Wal-Mart runs the country and the state of Vermont is the only holdout against the Big Brother of Walmartopia. Mother and daughter fight the system, do not succumb to the seduction of the smiling-singing Sam Walton (Scotty Watson), and return to 2007 to warn America about its fate. The characters were broad stereotypes, the plot a feeble series of exaggerated skits, and the score a bright and mindless set of songs that sounded familiar and forgettable. A show pointing out the bland and soulless world of Wal-Mart ended up being more dreary than any branch of the store chain. *Walmartopia* began as a forty-five minute piece that was presented in various theatres in Wisconsin. It was a full-length musical by the time it played at the New York International Fringe Festival in 2006, though expanding the little musical only weakened it further. The New York production was one of the most expensive yet seen Off Broadway with garish scenery, costumes, and props, as seen in a chorus line of dancing smile faces (the Wal-Mart logo). The cast was far better than the material they were given, and the only compliments *Walmartopia* got from the press was for Freeman, James, and their fellow performers. Playgoers were curious enough to let the musical run for four months. Will *Walmartopia* find life in the cities and suburbs where the stores proliferate? Only Dr. Normal's time machine knows.

CELIA: THE LIFE AND MUSIC OF CELIA CRUZ

[26 September 2007, World Stages 2, 269 performances] a musical play by Carmen Rivera, Candido Torado. *Score:* various. *Cast:* Xiomara Laugart, Modestp Lacén, Pedro Capó, Anissa Gathers, Selenis Leyva, Elvis Nolasco.

Although she had died in 2003 after a sixty-year career singing across the Western Hemisphere, the salsa singer Celia Cruz was not forgotten by Latino and other audiences, and the Off-Broadway musical about her was well attended for nine months before it toured U.S. and Latin American cities. Dubbed the Queen of Salsa, Cruz did not suffer a tragic or even a melodramatic life, but her story still made for an interesting biographical musical. Born in Havana in 1925 to a large family, Cruz (Xiomara Laugart) went against her father's wishes for her to become a school teacher and as a teenager began singing in clubs and on Cuban radio. By 1950 she was famous throughout Latin America, and when Castro took over Cuba in 1959, Cruz and her husband Pedro Knight (Modesto Lacén) settled in New Jersey. She toured and recorded (winning many Grammy Awards) for the next forty years. She then quietly died of a brain tumor at the age of seventy-seven. There were no broken marriages or other hardships to spice up the story, though there was a touching scene in which Cruz cannot get a visa to visit her dying mother in Cuba because she had spoken out against Castro. The show was also about Cruz's music, showing how she was influenced by other artists and eventually came to represent Cuban music, particularly salsa and bolero, to the rest of the world. Cruz's most popular hits were performed, including "La Vida es un Carnaval," "Yo Viviré (I Will Survive)," "La Negra Tiene Tumbao (The Black Lady Has Attitude)," and "Bemba Colorá." The Cuban singer Laugart was praised for her dramatic and singing performance, and the reviews also approved of the libretto that held the songs and story together. The musical was performed in Spanish for six performances each week and the other two performances were in English. With *Celia: The Life and Music of Celia Cruz* running Off Broadway and *In the Heights* still playing on Broadway, the Hispanic musical in New York was alive and well.

THREE MO' TENORS

[27 September 2007, Little Shubert Theatre, 142 performances] a musical revue by Marion J. Caffey. *Score:* various. *Cast:* Duane A. Moody, Victor Robertson, James N. Berger Jr., Kenneth D. Alston Jr., Ramone Diggs, Phumzile Sojola.

Although it was billed as a "musical revue," this dazzling little show was really a concert but on the intimate scale of an Off-Broadway musical. After the three world-famous opera tenors José Carreras, Placido Domingo, and Luciano Pavarotti teamed for a series of concerts in huge venues, the term "The Three Tenors" became very familiar even to those not interested in classical music. Director-choreographer Marion J. Caffey wanted to highlight the ability of African American tenors to sing classical as well as popular music, so he arranged a concert in Boston in 2000 titled *Three Mo' Tenors* and created a program featuring the classically trained tenors Victor Trent Cook, Roderick Dixon, and Thomas Young. It was a gimmick title, one that might be used for a spoof of the famous international trio, but it caught the attention of the public. The concert was so successful it was filmed for *Great Performances* on PBS and broadcast in 2001. For the Off-Broadway version, Caffey recruited two sets of African American tenors and alternated their performances in the very voice-demanding show. The reception by the New York press was exemplary and, unlike the cavernous stadiums that the opera trio had played, the Little Shubert was the ideal venue to enjoy *Three Mo' Tenors*. Over four hundred years of music was represented in the program, from traditional hymns, African chants, and folk songs to selections from opera and Broadway to gospel, soul, rhythm and blues, and even rock. The versatility of the three performers was overwhelming as numbers from *Les Misérables*, *Company*, and *Ragtime* were sung alongside passages from *Rigoletto* and *The Daughter of the Regiment*. The three harmonized through the African "Dali Wum," the gospel "No Way Tired," and the jazzy "Minnie the Moocher," then sang a montage of rock favorites by the group Queen. To say that there was something for every musical taste was surely an understatement. The two casts entertained New York audiences for eighteen weeks then took off on tour.

FRANKENSTEIN

[1 November 2007, 37 Arts, 45 performances] a musical play by Jeffrey Jackson. *Score:* Mark Baron (music), Jackson (lyrics). *Cast:* Hunter Foster, Christiane Noll, Steve Blanchard, Mandy Bruno, Jim Stanek.

A week before Mel Brooks's musical farce *Young Frankenstein* opened on Broadway, a much more earnest and faithful version of the Mary Shelley story was musicalized Off Broadway. The authors returned to Shelley's original novel rather than the more familiar movie and television versions of *Frankenstein* and came up with a father-son melodrama rather than a horror show. The musical was a memory piece, told in flashback by the aged Victor Frankenstein (Hunter Foster). The Creature (Steve Blanchard) he made was an intelligent talking and singing outcast instead of a grunting monster. The necessary romance was provided by Victor's fiancée Elizabeth (Christiane Noll), a girl from his hometown of Geneva, Switzerland. The narrative was not linear, allowing for scenes from the past to surface as needed, and culminated with the death of the Creature in Victor's arms, the scientist calling him his son. It was an intelligent libretto without a touch of camp or even humor. Unfortunately, the score was a pretentious example of the pop opera variety and the lyrics so banal that *Frankenstein* often came close to *Young Frankenstein* when the singing took over. Victor's howling "Birth to My Creation"; the Creature's angst-ridden "Walking Nightmare"; Victor and Elizabeth's mindless love duet "The Music of Love"; and the stirring, empty anthem "The Coming of the Dawn" were typical of the bloated score. Yet the cast of thirteen was so proficient that they pulled off most of the songs, and audiences cheered the show as if it were one of the overblown mega-musicals on Broadway. The critics were not impressed and said so, but the six-week run was well attended. Already productions have surfaced regionally and in England. Can Las Vegas be next?

THE GLORIOUS ONES

[5 November 2007, Mitzi E. Newhouse Theatre, 72 performances] a musical play by Lynn Ahrens from a novel by Francine Prose. *Score:* Stephen Flaherty (music), Ahrens (lyrics). *Cast:* Marc Kudisch, Natalie Venetia Belcon, John Kassir, Erin Davie, David Patrick Kelly, Jeremy Webb, Julyana Soelistyo.

The creation of the *commedia dell'arte* form of theatre in the sixteenth century was an encouraging idea for a musical, and the songwriting team of Stephen Flaherty and Lynn Ahrens seemed the right people to pull off the score for such a show, but *The Glorious Ones* was something of a disappointment. It was competently written, admirably scored, and beautifully performed, but the result was less than engaging. Ahrens's libretto, based on a novel by Francine Prose, concerned the boasting egomaniac Flamino Scala (Marc Kudisch), a Venetian actor who assembled a troupe of misfits, encouraged them in improvisation, and created the famous character types of the *commedia*. The musical was thin on plot and long on physical humor (as was the *commedia*), and there was infighting among the performers, a romance between the aristocrat-turned-actress Isabella (Erin Davie) and Flamino's protégé Francesco (Jeremy Webb), and a royal performance in Paris that turns into a fiasco. By the end of the musical, the *commedia* tradition has been established, and the players offer their gift to modern audiences. The trouble is most American playgoers have difficulty with the *commedia* style, finding it repetitive and obvious. One watched with an intellectual attitude, knowing how the *commedia* influenced comedy for the next three hundred years. *The Glorious Ones* was a similarly detached experience for most of the audience, and the mildly favorable reviews applauded the efforts more than the finished product. There was no scrimping on praise for the vigorous performances, particularly for the robust Kudisch, and there were many compliments on the score. There were some standout numbers, to be sure, but some of the songs were as tiresome as the endless pratfalls. Flaherty's music had a circuslike flavor, and Ahrens's lyrics were sometimes intoxicating, as in the ravishing duet "Opposite You," Flamino's "Madness to Act," and Isabella's "The World She Writes" about creating a story. "Absalom" was a pleasing narrative ballad, the plaintive "Armanda's Sack" was an accomplished list song about the remnants from the troupe's glory days, and "I Was Here" was a poignant plea to be remembered. *The Glorious Ones* had premiered at the Pittsburgh Public Theatre then was given a nine-week engagement at Lincoln Center. Its future is problematic. The small cast of seven and the simple stage-within-a-stage setting might be appealing to regional theatres, but do audiences really want to see *commedia dell'arte*? My guess is it will receive more productions at colleges where the academic interest in the past art form might be stronger.

MAKE ME A SONG: THE MUSIC OF WILLIAM FINN

[12 November 2007, New World Stages, 55 performances] a musical revue by Rob Ruggiero. *Score:* William Finn (music and lyrics). *Cast:* Sandy Binion, D. B. Bonds, Adam Heller, Sally Wilfert.

Having written eight sung-through musicals over the previous twenty-eight years, William Finn had amassed quite a catalogue of songs, so director Rob Ruggiero had much to choose from when he put together this revue at TheatreWorks in Hartford, Connecticut, in 2006. The cast of four performed some two dozen Finn songs taken from his hits and misses, and it was an impressive and thrilling journey. The "Falsettos Suite" represented his famous Marvin trilogy, and there were numbers from abandoned shows, musicals yet to be produced, and works that quickly closed. It was just as rewarding to hear the superior "All Fall Down" and "That's Enough for Me" from the failed *Romance in Hard Times* as it was to revisit favorites from *March of the Falsettos*, *Falsettoland*, and *A New Brain*. "Hitchhiking Across America," from a musical of the same name that was never completed, was one of the pleasant surprises of the evening, as was the very personal "You're Even Better Than You Think You Are" about the commitment to keep writing songs no matter what. The narration provided some background about each song, but there was no attempt to create a biography on stage; the songs told their own story. *Make Me a Song* opened Off Broadway to complimentary reviews and for seven weeks entertained both old and new Finn fans.

NEXT TO NORMAL

[13 February 2008, Second Stage Theatre, 38 performances; Booth Theatre, 733 performances] a musical play by Brian Yorkey. *Score:* Tom Kitt (music), Yorkey (lyrics). *Cast:* Alice Ripley, Brian d'Arcy James, Jennifer Damiano, Aaron Tveit, Adam Chanler-Berat.

A rock musical about mental illness, *Next to Normal* was never meant to be an escapist show. The characters were disturbed without being cute, issues were not easily resolved, the music attacked rather than seduced, and there was no happy resolution. Here was a musical whose heart (and head) was in the right place. But good intentions are more admirable than satisfying, and *Next to Normal* was a theatrical mess when it opened Off Broadway after a short stint at the New York Musical Theatre Festival in 2006. As fluctuating as its major character, the musical wanted to hit big issues and use rock music to reveal the dysfunctional nature of the family concerned. Yet the lyrics were often banal clichés and the music more repetitive than engrossing, resulting in a promising but flawed show. The plot was as simple as the neuroses were supposedly complex. Middle-aged housewife and mother Diana (Alice Ripley) suffers from bipolar swings of emotion and chronic depression. Eighteen years earlier her baby son died and, in the overly simple diagnosis by the writers, she never got over it. Her patient, dull husband Dan (Brian d'Arcy James) and their maladjusted teenage daughter Natalie (Jennifer Damiano) are used to Diana's problem and react to it in different but ineffective ways. A series of doctors puts Diana on different medications resulting in some surreal fantasies and bitter songs about the futility of modern psychotherapy. To add to the emotional jumble, Diana keeps seeing her dead son, now the eighteen-year-old Gabe (Aaron Tveit), and they perform some emotive duets together. In the end Diana leaves Dan, Jennifer commits to her boyfriend Henry (Adam Chanler-Berat), Dan confronts his dead/imaginary son and for the first time calls him by name, and all vow to continue on. What it all came down to was: Mother goes crazy because father won't mention dead baby by name. This may or may not have been bargain basement psychology, but it surely was bottom-drawer drama. Critics applauded the restrained performance by James, who found humanity in an underwritten role, and many commentators thought Ripley fierce and dynamic as Diana. Michael Greif directed the piece smashingly on the simple three-level setting which came alive with pop-art images reflecting Diana's mental state. The rock score received mixed notices, commentators pointing out the hackneyed lyric phrases but liking some of the lyric ideas and the driving music. The one-month run at the Second Stage Theatre did not garner much attention, but everyone involved with the show thought *Next to Normal* had a future.

The authors went to work revising both script and score, and the musical was scheduled for a month run as part of the next season at the Arena Stage in Washington, D.C. With some casting changes, Grief and the staff worked on *Next to Normal* during the run. The new version opened on Broadway in March 2009 and met with mostly enthusiastic reviews. While some critics thought Ripley's performance was one long, unipolar screech, most adulated her theatrics. Brian d'Arcy James went on to other projects, and J. Robert Spencer struggled with the problematic character of Dan. (During the long run, James returned to play Dan again.) The long first act was trimmed considerably, the act one finale "Feeling Electric" (which was the original title for the show) was cut and replaced by the duet "A Light in the Dark," the clichéd act two finale "Let There Be Light" was replaced by a similarly obtuse "There Will Be Light," the role of Natalie was solidified, and the presence of the dead Gabe was clarified. There were many other minor changes as well and, under Greif's polish, *Next to Normal* finally seemed to work. Too many of the lyrical gaffs remained, and the pounding rock music was up for grabs, critically speaking. But many playgoers felt they were seeing something bold and exciting, and business in the small Booth Theatre was steady. Diana may still be crazy, but at least *Next to Normal* had a happy ending.

ADDING MACHINE

[25 February 2008, Minetta Lane Theatre, 149 performances] a musical play by Jason Loewith, Joshua Schmidt based on Elmer Rice's play *The Adding Machine*. *Score:* Loewith (lyrics), Schmidt (music and lyrics). *Cast:* Joel Hatch, Cyrilla Baer, Amy Warren, Joe Farrell, Daniel Marcus, Niffer Clarke, Roger E. DeWitt, Jeff Still.

A musical that actually was bold and exciting was this uncompromising musicalization of Elmer Rice's 1923 expressionistic play *The Adding Machine*. The Broadway musical had recently gotten a healthy dose of German expressionism with *Spring Awakening*, but that audience-pleasing show was no preparation for the harsh music, lyrics, and dialogue of *Adding Machine*. Mr. Zero (Joel Hatch) has been numbed by his prattling wife Mrs. Zero (Cyrilla Baer) and his accountant job shuffling numbers in the basement of an impersonal corporation. The only spark of life left in him is his unexpressed affection for the secretary Daisy Devore (Amy Warren) who feels the same about him but is equally unable to pursue it. When Zero is told by his Boss (Jeff Still) on his twenty-fifth anniversary with the company that he is to be replaced by an adding machine, Zero finally experiences a surge of vitality and kills the Boss. Arrested and convicted of murder, Zero is executed and finds himself in a bleak underworld where he is united with Daisy, who has committed suicide. But soon Zero is told he is condemned to return to earth and live his dreary life all over again, just as he has done many times in the past. Rather than submit, he and Daisy jump into the gears of a giant adding machine and are ground to pieces, never to suffer life again. Rice's play was a cautionary tale about the mechanization of humanity, a common theme in expressionism, but the musical took the form of a nightmarish folk tale and placed the inhumanity of existence on people. All the same, there was a machine-like feel to the sights and sounds of *Adding Machine*. The score sometimes took its tempo from the routine calling of numbers, electronic sounds were heard during both the spoken and sung portions of the musical, and musical underscoring infiltrated scenes giving them an uncomfortably eerie feeling. Director David Cromer, who would have a series of critical triumphs starting with *Adding Machine*, staged the piece with precision and imagination, each scene meticulously set and polished like a fine pocket watch. The simple, stark sets and lights and the slightly cartoonish performances were also all of a whole, creating a world that echoed with artificiality yet was surprisingly tender at times. Hatch's performance was a marvel of understatement, while the scatterbrained chirping of Baer's Mrs. Zero and the aching charm of Warren's Daisy provided pathetic examples of people still clinging to life. Jason Loewith and Joshua Schmidt streamlined Rice's original into a long one-act and provided a score that sounded contemporary but not out of keeping with the 1920s costumes the characters wore. Many songs were brave experiments with words and notes battling each other. The recurring "In Numbers" was a hymnlike chant that had a foreboding subtext; "Office Reverie" revealed the inner thoughts of the frustrated Zero and Daisy as their ideas agreed and disagreed; "Something to Be Proud Of" jumped all over the musical scale just as Mrs. Zero's mind scrambled from one subject to another; "Harmony, Not Discord" was sung by three women in the office, each one reading off numbers at a different tempo and creating an appalling fugue; and the chatter at "The Party" turned into a carousel of banalities. "Zero's Confession" was a bitter list song in which his whole life came down to counting, be it numbers, days, or strikes at a baseball game. Daisy pathetically compared Zero to movie stars and concluded "I'd Rather Watch You." Zero and his wife had the reminiscing duet "Didn't We?" when she visited him in jail and what would have been a charm song in any other musical turned sour. By the finale, "The Music of the Machine," the music had such a grinding sound that anything lyrical in life seemed to be swallowed up by the giant adding machine. It was a score that continually surprised, disarmed, and dazzled. *Adding Machine* had originated at the Next Theatre in Evanston, Illinois, had a brief run in Chicago, then opened Off Broadway to auspicious reviews. Yet they were the kind of notices that would drive most playgoers in the opposite direction of the Minetta Lane Theatre because it was clear that this was a dark and oppressive piece of musical theatre. So it was surprising when business was healthy and the limited run was extended to five months. A London production was similarly successful, and ambitious regional theatres have started to produce the musical. *Adding Machine* will never find a wide audience. By its very nature it defies popularity. But for those who connect with it, the show is unforgettable.

BASH'D! A GAY RAP OPERA

[23 June 2008, Zipper Factory Theatre, c. 40 performances] a musical play by Chris Craddock, Nathan Cuckow. *Score:* Aaron Macri (music), Craddock, Cuckow (lyrics). *Cast:* Craddock, Cuckow.

Rap singing had slowly been making appearances in musicals, and most recently it had been used frequently throughout *In the Heights*, but this was the first show to embrace the form unapologetically, and very few of its seventy minutes was not rap with accompanying hip-hop movements to accentuate it. For some audiences those were sixty minutes too many, but for many *Bash'd! A Gay Rap Opera* was far from repetitive or monotonous. The show's creators, lyricists, and performers were two men from Alberta, Canada, who effectively used rap to tell a difficult story. The musical is narrated by two hip-hopping gays, T-Bag (Chris Craddock) and Feminem (Nathan Cuckow), and the story was about the courtship, wedding, and tragic end of two gay lovers, the naive country kid Dillon (Cuckow) and the streetwise city kid Jack (Craddock). The *Romeo and Juliet*-like tale was filled with humor as well as sex and love, so when one of the lovers is "bash'd," revenge flares up, only to end with regret and a plea for understanding. As disturbing as *Bash'd!* was at times, it rarely wallowed in bitterness or sentiment. Cuckow and Craddock also played all the supporting characters, from homophobes and parents to militant lesbians and support group workers. The lyrics were frank, sometimes crude, but a notch above most street rapping, and the music by Aaron Macri managed to deviate from the expected rap beat and find melodic moments here and there. *Bash'd!* was first presented in Alberta in 2006 and was first seen in Manhattan at the New York International Fringe Festival. The Off-Broadway production was favorably received by the press, and the five-week engagement was well attended by gay and straight audiences. Without getting preachy, the musical raised many questions about gay marriage, gay legislation, homophobia, heterophobia, and gay bashing. To do that and still entertain was no minor feat.

FELA!

[4 September 2008, 37 Arts, c. 32 performances; Eugene O'Neill Theatre, 468 performances] a musical play by Jim Lewis, Bill T. Jones. *Score:* Fela Anikulapo Kuti (music and lyrics). *Cast:* Sahr Ngaujah, Abena Koomson, Sparlha Swa, Calvin C. Booker, Ismael Kouyate.

Experiencing the passionate musical *Fela!* in a 299-seat Off-Broadway theatre was akin to being inside a pressure cooker: you could not stand back and observe but were drawn into the fury and excitement until it was difficult to judge what was going on. Most playgoers knew that they were captivated and energized by the experience but looking back wondered what hit them. Such was the hypnotic power of *Fela!*, the quasi-biographical musical about the Nigerian musician, songwriter, and activist Fela Anikulapo Kuti (Sahr Ngaujah). The plot began in 1978 with Fela's farewell performance at the Shrine, a performance space he created in the Kalakuta compound in the capital city of Lagos. The story then shifted back and forth through time. As a medical student in London and later a musician in Los Angeles and Brooklyn, Fela developed his unique Afrobeat style, a thrilling mix of jazz, funk, and African chants. Back in Nigeria, he turns Kalakuta into his home base and even declares the community an independent republic. Clashes with the military government and repeated police harassment climax when soldiers storm the compound and there is mass murder, including the death of Fela's aged mother Funmilayo (Abena Koomson), who is thrown out a second-story window. In grief and protest, Fela places his mother's coffin on the steps of the Nigerian capitol building. The plot tossed pieces of the story back and forth, not always with clarity but certainly with kinetic power, using Fela's music and vigorous dancing choreographed by coauthor and director Bill T. Jones.

The uneven chronicle did not conclude Fela's story (he died of an AIDS-related illness in 1997) but rather celebrated it. It was a celebration one was forced to participate in. For a number called "The Clock," the playgoers were told to stand and were instructed how to tell time using one's ass. Many of the songs were similarly involving, but audiences were usually so caught up in the vivacious music and dance that it was impossible not to react. There were a few quieter moments, such as the lovely lullaby "Trouble Sleep" sung by Funmilayo, but most of *Fela!* was either infectious, as in the spirited "I Got the Feeling," or abrasive and sarcastic, as in "Expensive Shit" about the police waiting for Fela to pass the cannabis he swallowed. The most potent numbers were "Sorrow, Tears and Blood" about the aftermath of the raid on Kalakuya, and the funeral dirge "Coffin for Head of State." Sahr Ngaujah was mesmerizing as Fela, conveying his power to seduce crowds and women (he had twenty-seven wives). Critics thought Jones's direction and choreography was quite accomplished, and there were many compliments for the design which included projections and lights splashed onto the shabby corrugated-iron walls of the compound. Even the reviews that praised and recommended *Fela!* admitted it was repetitious at times and, like the character of Fela, self-indulgent on occasion. But audience response was strong, and the one-month engagement sold out. With minor tinkering with the script and some recasting (the terrific Lillias White played Funmilayo and Kevin Mambo alternated with Ngaujah in the title role), *Fela!* opened on Broadway a year later where it received another round of raves. Some commentators noted that the show felt more like a large political rally in the Broadway venue and it was possible to distance oneself from the action, which was not possible Off Broadway. Yet audiences were just as energized by the musical which, while not for all tastes, was nevertheless a hit.

WHAT'S THAT SMELL: THE MUSIC OF JACOB STERLING

[10 September 2008, Atlantic Stage 2, c. 56 performances] a musical revue by David Pittu. *Score:* Randy Redd (music), Pittu (lyrics). *Cast:* Pittu, Peter Bartlett.

Just as *Gutenberg! The Musical!* proved bad art can make for fun theatre, this saucy little revue illustrated how nontalent could be equally entertaining. The show was about a fictional pretentious songwriter who has twenty years of flops but is still confident his work will soon be appreciated. Jacob Sterling

(David Littu) appears on the low-cost cable TV show called "Leonard Swagg's CLOT (Composers & Lyricists of Tomorrow)" and tells his host Leonard (Peter Bartlett) about his life and work, performing several of his atrocious songs and making snide comments about how show business has refused to acknowledge him. The character of the Jewish, gay, mother-obsessed Jacob may have sounded familiar, but Pittu's performance was original and sprightly. (Pittu wrote the script and the lyrics for Randy Redd's music.) He was ably supported by Bartlett as the smooth, artificial host, the two actors playing off each other superbly. Jacob's atrocious songs, with pompous music and forced lyrics, were so funny that one looked forward to each one with glee. "Shopping Out Loud" was an attack on consumerism, presented like a pop opera anthem. "Marty" was a tribute to Jacob's late lover whose greatest quality was adulating Jacob, "That Goddamned Day" was the lament of a dancer who was having a breast implant the day the World Trade Towers were attacked, "Mademoiselle Death" was a turgid aria from Jacob's musical version of *La Femme Nikita*, "He Died Inside Me" was the lament of a Jewish girl whose lover died right after she had an orgasm. "Let Me Taste the World" was the revelation number about a green Montana lad who discovers international take-out food in the city. "The Sounds of Human Loving" was about listening to his bisexual roommate noisily making love. Perhaps the funniest song was the title number, the musical complaint of Jacob's overbearing mother about her son, New York City, and the way both were living. Some critics and playgoers thought the thin premise for *What's That Smell: The Music of Jacob Sterling* could not sustain a full evening, while others found the revue a droll and merry entertainment.

THE MARVELOUS WONDERETTES

[14 September 2008, Westside Theatre, 545 performances] musical revue by Roger Bean. *Score:* various. *Cast:* Farah Alvin, Beth Malone, Bets Malone, Victoria Matlock.

A tongue-in-cheek revue dripping with nostalgia, *The Marvelous Wonderettes* seemed like a lot of other girl-group musicals but was so enjoyable that no one, including most of the critics, seemed to mind. The gym at Springfield High School is decorated for the 1958 prom, and four senior girls, calling themselves the Wonderettes, are hired to entertain. Each is also a contender for the title of Prom Queen, so between the 1950s pop songs a bit of rivalry is detected. This becomes more obvious by the end of Act One when one of the girls wins the crown. Act Two is set during the 1968 prom and the Wonderettes are back at their old high school to sing. The decade has taken a toll on the foursome as career and man problems are revealed. But the girls continue to sing the hits of the day, adding some 1960s favorites to their repertoire. The Wonderettes were each a stereotype (bossy diva, tomboy, meek underachiever, and bubblehead), but their chatter was enjoyable enough, and their singing was much more than that. The first act's score of such innocent hits as "Mr. Sandman," "Lollipop," "Sincerely," and "All I Have to Do Is Dream" gave way in the second act to more feminist numbers such as "Respect" and "You Don't Own Me." Yet *The Marvelous Wonderettes* never got too heavy, and the presentation of the jukebox hit parade was what really counted. The revue was written by Roger Bean, who first presented it in Milwaukee in 1999 and then again in 2001. After a run in Los Angeles, it opened Off Broadway where most critics declared it unpretentious fun. Audiences agreed, and the show ran a year and a half. Regional productions followed with many more to come. In 2003 there was a sequel version titled *Winter Wonderettes* that ran in Milwaukee, where it seems they just cannot get enough of the crooning foursome.

ROMANTIC POETRY

[28 October 2008, City Center Stage 1, c. 40 performances] a musical play by John Patrick Shanley. *Score:* Henry Krieger (music), Shanley (lyrics). *Cast:* Mark Linn-Baker, Jeb Brown, Jerry Dixon, Patina Renea Miller, Emily Swallow, Ivan Hernandez.

With so much talent attached on and off stage, the musical *Romantic Poetry* was indeed promising. The result was so disappointing that the Manhattan Theatre Club pulled the piece as soon as its subscription run was complete. Two mismatched married couples find they cannot live with each other nor can they live without each other. One of the wives is tormented by the clownish behavior of her two ex-husbands who got a few laughs out of the audience but seemed to drive her deeper into confusion. The dialogue was glib without being clever, and the score, consisting of more two dozen irritating songs, was a new low in lyric writing. All the critics gleefully quoted lines in their reviews because they spoke volumes for what was wrong with *Romantic Poetry*. The acclaimed playwright John Patrick Shanley, who had written excellent comedies, such as *Italian American Reconciliation*, and dramas, as the recent *Doubt*, wrote the book and lyrics and also directed the show. Henry Krieger, who had composed such first-rate scores as *Dreamgirls* and *Side Show*, wrote the music for *Romantic Comedy* in an old-fashioned, tuneful way, but every idea and every line of each song refused to fly. The gifted cast included Mark Linn-Baker and Jeb Brown as the farcical ex-husbands, and there was also commendable work by Jerry Dixon and Emily Swallow, all who labored in vain. *Romantic Comedy* was developed at a new works festival at Vassar College. The Manhattan Theatre Club, who had had great success with Shanley's plays, picked it up for Off Broadway. The press was unanimous in its disdain for the musical, and there were a lot of empty seats to go with the empty laughs during the five-week run.

ROAD SHOW

[18 November 2008, Public Theatre/Newman Theatre, c. 44 performances] a musical play by John Weidman. *Score:* Stephen Sondheim (music and lyrics). *Cast:* Michael Cerveris, Alexander Gemingnani, Alma Cuervo, Claybourne Elder, William Parry.

Stephen Sondheim's first wholly new work since *Passion* in 1994, *Road Show* garnered a lot of attention. It also was plagued by high expectations which it could not fulfill. But a secondary Sondheim musical is reason enough to rejoice, and there were plenty of good things in *Road Show* to make it memorable. The famous brothers Wilson (Michael Cerveris) and Addison Mizner (Alexander Gemignani) are first glimpsed after death, arguing with each other in the afterlife as they had in real life. A series of episodic flashbacks followed, with the boys' dying father (William Parry) urging them to grab opportunity by the throat and make their name in the exciting new twentieth century. The brothers do exactly that, Wilson looking for gold in the Yukon, making and losing a fortune, marrying for money, and becoming a crass but successful promoter of everything from boxers to real estate. Addison loses his money in bad business enterprises in Hawaii, India, Hong Kong, and Guatemala before finding his niche as an architect and interior designer for the mansions of the fabulously wealthy. The brothers unite on a scheme to build a new city called Boca Raton in Florida and lose another fortune even though the resort community lives on. It seems the two Mizners are their own worst enemies, and the musical ends back in limbo with the two looking back with sardonic awe, realizing that they have indeed lived a full life and that the journey was the destination. The fact-based libretto by John Weidman, Sondheim's collaborator on *Pacific Overtures* and *Assassins*, was competently written, but there was something in the Mizners that did not allow a musical about them to rise much beyond the mildly interesting. Wilson was slick, shameless, and often irritating; Addison was more gentle and loving, his relationships with his mother (Alma Cuervo) and the gay millionaire philanthropist Hollis Bessemer (Claybourne Elder) providing the only heart in the show. Their adventures were intriguing but far from gripping. Only in some of the musical numbers did *Road Show* take flight. The warm duet "The Best Thing That Ever Has Happened"; Mama Mizner's wry song of affection "Isn't He Something!"; the rousing number "Gold!"; and the oddly romantic sibling duet "Brotherly Love" were sterling examples of Sondheim's command of character. There were also times when the plot was carried on by a complex, narrative number, such as "The Game" and the cunning travelogue piece "Addison's Trip." Working in a quieter, more reflective mode than, say, *Assassins*, Sondheim demonstrated that his musical and lyrical powers were still acute and that time had not blurred his theatrical vision.

   Road Show was aptly titled since it had taken a very long journey to arrive Off Broadway. Although Sondheim had wanted to write a musical about the Mizners since the 1950s, it didn't happen until he and Weidman collaborated on an early version entitled *Wise Guys* which had a brief workshop production Off Off Broadway in 1999. A reworked version directed by Harold Prince opened in Chicago in 2003 under the title *Gold!* retitled *Bounce*, the show then opened in Washington, D.C., with Broadway plans. But the reviews were not encouraging, and although the production was recorded, *Bounce* closed in D.C. Further revisions, recasting, and with John Doyle now directing, the musical now named *Road Show* opened at the Public Theatre. The production, staged as a kind of vaudeville evening, was very presentational, and the episodic nature of the script was supported by Doyle's use of the supporting actors as commentators on the action, remaining on stage all evening and playing up the folklike quality of the story. *Road Show* met with mixed notices, the critics' compliments alongside their disappointment in the book. The changes Weidman had made over the years were mostly for the better, but commentators felt the Mizners still did not make for a satisfying musical. Because one can listen to the scores for both *Bounce* and *Road Show*, these changes can be identified. Also, it is interesting to see what songs Sondheim changed, dropped, or replaced during the journey to Off Broadway. It will take some time, but it is likely that *Road Show* will eventually join the list of other regularly produced Sondheim musicals in regional, community, and college theatres.

HAPPINESS

[30 March 2009, Mitzi E. Newhouse Theatre, c. 112 performances] a musical play by John Weidman. *Score:* Scott Frankel (music), Michael Korie (lyrics). *Cast:* Hunter Foster, Ken Page, Joanna Gleason, Fred Applegate, Miguel Cervantes, Robert Petkoff, Jenny Powers, Phyllis Somerville.

Two months after *Road Show* closed, librettist John Weidman had another new musical presented Off Broadway, and it too had script problems. Yet it also had its merits; just what they were differed according to the critics. An original piece, though the premise had been used in plays and films and television in the past, *Happiness* was a reflective musical that took the form of a fantasy parable. Ten New Yorkers riding the same subway car during morning rush hour are stalled between train stops. Subway conductor Stanley (Hunter Foster) appears, explains to the others that he was a money-grubbing investment banker in life, and now it is his job to help others prepare for the next life. The nine travelers soon realize that they have all died that morning and now must share with each other a moment of supreme happiness they experienced in life in order to move on. It was the kind of contrived situation that appealed to some playgoers and annoyed others. A doorman recalled a day at a baseball game with his young son, an elderly woman relived an evening in 1944 when she danced with a young soldier at a USO club, a salesgirl at a department store perfume counter remembered a day at Coney Island, a conservative radio personality thought back to her youth when she was a radical, a gay interior decorator wishes for any day he spent with his lover who died of AIDS, and so on. Each of the moments of happiness was told through song and, again, these feel-good memories were either inspirational or sentimental, depending on one's point of view. Most critics disparaged the musical, but most audiences were caught up in it. Both agreed that the production directed and choreographed by Susan Stroman was first class, from its revolving subway car to the superior ensemble cast. The songs by Scott Frankel and Michael Korie, who had written the impressive score for *Grey Gardens*, were similarly up for grabs, some reviews labeling them bland and others proclaiming them the best thing about *Happiness*. Inexplicably, the score has not been recorded, so theatre lovers cannot yet judge for themselves. The frantic opening number, "Just Not Right Now," was deemed the best song in the show according to some aisle-sitters; others cited it as bland. Most thought the doorman's "Best Seats in the Ballpark" to be genuinely touching, while most abhorred "The Tooth Fairy Song" sung by a divorced dad who sneaks into his sleeping daughter's bedroom at night dressed as the Tooth Fairy. Business was brisk during the fourteen-week run at Lincoln Center as audiences came and agreed or disagreed with the critics. Until *Happiness* is recorded and if and when it receives further productions, it is a debate limited to those who saw it.

THE TOXIC AVENGER

[6 April 2009, New World Stages, 279 performances] a musical satire by Joe DiPietro. *Score:* David Bryan (music, lyrics), DiPietro (lyrics). *Cast:* Nick Cordero, Sara Chase, Nancy Opel, Matthew Saldivar, Demond Green.

It is interesting, and a little disheartening, that twenty-seven years after *Little Shop of Horrors*, Off Broadway was still trying to recreate the critical and commercial success of that show by turning yet another cheaply made cult horror film into a hit musical. The latest attempt was the modestly successful *The Toxic Avenger*, based on the 1984 film and its sequels, all of which had developed quite a following over the years. The corrupt Mayor Babs Belgoody (Nancy Opel) of Tromaville, New Jersey, has been receiving kickbacks by allowing companies to dump toxic waste outside her town. Melvin Ferd the Third (Nick Cordero), a nerdy teenager who wants to be an environmental scientist, discovers the toxic dump site and threatens the mayor, who is running for governor of New Jersey, with the evidence. The mayor's henchmen throw Melvin into a vat of toxic goo to die, but instead he emerges from the slime as a deformed, green, muscular creature with superhuman strength. Calling himself the Toxic Avenger, he sets out to clean up Tromaville. He also seeks to win the heart of the blind librarian Sarah (Sara Chase); her inability to see his disgusting form gives him hope. The Avenger (Toxie to his friends) becomes a local superhero with the community, and Sarah falls in love with him. The mayor finds out that the only thing that can stop the Toxic Avenger is bleach, so she arranges to have him doused with the stuff. Luckily Melvin's mother Ma Ferd (Opel), an old rival of the mayor since school days, counteracts the bleach by drenching her son with filthy water from the Hudson River. Toxie wins the day, his sweetheart Sarah, and the state governorship, and all look forward to a toxic-free tomorrow. As in the *Toxic Avenger* movies, the violence was graphic and exaggerated, with the Avenger pulling off limbs of his enemies and his body festering with huge warts and slime. While not as gross as *Evil Dead*, the musical still enjoyed making the disgusting funny and letting the audience laugh at off-color jokes about everything from superhero sex to blindness. The script was uneven with some overlong unfunny sections, but mostly it moved along, thanks to the expert direction by John Rando and a skillful cast of four who played all the characters. The trite, comic book dialogue was repeated in the lyrics, where they seemed less effective. The cleverness needed to make the score soar wasn't there, so audiences had to be content with silly songs rather than pastiche gems as in *Little Shop of Horrors*. Joe DiPietro wrote the slapstick libretto and the lyrics with composer David Bryan, and their score was in the rock mode, heavy on rhythm and repetition and lacking in melody. Yet it was still a likable score that was not hard to listen to. The opening "Who Will Save New Jersey?" merrily set up the characters and situation; "Hot Toxic Love" was a muddle-headed romantic duet; "All Men Are Freaks" was a girl-group parody; "Thank God She's Blind" was a bizarre ballad; "Choose Me, Oprah!" was a risible cry for fame; and "You Tore My Heart Out" was a mock torch song. *The Toxic Avenger* premiered at the George Street Playhouse in New Jersey in 2008 then opened Off Broadway where it was greeted with mostly favorable notices. Fans of the movies combined with new admirers, and the musical ran nine months. A version in Toronto followed, and joining it will be, no doubt, many more productions.

POSTSCRIPT

Off Broadway continues to offer musicals lauded by the press as bold, intriguing new works, and some are popular enough to be extended to meet the demand of tickets. Predictably, plans to reopen on Broadway follow, and an open run Off Broadway is not considered. These days, a successful Off-Broadway musical cannot stay in the venue for which it was conceived and where it first found favor. This situation is akin to having the brightest and most prized citizens of a small community all leave town and seek their fortunes elsewhere. Yet if Off Broadway has been reduced to a testing ground for celebrity elsewhere, its importance is not diminished, only altered. The threat of extinction is an idle one because the American theatre still needs Off Broadway. But the species known as the Off Broadway musical is threatened in other ways. Success away from the Street is no longer considered valid; it is just a means to an end. The community once known as Off Broadway continually watches its favorite sons and daughters skip town. Home is not good enough for the insatiable needs for fame and wealth. All one can do is welcome unknown talent and nurture it until the inevitable day when it says farewell.

Appendix: Guide to Recordings

A . . . My Name Is Still Alice
1995 Great Barrington revival (CD) with Heather MacRae, Barbara Walsh, Marguerite MacIntyre.

Adding Machine
2008 Off Broadway (CD) with Joel Hatch, Cyrilla Baer, Amy Warren, Joe Farrell, Daniel Marcus, Niffer Clarke, Roger E. DeWitt, Jeff Still.

Adrift in Macao
2007 Off Broadway (CD) with Will Swenson, Michele Ragusa, Alan Campbell, Orville Mendoza, Rachel De Benedet, Jonathan Rayson, Elisa Van Duyne.

After the Fair
1999 Off Broadway (CD) with Michele Pawk, David Staller, James Ludwig, Jennifer Piech.

Ain't Misbehavin'
1978 Broadway (CD) with Nell Carter, Andre De Shields, Charlaine Woodard, Ken Page, Armelia McQueen.
1995 Tour recording (CD) with the Pointer Sisters, Michael-Leon Wooley, Eugene Barry-Hill.
2009 Tour recording (CD) with Ruben Studdard, Frenchie Davis, David Jennings, Patrice Covington, Trenyce Cobbins.

All in Love
1961 Off Broadway (LP) with David Atkinson, Mimi Randolph, Gaylea Byrne, Lee Cass, Christina Gillespie, Dom DeLuise, Michael Davis.

Altar Boyz
2005 Off Broadway (CD) with Scott Porter, David Josefsberg, Ryan Duncan, Tyler Maynard, Andy Karl.

Always . . . Patsy Cline
1994 Nashville (CD) with Mandy Barnett, Tere Myers.

And the World Goes 'Round
1991 Off Broadway (CD) with Bob Cuccioli, Karen Mason, Jim Walton, Karen Ziemba, Brenda Pressley.

Annie Warbucks
1993 Off Broadway (CD) with Harve Presnell, Donna McKechnie, Kathryn Zaremba, Marguerite MacIntyre, Arlene Robertson, Harvey Evans, Raymond Thorne.

Assassins
1991 Off Broadway (CD) with Victor Gerber, Jonathan Hadary, Terrence Mann, Debra Monk, Jace Alexander, Patrick Cassidy, Annie Golden, Greg Germann, William Parry, Eddie Korbich, Lee Wilkof.
2004 Broadway revival (CD) with Michael Cerveris, Neil Patrick Harris, Denis O'Hare, Marc Kudisch, Becky Ann Baker, James Barbour, Mario Cantone, Catherine Garrison, Alexander Gemignani, Jeffrey Kuhn.

Avenue Q
2003 Off Broadway/Broadway (CD) with John Tartaglia, Stephanie D'Abruzzo, Jordan Gelber, Rick Lyon, Ann Harada, Natalie Venetia Belcon, Jennifer Barnhart.

Balancing Act
1992 Off Broadway (CD) with Craig Wells, Diane Fratantoni, Christine Toy, J. B. Adams, Suzanne Hevner, Nancy E. Carroll.

Ballad for a Firing Squad See *Mata Hari*.

Ballad for Bimshire
1963 Off Broadway (LP) with Christine Spencer, Jimmy Randolph, Frederick O'Neal, Robert Hooks, Alyce Webb, Ossie Davis, Eugene Edwards.

bare
2007 Studio recording (CD) with Wade Muir, Graham Parkhurst, Alison O'Neill, Claire Rouleau, Nichola Lawrence.

Bat Boy: The Musical
2001 Off Broadway (CD) with Deven May, Kerry Butler, Kaitlin Hopkins, Sean McCourt, Richard Pruitt, Dick Storm, Trent Armand Kendall.
2004 London (CD) with Devon May, Rebecca Vere, John Barr, Emma Williams.

Beehive
1986 Off Broadway (LP) with Alison Fraser, Gina Taylor, Jasmine Guy, Pattie Darcy, Adriane Lenox, Laura Theodore.

The Believers
1968 Off Broadway (LP) with Josephine Jackson, Joseph A. Walker, Barry Hemphill, Anje Ray, Ron Steward, Benjamin Carter, Veronica Redd, Ladji Camara, Don Oliver.

Below the Belt
1966 Off Broadway (LP) with Madeline Kahn, Richard Blair, Lily Tomlin, Genna Carter, Robert Rovin, Judy Graubart.

Berlin to Broadway with Kurt Weill
1972 Off Broadway (LP) with Ken Kercheval, Jerry Lanning, Margery Cohen, Judy Lander, Hal Watters.

Bernarda Alba
2006 Off Broadway (CD) with Phylicia Rashad, Sally Murphy, Daphne Rubin-Vega, Judith Blazer, Saundra Santiago, Nikki M. James.

The Best Little Whorehouse in Texas
1978 Off Broadway/Broadway (CD) with Henderson Forsythe, Carlin Glynn, Jay Garner, Clint Allmon, Delores Hall, Pamela Blair, Susan Mansur.
1982 Film soundtrack (CD) with Dolly Parton, Burt Reynolds, Charles Durning, Jim Nabors, Dom DeLuise, Theresa Merritt. (Also on DVD.)

The Billy Barnes Revue
1959 Off Broadway/Broadway (LP) with Bob Rodgers. Bert Convy, Ann Guilbert, Ken Berry, Joyce Jameson, Jackie Joseph, Len Weinrib, Patti Regan.

Billy Noname
1970 Off Broadway (LP) with Donny Burks, Alan Weeks, Hattie Winston, Andrea Saunders, Charles Moore, Gory Van Scott.

Birds of Paradise
1987 Off Broadway (CD) with Todd Graff, John Cunningham, Crista Moore, Barbara Walsh, Donna Murphy, Mary Beth Peil, Andrew Hill Newman, J. K. Simmons.

Blues in the Night
1987 London (CD) with Carol Woods, Maria Friedman, Debbie Bishop, Clarle Peters.

Boobs! The Musical
2003 Off Broadway (CD) with Robert Hunt, Jenny Lynn Suckling, Rebecca Young, Max Perlman, J. Brandon Savage.

Boy Meets Boy
1975 Off Broadway (CD) with Joe Barrett, David Gallegly, Rita Gordon, Raymond Wood.

Bright Lights Big City
2005 Studio recording (CD) with Patrick Wilson, Jesse L. Martin, Eden Espinosa, Celia Keenan-Bolger, Sharon Leal, Anne Marie Milazzo, Gavin Creel, Sheri Rene Scott, Christine Ebersole.

Bring in 'da Noise Bring in 'da Funk
1995 Broadway (CD) with Savion Glover, Ann Duquesnay, Jeffrey Wright, Jared Crawford, Jimmy Tate, Dule Hill, Raymond King, Baakari Wilder, Vincent Bingham.

Brownstone
2003 Studio recording (CD) with Liz Callaway, Brian d'Arcy James, Rebecca Luker, Kevin Reed, Debbie Gravitte.

The Bubbly Black Girl Sheds Her Chameleon Skin
2000 Off Broadway (CD) with La Chanze, Darius de Haas, Duane Boutte, Jerry Dixon, Cheryl Alexander, Jonathan Dokuchitz.

Candide
1956 Broadway (CD) with Max Adrian, Barbara Cook, Robert Rounseville, Irra Petina.

1973 Off Broadway/Broadway (LP) with Lewis J. Stadlen, Mark Baker, Maureen Brennan, June Gable, Sam Freed, Deborah St. Darr.

1982 New York City Opera (CD) with John Lankston, Erie Mills, David Eisler, Joyce Castle.

1989 Studio recording (CD) with Jerry Hadley, June Anderson, Adolph Green, Christa Ludwig.

1997 Broadway (CD) with Jim Dale, Harolyn Blackwell, Jason Danieley, Andrea Martin.

1999 London (CD) with Simon Russell Beale, Daniel Evans, Alex Kelly, Beverly Klein.

Captain Louie

2005 Off Broadway (CD) with Jimmy Dieffenbach, Ronny Mercedes, Alexio Barboza, Sara Kapner, Kelsey Fatebene.

Caroline, or Change

2003 Off Broadway (CD) with Tonya Pinkins, Harrison Chad, Anika Noni Rose, Veanne Cox, David Costabile, Alice Playten, Reathel Bean, Larry Keith, Chuck Cooper.

Charlotte Sweet

1982 Off Broadway (CD) with Mara Beckerman, Christopher Seppe, Merle Louise, Lynn Eldridge, Jeffrey Keller, Timothy Lansfield, Michael McCormick, Polly Pen.

A Chorus Line

1975 Off Broadway/Broadway (CD) with Donna McKechnie, Robert LuPone, Wayne Cilento, Priscilla Lopez, Pamela Blair, Carole Bishop, Sammy Williams, Renee Baughman, Baayork Lee, Thomas J. Walsh.

1985 Film soundtrack (CD) with Alyson Reed, Yamil Borges, Gregg Burge, Terrence Mann, Vicki Frederick, Audrey Landers, Cameron English. (Also on DVD.)

2006 Broadway revival (CD) with Charlotte d'Amboise, Michael Berresse, Deidre Goodwin, Natalie Cortez, Jeffrey Schectet, Jason Tam, Yuka Takara.

Christy

1975 Off Broadway (LP) with Jimi Elmer, Betty Forsyth, Bea Swanson, John Canary, Alexander Sokoloff, Bruce Levitt.

Cindy

1964 Off Broadway (LP) with Jacqueline Mayro, Johnny Harmon, Joe Masiell, Thelma Oliver, Tommy Karaty, Mark Stone, Mike Sawyer, Sylvia Mann, Frank Nastasi.

A Class Act
2000 Off Broadway (CD) with Lonny Price, Randy Graff, Carolee Carmello, David Hibbard, Ray Wills, Jonathan Freeman, Nancy Anderson, Julia Murney.

Closer Than Ever
1989 Off Broadway (CD) with Sally Mayes, Lynne Wintersteller, Richard Muenz, Brent Barrett.

Colette
1970 Off Broadway (LP) with Zoe Caldwell, Ruth Nelson, Keith Charles, Holland Taylor, Tom Aldredge, Louis Turenne.
1994 Studio recording (CD) with Judy Blazer, Judy Kaye, George Lee Andrews, Rita Gardner, Jason Graae, Jonathan Freeman, Walter Willison. (Retitled *Colette Collage*)

Contact
1999 Off Broadway/Broadway (CD) Recorded music by Beach Boys, Benny Goodman and his Orchestra, Stephanie Grappelli, Al Cooper and his Savoy Sultans.

Cotton Patch Gospel
1988 Studio recording (CD) with Tom Key, Scott Ainslie, Pete Corum, Jim Lauderdale, Michael Mark.

Cowgirls
1996 Off Broadway (CD) with Betsy Howie, Mary Murfitt, Jackie Sanders, Rhonda Coullet, Mary Ehrlinger, Lori Fischer.

The Cradle Will Rock
1937 Off Broadway (CD) with Howard Da Silva, Olive Stanton, Jules Schmidt, Edward Fuller, Blanche Collins, Frank Marvel, John Adair, Peggy Coudray, Maynard Holmes, Bert Weston, Dulce Fox.
1964 Off Broadway (LP) with Jerry Orbach, Lauri Peters, Clifford David, Hal Buckley, Micki Grant, Rita Gardner, Gordon B. Clarke, Joseph Bova, Nancy Andrews, Dean Dittmann.
1985 London with several cast members of 1983 Off Broadway (CD) with Patti LuPone, Randle Mel, David Schramm, Mary Lou Rosato, Michele-Denise Woods, Henry Stram, Casey Biggs, Leslie Geraci, Brooks Baldwin.

Dames at Sea
1968 Off Broadway (CD) with Bernadette Peters, David Christmas, Tamara Long, Steve Elmore, Sally Stark, Joseph R. Sicari.
1971 Television soundtrack (LP) with Ann-Margaret, Ann Miller, Dick Shawn, Anne Meara, Fred Gwynne.
1989 British tour (CD) with Tina Doyle, Paul Robinson, Josephine Blake, Sandra Dickinson.

Das Barbecü
1994 Off Broadway (CD) with J. K. Simmons, Sally Mayes, Carolee Carmello, Julie Johnson, Jerry McGarity.

Debbie Does Dallas
2002 Off Broadway (CD) with Sherie René Scott, Jama Williamson, Caitlin Miller, John Patrick Walker, Paul Fitzgerald, Mary Catherine Garrison.

The Decline and Fall of the Entire World as Seen through the Eyes of Cole Porter Revisited
1965 Off Broadway (CD) with Kaye Ballard, Harold Lang, William Hickey, Carmen Alvarez, Elmarie Wendel.

Demi-Dozen
1958 Off Broadway (LP) with Ronny Graham, Jane Connell, Gerry Matthews, Jean Arnold, Ceil Cabot, Jack Fletcher, George Hall.

Dessa Rose
2005 Off Broadway (CD) with La Chanze, Rachel York, Michael Hayden, Norm Lewis, William Parry, Rebecca Eichenberger, Kecia Lewis, Eric Jordan Young, Tina Fabrique.

Dime a Dozen
1962 Off Broadway (LP) with Gerry Matthews, Mary Louise Wilson, Rex Robbins, Fredricka Weber, Susan Browning, Jack Fletcher.

Dinah Was
2005 Los Angeles (CD) with Yvette Freeman.

Doctor Selavy's Magic Theatre
1972 Off Broadway (LP) with George McGrath, Barry Primus, Denise Delapenha, Jessica Harper, Amy Taubin, Steve Menken.

Dressed to the Nines
1960 Off Broadway (LP) with Gerry Matthews, Gordon Connell, Bill Hinnant, Mary Louise Wilson, Ceil Calbot, Pat Ruhl.

Eating Raoul
1992 Off Broadway (CD) with Eddie Korbich, Courtenay Collins, Adrian Zmed, Susan Wood, M. W. Reid, Jonathan Brody, David Masenheimer, Cindy Benson, Lovette George.

Elegies: A Song Cycle
2003 Off Broadway (CD) with Betty Buckley, Michael Rupert, Carolee Carmello, Christian Borle, Keith Byron Kirk.

Ernest in Love
1960 Off Broadway (CD) with Sara Seegar, John Irving, Louis Edmonds, Leila Martin, Gerrianne Raphael, George Hall.

Evil Dead: The Musical
2006 Off Broadway (CD) with Ryan Ward, Jennifer Bryne, Darryl Winslow, Brandon Wardell, Jenna Coker, Renee Klapmeyer, Tom Walker, Ryan Williams.

The Faggot
1973 Off Broadway (LP) with Al Carmines, Julie Kurnitz, Essie Borden, Ira Siff, Lee Guilliatt, Frank Coppola.

Falsettoland
1990 Off Broadway (CD) with Michael Rupert, Faith Prince, Stephen Bogardus, Chip Zien, Danny Gerard, Heather MacRae, Janet Metz.

Fame on 42nd Street
2003 Off Broadway (CD) with José Vegas, Christopher J. Hanke, Sara Schmidt, Nicole Leach, Q. Smith, Cheryl Freeman.

The Fantasticks
1960 Off Broadway (CD) with Jerry Orbach, Rita Gardner, Kenneth Nelson, William Larsen, Hugh Thomas.
1993 Japan tour (CD) with Alfred Lakeman, Chiara Peacock, Sam Samuelson.
1995 Film (DVD) with Jonathan Morris, Joseph McIntyre, Jean Louisa Kelly, Joel Grey, Brad Sullivan, Barnard Hughes.

2000 Kings College Wimbledon (CD) with Andrew Nicolaides, Robin Chalk, Amber Sinclair, Ian Goodman, Mark Lowe.

2006 Off Broadway revival (CD) with Burke Moses, Santino Fontana, Sara Jean Ford, Leo Burmester, Martin Vidnovic.

Fashion
1974 California revival (CD) with Mary Jo Catlett, Frank Ferrante, Henrietta Valor, Christina Saffran, Jenifer Chatfield.

First Lady Suite
2002 Los Angeles (CD) with Evelyn Halus, Eydie Alyson, Paula Newsome, Heather Lee, Kate Shindle, Gregory Jbara, Mary-Pat Green, Irene Piccinni.

Five Course Love
2005 Off Broadway (CD) with Heather Ayers, John Bolton, Jeff Gurner.

Floyd Collins
1996 Off Broadway (CD) with Christopher Innvar, Jason Danieley, Theresa McCarthy, Martin Moran, Cass Morgan, Don Chastain, Brian d'Arcy James.

Fly Blackbird
1962 Off Broadway (LP) with Avon Long, Robert Guillaume, Mary Louise, Thelma Oliver, Micki Grant, Gilbert Price, Chele Abel.

Forbidden Broadway
1982 Off Broadway (CD) with Gerard Alessandrini, Fred Barton, Bill Carmichael, Nora Mae Lyng, Chloé Webb.

1991 Compilation recording (1985–1991) (CD) with Toni DiBuono, Kevin Ligon, Michael McGrath, Karen Murphy.

1993 Off Broadway (CD) with Suzanne Blakeslee, Craig Wells, John Freedson, Brad Oscar, Gina Kreizmar, Christine Pedi, Gerard Alessandrini, Carol Channing.

Forbidden Broadway Strikes Back!
1996 Off Broadway (CD) with Tom Plotkin, Christine Pedi, Donna English, Bryan Batt.

Forbidden Broadway Cleans Up Its Act
1998 Off Broadway (CD) with Bryan Batt, Lori Hammel, Matthew Ward, Kristine Zbornik, Edward Staudenmayer.

Forbidden Broadway 2001: A Spoof Odyssey
2000 Off Broadway (CD) with Danny Gurwin, Tony Nation, Christine Pedi, Catherine Stornetta, Felicia Finley.

Forbidden Broadway 20th Anniversary Edition
2000 Off Broadway (CD) with Toni DiBuono, Christine Pedi, Terri White.

Forbidden Broadway: Special Victims Unit
2005 Off Broadway (CD) with Jason Mills, Megan Lewis, Jennifer Simard, Ron Bohmer.

Forbidden Broadway: Rude Awakening
2008 Off Broadway (CD) with Valerie Fagan, James Donegan, Janet Dickson, Jared Bradshaw, Megan Lewis, William Selby, Michael West, Jeanne Montano.

Forbidden Broadway Goes to Rehab
2009 Off Broadway (CD) with Ed Staudenmayer, Gina Kreizmar, James Donegan, Kristen Mengelkoch, William Selby, Christina Bianco, Michael West.

Forever Plaid
1990 Off Broadway (CD) with Jason Graae, Guy Stroman, David Engel, Stan Chandler.
2005 Las Vegas (CD) with Ken Seiffert, David Kancsar, Bruce Ewing, Stan Sandish.

Four Below Strikes Back
1960 Off Broadway (LP) with Nancy Dussault, George Furth, Cy Young, Jenny Lou Law.

4 Guys Named José . . . and Una Mujer Named Maria!
2000 Off Broadway (CD) with Philip Anthony, Ricardo Puente, Lissette Gonzalez, Allen Hidalgo, Henry Gainza.

Frankenstein
2007 Off Broadway (CD) with Hunter Foster, Christiane Noll, Steve Blanchard, Mandy Bruno, Jim Stanek.

Gertrude Stein's First Reader
1969 Off Broadway (LP) with Ann Sternberg, Joy Garrett, Frank Giordano, Michael Anthony, Sandra Thornton.

The Gifts of the Magi
1984 Off Off Broadway (CD) with Scott Waara, Sarah Knapp, Eddie Korbich, Walter Charles, Donna Bullock, Gordon Stanley.

The Glorious Ones
2007 Off Broadway (CD) with Marc Kudisch, Natalie Venetia Belcon, John Kassir, Erin Davie, David Patrick Kelly, Jeremy Webb, Julyana Soelistyo.

Goblin Market
1986 Off Broadway (CD) with Terri Klausner, Ann Morrison.

Godspell
1971 Off Broadway (CD) with Stephen Nathan, David Haskell, Lamar Alford, Robin Lamont, Sonia Manzano, Herb Simon, Joanne Jonas, Peggy Gordon, Jeffrey Mylett, Gilmer McCormick.
1972 London (CD) with David Essex, Jeremy Irons, Julie Covington, Marti Webb, Verity-Anne Meldrum.
1973 Film soundtrack (CD) with Victor Garber, David Haskell, Lynn Thigpen, Gilmer McCormick, Merrell Jackson, Joanne Jonas, Robin Lamont, Jeffrey Mylett. (Also on DVD.)
1993 British studio recording (LP) with Darren Day, Glynn Kerslake, Ruthie Henshaw, John Barrowman, Paul Manuel, Clive Rowe.
2000 Off Broadway (CD) with Barrett Foa, Will Erat, Capathia Jenkins, Eliseo Roman, Catherine Carpenter, Shoshana Bean.
2001 National tour (CD) with Joe Carney, Michael Yuen, Sal Sabella, Jessica Carter.

The Golden Apple
1954 Off Broadway (CD) with Stephen Douglass, Priscilla Gillette, Kay Ballard, Jack Whiting, Bibi Osterwald, Portia Nelson, Jerry Stiller, Jonathan Lucas, Dean Michener.

The Golden Land
1985 Off Broadway (LP) with Bruce Adler, Neva Small, Avi Hoffman, Marc Krause, Phylis Berk, Joanne Borts.

The Great American Trailer Park Musical
2005 Off Broadway (CD) with Linda Hart, Shuler Hensley, Orfeh, Wayne Wilcox, Leslie Kritzer, Kaitlin Hopkins, Marya Grandy.

Greenwich Village, U.S.A.

1960 Off Broadway (LP) with Jane A. Johnston, Saralou Cooper, Jack Betts, Dawn Hampton, James Pompeii, Pat Finley, James Harwood, Burke McHugh.

Grey Gardens

2006 Off Broadway (CD) with Christine Ebersole, Mary Louise Wilson, Sara Gettelfinger, John McMartin, Matt Cavanaugh, Bob Stillman, Michael Potts.

2006 Broadway (CD) with Christine Ebersole, Mary Louise Wilson, Erin Davie, John McMartin, Matt Cavanaugh, Bob Stillman, Michael Potts.

Groucho: A Life in Revue

1995 studio recording (CD) with Frank Ferrante, Marguerite Lowell, Ray Abramsohn.

Gutenberg! The Musical!

2007 Off Broadway (CD) with Christopher Fitzgerald, Jeremy Shamos.

Hair

1967 Off Broadway (CD) with Gerome Ragni, Walker Daniels, Lynn Kellogg, Shelley Plimpton, Suzannah Evans, Linda Compton, Steve Dean, Sally Eaton, Jill O'Hara, Marijane Maricle.

1968 Broadway (CD) with Gerome Ragni, James Rado, Lynn Kellogg, Lamont Washington, Steve Curry, Sally Eaton, Shelley Plimpton, Melba Moore, Ronald Dyson, Diane Keaton.

1968 London (CD) with Paul Nicholas, Oliver Tobias, Annabel Leventon, Michael Feast, Marsha Hunt, Linda Kendrick, Sonja Kristina, Peter Straker.

1979 Film soundtrack (CD) with Treat Williams, John Savage, Beverly D'Angelo, Don Dacus, Annie Golden, Cheryl Barnes, Nell Carter, Melba Moore, Ronald Dyson, Ellen Foley. (Also on DVD.)

2005 Concert (CD) with Raul Esparza, Adam Pascal, Annie Golden, Lillias White, Gavin Creel, Shoshana Bean, Lea DeLaria, Chuck Cooper, Laura Benanti, Harvey Fierstein, Orfeh, Liz Callaway, Norm Lewis.

2009 Broadway revival (CD) with Gavin Creel, Will Swenson, Allison Case, Caissy Levy, Bryce Ryness, Sasha Allen, Darius Nichols, Kacie Sheik.

Half-Past Wednesday

1962 Off Broadway (LP) with David Winters, Dom DeLuise, Audre Johnston, Sean Garrison, Robert Fitch, Holly Sherwood.

Hank Williams: Lost Highway
2003 Off Broadway (CD) with Jason Petty, Michael P. Moran, Margaret Bowman, Michael J. Howell.

Hannah . . . 1939
1992 Studio recording (CD) with Julie Wilson, Neva Small, Peter Frechette, Yusef Bulos, Leigh Berry, Lori Wilner, Patti Perkins, Ann Talman.

Happy End
1995 Studio recording (CD) with Gabriele Ramm, Steven Kimbrough, Walter Raffeiner, Karin Ploog.
2006 San Francisco (CD) with Peter Macon, Charlotte Cohn, Steven Anthony Jones, Jack Willis, Sab Shimono, Brennan Leath.

Harlem Song
2002 Off Broadway (CD) with Queen Esther, B. J. Crosby, David St. Louis, Rosa Curry, Rosa Evangelina, Randy A. Davis.

Hedwig and the Angry Inch
1998 Off Broadway (CD) with John Cameron Mitchell, Miriam Shor.
2001 Film soundtrack (CD) with John Cameron Mitchell, Miriam Shor, Michael Pitt, Andrea Martin. (Also on DVD.)

Hello Again
1994 Off Broadway (CD) with Donna Murphy, Judy Blazer. John Dossett, Malcolm Gets, John Cameron Mitchell, Carolee Carmello, Dennis Parlato, Michele Pawk, Michael Park, David A. White.

The Housewives' Cantata
1980 Off Broadway (LP) with Sharon Talbot, Maida Meyers, Mira J. Spektor, Lawrence Chelsi.

How to Steal an Election
1968 Off Broadway (LP) with Bill McCutcheon, Carole Demas, D. R. Allen, Clifton Davis, Del Hinkley, Beverly Ballard, Ed Crowley, Barbara Anson, Thom Koutsoukos.

Howard Crabtree's Whoop-Dee-Doo!
1993 Off Broadway (CD) with Howard Crabtree, Peter Morris, Mark Waldrop, Keith Cromwell, Alan Tulin, Ron Skobel, Tommy Femia, David Lowenstein, Jay Rogers.

The Human Comedy
1983 Off Broadway/Broadway (CD) with Rex Smith, Bonnie Koloc, Mary Elizabeth Mastrantonio, Stephen Geoffreys, Delores Hall, Caroline Peyton, Laurie Franks, Josh Blake, Anne Marie Bobby.

I Can't Keep Running in Place
1981 Off Broadway (CD) with Helen Gallagher, Marcia Rodd, Joy Franz, Bev Larson, Evalyn Baron, Phyllis Newman, Mary Donnet.

I Love You Because
2006 Off Broadway (CD) with Colin Hanlon, Farah Alvin, Stephanie D'Abruzzo, David A. Austin, Jordan Leeds, Courtney Balan.

I Love You, You're Perfect, Now Change
1996 Off Broadway (CD) with Jennifer Simard, Danny Burnstein, Robert Roznowski, Melissa Weil.

If Love Were All
1999 Off Broadway (CD) with Harry Groener, Twiggy.

I'm Getting My Act Together and Taking It on the Road
1978 Off Broadway (CD) with Gretchen Cryer, Margot Rose, Betty Aberlin, Don Scardino.
1981 London cast (CD) with Diane Langton, Nicky Croydon, Megg Nicol, Greg Martin.

In Circles
1967 Off Broadway (LP) with Al Carmines, Elaine Summers, Arlene Rothlein, David Vaughn, Theo Barnes, Julie Kurnitz, George McGrath.

In the Heights
2007 Off Broadway (CD) with Lin-Manuel Miranda, Mandy Gonzalez, Christopher Jackson, Karen Olivo, Olga Meredez, Priscilla Lopez, Andrea Burns, Robin De Jesus.

In Trousers
1978 Off Broadway (CD) with Chip Zien, Alison Fraser, Mary Testa, Joanna Green.

The IT Girl
2001 Off Broadway (CD) with Jean Louise Kelly, Stephen DeRosa, Jessica Boevers, Jonathan Dokuchitz, Susan M. Haefner, Danette Holden, Monte Wheeler.

Jacques Brel Is Alive and Well and Living in Paris

1968 Off Broadway (CD) with Mort Shuman, Elly Stone, Shawn Elliott, Alice Whitfield.

1974 Film soundtrack (LP) with Mort Shuman, Elly Stone, Joe Masiell, Jacques Brel. (Also on DVD.)

2006 Off Broadway (CD) with Gay Marshall, Stephen Gilewski, Natascia Diaz, Robert Cuccioli, Brad Carbone, Sean McDaniel, Eric Svejcar, George Petit, Rodney Hicks.

1995 London (CD) with Allison Egan, Liz Greenaway, Michael Cahill, Stuart Pendred.

Jericho-Jim Crow

1964 Off Broadway (LP) with Gilbert Price, Micki Grant, Rosalie King, Joseph Attles, Dorothy Drake, William Cain, Metrogene Myles.

Joan

1972 Off Broadway (LP) with Lee Guilliatt, Essie Borden, Tracy Moore, Ira Siff, Julie Kurnitz, Emily Adams.

john & jen

1995 Off Broadway (CD) with James Ludwig, Carolee Carmello.

Johnny Guitar

2004 Off Broadway (CD) with Steve Blanchard, Ann Crumb, Judy McLane, Robert Evan, Ed Sala, David Sinkus, Robb Sapp, Jason Edwards, David Sinkus, Grant Norman.

Jolson and Company

2002 Off Broadway (CD) with Stephen Mo Hanan, Robert Ari, Nancy Anderson.

Joseph and the Amazing Technicolor Dreamcoat

1968 Concept Album (LP) with David Daltry, Tim Rice, Bryan Watson, Malcolm Parry.

1974 Studio recording (CD) with Gary Bond, Peter Reeves, Tim Rice, John Marson, Maynard Williams, Roger Watson.

1982 Off Broadway/Broadway (CD) with Bill Hutton, Laurie Beechman, Tom Carder, Steve McNaughton, Gordon Stanley.

1991 London (CD) with Jason Donovan, Linzi Hateley, David Easter, Jason Moore, Mark Frendo.

1992 Canadian Production (CD) with Donny Osmond, Janet Metz, Jeff Blumenkrantz, Johnny Seaton, Michael Fletcher.

1993 Los Angeles (CD) with Michael Damien, Kelli Rabke, Clifford David, Robert Torti.
1999 Video soundtrack (CD) with Donny Osmond, Maria Friedman. (Also on DVD.)

Joy
1970 Off Broadway (LP) with Oscar Brown Jr., Jean Pace, Sivuca, Norman Shobey.

Ka-Boom!
1980 Off Broadway (LP) with John Hall, Andrea Wright, Judith Bro, Ken Ward, Valerie Williams, Ben Agresti.

King of the Whole Damn World
1962 Off Broadway (LP) with Boris Aplon, Alan Howard, Tom Pedi, Francine Beers, Brendan Fay, Sheldon Golomb, Charlotte Whaley, Jerry Brent, Jackie Perkuhn.

Kuni-Leml
1998 Off Broadway revival (CD) with Jennifer Rosin, Danny Gurwin, Jonathan Hadley, David Brummel, Farah Alvin, Pul Harman, Joel Newsome, Jay Brian Winnick.

A Kurt Weill Cabaret (The World of Kurt Weill in Song)
1963 Off Broadway (LP) with Will Holt, Martha Schlamme.

The Last Five Years
2002 Off Broadway (CD) with Sherie René Scott, Norbert Leo Butz.

The Last Session
1997 Off Broadway (CD) with Bob Stillman, Grace Garland, Amy Coleman, Dean Bradshaw, Stephen Bienskie.

The Last Sweet Days of Isaac
1970 Off Broadway (LP) with Austin Pendleton, Fredricka Weber, John Long, Charles Collins, Louise Heath, C. David Colson.

Let My People Come
1974 Off Broadway (LP) with Tobie Columbus, Lorraine Davidson, Larry Paulette, Christine Rubens, Joe Jones.

Lies & Legends: The Musical Stories of Harry Chapin
1985 Off Broadway (LP) with Terri Klausner, Martin Vidnovic, John Herrera, Joanna Glushak, Ron Orbach.

Listen to My Heart: The Songs of David Friedman
2003 Off Broadway (CD) with David Friedman, Alix Korey, Joe Cassidy, Michael Hunsaker, Allison Briner, Anne Runolfsson.

Little Fish
2007 Los Angeles (CD) with Alice Ripley, Robert Torti, Dina Morishita, Chad Kimball, Samantha Shelton, Gregory Jbara, German Santiago.

Little Ham
2002 Off Broadway (CD) with André Garner, Monica L. Patton, Richard Vida, Brenda Braxton, Joe Wilson Jr.

Little Mary Sunshine
1959 Off Broadway (CD) with Eileen Brennan, William Graham, John Mc-Martin, Elizabeth Parrish, Elmarie Wendel, John Aniston, Mario Siletti.

Little Shop of Horrors
1982 Off Broadway (CD) with Lee Wilkof, Ellen Greene, Hy Anzell, Franc Luc, Leilani Jones, Jennifer Leigh Warren, Sheila Kay Davis, Ron Taylor.
1986 Film soundtrack (CD) with Rick Moranis, Ellen Greene, Vincent Gardenia, Steve Martin, Tisha Campbell, Tichina Arnold, Michelle Campbell, Levi Stubbs. (Also on DVD.)
1993 British studio recording (CD) with Harry Formby, Michaela Aughton, Charles de Trafford, Terry Totten, Wendy Wood, Christianne Lennox, Melinda Belter, Alex Hatchett.
1994 London revival (CD) with Su Pollard, Barbara Jaeson, Marc Joseph, Peter McNally, Lisa Daniel, Morgan Deare, Billy Miller.
2003 Broadway (CD) with Hunter Foster, Kerry Butler, Ron Bartlett, Douglas Sills, Carla J. Hargrove, De Quina Moore, Trisha Jeffrey, Michael-Leon Wooley.

The Littlest Revue
1956 Off Broadway (CD) with Charlotte Rae, Tammy Grimes, Joel Grey, Larry Storch, George Marcy, Beverly Bozeman, Dorothy Jarnac, Tommy Morton.

Love See *What about Luv?*

Lovers
1975 Off Broadway (LP) with Michael Cascone, John Ingle, Martin Rivera, Robert Sevra, Reathel Bean, Gary Sneed.

Lovesong
1976 Off Broadway (LP) with Jess Richards, Melanie Chartoff, Sigrid Heath, Robert Manzari.

Lucky Stiff
1994 studio recording (CD) with Evan Papas, Mary Testa, Jason Graae, Judy Blazer, Debbie Shapiro Gravitte, Paul Kandel, Patrick Quinn.
2003 Off Broadway (CD) with Malcolm Gets, Mary Testa, Janet Metz, Paul Kandel, Stuart Zagnit, Rob Faber, Rosena M. Hill.

The Mad Show
1966 Off Broadway (LP) with Linda Lavin, Dick Libertini, Jo Anne Worley, Paul Sand, MacIntyre Dixon.

Mahagonny See *The Rise and Fall of the City of Mahagonny.*

Make Me a Song: The Music of William Finn
2007 Off Broadway (CD) with Sandy Binion, D. B. Bonds, Adam Heller, Sally Wilfert.

A Man of No Importance
2002 Off Broadway (CD) with Roger Rees, Faith Prince, Steven Pasquale, Charles Keating, Jessica Molansky, Ronn Carroll.

Man with a Load of Mischief
1966 Off Broadway (LP) with Virginia Vestoff, Reid Shelton, Alice Cannon, Raymond Thorne, Tom Noel, Lesslie Nicol.

March of the Falsettos
1981 Off Broadway (CD) with Michael Rupert, Alison Fraser, Stephen Bogardus, Chip Zien, James Kushner.

Marry Me a Little
1981 Off Broadway (CD) with Craig Lucas, Suzanne Henry.

The Marvelous Wonderettes
2008 Off Broadway (CD) with Farah Alvin, Beth Malone, Bets Malone, Victoria Matlock.

Mata Hari
1996 Off Broadway (CD) with Robin Skye, Michael Zaslow, Kirk McDonald, Rosemarie Dama, Jack Fletcher, Karen Sanders (recorded in 2001).

Mayor
1985 Off Broadway (CD) with Lenny Wolpe, Ken Jennings, Kathryn Mc-Ateer, Ilene Kristen, Keith Curran, Nancy Giles, Douglas Bernstein, Marion J. Caffey.

The Me Nobody Knows
1970 Off Broadway (CD) with Irene Cara, Northern J. Calloway, Hattie Winston, Jose Fernandez, Gerri Dean, Laura Michaels, Melanie Henderson, Douglas Grant, Beverly Ann Bremers, Paul Mace, Kevin Lindsay, Carl Thomas.

Menopause: The Musical
2002 Off Broadway (CD) with Mary Jo McConnell, Joy Lynn Matthews, Joyce A. Presutti, Carolann Page.
2004 Studio recording (CD) with Catherine Thomas, Shelly Browne, Pammie O'Bannon, Wesley Williams.

Mixed Doubles
1966 Off Broadway (LP) with Madeline Kahn, Judy Graubart, Robert Rovin, Janie Sell, Gary Sneed, Larry Moss.

The Musical of Musicals—The Musical
2003 Off Broadway (CD) with Eric Rockwell, Joanne Bogart, Lovette George, Craig Fols.

My Life with Albertine
2003 Off Broadway (CD) with Brent Carver, Kelli O'Hara, Chad Kimball, Emily Skinner, Donna Lynne Champlin.

The Mystery of Edwin Drood
1985 Broadway (CD) with George Rose, Betty Buckley, Howard McGillin, Patti Cohenour, Cleo Laine, Jana Schneider, George N. Martin, John Herrera, Joe Grifasi.

Myths & Hymns (Saturn Returns)
1998 Studio recording (CD) with Bob Stillman, Theresa McCarthy, Adam Guettel, Mandy Patinkin, Audra McDonald, Annie Golden, Billy Porter, Jose Llana, Vivian Cherry, Lawrence Clayton.

Naked Boys Singing!

1998 Los Angeles (CD) with Christopher Gilbert, Tony Davis, Brian Beacock, Steve Gibson, Mike Haboush, Gabriel Colbert, Tod Macofsky.

2007 Los Angeles (DVD) with Kevin Shea, Joe Souza, Salvatore Vassallo, Jason Currie, Joseph Keane.

A New Brain

1998 Off Broadway (CD) with Malcolm Gets, Chip Zien, Norm Lewis, Penny Fuller, Mary Testa, Liz Larsen, Michael Mandell, Kristin Chenoweth.

Newsical

2004 Off Broadway (CD) with Todd Alan Johnson, Kim Cea, Stephanie Kurtzuba, Jeff Skowron.

Next to Normal

2009 Broadway (CD) with Alice Ripley, J. Robert Spencer, Jennifer Damiano, Aaron Tveit, Adam Chanler-Berat.

Nite Club Confidential

1984 Off Broadway (LP) with Stephen Berger, Fay DeWitt, Steve Gideon, Denise Nolin, Tom Spiroff.

No for an Answer

1941 Off Broadway (CD) with Carol Channing, Olive Deering, Bert Conway, Lloyd Gough, Martin Wolfson, Curt Conway.

No Way to Treat a Lady

1996 Off Broadway (CD) with Adam Grupper, Alix Korey, Paul Schoeffler, Marguerite McIntyre.

Now Is the Time for All Good Men

1967 Off Broadway (CD) with David Cryer, Sally Niven (pseudonym for Gretchen Cryer), Donna Curtis, Judy Frank, Anne Kaye, David Sabin, John Bennett Perry, Art Wallace, Steve Skiles.

Nunsense

1985 Off Broadway (CD) with Christine Anderson, Edwina Lewis, Marilyn Farina, Semina De Laurentis, Suzi Winson.

1987 London (CD) with Honor Blackman, Anna Sharkey, Bronwen Stanway, Louise Gold, Pip Hinton.

1997 Off Broadway (DVD) with Rue McClanahan, Christine L. Anderson, Semina De Laurentis, Christine Toy Johnson.

Nunsense II: The Second Coming
1994 Off Broadway (CD) with Christine Johnson, Semina De Laurentis, Lyn Vaux, Kathy Robinson, Mary Gillis.

O Marry Me!
1961 Off Broadway (LP) with Chevi Colton, Muriel Greenspon, Ted Van Griethuysen, Elly Stone, James Harwood, Joe Silver, Leonard Drum.

Oh! Calcutta!
1969 Off Broadway (CD) with The Open Window (Robert Dennis, Peter Schickele, Stanley Walden), Bill Macy, Margo Sappington, Mark Dempsey, Raina Barrett, George Welbes, Leon Russom, Alan Rachins, Boni Enten. (Also DVD version in 1971.)

Oh Coward!
1972 Off Broadway (LP) with Roderick Cook, Barbara Carson, Jamie Ross.

Oil City Symphony
1987 Off Broadway (CD) with Mike Craver, Debra Monk, Mary Murfitt, Mark Hardwick.

Olympus on My Mind
1986 Off Broadway (CD) with Martin Vidnovic, Joyce DeWitt, Susan Powell, Jason Graae, Nancy Johnston, Frank Kopyc.

Once on This Island
1990 Off Broadway/Broadway (CD) with La Chanze, Jerry Dixon, Sheila Gibbs, Gerry McIntyre, Kecia Lewis-Evans, Afi McClendon, Milton Craig Nealy, Andrea Frierson, Eric Riley.
1994 London (CD) with Lorna Brown, Anthony Corriette, Sharon Dee Clarke, P. P. Arnold, Clive Rowe, Monique Mason.

Once Upon a Mattress
1959 Off Broadway/Broadway (CD) with Carol Burnett, Jane White, Joe Bova, Jack Gilford, Anne Jones, Allen Case, Matt Mattox, Harry Snow.
1996 Broadway revival (CD) with Sarah Jessica Parker, David Aaron Baker, Mary Lou Rosato, Heath Lamberts, Lewis Cleale, Jane Krakowski, David Hibbard, Lawrence Clayton.

2005 television (DVD) with Carol Burnett, Tracey Ullman, Denis O'Hare, Matthew Morrison, Zooey Deschanel, Tom Smothers, Edward Hibbard.

One Mo' Time
1979 Off Broadway (LP) with Vernel Bagneris, Topsy Chapman, Sylvia "Kuumba" Williams, Thais Clark.

Parade
1960 Off Broadway (CD) with Dody Goodman, Charles Nelson Reilly, Lester James, Fia Karin, Richard Tone.

Passing Strange
2007 Broadway (CD) with Stew, Daniel Breaker, de'Adre Aziza, Eisa Davis, Colman Domingo, Chad Goodridge, Rebecca Naomi Jones. (Also on DVD.)

Peace
Off Broadway 1969 (LP) with Reathel Bean, Judy Kurnitz, George McGrath, Arlene Rothlein, Lee Crespi, David Pursley, David Tice, David Vaughan.

Personals
1998 London (CD) with Martin Callaghan, Summer Rognlie, Christina Fry, Marcus Allen Cooper, Ria Jones, David Bardsley.

Pete 'n' Keely
2000 Off Broadway (CD) with Sally Mayes, George Dvorsky.

Philemon
1975 Off Broadway (LP) with Dick Latessa, Leila Martin, Michael Glenn-Smith, Virginia Gregory, Howard Ross, Drew Katzman, Kathrin King Segal.

Piano Bar
1978 Off Broadway (LP) with Kelly Bishop, Steve Elmore, Karen De Vito, Richard Ryder, Joel Silberman.

Pieces of Eight
1959 Off Broadway (LP) with Jane Connell, Estelle Parsons, Gerry Matthews, Ceil Cabot, Del Close, Gordon Connell.

Pins and Needles
1962 Studio recording of 1937 score (CD) with Barbra Streisand, Jack Carroll, Alan Sokoloff, Rose Marie Jun, Harold Rome.

The Prince and the Pauper
2002 Off Broadway (CD) with Dennis Michael Hall, Gerard Canonico, Michael McCormick, Sally Wilfert, Allison Fisher, Kathy Brier, Rob Evan, Stephen Zinnato.

Privates on Parade
1982 film (DVD) with Denis Quilley, John Cleese, Patrick Pearson, Nicola Pagett, Michael Elphick.

Prom Queens Unchained
1991 Off Broadway (CD) with Dana Ertischek, Don Crosby, Mark Traxler, Susan Levine, Pamela Lloyd.

Promenade
1969 Off Broadway (CD) with Gilbert Price, Ty McConnell, Alice Playten, Madeline Kahn, Carrie Wilson, Margot Albert, Shannon Bolin, Sandra Schaeffer.

Pump Boys and Dinettes
1981 Off Broadway/Broadway (CD) with Jim Wann, Debra Monk, Mark Hardwick, Cass Morgan, John Schimmel, John Foley.

Putting It Together
1993 Off Broadway (CD) with Julie Andrews, Stephen Collins, Rachel York, Christopher Durang, Michael Rupert.
1999 Broadway (DVD) with Carol Burnett, George Hearn, Ruthie Henshaw, Bronson Pinchot, John Barrowman.

Radio Gals
1995 Pasadena (CD) with Helen Geller, Mike Craver, Mark Nadler, Eileen Barrett, Klea Blackhurst, Emily Mikesell, Lenny Wolpe.

Really Rosie
1975 Television (CD) with Carole King, Alice Playten, Dave Soules, Baille Gerstein, Mark Hampton.

Reefer Madness
1999 Los Angeles cast (CD) with Christian Campbell, Jolie Jenkins, Gregg Edelman, Erin Matthews, Robert Torti, Michele Pawk, John Kassir, Lori Alan, Kristen Bell, Harry S. Murphy.
2005 Television soundtrack (CD) with Christian Campbell, Kristen Bell, Alan Cummings, Robert Torti, Steven Weber, Amy Spangler, Ana Gasteyer, John Kassir. (Also on DVD.)

Rent
1996 Off Broadway/Broadway (CD) with Adam Pascal, Anthony Rapp, Daphne Rubin-Vega, Idina Menzel, Wilson Jermaine Heredia, Fredi Walker, Taye Diggs.
2005 Film soundtrack (CD) with Adam Pascal, Anthony Rapp, Rosario Dawson, Idina Menzel, Wilson Jermaine Heredia, Tracie Thoms, Taye Diggs. (Also on DVD.)
2008 Broadway cast (DVD) with Will Chase, Adam Kantor, Renee Goldsberry, Eden Espinosa, Justin Johnston, Michael McElroy, Tracie Thoms, Rodney Hicks.

Return to the Forbidden Planet
1989 London (CD) with John Ashby, Christian Roberts, Allison Harding, Matthew Devitt, Kraig Thornber, Patrick Moore.

The Rise and Fall of the City of Mahagonny
1958 German studio recording (CD) with Lotte Lenya, Heinz Sauerbaum, Gisela Litz.
1997 Salzburg Festival (DVD) with Jerry Hadley, Catherine Malfitano, Gwyneth Jones, Cornelius Smith, Wilbur Pauley.
2007 Los Angeles Opera (DVD) with Anthony Dean Griffey, Patti LuPone, Audra McDonald, James Conlon, Robert Worle.
2008 German studio recording (CD) with Frederic Mayer, Anja Silja, Anny Schlemn, Hans Franzen.

Riverwind
1962 Off Broadway (LP) with Lawrence Brooks, Elizabeth Parrish, Dawn Nickerson, Helon Blount, Martin J. Cassidy, Brooks Morton, Lovelady Powell.

Road Show
2008 Off Broadway (CD) with Michael Cerveris, Alexander Gemingnani, Alma Cuervo, Claybourne Elder, William Parry.

Roadside
2001 Off Broadway (CD) with Julie Johnson, Jonathan Beck Reed, G. W. Bailey, James Hindman, Tom Flagg, Steve Barcus, Ryan Appleby, Jennifer Allen, William Ryall.

Runaways
1978 Off Broadway/Broadway (CD) with Evan Miranda, Diane Lane, Josie De Guzman, David Schechter, Karen Evans, Trini Alvarado, Bernie Allison.

Ruthless!

1994 Los Angeles cast (CD) with Lindsay Ridgeway, Joan Ryan, Loren Freeman, Rita McKenzie, Joanne Baum, Nancy Linari.

Salad Days

1954 London cast (CD) with Eleanor Drew, John Warner, Dorothy Reynolds, Newton Blick, James Cairncross, Michael Meacham, Christine Finn.

1976 London revival (CD) with Elizabeth Seal, Adam Bareham, Sheila Steafel, Christina Matthews, Barry Martin, Malcolm Rennie.

1994 British studio recording (CD) with Leslie Phillips, Tony Slattery, Roy Hudd, Willie Rushton, Simon Green, Timothy West, Prunella Scales, Timothy West, Sara Crowe, Valerie Masterson.

Salvation

1969 Off Broadway (CD) with Peter Link, C. C. Courtney, Joe Morton, Yolande Bavan, Boni Enten, Marta Heflin, Annie Rachel, Chapman Roberts.

The Sap of Life

1961 Off Broadway (LP) with Kenneth Nelson, Jerry Dodge, Dina Paisner, Jack Bittner, Lilian Fields, Patricia Bruder, Lee Powell.

Sarafina!

1987 Off Broadway (CD) with Leleti Khumalo, Mhlathi Khuzwayo, Nhlanhla Ngema, Siboniso Khumalo, Baby Cele.

1992 Film soundtrack (CD) with Leleti Khumalo, Hugh Masekela, Sbasio Ngema, Thandi Zulu, James Ingram. (Also on DVD.)

Saturday Night

1998 London (CD) with Sam Newman, Anna Francolini, Maurice Yeoman, Simon Greiff, Jeremy David, Tracie Bennett, Gavin Lee, Ashleigh Sendin.

2000 Off Broadway (CD) with Michael Benjamin Washington, Kirk McDonald, Greg Zola, Lauren Ward, Joey Sorge, Christopher Fitzgerald, David Campbell, Andrea Burns, Clarke Thorell, Natascia A. Diaz.

Saturn Returns See Myths & Hymns.

Scrambled Feet

1979 Off Broadway (LP) with John Driver, Jeffrey Haddow, Evalyn Baron, Roger Neil.

The Secret Life of Walter Mitty
1964 Off Broadway (LP) with Marc London, Lorraine Serabian, Charles Rydell, Cathryn Damon, Rudy Tronto, Eugene Roche, Rue McClanahan, Rudy Tronto.

Secrets Every Smart Traveler Should Know
1999 Studio recording (CD) with Jay Lenohart, Denise Nolin, Charles Alterman, Maribeth Graham, Nick Santa Maria, Ray deMattis.

See What I Wanna See
2005 Off Broadway (CD) with Idina Menzel, Marc Kudisch, Aaron Lohr, Henry Stram, Mary Testa.

Seven Comes Eleven
1961 Off Broadway (LP) with Mary Louise Wilson, Rex Robbins, Philip Bruns, Ceil Cabot, Donna Sanders, Steve Roland.

Shockheaded Peter
1998 London (CD) with Julian Bleach, Anthony Cairns, Graeme Gilmour, Tamzin Griffin, Jo Pocock.

Shoestring '57 (Ben Bagley's Shoestring '57)
1959 Studio recording of 1956 Off Broadway revue (CD) with Dody Goodman, Beatrice Arthur, Fay DeWitt, Danny Carroll, Dorothy Greener, John Bartis.

Shoestring Revue (Ben Bagley's Shoestring Revue)
1959 Studio recording of 1955 Off Broadway revue (CD) with Beatrice Arthur, Dody Goodman, Bill McCutcheon, Fay DeWitt, Dorothy Greener.

Shout!
2001 London (CD) Denise Summerford, Erica Schroeder, Erin Crosby, Marie-France Arcilla, Julie Dingman Evans.

The Show Goes On
1998 Off Broadway (CD) with Tom Jones, JoAnn Cunningham, Emma Lambert, J. Mark McVey.

Shuffle Along
Studio reconstruction of 1921 production (LP) with Flournoy Miller, Aubrey Lyles, Noble Sissle, Eubie Blake, Gertrude Saunders.

Sing Muse!

1961 Off Broadway (LP) with Karen Morrow, Brandon Maggart, Bob Spencer, Paul Michael, Ralph Stantley, William Pierson.

Smiling the Boy Fell Dead

1961 Off Broadway (LP) with Danny Meehan, Phil Leeds, Claiborne Cary, Joseph Macaulay, Warren Wade, Louise Larabee, Justine Johnson.

Snoopy

1975 San Francisco (CD) with Don Porter, James Gleason, Pamela Myers, Jimmy Dodge, Carla Manning, Roxann Pyle, Alfred Mazza.

1983 London (CD) with Terry Kempner, Robert Locke, Nicky Croydon, Susie Blake, Mark Hadfield, Zoe Bright, Anthony Best.

1988 video (VHS) with Sean Colling, Cam Clarke, Kristie Baker, Tiffany Billings, Ami Foster.

Song of Singapore

1991 Off Broadway (CD) with Jacquey Maltby, Erik Frandsen, Michael Garin, Robert Hipkens, Cathy Foy, Francis Kane, Oliver Jackson Jr.

Songs for a New World

1995 Off Off Broadway (CD) with Jessica Molaskey, Brooks Ashmanskas, Billy Porter, Andrea Burns.

The Spitfire Grill

2001 Off Broadway (CD) with Garrett Long, Phyllis Somerville, Liz Callaway, Armand Schultz, Steven Pasquale, Mary Gordin Murray, Stephen Sinclair.

Spring Awakening

2006 Broadway (CD) with Jonathan Groff, John Gallagher Jr., Lea Michele, Stephen Spinella, Christine Estabrook, Lauren Pritchard, Jonathan B. Wright, Gideon Glick, Lilli Cooper.

Starting Here, Starting Now

1977 Off Broadway (CD) with Loni Ackerman, Margery Cohen, George Lee Andrews.

1993 London (CD) with Clare Burt, Michael Cantwell, Samantha Shaw.

The Streets of New York

1963 Off Broadway (CD) with Ralston Hill, Barbara Williams, David Cryer, Gail Johnson, Barry Alan Grael, Don Phelps.

Sunset
1983 Off Broadway (CD) with Tammy Grimes, Ronee Blakley, Walt Hunter, Kim Milford.

Swingtime Canteen
1997 Studio recording (CD) with Ruth Williamson, Marcy McGuigan, Amy Elizabeth Jones, Penny Ayn Maas, Kelli Maguire, Alison Fraser, Emily Loesser, Debra Barsha, Marcy McGuigan, Maxene Andrews.

The Taffetas
1988 Off Broadway (CD) with Jody Abrahams, Tia Speros, Melanie Mitchell, Karen Curlee.

Take Five
1957 Off Broadway (LP) with Ronny Graham, Ellen Hanley, Gerry Matthews, Jean Arnold, Ceil Cabot.

Taking a Chance on Love
2000 Off Broadway (CD) with Jerry Dixon, Donna English, Eddie Korbich, Terry Burrell.

Taking My Turn
1983 Off Broadway (CD) with Margaret Whiting, Marni Nixon, Tiger Haynes, Sheila Smith, Cissy Houston, Mace Barrett, Victor Griffin, Ted Thurston.
1984 video (VHS) with Margaret Whiting, Marni Nixon, Tiger Haynes, Sheila Smith, Cissy Houston, Mace Barrett, Victor Griffin, Ted Thurston.

Tallulah
1983 Off Broadway (CD) with Helen Gallagher, Russell Nype, Joel Craig.

Ten Percent Revue
1987 Studio recording (CD) with Lisa Bernstein, Paul Hardt, Jimmy Humphrey, Helena Snow, Jenifer Firestone, Tom Wilson Weinberg.

The Thing about Men
2003 Off Broadway (CD) with Marc Kudisch, Leah Hocking, Ron Bohmer, Daniel Reichard, Jennifer Simard.

3 Guys Naked from the Waist Down
1985 Off Broadway (CD) with Jerry Colker, Scott Bakula, John Kassir.

Three Mo' Tenors
2001 Concert (CD) with Victor Trent Cook, Roderick Dixon, Thomas Young.

The Threepenny Opera
1954 Off Broadway (CD) with Scott Merrill, Lotte Lenya, Jo Sullivan, Charlotte Rae, Beatrice Arthur, George Tyne, Gerald Price, John Astin, Martin Wolfson.
1976 Broadway (LP) with Raul Julia, Blair Brown, Ellen Greene, C. K. Alexander, Elizabeth Wilson, Caroline Kava, Tony Azito, Roy Brocksmith, David Sabin.
1990 Studio recording in German (CD) with René Rollo, Helga Dernesch, Rolf Boysen, Ute Lemper, Ario Adorf, Susanne Tremper, Wolfgang Reichmann.
1994 London revival (CD) with Tom Hollander, Sharon Small, Beverly Klein, Tara Hugo, Natasha Bain, Tom Mannion.

Tick, Tick . . . Boom!
2001 Off Broadway (CD) with Raúl Esparza, Amy Spanger, Jerry Dixon.

Tintypes
1980 Off Broadway/Broadway (CD) with Jerry Zaks, Lynne Thigpen, Carolyn Mignini, Trey Wilson, Mary Catherine Wright. (Also on DVD.)

[title of show]
2006 Off Broadway (CD) with Hunter Bell, Jeff Bowen, Heidi Blickenstaff, Susan Blackwell.

Touch
1970 Off Broadway (LP) with Kenn Long, Ava Rosenblum, Phyllis Gibbs, Barbara Ellis, Susan Rosenblum, Gerald S. Doff.

The Toxic Avenger
2009 Off Broadway (CD) with Nick Cordero, Sara Chase, Nancy Opel, Matthew Saldivar, Demond Green.

Tuscaloosa's Calling Me . . . But I'm Not Going!
1975 Off Broadway (LP) with Len Gochman, Patti Perkins, Renny Temple.

The 25th Annual Putnam County Spelling Bee
2005 Off Broadway (CD) with Dan Fogler, Celia Keenan-Bolger, Jose Llana, Sarah Saltzberg, Jesse Tyler Ferguson, Lisa Howard, Derrick Baskin, Deborah S. Craig, Jay Reiss.

Two Gentlemen of Verona
1971 Off Broadway (CD) with Raul Julia, Clifton Davis, Jonelle Allen, Carla Pinza, Alix Elias, Jerry Stiller, Frank O'Brien, Norman Matlock.

Upstairs at O'Neals'
1982 Off Broadway (CD) with Bebe Neuwirth, Sarah Weeks, Douglas Bernstein, Richard Ryder, Randall Edwards, Michon Peacock.

Urinetown
2001 Off Broadway (CD) with Hunter Foster, John Cullum, Jennifer Laura Thompson, Nancy Opel, Daniel Marcus, Jeff McCarthy.

Valmouth
1958 London (CD) with Cleo Laine, Barbara Couper, Doris Hare, Fenella Fielding, Denise Hirst, Alan Edwards, Aubrey Woods, Peter Gilmore, Geoffrey Dunn, Marcia Ashton, Patsy Rowlands.

1982 Chichester, UK (LP) with Bertice Reading, Femi Taylor, Robert Helpmann, Cheryl Kennedy, Fenella Fedling, Doris Hare, Marcis Ashton, Robert Meadmore, Judy Campbell, Mark Wynter.

Violet
1997 Off Broadway (CD) with Lauren Ward, Michael McElroy, Michael Park, Cass Morgan, Robert Westenberg.

Walmartopia
2007 Off Broadway (CD) with Cheryl Freeman, Nikki M. James, Bradley Dean, Stephen DeRosa, Brennen Leath, Scotty Watson.

Weird Romance
1992 Off Broadway (CD) with Ellen Greene, Jonathan Hadary, Danny Burstein, Jessica Molaskey, Valerie Pettiford, Sal Viviano, Eric Riley, Marguerite MacIntyre, William Youmans.

What about Luv?
1990 Studio recording (CD) with Judy Kaye, David Green, Simon Green.

When Pigs Fly
1996 Off Broadway (CD) with David Pevsner, Jay Rogers, Michael West, Stanley Bojarski, John Treacy Egan, Keith Cromwell.

Whoop-Dee-Doo! See *Howard Crabtree's Whoop-Dee-Doo!*

The Wild Party

2000 Off Broadway (CD) with Julia Murney, Brian d'Arcy James, Idina Menzel, Taye Diggs, Kena Tangi Dorsey, Alix Korey, Lawrence Keigwin, Raymond Jaramillo NcLeod, Jennifer Cody.

Wings

1995 Studio recording (CD) with Linda Stephens, William Brown, Hollis Resnik, Russ Thacker, Ora Jones.

The World of Kurt Weill in Song See A Kurt Weill Cabaret.

Your Own Thing

1968 Off Broadway (CD) with Leland Palmer, Tom Ligon, Marcia Rodd, Rusty Thacker, Danny Apolinar, John Kuhner, Michael Valenti, Igors Gavon, Imogene Bliss.

You're a Good Man, Charlie Brown

1966 Concept recording (LP) with Orson Bean, Barbara Minkus, Bill Hinnant, Clark Gesner.

1967 Off Broadway (CD) with Gary Burghoff, Bob Balaban, Reva Rose, Skip Hinnant, Bill Hinnant, Karen Johnson.

1973 Television soundtrack (LP) with Wendell Burton, Ruby Pearson, Barry Livingston, Bill Hinnant, Mark Montgomery, Noelle Matlovsky.

1999 Broadway (CD) with Adam Rapp, Ilana Levine, Roger Bart, Kristin Chenoweth, B. D. Wong, Stanley Wayne Mathis.

Yours, Anne

1985 Off Broadway (LP) with Trini Alvarado, George Guidall, David Cady, Betty Aberlin, Ann Talman, Dana Zeller-Alexis, Hal Robinson, Merwin Goldsmith.

Zanna, Don't!

2003 Off Broadway (CD) with Jai Rodriguez, Jared Zeus, Anika Larsen, Shelley Thomas, Robb Sharp, Enrico Rodriguez, Amanda Ryan, Darius Nichols.

Zombie Prom

1996 Off Broadway (CD) with Richard Roland, Jessica-Snow Wilson, Karen Murphy, Stephen Bienski, Richard Muenz, Marc Lovci, Rebecca Rich.

Bibliography

Banham, Martin, ed. *The Cambridge Guide to Theatre*. New York: Cambridge University Press, 1992.

Baral, Robert. *Revue: The Great Broadway Period*. New York: Fleet Press Corp., 1970.

Blum, Daniel C., ed. *Theatre World (1946–1964)*. New York: Norman McDonald Associate, 1946–1949.

Bordman, Gerald. *American Theatre Revue: From the Passing Show to Sugar Babies*. New York: Oxford University Press, 1985.

———. *American Musical Theatre: A Chronicle*. 3rd ed. New York: Oxford University Press, 2001.

Bordman, Gerald, and Thomas S. Hischak. *The Oxford Companion to American Theatre*. 3rd ed. New York: Oxford University Press, 2004.

Bottoms, Stephen J. *Playing Underground: A Critical History of the 1960s Off-Off-Broadway Movement*. Ann Arbor: University of Michigan Press, 2004.

Chapman, John, ed. *The Best Plays (1947–1952)*. New York: Dodd, Mead & Co., 1894–1988.

Crespy, David A. *Off-Off-Broadway Explosion*. New York: Back Stage Books, 2003.

Dietz, Dan. *The Off Broadway Musical, 1910–2007*. Jefferson, N.C.: McFarland & Co., 2010.

Farber, Donald C., and Robert Viagas. *The Amazing Story of* The Fantasticks. New York: Citadel Press, 1991.

Ganzl, Kurt. *Ganzl's Encyclopedia of the Musical Theatre*. New York: Schirmer Books, 2001.

Green, Stanley. *Broadway Musicals Show by Show* (revised and updated by Kay Green). 6th ed. Milwaukee: Hal Leonard Publishing Corp., 2008.

———. *The World of Musical Comedy*. New York: A. S. Barnes & Co.,1980.

Greenberger, Howard. *The Off Broadway Experience*. Englewood Cliffs, N.J.: Prentice-Hall, 1971.

Guernsey, Otis, Jr., ed. *The Best Plays (1964–2000)*. New York: Dodd, Mead & Co., 1894–1988; New York: Applause Theatre Book Publishers, 1988–1993; New York: Limelight Editions, 1994–2009.

Hewes, Henry, ed. *The Best Plays (1961–1964)*. New York: Dodd, Mead & Co., 1894–1988.

Himelstein, Morgan Y. *Drama Was a Weapon: The Left-Wing Theatre in New York, 1929–1941*. New Brunswick, N.J.: Rutgers University Press, 1963.

Hischak, Thomas S. *The Oxford Companion to the American Musical: Theatre, Film, and Television*. New York: Oxford University Press, 2008.

———. *Stage It with Music: An Encyclopedic Guide to the American Musical Theatre*. Westport, Conn.: Greenwood Press, 1993.

Jackson, Arthur. *The Best Musicals from* Show Boat *to* A Chorus Line. New York: Crown Publishers, 1977.

Jenkins, Jeffrey Eric, ed. *The Best Plays (2000–2009)*. New York: Limelight Editions, 1994–2009.

Jones, John Bush. *Our Musicals, Ourselves*. Lebanon, N.H.: University Press of New England, 2003.

Kantor, Michael, and Laurence Maslon. *Broadway: The American Musical*. New York: Bullfinch Press, 2004.

Kennedy, Michael Patrick, and John Muir. *Musicals*. Glasgow, U.K.: HarperCollins, 1997.

Kronenberger, Louis, ed. *The Best Plays (1952–1961)*. New York: Dodd, Mead & Co., 1894–1988.

Lamb, Andrew. *150 Years of Popular Musical Theatre*. New Haven, Conn.: Yale University Press, 2000.

Levine, Mindy. *New York's Other Theatre*. New York: Avon Books, 1981.

Little, Stuart. *Off Broadway: The Prophetic Theatre*. New York: Coward, McCann & Geoghegan, 1972.

Lynch, Richard Chigley. *Broadway, Movie, TV, and Studio Cast Musicals on Record*. Westport, Conn.: Greenwood Press, 1996.

———. *Broadway on Record: A Directory of New York Cast Recordings of Musical Shows, 1931–1986*. Westport, Conn.: Greenwood Press, 1987.

Mantle, Burns, ed. *The Best Plays (1919–1947)*. New York: Dodd, Mead & Co., 1894–1988.

Miller, Scott. *Rebels with Applause: Broadway's Groundbreaking Musicals*. Portsmouth, N.H.: Heinemann Drama, 2001.

Patinkin, Sheldon. *No Legs, No Jokes, No Chance: A History of the American Musical Theatre*. Evanston, Ill.: Northwestern University Press, 2008.

Portantier, Michael, ed. *The TheatreMania Guide to Musical Theatre Recordings*. New York: Backstage Books, 2004.

Price, Julia S. *The Off Broadway Theatre*. New York: Scarecrow Press, 1962.

Raymond, Jack. *Show Music on Record, From the 1890s to the 1980s*. New York: Frederick Ungar Publishing, 1982.

Sherwood, Garrison, and John Chapman, eds. *The Best Plays (1894–1919)*. New York: Dodd, Mead & Co., 1894–1988.

Sheward, David. *It's a Hit: The Back Stage Book of Longest-Running Broadway Shows, 1884 to the Present.* New York: Watson-Guptill Publications–BPI Communications, 1994.

Singer, Barry. *Ever After: The Last Years of Musical Theatre and Beyond.* New York: Applause Theatre and Cinema Books, 2004.

Smith, Cecil, and Glenn Litton. *Musical Comedy in America.* 2nd ed. New York: Theatre Arts Books, 1981.

Swain, Joseph P. *The Broadway Musical: A Critical and Musical Survey.* New York: Oxford University Press, 1990.

Willis, John, ed. *Theatre World (1964–2007).* New York: Crown Publishers: 1964–1991; New York: Applause Theatre Book Publishers, 1991–2008.

Willis, John, and Ben Hodges, eds. *Theatre World (2005–2008).* New York: Applause Theatre Book Publishers, 1991–2008.

Wilmeth, Don B., and Tice Miller, eds. *Cambridge Guide to American Theatre.* New York: Cambridge University Press, 1993.

Wollman, Elizabeth L. *The Theatre Will Rock: A History of the Rock Musical from Hair to Hedwig.* Ann Arbor: University of Michigan Press, 2006.

Index

Note: *Page numbers in bold indicate the main entry for an Off-Broadway musical. Only names in the text, not the boxes, are included below.*

About the Author

Thomas S. Hischak is the author of twenty-one books on popular music, theatre, and film, including such titles as *Theatre as Human Action*, *The Oxford Companion to the American Musical: Theatre, Film and Television*, *The Tin Pan Alley Encyclopedia*, *The Oxford Companion to the American Theatre* (with Gerald Bordman), *The Disney Song Encyclopedia* (with Mark A. Robinson), *Boy Meets Girl: Broadway Librettists*, and *Word Crazy: Broadway Lyricists from Cohan to Sondheim*. Hischak is professor of theatre at the State University of New York College at Cortland. He is also the author of twenty published plays.